PLOTINUS

The Enneads

PLOTINUS

TRANSLATED BY Stephen MacKenna

The Enneads

A new, definitive edition with comparisons to other translations on hundreds of key passages ∽

Published for the Paul Brunton Philosophic Foundation by

LARSON PUBLICATIONS

CLASSIC
REPRINT
SERIES

International Standard Book Number (cloth): 0-943914-55-8
International Standard Book Number (paper): 0-943914-59-0
Library of Congress Catalogue Card Number: 91-77117

Manufactured in the United States of America

Published for the
Paul Brunton Philosophic Foundation
by Larson Publications
4936 Route 414
Burdett, New York 14818 USA

99 98 97 96 95 94 93 92

10 9 8 7 6 5 4 3 2 1

Passages from the translation of A.H. Armstrong are reprinted by
permission of the publisher and the Loeb Classical Library from *Plotinus*
(in seven volumes), translated by A.H. Armstrong, Cambridge, Mass.:
Harvard University Press, volume 1 © 1966, volume 2 © 1966,
volume 3 © 1967, volume 4 © 1984, volume 5 © 1984,
volume 6 © 1988, volume 7 © 1988.

Book and cover design: Paperwork, Ithaca, New York

Dedicated to Anthony J. Damiani ∽
1922 - 1984

CONTENTS

THE FIRST ENNEAD

THE SECOND ENNEAD

THE THIRD ENNEAD

THE FOURTH ENNEAD

THE FIFTH ENNEAD

THE SIXTH ENNEAD

APPENDICES

FOREWORD

∾ THE *ENNEADS* of Plotinus transport the reader, by what Pierre Hadot has called "an irresistible movement that defies analysis," toward a fundamental but unutterable experience that transfigures everything. They are, as Hadot observes so beautifully, "spiritual exercises in which the soul sculpts herself—that is, purifies herself, simplifies herself, lifts herself to the plane of pure thought prior to transcending herself in ecstasy."

"Withdraw into yourself and look," Plotinus writes in *Ennead* I.6.9:

> And if you do not find yourself beautiful yet, act as does the creator of a statue that is to be made beautiful: he cuts away here, he smoothes there, he makes this line lighter, this other purer, until a lovely face has grown upon his work. So do you also: cut away all that is excessive, straighten all that is crooked, bring light to all that is overcast, labour to make all one glow of beauty and never cease chiselling your statue, until there shall shine out on you from it the godlike splendour of virtue, until you shall see the perfect goodness surely established in the stainless shrine.

> When you know that you have become this perfect work, when you are self-gathered in the purity of your being, nothing now remaining that can shatter that inner unity, nothing from without clinging to the authentic man, when you find yourself wholly true to your essential nature, wholly that only veritable Light which is not measured by space, not narrowed to any circumscribed form ... ever unmeasurable as something greater than all measure and more than all quantity—when you perceive that you have grown to this, you are now become very vision: now call up all your confidence, strike forward yet a step—you need a guide no longer—strain, and see.

Here, when one has become an eye adapted to (or of sufficient likeness with) what is to be seen, this unutterable "experience" may begin. "When this consciousness takes hold of a man," Paul Brunton writes, "it takes him by surprise. Infinity is so utterly different from what he was experiencing a few minutes earlier that its wonder, its truth, its love fill him abruptly, as if in descent from the skies." Stillness lends its eloquence to a mind struck speechless, and nothing can ever again be the same. Nothing is ever again devoid of the divine; yet neither does any *thing* fully capture or express the exquisite intimacy of this eternally new ever-presence that remains absolutely seamless, free, and beyond conception.

For most who glimpse it, the actual experience passes, but the urge to regain it—to make it an established state—becomes a driving force of their inner life. Communicating this unutterable state—at once immanent and transcendent—and forging a way to it for his readers, is Plotinus' sole purpose. To accomplish it, he summons all the possibilities of the language and thought of his epoch, developing a unique and incomparable tonality for which there is no substitute.

To experience the powerful cogency of his reasoning, even to be thrilled by the elegant beauty of his expositions, one need not share or even grant initial validity to his mystical—or paramystical—perceptions. Yet the cogency and beauty do lend wings to the rational mind. A process begins whereby that mind can convince itself, rationally, of the need for such perceptions—and gradually allow deeper levels of one's own being to emerge and deliver them.

Plotinus was vividly aware that the self, the true "I," is not essentially of our common sensible world: yet he was equally aware that we do not have to leave this world to reclaim the spiritual dimensions of our being. His "spiritual world" is not a supra-terrestrial or supra-cosmic place from which the vastness of extended space and the density of bodies separate the true self. It is the inner topography of that self, whose discontinuous levels can be revealed immediately through profound inward communion. As John Deck points out in *Nature, Contemplation, and the One,* this dimension of realization "is not, except metaphorically, a world above the everyday world. It *is* the everyday world—not as experienced by sense, by opinion, or by discursive reasoning—but as known . . . by the best knowing power." And Plotinus also knew, paradoxically, that he was most this (true) self when least his (ego) self.

Plotinus' uncanny ability to exhibit and map a course to this state of perception and—more importantly—to inspire us to pursue it, is what makes the *Enneads* of such inestimable value to contemporary seekers. It is, at the same time, what makes these writings such an astonishing challenge to translate. This issue deserves explanation, as it is the basis for structuring the present edition as we have.

One level of difficulty: Plotinus wrote mainly for his own students, who had distinct advantages in recognizing the nuances of his particular usage of certain terms. Another: his inspiration frequently stretches language toward nearly inexpressible profundities, invoking the poetic dimension and "violating" the grammar of linear thought. A third: the *Enneads* are not a step-by-step sequence of teachings readily reducible to a linear system of notions; rather, each seems to unfold a specific intuition that is itself an aspect of an underlying—and unwritable—grand insight; without access to this grand insight that makes ultimate sense of each of its intuited or reasoned elements, certain passages simply cannot be made to yield their full meaning. The reader will see, for example, several places in the present edition where major translators differ greatly: holding them all together, rather than trying to choose which is "right," will sometimes show a large idea of which each has grasped a legitimate and necessary part.

ABOUT THIS EDITION

Our inspiration for an edition such as this one comes from years of living with the *Enneads* as the core of a broadly diversified spiritual practice under the late Anthony Damiani (1922–1984), founder of Wisdom's Goldenrod Center for Philosophic Studies in Valois, New York. Time and again Anthony found in Plotinus ideas, or fertile perspectives on ideas, that resolved apparent conflicts in the teachings of sages from various traditions, teachings that—at least in their extant English texts—lacked the metaphysical or mystical detail Plotinus provides.

Stephen Clark, in *The Mysteries of Religion*, writes of how "Great critics sometimes seem to understand a text better than the words before them quite explain, better even than the author: they are, as we say, 'on the same wavelength'." In the case of Anthony Damiani and Plotinus, Anthony often discovered more in the text than seemed readily apparent from the words a given *translator* provided. Working with him often yielded glimpses of what Stephen Clark calls "the Angel of the Book"—an intelligence present with but slightly beyond the imperfect medium of the words, with revelatory power much greater than the intellect. When an author is inspired by and a reader tunes in to this "angel," the words become transparent. Where intellect may before have proffered a dozen possible meanings, the angel silences all but the one that mirrors its intent.

Anyone who has successfully translated inspired thought from one language to another knows that meeting a winged idea in its original language is often only half the task. The next is to fashion words in the new language that not only describe its body but also soar with its wings. The poetic dimension must be activated anew, perhaps with the help of the "angel" itself.

And this is where the Irish poet and self-taught Greek scholar Stephen MacKenna shines. More often than any of the other English translators, he speaks the "angel" of the *Enneads*. When he catches an exalted idea, he expresses it exquisitely. For this reason, Anthony Damiani nearly always chose the poet in MacKenna over all other translators as providing the words most fruitful to take into meditation. But it must also be admitted that when MacKenna missed, he often missed completely.

Stephen MacKenna, however, worked on only the first of the four editions that bear his name. The subsequent three editions include increasing numbers of changes made by B.S. Page and incorporated indistinguishably into the text. The vast majority of Page's changes are unquestionably improvements, and the fourth edition is deservedly most scholars' text of choice for the MacKenna translation of Plotinus.

Anthony Damiani generally preferred the fourth edition as well. Through my years of study with him, however, there were many times that he expressed a preference for MacKenna's original translation over Page's changes where the two men differ significantly on points of philosophical meaning. In many of these cases, the difference of meaning is quite dramatic; in others the meaning is the same, but some readers may find the first edition more clear.

With the MacKenna translation out of print, we decided not only to re-issue it but also to show what we consider some of the more significant—and debatable—differences between the original and fourth editions. This editorial dimension of the project began primarily for our own edification. In the process of a thorough line-by-line comparison of the first and fourth editions, however, we discovered many more noteworthy differences than we had expected. The importance of such an undertaking became increasingly obvious.

Each of the differences noted is one that merited discussion among the editors on the project. Though we did not always agree on whether or not to footnote a given passage, we ultimately took the fact of having such differences of opinion as reason enough to do so. In some cases we ultimately agree with Page, but think MacKenna's original thought worthy of consideration. In many others we firmly believe that MacKenna's translation is not only more profound but also more attuned with the Plotinian "grand insight."

Having found so many significant contrasts, we chose to take yet a further step toward creating the book that many serious students of Plotinus would most like to have. In most of the passages involving what we consider debatable differences between MacKenna and Page, we also show how the same ideas are handled by other major translators and interpreters: A.H. Armstrong, Thomas Taylor, K.S. Guthrie, and, occasionally, John Deck.

Each of the other translations has unique and laudable virtues, and the serious student will eventually want to read them all. Each also brings a wealth of scholarship bear on the text. In general, A.H. Armstrong is highly praised for his technical precision, fidelity to the Greek text in light of recent scholarship, clear explication of his reasons for occasionally introducing interpretive changes, and valuable commentary. Thomas Taylor is renowned for his philosophical profundity; though he translated only a third of the tractates, his footnotes firmly establish the overall Neoplatonic context of many important ideas. Kenneth Sylvan Guthrie is most generous in carefully spelling out his understanding of a given idea, and offers many valuable cross-references—both within the *Enneads* themselves and to other Platonic and Neoplatonic sources. And John Deck, though he translated only small sections of the writings, shows an astonishing grasp of the overall Plotinian vision in his own treatment of some difficult metaphysical details. Juxtaposing their various visions of debatable passages often rounds out an idea with a clarity that none delivers alone. In some cases, it simply puts the non-Greek reader in a more informed position to reflect upon what Plotinus may have intended.

As B.S. Page points out in his preface to the second edition of MacKenna's work, MacKenna "was no friend of the scholiast, and would not easily have consented to have his version of Plotinus used as itself a text for notes and variants." Footnoting the text could easily be, as Page observes, "strangely incompatible with MacKenna's ceaseless striving for lucidity and elegance of presentation." Agreeing with and trying to honor this perception, we have attempted to minimize our intrusion on MacKenna's magical spell.

We run the fourth edition as our main text. The reader may profitably ignore, on first reading, the vertical bars and tiny superscripts defining passages for which endnotes are to be found at the end of each tractate. We have also attempted to minimize the number of endnotes: the vast majority of Page's changes being unquestionably correct, we call attention only to a relatively small percentage of them. On more careful study in subsequent reading, however, the reader should find most of these endnotes helpful—some perhaps even illuminating.

The first three tractates of the sixth ennead have no notes at all. These sections were translated by B.S. Page even in the first edition; though there are many changes between the first and fourth editions, these are changes Page made in his own work, not in MacKenna's.

We hope that this edition will be a welcome contribution to the growing "Plotinian revival" and East-West spiritual dialogue. It has been a most satisfying project to work on. Much of which we were only partially aware through the years of working with Anthony Damiani has crystallized in the process of assembling it.

We offer it not as a be-all-and-end-all edition of Plotinus, simply as the most definitive edition of the MacKenna edition to date. The continuing dialogue of which it is a part is of inestimable value. Such dialogue, appropriately conducted, becomes a genuine spiritual practice in itself, expressing the ongoing life of the tradition of wisdom-knowledge.

In the spirit of further contributing to that dialogue, we have also added an appendix at the end of the book. It introduces key elements of one fertile perspective on the Plotinian "grand insight." We are most grateful to Anthony Damiani for having exposed us to this perspective, and hope that it will prove useful to others who approach the *Enneads* as one of the greatest literary and philosophical masterpieces of all time.

This edition has come about through the combined volunteer efforts of many people. I am most grateful to more than twenty individuals associated with Wisdom's Goldenrod and the Paul Brunton Philosophic Foundation for reproducing, carefully proofreading, and correcting the fourth-edition main text; for an exacting, line-by-line comparison of the first and fourth editions to identify all differences; for extensive and much-needed assistance in comparing these differences with those other translations and selecting which ones to footnote; and for essential financial assistance toward the cost of its publication. Thanks to this remarkable coming-together of so many highly motivated people, this edition has come to print despite the numerous difficulties besetting such idealistic publishing efforts at the present time.

I am also most grateful to James Hillman for his initial suggestion of comparing debatable differences to the A.H. Armstrong translation, which we subsequently developed to include other translations as well; to Huston Smith, Jacob Needleman, and Robert Bly for their enthusiastic support in the early stages of conceiving this project; to Anne Kilgore of Paperwork for skillful design and diligent production of the text and cover; and to George Whipple of Cornell University Press for valuable production advice and assistance.

PAUL CASH
Director, Larson Publications
January 1992

EXTRACTS FROM THE EXPLANATORY
MATTER IN THE FIRST EDITION

I. THE TEXT

THE TEXT on which this translation has been made is that of Richard Volkmann (Teubner, Leipzig, 1883): occasionally a reading has been adopted from the text variations or spacious commentary given in the three-volume edition of Friedrich Creuzer (Oxford, 1835): very rarely the translator has been driven to venture an emendation of his own.

II. PREVIOUS TRANSLATIONS

THE PRESENT translation has been scrupulously compared, clause by clause, over and over again, with those undermentioned:

THE LATIN OF FICINO (in Creuzer's edition).
THE FRENCH OF M.N. BOUILLET (three vols., Paris, 1875, &c.).
THE GERMAN OF HERMANN FRIEDRICH MUELLER (2 vols., Berlin: Weidmann, 1878-80)
THE GERMAN OF OTTO KIEFER (2 vols., Diederichs: Jena and Leipzig, 1905).

[The translator upon reading some of the treatises translated into English by Thomas Taylor decided, for reasons mainly literary, that the work of this devoted pioneer would not be helpful in the present undertaking: it has, therefore, not been used in any part of this work except possibly by indirect suggestion from the quotations made occasionally in the commentaries of Bouillet and Creuzer.]

[Editors' note: B.S. Page, in his revisions through the fourth edition, drew also upon the Henry-Schwyzer critical edition and the Beutler-Theiler revision of Harder's German translation, as well as the first three volumes of the Loeb translation by A.H. Armstrong.]

III. METHOD OF THE PRESENT TRANSLATION

INEVITABLY the present translator has sometimes differed from all his predecessors, as they have sometimes differed from all the others: he hopes it will not be thought an insolence in him to remark that his rendering of any given passage is not to be tested finally by the authority of any of these scholars, still less by any preconceived idea of Plotinus' meaning or by hasty memory of controversy and decisions as to the peculiar uses of words in Plato or Aristotle. The text of the

Enneads may be taken to be very fairly well established, but it would be absurd to suppose that as yet Plotinus, so little cautious or consistent in verbal expression, yields his precise meaning, or full content, as Plato, for example, may be supposed now to do after the scholarly scrutiny of generations. It may, indeed, be said with a rough truth that Plotinus' terms, shifting at best and depending upon context and again upon the context of the context, are never to be more carefully examined than when they seem to be most true to the Platonic or Aristotelian uses: the confusion is a constant pitfall: Plotinus was pouring a quite new wine into very old bottles. Plotinus is often to be understood rather by swift and broad rushes of the mind—the mind trained to his methods—than by laborious word-racking investigation: we must know him through and through before we can be quite sure of his minuter meanings anywhere: there must be many a scholar at work yet, many an order of mind, before we can hope to have a perfectly true translation of the Enneads in any language. The present worker must have made mistakes, some perhaps that to himself will one day appear inexcusable: his one consolation is that the thing he will that day welcome from other hands has most certainly passed through his own, and been deliberately rejected. Where he appears most surely to have sinned against the light, it is most sure that he has passed through an agony of hesitation.

People seem always anxious to know whether a work of translation is what they call literal; the important question is rather whether it is faithful: the present work pretends to be faithful—and, if we must be precise, literary rather than literal. This is not to say that it is a paraphrase.

Probably every translator from the classic tongues sets out gaily in the firm purpose of achieving the impossible, of making a crib that shall also be a piece of sound and flowing idiomatic writing; and certainly many critics demand the miracle. Some years ago, on the publication of a preliminary specimen of this present venture, one very highly accomplished scholar wrote complaining with utter seriousness of an English past tense which had dared to translate a 'frequentative aorist' of the Greek original; he had apparently never asked himself whether an English past may not be as frequentative as any Greek aorist: in any case, readers who desire their translations to serve as an unfailing treasury of illustrations to 'X. on Greek Idioms' are not asked to like this version.

Again, various arbitrary principles, laid down by translators of a formally precise school, have been quite ignored here. For example, it has been decreed that 'one word must translate one word', and this in a double application:

1. That if, for example, the word *phusis* is once translated Nature, *phusis* must stand as Nature at every repetition, never Kind or Essence, or Being or any other word which happens, in a particular context, to be equally clear and precise or even imperative in English to the sense and connexion of thought.

2. That *phusis*, for example, may never be translated by such a double as 'Nature or Hypostasis', *doxa*, for example never by such a double as 'Opinion or Seeming-Knowledge', still less, as several times here, by 'Ordinary Mentation', with or without an alternative or an addition.

All such bans have been treated here as belonging to the childish pedantry of a game of skill, not to the serious task of conveying to the reader a grave body of foreign thought. Probably in every writer—certainly in Plotinus—such a word as *phusis*, such a word as *theos*, or again *theios*, may carry in connotation not merely two but three or four or more notions, any one of which may at a given moment be the dominant, though not necessarily to the utter exclusion of the others. Plotinus has some score of words, technical terms, which he uses in very varying applications where no single fixed English word or even combination of words would always carry his meaning. The translator has in this whole matter adopted the principle of using such a variety of terms, single or double or upon occasion triple, as will exactly cover or carry the idea which appears in the original; he has arrogated to himself almost the entire freedom of a philosophic writer in English who uses his words with an absolute loyalty, of course, to his thought but with never a moment's scruple as to the terms in which he happened to convey or indicate a given notion five pages back. In other words the present translator has not thought of his probable readers as glossary-bound pedants but as possessed of the living vision which can follow a stream of thought by the light of its vivid movement.

Other theorists of translation desire that a version should represent the style of the original writer: this notion is tempting and may often be safely achieved but not, the present writer ventures to say, in the case of Plotinus, or perhaps in the case of any writer whose main preoccupation is less with artistic expression than with the enunciation of cardinal and gravely important ideas. Longinus, as may be learned from Porphyry's Life-sketch of Plotinus, so little grasped Plotinus' manner of expression as to judge ruinously erroneous the most faithful transcripts that could be: a version which should reproduce such a style as disconcerted and misled the most widely read contemporary critic of Greek letters would not be a translation in any useful sense of the word, or at least would not be English or would not be readable.

The present translation, therefore, has been executed on the basic ideal of carrying Plotinus' thought—its strength and its weakness alike—to the mind of the reader of English; the first aim has been the utmost attainable clearness in the faithful, full, and unalloyed expression of the meaning; the second aim, set a long way after the first, has been the reproduction of the splendid soaring passages with all their warmth and light. Nothing whatever has been, consciously, added or omitted with such absurd purpose as that of heightening either the force of the thought or the beauty of the expression—except in so far as force and beauty demand a clarity which sometimes must be, courageously, imposed upon the most negligent, probably, of the great authors of the world.

[*Added in volume 2 of the first edition:* In simple honesty to such readers as do not consult the original, the translator feels obliged to state that he does not pretend to be perfectly satisfied that he has himself understood every passage of which he has been obliged to present a rendering: he has in no case passed for publication any passage or phrase which does not appear to him to carry a clear sense in English and a sense possible in view at once of the text and of Plotinus' general thought; he has been scrupulous in frankly committing himself; but there are at least three or four places in which he feels himself to be as probably wrong as right, places in which either the text is disordered or Plotinus, as often, was inattentive to the normal sequence, or even—verbally at least—to the general consistency, of his thought.

For the present it appears that the best service to Plotinian studies is to dare to be tentative and to beg critics to collaborate in the clearing of dark passages: the notices the first volume of this series received were more flattering than helpful . . .]

PORPHYRY

On the Life of Plotinus and the Arrangement of his Work

1. PLOTINUS, the philosopher our contemporary, seemed ashamed of being in the body.

So deeply rooted was this feeling that he could never be induced to tell of his ancestry, his parentage, or his birthplace.

He showed, too, an unconquerable reluctance to sit to a painter or a sculptor, and when Amelius persisted in urging him to allow of a portrait being made he asked him, 'Is it not enough to carry about this image in which nature has enclosed us?' Do you really think I must also consent to leave, as a desirable spectacle to posterity, an image of the image?'

In view of this determined refusal Amelius brought his friend Carterius, the best artist of the day, to the Conferences, which were open to every comer, and saw to it that by long observation of the philosopher he caught his most striking personal traits. From the impressions thus stored in mind the artist drew a first sketch; Amelius made various suggestions towards bringing out the resemblance, and in this way, without the knowledge of Plotinus, the genius of Carterius gave us a lifelike portrait.

2. Plotinus was often distressed by an intestinal complaint, but declined clysters, pronouncing the use of such remedies unbecoming in an elderly man: in the same way he refused such medicaments as contain any substance taken from wild beasts or reptiles: all the more, he remarked, since he could not approve of eating the flesh of animals reared for the table.

He abstained from the use of the bath, contenting himself with a daily massage at home: when the terrible epidemic carried off his masseurs he renounced all such treatment: in a short while he contracted malign diphtheria.

During the time I was about him there was no sign of any such malady, but after I sailed for Sicily the condition grew acute: his intimate, Eustochius, who was with him till his death, told me, on my return to Rome, that he became hoarse, so that his voice quite lost its clear sonorous note, his sight grew dim and ulcers formed on his hands and feet.

As he still insisted on addressing everyone by word of mouth, his condition prompted his friends to withdraw from his society: he therefore left Rome for Campania, retiring to a property which had belonged to Zethos, an old friend of his at this time dead. His wants were provided in part out of Zethos' estate, and for the rest were furnished from Minturnae, where Castricius' property lay.

Of Plotinus' last moments Eustochius has given me an account.

He himself was staying at Puteoli and was late in arriving: when he at last came, Plotinus said: 'I have been a long time waiting for you; I am striving to give back the Divine in myself to the Divine in the All.' As he spoke a snake crept under the bed on which he lay and slipped away into a hole in the wall: at the same moment Plotinus died.

This was at the end of the second year of the reign of Claudius (A.D. 270), and, as Eustochius tells me, Plotinus was then sixty-six. I myself was at Lilybaeum at the time, Amelius at Apamea in Syria, Castricius at Rome; only Eustochius was by his side.

Counting sixty-six years back from the second year of Claudius, we can fix Plotinus' birth at the thirteenth year of Severus (A.D. 204^{8}5); but he never disclosed the month or day. This was because he did not desire any birthday sacrifice or feast; yet he himself sacrificed on the traditional birthdays of Plato and of Socrates, afterwards giving a banquet at which every member of the circle who was able was expected to deliver an address.

3. Despite his general reluctance to talk of his own life, some few details he did often relate to us in the course of conversation.

Thus he told how, at the age of eight, when he was already going to school, he still clung about his nurse and loved to bare her breasts and take suck: one day he was told he was a 'perverted imp', and so was shamed out of the trick.

At twenty-seven he was caught by the passion for philosophy: he was directed to the most highly reputed professors to be found at Alexandria; but he used to come from their lectures saddened and discouraged. A friend to whom he opened his heart divined his temperamental craving and suggested Ammonius, whom he had not yet tried. Plotinus went, heard a lecture, and exclaimed to his comrade: 'This was the man I was looking for.'

From that day he followed Ammonius continuously, and under his guidance made such progress in philosophy that he became eager to investigate the Persian methods and the system adopted among the Indians. It happened that the Emperor Gordian was at that time preparing his campaign against Persia; Plotinus joined the army and went on the expedition. He was then thirty-eight, for he had passed eleven entire years under Ammonius. When Gordian was killed in Mesopotamia, it was only with great difficulty that Plotinus came off safe to Antioch.

At forty, in the reign of Philip, he settled in Rome.

Erennius, Origen, and Plotinus had made a compact not to disclose any of the doctrines which Ammonius had revealed to them. Plotinus kept faith, and in all his intercourse with his associates divulged nothing of Ammonius' system. But the compact was broken, first by Erennius and then by Origen following suit: Origen, it is true, put in writing nothing but the treatise *On the Spirit-Beings*, and in Gallienus' reign that entitled *The King the Sole Creator*. Plotinus himself remained a long time without writing, but he began to base his Conferences on what he had gathered from his studies under Ammonius. In this way, writing nothing but constantly conferring with a certain group of associates, he passed ten years.

He used to encourage his hearers to put questions, a liberty which, as Amelius told me, led to a great deal of wandering and futile talk.

Amelius had entered the circle in the third year of Philip's reign, the third, too, of Plotinus' residence in Rome, and remained about him until the first year of Claudius, twenty-four years in all. He had come to Plotinus after an efficient training under Lysimachus: in laborious diligence he surpassed all his contemporaries; for example, he transcribed and arranged nearly all the works of Numenius, and was not far from having most of them off by heart. He also took notes of the Conferences and wrote them out in something like a hundred treatises which he has since presented to Hostilianus Hesychius of Apamea, his adopted son.

4. I myself arrived from Greece in the tenth year of Gallienus' reign, accompanied by Antonius of Rhodes, and found Amelius an eighteen-years' associate of Plotinus, but still lacking the courage to write anything except for the notebooks, which had not reached their century. Plotinus, in this tenth year of Gallienus, was about fifty-nine: when I first met him I was thirty.

From the first year of Gallienus Plotinus had begun to write upon such subjects as had arisen at the Conferences: when I first came to know him in this tenth year of the reign he had composed twenty-one treatises.

They were, as I was able to establish, by no means given about freely. In fact the distribution was still grudging and secret; those that obtained them had passed the strictest scrutiny.

Plotinus had given no titles to these treatises; everybody headed them for himself: I cite them here under the titles which finally prevailed, quoting the first words of each to facilitate identification.*

1. On Beauty (i. 6).
2. On the Immortality of the Soul (iv. 7).

* These first words are of course omitted and the Ennead reference is added.

3. On Fate (III. 1).
4. On the Essence of the Soul (IV.2).
5. On the Intellectual-Principle, on the Ideas, and on the Authentic-Existent (V. 9).
6. On the Descent of the Soul into Bodies (IV. 8).
7. How the Post-Primal derives from the Primal; and on The One (V. 4).
8. Whether all the Souls are One (IV. 9).
9. On the Good or the One (VI. 9).
10. On the Three Primal Hypostases (V. 1).
11. On the Origin and Order of the Post-Primals (V. 2).
12. On the Two Orders of Matter (II. 4).
13. Various Questions (III. 9).
14. On the Circular Movement (II. 2).
15. On our Tutelary Spirit (III. 4).
16. On the Reasoned Dismissal (I. 9).
17. On Quality (II. 6).
18. Whether there are Ideas even of Particulars (V. 7).
19. On the Virtues (I. 2).
20. On Dialectic (I. 3).
21. Why the Soul is described as Intermediate between the Existent having parts and the undisparted Existent (IV. 1).

These are the twenty-one treatises which, as I have said, Plotinus had already written, by his fifty-ninth year, when I first came to him.

5. I had been, it is true, in Rome a little before this tenth year of Gallienus, but at that time Plotinus was taking a summer holiday, engaging merely in conversation with his friends. After coming to know him I passed six years in close relation with him. Many questions were threshed out in the Conferences of those six years and, under persuasion from Amelius and myself, he composed two treatises to establish:

22, 23. That the Authentic-Existent is universally an integral, self-identical Unity (VI. 4, 5).

In immediate succession to these he composed two more: one is entitled:

24. That there is no Intellectual Act in the Principle which transcends the Authentic-Existent; and on the Nature that has the Intellectual Act Primally and that which has it Secondarily (V. 6);

The other:

25. On Potentiality and Actuality (II. 5).

After these come the following twenty:

26. On the Impassibility of the Bodiless (III. 6).
27. On the Soul, First (IV. 3).

28. On the Soul, Second (IV. 4).
29. On the Soul, Third; or, How We See (IV. 5).
30. On Contemplation (III. 8).
31. On Intellectual Beauty (V. 8).
32. That the Intelligibles are not outside the Intellectual-Principle; and on the Good (V. 5).
33. Against the Gnostics (II. 9).
34. On Numbers (VI. 6).
35. Why Distant Objects appear Small (II. 8).
36. Whether Happiness depends upon Extension of Time (I. 5).
37. On Coalescence (II. 7).
38. How the Multitude of Ideas I Exists'I; and on the Good (VI. 7).
39. On Free-Will (VI. 8).
40. On the World (II. 1).
41. On Sensation and Memory (IV. 6).
42. On the Kinds of Being, First (VI. 1).
43. On the Kinds of Being, Second (VI. 2).
44. On the Kinds of Being, Third (VI. 3).
45. On Eternity and Time (III. 7).

Thus we have twenty-four treatises composed during the six years of my association with him and dealing, as the titles indicate, with such problems as happened to arise at the Conferences; add the twenty-one composed before my arrival, and we have accounted for forty-five treatises.

6. The following five more Plotinus wrote and sent to me while I was living in Sicily, where I had gone about the fifteenth year of Gallienus:
46. On Happiness (I. 4).
47. On Providence, First (III. 2).
48. On Providence, Second (III. 3).
49. On the Conscious Hypostases and the All-Transcending (V. 3).
50. On Love (III. 5).
These five he sent me in the first year of Claudius: in the early months of the second year, shortly before his death, I received the following four:
51. On Evil (I. 8).
52. Whether the Stars have Causal Operation (II. 3).
53. On the Animate (I. 1).
54. On Happiness (I. 7).
Adding these nine to the forty-five of the first and second sets we have a total of fifty-four treatises.

According to the time of writing—early manhood, vigorous prime, worn-out constitution—so the tractates vary in power. The first twenty-one pieces manifest a slighter capacity, the talent being not yet matured to the fullness of nervous strength. The twenty-four produced in the mid-period display the utmost reach of the powers and, except for the short treatises among them, attain the highest perfection. The last nine were written when the mental strength was already waning, and of these the last four show less vigour even than the five preceding.

7. Plotinus had a large following. Notable among the more zealous students, really devoted to philosophy, was Amelius of Tuscany, whose family name was Gentilianus. Amelius preferred to call himself Amerius, changing L for R, because, as he explained, it suited him better to be named from Amereia, Unification, than from Ameleia, Indifference.

The group included also one Paulinus, a doctor of Scythopolis, whom Amelius used to call Mikkalos in allusion to his blundering habit of mind.

Among closer personal friends was Eustochius of Alexandria, also a doctor, who came to know Plotinus towards the end of his life, and attended him until his death: Eustochius consecrated himself exclusively to Plotinus' system and became a veritable philosopher.

Then there was Zoticus, at once critic and poet, who has amended the text of Antimachus' works and is the author of an exquisite poem upon the Atlantis story: his sight failed, and he died a little before Plotinus, as also did Paulinus.

Another friend was Zethos, an Arabian by descent, who married a daughter of Ammonius' friend Theodosius. Zethos, too, was a doctor: Plotinus was deeply attached to him and was always trying to divert him from the political career in which he stood high. Plotinus was on the most familiar terms with him, and used to stay with him at his country place, six miles from Minturnae, a property which had formerly belonged to Castricius Firmus.

Castricius was excelled by none of the group in appreciation of the finer side of life: he venerated Plotinus; he devoted himself in the most faithful comradeship to Amelius in every need, and was in all matters as loyal to myself as though I were his own brother.

This was another example of a politician venerating the philosopher. There were also among Plotinus' hearers not a few members of the Senate, amongst whom Marcellus Orontius and Sabinillus showed the greatest assiduity in philosophical studies.

Another Senator, Rogatianus, advanced to such detachment from political ambitions that he gave up all his property, dismissed all his slaves, renounced every dignity, and, on the point of taking up his praetorship, the lictors already at the door, refused to come out or to have anything to do with the office. He even abandoned his own house, spending his time here and there at his friends' and acquaintances', sleeping and eating with them and taking, at that, only one meal every other day. He had been a victim of gout, carried in a chair, but this new regime of abstinence and abnegation restored his health: he had been unable to stretch out his hands; he came to use them as freely as men living by manual labour. Plotinus took a great liking to Rogatianus and frequently praised him very highly, holding him up as a model to those aiming at the philosophical life.

Then there was Serapion, an Alexandrian, who began life as a professional orator and later took to the study of philosophy, but was never able to conquer the vices of avarice and usury.

I myself, Porphyry of Tyre, was one of Plotinus' very closest friends, and it was to me he entrusted the task of revising his writings.

8. Such revision was necessary: Plotinus could not bear to go back on his work even for one re-reading; and indeed the condition of his sight would scarcely allow it: his handwriting was slovenly; he misjoined his words; he cared nothing about spelling; his one concern was for the idea: in these habits, to our general surprise, he remained unchanged to the very end.

He used to work out his design mentally from first to last: when he came to set down his ideas, he wrote out at one jet all he had stored in mind as though he were copying from a book.

Interrupted, perhaps, by someone entering on business, he never lost hold of his plan; he was able to meet all the demands of the conversation and still keep his own train of thought clearly before him; when he was free again, he never looked over what he had previously written—his sight, it has been mentioned, did not allow of such re-reading—but he linked on what was to follow as if no distraction had occurred.

Thus he was able to live at once within himself and for others; he never relaxed from his interior attention unless in sleep; and even his sleep was kept light by an abstemiousness that often prevented him taking as much as a piece of bread, and by this unbroken concentration upon his own highest nature.

9. Several women were greatly attached to him, amongst them Gemina, in whose house he lived, and her daughter, called Gemina, too, after the mother, and Amphiclea, the wife of Ariston, son of Iamblichus; all three devoted themselves assiduously to philosophy.

Not a few men and women of position, on the approach of death, had left their boys and girls, with all their property, in his care, feeling that with Plotinus for guardian the children would be in holy hands. His house therefore was filled with lads and lasses, amongst them Potamon, in whose education he took such interest as often to hear the boy recite verses of his own composition.

He always found time for those that came to submit returns of the children's property, and he looked closely to the accuracy of the accounts: 'Until the young people take to philosophy,' he used to say, 'their fortunes and revenues must be kept intact for them.' And yet all this labour and thought over the worldly interests of so many people never interrupted, during waking hours, his intention towards the Supreme.

He was gentle, and always at the call of those having the slightest acquaintance with him. After spending twenty-six years in Rome, acting, too, as arbiter in many differences, he had never made an enemy of any citizen.

10. Among those making profession of Philosophy at Rome was one Olympius, an Alexandrian, who had been for a little while a pupil of Ammonius.

This man's jealous envy showed itself in continual insolence, and finally he grew so bitter that he even ventured sorcery, seeking to crush Plotinus by star-spells. But he found his experiments recoiling upon himself, and he confessed to his associates that Plotinus possessed 'a mighty soul, so powerful as to be able to hurl every assault back upon those that sought his ruin'. Plotinus had felt the operation and declared that at that moment Olympius' 'limbs were convulsed and his body shrivelling like a money-bag pulled tight'. Olympius, perceiving on several attempts that he was endangering himself rather than Plotinus, desisted.

In fact Plotinus possessed by birth something more than is accorded to other men. An Egyptian priest who had arrived in Rome and, through some friend, had been presented to the philosopher, became desirous of displaying his powers to him, and he offered to evoke a visible manifestation of Plotinus' presiding spirit. Plotinus readily consented and the evocation was made in the Temple of Isis, the only place, they say, which the Egyptian could find pure in Rome.

At the summons a Divinity appeared, not a being of the spirit-ranks, and the Egyptian exclaimed: 'You are singularly graced; the guiding-spirit within you is not of the lower degree but a God.' It was not possible, however, to interrogate or even to contemplate this God any further, for the priest's assistant, who had been holding the birds to prevent them flying away, strangled them, whether through jealousy or in terror. Thus Plotinus had for indwelling spirit a Being of the more divine degree, and he kept his own divine spirit unceasingly intent upon that inner presence. It was this preoccupation that led him to write his treatise upon *Our Tutelary Spirit,* an essay in the explanation of the differences among spirit-guides.

Amelius was scrupulous in observing the day of the New-Moon and other holy-days, and once asked Plotinus to join in some such celebration: Plotinus refused: 'It is for those Beings to come to me, not for me to go to them.'

What was in his mind in so lofty an utterance we could not explain to ourselves and we dared not ask him.

11. He had a remarkable penetration into character.

Once a valuable necklace was stolen from Chione, who was living in honourable widowhood with her children in the same house as Plotinus: the servants were called before him: he scrutinized them all, then indicated one: 'This man is the thief.' The man was whipped but for some time persisted in denial: finally, however, he confessed, and restored the necklace.

Plotinus foretold also the future of each of the children in the household: for instance, when questioned as to Polemon's character and destiny he said: 'He will be amorous and short-lived'; and so it proved.

I myself at one period had formed the intention of ending my life; Plotinus discerned my purpose; he came unexpectedly to my house where I had secluded myself, told me that my decision sprang not from reason but from mere melancholy and advised me to leave Rome. I obeyed and left for Sicily, which I chose because I heard that one Probus, a man of scholarly repute, was living there not far from Lilybaeum. Thus I was induced to abandon my first intention but was prevented from being with Plotinus between that time and his death.

12. The Emperor Gallienus and his wife Salonina greatly honoured and venerated Plotinus, who thought to turn their friendly feeling to some good purpose. In Campania there had once stood, according to tradition, a City of Philosophers, a ruin now; Plotinus asked the Emperor to rebuild this city and to make over the surrounding district to the new-founded state; the population was to live under Plato's laws: the city was to be called Platonopolis; and Plotinus undertook to settle down there with his associates. He would have had his way without more ado but that opposition at court, prompted by jealousy, spite, or some such paltry motive, put an end to the plan.

13. At the Conferences he showed the most remarkable power of going to the heart of a subject, whether in exposition or in explanation, and his phrasing was apt; but he made mistakes in certain words; for example, he said 'anamnemisketai' for 'anamimnesketai'—just such errors as he committed in his writing.

When he was speaking his intellect visibly illuminated his face: always of winning presence, he became at these times still more engaging: a slight moisture gathered on his forehead; he radiated benignity.

He was always as ready to entertain objections as he was powerful in meeting them. At one time I myself kept interrogating him during three days as to how the soul is associated with the body, and he continued explaining; a man called

Thaumasius entered in the midst of our discussions; the visitor was more interested in the general drift of the system than in particular points, and said he wished to hear Plotinus expounding some theory as he would in a set treatise, but that he could not endure Porphyry's questions and answers: Plotinus asked, 'But if we cannot first solve the difficulties Porphyry raises what could go into the treatise?'

14. In style Plotinus is concise, dense with thought, terse, more lavish of ideas than of words, most often expressing himself with a fervid inspiration. He followed his own path rather than that of tradition, but in his writings both the Stoic and Peripatetic doctrines are sunk; Aristotle's Metaphysics, especially, is condensed in them, all but entire.

He had a thorough theoretical knowledge of Geometry, Mechanics, Optics, and Music, though it was not in his temperament to go practically into these subjects.

At the Conferences he used to have treatises by various authors read aloud—among the Platonists it might be Severus or Cronius, Numenius, Gaius, or Atticus; and among the Peripatetics Aspasius, Alexander, Adrastus, or some such writer, at the call of the moment. But it was far from his way to follow any of these authors blindly; he took a personal, original view, applying Ammonius' method to the investigation of every problem.

He was quick to absorb; a few words sufficed him to make clear the significance of some profound theory and so to pass on. After hearing Longinus' work *On Causes* and his *Antiquary*, he remarked: 'Longinus is a man of letters, but in no sense a philosopher.'

One day Origen came to the conference-room; Plotinus blushed deeply and was on the point of bringing his lecture to an end; when Origen begged him to continue, he said: 'The zest dies down when the speaker feels that his hearers have nothing to learn from him.'

15. Once on Plato's feast I read a poem, 'The Sacred Marriage'; my piece abounded in mystic doctrine conveyed in veiled words and was couched in terms of enthusiasm; someone exclaimed: 'Porphyry has gone mad'; Plotinus said to me so that all might hear: 'You have shown yourself at once poet, philosopher and hierophant.'

The orator Diophanes one day read a justification of the Alcibiades of Plato's Banquet and maintained that the pupil, for the sake of advancement in virtue, should submit to the teacher without reserve, even to the extent of carnal commerce: Plotinus started up several times to leave the room but forced himself to remain; on the breaking up of the company he directed me to write a refutation.

Diophanes refused to lend me his address and I had to depend on my recollection of his argument; but my refutation, delivered before the same audience, delighted Plotinus so much that during the very reading he repeatedly quoted: 'So strike and be a light to men.'

When Eubulus, the Platonic Successor, wrote from Athens, sending treatises on some questions in Platonism, Plotinus had the writings put into my hands with instructions to examine them and report to him upon them.

He paid some attention to the principles of Astronomy though he did not study the subject very deeply on the mathematical side. He went more searchingly into Horoscopy; when once he was convinced that its results were not to be trusted he had no hesitation in attacking the system frequently both at the Conferences and in his writings.

16. Many Christians of this period—amongst them sectaries who had abandoned the old philosophy, men of the schools of Adelphius and Aquilinus—had possessed themselves of works by Alexander of Libya, by Philocomus, by Demostratus, and by Lydus, and exhibited also Revelations bearing the names of Zoroaster, Zostrianus, Nicotheus, Allogenes, Mesus, and others of that order. Thus they fooled many, themselves fooled first; Plato, according to them, had failed to penetrate into the depth of Intellectual Being.

Plotinus frequently attacked their position at the Conferences and finally wrote the treatise which I have headed *Against the Gnostics:* he left to us of the circle the task of examining what he himself passed over. Amelius proceeded as far as a fortieth treatise in refutation of the book of Zostrianus: I myself have shown on many counts that the Zoroastrian volume is spurious and modern, concocted by the sectaries in order to pretend that the doctrines they had embraced were those of the ancient sage.

17. Some of the Greeks began to accuse Plotinus of appropriating the ideas of Numenius.

Amelius, being informed of this charge by the Stoic and Platonist Trypho, challenged it in a treatise which he entitled *The Difference between the Doctrines of Plotinus and Numenius.* He dedicated the work to me, under the name of Basileus (or King). This really is my name; it is equivalent to Porphyry (Purplerobed) and translates the name I bear in my own tongue; for I am called Malchos, like my father, and 'Malchos' would give 'Basileus' in Greek. Longinus, in dedicating his work *On Impulse* to Cleodamus and myself, addressed us as 'Cleodamus and Malchus', just as Numenius translated the Latin 'Maximus' into its Greek equivalent 'Megalos'.

Here follows Amelius' letter:

'Amelius to Basileus, with all good wishes.

'You have been, in your own phrase, pestered by the persistent assertion that our friend's doctrine is to be traced to Numenius of Apamea.

'Now, if it were merely for those illustrious personages who spread this charge, you may be very sure I would never utter a word in reply. It is sufficiently clear that they are actuated solely by the famous and astonishing facility of speech of theirs when they assert, at one moment, that he is an idle babbler, next that he is a plagiarist, I and finally that his plagiarisms are feeble in the extreme.²I Clearly in all this we have nothing but scoffing and abuse.

'But your judgement has persuaded me that we should profit by this occasion firstly to provide ourselves with a useful memorandum of the doctrines that have won our adhesion, and secondly to bring about a more complete knowledge of the system—long celebrated though it be—to the glory of our friend, a man so great as Plotinus.

'Hence I now bring you the promised Reply, executed, as you yourself know, in three days. You must judge it with reasonable indulgence; this is no orderly and elaborate defence composed in step-by-step correspondence with the written indictment: I have simply set down, as they occurred to me, my recollections of our frequent discussions. You will admit, also, that it is by no means easy to grasp the meaning of a writer who (like Numenius), now credited with the opinion we also hold, varies in the terms he uses to express the one idea.

'If I have falsified any essential of the doctrine, I trust to your good nature to set me right: I am reminded of the phrase in the tragedy: A busy man and far from the teachings of our master I must needs correct and recant. Judge how much I wish to give you pleasure. Good health.'

18. This letter seemed worth insertion as showing, not merely that some contemporary judgement pronounced Plotinus to be parading on the strength of Numenius' ideas, but that he was even despised as a word-spinner.

The fact is that these people did not understand his teaching: he was entirely free from all the inflated pomp of the professor: his lectures had the air of conversation, and he never forced upon his hearers the severely logical substructure of his thesis.

I myself, when I first heard him, had the same experience. It led me to combat his doctrine in a paper in which I tried to show that the Intelligibles exist outside of the Intellectual-Principle. He had my work read to him by Amelius: at the end he smiled and said: 'You must clear up these difficulties, Amelius: Porphyry doesn't understand our position.' Amelius wrote a tract of considerable length *In Answer to Porphyry's Objections;* I wrote a reply to the reply: Amelius replied to my reply; at my third attempt I came, though even so with difficulty, to grasp the doctrine: then only, I was converted, wrote a recantation, and read it before the circle. From that time on I was entrusted with Plotinus' writings and sought to stir in the master himself the ambition of organizing his doctrine and setting it down in more extended form. Amelius, too, under my prompting, was encouraged in composition.

19. Longinus' estimate of Plotinus, formed largely upon indications I myself had given him in my letters, will be gathered from the following extract from one of his to me. He is asking me to leave Sicily and join him in Phoenicia, and to bring Plotinus' works with me. He says:

'And send them at your convenience or, better, bring them; for I can never cease urging you to give the road towards us the preference over any other. If there is no better reason—and what intellectual gain can you anticipate from a visit to us?—at least there are old acquaintances and the mild climate which would do you good in the weak state of health you report. Whatever else you may be expecting, do not hope for anything new of my own, or even for the earlier works which you tell me you have lost; for there is a sad dearth of copyists here. I assure you it has taken me all this time to complete my set of Plotinus, and it was done only by calling off my scribe from all his routine work, and keeping him steadily to this one task.

'I think that now, with what you have sent me, I have everything, though in a very imperfect state, for the manuscript is exceeding faulty. I had expected our friend Amelius to correct the scribal errors, but he evidently had something better to do. The copies are quite useless to me; I have been especially eager to examine the treatises *On the Soul* and *On the Authentic-Existent,* and these are precisely the most corrupted. It would be a great satisfaction to me if you would send me faithful transcripts for collation and return—though again I suggest to you not to send but to come in person, bringing me the correct copies of these treatises and of any that Amelius may have passed over. All that he brought with him I have been careful to make my own: how could I be content not to possess myself of all the writings of a man so worthy of the deepest veneration?

'I repeat, what I have often said in your presence and in your absence, as on that occasion when you were at Tyre, that while much of the theory does not convince me, yet I am filled with admiration and delight over the general character of the work, the massive thinking of the man, the philosophic handling of problems; in my judgement investigators must class Plotinus' work with that holding the very highest rank.'

20. This extended quotation from the most acute of the critics of our day—a writer who has passed judgement on nearly all his contemporaries—serves to

show the estimate he came to set upon Plotinus of whom, at first, misled by ignorant talk, he had held a poor opinion.

His notion, by the way, that the transcripts he acquired from Amelius were faulty sprang from his misunderstanding of Plotinus' style and phraseology; if there were ever any accurate copies, these were they, faithful reproductions from the author's own manuscript.

Another passage from the work of Longinus, dealing with Amelius, Plotinus, and other metaphysicians of the day, must be inserted here to give a complete view of the opinion formed upon these philosophers by the most authoritative and most searching of critics. The work was entitled *On the End: in Answer to Plotinus and Gentilianus Amelius.* It opens with the following preface:

'In our time, Marcellus, there have been many philosophers—especially in our youth—for there is a strange scarcity at present. When I was a boy, my parents' long journeys gave me the opportunity of seeing all the better-known teachers; and in later life those that still lived became known to me as my visits to this and that city and people brought me where they happened to live.

'Some of these undertook the labour of developing their theories in formal works and so have bequeathed to the future the means of profiting by their services. Others thought they had done enough when they had convinced their own immediate hearers of the truth of their theories.

'First of those that have written.

'Among the Platonists there are Euclides, Democritus, Proclinus the philosopher of the Troad, and the two who still profess philosophy at Rome, Plotinus and his friend Gentilianus Amelius. Among the Stoics there are Themistocles and Phoibion and the two who flourished only a little while ago, Annius and Medius. And there is the Peripatetic, Heliodorus of Alexandria.

'For those that have not written, there are among the Platonists Ammonius and Origen, two teachers whose lectures I myself attended during a long period, men greatly surpassing their contemporaries in mental power; and there are the Platonic Successors at Athens, Theodotus and Eubulus.

'No doubt some writing of a metaphysical order stands to the credit of this group: Origen wrote *On Spirit-Beings,* Eubulus *On the Philebus and Gorgias, and the objections urged by Aristotle to Plato's Republic;* but this is not enough to class either of them with systematic authors. This was side-play; authorship was not in the main plan of their careers.

'Among Stoic teachers that refrained from writing we have Herminus and Lysimachus, and the two living at Athens, Musonius and Athenaeus; among Peripatetics, Ammonius and Ptolemaeus.

'The two last were the most accomplished scholars of their time, Ammonius especially being unapproached in breadth of learning; but neither produced any systematic work; we have from them merely verses and duty-speeches; and these I cannot think to have been preserved with their consent; they did not concern themselves about formal statement of their doctrine, and it is not likely they would wish to be known in after times by compositions of so trivial a nature.

'To return to the writers; some of them, like Euclides, Democritus, and Proclinus, confined themselves to the mere compilation and transcription of passages from earlier authorities. Others diligently worked over various minor points in the investigations of the ancients, and put together books dealing with the same subjects. Such were Annius, Medius, and Phoibion, the last especially choosing to be distinguished for style rather than for systematic thinking. In the same class must be ranked Heliodorus; his writings contribute nothing to the organization of the thought which he found to his hand in the teaching of earlier workers.

'Plotinus and Gentilianus Amelius alone display the true spirit of authorship; they treat of a great number of questions and they bring a method of their own to the treatment.

'Plotinus, it would seem, set the principles of Pythagoras and of Plato in a clearer light than anyone before him; on the same subjects, Numenius, Cronius, Moderatus, and Thrasyllus fall far short of him in precision and fullness. Amelius set himself to walk in Plotinus' steps and adopted most of Plotinus' opinions; his method, however, was diffuse and, unlike his friend, he indulges in an extravagance of explanation.

'Only these two seem to me worth study. What profit can anyone expect from troubling the works of any of the others to the neglect of the originals on which they drew? They bring us nothing of their own, not even a novel argument, much less a leading idea, and are too unconcerned even to set side by side the most generally adopted theories or to choose the better among them.

'My own method has been different; as for example when I replied to Gentilianus upon Plato's treatment of Justice and in a review I undertook of Plotinus' work *On the Ideas*. This latter was in the form of a reply to Basileus of Tyre, my friend as theirs. He had preferred Plotinus' system to mine and had written several works in the manner of his master, amongst them a treatise supporting Plotinus' theory of the Idea against that which I taught. I endeavoured, not, I think, unsuccessfully, to show that his change of mind was mistaken.

'In these two essays I have ranged widely over the doctrines of this school, as also in my *Letter to Amelius* which, despite the simple title with which I contented myself, has the dimensions of a book, being a reply to a treatise he addressed to me from Rome under the title *On Plotinus' Philosophic Method*.'

21. This Preface leaves no doubt of Longinus' final verdict: he ranks Plotinus and Amelius above all authors of his time in the multitude of questions they discuss; he credits them with an original method of investigation: in his judgement they by no means took their system from Numenius or gave a first place to his opinions, but followed the Pythagorean and Platonic schools; finally he declares the writings of Numenius, Cronius, Moderatus, and Thrasyllus greatly inferior in precision and fullness to those of Plotinus.

Notice, by the way, that while Amelius is described as following in Plotinus' footsteps, it is indicated that his temperamental prolixity led him to delight in an extravagance of explanation foreign to his master: in the reference to myself, though I was then only at the beginning of my association with Plotinus— 'Basileus of Tyre, my friend as theirs, who has written a good deal, has taken Plotinus as his model'—Longinus recognizes that I entirely avoided Amelius' unphilosophical prolixity and made Plotinus' manner my standard.

Such a pronouncement upon the value of Plotinus' work, coming from so great an authority, the first of critics then as now, must certainly carry weight, and I may remark that if I had been able to confer with him, during such a visit as he proposed, he would not have written to combat doctrines which he had not thoroughly penetrated.

22. But why talk, to use Hesiod's phrase, 'About Oak and Rock'? If we are to accept the evidence of the wise—who could be wiser than a God? And here the witness is the same God that said with truth:

'I have numbered the sands and taken the measure of the sea; I understand the dumb and hear where there has been no speech.'

Apollo was consulted by Amelius, who desired to learn where Plotinus' soul had gone. And Apollo, who uttered of Socrates that great praise, 'Of all men, Socrates the wisest'—you shall hear what a full and lofty oracle Apollo rendered upon Plotinus.

I raise an undying song, to the memory of a gentle friend, a hymn of praise woven to the honey-sweet tones of my lyre under the touch of the golden plectrum.

The Muses, too, I call to lift the voice with me in strains of many-toned exultation, in passion ranging over all the modes of song:

even as of old they raised the famous chant to the glory of Aeacides in the immortal ardours of the Homeric line.

Come, then, Sacred Chorus, let us intone with one great sound the utmost of all song, I Phoebus, Bathychaites, singing in the midst.

Celestial! Man at first but now nearing the diviner ranks! the bonds of human necessity are loosed for you and, strong of heart, you beat your eager way from out the roaring tumult of the fleshly life to the shores of that wave-washed coast free from the thronging of the guilty, thence to take the grateful path of the sinless soul:

where glows the splendour of God, where Right is throned in the stainless place, far from the wrong that mocks at law.

Oft-times as you strove to rise above the bitter waves of this blood-drenched life, above the sickening whirl, toiling in the mid-most of the rushing flood and the unimaginable turmoil, oft-times, from the Ever-Blessed, there was shown to you the Term still close at hand:

Oft-times, when your mind thrust out awry and was like to be rapt down unsanctioned paths, the Immortals themselves prevented, guiding you on the straightgoing way to the celestial spheres, pouring down before you a dense shaft of light that your eyes might see from amid the mournful loom.

Sleep never closed those eyes: high above the heavy murk of the mist you held them; tossed in the welter, you still had vision; still you saw sights many and fair not granted to all that labour in wisdom's quest.

But now that you have cast the screen aside, quitted the tomb that held your lofty soul, you enter at once the heavenly consort:

where fragrant breezes play, where all is unison and winning tenderness and guileless joy, and the place is lavish of the nectar-streams the unfailing Gods bestow, with the blandishments of the Loves, and delicious airs, and tranquil sky:

where Minos and Rhadamanthus dwell, great brethren of the golden race of mighty Zeus; where dwell the just Aeacus, and Plato, consecrated power, and stately Pythagoras and all else that form the Choir of Immortal Love, that share their parentage with the most blessed spirits, there where the heart is ever lifted in joyous festival.

O Blessed One, you have fought your many fights; now, crowned with unfading life, your days are with the Ever-Holy.

Rejoicing Muses, let us stay our song and the subtle windings of our dance; thus much I could but tell, to my golden lyre, of Plotinus, the hallowed soul.

23. Good and kindly, singularly gentle and engaging: thus the oracle presents him, and so in fact we found him. Sleeplessly alert—Apollo tells—pure of soul, ever striving towards the divine which he loved with all his being, he laboured strenuously to free himself and rise above the bitter waves of this blood-drenched life: and this is why to Plotinus—God-like and lifting himself often,

by the ways of meditation and by the methods Plato teaches in the Banquet, to the first and all-transcendent God—that God appeared, the God who has neither shape nor form but sits enthroned above the Intellectual-Principle and all the Intellectual-Sphere.

'There was shown to Plotinus the Term ever near': for the Term, the one end, of his life was to become Uniate, to approach to the God over all: and four times, during the period I passed with him, he achieved this Term, by no mere latent fitness but by the ineffable Act.

To this God, I also declare, I Porphyry, that in my sixty-eighth year I too was once admitted and entered into Union.

We are told that often when he was leaving the way, the Gods set him on the true path again, pouring down before him a dense shaft of light; here we are to understand that in his writing he was overlooked and guided by the divine powers.

'In this sleepless vision within and without,' the oracle says, 'your eyes have beheld sights many and fair not vouchsafed to all that take the philosophic path': contemplation in man may sometimes be more than human, but compare it with the True-Knowing of the Gods and, wonderful though it be, it can never plunge into the depths their divine vision fathoms.

Thus far the Oracle recounts what Plotinus accomplished and to what heights he attained while still in the body: emancipated from the body, we are told how he entered the celestial circle where all is friendship, tender delight, happiness, and loving union with God, where Minos and Rhadamanthus and Aeacus, the sons of God, are enthroned as judges of souls—not, however, to hold him to judgement but as welcoming him to their consort to which are bidden spirits pleasing to the Gods—Plato, Pythagoras, and all the people of the Choir of Immortal Love, there where the blessed spirits have their birth-home and live in days filled full of 'joyous festival' and made happy by the Gods.

24. I have related Plotinus' life; something remains to tell of my revision and arrangement of his writings. This task he himself had imposed upon me during his lifetime and I had pledged myself to him and to the circle to carry it out.

I judged that in the case of treatises which, like these, had been issued without consideration of logical sequence it was best to disregard the time-order.

Apollodorus, the Athenian, edited in ten volumes the collected works of Epicharmus, the comedy writer; Andronicus, the Peripatetic, classified the works of Aristotle and of Theophrastus according to subject, bringing together the discussions of related topics: I have adopted a similar plan.

I had fifty-four treatises before me: I divided them into six sets of nine, an arrangement which pleased me by the happy combination of the perfect number six with the nines: to each such ennead I assigned matter of one general nature, leading off with the themes presenting the least difficulty.

The FIRST ENNEAD, on this method, contains the treatises of a more ethical tendency:

1. On the Animate and the Man.
2. On the Virtues.
3. On Dialectic.
4. On Happiness.
5. Whether Happiness depends on Extension of Time.
6. On Beauty.
7. On the Primal Good and Secondary forms of Good.
8. On Evil.
9. On the Reasoned Withdrawal from Life.

The SECOND ENNEAD, following the more strictly ethical First, is physical, containing the disquisitions on the world and all that belongs to the world:

1. On the World.
2. On the Circular Movement.
3. Whether the Stars have Causal Operation.
4. On the Two Orders of Matter.
5. On Potentiality and Actuality.
6. On Quality and Form.
7. On Coalescence.
8. Why Distant Objects appear Small.
9. Against those Declaring the Creator of the World, and the World itself, to be Evil.

The THIRD ENNEAD, still keeping to the World, discusses the philosophical implications of some of its features:

1. On Fate.
2. The First Treatise on Providence.
3. The Second Treatise on Providence.
4. On Our Tutelary Spirit.
5. On Love.
6. On the Impassibility of the Bodiless.
7. On Eternity and Time.
8. On Nature, Contemplation, and The One.
9. Various Questions.

25. These first three Enneads constitute in my arrangement one self-contained section.

The treatise on Our Tutelary Spirit is placed in the Third Ennead because this Spirit is not discussed as it is in itself, and the essay by its main content falls into the class dealing with the origin of man. Similar reasons determined the inclusion in this set of the treatise on Love. That on Eternity and Time is placed in this Third Ennead in virtue of its treatment of Time: that on Nature, Contemplation, and The One, because of the discussion of Nature contained in it.

Next to the two dealing with the world comes the FOURTH ENNEAD containing the treatises dealing with the Soul:

1. On the Essence of the Soul (I).
2. On the Essence of the Soul (II).
3. Questions referring to the Soul (I).
4. Questions referring to the Soul (II).
5. Questions referring to the Soul (III); or, On Vision.
6. On Sensation and Memory.
7. On the Immortality of the Soul.
8. On the Descent of the Soul into Bodies.
9. Whether all Souls are One.

The FIFTH ENNEAD —following upon that dealing with the Soul—contains the treatises upon the Intellectual-Principle, each of which has also some reference to the All-Transcending and to the Intellectual-Principle in the Soul, and to the Ideas:

1. On the three Primal Hypostases.
2. On the Origin and Order of the Post-Primals.
3. On the Conscious Hypostases and the All-Transcending.
4. How the Post-Primal derives from the Primal, and on the One.
5. That the Intelligibles are not outside the Intellectual-Principle, and on the Good.
6. That there is no Intellectual Act in the Principle which transcends the Authentic-Existent; and on the Nature that has the Intellectual Act Primally and that which has it Secondarily.
7. Whether there are Ideas even of Particulars.
8. On Intellectual Beauty.
9. On the Intellectual-Principle, on the Ideas, and on the Authentic-Existent.

26. These Fourth and Fifth Enneads, again, I have arranged in the form of one distinct section.

The last Ennead, the Sixth, constitutes one other section, so that we have the entire work of Plotinus in three sections, the first containing three Enneads, the second two, the third one Ennead.

The content of the third section, that is of the SIXTH ENNEAD, is as follows:

1, 2, 3. On the Kinds of Being.

4, 5. That the Authentic-Existent, one and identical, is everywhere present, integrally.

6. On Numbers.

7. How the Multitude of Ideas Exists; and on the Good.

8. On Free-Will and the Will of The One.

9. On The Good, or The One.

Thus, in sum, I have arranged the fifty-four treatises, constituting Plotinus' entire work, into six sets of nine: to some of the treatises I have further added commentaries—irregularly, as friends asked for enlightenment on this or that point; finally for all the treatises, except that on Beauty, which was not to hand, I have written Summaries which follow the chronological order: in this department of my work besides the Summaries will be found Developments; the numbering of these also adopts the chronological order.

Now I have only to go once more through the entire work, see to the punctuation, and correct any verbal errors; what else has solicited my attention, the reader will discover for himself.

NOTES TO PORPHYRY: ON THE LIFE OF PLOTINUS

1. FIRST EDITION: "How the multitude of Ideas *came into Being...*"

ARMSTRONG: "How the Multitude of the Forms came into being . . ."

TAYLOR: "How the multitude of Ideas subsists . . ."

COMMENT: "Being" and "existence," as technical terms in Platonism, connote different levels of reality. "Being" indicates an order at least logically prior to extension, "existence" an order involved with extension.

2. FIRST EDITION: ". . . and finally that *he bases his universe on the meanest of existents.*"

ARMSTRONG: ". . . that his fundamental principles are the meanest of realities."

GUTHRIE: ". . . that his opinions are impossible."

THE FIRST ENNEAD

FIRST TRACTATE

The Animate and the Man

1. PLEASURE and distress, fear and courage, desire and aversion, where have these affections and experiences their seat?

Clearly, either in the Soul alone, or in the Soul as employing the body, or in some third entity deriving from both. And for this third entity, again, there are two possible modes: it might be either a blend or a distinct form due to the blending.

And what applies to the affections applies also to whatsoever acts, physical or mental, spring from them.

We have, therefore, to examine discursive-reason and the ordinary mental action upon objects of sense, and inquire whether these have the one seat with the affections and experiences, or perhaps sometimes the one seat, sometimes another.

And we must consider also our acts of Intellection, their mode and their seat.

And this very examining principle, which investigates and decides in these matters, must be brought to light.

Firstly, what is the seat of Sense-Perception? This is the obvious beginning since the affections and experiences either are sensations of some kind or at least never occur apart from sensation.

2. This first inquiry obliges us to consider at the outset the nature of the Soul—that is whether a distinction is to be made between Soul and Essential Soul (between an individual Soul and the Soul-Kind in itself).

If such a distinction holds, then the Soul (in man) is some sort of a composite and at once we may agree that it is a recipient and—if only reason allows—that all the affections and experiences really have their seat in the Soul, and with the affections every state and mood, good and bad alike.

But if Soul (in man) and Essential Soul are one and the same, then the Soul will be an Ideal-Form unreceptive of all those activities which it imparts to another Kind but possessing within itself that native Act of its own I which reason manifests.[1]

If this be so, then, indeed, we may think of the Soul as an immortal—if the immortal, the imperishable, must be impassive, giving out something of itself but itself taking nothing from without except for what it receives from the Existents prior to itself, from which Existents, in that they are the nobler, it cannot be sundered.

Now what could bring fear to a nature thus unreceptive of all the outer? Fear demands feeling. Nor is there place for courage: courage implies the presence of danger. And such desires as are satisfied by the filling or voiding of the body, must be proper to something very different from the Soul, to that only which admits of replenishment and voidance.

And how could the Soul lend itself to any admixture? An essential is not mixed. Or to the intrusion of anything alien? If it did, it would be seeking the destruction of its own nature. Pain must be equally far from it. And Grief—how or for what could it grieve? Whatever possesses Existence unalloyed is supremely free, dwelling, unchangeable, within its own peculiar nature. And can any increase bring joy, where nothing, not even anything good, can accrue? What such an Existent is, it is unchangeably.

Thus assuredly Sense-Perception, Discursive-Reasoning, and all our ordinary mentation are foreign to the Essential-Existent: for sensation is a receiving—whether of an Ideal-Form or of a bodily affection—and reasoning and all ordinary mental action deal with sensation.

The question still remains to be examined in the matter of the intellections—whether these are to be assigned to the Soul—and as to Pure-Pleasure (pleasure apart from sense), whether this belongs to the Soul in its solitary state.

3. We may treat of the Soul as in the body—whether it be set above it or actually within it—since the association of the two constitutes the one thing called the living organism, the Animate.

Now from this relation, from the Soul using the body as an instrument, it does not follow that the Soul must share the body's experiences: a man does not himself feel all the experiences of the tools with which he is working.

It may be objected that the Soul must, however, have Sense-Perception since its use of its instrument must acquaint it with the external conditions, and such knowledge comes by way of sense. Thus, it will be argued, the eyes are the instrument of seeing, and seeing may bring distress to the Soul: hence the Soul may feel sorrow and pain and every other affection that belongs to the body; and from this again will spring desire, the Soul seeking the mending of its instrument.

But, we ask, how, possibly, can these affections pass from body to Soul? Body may communicate qualities or conditions to another body: but—body to Soul? Something happens to A; does that make it happen to B? As long as we have agent and instrument, there are two distinct entities; if the Soul uses the body it is separate from it.

But apart from the philosophical separation how does Soul stand to body?

Clearly there is a combination. And for this several modes are possible. There might be a complete coalescence: or Soul might be 'inter-woven' through the body: or it might be an Ideal-Form not separated from the body: or again, an Ideal-Form in governing contact like a pilot. Another possibility is that there might be part of the Soul related to body in one way and another part in another way—the one part separated like the agent or user, the other conjoined in some fashion and ranked with the instrument or thing used.

In this last case it will be the double task of philosophy to direct this lower Soul towards the higher, the agent, and except in so far as the conjunction is absolutely necessary, to sever the agent from the instrument, the body, so that it need not forever have its Act upon or through this inferior.

4. Let us consider, then, the hypothesis of a coalescence.

Now if there is a coalescence, the lower is ennobled, the nobler degraded; the body is raised in the scale of being as made participant in life; the Soul, as associated with death and unreason, is brought lower. How can a lessening of the life-quality produce an increase such as Sense-Perception?

No: the body has acquired life, it is the body that will acquire, with life, sensation and the affections coming by sensation. Desire, then, will belong to the body, as the objects of desire are to be enjoyed by the body. And fear, too, will belong to the body alone; for it is the body's doom to fail of its joys and to perish.

Then again we should have to examine how such a coalescence could be conceived: we might find it impossible: perhaps all this is like announcing the coalescence of things utterly incongruous in kind, let us say of a line with whiteness.

Next for the suggestion that the Soul is interwoven through the body: such a relation would not give woof and warp community of sensation: the inter-woven element might very well suffer no change: the permeating soul might remain entirely untouched by what affects the body—as light goes always free of all it floods—and all the more so, since, precisely, we are asked to consider it as (not confined to any one part but) diffused throughout the entire frame. Under such an interweaving, then, the Soul would not be subjected to the body's affections and experiences.

Let us then suppose Soul to be in body as Ideal-Form in Matter. Now if—the first possibility—the Soul is an essence, a self-existent, it can be present only as a separable form and will therefore all the more decidedly be the Using-Principle (and therefore unaffected).

Suppose, next, the Soul to be present like axe-form on iron: here, no doubt, the form is all important but it is still (not the one member but) the axe, the couplement of iron and form, that effects whatever is effected by the iron thus modified: on this analogy, therefore, we are even more strictly compelled to assign all the experiences of the combination I to the body: yet the body is of a particular kind—'a natural body, having organs (or faculty-instruments), and the potential recipient of life'.[2] I

Compare the passage where we read that 'it is absurd to suppose that the Soul weaves'; equally absurd to think of it as desiring, grieving. All this is rather in the province of something which we may call the Animate.

5. Now this Animate might be merely the body as having life: it might be the Couplement of Soul and body: it might be a third and different entity formed from both.

The Soul in turn—apart from the nature of the Animate—must be either impassive, merely causing Sense-Perception in its yoke-fellow, or sympathetic; and, if sympathetic, it may have identical experiences with its fellow or merely correspondent experiences: desire for example in the Animate may be something quite distinct from the accompanying movement or state in the desiring faculty.

The body, the live-body as we know it, we will consider later.

Let us take first the Couplement of body and Soul. How could suffering, for example, be seated in this Couplement?

It may be suggested that some unwelcome state of the body produces a distress which reaches to a Sensitive-Faculty which in turn merges into Soul. But this account still leaves the origin of the sensation unexplained.

Another suggestion might be that all is due to an opinion or judgement: some evil seems to have befallen the man or a member of his family and this conviction sets up a state of trouble in the body and in the entire Animate. But this account leaves still a question as to the source and seat of the judgement: does it belong to the Soul or to the Couplement? Besides, the judgement that evil is present does not involve the feeling of grief: the judgement might very well arise and the grief by no means follow: one may think oneself slighted and yet not be angry; and the appetite is not necessarily excited by the thought of a pleasure. We are, thus, no nearer than before to any warrant for assigning these affections to the Couplement.

Is it any explanation to say that desire is vested in a Faculty-of-desire and anger in the Irascible-Faculty and, collectively, that all tendency is seated in the Appetitive-Faculty? Such a statement of the facts does not make the affections common I to the Couplement but seats them in the Soul alone: yet the body also must be involved, because[3] if the appetite I is to be stirred, as in the carnal passion, there must be a heating of the blood and the bile, a well-defined state of the body. On the other hand, the impulse towards The Good cannot be a joint affection, but, like certain others too, it would belong necessarily to the Soul alone.

❚ There is, accordingly, a theory which refuses[4] to assign ❚ all the affections to the Couplement.

In the case of carnal desire, it will certainly be the Man that desires, and yet, on the other hand, there must be desire in the Desiring-Faculty as well. How can this be? Are we to suppose that, when the man originates the desire, the Desiring-Faculty moves to the order? How could the Man have come to desire at all unless through a prior activity in the Desiring-Faculty? Then it is the Desiring-Faculty that takes the lead? Yet how, unless the body be first in the appropriate condition?

6. It may seem reasonable to lay down as a law that when any powers are contained by a recipient, every action or state expressive of them must be the action or state of that recipient, they themselves remaining unaffected as merely furnishing efficiency.

But if this were so, then, since the Animate is the recipient of the Causing-Principle (i.e., the Soul) which brings life to the Couplement, this Cause must itself remain unaffected, all the experiences and expressive activities of the life being vested in the recipient, the Animate.

But this would mean that life itself belongs not to the Soul but to the Couplement; or at least the life of the Couplement would not be the life of the Soul; Sense-Perception would belong not to the Sensitive-Faculty but to the container of the faculty.

❚ But if sensation is a movement traversing the body and culminating in Soul, how can the Soul lack sensation? The very presence of the Sensitive-Faculty must assure sensation—

Yes, but not to the Soul: rather to the Couplement.[5]

Yet how ❚ can the Couplement have sensation independently of action in the Sensitive-Faculty, the Soul left out of count and the Soul-Faculty?

7. The truth lies in the consideration that the Couplement subsists by the virtue of the Soul's presence.

This, however, is not to say that the Soul gives itself as it is in itself to form either the Couplement or the body.

No; from the organized body and something else, let us say a light, which the Soul gives forth from itself, it forms a distinct Principle, the Animate; and in this Principle are vested Sense-Perception and all the other experiences found to belong to the Animate.

But the 'We'? How have We Sense-Perception?

By the fact that We are not separate from the Animate so constituted, even though certainly other and nobler elements go to make up the entire many-sided nature of Man.

The faculty of perception in the Soul cannot act by the immediate grasping of sensible objects, but only by the discerning of impressions printed upon the Animate by sensation: these impressions are already Intelligibles, while the outer sensation is a mere phantom of the other (of that in the Soul) which is nearer to Authentic-Existence as being an impassive reading of pure Ideal-Forms.

And by means of these Ideal-Forms, by which the Soul wields single lordship over the Animate, we have Discursive-Reasoning, Sense-Knowledge, and Intellection. From this moment we have peculiarly the We: before this there was only the 'Ours'; but at this stage stands the We (the authentic Human-Principle) loftily presiding over the Animate.

There is no reason why the entire compound entity should not be described as the Animate or Living-Being—mingled in a lower phase, but above that point the beginning of the veritable man, distinct from all that is kin to the lion, all that is of the order of the multiple brute. And since The Man, so understood, is essentially the associate of the reasoning Soul, in our reasoning it is this 'We' that reasons, in that the use and act of reason is a characteristic Act of the Soul.

8. And towards the Intellectual-Principle what is our relation? By this I mean, not that faculty in the soul which is one of the emanations from the Intellectual-Principle, but The Intellectual-Principle itself (Divine-Mind).

This also we possess as the summit of our being. And we have It either as common to all or as our own immediate possession: or again we may possess It in both degrees, that is in common, since It is indivisible—one, everywhere and always Its entire self—and severally in that each personality possesses It entire in the First-Soul (i.e., in the Intellectual as distinguished from the lower phase of the Soul).

Hence we possess the Ideal-Forms also after two modes: in the Soul, as it were unrolled and separate; in the Intellectual-Principle, concentrated, unified.

And how do we possess the Divinity?

In that the Divinity is poised upon the Intellectual-Principle and Authentic-Existence; and We come third in order after these two, for the We is constituted by a union of the supreme, the 'undivided essence' of Soul—we read—and that which is 'divided among bodies'. For, note, we inevitably think of the Soul as being present to bodies in division: in so far as any bodies are Animates, the Soul has given itself to each of the separate material masses, regardless of magnitude;

even in the whole universe it remains one and undivided: say rather that it appears to be present in the bodies by the fact that it shines into them: ⁶ ❙ it makes them living beings not by merging into body but by giving forth, without any change in itself, images or likenesses of itself like one face caught by many mirrors.

The first of these images is (the faculty of) Sense-Perception seated in the Couplement; and from this downwards all the successive images are to be recognized as phases of the Soul in lessening succession from one another, until the series ends in the faculties of generation and growth and of all production of offspring—offspring efficient in its turn, in contradistinction to the engendering Soul which (has no direct action within matter but) produces by mere inclination towards what it fashions.

. That Soul, then, in us, will in its nature stand apart from all that can cause any of the evils which man does or suffers; for all such evil, as we have seen, belongs only to the Animate, the Couplement.

But there is a difficulty in understanding how the Soul can go guiltless if our mentation and reasoning are vested in it: for all this lower kind of knowledge is delusion and is the cause of much of what is evil.

When we have done evil it is because we have been worsted by our baser side—for a man is many—by desire or rage or some evil image: the misnamed reasoning that takes up with the false, in reality fancy, has not stayed for the judgement of the Reasoning-Principle: we have acted at the call of the less worthy, just as in matters of the sense-sphere we sometimes see falsely because we credit only the lower perception, that of the Couplement, without applying the tests of the Reasoning-Faculty.

❙ The Intellectual-Principle either apprehends its object or does not: error is impossible. The same, we must admit, applies to ourselves: either we do or we do not put ourselves in touch with what is object to the Intellectual-Principle, or, more strictly, with the Intellectual-Realm within ourselves:⁷ for it is possible ❙ at once to possess and not to use.

Thus we have marked off what belongs to the Couplement from what stands by itself: the one group has the character of body and never exists apart from body, while all that has no need of body for its manifestation belongs peculiarly to Soul: and the Understanding, as passing judgement upon Sense-Impressions, is at the point of the vision of Ideal-Forms, seeing them as it were with an answering sensation (i.e., with consciousness); this last is at any rate true of the Understanding in the Veritable Soul. For Understanding, the true, is the Act of the Intellections: in many of its manifestations it is the assimilation and reconciliation of the outer to the inner.

Thus in spite of all, the Soul is at peace as to itself and within itself: all the changes and all the turmoil we experience are the issue of what is subjoined to the Soul, and are, as we have said, the states and experiences of this elusive 'Couplement'.

10. It will be objected, that if the Soul constitutes the We (the personality) and We are subject to these states, then the Soul must be subject to them, and similarly that what We do must be done by the Soul.

But it has been observed that the Couplement, too—especially before our emancipation—is a member of this total We, and in fact what the body experiences we say We experience. This We, then, covers two distinct notions; sometimes it includes the brute-part, sometimes it transcends the brute. Brute means body touched to life; the true man is the other, going pure of the body, natively endowed with the virtues which belong to the Intellectual-Activity, virtues whose seat is the Separate Soul, the Soul which even in its dwelling here may be kept apart. (This Soul constitutes the human being) for when it has wholly withdrawn, that other Soul which is a radiation (or emanation) from it withdraws also, drawn after it.

Those virtues, on the other hand, which spring not from contemplative wisdom but from custom or practical discipline belong to the Couplement: to the Couplement, too, belong the vices; they are its repugnances, desires, sympathies.

And Friendship?

This emotion belongs sometimes to the lower part, sometimes to the interior man.

11. In childhood the main activity is in the Couplement, and there is but little irradiation from the higher principles of our being: but when these higher principles act but feebly or rarely upon us their action is directed towards the Supreme; they work upon us only when they stand at the mid-point.

But does not the We include that phase of our being which stands above the mid-point?

It does, but on condition that we lay hold of it: our entire nature is not ours at all times but only as we direct the mid-point upwards or downwards, or lead some particular phase of our nature from potentiality or native character into act.

And the animals, in what way or degree do they possess the Animate?

If there be in them, as the opinion goes, human Souls that have sinned, then the Animating-Principle in its separable phase does not enter directly into the brute; it is there but not there to them; they are aware only of the image of the

Soul (only of the lower Soul) and of that only by being aware of the body organized and determined by that image.

If there be no human Soul in them, the Animate is constituted for them by a radiation from the All-Soul.

12. But if Soul is sinless, how come the expiations? Here surely is a contradiction; on the one side the Soul is above all guilt; on the other, we hear of its sin, its purification, its expiation; it is doomed to the lower world, it passes from body to body.

We may take either view at will: they are easily reconciled.

When we tell of the sinless Soul we make Soul and Essential-Soul one and the same: it is the simple unbroken Unity.

By the Soul subject to sin we indicate a groupment, we include that other, that phase of the Soul which knows all the states and passions: the Soul in this sense is compound, all-inclusive: it falls under the conditions of the entire living experience: this compound it is that sins, it is this, and not the other, that pays penalty.

It is in this sense that we read of the Soul: 'We saw it as those others saw the sea-god Glaukos.' 'And', reading on, 'if we mean to discern the nature of the Soul we must strip it free of all that has gathered about it, I must see into its love of wisdom,[8] examine I with what Existences it has touch and by kinship to what Existences it is what it is.'

Thus the life and activities of the Soul are not those of the Expiator. The retreat and sundering, then, must be not from this body only, but from every alien accruement. Such accruement takes place at birth; or rather birth is the coming-into-being of that other (lower) phase of the Soul. For the meaning of birth has been indicated elsewhere; it is brought about by a descent of the Soul, something being given off by the Soul and coming down in the declension.

Then the Soul has let this image fall? And this declension, is it not certainly sin?

If the declension is no more than the illuminating of an object beneath, it constitutes no sin: the shadow is to be attributed not to the luminary but to the object illuminated; if the object were not there, the light could cause no shadow.

And the Soul is said to go down, to decline, only in that the object it illuminates lives by its life. And it lets the image fall only if there be nothing near to take it up; and it lets it fall, not as a thing cut off, but as a thing that ceases to be: the image has no further being when the whole Soul is looking toward the Supreme.

The poet, too, in the story of Hercules, seems to give this image separate existence; he puts the shade of Hercules in the lower world and Hercules himself among the gods: treating the hero as existing in the two realms at once, he gives us a twofold Hercules.

It is not difficult to explain this distinction. Hercules was a hero of practical virtue. By his noble serviceableness he was worthy to be a God. On the other hand, his merit was action and not the Contemplation which would place him unreservedly in the higher realm. Therefore while he has place above, something of him remains below.

13. And the principle that reasons out these matters? Is it We or the Soul?

We, but by the Soul.

But how 'by the Soul'? I Does this mean that we reason by the fact of possessing Soul?[9]

No; by the fact I of being Soul. Its Act subsists without movement; or any movement that can be ascribed to it must be utterly distinct from all corporal movement and be simply the Soul's own life.

And Intellection in us is twofold: since the Soul is intellective, and Intellection is the highest phase of life, we have Intellection both by the characteristic Act of our Soul and by the Act of the Intellectual-Principle upon us—for this Intellectual-Principle is part of us no less than the Soul, and towards it we are ever rising.

NOTES TO ENNEAD I.1

1. FIRST EDITION: "... which *Reason* manifests." Apparently MacKenna hoped that the capital "R" would distinguish the classical Greek usage of reason as *dianoia* from the common contemporary usage that equates it with the mere exercise of logic.

2. FIRST EDITION: " ... to the body: *their natural seat is the material member, the instrument,* the potential recipient of life *(and not the Life-Principle itself)."*

ARMSTRONG: "... to the body, but to a body 'of a specific kind,' 'formed by nature,' 'adapted to the use of the soul,' 'having life potentially.'"

GUTHRIE: "... to the body, which is an organized physical tool possessing potential life."

3. FIRST EDITION: "... to the Couplement; *they might still be seated either* in the Soul alone *or in the body alone. On the one hand* if the appetite ..."

ARMSTRONG: "But then they are no longer common to body and soul but belong to soul alone. Or do they belong to the body too, because blood and bile ..."

GUTHRIE: "But even so, they will not be common, and they will belong exclusively to the soul, or to the body."

4. FIRST EDITION: "*Reason, then, does not permit us* to assign ..."

ARMSTRONG: "... a reasoned examination does not attribute them all to the joint entity."

GUTHRIE: "Reason, therefore, does not allow us ..."

5. FIRST EDITION: "But if sensation is a movement traversing the body and culminating in Soul, how can the soul lack sensation? The very presence of the Sensitive-Faculty must assure sensation *to the Soul.*

"*Once again, where is Sense-Perception seated?*

"*In the Couplement.*

"Yet how . . ."

ARMSTRONG: "But if sense-perception is a movement through the body which ends in the soul, how will the soul not perceive? When the power of sense-perception is present the compound will perceive whatever it perceives by its presence. But if the power is not going to be moved, how will it still be the compound that perceives if neither soul nor soul-power are reckoned as included in it?"

GUTHRIE: "If, however, sensation, which is no more than a corporeal emotion, finds its term in the soul, the soul must surely feel sensation; therefore it does not occur as an effect of the presence of the faculty of sensation, for this ignores the feeling agent back of it. Nor is it the conjunction of soul and body, for unless the faculty of sensation operate, that aggregate could not feel, and it would then no longer include as elements either the soul, or the faculty of sensation."

6. FIRST EDITION: "For, note, we inevitably think of the Soul, *though one and undivided in the All,* as being present to bodies in division: in so far as any bodies are Animates, the Soul has given itself to each of the separate material masses; [*omits section*] or rather it appears to be present in the bodies by the fact that it shines into them: . . ."

ARMSTRONG: ". . . we must consider this part of soul as being divided in bodies in the sense that it gives itself to the magnitudes of bodies, in proportion to the size of each living being, since it gives itself to the whole universe, though the soul is one: or because it is pictured as being present to bodies since it shines into them . . ."

GUTHRIE: "She is indeed divisible in regard to the bodies, since she permeates each of them as far as they live; but at the same time she is indivisible because she is one in the universe. She seems to be present in the bodies, and illuminates them, making living beings out of them."

COMMENT: Anthony Damiani's interpretation of this passage emphasizes the dimensionless omnipresence of soul for each and all of nature's manifestations. That is, just as the whole of the mind is present in each thought—whether the thought of a pinhead or the thought of the vast sky—so the whole of the soul is present in each living being. In this sense soul is both divided and undivided.

7. FIRST EDITION: "The Intellectual-Principle *has held aloof from the act and so is guiltless; or, as we may state it, all depends on whether we ourselves have or have not put ourselves in touch with the Intellectual-Realm either in the Intellectual-Principle or within ourselves;* for it is possible . . ."

ARMSTRONG: "The intellect is either in touch with the proceedings or it is not, and so is sinless: but we ought rather to say that we are in touch with the intelligible in the intellect or we are not—with the intelligible in ourselves;"

GUTHRIE: "In this case did the intellect grasp the object itself? Certainly not; and, therefore, it is not the intellect that is responsible for the error. We say as much for the 'we', according as we will or will not have perceived the object, either in the intellect, or in ourselves; . . ."

8. FIRST EDITION: ". . . must see into *the philosophy of it,* examine . . ."

ARMSTRONG: ". . . and 'look at its philosophy,' . . ."

GUTHRIE: ". . . especially consider her philosophic love for truth . . ."

9. FIRST EDITION: "Does this mean that *the Soul reasons by possession (by contact with the matters of enquiry)?*
"No; by the fact . . ."

GUTHRIE: "The cause of this is, not we who consider the soul because we possess her, but that the soul considers herself."

ARMSTRONG: "Did 'we' investigate by having soul? No, but in so far as we *are* soul."

SECOND TRACTATE

The Virtues

1. Since Evil is here, 'haunting this world by necessary law', and it is the Soul's design to escape from Evil, we must escape hence.

But what is this escape?

'In attaining Likeness to God', we read. And this is explained as 'becoming just and holy, living by wisdom', the entire nature grounded in Virtue.

But does not Likeness by way of Virtue imply Likeness to some being that has Virtue? To what Divine Being, then, would our Likeness be? To the Being— must we not think?—in Which, above all, such excellence seems to inhere, that is to the Soul of the I Cosmos[1]I and to the Principle ruling within it, the Principle endowed with a wisdom most wonderful. What could be more fitting than that we, living in this world, should become Like to its ruler?

But, at the beginning, we are met by the doubt whether even in this Divine-Being all the virtues find place—Moral-Balance (Sophrosyny), for example; or Fortitude where there can be no danger since nothing is alien; where there can be nothing alluring whose lack could induce the desire of possession.

If, indeed, that aspiration towards the Intelligible which is in our nature exists also in this Ruling-Power, then we need not look elsewhere for the source of order and of the virtues in ourselves.

But does this Power possess the Virtues?

We cannot expect to find There what are called the Civic Virtues, the Prudence which belongs to the reasoning faculty; the Fortitude which conducts the emotional and passionate nature; the Sophrosyny which consists in a certain pact, in a concord between the passionate faculty and the reason; or Rectitude which is the due application of all the other virtues as each in turn should command or obey.

Is Likeness, then, attained, perhaps, not by these virtues of the social order but by those greater qualities known by the same general name? And if so do the Civic Virtues give us no help at all?

It is against reason utterly to deny Likeness by these while admitting it by the greater: tradition at least recognizes certain men of the civic excellence as divine, and we must believe that these too had in some sort attained Likeness: on both levels there is virtue for us, though not the same virtue.

Now, if it be admitted that Likeness is possible, though by a varying use of different virtues and though the civic virtues do not suffice, there is no reason why we should not, by virtues peculiar to our state, attain Likeness to a model in which virtue has no place.

But is that conceivable?

When warmth comes in to make anything warm, must there needs be something to warm the source of the warmth?

If a fire is to warm something else, must there be a fire to warm that fire?

Against the first illustration it may be retorted that the source of the warmth does already contain warmth, not by an infusion but as an essential phase of its nature, so that, if the analogy is to hold, the argument would make Virtue something communicated to the Soul but an essential constituent of the Principle from which the Soul attaining Likeness absorbs it.

Against the illustration drawn from the fire, it may be urged that the analogy would make that Principle identical with virtue, whereas we hold it to be something higher.

The objection would be valid if what the Soul takes in were one and the same with the source, but in fact virtue is one thing, the source of virtue is quite another. The material house is not identical with the house conceived in the intellect, and yet stands in its likeness: the material house has distribution and order while the pure idea is not constituted by any such elements; distribution, order, symmetry are not parts of an idea.

So with us: it is from the Supreme that we derive order and distribution and harmony, which are virtues in this sphere: the Existences There, having no need of harmony, order, or distribution, have nothing to do with virtue; and, none the less, it is by our possession of virtue that we become like to Them.

Thus much to show that the principle that we attain Likeness by virtue in no way involves the existence of virtue in the Supreme. But we have not merely to make a formal demonstration: we must persuade as well as demonstrate.

2. First, then, let us examine those good qualities by which we hold Likeness comes, and seek to establish what is this thing which, as we possess it, in transcription, is virtue, but as the Supreme possesses it, is in the nature of an exemplar or archetype and is not virtue.

We must first distinguish two modes of Likeness.

There is the likeness demanding an identical nature in the objects which, further, must draw their likeness from a common principle: and there is the case in which B resembles A, but A is a Primal, not concerned about B and not said to resemble B. In this second case, likeness is understood in a distinct sense: we no longer look for identity of nature, but on the contrary, for divergence, since the likeness has come about by the mode of difference.

What, then, precisely is Virtue, collectively and in the particular? The clearer method will be to begin with the particular, for so the common element by which all the forms hold the general name will readily appear.

The Civic Virtues, on which we have touched above, are a principle of order and beauty in us as long as we remain passing our life here: they ennoble us by setting bound and measure to our desires and to our entire sensibility, and dispelling false judgement—and this by sheer efficacy of the better, by the very setting of the bounds, by the fact that the measured is lifted outside of the sphere of the unmeasured and lawless.

And, further, these Civic Virtues—measured and ordered themselves and acting as a principle of measure to the Soul which is as Matter to their forming— are like to the measure reigning in the over-world, and they carry a trace of that Highest Good in the Supreme; for, while utter measurelessness is brute Matter and wholly outside of Likeness, any participation in Ideal-Form produces some corresponding degree of Likeness to the formless Being There. And participation goes by nearness: the Soul nearer than the body, therefore closer akin, participates more fully and shows a godlike presence, almost cheating us into the delusion that in the Soul we see God entire.

This is the way in which men of the Civic Virtues attain Likeness.

3. We come now to that other mode of Likeness which, we read, is the fruit of the loftier virtues: discussing this we shall penetrate more deeply into the essence of the Civic Virtue and be able to define the nature of the higher kind whose existence we shall establish beyond doubt.

To Plato, unmistakably, there are two distinct orders of virtue, and the civic does not suffice for Likeness: 'Likeness to God', he says, 'is a flight from this world's ways and things': in dealing with the qualities of good citizenship he does not use the simple term Virtue but adds the distinguishing word 'civic': and elsewhere he declares all the virtues without exception to be purifications.

But in what sense can we call the virtues purifications, and how does purification issue in Likeness?

As the Soul is evil by being interfused with the body and by coming to share the body's states and to think the body's thoughts, so it would be good, it would be possessed of virtue, if it threw off the body's moods and devoted itself to its own Act—the state of Intellection and Wisdom—never allowed the passions of the body to affect it—the virtue of Sophrosyny—knew no fear at the parting from the body—the virtue of Fortitude—and if reason and the Intellectual-Principle ruled without opposition—in which state is Righteousness. Such a disposition in the Soul, become thus intellective and immune to passion, it would not be wrong to call Likeness to God; for the Divine, too, is pure and the Divine-Act is such that Likeness to it is Wisdom.

But would not this make virtue a state of the Divine also?

No: the Divine has no states; the state is in the Soul. The Act of Intellection in the Soul is not the same as in the Divine: I of things in the Supreme, one (the Intellectual-Principle) has a different mode of intellection (from that of Soul), the other (the Absolute One) has none at all.[2]I

Then yet again, the one word, Intellection, covers two distinct Acts?

Rather there is primal Intellection and there is Intellection deriving from the Primal and of other scope.

As speech is the echo of the thought in the Soul, so thought in the Soul is an echo from elsewhere: that is to say, as the uttered thought is an image of the soul-thought, so the soul-thought images a thought above itself and is the interpreter of the higher sphere.

Virtue, in the same way, is a thing of the Soul: it does not belong to the Intellectual-Principle or to the Transcendence.

4. We come, so, to the question whether Purification is the whole of this human quality, virtue, or merely the forerunner upon which virtue follows? Does virtue imply the achieved state of purification or does the mere process suffice to it, Virtue being something of less perfection than the accomplished pureness which is almost the Term?

To have been purified is to have cleansed away everything alien: but Goodness is something more.

If before the impurity entered there was Goodness, the cleansing suffices; but even so, not the act of cleansing but the cleansed thing that emerges will be The Good. And it remains to establish what (in the case of the cleansed Soul) this emergent is.

It can scarcely prove to be The Good: The Absolute Good cannot be thought to have taken up its abode with Evil. We can think of it only as something of the nature of good but paying a double allegiance and unable to rest in the Authentic Good.

The Soul's true Good is in devotion to the Intellectual-Principle, its kin; evil to the Soul lies in frequenting strangers. There is no other way for it than to purify itself and so enter into relation with its own; the new phase begins by a new orientation.

After the Purification, then, there is still this orientation to be made? No: by the purification the true alignment stands accomplished.

The Soul's virtue, then, is this alignment? No: it is what the alignment brings about within.

And this is . . . ?

That it sees; that, like sight affected by the thing seen, the Soul admits the imprint, graven upon it and working within it, of the vision it has come to.

But was not the Soul possessed of all this always, or had it forgotten?

What it now sees, it certainly always possessed, but as lying away in the dark, not as acting within it: to dispel the darkness, and thus come to the knowledge of its inner content, it must thrust towards the light.

Besides, it possessed not the originals but images, pictures; and these it must bring into closer accord with the verities they represent. And, further, if the Intellectual-Principle is said to be a possession of the Soul, this is only in the sense that It is not alien and that the link becomes very close when the Soul's sight is turned towards It: otherwise, ever-present though It be, It remains foreign, just as our knowledge, if it does not determine action, is dead to us.

5. So we come to the scope of the purification: that understood, the nature of Likeness becomes clear. Likeness to what principle? Identity with what God?

The question is substantially this: how far does purification dispel the two orders of passion—anger, desire, and the like, with grief and its kin—and in what degree the disengagement from the body is possible.

Disengagement means simply that the Soul withdraws to its own place.

It will hold itself above all passions and affections. Necessary pleasures and all the activity of the senses it will employ only for medicament and assuagement lest its work be impeded. Pain it may combat, but, failing the cure, it will bear meekly and ease it by refusing to assent to it. All passionate action it will check: the suppression will be complete if that be possible, but at worst the Soul will never itself take fire but will keep the involuntary and uncontrolled outside its own precincts and rare and weak at that. The Soul has nothing to dread, though no doubt the involuntary has some power here too: fear therefore must cease, except so far as it is purely monitory. What desire there may be can never be for the vile; even the food and drink necessary for restoration will lie outside the Soul's attention, and not less the sexual appetite: or if such desire there must be, it will turn upon the actual needs of the nature and be entirely under control; or if any uncontrolled motion takes place, it will reach no further than the imagination, be no more than a fleeting fancy.

The Soul itself will be inviolately free and will be working to set the irrational part of the nature above all attack, or if that may not be, then at least to preserve it from violent assault, so that any wound it takes may be slight and be healed at once by virtue of the Soul's presence; just as a man living next door to a ❙ Proficient³❙ would profit by the neighbourhood, either in becoming wise and good himself or, for sheer shame, never venturing any act which the nobler mind would disapprove.

There will be no battling in the Soul: the mere intervention of Reason is enough: the lower nature will stand in such awe of Reason that for any slightest movement it has made it will grieve, and censure its own weakness, in not having kept low and still in the presence of its lord.

6. In all this there is no sin—there is only matter of discipline—but our concern is not merely to be sinless but to be God.

As long as there is any such involuntary action, the nature is twofold, God and Demi-God, or rather God in association with a nature of a lower power: when all the involuntary is suppressed, there is God unmingled, a Divine Being of those that follow upon The First.

For, at this height, the man is the very being that came from the Supreme. The primal excellence restored, the essential man is There: entering this sphere, he has associated himself with a lower phase of his nature but even this he will lead up into likeness with his highest self, as far as it is capable, so that if possible it shall never be inclined to, and at the least never adopt, any course displeasing to its over-lord.

What form, then, does each virtue take in one so lofty?

❙ Wisdom and understanding consist in the contemplation of all that exists in the Intellectual-Principle, and the Intellectual-Principle itself apprehends this all (not by contemplation but) as an immediate presence.

And each of these has two modes according as it exists in the Intellectual-Principle and in the Soul: in the Soul it⁴ is Virtue, in the Supreme not Virtue. ❙

In the Supreme, then, what is it?

Its proper Act and Its Essence.

That Act and Essence of the Supreme, manifested in a new form, constitute the virtue of this sphere. For the Ideal-Form of Justice or of any other virtue is not itself a virtue, but, so to speak, an exemplar, the source of what in the Soul becomes virtue: for virtue is dependent, seated in something not itself; the Ideal-Form is self-standing, independent.

But taking Rectitude to be the due ordering of faculty, does it not always imply the existence of diverse parts?

No: there is a Rectitude of Diversity appropriate to what has parts, but there is another, not less Rectitude than the former though it resides in a Unity. And the authentic Absolute-Rectitude is the Act of a Unity upon itself, of a Unity in which there is no this and that and the other.

On this principle, the supreme Rectitude of the Soul is that it direct its Act towards the Intellectual-Principle: its Restraint (Sophrosyny) is its inward bending towards the Intellectual-Principle; its Fortitude is its being impassive in the likeness of That towards Which its gaze is set, Whose nature comports an impassivity which the Soul acquires by virtue and must acquire if it is not to be at the mercy of every state arising in its less noble companion.

7. The virtues in the Soul run in a sequence correspondent to that existing in the over-world, that is among their exemplars in the Intellectual-Principle.

In the Supreme, Intellection constitutes Knowledge and Wisdom; self-concentration is Sophrosyny; Its proper Act is Its Dutifulness; Its Immateriality, by which It remains inviolate within Itself, is the equivalent of Fortitude.

In the Soul, the direction of vision towards the Intellectual-Principle is Wisdom and Prudence, ❙ soul-virtues but not identified with Soul: the identification comes about in[5] the Supreme (where Thinker and Thought are identical).❙ All the other virtues have similar correspondences.

And if the term of purification is the production of a pure being, then the purification of the Soul must produce all the virtues; if any are lacking, then not one of them is perfect.

And to possess the greater is potentially to possess the minor, though the minor need not carry the greater with them.

Thus we have indicated the dominant note in the life of a Proficient; but whether with his possession of the major virtues he possesses also the minor either actually or in some other mode, must be decided afresh in each several case.

Take, for example, Contemplative-Wisdom. If other guides of conduct must be called in to meet a given need, can this virtue hold its ground even in mere potentiality?

And what happens when the virtues in their very nature differ in scope and province? Where, for example, one type of Sophrosyny would allow certain acts or emotions under due restraint and another would cut them off altogether? And is it not clear that the other virtues may similarly have to yield, once Contemplative-Wisdom comes into action?

The solution is in understanding the virtues and what each has to give: thus the man will learn to work with this or that as every several need demands. And as he reaches to loftier principles and other standards these in turn will define his conduct: for example, Restraint in its earlier form will no longer satisfy him; he will work for the final Disengagement; he will live, no longer, the human life of the good man—such as Civic Virtue commends—but, leaving this beneath him, will take up instead another life, that of the Gods.

For it is to the Gods, not to the good, that our Likeness must look: to model ourselves upon good men is to produce an image of an image: we have to fix our gaze above the image and attain Likeness to the Supreme Exemplar.

NOTES TO ENNEAD I.2

1. MACKENNA used spelling "Kosmos" throughout: was this an attempt to evoke an image of the entire intelligible order implicit in this manifest universe, over and above its quantifiable mass?

2. FIRST EDITION: "... of things in the Supreme, *Soul grasps some after a mode of its own, some not at all.*"

GUTHRIE: "... the soul does not think intelligible objects in the same manner as the divinity; what is contained in the divinity is contained within us in a manner entirely different, or even perhaps is not at all contained."

ARMSTRONG: "The soul's intellectual activity is different: but of the realities There one thinks differently, and the other does not think at all."

TAYLOR: "... of the things which subsist with him [divinity—ed.], some subsist differently from what they do with us, and others are not at all with him."

3. MACKENNA used the word "Sage" rather than "Proficient" throughout.

4. FIRST EDITION answers the preceding question ("What form, then ...") as follows: "*It appears as Wisdom, which consists* in the contemplation of all that exists in the Intellectual-Principle, and *as the immediate presence of the Intellectual-Principle itself.*

"And each of these has two modes *or aspects: there is Wisdom as it is in the Intellectual-Principle and as in the Soul; and there is the Intellectual-Principle as it is present to itself and as it is present to the Soul: this gives what in the Soul* is Virtue, in the Supreme not Virtue."

TAYLOR: "Wisdom, indeed, will consist in the contemplation of what intellect contains. But he will possess intellect by contact. Each of the virtues, however, is twofold; for each is both in intellect and in soul. And in intellect, indeed, each is not [properly] virtue, but virtue is in soul." Brackets are Taylor's.

ARMSTRONG: "Wisdom, theoretical and practical, consists in the contemplation of that which intellect contains; but intellect has it by immediate contact. There are two kinds of wisdom, one in intellect, one in soul. That which is There [in intellect] is not virtue, that in the soul is virtue." Brackets are Armstrong's.

GUTHRIE: "For him, wisdom consists in contemplating the (essences) possessed by Intelligence, and with which Intelligence is in contact. There are two kinds of wisdom, one being proper to intelligence, the other to the soul;"

5. FIRST EDITION: "... soul virtues *not appropriate to* the Supreme where Thinker and Thought are identical."

ARMSTRONG: "In the soul, sight directed towards intellect is wisdom, theoretical and practical; these are virtues belonging to soul; for it is not itself they, as is the case There ..."

GUTHRIE: "To contemplate intelligence will therefore, for the soul, constitute wisdom and prudence, which then become virtues, and no longer remain mere intellectual types. For the soul is not identical with the essences she thinks, as is intelligence."

THIRD TRACTATE

Dialectic [1]

1. What art is there, what method, what discipline to bring us there where we must go?

The Term at which we must arrive we may take as agreed: we have established elsewhere, by many considerations, that our journey is to the Good, to the Primal-Principle; and, indeed, the very reasoning which discovered the Term was itself something like an initiation.

But what order of beings will attain the Term?

Surely, as we read, those that have already seen all or most things, those who at their first birth have entered into the life-germ from which is to spring a metaphysician, a musician, or a born lover, the metaphysician taking to the path by instinct, the musician and the nature peculiarly susceptible to love needing outside guidance.

But how lies the course? Is it alike for all, or is there a distinct method for each class of temperament?

For all there are two stages of the path, as they are making upwards or have already gained the upper sphere.

The first degree is the conversion from the lower life; the second—held by those that have already made their way to the sphere of the Intelligibles, have set as it were a footprint there but must still advance within the realm—lasts until they reach the extreme hold of the place, the Term attained when the topmost peak of the Intellectual realm is won.

But this highest degree must bide its time: let us first try to speak of the initial process of conversion.

We must begin by distinguishing the three types. Let us take the musician first and indicate his temperamental equipment for the task.

The musician we may think of as being exceedingly quick to beauty, drawn in a very rapture to it: somewhat slow to stir of his own impulse, he answers at once to the outer stimulus: as the timid are sensitive to noise so he to tones and the beauty they convey; all that offends against unison or harmony in melodies or rhythms repels him; he longs for measure and shapely pattern.

This natural tendency must be made the starting-point to such a man; he must be drawn by the tone, rhythm, and design in things of sense: he must learn to distinguish the material forms from the Authentic-Existent which is the source of all these correspondences and of the entire reasoned scheme in the work of art: he must be led to the Beauty that manifests itself through these forms; he must be shown that what ravished him was no other than the

Harmony of the Intellectual world and the Beauty in that sphere, not some one shape of beauty but the All-Beauty, the Absolute Beauty; and the truths of philosophy must be implanted in him to lead him to faith in that which, unknowing it, he possesses within himself. What these truths are we will show later.

2. The born lover, to whose degree the musician also may attain—and then either come to a stand or pass beyond—has a certain memory of beauty but, severed from it now, he no longer comprehends it: spellbound by visible loveliness he clings amazed about that. His lesson must be to fall down no longer in bewildered delight before some one embodied form; he must be led, under a system of mental discipline, to **|** physical²**|** beauty everywhere and made to discern the One Principle underlying all, a Principle apart from the material forms, springing from another source, and elsewhere more truly present. The beauty, for example, in a noble course of life and in an admirably organized social system may be pointed out to him—a first training this in the loveliness of the immaterial—he must learn to recognize the beauty in the arts, sciences, virtues; then these severed and particular forms must be brought under the one principle by the explanation of their origin. From the virtues he is to be led to the Intellectual-Principle, to the Authentic-Existent; thence onward, he treads the upward way.

3. The metaphysician, equipped by that very character, winged already and not, like those others, in need of disengagement, stirring of himself towards the supernal but doubting of the way, needs only a guide. **|** He must be shown, then, and set free, willing by his very temperament and long practised in freedom.³**|**

Mathematics, which as a student by nature he will take very easily, will be prescribed to train him to abstract thought and to faith in the unembodied; a moral being by native disposition, he must be led to make his virtue perfect; after the Mathematics he must be put through a course in Dialectic and made an adept in the science.

4. But this science, this Dialectic essential to all the three classes alike, what, in sum, is it?

It is the Method, or Discipline, that brings with it the power of pronouncing with final truth upon the nature and relation of things—what each is, how it differs from others, what common quality all have, to what Kind each belongs and in what rank each stands in its Kind and whether its Being is Real-Being, and how many Beings there are, and how many non-Beings to be distinguished from Beings.

Dialectic treats also of the Good and the not-Good, and of the particulars that fall under each, and of what is the Eternal and what the not-Eternal—and of these, it must be understood, I not by seeming-knowledge (opinion)⁴I but with authentic science.

All this accomplished, it gives up its touring of the realm of sense and settles down in the Intellectual Cosmos and there plies its own peculiar Act: it has abandoned all the realm of deceit and falsity, and pastures the Soul in the 'Meadows of Truth': it employs the Platonic division to the discernment of the Ideal-Forms, of the Authentic-Existence, and of the First-Kinds (or Categories of Being): it establishes, in the light of Intellection, the affiliations of all that issues from these Firsts, until it has traversed the entire Intellectual Realm: then, by means of analysis, it takes the opposite path and returns once more to the First Principle.

Now it rests: caught up in the tranquillity of that sphere, it is no longer busy about many things: it has arrived at Unity and it contemplates: it leaves to another science all that coil of premises and conclusions called the art of reasoning, much as it leaves the art of writing: some of the matter of logic, no doubt, it considers necessary—to clear the ground—but it makes itself the judge, here as in everything else; where it sees use, it uses; anything it finds superfluous, it leaves to whatever department of learning or practice may turn that matter to account.

5. But whence does this science derive its own initial laws?

The Intellectual-Principle furnishes standards, the most certain for any soul that is able to apply them. What else is necessary Dialectic puts together for itself, combining and dividing, until it has reached perfect Intellection. 'For', we read, 'it is the purest (perfection) of Intellection and Contemplative-Wisdom.' And, being the noblest method and science that we have, it must needs deal with Authentic-Existence, The Highest there is: as Contemplative-Wisdom (or true-knowing) it deals with Being, as Intellection with what transcends Being.

What, then, is Philosophy?

Philosophy is the supremely precious.

Is Dialectic, then, the same as Philosophy?

It is the precious part of Philosophy. We must not think of it as the mere tool of the metaphysician: Dialectic does not consist of bare theories and rules: it deals with verities; Existences are, as it were, Matter to it, or at least it proceeds methodically towards Existences, and possesses itself, at the one step, of the notions and of the realities.

Untruth and sophism it knows, not directly, not of its own nature, but merely as something produced outside itself, something which it recognizes to be foreign to the verities laid up in itself; in the falsity presented to it, it perceives a clash with its own canon of truth. Dialectic, that is to say, has no knowledge of propositions—collections of words—but it knows the truth and, in that knowledge, knows what the schools call their propositions: it knows above all the operation of the Soul, and, by virtue of this knowing, it knows, too, what is affirmed and what is denied, whether the denial is of what was asserted or of something else, and whether propositions agree or differ; all that is submitted to it, it attacks with the directness of sense-perception and it leaves petty precisions of process to what other science may care for such exercises.

6. Philosophy has other provinces, but Dialectic is its precious part: in its study of the laws of the universe, Philosophy draws on Dialectic much as other studies and crafts use Arithmetic, though, of course, the alliance between Philosophy and Dialectic is closer.

And in morals, too, Philosophy uses Dialectic: by Dialectic it comes to contemplation, though it originates of itself the moral state or rather the discipline from which the moral state develops.

Our reasoning faculties employ the data of Dialectic almost as their proper possession, for their use of these data commonly involves Matter as well as Form.

And while the other virtues bring the reason to bear upon particular experiences and acts, the virtue of Wisdom (i.e., the virtue peculiarly induced by Dialectic) is a certain super-reasoning much closer to the Universal; for it deals with (such abstract ideas as) correspondence and sequence, the choice of time for action and inaction, the adoption of this course, the rejection of that other: Wisdom and Dialectic have the task of presenting all things as Universals and stripped of matter for treatment by the Understanding.

But can these inferior kinds of virtue exist without Dialectic and philosophy?

Yes—but imperfectly, inadequately.

And is it possible to be a Proficient,[5] a Master in Dialectic, without these lower virtues?

It would not happen: the lower will spring either before or together with the higher. And it is likely that everyone normally possesses the natural virtues from which, when Wisdom steps in, the perfected virtue develops. After the natural virtues, then, Wisdom, and so the perfecting of the moral nature. Once the natural virtues exist, both orders, the natural and the higher, ripen side by side to their final excellence: or as the one advances it carries forward the other towards perfection.

But, ever, the natural virtue is imperfect in vision and in strength—and to both orders of virtue the essential matter is from what principles we derive them.

NOTES TO ENNEAD I.3

1. FIRST EDITION title: "On Dialectic (The Upward Way)"

2. FIRST EDITION omits "physical."

ARMSTRONG, TAYLOR, and GUTHRIE, however, all support its insertion.

3. FIRST EDITION: "He must be shown, then, and *instructed, a willing wayfarer* by his very temperament, *all but self-directed.*"

TAYLOR: "The path, therefore, must be shown to him, and he must be liberated, since he is naturally willing, and was formerly freed [from the fetters of a corporeal nature]." Brackets are Taylor's.

ARMSTRONG: "So he must be shown and set free, with his own good will, he who has long been free by nature."

GUTHRIE: "He must therefore be shown the road; he must be helped to detach himself entirely from sense-objects, himself already possessing, as he does, the desire, being since a long while already detached therefrom by his nature."

4. FIRST EDITION: ". . . not by seeming-knowledge ('*sense-knowledge*') . . ."

COMMENT: "Opinion" is a technical term in Platonism, derived from Plato's 4-fold divided line. It corresponds to the level of "sense-knowledge," which is higher than fantasy and lower than both dianoetic reasoning and intellectual intuition. GUTHRIE, TAYLOR, and ARMSTRONG all use the term "opinion."

5. FIRST EDITION: "*Sage*"

FOURTH TRACTATE

Happiness[1]

1. Are we to make True Happiness one and the same thing with Welfare or Prosperity and therefore within the reach of the other living beings as well as ourselves?

There is certainly no reason to deny well-being to any of them as long as their lot allows them to flourish unhindered after their kind.

Whether we make Welfare consist in pleasant conditions of life, or in the accomplishment of some appropriate task, by either account it may fall to them as to us. For certainly they may at once be pleasantly placed and engaged about some function that lies in their nature: take for an instance such living beings as have the gift of music; finding themselves well off in other ways, they sing, too, as their nature is, and so their day is pleasant to them.

And if, even, we set Happiness in some ultimate Term pursued by inborn tendency, then on this head, too, we must allow it to animals from the moment of their attaining this Ultimate: the nature in them comes to a halt, having fulfilled its vital course from a beginning to an end.

It may be a distasteful notion, this bringing-down of happiness so low as to the animal world—making it over, as then we must, even to the vilest of them and not withholding it even from the plants, living they too and having a life unfolding to a Term.

But, to begin with, it is surely unsound to deny that good of life to animals only because they do not appear to man to be of great account. And as for plants, we need not necessarily allow to them what we accord to the other forms of life, since they have no feeling. It is true people might be found to declare prosperity possible to the very plants: they have life, and life may bring good or evil; the plants may thrive or wither, bear or be barren.

No: if Pleasure be the Term, if here be the good of life, it is impossible to deny the good of life to any order of living things; if the Term be inner-peace, equally impossible; impossible, too, if the good of life be to live in accordance with the purpose of nature.

2. Those that deny the happy life to the plants on the ground that they lack sensation are really denying it to all living things.

By sensation can be meant, only, perception of state, and the state of well-being must be a Good in itself quite apart from the perception: to be a part of the natural plan is good whether knowingly or without knowledge: there is good in the appropriate state even though there be no recognition of its fitness or desirable quality—for it must be in itself desirable.

This Good exists, then; is present: that in which it is present has well-being without more ado: what need then to ask for sensation into the bargain?

Perhaps, however, the theory is that the Good of any state consists not in the condition itself but in the knowledge and perception of it.

But at this rate the Good is nothing but the mere sensation, the bare activity of the sentient life. And so it will be possessed by all that feel, no matter what. Perhaps it will be said that two constituents are needed to make up the Good, that there must be both feeling and a given state felt: but how can it be maintained that the bringing together of two neutrals can produce the Good?

They will explain, possibly, that the state must be a state of Good and that such a condition constitutes well-being on the discernment of that present good; but then they invite the question whether the well-being comes by discerning the presence of the Good that is there, or whether there must further be the double recognition that the state is agreeable and that the agreeable state constitutes the Good.

If well-being demands this recognition, it depends no longer upon sensation but upon another, a higher faculty; and well-being is vested not in a faculty receptive of pleasure but in one competent to discern that pleasure is the Good.

Then the cause of the well-being is no longer pleasure but the faculty competent to pronounce as to pleasure's value. Now a judging entity is nobler than one that merely accepts a state: it is a principle of Reason or of Intellection: pleasure is a state: the reasonless can never be closer to the Good than reason is. How can reason abdicate and declare nearer to good than itself something lying in a contrary order?

No: those denying the good of life to the vegetable world, and those that make it consist in some precise quality of sensation, are in reality seeking a loftier well-being than they are aware of, and setting their highest in a more luminous phase of life.

Perhaps, then, those are in the right who found happiness not on the bare living or even on sensitive life but on the life of Reason?

But they must tell us why it should be thus restricted and why precisely they make Reason an essential to the happiness in a living being:

'When you insist on Reason, is it because Reason is resourceful, swift to discern and compass the primal needs of nature; or would you demand it, even though it were powerless in that domain?

'If you call it in as a provider, then the reasonless, equally with the reasoning, may possess happiness after their kind, as long as, without any thought of theirs, nature supplies their wants: Reason becomes a servant; there is no longer any worth in it for itself and no worth in that consummation of reason which, we hold, is virtue.

❙'If you say that reason is to be cherished for its own sake and not as²❙ supplying these human needs, you must tell us what other services it renders, what is its proper nature, and what makes it the perfect thing it is.'

For, on this admission, its perfection cannot reside in any such planning and providing: its perfection will be something quite different, something of quite another class: Reason cannot be itself one of those first needs of nature; it cannot even be a cause of those first needs of nature or at all belong to that order: it must be nobler than any and all of such things: otherwise it is not easy to see how we can be asked to rate it so highly.

Until these people light upon some nobler principle than any at which they still halt, they must be left where they are and where they choose to be, never understanding what the Good of Life is to those that can make it theirs, never knowing to what kind of beings it is accessible.

3. What then is happiness? Let us try basing it upon Life.

Now if we draw no distinction as to kinds of life, everything that lives will be capable of happiness, and those will be effectively happy who possess that one common gift of which every living thing is by nature receptive. We could not deny it to the irrational whilst allowing it to the rational. If happiness were inherent in the bare being-alive, the common ground in which the cause of happiness could always take root would be simply life.

Those, then, that set happiness not in the mere living but in the reasoning life seem to overlook the fact that they are not really making it depend upon life at all: they admit that this reasoning faculty, round which they centre happiness, is a property (not the subject of a property): the subject, to them, must be the Reasoning-Life since it is in this double term that they find the basis of the happiness: so that they are making it consist not in life but in a particular kind of life—not, of course, a species formally opposite but, in our terminology, standing as an 'earlier' to a 'later' in the one Kind.

Now in common use this word 'Life' embraces many forms which shade down from primal to secondary and so on, all massed under the common term—life of plant and life of animal—each phase brighter or dimmer than its next: and so it evidently must be with the Good-of-Life. And if thing is ever the image of thing, so every Good must always be the image of a higher Good.

If mere being is insufficient, if happiness demands fullness of life, and exists, therefore, where nothing is lacking of all that belongs to the idea of life, then happiness can exist only in a being that lives fully.

And such a one will possess not merely the good, but the Supreme Good if, that is to say, in the realm of existents the Supreme Good can be no other than the authentically living, no other than Life in its greatest plenitude, life in which the good is present as something essential not as something brought in from without, a life needing no foreign substance called in from a foreign realm, to establish it in good.

For what could be added to the fullest life to make it the best life? If anyone should answer 'The nature of Good' (The Good, as a Divine Hypostasis), the reply would certainly be near our thought, but we are not seeking the Cause but the main constituent.

It has been said more than once that the perfect life and the true life, the essential life, is in the Intellectual Nature beyond this sphere, and that all other forms of life are incomplete, are phantoms of life, imperfect, not pure, not more truly life than they are its contrary: here let it be said succinctly that since all living things proceed from the one principle but possess life in different degrees, this principle must be the first life and the most complete.

4. If, then, the perfect life is within human reach, the man attaining it attains

happiness: if not, happiness must be made over to the gods, for the perfect life is for them alone.

But since we hold that happiness is for human beings too, we must consider what this perfect life is. The matter may be stated thus:

❘It is beyond doubt[3]❘ that man when he commands not merely the life of sensation but also Reason and Authentic Intellection, has realized the perfect life.

But are we to picture this kind of life as something foreign imported into his nature?

No: there exists no single human being that does not possess this thing either potentially or effectively; to possess it effectively is what we mean by happiness.

But are we to think of man as including this form of life, the perfect, after the manner of a partial constituent of his entire nature?

We say, rather, that while in some men it is present as a mere portion of their total being—in those, namely, that have it potentially—there is, too, the man, already in possession of true felicity, who is this perfection realized, who has passed over into actual identification with it. All else is now mere clothing about the man, not to be called part of him since it lies about him unsought, not his because not appropriated to himself by any act of the will.

To the man in this state, what is the good?

He himself by what he has and is.

And the author and principle of what he is and holds is the Supreme (the One), which within Itself is the Good but manifests Itself within the human being after this other mode.

The sign that this state has been achieved is that the man seeks nothing else.

What indeed could he be seeking? Certainly none of the less worthy things; and the Best he carries always within him.

He that has such a life as this has all he needs in life.

Once the man is a❘Proficient,[4]❘ the means of happiness, the way to good, are within, for nothing is good that lies outside him. Anything he desires further than this he seeks as a necessity, and not for himself but for a subordinate, for the body bound to him, to which since it has life he must minister the needs of life, not needs, however, to the true man of this degree. He knows himself to stand above all such things, and what he gives to the lower he so gives as to leave his true life undiminished.

Adverse fortune does not shake his felicity: the life so founded is stable ever. Suppose death strikes at his household or at his friends; he knows what death is, as the victims, if they are among the wise, know too. And if death taking from him his familiars and intimates does bring grief, it is not to him, not to the true man, but to that in him which stands apart from Intellection, to that lower man in whose distress he takes no part.

5. But what of sorrows, illnesses, and all else that inhibits the native activity?

What of the suspension of consciousness which drugs or disease may bring about? Could either welfare or happiness be present under such conditions? And this is to say nothing of poverty and disgrace, which will certainly be urged against us, with undoubtedly also those never-failing 'Miseries of Priam'.

'The Proficient', we shall be told, 'may bear such afflictions and even take them lightly but they could never be his choice, and the happy life must be one that would be chosen. The Proficient, that is, cannot be thought of as simply a proficient soul, no count being taken of the bodily-principle in the total of the being.' Our critics will in fact profess to accept our teaching readily, provided that we make the body's appeals come up before the inner man, and, conversely, his longings and loathings depend upon the body. 'And since' (they will continue) 'pleasure must be counted in towards the happy life, how can one that thus knows the misery of ill fortune or pain be happy, however proficient he be? Such a state, of bliss self-contained, is for the Gods; men, because of the less noble part subjoined in them, must needs seek happiness throughout all their being and not merely in some one part; if the one constituent be troubled, the other, answering to its associate's distress, must perforce suffer hindrance in its own activity. There is nothing but to cut away the body or the body's sensitive life and so secure that self-contained unity essential to happiness.'

6. Now if happiness did indeed require freedom from pain, sickness, misfortune, disaster, it would be utterly denied to anyone confronted by such trials: but if it lies in the fruition of the Authentic Good, why turn away from this Term and look to means, imagining that to be happy a man must need a variety of things none of which enter into happiness? If, in fact, felicity were made up by heaping together things that are at once desirable and necessary—or perhaps even things that are called desirable without being necessary—we must bid for them all. But if the Term must be one and not many; if in other words our quest is of a Term and not of Terms; that only can be elected which is ultimate and noblest, that which calls to the tenderest longings of the Soul.

The quest and will of the Soul are not pointed directly towards freedom from this sphere: the reason which disciplines away our concern about this life has no fundamental quarrel with things of this order; it merely resents their interference; sometimes, even, it must seek them; essentially all the aspiration is not so much away from evil as towards the Soul's own highest and noblest:

this attained, all is won and there is rest—and this is the veritably willed state of life.

There can be no such thing as 'willing' the acquirement of necessaries, if Will is to be taken in its strict sense, and not misapplied to the mere recognition of need.

It is certain that we shrink from the unpleasant, and such shrinking is assuredly not what we should have willed; to have no occasion for any such shrinking would be much nearer to our taste; but the things we seek tell the story as soon as they are ours. For instance, health and freedom from pain; which of these has any great charm? As long as we possess them, we set no store upon them.

Anything which, present, has no charm and adds nothing to happiness, which when lacking is desired because of the presence of an annoying opposite, may reasonably be called a necessity but not a Good.

Such things can never make part of our final object: our Term must be such that though these pleasanter conditions be absent and their contraries present, it shall remain, still, intact.

7. Then why are these conditions sought and their contraries repelled by the man established in happiness?

Here is our answer:

These more pleasant conditions cannot, it is true, add any particle towards the Proficient's felicity: but they do serve towards the integrity of his being, while the presence of the contraries tends against his being or complicates the Term: it is not that the Proficient can be so easily deprived of the Term achieved but simply that he that holds the highest good desires to have that alone, not something else at the same time, something which, though it cannot banish the Good by its incoming, does yet take place by its side.

In any case if the man that has attained felicity meets some turn of fortune that he would not have chosen, there is not the slightest lessening of his happiness for that. If there were, his felicity would be veering or falling from day to day; the death of a child would bring him down, or the loss of some trivial possession. No: a thousand mischances and disappointments may befall him and leave him still in the tranquil possession of the Term.

But, they cry, great disasters, not the petty daily chances!

What human thing, then, is great, so as not to be despised by one who has mounted above all we know here, and is bound now no longer to anything below?

If the Proficient thinks all fortunate events, however momentous, to be no great matter—kingdom and the rule over cities and peoples, colonizations and the founding of states, even though all be his own handiwork—how can he take any great account of the vacillations of power or the ruin of his fatherland? Certainly if he thought any such event a great disaster, or any disaster at all, he must be of a very strange way of thinking. One that sets great store by wood and stones, or, Zeus! by mortality among mortals cannot yet be the Proficient, whose estimate of death, we hold, must be that it is better than life in the body.

But suppose that he himself is offered a victim in sacrifice?

Can he think it an evil to die beside the altars?

But if he go unburied?

Wheresoever it lie, under earth or over earth, his body will always rot.

But if he has been hidden away, not with costly ceremony but in an unnamed grave, not counted worthy of a towering monument?

The littleness of it!

But if he falls into his enemies' hands, into prison?

There is always the way towards escape, if none towards well-being.

But if his nearest be taken from him, his daughters and daughters-in-law dragged away to captivity?

What then, we ask, if he had died without witnessing the wrong? Could he have quitted the world in the calm conviction that nothing of all this could happen? He must be very shallow. Can he fail to see that it is possible for such calamities to overtake his household, and does he cease to be a happy man for the knowledge of what may occur? In the knowledge of the possibility he may be at ease; as, too, when the evil has come about.

He would reflect that the nature of this All is such as brings these things to pass and man must bow the head.

Besides in many cases captivity will certainly prove an advantage; and those that suffer have their freedom in their hands: if they stay, either there is reason in their staying, and then they have no real grievance, or they stay against reason, when they should not, and then they have themselves to blame. Clearly the absurdities of his neighbours, however near, cannot plunge the Proficient into evil: his state cannot hang upon the fortunes good or bad of any other men.

8. As for violent personal sufferings, he will carry them off as well as he can; if they overpass his endurance they will carry him off.

And so in all his pain he asks no pity: there is always the radiance in the inner soul of the man, untroubled like the light in a lantern when fierce gusts beat about it in a wild turmoil of wind and tempest.

But what if he be put beyond himself? What if pain grow so intense and so torture him that the agony all but kills? Well, when he is put to torture he will plan what is to be done: he retains his freedom of action.

Besides we must remember that the Proficient sees things very differently from the average man; neither ordinary experiences nor pains and sorrows, whether touching himself or others, pierce to the inner hold. To allow them any such passage would be a weakness in our soul.

And it is a sign of weakness, too, if we should think it gain not to hear of miseries, gain to die before they come: this is not concern for others' welfare but for our own peace of mind. Here we see our imperfection: we must not indulge it, we must put it from us and cease to tremble over what perhaps may be.

Anyone that says that it is in human nature to grieve over misfortune to our household must learn that this is not so with all, and that, precisely, it is virtue's use to raise the general level of nature towards the better and finer, above the mass of men. And the finer is to set at nought what terrifies the common mind.

We cannot be indolent: this is an arena for the powerful combatant holding his ground against the blows of fortune, and knowing that, sore though they be to some natures, they are little to his, nothing dreadful, nursery terrors.

So, the Proficient would have desired misfortune?

It is precisely to meet the undesired when it appears that he has the virtue which gives him, to confront it, his passionless and unshakeable soul.

9. But when he is out of himself, reason quenched by sickness or by magic arts?

If it be allowed that in this state, resting as it were in a slumber, he remains a Proficient, why should he not equally remain happy? No one rules him out of felicity in the hours of sleep; no one counts up that time and so denies that he has been happy all his life.

If they say that, failing consciousness, he is no longer the Proficient, then they are no longer reasoning about the Proficient: but we do suppose a Proficient, and are inquiring whether, as long as he is the Proficient, he is in the state of felicity.

'Well, a Proficient let him remain,' they say; 'still, having no sensation and not expressing his virtue in act, how can he be happy?'

But a man unconscious of his health may be, none the less, healthy: a man may not be aware of his personal attraction, but he remains handsome none the less: if he has no sense of his wisdom, shall he be any the less wise?

It may perhaps be urged that sensation and consciousness are essential to wisdom and that happiness is only wisdom brought to act.

Now, this argument might have weight if prudence, wisdom, were something fetched in from outside: but this is not so: wisdom is, in its essential nature, an

Authentic-Existence, or rather is The Authentic-Existent—and this Existent does not perish in one asleep or, to take the particular case presented to us, in the man out of his mind: the Act of this Existent is continuous within him; and is a sleepless activity: the Proficient, therefore, even unconscious, is still the Proficient in Act.

This activity is screened not from the man entire but merely from one part of him: we have here a parallel to what happens in the activity of the physical or vegetative life in us which is not made known by the sensitive faculty to the rest of the man: if our physical life really constituted the 'We', its Act would be our Act: but, in the fact, this physical life is not the 'We'; the 'We' is the activity of the Intellectual-Principle so that when the Intellective is in Act we are in Act.

10. Perhaps the reason this continuous activity remains unperceived is that it has no touch whatever with things of sense. No doubt action upon material things, or action dictated by them, must proceed through the sensitive faculty which exists for that use: but why should there not be an immediate activity of the Intellectual-Principle and of the soul that attends it, the soul that antedates sensation or any perception? For, if Intellection and Authentic-Existence are identical, this 'Earlier-than-perception' must be a thing having Act.

Let us explain the conditions under which we become conscious of this Intellective-Act:

❙The thought-object is deflected and the Intellectual-Principle which is active in the life of the Soul (i.e., the Rational Principle) is, so to speak, thrust back, as an image might be reflected in the smooth and shining and untroubled surface of a mirror; ⁵❙ in this illustration, when the mirror is in place the image appears but, though the mirror be absent or out of gear, all that would have acted and produced an image still exists; so in the case of the Soul; when there is peace in that within us which is capable of reflecting the images of the Rational and Intellectual-Principles these images appear. Then, side by side with the primal knowledge of the activity of the Rational and the Intellectual-Principles, we have also as it were a sense-perception of their operation.

When, on the contrary, the mirror within is shattered through some disturbance of the harmony of the body, Reason and the Intellectual-Principle act unpictured: intellection is unattended by imagination.

In sum we may safely gather that while the Intellective-Act may be attended by the Imaging Principle, it is not to be confounded with it.

And even in our conscious life we can point to many noble activities, of mind and of hand alike, which at the time in no way compel our consciousness. A reader will often be quite unconscious when he is most intent: in a feat of courage there can be no sense either of the brave action or of the fact that all that is done conforms to the rules of courage. And so in cases beyond number.

So that it would even seem that consciousness tends to blunt the activities upon which it is exercised, and that in the degree in which these pass unobserved they are purer and have more effect, more vitality, and that, consequently, the Proficient arrived at this state has the truer fullness of life, life not spilled out in sensation but gathered closely within itself.

11. We shall perhaps be told that in such a state the man is no longer alive: we answer that these people show themselves equally unable to understand his inner life and his happiness.

If this does not satisfy them, we must ask them to keep in mind a living Proficient and, under these terms, to inquire whether the man is in happiness: they must not whittle away his life and then ask whether he has the happy life; they must not take away the man and then look for the happiness of a man: once they allow that the Proficient lives within, they must not seek him among the outer activities, still less look to the outer world for the object of his desires. To consider the outer world to be a field to his desire, to fancy the Proficient desiring any good external, would be to deny Substantial-Existence to happiness; for the Proficient would like to see all men prosperous and no evil befalling anyone; but though it prove otherwise, he is still content.

If it be admitted that such a desire would be against reason, since evil cannot cease to be, there is no escape from agreeing with us that the Proficient's will is set always and only inward.

12. The pleasure demanded for the Proficient's life cannot be in the enjoyments of the licentious or in any gratifications of the body—there is no place for these, and they stifle happiness—nor in any violent emotions—what could so move the Proficient?—it can be only such pleasure as there must be where Good is, pleasure that does not rise from movement and is not a thing of process, for all that is good is immediately present to the Proficient and the Proficient is present to himself: his pleasure, his contentment, stands, immovable.

Thus he is ever cheerful, the order of his life ever untroubled: his state is fixedly happy and nothing whatever of all that is known as evil can set it awry—given only that he is and remains a Proficient.

If anyone seeks for some other kind of pleasure in the life of the Proficient, it is not the life of the Proficient he is looking for.

13. The characteristic activities are not hindered by outer events but merely adapt themselves, remaining always fine, and perhaps all the finer for dealing

with the actual. In the activities of the mind particular applications may find him in difficulties: he may not be able to put his vision into act without searching and thinking, but the one 'greatest principle of knowledge' (the Good) is ever present to him, like a part of his being—most of all present, should he be even a victim in the much-talked-of Bull of Phalaris. No doubt, despite all that has been said, it is idle to pretend that this is an agreeable lodging; but what cries in the Bull is the thing that feels the torture; I in the Proficient there is something else as well, something which associates with that other, but which, so long as the association is not of its own choice, can never be robbed[6]I of the vision of the All-Good.

14. For man, and especially the Proficient, is not the Couplement of Soul and body: the proof is that man can be disengaged from the body and disdain its nominal goods.

It would be absurd to think that happiness begins and ends with the living-body: happiness is the possession of the good of life: it is centred therefore in Soul, is an Act of the Soul—and not of all the Soul at that: for it certainly is not characteristic of the vegetative soul, the soul of growth; that would at once connect it with the body.

A powerful frame, a healthy constitution, even a happy balance of temperament, these surely do not make felicity; in the excess of these advantages there is, even, the danger that the man be crushed down and forced more and more within their power. There must be a sort of counter-pressure in the other direction, towards the noblest: the body must be lessened, reduced, that the veritable man may show forth, the man behind the appearances.

Let the earth-bound man be handsome and powerful and rich, and so apt to this world that he may rule the entire human race: still there can be no envying him, the fool of such lures. Perhaps such splendours could not, from the beginning even, have gathered to the Proficient; but if it should happen so, he of his own action will lower his state, if he has any care for his true life; the tyranny of the body he will work down or wear away by inattention to its claims; the rulership he will lay aside. While he will safeguard his bodily health, he will not wish to be wholly untried in sickness, still less never to feel pain: if such troubles should not come to him of themselves, he will wish to know them, during youth at least: in old age, it is true, he will desire neither pains nor pleasures to hamper him; he will desire nothing of this world, pleasant or painful; his one desire will be to know nothing of the body. If he should meet with pain he will pit against it the powers he holds to meet it; but pleasure and health and ease of life will not mean any increase of happiness to him nor will their contraries destroy or lessen it.

When in the one subject a positive can add nothing, how can the negative take away?

15. But suppose two wise men, one of them possessing all that is supposed to be naturally welcome, while the other meets only with the very reverse: do we assert that they have an equal happiness?

We do, if they are equally wise.

What though the one be favoured in body and in all else that does not help towards wisdom, still less towards virtue, towards the vision of the noblest, towards being the highest, what does all that amount to? The man commanding all such practical advantages cannot flatter himself that he is more truly happy than the man without them: the utmost profusion of such boons would not help even to make a flute-player.

We discuss the happy man after our own feebleness; we count alarming and grave what his felicity takes lightly: he would be neither wise nor in the state of happiness if he had not quitted all trifling with such things and become as it were another being, having confidence in his own nature, faith that evil can never touch him. In such a spirit he can be fearless through and through; where there is dread, there is not perfect virtue; the man is some sort of a half-thing.

As for any involuntary fear rising in him and taking the judgement by surprise, while his thoughts perhaps are elsewhere, the Proficient will attack it and drive it out; he will, so to speak, calm the refractory child within him, whether by reason or by menace, but without passion, as an infant might feel itself rebuked by a glance of severity.

This does not make the Proficient unfriendly or harsh: it is to himself and in his own great concern that he is the Proficient: giving freely to his intimates of all he has to give, he will be the best of friends by his very union with the Intellectual-Principle.

16. Those that refuse to place the Proficient aloft in the Intellectual Realm but drag him down to the accidental, dreading accident for him, have substituted for the Proficient we have in mind another person altogether; they offer us a tolerable sort of man and they assign to him a life of mingled good and ill, a case, after all, not easy to conceive. But admitting the possibility of such a mixed state, it could not be deserved to be called a life of happiness; it misses the Great, both in the dignity of Wisdom and in the integrity of Good. The life of true happiness is not a thing of mixture. And Plato rightly taught that he who is to be wise and to possess happiness draws his good from the Supreme, fixing his gaze on That, becoming like to That, living by That.

He can care for no other Term than That: all else he will attend to only as he might change his residence, not in expectation of any increase to his settled felicity, but simply in a reasonable attention to the differing conditions surrounding him as he lives here or there.

He will give to the body all that he sees to be useful and possible, but he himself remains a member of another order, not prevented from abandoning the body, and necessarily leaving it at nature's hour, he himself always the master to decide in its regard.

Thus some part of his life considers exclusively the Soul's satisfaction; the rest is not immediately for the Term's sake and not for his own sake, but for the thing bound up with him, the thing which he tends and bears with as the musician cares for his lyre, as long as it can serve him: when the lyre fails him, he will change it, or will give up lyre and lyring, as having another craft now, one that needs no lyre, and then he will let it rest unregarded at his side while he sings on without an instrument. But it was not idly that the instrument was given him in the beginning: he has found it useful until now, many a time.

NOTES TO ENNEAD I.4

1. FIRST EDITION title: "On True Happiness."

2. A typesetting error in the fourth edition resulted in the repetition here of the first line from the previous paragraph and omission of ". . . say that reason is to be cherished for its own sake and not as . . ." The line is correct as printed in the present edition.

3. FIRST EDITION: "*It has been shown elsewhere that man . . .*"

   GUTHRIE and ARMSTRONG support this original translation.

4. FIRST EDITION: "Sage" is used throughout rather than "Proficient"

5. FIRST EDITION paragraph begins as: "*When the Intellect is in upward orientation that (lower part of it) which contains (or, corresponds to) the life of the Soul, is, so to speak, flung down again and becomes like the reflection resting on* the smooth and shining surface of a mirror;"

   GUTHRIE: "It seems impossible for perception to arise except when thought reflects upon itself, and when the principle whose activity constitutes the life of the soul, so to speak, turns backwards, and reflects, as the image of an object placed before a brilliant polished mirror reflects itself therein."

   ARMSTRONG: "It seems as if awareness exists and is produced when intellectual activity is reflexive and when that in the life of the soul which is active in thinking is in a way projected back, as happens with a mirror-reflection when there is a smooth, bright, untroubled surface."

6. FIRST EDITION: ". . . in the *Sage* there is something else as well, *The Self-Gathered which, as long as it holds itself by main force within itself,* can never be robbed . . ."

   TAYLOR, ARMSTRONG, and GUTHRIE also emphasize the "dwelling within itself" nature of this "something else."

FIFTH TRACTATE

Happiness and Extension of Time

1. Is it possible to think that Happiness increases with Time, Happiness which is always taken as a present thing?

The memory of former felicity may surely be ruled out of count, for Happiness is not a thing of words, but a definite condition which must be actually present like the very fact and act of life.

2. It may be objected that our will towards living and towards expressive activity is constant, and that each attainment of such expression is an increase in Happiness.

But in the first place, by this reckoning every tomorrow's well-being will be greater than today's, every later installment successively larger than an earlier; at once time supplants moral excellence as the measure of felicity.

Then again the Gods today must be happier than of old: and their bliss, too, is not perfect, will never be perfect.

Further, when the will attains what it was seeking, it attains something present: the quest is always for something to be actually present until a standing felicity is definitely achieved. The will to life which is will to Existence aims at something present, since Existence must be a stably present thing. Even when the act of the will is directed towards the future, and the furthest future, its object is an actually present having and being: there is no concern about what is passed or to come: the future state a man seeks is to be a now to him; he does not care about the forever: he asks that an actual present be actually present.

3. Yes, but if the well-being has lasted a long time, if that present spectacle has been a longer time before the eyes?

If in the greater length of time the man has seen more deeply, time has certainly done something for him, but if all the process has brought him no further vision, then one glance would give all he has had.

4. Still the one life has known pleasure longer than the other?

But pleasure cannot be fairly reckoned in with Happiness—unless indeed by pleasure is meant the unhindered Act (of the true man), in which case this pleasure is simply our 'Happiness'. And even pleasure, though it exist continuously, has never anything but the present; its past is over and done with.

5. We are asked to believe, then, it will be objected, that if one man has been

happy from first to last, another only at the last, and a third, beginning with happiness, has lost it, their shares are equal?

This is straying from the question: we were comparing the happy among themselves: now we are asked to compare the not-happy at the time when they are out of happiness with those in actual possession of happiness. If these last are better off, they are so as men in possession of happiness against men without it and their advantage is always by something in the present.

6. Well, but take the unhappy man: must not increase of time bring an increase of his unhappiness? Do not all troubles—long-lasting pains sorrows, and everything of that type—yield a greater sum of misery in the longer time? And if thus in misery the evil is augmented by time why should not time equally augment happiness when all is well?

In the matter of sorrows and pains there is, no doubt, ground for saying that time brings increase: for example, in a lingering malady the evil hardens into a state, and as time goes on the body is brought lower and lower. But if the constitution did not deteriorate, if the mischief grew no worse, then, here too, there would be no trouble but that of the present moment: we cannot tell the past into the tale of unhappiness except in the sense that it has gone to make up an actually existing state—in the sense that, the evil in the sufferer's condition having been extended over a longer time, the mischief has gained ground. The increase of ill-being, then, is due to the aggravation of the malady, not to the extension of time.

It may be pointed out also that this greater length of time is not a thing existent at any given moment; and surely a 'more' is not to be made out by adding to something actually present something that has passed away.

No: true happiness is not vague and fluid: it is an unchanging state.

If there is in this matter any increase besides that of mere time, it is in the sense that a greater happiness is the reward of a higher virtue: this is not counting up to the credit of happiness the years of its continuance; it is simply noting the high-water mark once for all attained.

7. But if we are to consider only the present and may not call in the past to make the total, why do we not reckon so in the case of time itself, where, in fact, we do not hesitate to add the past to the present and call the total greater? Why not suppose a quantity of happiness equivalent to a quantity of time? This would be no more than taking it lap by lap to correspond with time-laps instead of choosing to consider it as an indivisible, measurable only by the content of a given instant.

There is no absurdity in taking count of time which has ceased to be: we are merely counting what is past and finished, as we might count the dead: but to treat past happiness as actually existent and as outweighing present happiness, that is an absurdity. For Happiness must be an achieved and existent state, whereas any time over and apart from the present is non-existent: I all progress of time means the dissipation of a unity whose existence is in the present.[1]I

Hence time is aptly described as a mimic of eternity that seeks to break up in its fragmentary flight the permanence of its exemplar. Thus whatever time seizes and seals to itself of what stands permanent in eternity is annihilated—saved only in so far as in some degree it still belongs to eternity, but wholly destroyed if it be unreservedly absorbed into time.

If Happiness demands the possession of the good of life, it clearly has to do with the life of Authentic-Existence, for that life is the Best. Now the life of Authentic-Existence is measurable not by time but by eternity; and eternity is not a more or a less or a thing of any magnitude but is the unchangeable, the indivisible, is timeless Being.

We must not muddle together Being and Non-Being, time and eternity, not even everlasting time with the eternal; we cannot make laps and stages of an absolute unity; all must be taken together, wheresoever and howsoever we handle it; and it must be taken at that, not even as an undivided block of time but as the Life of Eternity, a stretch not made up of periods but completely rounded, outside of all notion of time.

8. It may be urged that the actual presence of past experiences, kept present by Memory, gives the advantage to the man of the longer felicity.

But, Memory of what sort of experiences?

Memory either of formerly attained wisdom and virtue—in which case we have a better man and the argument from memory is given up—or memory of past pleasures, as if the man that has arrived at felicity must roam far and wide in search of gratifications and is not contented by the bliss actually within him.

And what is there pleasant in the memory of pleasure? What is it to recall yesterday's excellent dinner? Still more ridiculous, one of ten years ago. So, too, of last year's morality.

9. But is there not something to be said for the memory of the various forms of beauty?

That is the resource of a man whose life is without beauty in the present, so that, for lack of it now, he grasps at the memory of what has been.

10. But, it may be said, length of time produces an abundance of good actions missed by the man whose attainment of the happy state is recent—if indeed we

can think at all of a state of happiness where good actions have been few.

Now to make multiplicity, whether in time or in action, essential to Happiness is to put it together by combining non-existents, represented by the past, with some one thing that actually is. This consideration it was that led us at the very beginning to place Happiness in the actually existent and on that basis to launch our inquiry as to whether the higher degree was determined by the longer time. It might be thought that the Happiness of longer date must surpass the shorter by virtue of the greater number of acts it included.

But, to begin with, men quite outside of the active life may attain the state of felicity, and not in a less but in a greater degree than men of affairs.

Secondly, the good does not derive from the act itself but from the inner disposition which prompts the noble conduct: the wise and good man in his very action harvests the good not by what he does but by what he is.

A wicked man no less than a I Proficient[2]I may save the country, and the good of the act is for all alike, no matter whose was the saving hand. The contentment of the I Proficient[2]I does not hang upon such actions and events: it is his own inner habit that creates at once his felicity and whatever pleasure may accompany it.

To put Happiness in actions is to put it in things that are outside virtue and outside the Soul; for the Soul's expression is not in action but in wisdom, in a contemplative operation within itself; and this, this alone, is Happiness.

NOTES TO ENNEAD I.5

1. FIRST EDITION: ". . . all progress of time means the *extinction of all the time that has been*."

ARMSTRONG: "In general extension of time means the dispersal of a single present."

GUTHRIE: "Whatever might be the length of time that preceded the present, all that can be said of it is, that it is no more."

2. FIRST EDITION: "*Sage*"

SIXTH TRACTATE

Beauty

1. Beauty addresses itself chiefly to sight; but there is a beauty for the hearing too, as in certain combinations of words and in all kinds of music, for melodies and cadences are beautiful; and minds that lift themselves above the realm of sense to a higher order are aware of beauty in the conduct of life, in actions, in character, in the pursuits of the intellect; and there is the beauty of the virtues. What loftier beauty there may be, yet, our argument will bring to light.

What, then, is it that gives comeliness to material forms and draws the ear to the sweetness perceived in sounds, and what is the secret of the beauty there is in all that derives from Soul?

Is there some One Principle from which all take their grace, or is there a beauty peculiar to the embodied and another for the bodiless? Finally, one or many, what would such a Principle be?

Consider that some things, material shapes for instance, are gracious not by anything inherent but by something communicated, while others are lovely of themselves, as, for example, Virtue.

The same bodies appear sometimes beautiful, sometimes not; so that there is a good deal between being body and being beautiful.

What, then, is this something that shows itself in certain material forms? This is the natural beginning of our inquiry.

What is it that attracts the eyes of those to whom a beautiful object is presented, and calls them, lures them, towards it, and fills them with joy at the sight? If we possess ourselves of this, we have at once a standpoint for the wider survey.

Almost everyone declares that the symmetry of parts towards each other and towards a whole, with, besides, a certain charm of colour, constitutes the beauty recognized by the eye, that in visible things, as indeed in all else, universally, the beautiful thing is essentially symmetrical, patterned.

But think what this means.

Only a compound can be beautiful, never anything devoid of parts; and only a whole; the several parts will have beauty, not in themselves, but only as working together to give a comely total. Yet beauty in an aggregate demands beauty in details: it cannot be constructed out of ugliness; its law must run throughout.

All the loveliness of colour and even the light of the sun, being devoid of parts and so not beautiful by symmetry, must be ruled out of the realm of beauty. And how comes gold to be a beautiful thing? And lightning by night, and the stars, why are these so fair?

In sounds also the simple must be proscribed, though often in a whole noble composition each several tone is delicious in itself.

Again since the one face, constant in symmetry, appears sometimes fair and sometimes not, can we doubt that beauty is something more than symmetry, that symmetry itself owes its beauty to a remoter principle?

Turn to what is attractive in methods of life or in the expression of thought; are we to call in symmetry here? What symmetry is to be found in noble conduct, or excellent laws, in any form of mental pursuit?

What symmetry can there be in points of abstract thought?

The symmetry of being accordant with each other? But there may be accordance or entire identity where there is nothing but ugliness: the proposition that honesty is merely a generous artlessness chimes in the most perfect harmony with the proposition that morality means weakness of will; the accordance is complete.

Then again, all the virtues are a beauty of the Soul, a beauty authentic beyond any of these others; but how does symmetry enter here? The Soul, it is true, is not a simple unity, but still its virtue cannot have the symmetry of size or of number: what standard of measurement could preside over the compromise or the coalescence of the Soul's faculties or purposes?

Finally, how by this theory would there be beauty in the Intellectual-Principle, essentially the solitary?

2. Let us, then, go back to the source, and indicate at once the Principle that bestows beauty on material things.

Undoubtedly this Principle exists; it is something that is perceived at the first glance, something which the Soul names as from an ancient knowledge and, recognizing, welcomes it, enters into unison with it.

But let the Soul fall in with the Ugly and at once it shrinks within itself, denies the thing, turns away from it, not accordant, resenting it.

Our interpretation is that the Soul—by the very truth of its nature, by its affiliation to the noblest Existents in the hierarchy of Being—when it sees anything of that kin, or any trace of that kinship, thrills with an immediate delight, takes its own to itself, and thus stirs anew to the sense of its nature and of all its affinity.

But, is there any such likeness between the loveliness of this world and the splendours in the Supreme? Such a likeness in the particulars would make the two orders alike: but what is there in common between beauty here and beauty There?

We hold that all the loveliness of this world comes by communion in Ideal-Form.

All shapelessness whose kind admits of pattern and form, as long as it remains outside of Reason and Idea, is ugly by that very isolation from the Divine Reason-Principle. And this is the Absolute Ugly: an ugly thing is something that has not been entirely mastered by pattern, that is by Reason, the Matter not yielding at all points and in all respects to Ideal-Form.

But where the Ideal-Form has entered, it has grouped and co-ordinated what from a diversity of parts was to become a unity: it has rallied confusion into co-operation: it has made the sum one harmonious coherence: for the Idea is a unity and what it moulds must come to unity as far as multiplicity may.

And on what has thus been compacted to unity, Beauty enthrones itself, giving itself to the parts as to the sum: when it lights on some natural unity, a thing of like parts, then it gives itself to that whole. Thus, for an illustration, there is the beauty, conferred by craftsmanship, of all a house with all its parts, and the beauty which some natural quality may give to a single stone.

This, then, is how the material thing becomes beautiful—by communicating in the Reason-Principle that flows from the Divine.

3. And the Soul includes a faculty peculiarly addressed to Beauty—one incomparably sure I in the appreciation of its own, when Soul entire is enlisted to support its judgement.¹I

I Or perhaps the faculty² acts I immediately, affirming the Beautiful where it finds something accordant with the Ideal-Form within itself, using this Idea as a canon of accuracy in its decision.

But what accordance is there between the material and that which antedates all Matter?

On what principle does the architect, when he finds the house standing before him correspondent with his inner ideal of a house, pronounce it beautiful? Is it not that the house before him, the stones apart, is the inner idea stamped upon the mass of exterior matter, the indivisible exhibited in diversity?

So with the perceptive faculty: discerning in certain objects the Ideal-Form which has bound and controlled shapeless matter, opposed in nature to Idea, seeing further stamped upon the common shapes some shape excellent above the common, it gathers into unity what still remains fragmentary, catches it up and carries it within, no longer a thing of parts, and presents it to the inner Ideal-Principle as something concordant and congenial, a natural friend: the joy here is like that of a good man who discerns in a youth the early signs of a virtue consonant with the achieved perfection within his own soul.

The beauty of colour is also the outcome of a unification: it derives from shape, from the conquest of the darkness inherent in Matter by the pouring-in of light, the unembodied, which is a Rational-Principle and an Ideal-Form.

Hence it is that Fire itself is splendid beyond all material bodies, holding the rank of Ideal-Principle to the other elements, making ever upwards, the subtlest and sprightliest of all bodies, as very near to the unembodied; itself alone admitting no other, all the others penetrated by it: for they take warmth but this is never cold; it has colour primally; they receive the Form of colour from it: hence the splendour of its light, the splendour that belongs to the Idea. And all that has resisted and is but uncertainly held by its light remains outside of beauty, as not having absorbed the plenitude of the Form of colour.

And harmonies unheard in sound create the harmonies we hear and wake the Soul to the consciousness of beauty, showing it the one essence in another kind: for the measures of our sensible music are not arbitrary but are determined by the Principle whose labour is to dominate Matter and bring pattern into being.

Thus far of the beauties of the realm of sense, images and shadow-pictures, fugitives that have entered into Matter—to adorn, and to ravish, where they are seen.

4. But there are earlier and loftier beauties than these. In the sense-bound life we are no longer granted to know them, but the Soul, taking no help from the organs, sees and proclaims them. To the vision of these we must mount, leaving sense to its own low place.

As it is not for those to speak of the graceful forms of the material world who have never seen them or known their grace—men born blind, let us suppose—in the same way those must be silent upon the beauty of noble conduct and of learning and all that order who have never cared for such things, nor may those tell of the splendour of virtue who have never known the face of Justice and of Moral-Wisdom beautiful beyond the beauty of Evening and of Dawn.

Such vision is for those only who see with the Soul's sight—and at the vision, they will rejoice, and awe will fall upon them and a trouble deeper than all the rest could ever stir, for now they are moving in the realm of Truth.

This is the spirit that Beauty must ever induce, wonderment and a delicious trouble, longing and love and a trembling that is all delight. For the unseen all this may be felt as for the seen; and this the Souls feel for it, every Soul in some degree, but those the more deeply that are the more truly apt to this higher love—just as all take delight in the beauty of the body but all are not stung as sharply, and those only that feel the keener wound are known as Lovers.

5. These Lovers, then, lovers of the beauty outside of sense, must be made to declare themselves.

What do you feel in presence of the grace you discern in actions, in manners, in sound morality, in all the works and fruits of virtue, in the beauty of Souls?

When you see that you yourselves are beautiful within, what do you feel? What is this Dionysiac exultation that thrills through your being, this straining upwards of all your soul, this longing to break away from the body and live sunken within the veritable self?

These are no other than the emotions of Souls under the spell of love.

But what is it that awakens all this passion? No shape, no colour, no grandeur of mass: all is for a Soul, something whose beauty rests upon no colour, for the moral wisdom the Soul enshrines and all the other hueless splendour of the virtues. It is that you find in yourself, or admire in another, loftiness of spirit; righteousness of life; disciplined purity; courage of the majestic face; gravity, modesty that goes fearless and tranquil and passionless; and, shining down upon all, the light of godlike Intellection.

All these noble qualities are to be reverenced and loved, no doubt, but what entitles them to be called beautiful?

They exist: they manifest themselves to us: anyone that sees them must admit that they have reality of Being; and is not Real-Being really beautiful?

But we have not yet shown by what property in them they have wrought the Soul to loveliness: what is this grace, this splendour as of Light, resting upon all the virtues?

Let us take the contrary, the ugliness of the Soul, and set that against its beauty: to understand, at once, what this ugliness is and how it comes to appear in the Soul will certainly open our way before us.

Let us then suppose an ugly Soul, dissolute, unrighteous: teeming with all the lusts; torn by internal discord; beset by the fears of its cowardice and the envies of its pettiness; thinking, in the little thought it has, only of the perishable and the base; perverse in all its impulses; the friend of unclean pleasures; living the life of abandonment to bodily sensation and delighting in its deformity.

What must we think but that all this shame is something that has gathered about the Soul, some foreign bane outraging it, soiling it, so that, encumbered with all manner of turpitude, it has no longer a clean activity or a clean sensation, but commands only a life smouldering dully under the crust of evil; that, sunk in manifold death, it no longer sees what a Soul should see, may no longer rest in its own being, dragged ever as it is towards the outer, the lower, the dark?

An unclean thing, I dare to say; flickering hither and thither at the call of objects of sense, deeply infected with the taint of body, occupied always in Matter, and absorbing Matter into itself; in its commerce with the Ignoble it has trafficked away for an alien nature **I** its own essential form.[3]**I**

If a man has been immersed in filth or daubed with mud, his native comeliness disappears and all that is seen is the foul stuff besmearing him: his ugly condition is due to alien matter that has encrusted him, and if he is to win back his grace it must be his business to scour and purify himself and make himself what he was.

So, we may justly say, a Soul becomes ugly—by something foisted upon it, by sinking itself into the alien, by a fall, a descent into body, into Matter. The dishonour of the Soul is in its ceasing to be clean and apart. Gold is degraded when it is mixed with earthy particles; if these be worked out, the gold is left and is beautiful, isolated from all that is foreign, gold with gold alone. And so the Soul; let it be but cleared of the desires that come by its too intimate converse with the body, emancipated from all the passions, purged of all that embodiment has thrust upon it, withdrawn, a solitary, to itself again—in that moment the ugliness that came only from the alien is stripped away.

6. For, as the ancient teaching was, moral-discipline and courage and every virtue, not even excepting Wisdom itself, all is purification.

Hence the Mysteries with good reason adumbrate the immersion of the unpurified in filth, even in the Nether-World, since the unclean loves filth for its very filthiness, and swine foul of body find their joy in foulness.

What else is Sophrosyny, rightly so-called, but to take no part in the pleasures of the body, to break away from them as unclean and unworthy of the clean? So too, Courage is but being fearless of the death which is but the parting of the Soul from the body, an event which no one can dread whose delight is to be his unmingled self. And Magnanimity is but disregard for the lure of things here. And Wisdom is but the Act of the Intellectual-Principle withdrawn from the lower places and leading the Soul to the Above.

The Soul thus cleansed is all Idea and Reason, wholly free of body, intellective, entirely of that divine order from which the wellspring of Beauty rises and all the race of Beauty.

Hence the Soul heightened to the Intellectual-Principle is beautiful to all its power. For Intellection and all that proceeds from Intellection are the Soul's beauty, a graciousness native to it and not foreign, for only with these is it truly Soul. And it is just to say that in the Soul's becoming a good and beautiful thing is its becoming like to God, for from the Divine comes all the Beauty and all the Good in beings.

We may even say that Beauty *is* the Authentic-Existents and Ugliness is the Principle contrary to Existence: and the Ugly is also the primal evil; therefore its contrary is at once good and beautiful, or is Good and Beauty: and hence the one method will discover to us the Beauty-Good and the Ugliness-Evil.

And Beauty, this Beauty which is also The Good, must be posed as The First: directly deriving from this First is the Intellectual-Principle which is pre-eminently the manifestation of Beauty; through the Intellectual-Principle Soul is beautiful. The beauty in things of a lower order—actions and pursuits for instance—comes by operation of the shaping Soul which is also the author of the beauty found in the world of sense. For the Soul, a divine thing, a fragment as it were of the Primal Beauty, makes beautiful to the fullness of their capacity all things whatsoever that it grasps and moulds.

7. Therefore we must ascend again towards the Good, the desired of every Soul. Anyone that has seen This, knows what I intend when I say that it is beautiful. ❙ It is desired as the goal of desire.⁴❙ To attain it is for those that will take the upward path, who will set all their forces towards it, who will divest themselves of all that we have put on in our descent: so, to those that approach the Holy Celebrations of the Mysteries, there are appointed purifications and the laying aside of the garments worn before, and the entry in nakedness—until, passing, on the upward way, all that is other than the God, each in the solitude of himself shall behold that solitary-dwelling Existence, the Apart, the Unmingled, the Pure, that from Which all things depend, for Which all look and live and act and know, the Source of Life and of Intellection and of Being.

And one that shall know this vision—with what passion of love shall he not be seized, with what pang of desire, what longing to be molten into one with This, what wondering delight! If he that has never seen this Being must hunger for It as for all his welfare, he that has known must love and reverence It as the very Beauty; he will be flooded with awe and gladness, stricken by a salutary terror; he loves with a veritable love, with sharp desire; all other loves than this he must despise, and disdain all that once seemed fair.

This, indeed, is the mood even of those who, having witnessed the manifestation of Gods or Supernals, can never again feel the old delight in the comeliness of material forms: what then are we to think of one that contemplates Absolute Beauty in Its essential integrity, no accumulation of flesh and matter, no dweller on earth or in the heavens—so perfect Its purity—far above all such things in that they are nonessential, composite, not primal but descending from This?

Beholding this Being—the Choragus of all Existence, the Self-Intent that ever gives forth and never takes—resting, rapt, in the vision and possession of so lofty a loveliness, growing to Its likeness, what Beauty can the Soul yet lack? For This, the Beauty supreme, the absolute, and the primal, fashions Its lovers to Beauty and makes them also worthy of love.

And for This, the sternest and the uttermost combat is set before the Souls; all our labour is for This, lest we be left without part in this noblest vision, which to attain is to be blessed in the blissful sight, which to fail of is to fail utterly.

For not he that has failed of the joy that is in colour or in visible forms, not he that has failed of power or of honours or of kingdom has failed, but only he that has failed of only This, for Whose winning he should renounce king-doms and command over earth and ocean and sky, if only, spurning the world of sense from beneath his feet, and straining to This, he may see.

8. But what must we do? How lies the path? How come to vision of the inaccessible Beauty, dwelling as if in consecrated precincts, apart from the common ways where all may see, even the profane?

He that has the strength, let him arise and withdraw into himself, foregoing all that is known by the eyes, turning away for ever from the material beauty that once made his joy. When he perceives those shapes of grace that show in body, let him not pursue: he must know them for copies, vestiges, shadows, and hasten away towards That they tell of. For if anyone follow what is like a beautiful shape playing over water—is there not a myth telling in symbol of such a dupe, how he sank into the depths of the current and was swept away to nothingness? So too, one that is held by material beauty and will not break free shall be precipitated, not in body but in Soul, down to the dark depths loathed of the Intellective-Being, where, blind even in the Lower-World, he shall have commerce only with shadows, there as here.

'Let us flee then to the beloved Fatherland': this is the soundest counsel. But what is this flight? How are we to gain the open sea? For Odysseus is surely a parable to us when he commands the flight from the sorceries of Circe or Calypso—not content to linger for all the pleasure offered to his eyes and all the delight of sense filling his days.

The Fatherland to us is There whence we have come, and There is The Father.

What then is our course, what the manner of our flight? This is not a journey for the feet; the feet bring us only from land to land; nor need you think of coach or ship to carry you away; all this order of things you must set aside and refuse to see: you must close the eyes and call instead upon another vision which is to be waked within you, a vision, the birth-right of all, which few turn to use.

9. And this inner vision, what is its operation?

Newly awakened it is all too feeble to bear the ultimate splendour. Therefore the Soul must be trained—to the habit of remarking, first, all noble pursuits, then the works of beauty produced not by the labour of the arts but by the virtue of men known for their goodness: lastly, you must search the souls of those that have shaped these beautiful forms.

But how are you to see into a virtuous Soul and know its loveliness?

Withdraw into yourself and look. And if you do not find yourself beautiful yet, act as does the creator of a statue that is to be made beautiful: he cuts away here, he smoothes there, he makes this line lighter, this other purer, until a love-ly face has grown upon his work. So do you also: cut away all that is excessive, straighten all that is crooked, bring light to all that is overcast, labour to make all one glow of beauty and never cease chiselling your statue, until there shall shine out on you from it the godlike splendour of virtue, until you shall see the perfect goodness surely established in the stainless shrine.

When you know that you have become this perfect work, when you are self-gathered in the purity of your being, nothing now remaining that can shatter that inner unity, nothing from without clinging to the authentic man, when you find yourself wholly true to your essential nature, wholly that only veritable Light which is not measured by space, not narrowed to any circumscribed form nor again diffused as a thing void of term, but ever unmeasurable as something greater than all measure and more than all quantity—when you perceive that you have grown to this, you are now become very vision: now call up all your confidence, strike forward yet a step—you need a guide no longer—strain, and see.

This is the only eye that sees the mighty Beauty. If the eye that adventures the vision be dimmed by vice, impure, or weak, and unable in its cowardly blenching to see the uttermost brightness, then it sees nothing even though another point to what lies plain to sight before it. To any vision must be brought an eye adapted to what is to be seen, and having some likeness to it. Never did eye see the sun unless it had first become sun-like, and never can the Soul have vision of the First Beauty unless itself be beautiful.

Therefore, first let each become godlike and each beautiful who cares to see God and Beauty. So, mounting, the Soul will come first to the Intellectual-Principle and survey all the beautiful Ideas in the Supreme and will avow that this is Beauty, that the Ideas are Beauty. For by their efficacy comes all Beauty else, I by the offspring of Being and of the Intellectual-Principle.[5]I What is be-yond the Intellectual-Principle we affirm to be the nature of Good radiating Beauty before it. So that, treating the Intellectual-Cosmos as one, the first is the Beautiful: if we make distinction there, the Realm of Ideas constitutes the Beauty of the Intellectual Sphere; and The Good, which lies beyond, is the Fountain at once and Principle of Beauty: the Primal Good and the Primal Beauty have the one dwelling-place and, thus, always, Beauty's seat is There.

NOTES TO ENNEAD I.6

1. FIRST EDITION: "... in the appreciation of its own, *never in doubt whenever any lovely thing presents itself for* judgement."

GUTHRIE: ". . . an especially ordered faculty, whose sole function it is to appreciate all that concerns beauty, even when the other faculties take part in this judgement."

ARMSTRONG: ". . . and there is nothing more effective for judging its own subject-matter, when the rest of the soul judges along with it;"

2. FIRST EDITION: "Or perhaps the *soul itself* acts . . ."

GUTHRIE: "Often the soul makes her (aesthetic) decisions . . ."

ARMSTRONG: "Or perhaps the rest of the soul too pronounces the judgement . . ."

3. FIRST EDITION: ". . . its own essential *Idea.*"

GUTHRIE: ". . . has changed form by her admixture with an inferior nature."

ARMSTRONG: ". . . and receiving a form other than its own it has changed by a mixture which makes it worse;"

4. FIRST EDITION: "*Even the desire of it is to be desired as a Good.*"

ARMSTRONG: "It is desired as good, and the desire for it is directed to good . . ."

GUTHRIE: ". . . the Good is desirable for its own sake; it is the goal of our desires."

5. FIRST EDITION: ". . . by the offspring *and essence of the Intellectual-Being.*"

GUTHRIE: ". . . the daughters and the very essence of Intelligence.

ARMSTRONG: ". . . by the products and essence of intellect."

SEVENTH TRACTATE

The Primal Good and Secondary Forms of Good

1. We can scarcely conceive that for any entity the Good can be other than the natural Act expressing its life-force, or in the case of an entity made up of parts the Act, appropriate, natural, and complete, expressive of that in it which is best.

For the Soul, then, the Good is its own natural Act.

But the Soul itself is natively a 'Best'; if, further, its Act be directed towards the Best, the achievement is not merely the 'Soul's good' but 'The Good' without qualification.

Now, given an Existent which—as being itself the best of existences and even transcending the existences—directs its Act towards no other, but is the object to which the Act of all else is directed, it is clear that this must be at once the Good and the means through which all else may participate in Good.

This Absolute Good other entities may possess in two ways—by becoming like to It and by directing the Act of their being towards It.

Now, if all aspiration and Act whatsoever are directed towards the Good, it follows that the Essential-Good neither need nor can look outside itself or aspire to anything other than itself: it can but remain unmoved, as being, in the constitution of things, the wellspring and first-cause of all Act: whatsoever in other entities is of the nature of Good cannot be due to any Act of the Essential-Good upon them; it is for them on the contrary to act towards their source and cause. The Good must, then, be the Good not by any Act, not even by virtue of its Intellection, but by its very rest within Itself.

Existing beyond and above Being, I it must be beyond and above Act and beyond and above the Intellectual-Principle and[1] all Intellection.

For, again, that only can be named the Good to which all is bound and itself to none: for only thus is it veritably the object of all aspiration. It must be unmoved, while all circles around it, as a circumference around a centre from which all the radii proceed. Another example would be the sun, central to the light which streams from it and is yet linked to it, or at least is always about it, irremovably; try all you will to separate the light from the sun, or the sun from its light, for ever the light is in the sun.

2. But the Universe outside; how is it aligned towards the Good?

The soul-less by direction toward Soul: Soul towards the Good itself, through the Intellectual-Principle.

Everything has something of the Good, by virtue of possessing a certain degree of unity and a certain degree of Existence and by participation I in Form:[2] to the extent of the Unity, Being, and Form which are present, I there is a sharing in the Good, or rather in an image of the Good; for the Unity and Existence in which there is participation are no more than images, and the same is true of the Form.[3]

With Soul it is different; the First-Soul, that which follows upon the Intellectual-Principle, possesses a life nearer to the Verity and through that Principle is of the nature of good; it will actually possess the Good if it orientate itself towards the Intellectual-Principle since this follows immediately upon the Good.

In sum, then, life is the Good to the living, and the Intellectual-Principle to what is intellective; so that where there is life with intellection there is a double contact with the Good.

3. But if life is a good, is there good for all that lives?

No: in the vile, life limps: it is like the eye to the dim-sighted; it fails of its task.

But if the mingled strand of life is to us, though entwined with evil, still in the total a good, must not death be an evil?

Evil to what? There must be a subject for the evil: but if the possible subject is no longer among beings, or, still among beings, is devoid of life—why, a stone is not more immune.

If, on the contrary, after death life and Soul continue, then death will be no evil but a good; Soul, disembodied, is the freer to ply its own Act.

If it be taken into the All-Soul—what evil can reach it there? And as the Gods are—possessed of Good and untouched by evil—so, certainly, is the Soul that has preserved its essential character. And if it should lose its purity, the evil it experiences is not in its death but in its life. Suppose it to be under punishment in the lower world, even there the evil thing is its life and not its death; the misfortune is still life, a life of a definite character.

Life is a partnership of a Soul and body; death is the dissolution; in either life or death, then, the Soul will feel itself at home.

But, again, if life is good, how can death be anything but evil?

Remember that the good of life, where it has any good at all, is not due to anything in the partnership but to the repelling of evil by virtue; death, then, must be the greater good.

In a word, life in the body is of itself an evil but the Soul enters its Good through Virtue, not living the life of the Couplement but holding itself apart, even here.

NOTES TO ENNEAD I.7

1. FIRST EDITION omits section bracketed here: "... it must be beyond and above [Act and beyond and above] the Intellectual-Principle and ..."

GUTHRIE handles the ideas as follows: "Only by permanence—not by action, nor even by thought—is this principle the Good. For if it be super-Being, it must also be super-Activity, super-Intelligence, and Thought."

ARMSTRONG: "For because it is 'beyond being,' it transcends activity and transcends mind and thought."

2. FIRST EDITION: "... in *Ideal*-Form:"

3. FIRST EDITION omits bracketed words and differs also as shown by italics: "... there is a sharing in [the Good, or rather in] an image [of the Good], for the Unity and Existence in which there is participation are no more than images *of the Ideal-Form*."

ARMSTRONG: "... so they share in the Good. In an image of the Good, that is to say; for what they share in are images of existence and the One, and their form is an image too."

GUTHRIE: "By its participation in unity, essence and form each being participates in the Good, even though the latter be only an image, for the things in which it participates are only images of unity, essence, and form."

EIGHTH TRACTATE

The Nature and Source of Evil

1. Those inquiring whence Evil enters into beings, or rather into a certain order of beings, would be making the best beginning if they established, first of all, what precisely Evil is, what constitutes its Nature. At once we should know whence it comes, where it has its native seat, and where it is present merely as an accident; and there would be no further question as to whether it has Authentic-Existence.

But a difficulty arises. By what faculty in us could we possibly know Evil?

All knowing comes by likeness. The Intellectual-Principle and the Soul, being Ideal-Forms, would know Ideal-Forms and would have a natural tendency towards them; but who could imagine Evil to be an Ideal-Form, seeing that it manifests itself as the very absence of Good?

If the solution is that the one act of knowing covers contraries, and that as Evil is the contrary to Good the one act would grasp Good and Evil together, then to know Evil there must be first a clear perception and understanding of Good, since the nobler existences precede the baser and are Ideal-Forms while the less good hold no such standing, are nearer to Non-Being.

No doubt there is a question in what precise way Good is contrary to Evil—whether it is as First-Principle to last of things or as Ideal-Form to utter Lack (to Non-entity): but this subject we postpone.

2. For the moment let us define the Nature of the Good as far as the immediate purpose demands.

The Good is that on which all else depends, towards which all Existences aspire as to their source and their need, while Itself is without need, sufficient to Itself, aspiring to no other, the measure and Term of all, giving out from itself the Intellectual-Principle and Existence and Soul and Life and all Intellective-Act.

All until The Good is reached is beautiful; The Good is beyond-beautiful, beyond the Highest, holding kingly state in the Intellectual-Cosmos, that sphere constituted by a Principle wholly unlike what is known as Intelligence in us. Our intelligence is nourished on the propositions of logic, is skilled in following discussions, works by reasonings, examines links of demonstration, and comes to know the world of Being also by the steps of logical process, having no prior grasp of Reality but remaining empty, all Intelligence though it be, until it has put itself to school.

The Intellectual-Principle we are discussing is not of such a kind: It possesses all: It is all: It is present to all by Its self-presence: It has all by other means
than having, for what It possesses is still Itself, nor does any particular of all
within It stand apart; for every such particular is the whole and in all respects all,
while yet not confused in the mass but still distinct, apart to the extent that any
participant in the Intellectual-Principle participates not in the entire as one
thing but in whatsoever lies within its own reach.

❙ The Intellectual-Principle is the first Act of The Good and the first Existence; The Good remains stationary within itself, but the Intellectual-Principle
acts in relation to It and, as it were, lives about It.[1]❙

And the Soul, outside, circles around the Intellectual-Principle, and by
gazing upon it, seeing into the depths of It, through It sees God.

Such is the untroubled, the blissful, life of divine beings, and Evil has no place
in it; if this were all, there would be no Evil but Good only, the first, the second,
and the third Good. 'All', thus far, 'is with the King of All, unfailing Cause of
Good and Beauty and controller of all; and what is Good in the second degree
depends upon the Second-Principle and tertiary Good upon the Third.'

3. If such be the Nature of Beings and of That which transcends all the realm
of Being, Evil cannot have place among Beings or in the Beyond-Being; these
are good.

There remains, only, if Evil exist at all, that it be situate in the realm of
Non-Being, that it be some form or mode, as it were, of the Non-Being, that
it have its seat in something in touch with Non-Being or to a certain degree
communicate in Non-Being.

By this Non-Being, of course, we are not to understand something that
simply does not exist, but only something of an utterly different order from
Authentic-Being: there is no question here of movement or rest with regard to
Being; the Non-Being we are thinking of is, rather, an image of Being or perhaps something still further removed than even an image.

Now this (the required faint image of Being) might be the sensible universe
with all the properties it possesses, or it might be something of even later
derivation, accidental to the realm of sense, or again, it might be the source of
the sense-world or something entering into it to complete its character.

Some conception of it would be reached by thinking of measurelessness as
opposed to measure, of the unbounded against bound, the unshaped against a
principle of shape, the ever-needy against the self-sufficing: think of the ever-
undefined, the never at rest, the all-accepting but never sated, utter poverty
(Penia); and make all this character not mere accident in it but its equivalent
for essential-being, so that, whatsoever fragment of it be taken, that part is all

lawless void, while whatever participates in it and resembles it becomes evil, though not of course to the point of being, as itself is, Evil-Absolute.

In what substantial-form (hypostasis) then is all this to be found—not as accident but as the very substance itself?

For if Evil can enter into other things, it must have in a certain sense a prior existence, even though it may not be an essence. As there is Good, the Absolute, as well as Good, the quality, so, together with the derived evil entering into something not itself, there must be the Absolute Evil.

But how? Can there be Unmeasure apart from an unmeasured object?

Yes: precisely as there is Measure apart from anything measured, so there is Unmeasure apart from the unmeasured. If Unmeasure could not exist independently, it must exist either in an unmeasured object or in something measured; but the unmeasured could not need Unmeasure and the measured could not contain it.

There must, then, be some Undetermination-Absolute, some Absolute Formlessness; all the qualities cited as characterizing the Nature of Evil must be summed under an Absolute Evil; and every evil thing outside of this must either contain this Absolute by saturation or have taken the character of evil and become a cause of evil by consecration to this Absolute.

What will this be?

That Kind (Matter) whose place is below all the patterns, forms, shapes, measurements, and limits, that which has no trace of good by any title of its own, but (at best) takes order and grace from some Principle outside itself, a mere image as regards Absolute-Being but the Authentic Essence of Evil—in so far as Evil can have Authentic Being. In such a Kind Reason recognizes the Primal Evil, Evil Absolute.

4. The bodily Kind, in that it partakes of Matter, is an evil thing. What form is in bodies is an untrue form: they are without life: by their own natural disorderly movement they make away with each other; they are hindrances to the Soul in its proper Act; in their ceaseless flux they are always slipping away from Being.

Soul, on the contrary, since not every soul is evil, is not an evil Kind.

What, then, is the evil Soul?

It is, we read, the Soul that has entered into the service of that in which soul-evil is implanted by nature, in whose service the unreasoning phase of the Soul accepts evil—unmeasure, excess, and shortcoming, which bring forth licentiousness, cowardice, and all other flaws of the Soul, all the states, foreign to the true nature, which set up false judgements, so that the Soul comes to name things good or evil not by their true value but by the mere test of like and dislike.

But what is the root of this evil state? how can it be brought under the causing principle indicated?

Firstly, such a Soul is not apart from Matter, is not purely itself. That is to say, it is touched with Unmeasure, it is shut out from the Forming-Idea that orders and brings to measure, and this because it is merged into a body made of Matter.

Then if the Reasoning-Faculty too has taken hurt, the Soul's seeing is baulked by the passions and by the darkening that Matter brings to it, by its decline into Matter, by its very attention no longer to Essence but to Process—whose principle or source is, again, Matter, the Kind so evil as to saturate with its own pravity even that which is not in it but merely looks towards it.

For, wholly without part in Good, the negation of Good, unmingled Lack, this Matter-Kind makes over to its own likeness whatsoever comes in touch with it.

The Soul wrought to perfection, addressed towards the Intellectual-Principle is steadfastly pure: it has turned away from Matter; all that is undetermined, that is outside of measure, that is evil, it neither sees nor draws near; it endures in its purity, only, and wholly, determined by the Intellectual-Principle.

The Soul that breaks away from this source of its reality, in so far as it is not perfect or primal, is, as it were, a secondary, an image, to the loyal Soul. By its falling-away—and to the extent of the fall—it is stripped of Determination, becomes wholly indeterminate, sees darkness. Looking to what repels vision, as we look when we are said to see darkness, it has taken Matter into itself.

5. But, it will be objected, if this seeing and frequenting of the darkness is due to the lack of good, the Soul's evil has its source in that very lack; the darkness will be merely a secondary cause—and at once the Principle of Evil is removed from Matter, is made anterior to Matter.

No: Evil is not in any and every lack; it is in absolute lack. What falls in some degree short of the Good is not Evil; considered in its own kind it might even be perfect, but where there is utter dearth, there we have Essential Evil, void of all share in Good; this is the meaning of Matter.

Matter has not even existence whereby to have some part in Good: Being is attributed to it by an accident of words: the truth would be that it has Non-Being.

Mere lack brings merely Not-Goodness: Evil demands the absolute lack—though, of course, any very considerable shortcoming makes the ultimate fall possible and is already, in itself, an evil.

In fine, we are not to think of Evil as some particular bad thing—injustice, for example, or any other ugly trait—but as a principle distinct from any of the particular forms in which, by the addition of certain elements, it becomes manifest. Thus there may be wickedness in the Soul; the forms this general wickedness is to take will be determined by the environing Matter, by the faculties of the Soul that operate, and by the nature of their operation, whether seeing, acting, or merely admitting impression.

But supposing things external to the Soul are to be counted Evil—sickness, poverty, and so forth—how can they be referred to the principle we have described?

Well, sickness is excess or defect in the body, which as a material organism rebels against order and measure; ugliness is but matter not mastered by Ideal-Form; poverty consists in our need and lack of goods made necessary to us by our association with Matter whose very nature is to be one long want.

If all this be true, we cannot be, ourselves, the source of Evil, we are not evil in ourselves; Evil was before we came to be; the Evil which holds men down binds them against their will; and for those that have the strength—not found in all men, it is true—there is a deliverance from the evils that have found lodgement in the Soul.

❙ The gods of heaven (the star-souls) have Matter, but are free from Evil, free from the vice in men.[2]❙ Not all men are vicious; some overcome vice, some, the better sort, are never attacked by it; and those who master it win by means of that in them which is not material.

6. If this be so, how do we explain the teaching that evils can never pass away but 'exist of necessity', that 'while evil has no place in the divine order, it haunts mortal nature and this place for ever'?

Does this mean that heaven is clear of evil, ever moving its orderly way, spinning on the appointed path, no injustice There or any flaw, no wrong done by any power to any other but all true to the settled plan, while injustice and disorder prevail on earth, designated as 'the mortal kind and this place'?

Not quite so: for the precept to 'flee hence' does not refer to earth and earthly life. The flight we read of consists not in quitting earth but in living our earth-life 'with justice and piety in the light of philosophy'; it is vice we are to flee, so that clearly to the writer Evil is simply vice with the sequels of vice. And when the disputant in that dialogue says that, if men could be convinced of the doctrine advanced, there would be an end of Evil, he is answered, 'That can never be: Evil is of necessity, for there must be a contrary to good.'

Still we may reasonably ask how can vice in man be a contrary to The Good in the Supernal: for vice is the contrary to virtue and virtue is not The Good but merely the good thing by which Matter is brought to order.

How can there be any contrary to the Absolute Good, when the absolute has no quality?

Besides, is there any universal necessity that the existence of one of two contraries should entail the existence of the other? Admit that the existence of one is often accompanied by the existence of the other—sickness and health, for example—yet there is no universal compulsion.

Perhaps, however, our author did not mean that this was universally true; he is speaking only of The Good.

But then, if The Good is an essence, and still more, if It is that which transcends all existence, how can It have any contrary?

That there is nothing contrary to essence ∎ (or substance)³∎ is certain in the case of particular existences—established by practical proof—but not ∎ in the quite different case of essential existence in general.⁴∎

But of what nature would this contrary be, the contrary to universal existence and in general to the Primals?

To essential existence would be opposed the non-existence; to the nature of Good, some principle and source of evil. Both these will be sources, the one of what is good, the other of what is evil; and all within the domain of the one principle being opposed, as contrary, to the entire domain of the other, the totals are contrary, and this in a contrariety more violent than any existing between secondary things.

For these last are opposed as members of one species or of one genus, and, within that common ground, they participate in some common quality.

In the case of the Primals or Universals there is such complete separation that what is the exact negation of one group constitutes the very nature of the other; we have diametric contrariety if by contrariety we mean the extreme of remoteness.

Now to the content of the divine order, the fixed quality, the measuredness, and so forth—there is opposed the content of the evil principle, its unfixedness, measurelessness, and so forth: total is opposed to total. The existence of the one Kind is a falsity, primarily, essentially, a falseness: the other Kind has Essence-Authentic: the opposition is of truth to lie; essence is opposed to essence.

Thus we see that it is not universally true that an Essence (or substance) can have no contrary.

In the case of fire and water we would admit contrariety if it were not for their common element, the Matter, about which are gathered the warmth and dryness of one and the dampness and cold of the other: if there were only present what constitutes their distinct kinds, the common ground being absent, there would be, here also, essence contrary to essence.

In sum, things utterly sundered, having nothing in common, standing at the remotest poles, are opposites in nature: the contrariety does not depend upon quality or upon any other generic type, but upon the utmost difference, clash in content, clash in effect.

7. But why does the existence of the Principle of Good necessarily comport the existence of the Principle of Evil? Is it because the All necessarily comports the existence of Matter? Yes: for necessarily this All is made up of contraries: it could not exist if Matter did not. The Nature of this Cosmos is, therefore, a blend; it is 'blended from the Intellectual-Principle and Necessity': what comes into it from God is good; evil is from 'the Ancient Kind'—a phrase which means the underlying Matter not yet brought to order by the Ideal-Form.

But, since the expression 'this place' must be taken to mean the All, how explain the words 'mortal nature'?

The answer is in the passage (in which the Father of Gods addresses the Divinities of the lower sphere), 'Since you possess only a derivative being, you are not immortals—but by my power you shall escape dissolution'. On this reckoning it can be said with truth that Evil will never perish.

The 'flight hence', we read, is not a matter of place, but of acquiring virtue, of disengaging the self from the body; this is the escape from Matter, since association with the body implies association with Matter. Plato explains somewhere how a man frees himself and how he remains bound; and the phrase 'to live among the gods' means to live among the Intelligible-Existents, for these are the Immortals.

There is another consideration establishing the necessary existence of Evil.

Given that The Good is not the only existent thing, it is inevitable that, by the outgoing from it or, if the phrase be preferred, the continuous down-going or away-going from it, there should be produced a Last, something after which nothing more can be produced: this will be Evil.

As necessarily as there is Something after the First, so necessarily there is a Last: this Last is Matter, the thing which has no residue of good in it: here is the necessity of Evil.

8. But there will still be some to deny that it is through this Matter that we ourselves become evil.

They will say that neither ignorance nor wicked desires arise in Matter. Even if they admit that the unhappy condition within us is due to the pravity inherent in body, they will urge that still the blame lies not in the Matter itself but with the Form present in it—such Form as heat, cold, bitterness, saltness, and all other conditions perceptible to sense, or again such states as being full or void—not in the concrete signification but in the presence or absence of just such forms. In a word, they will argue, all particularity in desires and even in perverted judgements upon things can be referred to such causes, so that Evil lies in this Form much more than in the mere Matter.

Yet, even with all this, they can be compelled to admit that Matter is the Evil.

For, the quality (Form) that has entered into Matter does not act as an entity apart from the Matter, any more than axe-shape will cut apart from iron. Further, Forms lodged in Matter are not the same as they would be if they remained within themselves; they are Reason-Principles Materialized, they are corrupted in the Matter, they have absorbed its nature: essential fire does not burn, nor do any of the essential entities effect, of themselves alone, the operation which, once they have entered into Matter, is traced to their action.

Matter becomes mistress of what is manifested through it: it corrupts and destroys the incomer, it substitutes its own opposite character and kind, not in the sense of opposing, for example, concrete cold to concrete warmth, but by setting its own formlessness against the Form of heat, shapelessness to shape, excess and defect to the duly ordered. Thus, in sum, what enters into Matter ceases to belong to itself, comes to belong to Matter, just as, in the nourishment of living beings, what is taken in does not remain as it came, but is turned into, say, dog's blood and all that goes to make a dog, becomes, in fact, any of the humours of any recipient.

No, if body is the cause of Evil, then there is no escape; the cause of Evil is Matter.

Still, it will be urged, the incoming Idea should have been able to conquer the Matter.

The difficulty is that Matter's master cannot remain pure itself except by avoidance of Matter.

Besides, the constitution determines both the desires and their violence, so that there are bodies in which the incoming idea cannot hold sway: there is a vicious constitution which chills and clogs the activity and inhibits choice; a contrary bodily habit produces frivolity, lack of balance. The same fact is indicated by our successive variations of mood: when we are full, we are not the same—either in desires or in ideas—as when we are empty, and we differ again according to what has satisfied our appetite.

To resume: the Measureless is evil primarily; whatever, either by resemblance or participation, exists in the state of unmeasure, is evil secondarily, its unmeasure being but an attribute—primarily, the darkness; secondarily, the darkened. Now, Vice, being an ignorance and a lack of measure in the Soul, is secondarily evil, not the Essential Evil, just as Virtue is not the Primal Good but is Likeness to The Good, or participation in it.

9. But what approach have we to the knowing of Good and Evil?

And first of the Evil of soul: Virtue we may know by the Intellectual-Principle and by means of the philosophic habit; it recognizes itself: but Vice?

As a ruler marks off straight from crooked, so Vice is known by its divergence from the line of Virtue.

But are we able to affirm Vice by any vision we can have of it, or is there some other way of knowing it?

Utter viciousness, certainly not by any vision, for it is utterly outside of bound and measure; this thing which is nowhere can be seized only by abstraction; but any degree of evil falling short of The Absolute is knowable by the extent of that falling short.

We see partial goodness; from what is before us we divine that which is lacking to the entire form—that which the completed Kind (Virtue) contains but which does not appear in the present instance; this we call Vice, and leave Virtue's deprivation undetermined. In the same way when we observe what we feel to be an ugly appearance in Matter—left there because the Reason-Principle has not become so completely the master as to cover over the unseemliness—we recognize Ugliness by the falling-short from Ideal-Form.

But how can we identify what has never had any touch of Form?

We utterly eliminate every kind of Form; and the object in which there is none whatever we call Matter: if we are to see Matter we must so completely abolish Form that we take shapelessness into our very selves.

In fact it is another Intellectual-Principle, not the true, this which ventures a vision so uncongenial.

To see darkness the eye withdraws from the light; it is striving to cease from seeing, therefore it abandons the light which would make the darkness invisible; away from the light its power is rather that of not-seeing than of seeing and this not-seeing is its nearest approach to seeing Darkness. So the Intellectual-Principle, in order to see its contrary (Matter), must leave its own light locked up within itself, and as it were go forth from itself into an outside realm; it must ignore its native brightness, and submit itself to the very contradiction of its being.

10. But if Matter is devoid of quality how can it be evil?

It is described as being devoid of quality in the sense only that it does not essentially possess any of the qualities which it admits and which enter into it as into a substratum. No one says that it has no nature; and if it has any nature at all, why may not that nature be evil though not in the sense of quality?

Quality qualifies something not itself: it is therefore an accidental; it resides in some other object. Matter does not exist in some other object but is the substratum in which the accidental resides. Matter, then, is said to be devoid of

Quality in that it does not in itself possess this thing which is by nature an accidental. If, moreover, Quality itself be devoid of Quality, how can Matter, which is the unqualified, be said to have it?

Thus, it is quite correct to say at once that Matter is without Quality and that it is evil: it is Evil not in the sense of having Quality but, precisely, in not having it; give it Quality and in its very Evil it would almost be a Form, whereas in truth it is a Kind contrary to Form.

11. 'But', it may be said, 'the Kind opposed to all Form is Privation or Negation, and this necessarily belongs to something other than itself, it is no Substantial-Existence: therefore if Evil is Privation or Negation it must be lodged in a subject deprived of Form: there will be no Self-Existent Evil.'

This objection may be answered by applying the principle to the case of Evil in the Soul; the Evil, the Vice, will be a Negation and not anything having a separate existence; we come to the doctrine which denies Matter or, admitting it, denies its Evil; we need not seek elsewhere; we may at once place Evil in the Soul, recognizing it as the mere absence of Good. But if the negation is the negation of something that ought to become present, if it is a denial of the Good by the Soul, then the Soul produces vice within itself by the operation of its own nature, and is devoid of good and, therefore, Soul though it be, devoid of life: the Soul, if it has no life, is soulless; the Soul is no Soul.

No; the Soul has life by its own nature and therefore does not, of its own nature, contain this negation of The Good: it has much good in it; it carries a happy trace of the Intellectual-Principle and is not essentially evil: neither is it primally evil nor is that Primal Evil present in it even as an accidental, for the Soul is not wholly apart from the Good.

12. Perhaps Vice and Evil as in the Soul should be described not as an entire, but as a partial, negation of good.

▌But if this were so, the Soul must possess some part of The Good and be deprived of the rest; it[5] will have ▌ a mingled nature and the Evil within it will not be unblended: we have not yet lighted on the Primal, unmingled Evil. The Soul would possess the Good as its Essence, the Evil as an Accidental.

13. Perhaps Evil is merely an impediment to the Soul like something affecting the eye and so hindering sight.

But such an evil in the eyes is no more than an occasion of evil, the Absolute Evil is something quite different. If then Vice is an impediment to the Soul, Vice is an occasion of evil but not Evil-Absolute. Virtue is not the Absolute Good, but a co-operator with it; and if Virtue is not the Absolute Good, neither is Vice the Absolute Evil. Virtue is not the Absolute Beauty or the Absolute Good; neither, therefore, is Vice the Essential Ugliness or the Essential Evil.

We have said that Virtue is not the Absolute Good and Beauty, because we know that these are earlier than Virtue and transcend it, and that it is good and beautiful by some participation in them. Now, as going upward from Virtue, we come to the Beautiful and to the Good, so, going downward from Vice, we reach Essential Evil: from Vice as the starting-point we come to vision of Evil, as far as such vision is possible, and we become evil to the extent of our participation in it. We are become dwellers in the Place of Unlikeness, where, fallen from all our resemblance to the Divine, we lie in gloom and mud: for if the Soul abandons itself unreservedly to the extreme of viciousness, it is no longer a vicious Soul merely, for mere vice is still human, still carries some trace of good: it has taken to itself another nature, the Evil, and as far as Soul can die it is dead. And the death of Soul is twofold: while still sunk in body to lie down in Matter and drench itself with it; when it has left the body, to lie in the other world until, somehow, it stirs again and lifts its sight from the mud: and this is our 'going down to Hades and slumbering there'.

14. It may be suggested that Vice is feebleness in the Soul.

We shall be reminded that the Vicious Soul is unstable, swept along from every ill to every other, quickly stirred by appetites, headlong to anger, as hasty to compromises, yielding at once to obscure imaginations, as weak, in fact, as the weakest thing made by man or nature, blown about by every breeze, burned away by every heat.

Still the question must be faced what constitutes this weakness in the Soul, whence it comes.

For weakness in the body is not like that in the Soul: the word weakness, which covers the incapacity for work and the lack of resistance in the body, is applied to the Soul merely by analogy—unless, indeed, in the one case as in the other, the cause of the weakness is Matter.

But we must go more thoroughly into the source of this weakness, as we call it, in the Soul, which is certainly not made weak as the result of any density or rarity, or by any thickening or thinning or anything like a disease, like a fever.

Now this weakness must be seated either in souls utterly disengaged or in souls bound to Matter or in both.

It cannot exist in those apart from Matter, for all these are pure and, as we read, winged and perfect and unimpeded in their task: there remains only that the weakness be in the fallen souls, neither cleansed nor clean; and in them the weakness will be, not in any privation but in some hostile presence, like that of phlegm or bile in the organs of the body.

If we form an acute and accurate notion of the cause of the fall we shall understand the weakness that comes by it.

Matter exists; Soul exists; and they occupy, so to speak, one place. There is not one place for Matter and another for Soul—Matter, for instance, kept to earth, Soul in the air: the Soul's 'separate place' is simply its not being in Matter; that is, its not being united with it; that is that there be no compound unit consisting of Soul and Matter; that is that Soul be not moulded in Matter as in a matrix; this is the Soul's apartness.

But the faculties of the Soul are many, and it has its beginning, its intermediate phases, its final fringe. Matter appears, importunes, raises disorders, seeks to force its way within; but all the ground is holy, nothing there without part in Soul. Matter therefore submits, and takes light: but the source of its illumination it cannot attain to, for the Soul cannot tolerate this foreign thing close by, since the evil of it makes it invisible. On the contrary the illumination, the light streaming from the Soul, is dulled, is weakened, as it mixes with Matter which offers Birth to the Soul, providing the means by which it enters into generation, impossible to it if no recipient were at hand.

This is the fall of the Soul, this entry into Matter: thence its weakness: not all the faculties of its being retain free play, for Matter hinders their manifestation; it encroaches upon the Soul's territory and, as it were, crushes the Soul back; and it turns to evil all that it has stolen, until the Soul finds strength to advance again.

Thus the cause, at once, of the weakness of Soul and of all its evil is Matter.

The evil of Matter precedes the weakness, the vice; it is Primal Evil. Even though the Soul itself submits to Matter and engenders it; if it becomes evil within itself by its commerce with Matter, the cause is still the presence of Matter: the Soul would never have approached Matter but that the presence of Matter is the occasion of its earth-life.

15. If the existence of Matter be denied, the necessity of this Principle must be demonstrated from the treatises 'On Matter' where the question is copiously treated.

To deny Evil a place among realities is necessarily to do away with the Good as well, and even to deny the existence of anything desirable; it is to deny desire, avoidance, and all intellectual act; for desire has Good for its object, aversion looks to Evil, all intellectual act, all Wisdom, deals with Good and Bad, and is itself one of the things that are good.

There must then be The Good—good unmixed—and the Mingled Good and Bad, and the Rather Bad than Good, this last ending with the Utterly Bad we have been seeking, just as that in which Evil constitutes the lesser part tends, by that lessening, towards the Good.

What, then, must Evil be to the Soul?

What soul could contain Evil unless by contact with the lower Kind? There could be no desire, no sorrow, no rage, no fear: fear touches the compounded dreading its dissolution; pain and sorrow are the accompaniments of the dissolution; desires spring from something troubling the grouped being or are a provision against trouble threatened; all impression is the stroke of something unreasonable outside the Soul, accepted only because the Soul is not devoid of parts or phases; the Soul takes up false notions through having gone outside of its own truth by ceasing to be purely itself.

One desire or appetite there is which does not fall under this condemnation; it is the aspiration towards the Intellectual-Principle: this demands only that the Soul dwell alone enshrined within that place of its choice, never lapsing towards the lower.

Evil is not alone: by virtue of the nature of Good, the power of Good, it is not Evil only: it appears, necessarily, bound around with bonds of Beauty, like some captive bound in fetters of gold; and beneath these it is hidden so that, while it must exist, it may not be seen by the gods, and that men need not always have evil before their eyes, but that when it comes before them they may still be not destitute of Images of the Good and Beautiful for their Remembrance.

NOTES TO ENNEAD I.8

1. FIRST EDITION has this paragraph as follows: "*And the First Act is the Act of the Good stationary within Itself, and the First Existence is the self-contained Existence of The Good; but there is also an Act upon It, that of the Intellectual-Principle which,* as it were, lives about it."

TAYLOR: "... it is the first energy of intellect, and the first essence, intellect in the mean time abiding in itself; and it energizes, indeed, about intellect, as if living by an energy of this kind."

GUTHRIE: "She is the first actualization of Intelligence, the first being that Intelligence, though remaining within itself, begets. She directs her whole activity towards supreme Intelligence, and lives exclusively thereby."

ARMSTRONG: "That intellect is the first act of the Good and the first substance; the Good stays still in himself; but intellect moves about him in its activity, as also it lives around him."

COMMENT: The issue of whether the first "double act" in Plotinian metaphysics (cf. also Ennead V.4.2) is logically prior to, or is the self-establishing act of, Intellectual-Principle, is key to radically different interpretations of the Plotinian opus. The interpretation of this passage also concerns the issue of whether or not Plotinus conceives a "super-intelligence" in the One itself, prior to the self-establishing of Intellectual-Principle.

Much of Anthony Damiani's *Astronoesis* is devoted to supporting the idea expressed in MacKenna's original translation here. On this idea, see also the chapter on the One in

Nature, Contemplation, and the One, by John Deck (Larson Publications, 1991), particularly page 28 where Mr. Deck writes: "The One, remaining in itself, in its own proper seat, has its perfection in itself and exercises its own co-subsistent act, which is itself. The Nous [Intellectual-Principle, ed.] necessarily takes its hypostasis *from* this intimate act of the One, and in doing so comes to being and entity. Thus the doctrine has been expressed with precision. The self-act of the One is and remains complete in itself; the Nous is the act *from* the self-contained act of the One as from an originative source. The act *from* the entity is necessary when the act *of* the entity is exercising itself."

2. FIRST EDITION begins this paragraph as follows: "*In a word since Matter belongs only to the sensible world,* vice in men *is not the absolute evil.*"

GUTHRIE: "Evil, therefore, is caused by the presence of matter in sense-objects, and is not identical with the wickedness of men."

TAYLOR: "But the matter of bodies is the evil of our present nature; nor is the depravity of men evil itself;"

ARMSTRONG translates the whole paragraph as follows: "Though there is matter with the visible gods, evil is not there, not the vice which men have—since not even all men have it; the visible gods master matter,—yet the gods with whom there is no matter are better—and they master it by that in them which is not material." This interpretation footnoted by Armstrong as follows: *theois* (Heintz) seems a certain correction for the MSS *thesis* or *theseis.*"

3. FIRST EDITION omits "(or substance)"

4. FIRST EDITION: ". . . in the quite different case of *the Universal.*"

GUTHRIE: ". . . but the proposition has not been demonstrated as regards universal Being."

ARMSTRONG: ". . . but it has not been demonstrated that this applies in general."

TAYLOR: ". . . but whether or not there is something contrary to essence, simply considered, is not yet demonstrated."

5. FIRST EDITION: "But if this were so *part of the Soul must possess The Good, part be without it; the Soul* will have . . ."

ARMSTRONG: "In this case, if it has some good and is deprived of some . . ."

TAYLOR: ". . . if this is the case, the soul, partly possessing, and partly destitute of good, will have . . ."

GUTHRIE: ". . . in this case, if the soul simultaneously, contain possession and privation of good . . ."

COMMENT: For a part of the soul to possess The Good and another part of the soul to be without it does not imply that The Good lends itself to partition; the "partition" may then be seen as in the nature of soul, rather than in the nature of The Good itself.

NINTH TRACTATE

'The Reasoned Dismissal'

'You will not dismiss your Soul lest it go forth taking something with it.'

Your dismissal will ensure that it must go forth taking something (corporeal) with it, and its going forth is to some new place. The Soul will wait for the body to be completely severed from it; then it makes no departure; it simply finds itself free.

But how does the body come to be separated?

The separation takes place when nothing of Soul remains bound up with it: the harmony within the body, by virtue of which the Soul was retained, is broken and it can no longer hold its guest.

But when a man contrives the dissolution of the body, it is he that has used violence and torn himself away, not the body that has let the Soul slip from it. And in loosing the bond he has not been without passion; there has been revolt or grief or anger, movements which it is unlawful to indulge.

But if a man feel himself to be losing his reason?

That is not likely in the Proficient, but if it should occur, it must be classed with the inevitable, to be welcome at the bidding of the fact though not for its own sake. To call upon drugs to the release of the Soul seems a strange way of assisting its purposes.

And if there be a period allotted to all by fate, to anticipate the hour could not be a happy act, unless, as we have indicated, under stern necessity.

If everyone is to hold in the other world a standing determined by the state in which he quitted this, there must be no withdrawal as long as there is any hope of progress.

THE SECOND ENNEAD

FIRST TRACTATE

The Heavenly System

1. WE HOLD that the ordered universe, in its material mass, has existed for ever and will for ever endure: but simply to refer this perdurance to the Will of God, however true an explanation, is utterly inadequate.

The elements of this sphere change; the living beings of earth pass away; only the Ideal-form (the species) persists: possibly a similar process obtains in the All.

The Will of God is able to cope with the ceaseless flux and escape of body stuff by ceaselessly reintroducing the known forms in new substances, thus ensuring perpetuity not to the particular item but to the unity of Idea: now, seeing that objects of this realm possess no more than duration of form, why should celestial objects, and the celestial system itself, be distinguished by duration of the particular entity?

Let us suppose this persistence to be the result of the all-inclusiveness of the celestial and universal—with its consequence, the absence of any outlying matter into which change could take place or which could break in and destroy.

This explanation would, no doubt, safeguard the integrity of the Whole, of the All; but our sun and the individual being of the other heavenly bodies would not on these terms be secured in perpetuity: they are parts; no one of them is in itself the whole, the all; it would still be probable that theirs is no more than that duration in form which belongs to fire and such entities.

This would apply even to the entire ordered universe itself. For it is very possible that this too, though not in process of destruction from outside, might have only formal duration; its parts may be so wearing each other down as to keep it in a continuous decay while, amid the ceaseless flux of the Kind constituting its base, an outside power ceaselessly restores the form: in this way the living All may lie under the same conditions as man and horse and the rest—man and horse persisting but not the individual of the type.

With this, we would have no longer the distinction of one order, the heavenly system, stable for ever, and another, the earthly, in process of decay: all would be alike except in the point of time; the celestial would merely be longer lasting. If, then, we accepted this duration of type alone as a true account of the All equally with its partial members, our difficulties would be eased—or indeed we should have no further problem—once the Will of God were shown to be capable, under these conditions and by such communication, of sustaining the Universe.

But if we are obliged to allow individual persistence to any entity, whatever its size, within the Cosmos, then, firstly, we must show that the Divine Will is adequate to make it so; secondly, we have to face the question, What accounts for some things having individual persistence and others only the persistence of type? and, thirdly, we ask how the partial entities of the celestial system hold a real duration which would thus appear possible to all partial things.

2. Supposing we accept this view and hold that, while things below the moon's orb have merely type-persistence, the celestial realm and all its several members possess individual eternity; it remains to show how this strict permanence of the individual identity—the actual item eternally unchangeable—can belong to what is certainly corporeal, seeing that bodily substance is characteristically a thing of flux.

The theory of bodily flux is held by Plato no less than by the other philosophers who have dealt with physical matters, and is applied not only to ordinary bodies but to those also of the heavenly sphere.

'How', he asks, 'can these corporeal and visible entities continue eternally unchanged in identity?'—evidently agreeing, in this matter also, with Heraclitus who maintained that even the sun is perpetually coming anew into being. To Aristotle there would be no problem; it is only accepting his theories of a fifth-substance.

But to those who reject Aristotle's Quintessence and hold the material mass of the heavens to consist of the elements underlying the living things of this sphere, how is individual permanence possible? And the difficulty is still greater for the parts (than for the whole), for the sun and the heavenly bodies (than for the celestial sphere as a unit).

Every living thing is a combination of Soul and body-kind: the celestial sphere, therefore, if it is to be everlasting as an individual entity, must be so in virtue either of both these constituents or of one of them, by the combination of Soul and body or by Soul only or by body only.

Of course anyone that holds body to be incorruptible secures the desired permanence at once; no need, then, to call on a Soul or on any perdurable conjunction to account for the continued maintenance of a living being.

But the case is different when one holds that body is, of itself, perishable and that Soul is the principle of permanence: this view obliges us to the proof that the character of body is not in itself fatal either to the coherence or to the lasting stability which are imperative: it must be shown that the two elements of the union envisaged are not inevitably hostile, but that on the contrary (in the heavens) even Matter must conduce to the scheme of the standing result.

3. We have to ask, that is, how Matter, this entity of ceaseless flux constituting the physical mass of the universe, could serve towards the immortality of the Cosmos.

And our answer is, 'Because the flux is not outgoing': where there is motion within but not outwards and the total remains unchanged, there is neither growth nor decline, and thus the Cosmos never ages.

We have a parallel in our earth, constant from eternity to pattern and to mass; the air, too, never fails; and there is always water: all the changes of these elements leave unchanged the Principle of the total living thing, our world. In our own constitution, again, there is a ceaseless shifting of particles—and that with outgoing loss—and yet the individual persists for a long time; where (as in the case of the All) there is no question of an outside region, the body-principle cannot clash with Soul as against the identity and endless duration of the living thing.

Of these material elements—for example—fire, the keen and swift, co-operates by its upward tendency as earth by its lingering below; for we must not imagine that the fire, once it finds itself at the point where its ascent must stop, settles down as in its appropriate place, no longer seeking, like all the rest, to expand in both directions. No: but higher is not possible; lower is repugnant to its Kind; all that remains for it is to be tractable and, answering to a need of its nature, to be drawn by the Soul to the activity of life, and so to move—to move in a glorious place, in the Soul. Anyone that dreads its falling may take heart: the circuit of the Soul provides against any declination, embracing, sustaining; and since fire has of itself no downward tendency it accepts that guiding without resistance. The partial elements constituting our persons do not suffice for their own cohesion; once they are brought to human shape, they must borrow elsewhere if the organism is to be maintained: but in the upper spheres since there can be no loss by flux no such replenishment is needed.

Suppose such loss, suppose fire extinguished there, then a new fire must be kindled; so also if such loss by flux could occur in some of the superiors from which the celestial fire depends, that too must be replaced: but with such transmutations, while there might be something continuously similar, there would be, no longer, a Living All abidingly self-identical.

4. But matters are involved here which demand specific investigation and cannot be treated as incidental merely to our present problem. We are faced with

several questions: Is the heavenly system exposed to any such flux as would occasion the need of some restoration corresponding to nourishment; or do its members, once set in their due places, suffer no loss of substance, permanent by Kind? Does it consist of fire only, or is it mainly of fire with the other elements, as well, taken up and carried in the circuit by the dominant Principle?

(For the present we may say that) Our doctrine of the immortality of the heavenly system rests on the firmest foundation once we have cited the sovereign agent, the Soul, and considered, besides, the peculiar excellence of the bodily substance constituting the stars, a material so pure, so entirely the noblest, and chosen by the Soul as, in all living beings, the determining principle appropriates to itself the choicest among their characteristic parts. No doubt Aristotle is right in speaking of flame as a turmoil, fire insolently rioting; but the celestial fire is equable, placid, docile to the purposes of the stars.

Still, the great argument remains, the Soul, moving in its marvellous might second only to the very loftiest Existents—how could anything once placed within this Soul break away from it into non-being? No one that understands this principle, the support of all things, can fail to see that, sprung from God, it is a stronger stay than any bonds.

And is it conceivable that the Soul, valid to sustain for a certain space of time, could not so sustain for ever? This would be to assume that it holds things together by violence; that there is a 'natural course' at variance with what actually exists in the nature of the universe and in these exquisitely ordered beings; and that there is some power able to storm the established system and destroy its ordered coherence, some kingdom or dominion that may shatter the order founded by the Soul.

Further: the Cosmos has had no beginning—the impossibility has been shown elsewhere—and this is warrant for its continued existence. Why should there be in the future a change that has not yet occurred? The elements there are not worn away like beams and rafters: they hold sound for ever, and so the All holds sound. And even supposing these elements to be in ceaseless transmutation, yet the All persists: the ground of all the change must itself be changeless.

As to any alteration of purpose in the Soul (such as might lead it to bring the Cosmos to an end) we have already shown the emptiness of that fancy: the administration of the universe entails neither labour nor loss; and, even supposing the possibility of annihilating all that is material, the Soul would be no whit the better or the worse.

5. But how explain the permanence There, while the content of this sphere—its elements and its living things alike—are passing?

The reason is given by Plato: the celestial order is from God, the living things of earth are from the gods sprung from God; and it is law that the offspring of God endures.

In other words, the celestial Soul—and our souls with it—springs directly next from the Creator, while the animal life of this earth is produced by an image which goes forth from that celestial Soul and may be said to flow downwards from it.

A Soul, then, of the minor degree—reproducing, indeed, that of the Divine sphere but lacking in power inasmuch as it must exercise its creative act upon inferior stuff in an inferior region—the substances taken up into the fabric being of themselves repugnant to duration; with such an origin the living things of this realm cannot be of strength to last for ever; the material constituents are not as firmly held and controlled as if they were ruled immediately by a Principle of higher potency.

The heavens, on the contrary, must have persistence as a whole, and this entails the persistence of the parts, of the stars they contain: we could not imagine that whole to endure with the parts in flux—though, of course, we must distinguish things sub-celestial from the heavens themselves whose region does not in fact extend below the moon.

Our own case is different: physically we are formed by that (inferior) soul, given forth (not directly from God but) from the divine beings in the heavens and from the heavens themselves; it is by way of that inferior soul that we are associated with the body (which therefore will not be persistent); for the higher soul which constitutes the We is the principle not of our existence but of our excellence—or, if also of our existence, then only in the sense that, when the body is already constituted, it enters I bringing with it some small influence through the exercise of reasoning.[1]I

6. We may now consider the question whether fire is the sole element existing in that celestial realm and whether there is any outgoing thence with the consequent need of renewal.

Timaeus pronounced the material frame of the All to consist primarily of earth and fire—fire for visibility, earth for solidity—and deduced that the stars must be mainly composed of fire, but not solely since there is no doubt they are solid.

And this is probably a true account. Plato accepts it as indicated by all the appearances. And, in fact, to all our perception—as we see them and derive from them the impression of illumination—the stars appear to be mostly, if not exclusively, fire: but on reasoning into the matter we judge that since solidity cannot exist apart from earth, they must contain earth as well.

But what place could there be for the other elements? It is impossible to imagine water amid so vast a conflagration; and if air were present it would be continually changing into fire.

Admitting (with Timaeus as a logical truth) that two solid figures, standing as extremes to each other, need for their coherence two intermediaries; we may still question whether this holds good with regard to physical bodies. Certainly water and earth can be mixed without any such intermediate. It might seem valid to object that the intermediates are already present in the earth and the water; but a possible answer would be, 'Yes, but not as agents whose meeting is necessary to the coherence of those extremes.'

None the less we will take it that the coherence of extremes is produced by virtue of each I possessing all the other elements.²I It is still not proven that fire is necessary to the visibility of earth and earth to the solidarity of fire.

On this principle, nothing possesses an essential-nature of its very own; every several thing is a blend, and its name is merely an indication of the dominant constituent.

Thus we are told that earth cannot have concrete existence without the help of some moist element—the moisture in water being the necessary adhesive—but admitting that we so find it, there is still a contradiction in pretending that any one element has a being of its own and in the same breath denying its self-coherence, making its subsistence depend upon others, and so, in reality, reducing the specific element to nothing. How can we talk of the existence of the definite Kind, earth—earth essential—if there exists no single particle of earth which actually is earth without any need of water to secure its self-cohesion? What has such an adhesive to act upon if there is absolutely no given magnitude of real earth to which it may bind particle after particle in its business of producing the continuous mass? If there is any such given magnitude, large or small, of pure earth, then earth can exist in its own nature, independently of water: if there is no such primary particle of pure earth, then there is nothing whatever for the water to bind. As for air—air unchanged, retaining its distinctive quality—how could it conduce to the subsistence of a dense material like earth?

Similarly with fire. No doubt Timaeus speaks of it as necessary not to the existence but to the visibility of earth and the other elements; and certainly light is essential to all visibility—we cannot say that we see darkness, which implies, precisely, that nothing is seen, as silence means nothing being heard.

But all this does not assure us that the earth to be visible must contain fire: light is sufficient: snow, for example, and other extremely cold substances gleam without the presence of fire—though of course it might be said that fire was once there and communicated colour before disappearing.

As to the composition of water, we must leave it an open question whether there can be such a thing as water without a certain proportion of earth.

But how can air, the yielding element, contain earth?

Fire, again: is earth perhaps necessary there since fire is by its own nature devoid of continuity and not a thing of three dimensions?

Supposing it does not possess the solidity of the three dimensions, it has that of its thrust; now, cannot this belong to it by the mere right and fact of its being one of the corporeal entities in nature? Hardness is another matter, a property confined to earth-stuff. Remember that gold—which is water—becomes dense by the accession not of earth but of denseness or consolidation: in the same way fire, with Soul present within it, may consolidate itself upon the power of the Soul; I and there are living beings of fire, the Celestials.³I

But, in sum, do we abandon the teaching that all the elements enter into the composition of every living thing?

For this sphere, no: but to lift clay into the heavens is against nature, contrary to the laws of her ordaining: it is difficult, too, to think of that swiftest of circuits bearing along earthly bodies in its course—nor could such material conduce to the splendour and white glint of the celestial fire.

7. We can scarcely do better, in fine, than follow Plato.

Thus:

In the universe as a whole there must necessarily be such a degree of solidity, that is to say, of resistance, as will ensure that the earth, set in the centre, be a sure footing and support to the living beings moving over it, and inevitably communicate something of its own density to them: the earth will possess coherence by its own unaided quality, but visibility by the presence of fire: it will contain water against the dryness which would prevent the cohesion of its particles; it will hold air to lighten its bulky matters; it will be in contact with the celestial fire—not as being a member of the sideral system but by the simple fact that the fire there and our earth both belong to the ordered universe, so that something of the earth is taken up by the fire as something of the fire by the earth and something of everything by everything else.

This borrowing, however, does not mean that the one thing taking-up from the other enters into a composition, becoming an element in a total of both: it is simply a consequence of the cosmic fellowship; the participant retains its own being and takes over not the thing itself but some property of the thing, not air but air's yielding softness, not fire but fire's incandescence: the mixing determines all the properties, and it is the resultant compound, and not merely earth and fire, which exhibits the solidity we know and the fieriness.

We have authority for this where we read:

'At the second circuit from the earth, God kindled a light': he is speaking of the sun which, elsewhere, he calls the all-glowing and, again, the all-gleaming: thus he prevents us imagining it to be anything else but fire, though of a peculiar kind; in other words it is light, which he distinguishes from flame as being only modestly warm: this light is a corporeal substance but from it there shines forth that other 'light' which, though it carries the same name, we pronounce incorporeal, given forth from the first as its flower and radiance, the veritable 'incandescent body'. Plato's word 'earthy' is commonly taken in too depreciatory a sense: he is thinking of earth as the principle of solidity; we are apt to ignore his distinctions and think of the concrete clay.

Fire of this order, giving forth this purest light, belongs to the upper realm, and there its seat is fixed by nature; but we must not, on that account, suppose the flame of earth to be associated with the beings of that higher sphere.

No: the flame of this world, once it has attained a certain height, is extinguished by the currents of air opposed to it. Moreover, as it carries an earthy element on its upward path, it is weighed downwards and cannot reach those loftier regions. It comes to a stand somewhere below the moon—making the air at that point subtler—and its flame, if any flame can persist, is subdued and softened, and no longer retains its first intensity, but gives out only what radiance it reflects from the light above.

And it is that loftier light—falling variously upon the stars, to each in a certain proportion—that gives them their characteristic differences, as well in magnitude as in colour; just such light constitutes also the still higher heavenly bodies which, however, like clear air, are invisible because of the subtle texture and unresisting transparency of their material substance and also by their very distance.

8. Now: given a light of this degree, remaining in the upper sphere at its appointed station, pure light in purest place, what mode of outflow from it can be conceived possible?

Such a Kind is not so constituted as to flow downwards of its own accord; and there exists in those regions no power to force it down. Again, body in contact with Soul must always be very different from body left to itself; the bodily substance of the heavens has that contact and will show that difference.

Besides, the corporeal substance nearest to the heavens would be air or fire: air has no destructive quality; fire would be powerless there since it could not enter into effective contact: in its very rush it would change before its attack could be felt; and, apart from that, it has less strength and would be no match for what it would be opposing in these lower regions.

Again, fire acts by imparting heat: now it cannot be the source of heat to what is already hot by nature; and anything it is to destroy must as a first condition be heated by it, must be brought to a pitch of heat fatal to the nature concerned.

In sum, then, no outside body is necessary to the heavens to ensure their permanence—or to produce their circular movement, for it has never been shown that their natural path would be the straight line; on the contrary the heavens, by their nature, will either be motionless or move by circle; all other movement indicates outside compulsion. We cannot think, therefore, that the heavenly bodies stand in need of replenishment; we must not argue from earthly frames to those of the celestial system whose sustaining Soul is not the same, whose space is not the same, whose conditions are not those which make restoration necessary in this realm of composite bodies always in flux: we must recognize that the changes that take place in bodies here represent a slipping-away from the being (a phenomenon not incident to the celestial sphere) and take place at the dictate of a Principle not dwelling in the higher regions, one not powerful enough to ensure the permanence of the existences in which it is exhibited, one which in its coming into being and in its generative act is but an imitation of an antecedent Kind, and, as we have shown, cannot at every point possess the unchangeable identity of the Intellectual Realm.

NOTES TO ENNEAD II.1

1. FIRST EDITION: ". . . bringing with it some *effluence from the Divine Reason in support of the existence.*"

  GUTHRIE: ". . . and contributes to our being only by one part, by giving us reason (in making of us reasonable beings, and men)."

  ARMSTRONG: ". . . making only minor contributions from reasoning to our being."

2. FIRST EDITION: ". . . possessing all the *intermediates.*"

  ARMSTRONG: ". . . they are joined because each of them contains all things."

  GUTHRIE: ". . . each of these two elements contains all the others."

3. FIRST EDITION: ". . . and there are living beings of fire *among* the Celestials."

  ARMSTRONG: "There are, in fact, fiery living beings among the spirits."

  GUTHRIE: "The bodies of (certain among) the guardian spirits consist of fire."

SECOND TRACTATE

The Heavenly Circuit

1. But whence that circular movement?

In imitation of the Intellectual-Principle.

And does this movement belong to the material part or to the Soul? Can we account for it on the ground that the Soul has itself at once for centre and for the goal to which it must be ceaselessly moving; or that, being self-centred, it is not of unlimited extension (and consequently must move ceaselessly to be omnipresent), and that its revolution carries the material mass with it?

If the Soul had been the moving power (by any such semi-physical action) it would be so no longer; it would have accomplished the act of moving and have brought the universe to rest; there would be an end of this endless revolution.

In fact the Soul must be in repose or at least cannot have spatial movement; how then, having itself a movement of quite another order, could it communicate spatial movement?

But perhaps the circular movement (of the Cosmos as Soul and body) is not spatial or is spatial not primarily but only incidentally.

What, by this explanation, would be the essential movement of the cosmic Soul?

A movement towards itself, the movement of self-awareness, of self-intellection, of the living of its life, the movement of its reaching to all things so that nothing shall lie outside of it, nothing anywhere but within its scope.

The dominant in a living thing is what compasses it entirely and makes it a unity.

If the Soul has no motion of any kind, it would not vitally compass the Cosmos nor would the Cosmos, a thing of body, keep its content alive, for the life of body is movement.

Any spatial motion there is will be limited; it will be not that of Soul untrammelled but that of a material frame ensouled, an animated organism; the movement will be partly of body, partly of Soul, the body tending to the straight line which its nature imposes, the Soul restraining it; the resultant will be the compromise movement of the thing at once carried forward and at rest.

But supposing that the circular movement is to be attributed to the body, how is it to be explained, since all body, including fire (which constitutes the heavens), has straightforward motion?

The answer is that forthright movement is maintained only pending arrival at the place for which the moving thing is destined: where a thing is ordained to be, there it seeks, of its nature, to come for its rest; its motion is its tendence to its appointed place.

Then, since the fire of the sidereal system has attained its goal, why does it not stay at rest?

Evidently because the very nature of fire is to be mobile: if it did not take the curve, its straight line would finally fling it outside the universe: the circular course, then, is imperative.

But this would imply an act of providence?

Not quite: rather its own act under providence; attaining to that realm, it must still take the circular course by its indwelling nature; for it seeks the straight path onwards but finds no further space and is driven back so that it recoils on the only course left to it: there is nothing beyond; it has reached the ultimate; it runs its course in the regions it occupies, itself its own sphere, not destined to come to rest there, existing to move.

Further, the centre of a circle (and therefore of the Cosmos) is distinctively a point of rest: if the circumference outside were not in motion, the universe would be no more than one vast centre. And movement around the centre is all the more to be expected in the case of a body which has life and follows the order of nature.[1] Such motion alone can constitute its impulse towards its centre: it cannot coincide with the centre, for then there would be no circle; since this may not be, it whirls about it; so only can it indulge its tendence.

If, on the other hand, the cosmic circuit is due to the Soul, we are not to think of a painful driving (wearing it down at last); the Soul does not use violence or in any way thwart nature, for 'Nature' is no other than the custom the All-Soul has established. Omnipresent in its entirety, incapable of division, the Soul of the universe communicates that quality of universal presence to the heavens, too, in their degree, the degree, that is, of pursuing universality and advancing towards it.

If the Soul halted anywhere, there the Cosmos, too, brought so far, would halt: but the Soul encompasses all, and so the Cosmos moves, seeking everything.

Yet never to attain?

On the contrary this very motion is its eternal attainment.

Or, better; the Soul is ceaselessly leading the Cosmos towards itself: the continuous attraction communicates a continuous movement—not to some outside space but towards the Soul and in the one sphere with it, not in the straight line (which would ultimately bring the moving body outside the Soul), but in the curving course in which the moving body at every stage possesses the Soul that is attracting it and bestowing itself upon it.

If the Soul were stationary, that is if (instead of presiding over a Cosmos) it dwelt wholly and solely in the realm in which every member is at rest, motion would be unknown; but, since the Soul is not fixed in some one station There, the Cosmos must travel to every point in quest of it, and never outside it: in a circle, therefore.

2. And what of lower things? (Why have they not this motion?)

(Their case is very different:) the single thing here is not an all but a part and limited to a given segment of space; that other realm is all, is space, so to speak, and is subject to no hindrance or control, for in itself it is all that is.

And men?

As a self, each is a personal whole, no doubt; but as member of the universe, each is a partial thing.

But if, wherever the **I** circling universe[2] may be, it **I** possesses the Soul, what need of the circling?

I Because it possesses the Soul not only at that point.[3]**I**

The circular movement would be explained, too, if the Soul's power may be taken as resident at its centre.

Here, however, we must distinguish between a centre in reference to the two different natures, body and Soul.

In body, centre is a point of place; in Soul it is a source, the source of some other nature. The word, which without qualification would mean the midpoint of a spheric mass, may serve in the double reference; and, as in a material mass so in the Soul, there must be a centre, that around which the object, Soul or material mass, revolves.

The Soul exists in revolution around God to whom it clings in love, holding itself to the utmost of its power near to Him as the Being on which all depends; and since it cannot coincide with God it circles about Him.

Why then do not all souls (i.e., the lower, also, as those of men and animals) thus circle about the Godhead?

Every soul does in its own rank and place.

And why not our very bodies also?

Because the forward path is characteristic of body and because all the body's impulses are to other ends and because what in us is of this circling nature (the Soul) is hampered in its motion by the clay it bears with it, while in the higher realm everything flows on its course, lightly and easily, with nothing to check it, once there is any principle of motion in it at all.

And it may very well be that even in us the Spirit (Pneuma) which dwells with the Soul does thus circle about the divinity. For since God is omnipresent the Soul desiring perfect union must take the circular course: God is not stationed.

Similarly Plato attributes to the stars not only the spheric movement belonging to the universe as a whole but also to each a revolution around their common centre; each—not by way of thought but by links of natural necessity—has in its own place taken hold of God and exults.

3. The truth may be resumed in this way:

There is a lowest power of the Soul, a nearest to earth, and this is interwoven throughout the entire universe: another phase possesses sensation, while yet another includes the Reason which is concerned with judgement: this higher phase holds itself to the spheres, poised towards the Above but hovering over the lesser Soul and giving forth to it an effluence which makes it more intensely vital.

The lower Soul is moved by the higher which, besides encircling and supporting it, actually resides in whatsoever part of it has thrust upwards and attained the spheres. The lower then, ringed round by the higher and answering its call, turns and tends towards it; and this upward tension communicates motion to the material frame in which it is involved: for if a single point in a spheric mass is in any degree moved, without being drawn away from the rest, it moves the whole, and the sphere is set in motion. Something of the same kind happens in the case of our bodies: the unspatial movement of the Soul—in happiness, for instance, or at the idea of some pleasant event—sets up a spatial movement in the ❙ body. Similarly, the universal Soul,[4] attaining ❙ in its own region some good which increases its sense of life, moves towards what pleases it; and so, by force of the union established in the order of nature, it moves the body, in the body's region, that is in space.

As for that phase of the Soul in which sensation is vested, it, too (like the higher), takes its good from the Supreme above itself and moves, rejoicingly, in quest of it: and since the object of its desire is everywhere, it too ranges always through the entire scope of the universe.

The Intellectual-Principle has no such progress in any region; its movement is a stationary act, for it turns upon itself.

And this is why the All, circling as it does, is at the same time at rest.

NOTES TO ENNEAD II.2

1. FIRST EDITION: ". . . in the case of a *living thing whose nature binds it within a body.*"

GUTHRIE: ". . . in this living and naturally organized body."

ARMSTRONG: ". . . in the case of a living body in its natural state . . ."

2. FIRST EDITION: ". . . circling *body* be, it . . ."

ARMSTRONG: "heaven"

GUTHRIE: "heavens"

3. FIRST EDITION has this sentence as: "Because *everywhere it finds something else besides the Soul (which it desires to possess alone)*."

> GUTHRIE: "...because the Soul is not exclusively in a determinate place (and the world does not exclusively in one place desire to possess her)."

> ARMSTRONG: "Because it does not possess it only in that particular place."

4. FIRST EDITION: "... body: *the Soul*, attaining ..."

> ARMSTRONG: "... the soul ..."

> GUTHRIE: "... the universal Soul ..."

THIRD TRACTATE

Are the Stars Causes?

1. That the circuit of the stars indicates definite events to come but without being the cause direct (as the general opinion holds) of all that happens, has been elsewhere affirmed, and proved by some modicum of argument: but the subject demands more precise and detailed investigation, for to take the one view rather than the other is of no small moment.

The belief is that the planets in their courses actually produce not merely such conditions as poverty, wealth, health, and sickness, but even ugliness and beauty and, gravest of all, vices and virtue and the very acts that spring from these qualities, the definite doings of each moment of virtue or vice. We are to suppose the stars to be annoyed with men—and upon matters in which men, moulded to what they are by the stars themselves, can surely do them no wrong.

They will be distributing what pass for their good gifts, not out of kindness towards the recipients but as they themselves are affected pleasantly or disagreeably at the various points of their course; so that they must be supposed to change their plans as they stand at their zeniths or are declining.

More absurdly still, some of them are supposed to be malicious and others to be helpful, and yet the evil stars will (in certain positions) bestow favours and the benevolent act harshly: further, their action alters as they see each other or not, so that, after all, they possess no definite nature but vary according to their angles of aspect; a star is kindly when it sees one of its fellows but changes at sight of another: and there is even a distinction to be made in the seeing as it occurs in this figure or in that. Lastly, all acting together, the fused influence is different again from that of each single star, just as the blending of distinct fluids gives a mixture unlike any of them.

Since these opinions and others of the same order are prevalent, it will be well to examine them carefully one by one, beginning with the fundamental question:

2. Are these planets to be thought of as soulless or ensouled?

Suppose them, first, to be without Soul.

In that case they can purvey only heat or cold—if cold from the stars can be thought of—that is to say, any communication from them will affect only our bodily nature, since all they have to communicate to us is merely corporeal. This implies that no considerable change can be caused in the bodies affected, since emanations merely corporeal cannot differ greatly from star to star, and must, moreover, blend upon earth into one collective resultant: at most the differences would be such as depend upon local position, upon nearness or farness with regard to the centre of influence. This reasoning, of course, is as valid of any cold emanation there may be as of the warm.

Now, what is there in such corporeal action to account for the various classes and kinds of men, learned and illiterate, scholars as against orators, musicians as against people of other professions? Can a power merely physical make rich or poor? Can it bring about such conditions as in no sense depend upon the interaction of corporeal elements? Could it, for example, bring a man such and such a brother, father, son, or wife, give him a stroke of good fortune at a particular moment, or make him generalissimo or king?

Next, suppose the stars to have life and mind and to be effective by deliberate purpose.

In that case, what have they suffered from us that they should, in free will, do us hurt, they who are established in a divine place, themselves divine? There is nothing in their nature of what makes men base, nor can our weal or woe bring them the slightest good or ill.

3. Possibly, however, they act not by choice but under stress of their several positions and collective figures?

But if position and figure determined their action each several one would necessarily cause identical effects with every other on entering any given place or pattern.

And that raises the question what effect for good or bad can be produced upon any one of them by its transit in the parallel of this or that section of the Zodiac circle—for they are not in the Zodiacal figure itself but considerably beneath it—especially since, whatever point they touch, they are always in the heavens.

It is absurd to think that the particular grouping under which a star passes can modify either its character or its earthward influences. And can we imagine it altered by its own progression as it rises, stands at centre, declines? Exultant when at centre; dejected or enfeebled in declension; some raging as they rise and growing benignant as they set, while declension brings out the best in one among them; surely this cannot be?

We must not forget that invariably every star, considered in itself, is at centre with regard to some one given group and in decline with regard to another and vice versa; and, very certainly, it is not at once happy and sad, angry and kindly. There is no reasonable escape in representing some of them as glad in their setting, others in their rising: they would still be grieving and glad at one and the same time.

Further, why should any distress of theirs work harm to us?

No: we cannot think of them as grieving at all or as being cheerful upon occasions: they must be continuously serene, happy in the good they enjoy and the vision before them. Each lives its own free life; each finds its Good in its own Act; and this Act is not directed towards us.

Like the birds of augury, the living beings of the heavens, having no lot or part with us, may serve incidentally to foreshow the future, but they have absolutely no main function in our regard.

4. It is again not in reason that a particular star should be gladdened by seeing this or that other while, in a second couple, such an aspect is distressing: what enmities can affect such beings? what causes of enmity can there be among them?

And why should there be any difference as a given star sees certain others from the corner of a triangle or in opposition or at the angle of a square?

Why, again, should it see its fellow from some one given position and yet, in the next Zodiacal figure, not see it, though the two are actually nearer?

And, the cardinal question: by what conceivable process could they effect what is attributed to them? How explain either the action of any single star independently or, still more perplexing, the effect of their combined intentions?

We cannot think of them entering into compromises, each renouncing something of its efficiency, and their final action in our regard amounting to a concerted plan.

No one star would suppress the contribution of another, nor would star yield to star and shape its conduct under suasion.

As for the fancy that while one is glad when it enters another's region, the second is vexed when in its turn it occupies the place of the first, surely this is like starting with the supposition of two friends and then going on to talk of one being attracted to the other who, however, abhors the first.

5. When they tell us that a certain cold star is more benevolent to us in proportion as it is further away, they clearly make its harmful influence depend upon the coldness of its nature; and yet it ought (by this reasoning) to be beneficent to us when it is in the opposed Zodiacal figures.

When the cold planet, we are told, is in opposition to the hot, both become menacing: but the natural effect would be a compromise.

And we are asked to believe that one of them is happy by day and grows kindly under the warmth, while another, of a fiery nature, is most cheerful by night—as if it were not always day to them, light to them, and as if the first one could be darkened by night at that great distance above the earth's shadow.

Then there is the notion that the moon, in conjunction with a certain star, is softened at her full but is malignant in the same conjunction when her light has waned; yet, if anything of this order could be admitted, the very opposite would be the case. For when she is full to us she must be dark on the further hemisphere, that is to that star which stands above her; and when dark to us she is full to that other star, and then her influence must be reversed. To the moon itself, in fact, it can make no difference in what aspect she stands, for she is always lit on the upper or on the under half: to the other star, the warmth from the moon, of which they speak, might make a difference; but that warmth would reach it precisely when the moon is without light to us; at its darkest to us it is full to that other, and therefore (by the theory) beneficent. The darkness of the moon to us is of moment to the earth, but brings no trouble to the planet above. That planet, it is alleged, can give no help on account of its remoteness and therefore seems less well disposed; but the moon at its full suffices to the lower realm so that the distance of the other is of no importance. When the moon, though dark to us, is in aspect with the Fiery Star she is held to be favourable: the reason alleged is that the force of Mars is all-sufficient since it contains more fire than it needs.

The truth is that while the material emanations from the living beings of the heavenly system are of various degrees of warmth—planet differing from planet in this respect—no cold comes from them: the nature of the space in which they have their being is voucher for that.

The star known as Jupiter includes a due measure of fire (and warmth), in this resembling the Morning-star and therefore seeming to be in alliance with it. In aspect with what is known as the Fiery Star, Jupiter is unfriendly by virtue of the mixing of influences: in aspect with Saturn unfriendly by dint of distance. Mercury, it would seem, is (in itself) indifferent whatever stars it be in aspect with; for it adopts any and every character.

But (again, the truth is that) all the stars are serviceable to the Universe, and therefore can stand to each other only as the service of the Universe demands, in a harmony like that observed in the members of any one animal form. They exist essentially for the purpose of the Universe, just as the gall exists for the purposes of the body as a whole not less than for its own immediate function: it is to be the inciter of the animal spirits but without allowing the entire organism and its own especial region to run riot. Some such balance of function was indispensable in the All—bitter with sweet. There must be differentiation—eyes and so forth—but all the members will be in sympathy with the entire animal frame to which they belong. Only so can there be a unity and a total harmony.

And in such a total, analogy will make every part a Sign.

6. But that this same Mars, or Venus, in certain aspects should cause adulteries—as if they could thus, through the agency of human incontinence, satisfy their own mutual desires—is not such a notion the height of unreason? And who could accept the fancy that their happiness comes from their seeing each other in this or that I relative position even if they achieve nothing by doing so?'I

Again: countless myriads of living beings are born and continue to be: to minister continuously to every separate one of these; to make them famous, rich, poor, lascivious; to shape the active tendencies of every single one—what kind of life is this for the stars, how could they possibly handle a task so huge?

They are to watch, we must suppose, the rising of each several constellation and upon that signal to act; such a one, they see, has risen by so many degrees, representing so many of the periods of its upward path; they reckon on their fingers at what moment they must take the action which, executed prematurely, would be out of order: and in the sum, there is no One Being controlling the entire scheme; all is made over to the stars singly, as if there were no Sovereign Unity, standing as source of all the forms of Being in subordinate association with it, and delegating to the separate members, in their appropriate Kinds, the task of accomplishing its purposes and bringing its latent potentiality into act.

This is a separatist theory, tenable only by minds ignorant of the nature of a Universe which has a ruling principle and a first cause operative downwards through every member.

7. But, if the stars announce the future—as we hold of many other things also—what explanation of the cause have we to offer? What explains the purposeful arrangement thus implied? Obviously, unless the particular is included under some general principle of order, there can be no signification.

We may think of the stars as letters perpetually being inscribed on the heavens or inscribed once for all and yet moving as they pursue the other tasks allotted to them: upon these main tasks will follow the quality of signifying, just as the one principle underlying any living unit enables us to reason from member to member, so that for example we may judge of character and even of perils and safeguards by indications in the eyes or in some other part of the body. If these parts of us are members of a whole, so are we: in different ways the one law applies.

All teems with symbol; the wise man is the man who in any one thing can read another, a process familiar to all of us in not a few examples of everyday experience.

But what is the comprehensive principle of co-ordination? Establish this and we have a reasonable basis for the divination, not only by stars but also by birds and other animals, from which we derive guidance in our varied concerns.

All things must be enchained; and the sympathy and correspondence obtaining in any one closely knit organism must exist, first, and most intensely, in the All. There must be one principle constituting this unit of many forms of life and enclosing the several members within the unity, while at the same time, precisely as in each thing of detail the parts too have each a definite function, ∣ so in the All[2] each ∣ several member must have its own task—but more markedly so since in this case the parts are ∣ not merely members but themselves alls and of greater power.[3] ∣

Thus each entity takes its origin from one principle and, therefore, while executing its own function, works in with every other member of that All from which its distinct task has by no means cut it off: each performs its act, each receives something from the others, every one at its own moment bringing its touch of sweet or bitter. And there is nothing undesigned, nothing of chance, in all the process: all is one scheme of differentiation, starting from the Firsts and working itself out in a continuous progression of Kinds.

8. ∣ Soul, then, in the same way, is intent upon a task of its own; in everything it does it counts as an independent source of motion; it may take a direct course or it may divagate, but a Law of Justice goes with every action in the Universe[4] ∣ which, otherwise, would be dissolved and is perdurable because the entire fabric is guided as much by the orderliness as by the power of the controlling force. And in this order the stars, as being no minor members of the heavenly system, are co-operators contributing through their radiance to its symbolic function. Their symbolic power extends to the entire realm of sense, their efficacy only to what they patently do.

For our part nature keeps us upon the work of the Soul as long as we are not wrecked in the multiplicity of the Universe: once thus sunk and held we pay the penalty, which consists both in the fall itself and in the lower rank thus entailed upon our future: riches and poverty are caused (not by the stars but) by the combinations of external fact.

And what of virtue and vice?

That question has been amply discussed elsewhere: in a word, virtue is ours by the ancient staple of the Soul; vice is due to the commerce of a Soul with the outer world.

9. This brings us to the Spindle-destiny, spun according to the ancients by the Fates. To Plato the Spindle represents the co-operation of the moving and the stable elements of the cosmic circuit: the Fates with Necessity, Mother of the Fates, manipulate it and spin at the birth of every being, so that all comes into existence through Necessity.

In the Timaeus the creating God bestows the essential of the Soul, but it is the divinities moving in the Cosmos (the stars) that infuse the powerful affections holding from Necessity—our impulse and our desire, our sense of pleasure and of pain—and that lower phase of the Soul in which such experiences originate. By this statement our personality is bound up with the stars, | whence our Soul[5] takes shape; | and we are set under necessity at our very entrance into the world: our temperament will be of the stars' ordering, and so, therefore, the actions which derive from temperament, and all the experiences of a nature shaped to impressions.

What, after all this, remains to stand for the 'We'?

The 'We' is the actual resultant of a Being whose nature includes, with certain sensibilities, the power of governing them. Cut off as we are by the nature of the body, God has yet given us, in the midst of all this evil, 'virtue the unconquerable', meaningless in a state of tranquil safety but everything where its absence would be peril of fall.

Our task, then, is to work for our liberation from this sphere, severing ourselves from all that has gathered about us; the total man is to be something better than a body ensouled—the bodily element dominant with a trace of Soul running through it and a resultant life-course mainly of the body—for in such a combination all is, in fact, bodily. There is another life, emancipated, whose quality is progression towards the higher realm, towards the good and divine, towards that Principle which no one possesses except by deliberate usage but so may appropriate, becoming, each personally, the higher, the beautiful, the Godlike, and living, remote, in and by It—unless one choose to go bereaved of that higher Soul and therefore, to live fate-bound, no longer profiting, merely, by the significance of the sidereal system but becoming as it were a part sunken in it and dragged along with the whole thus adopted.

For every human Being is of twofold character; there is that compromise-total and there is the Authentic Man: and it is so with the Cosmos as a whole; it is in the one phase a conjunction of body with a certain form of the Soul bound up in body; in the other phase it is the Universal Soul, that which is not itself embodied but flashes down its rays into the embodied Soul: and the same twofold quality belongs to the Sun and the other members of the heavenly system.

To the remoter Soul, the pure, sun and stars communicate no baseness. In their efficacy upon the (material) All, they act as parts of it, as ensouled bodies within it; and they act only upon what is partial; body is the agent while, at the same time, it becomes the vehicle through which is transmitted something of the star's will and of that authentic Soul in it which is steadfastly in contemplation of the Highest.

But (with every allowance to the lower forces) all follows either upon that Highest or rather upon the Beings about It—we may think of the Divine as a fire whose outgoing warmth pervades the Universe—or upon whatsoever is transmitted by the one Soul (the divine first Soul) to the other, its Kin (the Soul of any particular being). All that is graceless is admixture. For the Universe is in truth a thing of blend, and if we separate from it that separable Soul, the residue is little. The All is a God when the divine Soul is counted in with it; the rest, we read, is 'a mighty spirit' and its ways are subdivine.

10. If all this be true, we must at once admit signification, but efficacy we must not admit without reservation or ascribe it to the stars in their wholeness, except in what concerns the (material) All and in what is of their own residuary function.

We must admit that the Soul before entering into birth presents itself bearing with it something of its own, for it could never I touch body without a large capacity for submission;[6] I we must admit some element of chance around it from its very entry, since the moment and conditions are determined by the cosmic circuit: and we must admit some effective power in that circuit itself; it is co-operative, and completes of its own act the task that belongs to the All of which everything in the circuit takes the rank and function of a part.

11. And we must remember that what comes from the supernals (stars) does not enter into the recipients as it left the source; fire, for instance, will be duller; the loving instinct will degenerate and issue in ugly forms of the passion; the vital energy in a subject not so balanced as to display the mean of manly courage, will come out as either ferocity or faintheartedness; I and ambition filled with desire and with honour for its goal will set up the pursuit of specious values; intellectual power[7] I at its lowest produces the extreme of wickedness, for wickedness is a miscalculating effort towards Intelligence.

Any such quality, modified at best from its supreme form, deteriorates again within ourselves: things of any kind that approach from above, altered by merely leaving their source, change further still by their blending with bodies, with Matter, with each other.

12. All that thus proceeds from the supernal combines into a unity (in the subject concerned) and every existing entity takes something from this blended infusion so that the result is the thing itself plus some quality. The effluence does not make the horse but adds something to it; for horse comes by horse, and man by man: the sun plays its part no doubt in the shaping, but the man has his origin in the Human-Principle. Outer things have their effect, sometimes to hurt and sometimes to help; like a father, they often contribute to good but sometimes also to harm; but they do not wrench the human being from the foundation of its nature; though sometimes Matter is the dominant, and the human principle takes the second place so that there is a failure to achieve perfection; the Ideal has been attenuated.

13. Of phenomena of this sphere some derive from the cosmic circuit and some not: we must take them singly and mark them off, assigning to each its origin.

The gist of the whole matter lies in the consideration that Soul governs this All by the plan contained in the Reason-Principle and plays in the All exactly the part of the particular principle which in every living-thing forms the members of the organism and adjusts them to the unity of which they are portions; the entire force of the Soul is represented in the All but, in the parts, Soul is present only in proportion to the degree of essential reality held by each of such partial objects. Surrounding every separate entity there are other entities, whose approach will sometimes be hostile and sometimes helpful to the purpose of its nature; but to the All taken in its length and breadth each and every separate existent is an adjusted part, holding its own characteristic and yet contributing by its own native tendency to the entire life-history of the Universe.

The soulless parts of the All are merely instruments; all their action is effected, so to speak, under a compulsion from outside themselves.

The ensouled fall into two classes. The one kind has a motion of its own, but haphazard like that of horses between the shafts but before their driver sets the course; they are set right by the whip. In the Living-Being possessed of Reason, the nature-principle includes the driver; where the driver is intelligent, it takes in the main a straight path to a set end. But both classes are members of the All and co-operate towards the general purpose.

The greater and most valuable among them have an important operation over a wide range: their contribution towards the life of the whole consists in acting, not in being acted upon; others, but feebly equipped for action, are

almost wholly passive; there is an intermediate order whose members contain
within themselves a principle of productivity and activity and make themselves
very effective in many spheres or ways and yet serve also by their passivity.

Thus the All stands as one all-complete Life, whose members, to the measure
in which each contains within itself the Highest, effect all that is high and noble:
and the entire scheme must be subordinate to its Dirigeant as an army to its
general, 'following upon Zeus'—it has been said—as he proceeds towards the
Intelligible Kind.

Secondary in the All are those of its parts which possess a less exalted nature
just as in us there are the secondary faculties of the Soul; and so all through, there
is a general analogy between the things of the All and our own members—none
of quite equal rank.

All living things, then—all in the heavens and all elsewhere—fall under the
general Reason-Principle of the All—they have been made parts with a view to
the whole: not one of these parts, however exalted, has power to effect any
alteration of these Reason-Principles or of things shaped by them and to them;
some modification one part may work upon another, whether for better or for
worse; but there is no power that can wrest anything outside of its distinct
nature.

The part effecting such a modification for the worse may act in several ways.

It may set up some weakness restricted to the material frame. Or it may carry
the weakness through to the sympathetic Soul which it has delivered over,
though never in its essence, to the inferior order of being. Or, in the case of a
material frame ill organized, it may check all such action (of the Soul) upon the
material frame as demands a certain collaboration in the part acted upon: thus
a lyre may be so ill strung as to be incapable of the melodic exactitude necessary to musical effect.

14. What of poverty and riches, glory and power?

In the case of inherited fortune, the stars merely announce a rich man,
exactly as they announce the high social standing of the child born to a distinguished house.

Wealth may be due to personal activity: in this case if the body has contributed, part of the effect is due to whatever has contributed towards the physical
powers, first the parents and then, if place has had its influence, sky and earth;
if the body has borne no part of the burden, then the success, and all the splendid accompaniments added by the Recompensers, must be attributed to virtue
exclusively. If fortune has come by gift from the good, then the source of the
wealth is, again, virtue: if by gift from the evil, but to a meritorious recipient,
then the credit must be given to the action of the best in them: if the recipient

is himself unprincipled, the wealth must be attributed primarily to the very wickedness and to whatsoever is responsible for the wickedness, while the givers bear an equal share in the wrong.

When the success is due to labour, tillage for example, it must be put down to the tiller, with all his environment as contributory. In the case of treasure trove, something from the All has entered into action; and if this be so, it will be foreshown—since all things make a chain, so that we can speak of things universally. Money is lost: if by robbery, the blame lies with the robber and the native principle guiding him: if by shipwreck, the cause is the chain of events. As for good fame, it is either deserved and then is due to the services done and to the merit of those appraising them, or it is undeserved, and then must be attributed to the injustice of those making the award. And the same principle holds as regards power—for this also may be rightly or unrightly placed—it depends either upon the merit of the dispensers of place or upon the man himself who has effected his purpose by the organization of supporters or in many other possible ways. Marriages, similarly, are brought about either by choice or by chance interplay of circumstance. And births are determined by marriages: the child is moulded true to type when all goes well; otherwise it is marred by some inner detriment, something due to the mother personally or to an environment unfavourable to that particular conception.

15. According to Plato lots and choice play a part (in the determination of human conditions) before the Spindle of Necessity is turned; that once done, only the Spindle-destiny is valid; it fixes the chosen conditions irretrievably since the elected guardian-spirit becomes accessory to their accomplishment.

But what is the significance of the Lots?

By the Lots (implying the unchosen element) we are to understand birth into the conditions actually existent in the All at the particular moment of each entry into body, birth into such and such a physical frame, from such and such parents, in this or that place, and generally all that in our phraseology is the External.

For Particulars and Universals alike it is established that to the first of those known as the Fates, to Clotho the Spinner, must be due the unity and as it were interweaving of all that exists: Lachesis (the Apportioner) presides over the Lots: to Atropos (the Inflexible) must necessarily belong the conduct of mundane events.

Of men, some enter into life as fragments of the All, bound to that which is external to themselves: they are victims of a sort of fascination, and are hardly, or not at all, themselves: but others mastering all this—straining, so to speak, by the head towards the Higher, to what is outside even the Soul—preserve still the nobility and the ancient privilege of the Soul's essential being.

For certainly we cannot think of the Soul as a thing whose nature is just a sum of impressions from outside—as if it, alone, of all that exists, had no native character.

No: much more than all else, the Soul, a Principle in its own right, must have as its native wealth many powers serving to the activities of its Kind. It is an Essential-Existent and with this Existence must go desire and act and the tendency towards some good.

While body and soul stand one combined thing, there is a joint nature, a definite entity having definite functions and employments; but as soon as any soul is detached, its employments are kept apart, its very own: it ceases to take the body's concerns to itself: it has vision now: body and soul stand widely apart.

16. The question arises what phase of the Soul enters into the union for the period of embodiment and what phase remains distinct, what is separable and what necessarily interlinked, and in general what the Living-Being is.

On all this there has been a conflict of teaching: the matter must be examined later on from quite other considerations than occupy us here. For the present let us explain in what sense we have affirmed that 'Soul governs the All by the plan contained in the Reason-Principle'.

One theory might be that the Soul creates the particular entities in succession—man followed by horse and other animals domestic or wild: fire and earth, though, first of all—that it watches these creations acting upon each other whether to help or to harm, observes, and no more, the tangled web formed of all these strands, and their unfailing sequences; and that it makes no concern of the result beyond securing the reproduction of the primal living-beings, leaving them for the rest to act upon each other according to their definite natures.

Another view makes the Soul answerable for all that thus comes about, since its first creations have set up the entire enchainment.

No doubt the Reason-Principle (conveyed by the Soul) covers all the action and experience of this realm: nothing happens, even here, by any form of hazard; all follows a necessary order.

Is everything, then, to be attributed to the act of the Reason-Principles?

To their existence, no doubt, but not to their effective action; they exist and they know; or better, the Soul, which contains the engendering Reason-Principle, knows the results of all it has brought to pass. For whensoever similar factors meet and act in relation to each other, similar consequences must inevitably ensue: the Soul adopting or fore-planning the given conditions accomplishes the due outcome and links all into a total.

All, then, is antecedent and resultant, each sequent becoming in turn an antecedent once it has taken its place among things. And perhaps this is a cause of progressive deterioration: men, for instance, are not as they were of old; by dint of interval and of the inevitable law, the Reason-Principles (constituting man) have ceded something to the characteristics of the Matter.

But:

The Soul watches the ceaselessly changing universe and follows all the fate of all its works: this is its life, and it knows no respite from this care, but is ever labouring to bring about perfection, planning to lead all to an unending state of excellence—like a farmer, first sowing and planting and then constantly setting to rights where rainstorms and long frosts and high gales have played havoc.

If such a conception of Soul be rejected as untenable we are obliged to think that the Reason-Principles themselves foreknew or even contained the ruin and all the consequences of flaw.

But then we would be imputing the creation of evil to the Reason-Principles, though (we ought to be saved from this by reflecting that) the arts and their guiding principles do not include blundering, do not cover the inartistic, the destruction of the work of art.

And here it will be objected that in the All there is nothing contrary to nature, nothing evil.

Still, by the side of the better there exists also what is less good.

Well, perhaps even the less good has its contributory value in the All. Perhaps there is no need that everything be good. Contraries may co-operate; and without opposites there could be no ordered Universe: all living-beings of the partial realm include contraries. The better elements are compelled into existence and moulded to their function by the Reason-Principle directly; the less good are potentially present in the Reason-Principles, actually present in the phenomena themselves; the Soul's power had reached its limit, and failed to bring the Reason-Principles into complete actuality since, amid the clash of these antecedent Principles, Matter had already from its own stock produced the less good.

Yet, with all this, Matter is continuously overruled towards the better; so that out of the total of things—modified by Soul on the one hand and by Matter on the other hand, and on neither hand as sound as in the Reason-Principles—there is, in the end, a Unity.

17. But these Reason-Principles, contained in the Soul, are they Thoughts?

And if so, by what process does the Soul create in accordance with these Thoughts?

It is upon Matter that this act of the Reason is exercised; and what acts physically is not an intellectual operation or a vision, but a power modifying matter, not conscious of it but merely acting upon it: the Reason-Principle, in other words, acts much like a force producing a figure or pattern ❙ upon water, but distinct from what we call the vegetative or generative faculty is another principle which provides the stimulus for the physical action.

If this is so, the leading principle of the Soul must act (not directly but) by manipulating the other (lower) phase,[8] that which is united with Matter and has the generative function. ❙

But is this handling the result of calculation?

Calculation implies reference. Reference, then, to something outside or to something contained within itself? If to its own content, there is no need of reasoning, which could not itself perform the act of creation; creation is the operation of that phase of the Soul which contains Reason-Principles; for that is its stronger puissance, its creative part.

It creates, then, on the model of the Ideas; for, what it has received from the Intellectual-Principle it must pass on in turn.

In sum, then, the Intellectual-Principle gives from itself to the Soul of the All which follows immediately upon it: this again gives forth from itself to its next, illuminated and imprinted by it; and that secondary Soul at once begins to create, as under order, unhindered in some of its creations, striving in others against the repugnance of Matter.

It has a creative power, derived; it is stored with Reason-Principles not the very originals: therefore it creates, but not in full accordance with the Principles from which it has been endowed: something enters from itself; and, plainly, this is inferior. The issue then is something living, yes; but imperfect, discontented with its own life, something very poor and reluctant and crude, formed in a Matter that is the fallen sediment of the Higher Order, bitter and embittering. This is the Soul's contribution to the All.

18. Are the evils in the Universe necessary because it is of later origin than the Higher Sphere?

Perhaps rather because without evil the All would be incomplete. For most or even all forms of evil serve the Universe—much as the poisonous snake has its use—though in most cases their function is unknown. Vice itself has many useful sides: it brings about much that is beautiful, in artistic creations for example, and its stirs us to thoughtful living, not allowing us to drowse in security.

If all this is so, then (the secret of creation is that) the Soul of the All abides in contemplation of the Highest and Best, ceaselessly striving towards the

Intelligible Kind and towards God: but, thus absorbing and filled full, it overflows—so to speak—and the image it gives forth, its last utterance towards the lower, will be the creative puissance.

This, then, is the ultimate Maker, secondary to that aspect of the Soul which is primarily saturated from the Divine Intelligence. But the Creator above all is the Intellectual-Principle, as giver, to the Soul that follows it, of those gifts whose traces exist in the Third Kind.

Rightly, therefore, is this Cosmos described as an image continuously being imaged, the First and the Second Principles immobile, the Third, too, immobile essentially, but, accidentally and in Matter, having motion.

For as long as divine Mind and Soul exist, the divine Thought-Forms (Reason-Principles) will pour forth into that phase of the Soul: as long as there is a sun, all that streams from it will be some form of Light.

NOTES TO ENNEAD II.3

1. FIRST EDITION: ". . . relative position *and not from their own settled nature?*"

GUTHRIE: ". . . how could we believe that the aspects of planets is favorable when they regard each other in a certain manner? How can we avoid believing that their nature is determinate?"

ARMSTRONG: ". . . how could anyone accept that the sight of each other, in a particular aspect, gives them pleasure, but they have no limit?"

2. FIRST EDITION: ". . . so in the All (*the higher All*) each . . ." MACKENNA is alone in offering this clarification. ARMSTRONG has simply "the All"; GUTHRIE has "the universe."

3. FIRST EDITION: ". . . not merely members but themselves *Alls, members of the loftier Kind.*"

ARMSTRONG: ". . . not merely members but wholes, and more important than the members of particular things."

GUTHRIE: ". . . that they not only form part of the universe, but that they themselves also form universes not without importance." Guthrie also adds a footnote here to see Ennead IV.4.32.

4. FIRST EDITION: "Soul, then, in the same way, is intent upon a task of its own; *alike in its direct course (its tendence towards the divine?) and in its divagation (its activity towards the lower?) it is the cause of all by its possession of the Thought of the First Principle: thus* a Law of Justice goes with *all that exists* in the Universe . . ."

ARMSTRONG: "Soul, then, is set upon doing its own work—for soul, since it has the status of a principle, does everything—and it may keep to the straight path and it may also be led astray; and just payment follows upon what is done in the All;"

GUTHRIE: "When the soul applies herself to carry out her proper function—for the soul effects everything, as far as she plays the part of a principle—she follows the straight road; when she loses her way the divine justice subjugates her to the physical order which reigns in the universe, unless the soul succeed in liberating herself."

5. FIRST EDITION: ". . . whence our Soul *(as total of Principle and affections)* takes shape;"

6. FIRST EDITION: ". . . touch body *except under stress of a powerful inner impulse;*"

ARMSTRONG: ". . . come into body unless it had a large part subject to affections."

GUTHRIE: ". . . enter into a body unless she had a great disposition to suffer. (That is, to share the passions of the bodies; see III.1.2)"

7. FIRST EDITION (ellipses here are MacKenna's): "and ambition . . . *in love . . .; and the instinct towards good sets up the pursuit of semblant beauty;* intellectual power . . ."

ARMSTRONG: ". . . and that which belongs to honour in love and is concerned with beauty produces desire of what only seems to be beautiful . . ."

GUTHRIE: "Love of the beautiful and good thus becomes the search for what only appears so."

8. FIRST EDITION: ". . . upon water—*that of a circle, suppose, where the formation of the ring is conditioned by something distinct from that force itself (i.e., by the existence and nature of the water).*

"If this is so, the *prior puissance* of the Soul *(that which conveys the Reason-Principles)* must act (not directly but) by manipulating the other *Soul,* that which is united with matter and has the generative function."

ARMSTRONG: ". . . in water; something else, different from what is called the power of growth and generation, gives it what is required for this making. If this is so, the ruling principle of the soul will make by manipulating the generative soul in matter."

GUTHRIE: ". . . just as a circle gives water a circular figure and impression. Indeed, the natural generative power has the function of production; but it needs the co-operation of the governing (principle) of the Soul, which forms and which causes the activity of the generative soul engaged in matter."

FOURTH TRACTATE
Matter [1]

1. By common agreement of all that have arrived at the conception of such a Kind, what is known as Matter is understood to be a certain base, a recipient of Form-Ideas. Thus far all go the same way. But departure begins with the attempt to establish what this basic Kind is in itself, and how it is a recipient and of what.

To a certain school, body-forms exclusively are the Real Beings; existence is limited to bodies; there is one only Matter, the stuff underlying the primal-constituents of the Universe: existence is nothing but this Matter: everything is some modification of this; the elements of the Universe are simply this Matter in a certain condition.

The school has even the audacity to foist Matter upon the divine beings so that, finally, God himself becomes a mode of Matter—and this though they make it corporeal, describing it as a body void of quality, but a magnitude.

Another school makes it incorporeal: among these, not all hold the theory of one only Matter; some of them while they maintain the one Matter, in which the first school believes, the foundation of bodily forms, admit another, a prior, existing in the divine-sphere, the base of the Ideas there and of the unembodied Beings.

2. We are obliged, therefore, at the start, both to establish the existence of this other Kind and to examine its nature and the mode of its Being.

Now (it will be reasoned) if Matter must characteristically be undetermined, void of shape, while in that sphere of the Highest there can be nothing that lacks determination, nothing shapeless, there can be no Matter there. Further, if all that order is simplex, there can be no need of Matter, whose function is to join with some other element to form a compound: it will be found of necessity in things of derived existence and shifting nature—the signs which lead us to the notion of Matter—but it is unnecessary to the primal.

And again, where (it will be asked) could it have come from? whence did it take its being? If it is derived, it has a source: if it is eternal, then the Primal-Principles are more numerous than we thought, the Firsts are a meeting-ground. Lastly, if that Matter has been entered by Idea, the union constitutes a body; and, so, there is Body in the Supreme.

3. Now it may be observed, first of all, that we cannot hold utterly cheap either the indeterminate, or even a Kind whose very idea implies absence of form, provided only that it offer itself to its Priors, to the Highest Beings. We have the example of the Soul itself in its relation to the Intellectual-Principle and the Divine Reason, taking shape by these and led so to a nobler principle of form.

Further, a compound in the Intellectual order is not to be confounded with a compound in the physical realm; the Divine Reasons are compounds and their Act is to produce a compound, namely that (lower) Nature which works towards Idea and whose first state and last confirm its composite character.[2] Then, too, the Matter of the realm of process ceaselessly changes its form: in the eternal, Matter is immutably one and the same, so that the two are diametrically opposites. The Matter of this realm is all things in turn, a new entity in every separate case, so that nothing is permanent and one thing ceaselessly pushes another out of being: Matter has no identity here. In the Intellectual it is all things at once: and therefore has nothing to change into: it already and ever contains all. This means that not even in its own Sphere is the Matter there at any moment shapeless: no doubt that is true of the Matter here as well; but shape is held by a very different right in the two orders of Matter.

As to whether Matter is eternal or a thing of process, this will be clear when we are sure of its precise nature.

4. The existence of the Ideal-Forms has been demonstrated elsewhere: we take up our argument from that point.

If, then, there is more than one of such forming Ideas, there must of necessity be some character common to all and equally some peculiar character in each keeping them distinct.

This peculiar characteristic, this distinguishing difference, is the individual shape. But if shape, then there is the shaped, that in which the difference is lodged.

There is, therefore, a Matter accepting the shape, a permanent substratum.

Further, admitting that there is an Intelligible Realm beyond, of which this world is an image, then, since this world-compound is based on Matter, there must be Matter there also.

And how can you predicate an ordered system without thinking of form, and how think of form apart from the notion of something in which the form is lodged?

No doubt that Realm is, in the strict fact, utterly without parts, but in some sense there is part there too. And in so far as these parts are really separate from each other, any such division and difference can be no other than a condition of Matter, of a something divided and differentiated: in so far as that realm, though without parts, yet consists of a variety of entities, these diverse entities, residing in a unity of which they are variations, reside in a Matter; for this unity, since it is also a diversity, must be conceived of as varied and multiform; it must have been shapeless before it took the form in which variation occurs. For if we abstract from the unity the variety and the particular shapes, the Reason-Principles and the Thoughts, what precedes these was something shapeless and undetermined, nothing of what is actually present there.

5. It may be objected that the Intellectual-Principle possesses its content in an eternal conjunction so that the two make a perfect unity, and that thus there is no Matter there.

But that argument would equally cancel the Matter present in the bodily forms of this realm: body without shape has never existed, always body achieved and yet always the two constituents. We discover these two—Matter and Form—by sheer force of our reasoning which distinguishes continually in pursuit of the simplex, the irreducible, working on, until it can go no further, towards the ultimate in the subject of inquiry. And the ultimate of every partial-thing is its Matter, which, therefore, must be all darkness since the light is the

Reason-Principle. I The mind, therefore,[3] sees only I in each particular object the Reason-Principle lodging there; anything lying below that it declares to lie below the light, to be therefore a thing of darkness, just as the eye, a thing of light, seeks light and colours which are modes of light, and dismisses all that is below the colours and hidden by them, as belonging to the order of the darkness, which is the order of Matter.

The dark element in the Intelligible, however, differs from that in the sense-world: so therefore does the Matter—as much as the forming-Idea presiding in each of the two realms. The Divine Matter, though (like the Matter here) it is the object of determination, has, of its own nature, a life defined and intellectual; the Matter of this sphere while it does accept determination is not living or intellective, but a dead thing decorated: any shape it takes is an image, exactly as the Base is an image. There on the contrary the shape is a real-existent as is the Base. Those that ascribe Real Being to Matter must be admitted to be right as long as they keep to the Matter of the Intelligible Realm: for the Base there is Being, or even, taken as an entirety with the higher that accompanies it, is illuminated Being.

But does this Base, of the Intellectual Realm, possess eternal existence?

The solution of that question is the same as for the Ideas.

Both are engendered, in the sense that they have had a beginning, but unengendered in that this beginning is not in Time: they have a derived being but by an eternal derivation: they are not, like the (physical) Cosmos, always in process but, in the character of the Intelligible Cosmos, have their Being permanently. For that differentiation within the Intelligible which produces Matter has always existed and it is this cleavage which produces the Matter there: it is the first movement; and movement and differentiation are convertible terms since the two things arose as one: this motion, this cleavage, away from The First is indetermination (= Matter), needing The First to its determination which it achieves by its Return, remaining, until then, an Alienism, still lacking good; unlit by the Supernal. It is from The First that all light comes, and, until this be absorbed, no light in any recipient of light can be authentic; the recipient is itself without light since light is from elsewhere.

About Matter in the Intelligible Realm we have exposed more than our purpose demanded.

6. We are led thus to the question of receptivity in things of body.

A proof that bodies must have some substratum different from themselves is found in the changing of the basic-constituents into one another. Notice that the destruction of the elements passing over is not complete—if it were we would have a Principle of Being wrecked in Non-being—nor does an en-

gendered thing pass from utter non-being into Being: what happens is that a
new form takes the place of an old. There is, then, a stable element, that which
puts off one form to receive the form of the incoming entity.

The same fact is clearly established by decay, a process implying a compound
object; in the compound there is a distinction between Matter and Form.

And the reasoning which shows the destructible to be a compound is borne
out by practical examples of reduction: a drinking vessel is reduced to its gold,
the gold to liquid; analogy forces us to believe that the liquid too is reducible.

The basic-constituents of things must be either Form or Primal Matter or a
compound of the Form and Matter.

Form-Idea, pure and simple, they cannot be: for without Matter how could
things stand in their mass and magnitude?

Neither can they be that Primal Matter, for they are not indestructible.

They must, therefore, consist of Matter and Form-Idea—Form for quality
and shape, Matter for the base, indeterminate as being other than Idea.

7. Empedocles in identifying his 'elements' with Matter is refuted by their decay.

Anaxagoras, in identifying his 'primal-combination' with Matter—to which
he allots no mere aptness to any and every nature or quality but the effective
possession of all—withdraws in this way the very Intellectual-Principle he had
introduced; for this Mind is not to him the bestower of shape, of Forming Idea;
and it is coeval with Matter, not its prior. But this simultaneous existence is
impossible: for if the combination derives Being by participation, Being is the
prior; if both (the combination and Being) are Authentic Existents, then an
additional Principle, a third, is imperative (a ground of unification). And if this
Creator, Mind, must pre-exist, why need Matter contain the Forming-Ideas
parcelwise for the Mind, with unending labour, to assort and allot? Surely the
undetermined could be brought to quality and pattern in the one comprehensive act?

As for the notion (of Anaxagoras) that all is in all, this clearly is impossible.

Those who (with Anaximander) make the base to be 'the infinite' must define
the term.

If this 'infinite' means 'of endless extension' there is no infinite among
beings; there is neither an infinity-in-itself (Infinity Abstract) nor an infinity as
an attribute to some body; for in the first case every part of that infinity would
be infinite and in the second an object in which the infinity was present as an
attribute could not be infinite apart from that attribute, could not be simplex,
could not therefore be Matter.

Atoms again (Democritus) cannot meet the need of a base.

There are no atoms; all body is divisible endlessly: besides, neither the continuity nor the ductility of corporeal things is explicable apart from Mind, or apart from the Soul which cannot be made up of atoms; and, again, out of atoms creation could produce nothing but atoms: a creative power could produce nothing from a material devoid of continuity. Any number of reasons might be brought, and have been brought, against this hypothesis and it need detain us no longer.

8. What, then, is this Kind, this Matter, described as one stuff, continuous and without quality?

Clearly since it is without quality it is incorporeal; bodiliness would be quality.

It must be the basic stuff of all the entities of the sense-world and not merely base to some while being to others achieved form.

Clay, for example, is matter to the potter but is not Matter pure and simple. Nothing of this sort is our object: we are seeking the stuff which underlies all alike. We must therefore refuse to it all that we find in things of sense—not merely such attributes as colour, heat, or cold, but weight or weightlessness, thickness or thinness, shape and therefore magnitude; for magnitude and shape cannot be identified with subjects possessing these properties.

It cannot be a compound, it must be a simplex, one distinct thing in its nature; only so can it be void of all quality. The Principle which gives it form gives this as something alien: so with magnitude and all really-existent things bestowed upon it. If, for example, it possessed a magnitude of its own, the Principle giving it form would be at the mercy of that magnitude and must produce not at will, but only within the limit of the Matter's capacity: to imagine that Will keeping step with its material is fantastic.

The Matter must be of later origin than the forming-power, and therefore must be at its disposition throughout, ready to become anything, ready therefore to any bulk; besides, if it possessed magnitude, it would necessarily possess shape also: it would be doubly inductile.

No: all that ever appears upon it is brought in by the Idea: the Idea alone possesses: to it belongs the magnitude and all else that goes with the Reason-Principle or follows upon it. Quantity is given with the Ideal-Form in all the particular species—man, bird, and particular kind of bird.

The imaging of Quantity upon Matter by an outside power is not more surprising than the imaging of Quality; Quality is no doubt a Reason-Principle, but Quantity also—being measure, number—is equally so.

9. But how can we conceive a thing having existence without having magnitude?

We have only to think of things whose identity does not depend on their quantity—for certainly magnitude can be distinguished I from existence as it can from many other forms⁴I and attributes.

In a word, every unembodied Kind must be classed as without quantity, and Matter is unembodied.

Besides, quantitativeness itself (the Absolute-Principle) does not possess quantity, which belongs only to things participating in it, a consideration which shows that Quantitativeness is an Idea-Principle. A white object becomes white by the presence of whiteness; what makes an organism white or of any other variety of colour is not itself a specific colour but, so to speak, a specific Reason-Principle: in the same way what gives an organism a certain bulk is not itself a thing of magnitude but is Magnitude itself, the abstract Absolute, or the Reason-Principle.

This Magnitude-Absolute, then, enters and beats the Matter out into Magnitude?

Not at all: the Matter was not previously shrunken small: there was no littleness or bigness: the Idea gives Magnitude exactly as it gives every other quality not previously present.

10. 'But how can I form the conception of the sizelessness of Matter?'

How do you form the concept of any absence of quality? What is the Act of the Intellect, what is the mental approach, in such a case?

The secret is Indetermination.

Likeness knows its like: the indeterminate knows the indeterminate. Around this indefinite a definite conception will be realized, but the way lies through indefiniteness.

All knowledge comes by Reason and the Intellectual Act; in this case Reason conveys information in any account it gives, but the act which aims at being intellectual is, here, not intellection but rather its failure: therefore (in this crippled approach) the representation of Matter must be spurious, unreal, something sprung of the Alien (the unreal) and of the conception bound up with this Alien.

This, we may take it, is Plato's meaning where he says that Matter is apprehended by a sort of spurious reasoning.

What, then, is this indetermination in the Soul? Does it amount to an utter absence of Knowledge, as if the Soul or Mind had withdrawn?

No: the indeterminate has some footing in the sphere of affirmation. The eye is aware of darkness as a base capable of receiving any colour not yet seen against it: so the Mind, putting aside all attributes perceptible to sense—all that corresponds to light—comes upon a residuum which it cannot bring under determination: it is thus in the state of the eye which, when directed towards darkness, has become in some way identical with the object of its spurious vision.

There is vision, then, in this approach of the Mind towards Matter?

Some vision, yes; of shapelessness, of colourlessness, of the unlit, and therefore of the sizeless. More than this would mean that the Soul is already bestowing Form.

But is not such a void precisely what the Soul experiences when it has no intellection whatever?

No: in that case it affirms nothing, or rather has no experience: but in knowing Matter, it has an experience, what may be described as the impact of the shapeless; for in its very consciousness of objects that have taken shape and size it knows them as compounds (i.e. as possessing with these forms a formless base), for they appear as things that have accepted colour and other quality.

It knows, therefore, a whole which includes two components; it has a clear knowledge or perception of the overlie (the Ideas) but only a dim awareness of the underlie, the shapeless which is not an Ideal-Principle.

I With what is perceptible to it there are presented in the composite total the overlying properties which it separates and sets aside; and what is left from the process of abstraction, this, the dim,⁵I it knows dimly, this, the dark, it knows darkly, this it knows in a sort of non-knowing.

And just as even Matter itself is not stably shapeless but, in things, is always shaped, the Soul also is eager to throw over it the thing-form; for the Soul recoils from the indefinite, dreads, almost, to be outside of reality, does not endure to linger about Non-Being.

11. 'But, given Magnitude and the properties we know, what else can be necessary to the existence of body?'

Some base to be the container of all the rest.

'A certain mass then; and if mass, then Magnitude? Obviously if your Base has no Magnitude it offers no footing to any entrant. And suppose it sizeless; then, what end does it serve? It never helped Idea or quality; now it ceases to account for differentiation or for magnitude, though the last, wheresoever it resides, seems to find its way into embodied entities by way of Matter.

'Or, taking a larger view, observe that actions, productive operations, periods of time, movements, none of these have any such substratum and yet are real things; in the same way the most elementary body has no need of Matter; things may be, all, what they are, each after its own kind, in their great variety, deriving the coherence of their being from the blending of the various Ideal-Forms. This Matter with its sizelessness seems, then, to be a name without a content.'

Now, to begin with: extension is not an imperative condition of being a recipient; it is necessary only where it happens to be a property inherent to the recipient's peculiar mode of being. The Soul, for example, contains all things but holds them all in an unextended unity; if magnitude were one of its attributes it would contain things in extension. Matter does actually contain in spatial extension what it takes in; but this is because itself is a potential recipient of spatial extension: animals and plants, in the same way, as they increase in size, take quality in parallel development with quantity, and they lose in the one as the other lessens.

No doubt in the case of things as we know them there is a certain mass lying ready beforehand to the shaping power: but that is no reason for expecting bulk in Matter strictly so called; for in such cases Matter is not the absolute; it is that of some definite object; the Absolute Matter must take its magnitude, as every other property, from outside itself.

A thing then need not have magnitude in order to receive form: it may receive mass with everything else that I comes to it:[6] a phantasm I of mass is enough, a primary aptness for extension, a magnitude of no content—whence the identification that has been made of Matter with The Void.

But I prefer to use the word phantasm as hinting the indefiniteness into which the Soul spills itself when it seeks to communicate with Matter, finding no possibility of delimiting it, neither encompassing it nor able to penetrate to any fixed point of it, either of which achievements would be an act of delimitation.

In other words we have something which is to be described not as small or great but as the great-and-small: for it is at once a mass and a thing without magnitude, in the sense that it is the Matter on which Mass is based and that, as it changes from great to small and small to great, it traverses magnitude. Its very undeterminateness is a mass in the same sense—that of being a recipient of Magnitude: but it is pictured in the way we have described it.

In the order of things without Mass, all that is Ideal-Principle possesses delimitation, each entity for itself, so that the conception of Mass has no place in them: Matter, not delimited, having in its own nature no stability, swept into any or every form by turns, ready to go here, there, and everywhere, becomes a thing of multiplicity: driven into all shapes, becoming all things, it has that much of the character of mass.

12. I Matter, then, plays a decisive part in the constitution of bodies:[7] the Ideal-Forms I of body are installed in Mass.

But these Forms enter, not into Magnitude itself but into some subject that has been brought to Magnitude. For to suppose them entering into Magnitude—and not into Matter—I is to represent them as being without Magnitude and without Real-Existence, nothing but Reason-Principles whose sphere could only be Soul; at this, there would be no such thing as body.[8] ¶

The multiplicity here must be based upon some unity which, since it has been brought to Magnitude, must be, itself, distinct from Magnitude. Matter is the base of Identity to all that is composite: once each of the constituents comes bringing its own Matter with it, there is no need of any other base. No doubt there must be a container, as it were a place, to receive what is to enter, but Matter and even body precede place and space; the primal necessity, in order to the existence of body, is Matter.

There is no force in the suggestion that since production and act are immaterial, corporeal entities also must be immaterial.

Bodies are compound, actions not. Further, Matter does in some sense underlie action; it supplies the substratum to the doer: it is permanently within him though it does not enter as a constituent into the act where, indeed, it would be a hindrance. Doubtless, one act does not change into another—as would be the case if there were a specific Matter of actions—but the doer directs himself from one act to another so that he is the Matter, himself, to his varying actions.

Matter, in sum, is necessary to quality and to quantity, and, therefore, to body.

It is, thus, no name void of content; we know there is such a base, invisible and without bulk though it be.

If we reject it, we must by the same reasoning reject qualities and mass: for quality, or mass, or any such entity, taken by itself apart, might be said not to exist. But these do exist, though in an obscure existence: there is much less ground for rejecting Matter, however it lurks, discerned by none of the senses.

It eludes the eye, for it is utterly outside of colour: it is not heard, for it is no sound: it is no flavour or savour for nostrils or palate: can it, perhaps, be known to touch? No: for neither is it corporeal; and touch deals with body, which is known by being solid, fragile, soft, hard, moist, dry—all properties utterly lacking in Matter.

It is grasped only by a mental process, though that not an act of the intellective mind but a reasoning that finds no subject; and so it stands revealed as the spurious thing it has been called. No bodiliness belongs to it; bodiliness is itself a phase of Reason-Principle and so is something different from Matter, as Matter, therefore, from it: bodiliness already operative and so to speak made concrete would be body manifest and not Matter unelaborated.

13. Are we asked to accept as the substratum some attribute or quality present to all the elements in common?

Then, first, we must be told what precise attribute this is and, next, how an attribute can be a substratum. How conceive an attribute where there is neither base nor bulk?

Again, if the quality possesses determination, it is not Matter the undetermined; and anything without determination is not a quality but is the substratum—the very Matter we are seeking.

It may be suggested that perhaps this absence of quality means simply that, of its own nature, it has no participation in any of the set and familiar properties, but takes quality by this very non-participation, holding thus an absolutely individual character, marked off from everything else, being as it were the negation of those others. Deprivation, we will be told, comports quality: a blind man has the quality of his lack of sight. If then—it will be urged—Matter exhibits such a negation, surely it has a quality, all the more so, assuming any deprivation to be a quality, in that here the deprivation is all-comprehensive.

But this notion reduces all existence to qualified things or qualities: Quantity itself becomes a Quality and so does even ∣ Substance.⁹∣ Now this cannot be: if such things as Quantity and ∣ Substance⁹∣ are qualified, they are, by that very fact, not qualities: Quality is an addition to them; we must not commit the absurdity of giving the name Quality to something distinguishable from Quality, something therefore that is not Quality.

Is it suggested that its mere Alienism is a quality in Matter?

If this Alienism is difference-absolute (the abstract entity) it possesses no Quality: absolute Quality cannot be itself a qualified thing.

If the Alienism is to be understood as meaning only that Matter is differentiated, then it is different not by itself (since it is certainly not an absolute) but by this Difference, just as all identical objects are so (not by themselves but) by virtue of Identicalness (the Absolute principle of Identity).

An absence is neither a Quality nor a qualified entity; it is the negation of a Quality or of something else, as noiselessness is the negation of noise and so on. A lack is negative; Quality demands something positive. The distinctive character of Matter is unshape, the lack of qualification and of form; surely then it is absurd to pretend that it has Quality in not being qualified; that is like saying that sizelessness constitutes a certain size.

The distinctive character of Matter, then, is simply its manner of being—not something definite inserted in it but, rather a relation towards other things, the relation of being distinct from them.

Other things possess something besides this relation of Alienism: their form makes each an entity. Matter may with propriety be described as merely alien; perhaps, even, we might describe it as 'The Aliens', for the singular suggests a certain definiteness while the plural would indicate the absence of any determination.

14. But is Matter this Privation itself, or something in which this Privation is lodged?

Anyone maintaining that Matter and Privation are one and the same in substratum but stand I separable in definition[10]I cannot be excused from assigning to each the precise principle which distinguishes it in reason from the other: that which defines Matter must be kept quite apart from that defining the Privation and vice versa.

There are three possibilities: Matter is not in Privation and Privation is not in Matter; or each is in each; or one is in the other but not conversely (e.g., heat in fire).

Now if they should stand quite apart, neither calling for the other, they are two distinct things: Matter is something other than Privation even though Privation always goes with it: into the principle of the one the other cannot enter even potentially.

If their relation to each other is that of a snubnose to snubness, here also there is a double concept; we have two things.

If they stand to each other as fire to heat—heat in fire, but fire not included in the concept of heat—if Matter is Privation in the way in which fire is heat, then the Privation is a form under which Matter appears but there remains a base distinct from the Privation and this base must be the Matter. Here, too, they are not one thing.

Perhaps the identity in substance with differentiation in reason will be defended on the ground that Privation does not point to something present but precisely to an absence, to something absent, to the negation or lack of Real-being: the case would be like that of the affirmation of non-existence, where there is no real predication but simply a denial.

Is, then, this Privation simply a non-existence?

If a non-existence in the sense that it is not a thing of Real-being but belongs to some other Kind of existent, we have still two Principles, one referring directly to the substratum, the other merely exhibiting the relation of the Privation to other things (as their potentiality).

Or we might say that the one concept defines the relation of substratum to what is not substratum (but realized entity) while that of Privation, in bringing out the indeterminateness of Matter, applies to the Matter in itself (and not in its relationships): but this still makes Privation and Matter two in definition though one in substratum.

If, however, Privation is identical with Matter in being indeterminate, unfixed, and without quality, how can there be two definitions?

15. The further question, therefore, is raised whether boundlessness and

indetermination are things lodging in something other than themselves as a sort of attribute and whether Privation (or Negation of quality) is also an attribute residing in some separate substratum.

Now all that is Number and Reason-Principle is outside of boundlessness (is fully delimited): these (Number and Reason) bestow bound and settlement and order in general upon all else: neither anything that has been brought under order nor any Order-Absolute (apart from themselves) is needed to bring them under order. The thing that has to be brought under order (e.g. Matter) is other than the Ordering Principle which is Limit and Definiteness and Reason-Principle. Therefore, necessarily, the thing to be brought under order and to definiteness must be in itself a thing lacking delimitation.

Now Matter is a thing that is brought under order—like all that shares its nature by participation or by possessing the same principle—therefore, necessarily, Matter is The Undelimited (the Absolute Indefiniteness) and not merely the recipient of a non-essential quality of Indefiniteness entering as an attribute.

For, first, any attribute to any subject must be a Reason-Principle; and Indefiniteness is not a Reason-Principle.

Secondly, what must a thing be to take Indefiniteness as an attribute? Obviously it must, beforehand, be either Definiteness (the Principle) or a defined thing. But Matter is neither.

Then again Indefiniteness entering as an attribute into the definite must cease to be indefinite: but (since Matter remains true to its Kind, i.e. is indefinite as long as it is Matter) Indefiniteness has not entered as an attribute into Matter: that is, Matter is essentially Indefiniteness.

The Matter even of the Intellectual Realm is the Indefinite (the undelimited); it must be a thing generated by the undefined nature, the illimitable nature, of the Eternal Being, The One—an illimitableness, however, not possessing native existence There (not inherent) but engendered by The One.

But how can Matter be common to both spheres, be here and be There?

Because even Indefiniteness has two phases.

But what difference can there be between phase and phase of Indefiniteness?

The difference of archetype and image.

So that Matter here (as only an image of Indefiniteness) would be less indefinite?

On the contrary, more indefinite as an Image-thing remote from true being. Indefiniteness is the greater in the less ordered object; the less deep in good, the deeper in evil. The Indeterminate in the Intellectual Realm, where there is truer being, might almost be called merely an Image of Indefiniteness: in this lower Sphere where there is less Being, where there is a refusal of the Authentic, and an adoption of the Image-Kind, Indefiniteness is more authentically indefinite.

But this argument seems to make no difference between the indefinite object and Indefiniteness-essential. Is there none?

In any object in which Reason and Matter co-exist we distinguish between Indeterminateness and the indeterminate subject: but where Matter stands alone we make them identical, or, better, we would say right out that in that case essential Indeterminateness is not present; for it is a Reason-Principle and could not lodge in the indeterminate object without at once annulling the indeterminateness.

Matter, then, must be described as Indefinite of itself, by its natural opposition to Reason-Principle. Reason is Reason and nothing else; just so Matter, opposed by its indeterminateness to Reason, is Indeterminateness and nothing else.

16. Then Matter is simply Alienism (the Principle of Difference)?

No: it is merely that part of Alienism which stands in contradiction with the Authentic Existents which are Reason-Principles. So understood, this non-existent has a certain measure of existence; it is identical with Privation, which may be considered as a thing standing in opposition to the things that exist in Reason.

But must not Privation cease to have existence, when what has been lacking is present at last?

By no means: the recipient of a state or character is not a state but the (negation or) Privation of the state; and that into which determination enters is neither a determined object nor determination itself, but simply the wholly or partly undetermined.

Still, must not the nature of this Undetermined be annulled by the entry of Determination, especially where (as in Matter) this is no mere attribute (but the very nature of the recipient)?

No doubt to introduce quantitative determination into an undetermined object would annul the original state; but in the particular case, the introduction of determination only confirms the original state, bringing it into actuality, into full effect, as sowing brings out the natural quality of land or as a female organism impregnated by the male is not defeminized but becomes more decidedly of its sex; the thing becomes more emphatically itself.

But on this reasoning must not Matter owe its evil to having in some degree participated in good?

No: its evil is in its first lack: it was not a possessor (as the land or the female organism are, of some specific character).

To lack one thing and to possess another, in something like equal proportions, is to hold a middle state of good and evil: but whatsoever (like this substratum) possesses nothing and so is in destitution—and especially what is essentially destitution—must be evil in its own kind.

For in Matter we have no mere absence of means or of strength; it is utter destitution—of sense, of virtue, of beauty, of pattern, of Ideal principle, of quality. This is surely ugliness, utter disgracefulness, unredeemed evil.

The Matter in the Intellectual Realm is an Existent, for there is nothing previous to it except the Beyond-Existence; but what precedes the Matter of this sphere is Existence; by its alienism in regard to the beauty and good of Existence, Matter is therefore a non-existent.

NOTES TO ENNEAD II.4

1. FIRST EDITION title: "Matter *In Its Two Kinds*"

2. FIRST EDITION: ". . . towards Idea. *And there is not only a difference of function; there is a still more notable difference of source. Then, too* . . ."

ARMSTRONG: "But if this [lower—ed.] nature both works on and derives from something other than itself, it is composite to an even higher degree."

GUTHRIE puts a different spin on the whole thought: "Besides, when we say that intelligible things are composite (of matter and form), this is not in the sense in which the word is used of bodies. Even reasons would thus be called composite, and by their actualization form another alleged composite, nature, which aspires to form. If, in the intelligible world, the composite tend toward some other principle, or depend thereon, the difference between this composite and bodies is still better marked."

3. FIRST EDITION: "The *Mind, too, as also a Reason-Principle,* sees only . . ."

ARMSTRONG: "Now intellect too is rational principle. So intellect sees the forming principle..."

TAYLOR: ". . . reason is light, and intellect is reason. Hence, too, intellect beholding the nature of each [i.e., of intelligible and sensible matter], conceives . . ." Brackets are Taylor's.

4. FIRST EDITION: ". . . from existence as *can many* other forms . . ."

ARMSTRONG: ". . . and there are many other things which are different from that which has quantity."

GUTHRIE: "Essence is distinct from quantity; for many other things beside it exist."

TAYLOR: "For being and a certain quantity are not the same; since there are many other things besides a definite quantity."

5. FIRST EDITION: "With what is perceptible to it there *is presented something else: what it can directly apprehend it sets on one side as its own; but the something else which Reason rejects,* this, the dim . . ."

TAYLOR: "When, therefore, in the whole and composite, she receives the subject together with its inherent properties, and analyzes and separates them, then she understands obscurely that which reason leaves, darkly that which is dark, and sees intellectually, not understanding."

ARMSTRONG: "That, then, which it apprehends in the composite whole along with the overlying elements, when it has analysed these out and separated them, that which reason leaves over, this is what it thinks, a dim thing dimly and a dark thing darkly, and it thinks it without thinking."

6. FIRST EDITION: ". . . comes to it *at the moment of becoming what it is to be:* a phantasm . . ."

ARMSTRONG: ". . . that which is going to receive the form must not be a mass, but it must receive the rest of its qualities as well at the same time as it becomes a mass."

TAYLOR: ". . . it is not necessary that the recipient of form should be bulk, but that at the same time it becomes bulk, it should receive another quality;"

7. FIRST EDITION begins the sentence: "*It is the corporeal, then, that demands magnitude:* the Ideal-Forms . . ."

TAYLOR: "Magnitude, therefore, contributes something to bodies; for the forms of bodies, are in dimensions."

GUTHRIE: "Extensions therefore contribute to the constitutions of bodies; for the forms of bodies are in extensions."

ARMSTRONG: "Matter, then, makes the greatest contribution to the formation of bodies; for the forms of bodies are in sizes."

8. FIRST EDITION: ". . . is to represent them as being *either* without Magnitude and without Real-Existence *(and therefore undistinguishable from the Matter)* or not Ideal-Forms *(apt to body)* but Reason-Principles *(utterly removed)* whose sphere could only be Soul; at this, there would be no such thing as body *(i.e., instead of Ideal-Forms shaping Matter and so producing body, there would be merely Reason-Principles dwelling remote in Soul.)*"

9. FIRST EDITION: "Existence."

ARMSTRONG: "substance"; TAYLOR: "essence"; GUTHRIE: "being."

10. FIRST EDITION: ". . . separable in *reason* . . ."

ARMSTRONG: "in rational definition"; GUTHRIE: "though logically distinct"; TAYLOR: "in definition."

FIFTH TRACTATE

Potentiality and Actuality

1. A distinction is made between things existing actually and things existing potentially; Actuality, also, is spoken of as a really existent entity. We must consider what content there is in these terms.

Can we distinguish between **I** Actuality[1] and the **I** state of being-in-act? And if there is such an Actuality, is this itself in Act, or are the two quite distinct so that this actually existent thing need not be, itself, an Act?

It is indubitable that Potentiality exists in the Realm of Sense: but does the

Intellectual Realm similarly include the potential or only the actual? and if the potential exists there, does it remain merely potential for ever? And, if so, is this resistance to actualization due to its being precluded (as a member of the Divine or Intellectual world) from time-processes?

First we must make clear what potentiality is.

We cannot think of potentiality as standing by itself; there can be no potentiality apart from something which a given thing may be or become. Thus bronze is the potentiality of a statue: but if nothing could be made out of the bronze, nothing wrought upon it, if it could never be anything as a future to what it has been, if it rejected all change, it would be bronze and nothing else: its own character it holds already as a present thing, and that would be the full of its capacity: it would be destitute of potentiality. Whatsoever has a potentiality must first have a (definite) character of its own; and its potentiality will consist in its having a reach beyond that character to some other.

Sometimes after it has turned its potentiality into actuality it will remain what it was; sometimes it will sink itself to the fullest extent in the new form and itself disappear: these two different modes are exemplified in (1) bronze as potentially a statue and (2) water (= primal-liquid) as potentially bronze or, again, air as potentially fire.

But if this be the significance of potentiality, may we describe it as a Power towards the thing that is to be? Is the bronze a power towards a statue?

Not in the sense of an effectively productive force: such a power could not be called a potentiality. I Of course we may consider Potentiality as a power when we are comparing it not merely with the Actuality but with the process of Actualization: but it is better, as more conducive to clarity, to compare a Potentiality with an Actuality and Power with Actualization.[2] I

Potentiality may be thought of as a Substratum to states and shapes and forms which are to be received, which it welcomes by its nature and even strives for—sometimes in gain but sometimes, also, to loss, to the annulling of some distinctive manner of being already actually achieved.

2. Then the question rises whether Matter—potentially what it becomes by receiving shape—is actually something else or whether it has no actuality at all. In general terms: When a potentiality has taken a definite form, does it retain its being? Does the potentiality, itself, pass into actuality? The alternative is that, when we speak of the 'Actual Statue' and of the 'Potential Statue', the Actuality is not predicated of the same subject as the Potentiality. If we have really two different subjects, then the potential does not really become the actual: all that happens is that an actual entity takes the place of a potential.

The actualized entity is not the Matter (the Potentiality merely) but a combination, including the Form-Idea upon the Matter.

This is certainly the case when a quite different thing results from the actualization—the statue, for example, the combination, is distinctly different from the bronze, the base; where the resultant is something quite new, the Potentiality has clearly not, itself, become what is now actualized. But take the case where a person with a capacity for education becomes in fact educated: is not potentiality, here, identical with actualization? Is not the potentially wise Socrates the same man as the Socrates actually wise?

But is an ignorant man a being of knowledge because he is so potentially? Is he, in virtue of his non-essential ignorance, potentially an instructed being?

It is not because of his accidental ignorance that he is a being of Knowledge: it is because, ignorant though he be by accident, his mind, apt to knowledge, is the potentiality through which he may become so. Thus, in the case of the potentially instructed who have become so in fact, the potentiality is taken up into the actual; or, if we prefer to put it so, there is on the one side the mere potentiality while, on the other, the potentiality has taken form.

If, then, the Potentiality is the Substratum while the thing in actualization—the statue for example—is a combination, how are we to describe the form that has entered the bronze?

There will be nothing unsound in describing this shape, this Form which has brought the entity from potentiality to actuality, as the actualization; but of course as the actualization of the definite particular entity, not as Actuality the abstract: we must not confuse it with the other actualization, strictly so called, that which is contrasted with the power producing actualization. The potential is led out into realization by something other than itself; power accomplishes, of itself, what is I within its scope, and the accomplishment is the actuality:[3] the relation I is that existing between a temperament and its expression in act, between courage and courageous conduct. So far so good:

3. We come now to the purpose of all this discussion; to make clear in what sense or to what degree Actualization is predicable in the Intellectual Realm and whether all is in Actualization there, each and every member of that realm being an Act, or whether Potentiality also has place there.

Now: if there is no Matter there to harbour potentiality: if nothing there has any future apart from its actual mode: if nothing there generates, whether by changes or in the permanence of its identity; if nothing goes outside of itself to give being to what is other than itself; then, potentiality has no place there: the Beings there possess actuality, as belonging to eternity, not to time.

Those, however, who (with us) assert Matter in the Intellectual Realm will be asked whether the existence of that Matter does not imply the potential there too; for even if Matter there exists in another mode than here, every Being there will have its Matter, its form, and the union of the two (and therefore the potential, separable from the actual). What answer is to be made?

I Simply, that even the 'Matter' there is Form, just as the Soul, a Form-Idea, is Matter to another (a higher) Being.

Is, then, this Matter relative to a higher Being and so a potentiality?

No: for the Form (to which it is Matter) is integral to it and does not arise in a future: the distinction between Form and Matter is purely mental: the Form and the Matter it includes are conceived as a conjunction but are essentially one kind:[4] I remember that Aristotle makes his Fifth Body immaterial.

But surely Potentiality exists in the Soul? Surely the Soul is potentially the living-being of this world before it has become so? Is it not potentially musical, and everything else that it has not been and becomes? Does not this imply potentiality even in the Intellectual Existences?

No: the Soul is not potentially these things; it is a Power towards them.

But after what mode does Actualization exist in the Intellectual Realm?

Is it the Actualization of a statue, where the combination is realized because the Form-Idea has mastered each separate constituent of the total?

No: it is that every constituent there is a Form-Idea and, thus, is perfect in its Being.

There is in the Intellectual Principle no progression from some power capable of intellection to the Actuality of intellection: such a progression would send us in search of a Prior Principle not progressing from Power to Act; there all stands ever realized. Potentiality requires an intervention from outside itself to bring it to the actualization which otherwise cannot be; but what possesses, of itself, identity unchangeable for ever is an actualization: all the Firsts then are actualizations, simply because eternally and of themselves they possess all that is necessary to their completion.

This applies equally to the Soul, not to that in Matter but to that in the Intellectual Sphere; and even that other Soul in Matter, the Soul of Growth, is an actualization; it possesses actually (and not, like material things, merely in image) the Being that belongs to it.

Then, everything in the intellectual is in actualization and so all There is Actuality?

Why not? If that Nature is rightly said to be 'Sleepless', and to be Life and the noblest mode of Life, the noblest Activities must be there; all then is actualization there, everything is an Actuality, for everything is a Life, and all Place there is the Place of Life, in the true sense the ground and spring of Soul and of the Intellectual Principle.

4. Now, in general, anything that has a potentiality is actually something else, and this potentiality of the future mode of being is an existing mode.

But what we think of as Matter, what we assert to be the potentiality of all things, cannot be said to be actually any one being among beings: if it were of itself any definite being, it could not be potentially all.

If, then, it is not among existences, it must necessarily be without existence.

How, therefore, can it be actually anything?

The answer is that while Matter cannot be any of the things which are founded upon it, it may quite well be something else, admitting that all existences are not rooted in Matter.

But once more, if it is excluded from the entities founded upon it and all these are Beings, it must itself be a Non-Being.

It is, further, in our conception, formless and therefore not an Idea: it cannot then be classed among things of the Intellectual Realm, and so is, once more, a Non-Being. Falling, as regards both worlds, under Non-Being, it is all the more decidedly the Non-Being.

It has eluded the Nature of the Authentic Existences; it has even failed to come up with the things to which a spurious existence can be attributed—for it is not even a phantasm of Reason as these are—how is it possible to include it under any mode of Being?

And if it falls under no mode of Being, what can it actually be?

5. How can we talk of it? How can it be the Matter of real things?

It is talked of, and it serves, precisely, as a Potentiality.

And, as being a Potentiality, it is not of the order of the thing it is to become: its existence is no more than an announcement of a future, as it were a thrust forward to what is to come into existence.

As Potentiality, then, it is not any definite thing but the potentiality of everything: being nothing in itself—beyond what being Matter amounts to—it is not in actualization. For if it were actually something, that actualized something would not be Matter, or at least not Matter out and out, but merely Matter in the limited sense in which bronze is the matter of the statue.

And its Non-Being must be no mere difference from Being.

Motion, for example, is different from Being, but plays about it, springing from it and living within it: Matter is, so to speak, the outcast of Being, it is utterly removed, irredeemably what it was from the beginning: in origin it was Non-Being and so it remains.

Nor are we to imagine that, standing away at the very beginning from the universal circle of Beings, it was thus necessarily an active Something or that it became a Something. It has never been able to annex for itself even a visible outline from all the forms under which it has sought to ▌ creep: remaining always the alien,[5] it was ▌ never more than a Potentiality towards its next: where all the circle of Being ends, there only is it manifest; discerned underneath things produced after it, it is remoter (from Real-Being) even than they.

Grasped, then, as an underlie in each order of Being, it can be no actualization of either: all that is allowed to it is to be a Potentiality, a weak and blurred phantasm, a thing incapable of a shape of its own.

Its actuality is that of being a phantasm, the actuality of being a falsity; and the false in actualization is the veritably false, which again is Authentic Non-Existence.

So that Matter, as the Actualization of Non-Being, is all the more decidedly Non-Being, is Authentic Non-Existence.

Thus, since the very reality of its Nature is situated in Non-Being, it is in no degree the Actualization of any definite Being.

If it is to be present at all, it cannot be an Actualization, for then it would not be the stray from Authentic Being which it is, the thing having its Being in Non-Beingness: for, note, in the case of things whose Being is a falsity, to take away the falsity is to take away what Being they have, and if we introduce actualization into things whose Being and Essence is Potentiality, we destroy the foundation of their nature since their Being is Potentiality.

If Matter is to be kept as the unchanging substratum, we must keep it as Matter: that means—does it not?—that we must define it as a Potentiality and nothing more—or refute these considerations.

NOTES TO ENNEAD II.5

1. FIRST EDITION: ". . . Actuality *(an absolute, abstract Principle)* and the . . ."

2. FIRST EDITION: "Of course *Potentiality may be* a power, *as, for instance, when we are referring not merely to a thing which may be brought into actualisation but to Actuality itself (the Principle or Abstract in which potentiality and the power of realising potentiality may be thought of as identical)*: but it is better, as more conducive to clarity, to use 'Potentiality' *in regard to the process of Actualisation and 'Power' in regard to the Principle, Actuality.*"

3. FIRST EDITION: ". . . within its scope, *but by virtue of Actuality (the abstract)*: the relation . . ."

4. FIRST EDITION has these three paragraphs as: "Simply, that even the *Matter* there is Idea, just as Soul, an Idea, is Matter to another (a higher) Being.

"*But relatively to that higher, the Soul is* a potentiality?

"No: for the *Idea* (to which it is Matter) is integral to *the Soul* and does not *look to* a future; the distinction between *the Soul and its Idea* is purely mental: the *Idea* and the Matter it includes are conceived as a conjunction but are essentially one *Kind*: . . ."

ARMSTRONG: ". . . the something like matter There is form, since the soul too, which is form, can be matter to something else. Then does it exist potentially in relation to that something else? No; for then the something else would be its form, and the form does not come to it afterwards and is not separated except by rational abstraction: it has matter in the sense that it is thought of as double, but both form and matter are one nature;"

GUTHRIE: ". . . in intelligible things, what plays the part of matter is a form, and that the soul, by herself, is form; but, in relation to something else, is matter. Is the soul then potential in respect of this other thing? Hardly, for the soul possesses the form, and possesses it at present, without regard to the future, and she is divisible in form and matter only for reason; if she contain matter, it is only because thought conceives of her as double (by distinguishing form and matter in her). But these two things form a single nature . . ."

5. FIRST EDITION: ". . . creep: *it has always pursued something other than itself;* it was . . ."

GUTHRIE: "Its permanent condition is to trend towards something else, to exist potentially in respect of the things that are to follow."

ARMSTRONG: ". . . remaining directed to something else it exists potentially to what comes next;"

SIXTH TRACTATE

Quality

1. Are not Being and Reality (*to on* and *hê ousia*) distinct; must we not envisage Being as the substance stripped of all else, while Reality is this same thing, Being, accompanied by the others—Movement, Rest, Identity, Difference—so that these are the specific constituents of Reality?

The universal fabric, then, is Reality in which Being, Movement, and so on are separate constituents.

Now Movement has Being (not essentially but) as an accident and therefore should have Reality as an accident; or is it something serving to the completion of Reality?

No: Movement is a Reality; everything in the Supreme is a Reality.

Why, then, does not Reality reside, equally, in this sphere?

In the Supreme there is Reality because all things are one; ours is the sphere of images whose separation produces grades of difference. Thus in the spermatic unity all the human members are present undistinguishably; there is no separation of head and hand: their distinct existence begins in the life here, whose content is image, not Authentic Existence.

And are the distinct Qualities in the Authentic Realm to be explained in the same way? Are they differing Realities centred in one Reality or gathered round

Being—differences which constitute Realities distinct from each other within the common fact of Reality?

This is sound enough; but it does not apply to all the qualities of this sphere, some of which, no doubt, are differentiations of Reality—such as the quality of two-footedness or four-footedness—but others are not such differentiations of Reality and, because they are not so, must be called qualities and nothing more.

On the other hand, one and the same thing may be sometimes a differentiation of Reality and sometimes not—a differentiation when it is a constitutive element, and no differentiation in some other thing, where it is not a constitutive element but an accidental. The distinction may be seen in the (constitutive) **whiteness of snow¹** or of ceruse and the whiteness which in a man is an accidental.

Where whiteness belongs to the very Reason-Form of the thing it is a constitutive element and not a quality; where it is a superficial appearance it is a quality.

In other words, qualification may be distinguished. We may think of a qualification that is of the very substance of the thing, something exclusively belonging to it. And there is a qualifying that is nothing more, (not constituting but simply) giving some particular character to the real thing; in this second case the qualification does not produce any alteration towards Reality or away from it; the Reality has existed fully constituted before the incoming of the qualification which—whether in soul or body—merely introduces some state from outside, and by this addition elaborates the Reality into the particular thing.

But what if (the superficial appearance such as) the visible whiteness in ceruse is constitutive? In the swan the whiteness is not constitutive since a swan need not be white: it is constitutive in ceruse, just as warmth is constitutive of the Reality, fire.

No doubt we may be told that the Reality in fire is (not warmth but) fieriness and in ceruse an analogous abstraction: yet the fact remains that in visible fire warmth or fieriness is constitutive and in the ceruse whiteness.

Thus the same entities (warmness, whiteness, and fieriness) are represented at once as being not qualities but constituents of Reality and not constituents but qualities.

Now it is absurd to talk as if one identical thing (warmth, whiteness, or the like) changed its own nature according to whether it is present as a constituent or as an accidental.

The truth is that while the Reason-Principles producing these entities contain nothing but what is of the nature of Reality, yet only in the Intellectual Realm do the produced things possess real existence: here they are not real; they are qualified.

And this is the starting-point of an error we constantly make: in our inquiries into things we let realities escape us and fasten on what is mere quality. Thus fire is not the thing we so name from the observation of certain qualities present; fire is a Reality (not a combination of material phenomena); the phenomena observed here and leading us to name fire call us away from the authentic thing; a quality is erected into the very matter of definition—a procedure, however, reasonable enough in regard to things of the realm of sense which are in no case realities but accidents of Reality.

And this raises the question how Reality can ever spring from what are not Realities.

It has been shown that a thing coming into being cannot be identical with its origins: it must here be added that nothing thus coming into being (no 'thing of process') can be a Reality.

Then how do we assert the rising in the Supreme of what we have called Reality from what is not Reality?

The Reality there—possessing Authentic Being in the strictest sense, with the least admixture—is Reality (not so much by being produced as) by existing among the differentiations of the Authentic Being; or, better, Reality is affirmed in the sense that with the existence of the Supreme is included its Act so that Reality seems to be a perfectionment of the Authentic Being, though in truth it is a diminution; the produced thing is deficient by the very addition, by being less simplex, by standing one step away from the Authentic.

2. But we must inquire into Quality in itself: to know its nature is certainly the way to settle our general question.

The first point is to assure ourselves whether or not one and the same thing may be held to be sometimes a mere qualification and sometimes a constituent of Reality—not staying on the point that qualification could not be constitutive of a Reality but of a qualified Reality only.

Now in a Reality possessing a determined quality, I the Reality and the essence[2] precedel the qualified Reality.

What, then, in the case of fire is the Reality which precedes the qualified Reality?

Its mere body, perhaps? If so, body being the Reality, fire is a warmed body; and the total thing is not the Reality; and the fire has warmth (not essentially but) as a man might have a snub nose.

Rejecting its warmth, its glow, its lightness—all which certainly do seem to be qualities—and its resistance, there is left only its extension by three dimensions: in other words, its Matter is its Reality.

But that cannot be held: surely the Form is much more likely than the Matter to be the Reality.

But is not the Form a Quality (and not therefore a Reality)?

No, the Form is not a Quality: it is a Reason-Principle.

And the outcome of this Reason-Principle entering into the underlying Matter, what is that?

Certainly not what is seen and burns, for that is the something in which these qualities inhere.

We might define the burning as an Act springing from the Reason-Principle: then the warming and lighting and other effects of fire will be its Acts and we still have found no foothold for its quality.

Such completions of a Reality cannot be called qualities since they are its Acts emanating from the Reason-Principles and from the essential powers. A quality is something persistently outside Reality; it cannot appear as a non-quality in one place after having figured in another as quality; its function is to bring in the something more after the Reality is established, such additions as virtue, vice, ugliness, beauty, health, a certain shape. On this last, however, it may be remarked that triangularity and quadrangularity are not in themselves qualities, but there is quality when a thing is triangular by having been brought to that shape; the quality is not the triangularity but the patterning to it. The case is the same with the arts and avocations (by which human beings take the quality of being instructed, &c.).

Thus: Quality is a condition superadded to a Reality whose existence does not depend upon it, whether this something more be a later acquirement or an accompaniment from the first; it is something in whose absence the Reality would still be complete. It will sometimes come and go, sometimes be inextricably attached, so that there are two forms of Quality, the movable and the fixed.

3. The whiteness, therefore, in a human being is, clearly, to be classed not as a quality but as an activity—the act of a power which can make white; and similarly what we think of as qualities in the Intellectual Realm should be known as activities; they are activities which to our minds take the appearance of quality from the fact that, differing in character among themselves, each of them is a particularity which, so to speak, distinguishes those Realities from each other.

What, then, distinguishes Quality in the Intellectual Realm from that here, if both are Acts?

❙ The difference is that the Qualities in the Sensible Realm do not indicate the very nature of the Reality (as do the corresponding Activities in the Intellectual) nor do they[3]❙ indicate variations of substance or of (essential) character; they merely indicate what we think of as Quality but in the Intellectual Realm must still be Activity.

In other words this thing, considered in its aspect as possessing the characteristic property of Reality, is by that alone recognized as no mere Quality. But when our reason separates what is distinctive in these ('Quality-Activities')— not in the sense of abolishing them but rather as taking them to itself and making something new of them—this new something is Quality: reason has, so to speak, appropriated a portion of Reality, that portion manifest to it on the surface.

By this analogy, warmth, as a concomitant of the specific nature of fire, may very well be no quality in fire but an Idea-Form belonging to it, one of its activities, while being merely a Quality in other things than fire: as it is manifested in any warm object, it is not a mode of Reality but merely a trace, a shadow, an image, something that has gone forth from its own Reality—where it was an Act—and in the warm object is a quality.

All, then, that is accident and not Act; all but what is Idea-Form of the Reality; all that merely confers pattern; all this is Quality: qualities are characteristics and modes which are distinct from a thing's substratum.

But the Archetypes of all such qualities, the foundation in which they exist primarily, these are (not qualities but) Activities of the Intellectual Beings.

And; one and the same thing cannot be both Quality and non-quality: the thing void of Real-Existence is Quality; but the thing accompanying the Real is Reality or Form or Activity: there is no longer self-identity when, from having its being in itself, anything comes to be in something else with a fall from its standing as Form and Activity.

Finally, anything which is never Form but always accidental to something else is Quality unmixed and nothing more.

NOTES TO ENNEAD II.6

1. FIRST EDITION: ". . . whiteness of *a swan . . .*" ARMSTRONG and GUTHRIE also have "swan."

2. FIRST EDITION: ". . . the Reality and the *fact of existence* precede . . ."

ARMSTRONG: ". . . the substance, the specific essence . . ."

GUTHRIE: "The suchness of being implies a previously existing being and quiddity."

3. FIRST EDITION: "The difference is that *these ('Quality-Activities')* in the *Supreme* do not indicate the very nature of the Reality (as do the corresponding Activities *here*) nor do they . . ."

ARMSTRONG: "The qualities in the intelligible world do not indicate what sort of things their underlying realities are . . ."

GUTHRIE: "The sense-quality does not show the essential quality of every being . . ."

SEVENTH TRACTATE

'Complete Transfusion'

1. Some inquiry must be made into what is known as the complete transfusion of material substances.

Is it possible that fluid be blended with fluid in such a way that each penetrate the other through and through? or—a difference of no importance if any such penetration occurs—that one of them pass completely through the other?

Those that admit only contact need not detain us. They are dealing with mixture, not with the coalescence which makes the total a thing of like parts, each minutest particle being composed of all the combined elements.

But there are those who, admitting coalescence, confine it to the qualities: to them the material substances of two bodies are in contact merely, but in this contact of the matter they find footing for the qualities of each.

Their view is plausible because it rejects the notion of total admixture and because it recognizes that the masses of the mixing bodies must be whittled away if there is to be mixture without any gap, if, that is to say, each substance must be divided within itself through and through for complete interpenetration with the other. Their theory is confirmed by the cases in which two mixed substances occupy a greater space than either singly, especially a space equal to the conjoined extent of each: for, as they point out, in an absolute interpenetration the infusion of the one into the other would leave the occupied space exactly what it was before and, where the space occupied is not increased by the juxtaposition, they explain that some expulsion of air has made room for the incoming substance. They ask further, how a minor quantity of one substance can be spread out so as to interpenetrate (speck by speck or drop by drop) a major quantity of another. In fact they have a multitude of arguments.

Those, on the other hand, that accept 'complete transfusion', might object that it does not require the reduction of the mixed things to fragments, a certain cleavage being sufficient: thus, for instance, sweat does not split up the body or even pierce holes in it. And if it is answered that this may well be a special decree of Nature to allow of the sweat exuding, there is the case of those manufactured articles, slender but without puncture, in which we can see a liquid wetting them through and through so that it runs down from the upper to the under surface. How can this fact be explained, since both the liquid and the solid are bodily substances? Interpenetration without disintegration is difficult to conceive, and if there is such mutual disintegration the two must obviously destroy each other.

When they urge that often there is a mixing without augmentation their adversaries can counter at once with the exit of air.

When there is an increase in the space occupied, nothing refutes the explanation—however unsatisfying—that this is a necessary consequence of two bodies bringing to a common stock their magnitude equally with their other attributes: size is as permanent as any other property; and, exactly as from the blending of qualities there results a new form of thing, the combination of the two, so we find a new magnitude; the blending gives us a magnitude representing each of the two. But at this point the others will answer, 'If you mean that substance lies side by side with substance and mass with mass, each carrying its quantum of magnitude, you are at one with us: if there were complete transfusion, one substance sinking its original magnitude in the other, we would have no longer the case of two lines joined end to end by their terminal points and thus producing an increased extension; we would have line superimposed upon line with, therefore, no increase.'

But a lesser quantity permeates the entire extent of a larger; the smallest is sunk in the greatest; transfusion is exhibited unmistakably. In certain cases it is possible to pretend that there is no total penetration, but there are manifest examples leaving no room for the pretence. In what they say of the spreading out of masses they cannot be thought very plausible; the extension would have to be considerable indeed in the case of a very small quantity (to be in true mixture with a very large mass); for they do not suggest any such extension by change as that of water into air.

2. This, however, raises a problem deserving investigation in itself: what has happened when a definite magnitude of water becomes air, and how do we explain the increase of volume? But for the present we must be content with the matter thus far discussed out of all the varied controversy accumulated on either side.

It remains for us to make out on our own account the true explanation of the phenomenon of mixing, without regard to the agreement or disagreement of that theory with any of the current opinions mentioned.

When water runs through wool or when papyrus-pulp gives up its moisture, why is not the moist content expressed to the very last drop, or even, without question of outflow, how can we possibly think that in a mixture the relation of matter with matter, mass with mass, is contact and that only the qualities are fused? The pulp is not merely in touch with water outside it or even in its pores; it is wet through and through so that every particle of its matter is drenched in that quality. Now if the matter is soaked all through with the quality, then the water is everywhere in the pulp.

'Not the water; the quality of the water.'

But then, where is the water? and (if only a quality has entered) why is there a change of volume? The pulp has been expanded by the addition: that is to say it has received magnitude from the incoming substance—but if it has received the magnitude, magnitude has been added; and a magnitude added has not been absorbed; therefore the combined matter must occupy two several places. And as the two mixing substances communicate quality and receive matter in mutual give and take, so they may give and take magnitude. Indeed when a quality meets another quality it suffers some change; it is mixed, and by that admixture it is no longer pure and therefore no longer itself but a blunter thing, whereas magnitude joining magnitude retains its full strength.

But let it be understood how we came to say that body passing through and through another body must produce disintegration, while we make qualities pervade their substances without producing disintegration: the bodilessness of qualities is the reason. Matter, too, is bodiless: it may, then, be supposed that as Matter pervades everything, so the bodiless qualities associated with it—as long as they are few—have the power of penetration without disintegration. Anything solid would be stopped either in virtue of the fact that a solid has the precise quality which forbids it to penetrate or in that the mere coexistence of too many qualities in Matter (constitutes density and so) produces the same inhibition.

If, then, what we call a dense body is so by reason of the presence of many qualities, that plenitude of qualities will be the cause (of the inhibition).

If on the other hand density is itself a quality like what they call corporeity, then the cause will be that particular quality.

This would mean that the qualities of two substances do not bring about the mixing by merely being qualities but by being apt to mixture; nor does Matter refuse to enter into a mixing as Matter but as being associated with a quality repugnant to mixture; and this all the more since it has no magnitude of its own but only does not reject magnitude.

3. We have thus covered our main ground, but since corporeity has been mentioned, we must consider its nature: is it the conjunction of all the qualities or is it an Idea, or Reason-Principle, whose presence in Matter constitutes a body?

Now if body is the compound, the thing made up of all the required qualities plus Matter, then corporeity is nothing more than their conjunction.

And if it is a Reason-Principle, one whose incoming constitutes the body, then clearly this Principle contains embraced within itself all the qualities. If this Reason-Principle is to be no mere principle of definition exhibiting the nature of a thing but a veritable Reason constituting the thing, then it cannot itself contain Matter but must encircle Matter, and by being present to Matter elaborate the body: thus the body will be Matter associated with an indwelling Reason-Principle which will be in itself immaterial, pure Form, even though irremovably attached to the body. It is not to be confounded with that other Principle—treated elsewhere—which dwells in the Intellectual World by right of being itself an Intellectual Principle.

EIGHTH TRACTATE

Why Distant Objects Appear Small

1. Seen from a distance, objects appear reduced and close together, however far apart they be: within easy range, their sizes and the distances that separate them are observed correctly.

Distant objects show in this reduction because they must be drawn together for vision and the light must be concentrated to suit the size of the pupil; besides, as we are placed farther and farther away from the material mass under observation, it is more and more the bare form that reaches us, stripped, so to speak, of magnitude as of all other quality.

Or it may be that we appreciate the magnitude of an object by observing the salience and recession of its several parts, so that to perceive its true size we must have it close at hand.

Or again, it may be that magnitude is known incidentally (as a deduction) from the observation of colour. With an object at hand we know how much space is covered by the colour; at a distance, only that something is coloured, for the parts, quantitatively reduced, do not give us the precise knowledge of that quantity, the colours themselves reaching us only in a blurred impression.

What wonder, then, if size be like sound—reduced when the form reaches us but faintly—for in sound the hearing is concerned only about the form; magnitude is not discerned except incidentally.

Well, in hearing magnitude is known incidentally; but how? Touch conveys a direct impression of a visible object; what gives us the same direct impression of an object of hearing?

The magnitude of a sound is known not by actual quantity but by degree of impact, by intensity—and this in no indirect knowledge; the ear appreciates a certain degree of force, exactly as the palate perceives, by no indirect knowledge, a certain degree of sweetness. But the true magnitude of a sound is its extension; this the hearing may define to itself incidentally by deduction from the degree of intensity but not to the point of precision. The degree of intensity is fixed for each sound, but its extension is measured by the sum of space occupied.

Still (it will be objected) the colours seen from a distance are faint; but they are not small as the masses are.

True; but there is the common fact of diminution. There is colour with its diminution, faintness; there is magnitude with its diminution, smallness; and magnitude follows colour diminishing stage by stage with it.

But, the phenomenon is more easily explained by the example of things of wide variety. Take mountains dotted with houses, woods, and other landmarks; the observation of each detail gives us the means of calculating, by the single objects noted, the total extent covered: but, where no such detail of form reaches us, our vision, which deals with detail, has not the means towards the knowledge of the whole by measurement of any one clearly discerned magnitude. This applies even to objects of vision close at hand: where there is variety and the eye sweeps over all at one glance so that the forms are not all caught, the total appears the less in proportion to the detail which has escaped the eye; observe each single point and then you can estimate the volume precisely. Again, magnitudes of one colour and unbroken form trick the sense of quantity: the vision can no longer estimate by the particular; it slips away, not finding the stand-by of the difference between part and part.

❙ The distant object shows near at hand for the same reason: the intervening space is contracted; for though the nearer part is not subject to this deception, as soon as the eye reaches that part which is more remote, it no longer passes through it stage by stage so as to note its forms, and therefore finds itself unable to report its magnitude.[1]❙

2. The explanation by lesser angle of vision has been elsewhere dismissed; one point, however, we may urge here.

Those attributing the reduced appearance to the lesser angle occupied allow by their very theory that the unoccupied portion of the eye still sees something beyond or something quite apart from the object of vision, if only air-space.

Now consider some very large object of vision, that mountain for example. No part of the eye is unoccupied; the mountain adequately fills it so that it can take in nothing beyond, for the mountain as seen either corresponds exactly to the eye-space or stretches away out of range to right and to left. How does the explanation by lesser angle of vision hold good in this case, where the object still appears smaller, far, than it is and yet occupies the eye entire?

Or look up to the sky and no hesitation can remain. Of course we cannot take in the entire hemisphere at one glance; the eye directed to it could not cover so vast an expanse. But suppose the possibility: the entire eye, then, embraces the hemisphere entire; but the expanse of the heavens is far greater than it appears; how can its appearing far less than it is be explained by a lessening of the angle of vision?

NOTE TO ENNEAD II.8

1. FIRST EDITION has paragraph as: "*It was the detail that prevented a near object deceiving our sense of magnitude: in the case of the distant object, because the eye does not pass stage by stage through the stretch of intervening space so as to note its forms, therefore it cannot report the magnitude of that space.*"

ARMSTRONG: "And things far off appear near because the real extent of the distance between is contracted for the same reason. The near part of the distance appears in its true extent, from the same causes; but the sight cannot go through the far part of the distance and see its forms as they really are, and so it is not able to say how great in magnitude it really is."

GUTHRIE: "The distant object seems to us close because our inability to distinguish the parts of the intervening space does not permit us to determine exactly its magnitude. When sight can no longer traverse the length of an interval by determining its quality, in respect to its form, neither can it any longer determine its quantity in respect to magnitude."

NINTH TRACTATE [1]

Against the Gnostics; or Against Those that Affirm the Creator of the Cosmos and the Cosmos Itself to be Evil

1. We have seen that the Good, the Principle, is simplex, and, correspondingly, primal—for the secondary can never be simplex: that it contains nothing: that it is an integral Unity.

Now the same nature belongs to the Principle we know as The One. Just as the goodness of The Good is essential and not the outgrowth of some prior substance so the Unity of The One is its essential.

Therefore:

When we speak of The One and when we speak of The Good we must recognize an identical nature; we must affirm that they are the same—not, it is true, as venturing any predication with regard to that (unknowable) Hypostasis but simply as indicating it to ourselves in the best terms we find.

Even in calling it The First we mean no more than to express that it is the most absolutely simplex: it is the Self-Suffing only in the sense that it is not of that compound nature which would make it dependent upon any constituent; it is the Self-Contained because everything contained in something alien must also exist by that alien.

Deriving then from nothing alien, entering into nothing alien, in no way a made-up thing, there can be nothing above it.

We need not, then, go seeking any other Principles; this—the One and the Good—is our First, next to it follows the Intellectual Principle, the Primal Thinker, and upon this follows Soul. Such is the order in nature. The Intellectual Realm allows no more than these and no fewer.

Those who hold to fewer Principles must hold the identity of either Intellectual-Principle and Soul or of Intellectual-Principle and The First; but we have abundantly shown that these are distinct.

It remains for us to consider whether there are more than these Three.

Now what other (Divine) Kinds could there be? No Principles of the universe could be found at once simpler and more transcendent than this whose existence we have affirmed and described.

They will scarcely urge upon us the doubling of the Principle in Act by a Principle in Potentiality. It is absurd to seek such a plurality by distinguishing between potentiality and actuality in the case of immaterial beings whose existence is in Act—even in lower forms no such division can be made—and we cannot conceive a duality in the Intellectual-Principle, one phase in some vague calm, another all astir. Under what form can we think of repose in the Intellectual Principle as contrasted with its movement or utterance? What would the quiescence of the one phase be as against the energy of the other?

No: the Intellectual-Principle is continuously itself, unchangeably constituted in stable Act. With movement—towards it or around it—we are in the realm of the Soul's operation: such act is a Reason-Principle emanating from it and entering into soul, thus made an Intellectual Soul, but in no sense creating an intermediate Principle to stand between the two.

Nor are we warranted in affirming a plurality of Intellectual Principles on the ground that there is one that knows and thinks and another knowing that it knows and thinks. For whatever distinction be possible in the Divine between its Intellectual Act and its Consciousness of that Act, still all must be one projection not unaware of its own operation: it would be absurd to imagine any such unconsciousness in the Authentic Intelligence; the knowing principle must be one and the selfsame with that which knows of the knowing.

The contrary supposition would give us two beings, one that merely knows, and another—a separate being—that knows of the act of knowing.

If we are answered that the distinction is merely a process of our thought, then, at once, I the theory of a further hypostasis[2] is abandoned: I further, the question is opened whether our thought can entertain a knowing principle so narrowed to its knowing as not to know that it knows—a limitation which would be charged as imbecility even in ourselves, who if but of very ordinary moral force are always master of our emotions and mental processes.

No: the Divine Mind in its mentation thinks itself; the object of the thought is nothing external: Thinker and Thought are one; therefore in its thinking and knowing it possesses itself, observes itself and sees itself not as something unconscious but as knowing: in this Primal Knowing it must include, as one and the same Act, the knowledge of the knowing; and even the logical distinction mentioned above cannot be I made the case[3] I of the Divine; the very eternity of its self-thinking precludes any such separation between that intellective act and the consciousness of the act.

The absurdity becomes still more blatant if we introduce yet a further distinction—after that which affirms the knowledge of the knowing, a third distinction affirming the knowing of the knowledge of the knowing: yet there is no reason against carrying on the division for ever and ever.

To increase the Primals by making the Supreme Mind engender the Reason-Principle, and this again engender in the Soul a distinct power to act as mediator between Soul and the Supreme Mind, this is to deny intellection to the Soul, which would no longer derive its Reason from the Intellectual-Principle but from an intermediate: the Soul then would possess not the Reason-Principle but an image of it: the Soul could not know the Intellectual-Principle; it could have no intellection.

2. Therefore we must affirm no more than these three Primals: we are not to introduce superfluous distinctions which their nature rejects. We are to proclaim one Intellectual-Principle unchangeably the same, in no way subject to decline, acting in imitation, as true as its nature allows, of the Father.

And as to our own Soul we are to hold that it stands, in part, always in the presence of the Divine Beings, while in part it is concerned with the things of this sphere and in part occupies a middle ground. It is one nature in graded powers; and sometimes the Soul in its entirety is borne along by the loftiest in itself and in the Authentic Existent; sometimes the less noble part is dragged down and drags the mid-soul with it, though the law is that the Soul may never succumb entire.

The Soul's disaster falls upon it when it ceases to dwell in the perfect Beauty—the appropriate dwelling-place of that Soul which is no part and of which we too are no part—thence to pour forth into the frame of the All whatsoever the All can hold of good and beauty. There that Soul rests, free from all solicitude, not ruling by plan or policy, not redressing, but establishing order by the marvellous efficacy of its contemplation of the things above it.

For the measure of its absorption in that vision is the measure of its grace and power, and what it draws from this contemplation it communicates to the lower sphere, illuminated and illuminating always.

3. Ever illuminated, receiving light unfailing, the All-Soul imparts it to the entire series of later Being which by this light is sustained and fostered and endowed with the fullest measure of life that each can absorb. It may be compared with a central fire warming every receptive body within range.

Our fire, however, is a thing of limited scope: given powers that have no limitation and are never cut off from the Authentic Existences, how imagine anything existing and yet failing to receive from them?

It is of the essence of things that each gives of its being to another: without this communication, The Good would not be Good, nor the Intellectual-Principle an Intellective Principle, nor would Soul itself be what it is: the law is, 'some life after the Primal Life, a second where there is a first; all linked in one unbroken chain; all eternal; divergent types being engendered only in the sense of being secondary'.

In other words, things commonly described as generated have never known a beginning: all has been and will be. Nor can anything disappear unless where a later form is possible: without such a future there can be no dissolution.

If we are told that there is always Matter as a possible term, we ask why then should not Matter itself come to nothingness. If we are told it may, then we ask why it should ever have been generated. If the answer comes that it had its necessary place as the ultimate of the series, we return that the necessity still holds.

With Matter left aside as wholly isolated, the Divine Beings are not everywhere but in some bounded place, walled off, so to speak; if that is not possible, Matter itself must receive the Divine light (and so cannot be annihilated).

4. To those who assert that creation is the work of the Soul 'after the failing of its wings', we answer that no such disgrace could overtake the Soul of the All. If they tell us of its falling, they must tell us also what caused the fall. And when did it take place? If from eternity, then the Soul must be essentially a fallen thing: if at some one moment, why not before that?

We assert its creative act to be a proof not of decline but rather of its steadfast hold. Its decline could consist only in its forgetting the Divine: but if it forgot, how could it create? Whence does it create but from the things it knew in the Divine? If it creates from the memory of that vision, it never fell. Even supposing it to be in some dim intermediate state, it need not be supposed more likely to decline: any inclination would be towards its Prior, in an effort to the clearer vision. If any memory at all remained, what other desire could it have than to retrace the way?

What could it have been planning to gain by world-creating? Glory? That would be absurd—a motive borrowed from the sculptors of our earth.

Finally, if the Soul created by policy and not by sheer need of its nature, by being characteristically the creative power—how explain the making of this universe?

And when will it destroy the work? If it repents of its work, what is it waiting for? If it has not yet repented, then it will never repent: it must be already accustomed to the world, must be growing more tender towards it with the passing of time.

Can it be waiting for certain souls still here? Long since would these have ceased returning for such rebirth, having known in former life the evils of this sphere; long since would they have foreborne to come.

Nor may we grant that this world is of unhappy origin because there are many jarring things in it. Such a judgement would rate it too high, treating it as the same with the Intelligible Realm and not merely its reflection.

And yet—what reflection of that world could be conceived more beautiful than this of ours? What fire could be a nobler reflection of the fire there than the fire we know here? Or what other earth than this could have been modelled after that earth? And what globe more minutely perfect than this, or more admirably ordered in its course, could have been conceived in the image of the self-centred circling of the World of Intelligibles? And for a sun figuring the Divine sphere, if it is to be more splendid than the sun visible to us, what a sun it must be!

5. Still more unreasonably:

There are men, bound to human bodies and subject to desire, grief, anger, who think so generously of their own faculty that they declare themselves in contact with the Intelligible World, but deny that the sun possesses a similar faculty less subject to influence, to disorder, to change; they deny that it is any wiser than we, the late born, hindered by so many cheats on the way towards truth.

Their own soul, the soul of the least of mankind, they declare deathless, divine; but the entire heavens and the stars within the heavens have had no communion with the Immortal Soul, though these are of far finer and purer grain than themselves—yet they are not blind to the order, the shapely pattern, the discipline prevailing in the heavens, since they are the loudest in complaint of the disorder that troubles our earth. We are to imagine the deathless Soul choosing of design the less worthy place, and preferring to abandon the nobler to the Soul that is to die.

Equally unreasonable is their introduction of that other Soul which they piece together from the elements.

How could any form or degree of life come about by a blend of the elements? Their conjunction could produce only a warm or cold or an intermediate substance, something dry or wet or intermediate.

Besides, how could such a soul be a bond holding the four elements together when (by the hypothesis) it is a later thing and rises from them? And this element-soul is described as possessing consciousness and will and the rest—what can we think?

Furthermore, these teachers, in their contempt for this creation and this earth, proclaim that another earth has been made for them into which they are to enter when they depart. Now this new earth is the Reason-Form (the Logos) of our world. Why should they desire to live in the archetype of a world abhorrent to them?

Then again, what is the origin of that pattern world? It would appear, from the theory, that the Maker had already declined towards the things of this sphere before that pattern came into being.

Now let us suppose the Maker craving to construct such an Intermediate World—though what motive could He have?—in addition to the Intellectual world which He eternally possesses. If He made the mid-world first, what end was it to serve?

To be a dwelling-place for souls?

How then did they ever fall from it? It exists in vain.

If He made it later than this world—abstracting the formal-idea of this world and leaving the Matter out—the souls that have come to know that intermediate sphere would have experienced enough to keep them from entering this. If the meaning is simply that souls exhibit the Ideal-Form of the Universe, what is there distinctive in the teaching?

6. And, what are we to think of the new forms of being they introduce—their 'Exiles' and 'Impressions' and 'Repentings'?

If all comes to states of the Soul—'Repentance' when it has undergone a change of purpose; 'Impressions' when it contemplates not the Authentic Existences but their simulacra—there is nothing here but a jargon invented to make a case for their school: all this terminology is piled up only to conceal their debt to the ancient Greek philosophy which taught, clearly and without bombast, the ascent from the cave and the gradual advance of souls to a truer and truer vision.

For, in sum, a part of their doctrine comes from Plato; all the novelties through which they seek to establish a philosophy of their own have been picked up outside of the truth.

From Plato come their punishments, their rivers of the underworld, and the changing from body to body; as for the plurality they assert in the Intellectual Realm—the Authentic Existent, the Intellectual-Principle, the Second Creator, and the Soul—all this is taken over from the Timaeus, where we read:

'As many Ideal-Forms as Mind beheld dwelling within the Veritably Living Being, so many the Maker resolved should be contained in this All.'

Misunderstanding their text, they conceived one Mind passively including within itself all that has being, another mind, a distinct existence, having vision, and a third planning the Universe—though often they substitute Soul for this planning Mind as the creating Principle—and they think that this third being is the Creator according to Plato.

They are in fact quite outside of the truth in their identification of the Creator.

In every way they misrepresent Plato's theory as to the method of creation as in many other respects they dishonour his teaching: they, we are to understand, have penetrated the Intellectual Nature, while Plato and all those other illustrious teachers have failed.

They hope to get the credit of minute and exact identification by setting up a plurality of intellectual Essences; but in reality this multiplication lowers the Intellectual Nature to the level of the Sense-Kind: their true course is to seek to reduce number to the least possible in the Supreme, simply referring all things to the second Hypostasis—which is all that exists as it is Primal Intellect and Reality and all else that is good after the First Nature—and to recognize Soul as the third Principle, accounting for the difference among souls merely by diversity of experience and character. Instead of insulting those venerable teachers they should receive their doctrine with the respect due to the older thought and honour all that noble system—an immortal Soul, an Intellectual and Intelligible Realm, the Supreme God, the Soul's need of emancipation from all intercourse with the body, the fact of separation from it, the escape from the world of process to the world of essential-being. These doctrines, all emphatically asserted by Plato, they do well to adopt: where they differ, they are at full liberty to speak their minds, but not to procure assent for their own theories by flaying and flouting the Greeks: where they have a divergent theory to maintain they must establish it by its own merits, declaring their own opinions with courtesy and with philosophical method and stating the controverted opinion fairly; they must point their minds towards the truth and not hunt fame by insult, reviling and seeking in their own persons to replace men honoured by the fine intelligences of ages past.

As a matter of fact the ancient doctrine of the Divine Essences was far the sounder and more instructed, and must be accepted by all not caught in the delusions that beset humanity: it is easy also to identify what has been conveyed in these later times from the ancients with incongruous novelties—how for example, where they must set up a contradictory doctrine, they introduce a medley of generation and destruction, how they cavil at the Universe, how they make the Soul blameable for the association with body, how they revile the Administrator of this All, how they ascribe to the Creator, identified with the Soul, the character and experiences appropriate to partial beings.

7. That this world has neither beginning nor end but exists for ever as long as the Supreme stands is certainly no novel teaching. And before this school rose it had been urged that commerce with the body is no gain to a soul.

But to treat the human Soul as a fair presentment of the Soul of the Universe is like picking out potters and blacksmiths and making them warrant for discrediting an entire well-ordered city.

We must recognize how different is the governance exercised by the All-Soul; the relation is not the same: it is not in fetters. Among the very great number of differences to which attention has been called it should not have been overlooked that we (the human Soul) lie under fetter;[4] and this in a second limitation, for the Body-Kind, already fettered within the All-Soul, imprisons all that it grasps.

But the Soul of the Universe cannot be in bond to what itself has bound: it is sovereign and therefore immune of the lower things, over which we on the contrary are not masters. That in it which is directed to the Divine and Transcendent is ever unmingled, knows no encumbering; that in it which imparts life to the body admits nothing bodily to itself. It is the general fact that an inset (as the Body) necessarily shares the conditions of its containing principle (as the Soul), and does not communicate its own conditions where that principle has an independent life: thus a graft will die if the stock dies, but the stock will live on by its proper life though the graft wither. The fire within your own self may be quenched, but the thing, fire, will exist still; and if fire itself were annihilated that would make no difference to the Soul, the Soul in the Supreme, but only to the plan of the material world; and if the other elements sufficed to maintain a Cosmos, the Soul in the Supreme would be unconcerned.

The constitution of the All is very different from that of the single, separate forms of life: there, the established rule commanding to permanence is sovereign; here things are like deserters kept to their own place and duty by a double bond; there is no outlet from the All, and therefore no need of restraining or of driving errants back to bounds: all remains where from the beginning the Soul's nature appointed.

The natural movement within the plan will be injurious to anything whose natural tendency it opposes: one group will sweep bravely onward with the great total to which it is adapted; the others, not able to comply with the larger order, are destroyed. A great choral is moving to its concerted plan; midway in the march, a tortoise is intercepted; unable to get away from the choral line it is trampled under foot; but if it could only range itself within the greater movement it too would suffer nothing.

8. To ask why the Soul has created the Cosmos, is to ask why there is a Soul and why a Creator creates. The question, also, implies a beginning in the eternal and, further, represents creation as the act of a changeful Being who turns from this to that.

Those that so think must be instructed—if they would but bear with correction—in the nature of the Supernals, and brought to desist from that blasphemy of majestic powers which comes so easily to them, where all should be reverent scruple.

Even in the administration of the Universe there is no ground for such attack, for it affords manifest proof of the greatness of the Intellectual Kind.

This All that has emerged into life is no amorphous structure—like those lesser forms within it which are born night and day out of the lavishness of its vitality—the Universe is a life organized, effective, complex, all-comprehensive, displaying an unfathomable wisdom. How, then, can anyone deny that it is a clear image, beautifully formed, of the Intellectual Divinities? No doubt it is copy, not original; but that is its very nature; it cannot be at once symbol and reality. But to say that it is an inadequate copy is false; nothing has been left out which a beautiful representation within the physical order could include.

Such a reproduction there must necessarily be—though not by deliberation and contrivance—for the Intellectual could not be the last of things, but must have a double Act, one within itself and one outgoing; there must, then, be something later than the Divine; for only the thing with which all power ends fails to pass downwards something of itself. In the Supreme there flourishes a marvellous vigour and therefore it produces.

If (as this doctrine maintains) there is another Universe, nobler than this, we must be told what it is; but if there is no other Cosmos, and a representation carrying down the features of the Intellectual Realm is necessary, this world of ours is such a representation.

This earth is full of varied life-forms and of immortal beings; to the very heavens it is crowded. And the stars, those of the upper and the under spheres, moving in their ordered path, fellow travellers with the universe, how can they be less than gods? Surely they must be morally good: what could prevent them? All that occasions vice here below is unknown there—no evil of body, perturbed and perturbing.

Knowledge, too; in their unbroken peace, what hinders them from the intellectual grasp of the God-Head and the Intellectual Gods? What can be imagined to give us a wisdom higher than belongs to the Supernals? Could anyone, not fallen to utter folly, bear with such an idea?

Admitting that human souls have descended under constraint of the All-Soul, are we to think the constrained the nobler? Among souls, what commands must be higher than what obeys. And if the coming was unconstrained, why find fault with a world you have chosen and can quit if you dislike it?

And further, if the order of this Universe is such that we are able, within it, to practise wisdom and to live our earthly course by the Supernal, does not that prove it a dependency of the Divine?

9. Wealth and poverty, and all inequalities of that order are made ground of complaint. But this is to ignore that the Sage demands no equality in such matters: he cannot think that to own many things is to be richer or that the powerful have the better of the simple; he leaves all such preoccupations to another kind of man. He has learned that life on earth has two distinct forms, the way of the Sage and the way of the mass, the Sage intent upon the sublimest, upon the realm above, while those of the more strictly human type fall, again, under two classes, the one reminiscent of virtue and therefore not without touch with good, the other mere populace, serving to provide necessaries to the better sort.

But what of murder? What of the feebleness that brings men under slavery to the passions?

Is it any wonder that there should be failing and error, not in the highest, the intellectual, Principle but in souls that are like undeveloped children? And is not life justified even so if it is a training ground with its victors and its vanquished?

You are wronged; need that trouble an immortal? You are put to death; you have attained your desire. And from the moment your citizenship of the world becomes irksome you are not bound to it.

Our adversaries do not deny that even here there is a system of law and penalty: and surely we cannot in justice blame a dominion which awards to every one his due, where virtue has its honour, and vice comes to its fitting shame, in which there are not merely representations of the gods, but the gods themselves, watchers from above, and—as we read—easily rebutting human reproaches, since they lead all things in order from a beginning to an end, allotting to each human being, as life follows life, a fortune shaped to all that has preceded—the destiny which, to those that do not penetrate it, becomes the matter of boorish insolence upon things divine.

A man's one task is to strive towards making himself perfect—though not in the idea—really fatal to perfection—that to be perfect is possible to himself alone.

We must recognize that other men have attained the heights of goodness; we must admit the goodness of the celestial spirits, and above all of the gods—those whose presence is here but their contemplation in the Supreme, and loftiest of them, the lord of this All, the most blessed Soul. Rising still higher, we hymn the divinities of the Intellectual Sphere, and, above all these, the mighty King of that dominion, whose majesty is made patent in the very multitude of the gods.

It is not by crushing the divine into a unity but by displaying its exuberance— as the Supreme himself has displayed it—that we show knowledge of the might of God, who, abidingly what He is, yet creates that multitude, all dependent on Him, existing by Him and from Him.

This Universe, too, exists by Him and looks to Him—the Universe as a whole and every god within it—and tells of Him to men, all alike revealing the plan and will of the Supreme.

These, in the nature of things, cannot be what He is, but that does not justify you in contempt of them, in pushing yourself forward as not inferior to them.

The more perfect the man, the more compliant he is, even towards his fellows; we must temper our importance, not thrusting insolently beyond what our nature warrants; we must allow other beings, also, their place in the presence of the Godhead; we may not set ourselves alone next after the First in a dream-flight which deprives us of our power of attaining identity with the Godhead in the measure possible to the human Soul, that is to say, to the point of likeness to which the Intellectual-Principle leads us; to exalt ourselves above the Intellectual-Principle is to fall from it.

Yet imbeciles are found to accept such teaching at the mere sound of the words 'You yourself are to be nobler than all else, nobler than men, nobler than even gods'. Human audacity is very great: a man once modest, restrained, and simple hears, 'You, yourself, are the child of God; those men whom you used to venerate, those beings whose worship they inherit from antiquity, none of these are His children; you without lifting hand are nobler than the very heavens'; others take up the cry: the issue will be much as if in a crowd all equally ignorant of figures, one man were told that he stands a thousand cubits; he will naturally accept his thousand cubits even though the others present are said to

measure only five cubits; he will merely tell himself that the thousand indicates a considerable figure.

Another point: (you hold that) God has care for you; how then can He be
indifferent to the entire Universe in which you exist?

We may be told that He is too much occupied to look upon the Universe, and
that it would not be right for Him to do so; yet when He looks down and upon
these people, is He not looking outside Himself and upon the Universe in which
they exist? If He cannot look outside Himself so as to survey the Cosmos, then
neither does He look upon them.

But they have no need of Him?

The Universe has need of Him, and He knows its ordering and its indwellers
and how far they belong to it and how far to the Supreme, and which of the men
upon it are friends of God, mildly acquiescing with the cosmic dispensation
when in the total course of things some pain must be brought to them—for we
are to look not to the single will of any man but to the universe entire, regarding
every one according to worth but not stopping for such things where all that
may is hastening onward.

Not one only kind of being is bent upon this quest, which brings bliss to
whatsoever achieves, and earns for the others a future destiny in accord with
their power. No man, therefore, may flatter himself that he alone is competent;
a pretension is not a possession; many boast though fully conscious of their
lack and many imagine themselves to possess what was never theirs and even
to be alone in possessing what they alone of men never had.

10. Under detailed investigation, many other tenets of this school—indeed we
might say all—could be corrected with an abundance of proof. But I am
withheld by regard for some of our own friends who fell in with this doctrine
before joining our circle and, strangely, still cling to it.

The school, no doubt, is free-spoken enough—whether in the set purpose of
giving its opinions a plausible colour of verity or in honest belief—but we are
addressing here our own acquaintances, not those people with whom we could
make no way. We have spoken in the hope of preventing our friends from being
perturbed by a party which brings, not proof—how could it?—but arbitrary,
tyrannical assertion; another style of address would be applicable to such as have
the audacity to flout the noble and true doctrines of the august teachers of
antiquity.

That method we will not apply; anyone that has fully grasped the preceding
discussion will know how to meet every point in the system.

Only one other tenet of theirs will be mentioned before passing the matter;

it is one which surpasses all the rest in sheer folly, if that is the word.

They first maintain that the Soul and a certain 'Wisdom' (Sophia) declined and entered this lower sphere—though they leave us in doubt of whether the movement originated in Soul or in this Sophia of theirs, or whether the two are the same to them—then they tell us that the other souls came down in the descent and that these members of Sophia took to themselves bodies, human bodies, for example.

Yet in the same breath, that very Soul which was the occasion of descent to the others is declared not to have descended. 'It knew no decline', but merely illuminated the darkness in such a way that an image of it was formed upon the Matter. Then, they shape an image of that image somewhere below—through the medium of Matter or of Materiality or whatever else of many names they choose to give it in their frequent change of terms, invented to darken their doctrine—and so they bring into being what they call the Creator or Demiurge, then this lower is severed from his Mother (Sophia) and becomes the author of the Cosmos down to the latest of the succession of images constituting it.

Such is the blasphemy of one of their writers.

11. Now, in the first place, if the Soul has not actually come down but has illuminated the darkness, how can it truly be said to have declined? The outflow from it of something in the nature of light does not justify the assertion of its decline; for that, it must make an actual movement towards the object lying in the lower realm and illuminate it by contact.

If, on the other hand, the Soul keeps to its own place and illuminates the lower without directing any act towards that end, why should it alone be the illuminant? Why should not the Cosmos draw light also from the yet greater powers contained in the total of existence?

Again, if the Soul possesses the plan of a Universe, and by virtue of this plan illuminates it, why do not that illumination and the creating of the world take place simultaneously? Why must the Soul wait till the representations of the plan be made actual?

Then again this Plan—the 'Far Country' of their terminology—brought into being, as they hold, by the greater powers, could not have been the occasion of decline to the creators.

Further, how explain that under this illumination the Matter of the Cosmos produces images of the order of Soul instead of mere bodily-nature? An image of Soul could not demand darkness or Matter, but wherever formed it would exhibit the character of the producing element and remain in close union with it.

Next, is this image a real-being, or, as they say, an Intellection?

If it is a reality, in what way does it differ from its original? By being a distinct form of the Soul? But then, since the original is the reasoning Soul, this secondary form must be the vegetative and generative Soul; and then, what becomes of the theory that it is produced for glory's sake, what becomes of the creation in arrogance and self-assertion? The theory puts an end also to creation by representation and, still more decidedly, to any thinking in the act; and what need is left for a creator creating by way of Matter and Image?

If it is an Intellection, then we ask first, What justifies the name? I and next, What does it signify, unless the Soul gives this Intellection creative power? and how, even if we allow this fictitious Intellection—how does it exercise the creative act?⁵I Are we to be told that it is a question (not so much of creation as) of a first Image followed by a second? But this is quite arbitrary. And why is fire the first creation?

12. And how does this Image set to its task immediately after it comes into being?

By memory of what it has seen?

But it was utterly non-existent, it could have no vision, either it or the Mother they bestow upon it.

Another difficulty: these people (tell us that they) come upon earth not as Soul-Images but as veritable Souls; yet, by great stress and strain, one or two of them are able to stir beyond the limits of the world, and when they do attain Reminiscence barely carry with them some slight recollection of the Sphere they once knew: on the other hand, this Image, a new-comer into being, is able, they tell us—as also is its Mother—to form at least some dim representation of the celestial world. It is an Image, stamped in Matter, yet it not merely has the conception of the Supreme and adopts from that world the plan of this, but knows what elements serve the purpose. How, for instance, did it come to make fire before anything else? What made it judge fire a better first than some other object?

Again, if it created the fire of the Universe by thinking of fire, why did it not make the Universe at a stroke by thinking of the Universe? It must have conceived the product complete from the first; the constituent elements would be embraced in that general conception.

The creation must have been in all respects more according to the way of Nature than to that of the arts—for the arts are of later origin than Nature and the Universe, and even at the present stage the partial things brought into being by the natural Kinds do not follow any such order—first fire, then the several other elements, then the various blends of these—on the contrary the living organism entire is encompassed and rounded off within the uterine germ. Why should not the material of the Universe be similarly embraced in a Cosmic Type in which earth, fire, and the rest would be included? We can only suppose that these people themselves, acting by their more authentic Soul, would have produced the world by such a process, but that the Creator had not wit to do so.

And yet to conceive the vast span of the Heavens—to be great in that degree—to devise the obliquity of the Zodiac and the circling path of all the celestial bodies beneath it, and this earth of ours—and all in such a way that reason can be given for the plan—this could never be the work of an Image; it tells unmistakably of the Power that issues from the very Highest Beings.

Against their will, they themselves admit this: their 'outshining upon the darkness', if the doctrine is sifted, makes it impossible to deny the true origins of the Cosmos.

Why should this down-shining take place unless such a process belonged to a universal law?

Either the process is in the order of Nature or against that order. If it is in the nature of things, it must have taken place from eternity; if it is against the nature of things, then the breach of natural right exists in the Supreme also; evil antedates this world; the cause of evil is not the world; on the contrary the Supreme is the evil to us; instead of the Soul's harm coming from this sphere, we have this sphere harmed by the Soul.

In fine, the theory amounts to making evil[6] one of the Primals, and with it the Matter from which it emerges.

The Soul that declined, they tell us, saw and illuminated the already existent Darkness. Now whence came that Darkness?

If they tell us that the Soul created the Darkness by its decline, then, obviously, there was nowhere for the Soul to decline to; the cause of the decline was not the Darkness but the very nature of the Soul. The theory, therefore, refers the entire process to pre-existing compulsions: the guilt inheres in the Primal Beings.

13. Those, then, that censure the constitution of the Cosmos do not understand what they are doing or where this audacity leads them. They do not understand that there is a successive order of Primals, Secondaries, Tertiaries, and so on continuously to the Ultimates; that nothing is to be blamed for being inferior to the First; that we can but accept, meekly, the constitution of the total, and make our best way towards the Primals, withdrawing from the tragic spectacle, as they see it, of the cosmic spheres—which in reality are 'all suave graciousness'.

And what, after all, is there so terrible in these spheres with which it is sought to frighten people unaccustomed to thinking, never trained in an instructive and coherent gnosis?

Even the fact that their material frame is of fire does not make them dreadful; their movements are in keeping with the All and with the Earth: but what we must consider in them is the Soul, that on which these people base their own title to honour.

And, yet, again, their material frames are pre-eminent in vastness and beauty, as they co-operate in act and in influence with the entire order of Nature, and can never cease to exist as long as the Primals stand; they enter into the completion of the All of which they are major parts.

If men rank highly among other living Beings, much more do these, whose office in the All is not to play the tyrant but to serve towards beauty and order. The action attributed to them must be understood as a foretelling of coming events, while the causing of all the variety is due, in part to diverse destinies— for there cannot be one lot for the entire body of men—in part to the birth moment, in part to wide divergencies of place, in part to states of the souls.

Once more, we have no right to ask that all men shall be good, or to rush into censure because such universal virtue is not possible: this would be repeating the error of confusing our sphere with the Supreme and treating evil as a nearly negligible failure in wisdom—as good lessened and dwindling continuously, a continuous fading out: it would be like calling the Nature-Principle evil because it is not Sense-Perception and the Sense-Faculty evil for not being the Reason. If evil is no more than that, we will be obliged to admit evil in the Supreme also, for there, too, Soul is less exalted than the Intellectual-Principle, and That too has its Superior.

14. In yet another way they infringe still more gravely upon the inviolability of the Supreme.

In the sacred formulas they inscribe, purporting to address the Supernal Beings—not merely the Soul but even the Transcendents—they are simply uttering spells and appeasements and evocations in the idea that these Powers will obey a call and be led about by a word from any of us who is in some degree trained to use the appropriate forms in the appropriate way—certain melodies, certain sounds, specially directed breathings, sibilant cries, and all else to which is ascribed magic potency upon the Supreme. Perhaps they would repudiate any such intention: still they must explain how these things act upon the unem- bodied: they do not see that the power they attribute to their own words is so much taken away from the majesty of the divine.

They tell us they can free themselves of diseases.

If they meant, by temperate living and an appropriate regime, they would be right and in accordance with all sound knowledge. But they assert diseases to be Spirit-Beings and boast of being able to expel them by formula: this pretension may enhance their importance with the crowd, gaping upon the powers of magicians; but they can never persuade the intelligent that disease arises otherwise than from such causes as overstrain, excess, deficiency, putrid decay, in a word some variation whether from within or from without.

The nature of illness is indicated by its very cure. A motion, a medicine, the letting of blood, and the disease shifts down and away; sometimes scantiness of nourishment restores the system: presumably the Spiritual power gets hungry or is debilitated by the purge. Either this Spirit makes a hasty exit or it remains within. If it stays, how does the disease disappear, with the cause still present? If it quits the place, what has driven it out? Has anything happened to it? Are we to suppose it throve on the disease? In that case the disease existed as something distinct from the Spirit-Power. Then again, if it steps in where no cause of sickness exists, why should there be anything else but illness? If there must be such a cause, the Spirit is unnecessary: that cause is sufficient to produce that fever. As for the notion, that just when the cause presents itself, the watchful Spirit leaps to incorporate itself with it, this is simply amusing.

But the manner and motive of their teaching have been sufficiently exhibited; and this was the main purpose of the discussion here upon their Spirit-Powers. I leave it to yourselves to read the books and examine the rest of the doctrine: you will note all through how our form of philosophy inculcates simplicity of character and honest thinking in addition to all other good qualities, how it cultivates reverence and not arrogant self-assertion, how its boldness is balanced by reason, by careful proof, by cautious progression, by the utmost circumspection—and you will compare those other systems to one proceeding by this method. You will find that the tenets of their school have been huddled together under a very different plan: they do not deserve any further examination here.

15. There is, however, one matter which we must on no account overlook—the effect of these teachings upon the hearers led by them into despising the world and all that is in it.

There are two theories as to the attainment of the End of life. The one proposes pleasure, bodily pleasure, as the term; the other pronounces for good and virtue, the desire of which comes from God and moves, by ways to be studied elsewhere, towards God.

Epicurus denies a Providence and recommends pleasure and its enjoyment, all that is left to us: but the doctrine under discussion is still more wanton; it carps at Providence and the Lord of Providence; it scorns every law known to us; immemorial virtue and all restraint it makes into a laughing stock, lest any loveliness be seen on earth; it cuts at the root of all orderly living, and of the righteousness which, innate in the moral sense, is made perfect by thought and by self-discipline: all that would give us a noble human being is gone. What is left for them—except where the pupil by his own character betters the teaching—comes to pleasure, self-seeking, the grudge of any share with one's fellows, the pursuit of advantage.

Their error is that they know nothing good here: all they care for is something else to which they will at some future time apply themselves: yet, this world, to those that have known it once, must be the starting-point of the pursuit: arrived here from out of the divine nature, they must inaugurate their effort by some earthly correction. The understanding of beauty is not given except to a nature scorning the delight of the body, and those that have no part in well-doing can make no step towards the Supernal.

This school, in fact, is convicted by its neglect of all mention of virtue: any discussion of such matters is missing utterly: we are not told what virtue is or under what different kinds it appears; there is no word of all the numerous and noble reflections upon it that have come down to us from the ancients; we do not learn what constitutes it or how it is acquired, how the Soul is tended, how it is cleaned. For to say 'Look to God' is not helpful without some instruction as to what this looking imports: it might very well be said that one can 'look' and still sacrifice no pleasure, still be the slave of impulse, repeating the word 'God' but held in the grip of every passion and making no effort to master any. Virtue, advancing towards the Term and, linked with thought, occupying a soul, makes God manifest: 'God' on the lips without a good conduct of life, is a word.

16. On the other hand, to despise this sphere, and the Gods within it, or anything else that is lovely, is not the way to goodness.

Every evildoer began by despising the Gods; and one not previously corrupt, taking to this contempt, even though in other respects not wholly bad, becomes an evildoer by the very fact.

Besides, in this slighting of the Mundane Gods and the world, the honour they profess for the gods of the Intellectual Sphere becomes an inconsistency; where we love, our hearts are warm also to the kin of the beloved; we are not indifferent to the children of our friend. Now every soul is a child of that Father; but in the heavenly bodies there are souls, intellective, holy, much closer to the Supernal Beings than are ours; for how can this Cosmos be a thing cut off from That and how imagine the gods in it to stand apart?

But of this matter we have treated elsewhere: here we urge that where there is contempt for the Kin of the Supreme the knowledge of the Supreme itself is merely verbal.

What sort of piety can make Providence stop short of earthly concerns or set any limit whatsoever to it?

And what consistency is there in this school when they proceed to assert that Providence cares for them, though for them alone?

And is this Providence over them to be understood of their existence in that other world only or of their lives here as well? If in the other world, how came they to this? If in this world, why are they not already raised from it?

Again, how can they deny that the Lord of Providence is here? How else can He know either that they are here, or that in their sojourn here they have not forgotten Him and fallen away? And if He is aware of the goodness of some, He must know of the wickedness of others, to distinguish good from bad. That means that He is present to all, is, by whatever mode, within this Universe. The Universe, therefore, must be participant in Him.

If He is absent from the Universe, He is absent from yourselves, and you can have nothing to tell about Him or about the powers that come after Him.

But, allowing that a Providence reaches to you from the world beyond—making any concession to your liking—it remains none the less certain that this world holds from the Supernal and is not deserted and will not be: a Providence watching entires is even more likely than one over fragments only; and similarly, Participation is more perfect in the case of the All-Soul—as is shown, further, by the very existence of things and the wisdom manifest in their existence. Of those that advance these wild pretensions, who is so well ordered, so wise, as the Universe? The comparison is laughable, utterly out of place; to make it, except as a help towards truth, would be impiety.

The very question can be entertained by no intelligent being but only by one so blind, so utterly devoid of perception and thought, so far from any vision of the Intellectual Universe as not even to see this world of our own.

For who that truly perceives the harmony of the Intellectual Realm could fail, if he has any bent towards music, to answer to the harmony in sensible sounds? What geometrician or arithmetician could fail to take pleasure in the symmetries, correspondences, and principles of order observed in visible things? Consider, even, the case of pictures: those seeing by the bodily sense the productions of the art of painting do not see the one thing in the one only way; they are deeply stirred by recognizing in the objects depicted to the eyes the presentation of what lies in the idea, and so are called to recollection of the truth—the very experience out of which Love rises. Now, if the sight of Beauty excellently reproduced upon a face hurries the mind to that other Sphere, surely no one seeing the loveliness lavish in the world of sense—this universal symmetry, this vast orderliness, the Form which the stars even in their remoteness display—no one could be so dull-witted, so immovable, as not to be carried by all this to recollection, and gripped by reverent awe in the thought of all this, so great, sprung from that greatness. Not to answer thus could only be to have neither fathomed this world nor had any vision of that other.

17. Perhaps the hate of this school for the corporeal is due to their reading of Plato who inveighs against body as a grave hindrance to Soul and pronounces the corporeal to be characteristically the inferior.

Then let them for the moment pass over the corporeal element in the Universe and study all that still remains.

They will think of the Intellectual Sphere which includes within itself the Ideal-Form realized in the Cosmos. They will think of the souls, in their ordered rank, that produce incorporeal magnitude and lead the Intelligible out towards spatial extension, so that finally the thing of process becomes, by its magnitude, as adequate a representation as possible of the principle void of parts which is its model—the greatness of power there being translated here into greatness of bulk. Then whether they think of this (Intellectual) Sphere as already in movement under the guidance of that power of God which holds it through and through, beginning and middle and end, or whether they consider it as in rest and exercising as yet no outer governance: either approach will lead to a true appreciation of the Soul that conducts this Universe.

Now let them set body within it—not in the sense that Soul suffers any change but that, since in the Gods there can be no grudging, it gives to its inferior all that any partial thing has strength to receive—and at once their conception of the Cosmos must be revised; they cannot deny that the Soul of the Cosmos has exercised such a weight of power as to have brought the corporeal-principle, in itself unlovely, to partake of good and beauty to the utmost of its receptivity—and to a pitch which stirs souls, beings of the divine order.

These people may no doubt say that they themselves feel no such stirring, and that they see no difference between beautiful and ugly forms of body; but, at that, they can make no distinction between the ugly and the beautiful in conduct; sciences can have no beauty; there can be none in thought; and none, therefore, in God. This world descends from the Firsts: if this world has no beauty, neither has its Source; springing thence, this world, too, must have its beautiful things. And while they proclaim their contempt for earthly beauty, they would do well to ignore that of youths and women so as not to be overcome by incontinence.

In fine, we must consider that their self-satisfaction could not turn upon a contempt for anything indisputably base; theirs is the perverse pride of despising what was once admired.

We must always keep in mind that the beauty in a partial thing cannot be identical with that in a whole; nor can any several objects be as stately as the total.

And we must recognize, that even in the world of sense and part, there are things of a loveliness comparable to that of the Celestials—forms whose beauty must fill us with veneration for their creator and convince us of their origin in the divine, forms which show how ineffable is the beauty of the Supreme since they cannot hold us but we must, though in all admiration, leave these for those. Further, wherever there is interior beauty, we may be sure that inner and outer correspond; where the interior is vile, all is brought low by that flaw in the dominants.

Nothing truly beautiful without can be base within, for a good exterior springs from a beauty dominant within; people passing as handsome but essentially base have a spurious and superficial beauty: if anyone tells me he has seen people really fine-looking but interiorly vile, I can only deny it; we have here simply a false notion of personal beauty; unless, indeed, the inner vileness were an accident in a nature essentially fine; in this Sphere there are many obstacles to self-realization.

In any case the All is beautiful, and there can be no obstacle to its inner goodness: where the nature of a thing does not comport perfection from the beginning, there may be a failure in complete expression; there may even be a fall to vileness, but the All never knew a childlike immaturity; it never experienced a progress bringing novelty into it; it never had bodily growth: there was nowhere from whence it could take such increment; it was always the All-Container.

And even for its Soul no one could imagine any such a path of process: or, if this were conceded, certainly it could not be towards evil.

18. But perhaps this school will maintain that, while their teaching leads to a hate and utter abandonment of the body, ours binds the Soul down in it.

In other words: two people inhabit the one stately house; one of them declaims against its plan and against its Architect, but none the less maintains his residence in it; the other makes no complaint, asserts the entire competency of the Architect, and waits cheerfully for the day when he may leave it, having no further need of a house: the malcontent imagines himself to be the wiser and to be the readier to leave because he has learned to repeat that the walls are of soulless stone and timber and that the place falls far short of a true home; he does not see that his only distinction is in not being able to bear with necessity—assuming that his conduct, his grumbling, does not cover a secret admiration for the beauty of those same 'stones'. As long as we have bodies we must inhabit the dwellings prepared for us by our good sister soul (the All-Soul) in her vast power of labourless creation.

Or would this school reject the word 'sister'? They are willing to address the lowest of men as brothers; are they capable of such raving as to disown the tie with the Sun and the powers of the Heavens and the very Soul of the Cosmos? Such kinship, it is true, is not for the vile; it may be asserted only of those that have become good and are no longer body but embodied soul and of a quality to inhabit the body in a mode very closely resembling the indwelling of the All-Soul in the universal frame. And this means continence, self-restraint, holding staunch against outside pleasure and against outer spectacle, allowing no hardship to disturb the mind. The All-Soul is immune from shock; there is nothing that can affect it: but we, in our passage here, must call on virtue in repelling these assaults, reduced for us from the beginning by a great conception of life, annulled by matured strength.

Attaining to something of this immunity, we begin to reproduce within ourselves the Soul of the vast All and of the heavenly bodies: when we are come to the very closest resemblance, all the effort of our fervid pursuit will be towards that goal to which they also tend; their contemplative vision becomes ours, prepared as we are, first by natural disposition and afterwards by all this training, I for that state which is theirs from the beginning.[7]I

This school may lay claim to vision as a dignity reserved to themselves, but they are not any the nearer to vision by the claim—or by the boast that while the celestial powers, bound for ever to the ordering of the Heavens, can never stand outside the material universe, they themselves have their freedom in their death. This is a failure to grasp the very notion of 'standing outside', a failure to appreciate the mode in which the All-Soul 'cares for the unensouled'.

No: it is possible to go free of love for the body; to be clean-living, to disregard death; to know the Highest and aim at that other world; not to slander, as negligent in the quest, others who are able for it and faithful to it; and not to err with those that deny vital motion to the stars because to our sense they stand still—the error which in another form leads this school I to deny to the Star-Nature the vision of what lies outside the material universe, only because they do not see that the Star-Soul itself arises in that non-material sphere.[8]I

NOTES TO ENNEAD II.9

1. In his introductory note to Ennead II.9, Armstrong points out that this treatise (thirty-third in Porphyry's chronological order) was originally part of a larger piece that Porphyry "hacked roughly into four parts" and placed into different Enneads. The other three parts of the originally continuous single piece are III.8 (chronological number 30), V.8 (chronological number 31) and V.5 (chronological number 32).

2. FIRST EDITION: "... the theory of a *plurality in the Divine Hypostasis* is abandoned."

ARMSTRONG: "... they will be abandoning the idea of a plurality of hypostases."

GUTHRIE: "A mere logical distinction between thought and consciousness of thought would not establish the (actual) differences between two (hypostatic substances)."

TAYLOR: "If, however, they say that these two [only] differ from each other in conceptions, in the first place indeed, they will be deprived of many hypostases;" Brackets are Taylor's.

3. FIRST EDITION: "... made *in* the case ..."

4. FIRST EDITION: "... overlooked that *the We* (the human Soul) lies under fetter;" MacKenna is alone in making this distinction:

ARMSTRONG, TAYLOR, and GUTHRIE all use simply "we."

5. FIRST EDITION: "... and next, *How does anything come into being* unless the Soul *give* this Intellection creative power and how, *after all, can creative power reside in a created thing?*"

ARMSTRONG: "... and then how it exists, unless Soul is going to give the thought power to make. But, over and above the fact that this is pure fiction, how does the making work?"

TAYLOR: "... and in the next place how it produces, unless it imparts to the conception a fabricative power. But how can there be production with a fiction?"

GUTHRIE: "... then, unless a creative force be predicated of this conception, it would be necessary to show how a conception can constitute a real being. But what creative force can be inherent in this imaginary being?"

6. FIRST EDITION: "... amounts to making *the world* one of the Primals ..."

ARMSTRONG: "... will lead to the attribution of responsibility for the universe to the first principles:"

TAYLOR: "... we are led to refer the world to the first of things."

GUTHRIE: "... reason will relate this world to the primary principles. If matter is also said to be the cause of evil, where does it originate?"

7. FIRST EDITION: "... for that state which is theirs *by the Principle of their Being.*"

TAYLOR: "Then also those things which were the objects of their vision from the first, will be ours ..."

GUTHRIE and ARMSTRONG both have from "the beginning."

8. FIRST EDITION: "... to deny *outer vision to the Star-Nature,* only because they do not see *the Star-Soul in outer manifestation.*"

GUTHRIE: "Let us not act as do the (Gnostics), who believe that the nature of the stars does not see what is external, because they themselves do not see that their own souls are outside."

TAYLOR: "For on this account also, the Gnostics fancy, that the nature of the stars does not survey the intelligibles that are as it were external to them, because they themselves do not see the soul of them externally subsisting."

ARMSTRONG: "... the Gnostics, too, do not think that the nature of the stars sees what is outside the material universe, because they do not see that their souls come from outside."

THE THIRD ENNEAD

FIRST TRACTATE

Fate

1. IN THE TWO orders of things—those whose existence is that of process and those in whom it is Authentic Being—there is a variety of possible relation to Cause.

Cause might conceivably underlie all the entities in both orders or none in either. It might underlie some, only, in each order, the others being causeless. It might, again, underlie the Realm of Process universally while in the Realm of Authentic Existence some things were caused, others not, or all were causeless. Conceivably, on the other hand, the Authentic Existents are all caused while in the Realm of Process some things are caused and others not, or all are causeless.

Now, to begin with the Eternal Existents:

The Firsts among these, by the fact that they are Firsts, cannot be referred to outside Causes; but all such (Eternals) as depend upon those Firsts may be admitted to derive their Being from them.

And in all cases the Act may be referred to the Essence (as its cause), for their Essence consists, precisely, in giving forth an appropriate Act.

As for Things of Process—or for Eternal Existents whose Act is not eternally invariable—we must hold that these are due to Cause; causelessness is quite inadmissible; we can make no place here for unwarranted 'slantings', for sudden movement of bodies apart from any initiating power, for precipitate spurts in a soul with nothing to drive it into the new course of action. Such causelessness would bind the Soul under an even sterner compulsion, no longer master of itself, but at the mercy of movements apart from will and cause. Something willed—within itself or without—something desired, must lead it to action; without motive it can have no motion.

On the assumption that all happens by Cause, it is easy to discover the nearest determinants of any particular act or state and to trace it plainly to them.

The cause of a visit to the centre of affairs will be that one thinks it necessary to see some person or to receive a debt, or, in a word, that one has some definite motive or impulse confirmed by a judgement of expediency. Sometimes a condition may be referred to the arts, the recovery of health for instance to medical science and the doctor. Wealth has for its cause the discovery of a treasure or the receipt of a gift, or the earning of money by manual or intellectual labour. The child is traced to the father as its Cause and perhaps to a chain of favourable outside circumstances such as a particular diet or, less immediately, a special organic aptitude, or a wife apt to childbirth.

And the general cause of all is Nature.

2. But to halt at these nearest determinants, not to be willing to penetrate deeper, indicates a sluggish mind, a dullness to all that calls us towards the primal and transcendent causes.

How comes it that the same surface causes produce different results? There is moonshine, and one man steals and the other does not: under the influence of exactly similar surroundings one man falls sick and the other keeps well; an identical set of operations makes one rich and leaves another poor. The differences amongst us in manners, in characters, in success, force us to go still further back.

Men therefore have never been able to rest at the surface causes.

One school postulates material principles, such as atoms; from the movement, from the collisions and combinations of these, it derives the existence and the mode of being of all particular phenomena, supposing that all depends upon how these atoms are agglomerated, how they act, how they are affected; our own impulses and states, even, are supposed to be determined by these principles.

Such teaching, then, obtrudes this compulsion, an atomic Anangke, even upon Real Being. Substitute, for the atoms, any other material entities as principles and the cause of all things, and at once Real Being becomes servile to the determination set up by them.

Others rise to the first-principle of all that exists and from it derive all; they tell of a cause penetrating all things, not merely moving all but making each and everything; but they pose this as a fate and a supremely dominating cause, which is in fact the universe itself; not merely all else that comes into being, but even our own thinking and thoughts would spring from its movement, just as the several members of an animal move not at their own choice but at the dictation of the leading principle which animal life presupposes.

Yet another school fastens on the universal Circuit as embracing all things and producing all by its motion and by the positions and mutual aspect of the planets and fixed stars in whose power of foretelling they find warrant for the belief that this Circuit is the universal determinant.

Finally, there are those that dwell on the interconnexion of the causative forces and on their linked descent—every later phenomenon following upon an earlier, one always leading back to others by which it arose and without which it could not be, and the latest always subservient to what went before them—but this is obviously to bring in fate by another path. This school may be fairly distinguished into two branches; a section which makes all depend upon some one principle and a section which ignores such a unity.

Of this last opinion we will have something to say, but for the moment we will deal with the former, taking the others in their turn.

3. 'Atoms' or 'elements'—it is in either case an absurdity, an impossibility, to hand over the universe and its contents to material entities, and out of the disorderly swirl thus occasioned to call order, reasoning, and the governing soul into being; but the atomic origin is, if we may use the phrase, the most impossible.

A good deal of truth has resulted from the discussion of this subject; but, even to admit such principles does not compel us to admit universal compulsion or any kind of 'fate'.

Suppose the atoms to exist:

These atoms are to move, some downwards—admitting a down and an up (in the Universe or before the Universe is in being)—others slantwise, all at haphazard, in a confused conflict. Nothing here is orderly; order has not come into being, though the outcome, this Universe, when it achieves existence, is all order; and thus prediction and divination are utterly impossible, whether by the laws of the science—what science can operate where there is no order?—or by divine possession and inspiration, which no less require that the future be something regulated.

Material entities exposed to all this onslaught may very well be under compulsion to yield to whatsoever the atoms may bring: but would anyone pretend that the acts and states of a soul or mind could be explained by any atomic movements? How can we imagine that the onslaught of an atom, striking downwards or dashing in from any direction, could force the soul to definite and necessary reasonings or impulses or into any reasonings, impulses, or thoughts at all, necessary or otherwise? And what of the soul's resistance to bodily states? What movement of atoms could compel one man to be a geometrician, set another studying arithmetic or astronomy, lead a third to the philosophic life? In a word, if we must go, like soulless bodies, wherever bodies push and drive us, there is an end to our personal act and to our very existence as living beings.

The School that erects other material forces (such as 'the elements') into universal causes is met by the same reasoning: we say that while these can warm us and chill us, and destroy the weaker part of us (the body), they can be causes of nothing that is done in the sphere of mind or soul: all this must be traceable to quite another kind of Principle.

4. Another theory:

The Universe is permeated by one Soul, Cause of all things and events; every separate phenomenon as a member of a whole moves in its place with the general movement; all the various causes spring into action from one source: therefore, it is argued, the entire descending chain of causes and all their interaction must follow inevitably and so constitute a universal determination. A plant rises from a root, and we are asked on that account to reason that not only the interconnexion linking the root to all the members and every member to every other but the entire activity and experience of the plant, as well, must be one organized overruling, a 'destiny' of the plant.

But such an extremity of determination, a destiny so all-pervasive, does away with the very destiny that is affirmed: it shatters the sequence and co-operation of causes.

It would be unreasonable to attribute to destiny the movement of our limbs dictated by the mind and will: this is no case of something outside (some destiny) bestowing motion while another thing (mind) accepts it and is thus set into action; the mind itself (and not destiny) is the prime mover.

Similarly in the case of the universal system; if all that performs act and is subject to experience constitutes one substance, if one thing does not really produce another thing under causes leading back continuously one to another, then it is not a truth that all happens by causes, there is nothing but a rigid unity. We are no 'We': nothing is our act; our thought is not ours; our decisions are the reasoning of something outside ourselves; we are no more agents than our feet are kickers when we use them to kick with.

No; each several thing must be a separate thing; there must be acts and thoughts that are our own; the good and evil done by each human being must be his own; and it is quite certain that we must not lay any vileness to the charge of the All.

5. But perhaps the explanation of every particular act or event is rather that they are determined by the spheric movement—the Phora—and by the changing position of the heavenly bodies as these stand at setting or rising or in mid course and in various aspects with each other.

Augury, it is urged, is able from these indications to foretell what is to happen not merely to the universe as a whole, but even to individuals, and this not merely as regards external conditions of fortune but even as to the events of the mind. We observe, too, how growth or check in other orders of beings—animals and plants—is determined by their sympathetic relations with the heavenly bodies and how widely they are influenced by them, how, for example, the various countries show a different produce according to their situation on the earth and especially their lie towards the sun. And the effect of place is not limited to plants and animals; it rules human beings too, determining their appearance, their height and colour, their mentality and their desires, their pursuits and their moral habit. Thus the universal circuit would seem to be the monarch of the All.

Now a first answer to this theory is that its advocates have merely devised another shift to immolate to the heavenly bodies all that is ours, our acts of will and our states, all the evil in us, our entire personality; nothing is allowed to us; we are left to be stones set rolling, not men, not beings whose nature implies a task.

But we must be allowed our own—with the understanding that to what is primarily ours, our personal holding, there is added some influx from the All—the distinction must be made between our individual act and what is thrust upon us: we are not to be immolated to the stars.

Place and climate, no doubt, produce constitutions warmer or colder; and the parents tell on the offspring, as is seen in the resemblance between them, very general in personal appearance and noted also in some of the unreflecting states of the mind.

None the less, in spite of physical resemblance and similar environment, we observe the greatest difference in temperament and in ideas: this side of the human being, then, derives from some quite other Principle (than any external causation or destiny). A further confirmation is found in the efforts we make to correct both bodily constitution and mental aspirations.

If the stars are held to be causing principles on the ground of the possibility of foretelling individual fate or fortune from observation of their positions, then the birds and all the other things which the soothsayer observes for divination must equally be taken as causing what they indicate.

Some further considerations will help to clarify this matter:

The heavens are observed at the moment of a birth and the individual fate is thence predicted in the idea that the stars are no mere indications, but active causes, of the future events. Sometimes the Astrologers tell of noble birth: 'the child is born of highly placed parents'; yet how is it possible to make out the stars (of the natal chart) to be causes of a condition which existed in the father and mother previously to that star pattern on which the prediction is based?

And consider still further:

They are really announcing the fortunes of parents from the horoscope of children; the character and career of children are included in the predictions as to the parents—they predict for the yet unborn!; in the lot of one brother they are foretelling the death of another; a girl's fate includes that of a future husband, a boy's that of a wife.

Now, can we think that the star-grouping over any particular birth can be the cause of what stands already announced in the facts about the parents? Either the previous star-groupings were the determinants of the child's future career or, if they were not, then neither is the immediate grouping. And notice further that physical I likeness to the parents implies that ugliness and beauty are of purely domestic origin and not caused[1] by astral movements. I

Again, there must at one and the same time be a widespread coming to birth—men, and the most varied forms of animal life at the same moment— and these should all be under the one destiny since the one pattern rules at the moment; how explain that identical star-groupings give here the human form, there the animal?

6. But in fact everything follows its own Kind; the birth is a horse because it comes from the Horse Kind, a man by springing from the Human Kind; offspring answers to species. Allow the cosmic circuit its part, a very powerful influence upon the thing brought into being: allow the stars a wide material action upon the bodily part of the man, producing heat and cold and their natural resultants in the physical constitution; still does such action explain character, vocation, and especially all that seems quite independent of material elements, a man taking to letters, to geometry, to gambling, and becoming an originator in any of these pursuits? And can we imagine the stars, divine beings, bestowing wickedness? And what of a doctrine that makes them wreak vengeance, as for a wrong, because they are in their decline or are being carried to a position beneath the earth—as if a decline from our point of view brought any change to themselves, as if they ever ceased to traverse the heavenly spheres and to make the same figure around the earth.

Nor may we think that these divine beings lose or gain in goodness as they see this one or another of the company in various aspects, and that in their happier position they are benignant to us and, less pleasantly situated, turn maleficent. We can but believe that their circuit is for the protection of the entirety of things while they furnish the incidental service of being letters on which the augur, acquainted with that alphabet, may look and read the future from their pattern—arriving at the thing signified by such analogies as that a soaring bird tells of some lofty event.

7. It remains to notice the theory of the one Causing-Principle alleged to interweave everything with everything else, to make things into a chain, to determine the nature and condition of each phenomenon—a Principle which, acting through seminal (operatively productive) Reason-Forms—*logoi spermatikoi*— elaborates all that exists and happens.

The doctrine is close to that which makes the Soul of the Universe the source and cause of all condition and of all movement whether without or—supposing that we are allowed as individuals some little power towards personal act—within ourselves.

But it is the theory of the most rigid and universal Necessity: all the causative forces enter into the system, and so every several phenomenon rises necessarily; where nothing escapes Destiny, nothing has power to check or to change. Such forces beating upon us, as it were, from one general cause leave us no resource but to go where they drive. All our ideas will be determined by a chain of previous causes; our doings will be determined by those ideas; personal action becomes a mere word. That we are the agents does not save our freedom when our action is prescribed by those causes; we have precisely what belongs to everything that lives, to infants guided by blind impulses, to lunatics; all these act; why, even fire acts; there is act in everything that follows the plan of its being, servilely.

No one that sees the implications of this theory can hesitate: unable to halt at such a determinant principle, we seek for other explanations of our action.

8. What can this other cause be; one standing above those treated of; one that leaves nothing causeless, that preserves sequence and order in the Universe and yet allows ourselves some reality and leaves room for prediction and augury?

I Soul we must bring into the world of things as a separate principle (a separate source of motion), not merely the Soul of the Universe but, accompanying it,[2] the Soul of the individual: I this, no mean Principle, is needed to be the bond of union in the total of things, not, itself, a thing sprung like things from life-seeds, but a first-hand Cause, bodiless and therefore supreme over itself, free, beyond the reach of cosmic Cause: though, brought into body, it will not be unrestrictedly sovereign; it will hold rank in a series.

Now the environment into which this independent principle enters, when it comes to this midpoint, will be largely led by secondary causes (or, by chance-causes): there will therefore be a compromise; the action of the Soul will be in part guided by this environment while in other matters it will be sovereign, leading the way where it will. The nobler Soul will have the greater power; the poorer Soul, the lesser. A soul which defers to the bodily temperament cannot escape desire and rage and is abject in poverty, overbearing in wealth, arbitrary in power. The soul of nobler nature holds good against its surroundings; it is more apt to change them than to be changed, so that often it improves the environment and, where it must make concession, at least keeps its innocence.

9. We admit, then, a Necessity in all that is brought about by this compromise between will and accidental circumstance: what room was there for anything else than the thing that is? Given all the causes, all must happen beyond aye or

nay—that is, all the external and whatever may be due to the sidereal circuit— therefore when the Soul has been modified by outer forces and acts under that pressure so that what it does is no more than an unreflecting acceptance of stimulus, neither the act nor the state can be described as voluntary: so, too, when even from within itself, it falls at times below its best and ignores the true, the highest, laws of action.

But when our Soul holds to its Reason-Principle, to the guide, pure and detached and native to itself, only then can we speak of personal operation, of voluntary act. Things so done may truly be described as our doing, for they have no other source; they are the issue of the unmingled Soul, a Principle that is a First, a leader, a sovereign not subject to the errors of ignorance, not to be over- thrown by the tyranny of the desires which, where they can break in, drive and drag, so as to allow of no act of ours, but mere answer to stimulus.

10. To sum the results of our argument: All things and events are foreshown and brought into being by causes; but the causation is of two kinds; there are results originating from the Soul and results due to other causes, those of the environment.

In the action of our souls all that is done of their own motion in the light of sound reason is the Soul's work, while what is done where they are hindered from their own action is not so much done as suffered. Unwisdom, then, is not due to the Soul, and, in general—if we mean by Fate a compulsion outside ourselves—an act is fated when it is contrary to wisdom.

But all our best is of our own doing: such is our nature as long as we remain detached. The wise and good do perform acts; their right action is the expres- sion of their own power: in the others it comes in the breathing spaces when the passions are in abeyance; but it is not that they draw this occasional wisdom from outside themselves; simply, they are for the time being unhindered.

NOTES TO ENNEAD III.1

1. FIRST EDITION: ". . . likeness to the parents—*the Astrologers hold*—*is* of purely domestic origin: *this* implies that ugliness and beauty are *so caused* and not by astral movements." Neither ARMSTRONG nor GUTHRIE references this position as the astrologers' own.

2. FIRST EDITION: "Soul: we must *place at the crest of* the world of *beings, this other Principle,* not merely the Soul of the Universe but, *included in it,* the Soul of the individual:" ARMSTRONG: "Soul, surely, is another principle which we must bring into reality—not only the Soul of the All but also the individual soul along with it as a principle of no small importance;" GUTHRIE: "We shall have to introduce among the number of beings another principle, namely: the soul; and not only the World-soul, but even the individual soul of every person. In the universal concatenation of causes and effects, this soul is a principle of no little importance, because, instead of, like all other things, being born of a 'seminal reason,' it constitutes a 'primary cause.' "

SECOND TRACTATE

Providence: First Treatise

1. To make the existence and coherent structure of this Universe depend upon automatic activity and upon chance is against all good sense.

Such a notion could be entertained only where there is neither intelligence nor even ordinary perception; and reason enough has been urged against it, though none is really necessary.

But there is still the question as to the process by which the individual things of this sphere have come into being, how they were made.

Some of them seem so undesirable as to cast doubts upon a Universal Providence; and we find, on the one hand, the denial of any controlling power, on the other the belief that the Cosmos is the work of an evil creator.

This matter must be examined through and through from the very first principles. We may, however, omit for the present any consideration of the particular providence, that beforehand decision which accomplishes or holds things in abeyance to some good purpose and gives or withholds in our own regard: when we have established the Universal Providence which we affirm, we can link the secondary with it.

Of course the belief that after a certain lapse of time a Cosmos previously non-existent came into being would imply a foreseeing and a reasoned plan on the part of God providing for the production of the Universe and securing all possible perfection in it—a guidance and partial providence, therefore, such as is indicated. But since we hold the eternal existence of the Universe, the utter absence of a beginning to it, we are forced, in sound and sequent reasoning, to explain the providence ruling in the Universe as a universal consonance with the divine Intelligence to which the Cosmos is subsequent not in time but in the fact of derivation, in the fact that the Divine Intelligence, preceding it in kind, is its cause as being the Archetype and Model which it merely images, the primal by which, from all eternity, it has its existence and subsistence.

The relationship may be presented thus:

The authentic and primal Cosmos is the Being of the Intellectual Principle and of the Veritable Existent. This contains within itself no spatial distinction, and has none of the feebleness of division, and even its parts bring no incompleteness to it since here the individual is not severed from the entire. In this nature inheres all life and all intellect, a life living and having intellection as one act within a unity: every part that it gives forth is a whole; all its content is its very own, for there is here no separation of thing from thing, no part standing in isolated existence estranged from the rest, and therefore nowhere is there any wronging of any other, even among contraries. Everywhere one and complete, it is at rest throughout and invites difference at no point; it does not make over any of its content into any new form; there can be no reason for changing what is everywhere perfect.

Why should Reason elaborate yet another Reason, or Intelligence another Intelligence? An indwelling power of making things is in the character of a being not at all points as it should be but making, moving, by reason of some failure in quality. Those whose nature is all blessedness have no more to do than to repose in themselves and be their being.

A widespread activity is dangerous to those who must go out from themselves to act. But such is the blessedness of this Being that in its very non-action it magnificently operates and in its self-dwelling it produces mightily.

2. By derivation from that I Authentic Cosmos, one within itself, there subsists this lower Cosmos,[1] I no longer a true unity.

It is multiple, divided into various elements, thing standing apart from thing in a new estrangement. No longer is there concord unbroken; hostility, too, has entered as the result of difference and distance; imperfection has inevitably introduced discord; for a part is not self-sufficient, it must pursue something outside itself for its fulfillment, and so it becomes the enemy to what it needs.

This Cosmos of parts has come into being not as the result of a judgement establishing its desirability, but by the sheer necessity of a secondary Kind.

The Intellectual Realm was not of a nature to be the ultimate of existents. I It was the first[2] and I it held great power, all there is of power; this means that it is productive without seeking to produce; for if effort and search were incumbent upon it, the Act would not be its own, would not spring from its essential nature; it would be, like a craftsman, producing by a power not inherent but acquired, mastered by dint of study.

The Intellectual Principle, then, in its unperturbed serenity has brought the universe into being, by communicating from its own store to Matter: and this gift is the Reason-Form flowing from it. For the Emanation of the Intellectual Principle is Reason, an emanation unfailing as long as the Intellectual Principle continues to have place among beings.

The Reason-Principle within a seed contains all the parts and qualities concentrated in identity; there is no distinction, no jarring, no internal hindering; then there comes a pushing out into bulk, part rises in distinction with part, and at once the members of the organism stand in each other's way and begin to wear each other down.

So from this, the one Intellectual Principle, and the Reason-Form emanating from it, our Universe rises and develops part, and inevitably are formed groups concordant and helpful in contrast with groups discordant and combative;

sometimes of choice and sometimes incidentally, the parts maltreat each other; engendering proceeds by destruction.

Yet: from all that they effect and accept, the one harmonious act ensues; each utters its own voice, but all is brought into accord, into an ordered system, for the universal purpose, by the ruling Reason-Principle. This Universe is not Intelligence and Reason, like the Supernal, but participant in Intelligence and Reason: it stands in need of the harmonizing because it is the meeting ground of Necessity and divine Reason—Necessity pulling towards the lower, towards the unreason which is its own characteristic, while yet the Intellectual Principle remains sovereign over it.

The Intellectual Sphere (the Divine) alone is Reason, and there can never be another Sphere that is Reason and nothing else; so that, given some other system, it cannot be as noble as that first; it cannot be Reason: yet since such a system cannot be merely Matter, which is the utterly unordered, it must be a mixed thing. Its two extremes are Matter and the Divine Reason; its governing principle is Soul, presiding over the conjunction of the two, and to be thought of not as labouring in the task but as administering serenely by little more than an act of presence.

3. Nor would it be sound to condemn this Cosmos as less than beautiful, as less than the noblest possible in the corporeal; and neither can any charge be laid against its source.

The world, we must reflect, is a product of Necessity, not of deliberate purpose: it is due to a higher Kind engendering in its own likeness by a natural process. And none the less, a second consideration, if a considered plan brought it into being it would still be no disgrace to its maker—for it stands a stately whole, complete within itself, serving at once its own purpose and that of all its parts which, leading and lesser alike, are of such a nature as to further the interests of the total. It is, therefore, impossible to condemn the whole on the merits of the parts which, besides, must be judged only as they enter harmoniously or not into the whole, the main consideration, quite overpassing the members which thus cease to have importance. To linger about the parts is to condemn not the Cosmos but some isolated appendage of it; in the entire living Being we fasten our eyes on a hair or a toe neglecting the marvellous spectacle of the complete Man; we ignore all the tribes and kinds of animals except for the meanest; we pass over an entire race, humanity, and bring forward—Thersites.

No: this thing that has come into being is (not a mass of fragments, but) the Cosmos complete: do but survey it, and surely this is the pleading you will hear:

I am made by a God: from that God I came endowed with every form[3] of life, I adequate to my function, self-sufficing, lacking nothing: for I am the container of all, that is, of every plant and every animal, of all the Kinds of created things, and many Gods and nations of Spirit-Beings and lofty souls and men happy in their goodness.

And do not think that, while earth is ornate with all its growths and with living things of every race, and while the very sea has answered to the power of Soul, do not think that the great air and the ether and the far-spread heavens remain void of it: there it is that all good Souls dwell, infusing life into the stars and into that orderly eternal circuit of the heavens which in its conscious movement ever about the one centre, seeking nothing beyond, is a faithful copy of the divine Mind. And all that is within me strives towards the Good; and each, to the measure of its faculty, attains. For from that Good all the heavens depend, with all my own Soul and the Gods that dwell in my every part, and all that lives and grows, and even all in me that you may judge inanimate.

There are, it would seem, degrees of participation: here no more than Existence, elsewhere Life; and, in Life, sometimes mainly that of Sensation, higher again that of Reason, finally Life in all its fullness. We have no right to demand equal powers in the unequal: the finger is not to be asked to see; there is the eye for that; a finger has its own business—to be finger and have finger power.

4. That water extinguishes fire and fire consumes other things should not astonish us. The thing destroyed derived its being from outside itself: this is no case of a self-originating substance being annihilated by an external; it rose on the ruin of something else, and thus in its own ruin it suffers nothing strange; and for every fire quenched, another is kindled.

In the immaterial heaven every member is unchangeably itself for ever; in the heavens of our universe, while the whole has life eternally and so too all the nobler and lordlier components, the souls pass from body to body entering into varied forms—and, when it may, a soul will rise outside of the realm of birth I and dwell with the All-Soul. The life of bodies is specific (rather than individual): each species (i.e., each of the four elements) lives as a whole and thus can give life and sustenance to the living beings within it:[4] for life here I is a thing of change; only in that prior realm is it unmoving. From that unchangingness change had to emerge and from that self-cloistered Life its derivative, this which breathes and stirs, the respiration of the still life of the divine.

The conflict and destruction that reign among living beings are inevitable, since things here are derived, brought into existence because the Divine Reason which contains all of them in the upper Heavens—how could they come here unless they were There?—must outflow over the whole extent of Matter.

Similarly, the very wronging of man by man may be derived from an effort towards the Good; foiled, in their weakness, of their true desire, they turn against each other: still, when they do wrong, they pay the penalty—that of having hurt their souls by their evil conduct and of degradation to a lower place—for nothing can ever escape what stands decreed in the law of the Universe.

This is not to accept the idea, sometimes urged, that order is an outcome of disorder and law of lawlessness, as if evil were a necessary preliminary to their existence or their manifestation: on the contrary order is the original and enters this sphere as imposed from without: it is because order, law, and reason exist that there can be disorder; breach of law and unreason exist because Reason exists—not that these better things are directly the causes of the bad but simply that what ought to absorb the Best is prevented by its own nature, or by some accident, or by foreign interference. An entity which must look outside itself for a law may be foiled of its purpose by either an internal or an external cause; there will be some flaw in its own nature, or it will be hurt by some alien influence, for often harm follows, unintended, upon the action of others in the pursuit of quite unrelated aims. Such living beings, on the other hand, as have freedom of motion under their own will sometimes take the right turn, sometimes the wrong.

Why the wrong course is followed is scarcely worth inquiring: a slight deviation at the beginning develops with every advance into a continuously wider and graver error—especially since there is the attached body with its inevitable concomitant of desire—and the first step, the hasty movement not previously considered and not immediately corrected, ends by establishing a set habit where there was at first only a fall.

Punishment naturally follows: there is no injustice in a man suffering what belongs to the condition in which he is; nor can we ask to be happy when our actions have not earned us happiness; the good, only, are happy; divine beings are happy only because they are good.

5. Now, once Happiness is possible at all to souls in this Universe, if some fail of it, the blame must fall not upon the place but upon the feebleness insufficient to the staunch combat in the one arena where the rewards of excellence are offered. Men are not born divine; what wonder that they do not enjoy a divine life. And poverty and sickness mean nothing to the good, while to the evil they bring benefit: where there is body there must be ill health.

Besides, these accidents are not without their service in the co-ordination and completion of the Universal system.

One thing perishes, and the Cosmic Reason—whose control nothing anywhere eludes—employs that ending to the beginning of something new; and, so, when the body suffers and the Soul, under the affliction, loses power, all that has been bound under illness and evil is brought into a new set of relations, into another class or order. Some of these troubles are helpful to the very sufferers—poverty and sickness, for example—and as for vice, even this brings something to the general service: it acts as a lesson in right-doing, and, in many ways even, produces good; thus, by setting men face to face with the ways and consequences of iniquity, it calls them from lethargy, stirs the deeper mind, and sets the understanding to work; by the contrast of the evil under which wrong-doers labour it displays the worth of the right. Not that evil exists for this purpose; but, as we have indicated, once the wrong has come to be, the Reason of the Cosmos employs it to good ends; and, precisely, the proof of the mightiest power is to be able to use the ignoble nobly and, given formlessness, to make it the material of unknown forms.

The principle is that evil by definition is a falling short in good, and good cannot be at full strength in this Sphere where it is lodged in the alien: the good here is in something else, in something distinct from the Good, and this something else constitutes the falling short, for it is not good. And this is why 'evil is ineradicable': there is, first, the fact that in relation to this principle of Good, thing will always stand less than thing, and, besides, all things come into being through it, and are what they are by standing away from it.

6. As for the disregard of desert—the good afflicted, the unworthy thriving—it is a sound explanation no doubt that to the good nothing is evil and to the evil nothing can be good: still the question remains, why should what essentially offends our nature fall to the good while the wicked enjoy all it demands? How can such an allotment be approved?

No doubt since pleasant conditions add nothing to true happiness and the unpleasant do not lessen the evil in the wicked, the conditions matter little: as well complain that a good man happens to be ugly and a bad man handsome.

Still, under such a dispensation, there would surely be a propriety, a reasonableness, a regard to merit which, as things are, do not appear, though this would certainly be in keeping with the noblest Providence: even though external conditions do not affect a man's hold upon good or evil, none the less it would seem utterly unfitting that the bad should be the masters, be sovereign in the state, while honourable men are slaves: a wicked ruler may commit the most lawless acts; and in war the worst men have a free hand and perpetrate every kind of crime against their prisoners.

We are forced to ask how such things can be, under a Providence. Certainly a maker must consider his work as a whole, but none the less he should see to the due ordering of all the parts, especially when these parts have Soul, that is, are Living and Reasoning Beings: the Providence must reach to all the details; its functioning must consist in neglecting no point.

Holding, therefore, as we do, despite all, that the Universe lies under an Intellectual Principle whose power has touched every existent, we cannot be absolved from the attempt to show in what way the detail of this sphere is just.

7. A preliminary observation: in looking for excellence in this thing of mixture, the Cosmos, we cannot require all that is implied in the excellence of the un-mingled; it is folly to ask for Firsts in the Secondary, and since this Universe contains body, we must allow for some bodily influence upon the total and be thankful if the mingled existent lack nothing of what its nature allowed it to receive from the Divine Reason.

Thus, supposing we were inquiring for the finest type of the human being as known here, we would certainly not demand that he prove identical with Man as in the Divine Intellect; we would think it enough in the Creator to have so brought this thing of flesh and nerve and bone under Reason as to give grace to these corporeal elements and to have made it possible for Reason to bloom on the surface of Matter.

Our progress towards the object of our investigation must begin from this principle of gradation which will open to us the wonder of the Providence and of the power by which our universe holds its being.

We begin with evil acts entirely dependent upon the souls which perpetrate them—the harm, for example, which perverted souls do to the good and to each other. Unless the fore-planning power alone is to be charged with the vice in such souls, we have no ground of accusation, no claim to redress: 'the blame lies on the Soul exercising its choice'. Even a soul, we have seen, must have its individual movement; it is not pure Soul; the first step towards animal life has been taken and the conduct will naturally be in keeping with that character.

It is not because the world existed that souls are here: before the world was, they had it in them to be of the world, to concern themselves with it, to pre-suppose it, to administer it: it was in their nature to produce it—by what ever method, whether by giving forth some emanation while they themselves re-mained above, or by an actual descent, or in both ways together, some presiding from above, others descending; for we are not at the moment concerned about the mode of creation but are simply urging that, however the world was pro-duced, no blame falls on Providence for what exists within it.

There remains the other phase of the question—the distribution of evil to the opposite classes of men: the good go bare while the wicked are rich: all that human need demands, the least deserving have in abundance; it is they that rule; peoples and states are at their disposal. Would not all this imply that the divine power does not reach to earth?

That it does is sufficiently established by the fact that Reason rules in the lower things: animals and plants have their share in Reason, Soul, and Life.

Perhaps, then, it reaches to earth but is not master over all?

We answer that the universe is one living organism: as well maintain that while human head and face are the work of nature and of the ruling reason-principle, the rest of the frame is due to other agencies—accident or sheer necessity—and owes its inferiority to this origin, or to the incompetence of unaided Nature. And even granting that those less noble members are not in themselves admirable it would still be neither pious nor even reverent to censure the entire structure.

8. Thus we come to our inquiry as to the degree of excellence found in such members, and how far they belong to an ordered system or in what degree they are, at least, not evil.

Now in every living being the upper parts—head, face—are the most beautiful, the mid and lower members inferior. In the Universe the middle and lower members are human beings; above them, the Heavens and the Gods that dwell there; these Gods with the entire circling expanse of the heavens constitute the greater part of the Cosmos: I the earth is but a point, and corresponds to one only[5] among the stars. I Yet human wrongdoing is made a matter of wonder; we are evidently asked to take humanity as the choice member of the Universe, nothing wiser existent!

But humanity, in reality, is poised midway between gods and beasts, and inclines now to the one order, now to the other; some men grow like to the divine, others to the brute, the greater number stand neutral. But those that are corrupted to the point of approximating to irrational animals and wild beasts pull the mid-folk about and inflict wrong upon them; the victims are no doubt better than the wrongdoers, but are at the mercy of their inferiors in the field in which they themselves are inferior, where, that is, they cannot be classed among the good since they have not trained themselves in self-defence.

A gang of lads, morally neglected, and in that respect inferior to the intermediate class, but in good physical training, attack and throw another set, trained neither physically nor morally, and make off with their food and their dainty clothes. What more is called for than a laugh?

And surely even the lawgiver would be right in allowing the second group to suffer this treatment, the penalty of their sloth and self-indulgence: the gymnasium lies there before them, and they, in laziness and luxury and listlessness, have allowed themselves to fall like fat-loaded sheep, a prey to the wolves.

But the evildoers also have their punishment: first they pay in that very wolfishness, in the disaster to their human quality: and next there is laid up for them the due of their kind; living ill here, they will not get off by death; on every precedent through all the line there waits its sequent, reasonable and natural—worse to the bad, better to the good.

This at once brings us outside the gymnasium with its fun for boys; they must grow up, both kinds, amid their childishness and both one day stand girt and armed. Then there is a finer spectacle than is ever seen by those that train in the ring. But at this stage some have not armed themselves—and the duly armed win the day.

Not even a God would have the right to deal a blow for the unwarlike: the law decrees that to come safe out of battle is for fighting men, not for those that pray. The harvest comes home not for praying but for tilling; healthy days are not for those that neglect their health: we have no right to complain of the ignoble getting the richer harvest if they are the only workers in the fields, or the best.

Again: it is childish, while we carry on all the affairs of our life to our own taste and not as the Gods would have us, to expect them to keep all well for us in spite of a life that is lived without regard to the conditions which the Gods have prescribed for our well-being. Yet death would be better for us than to go on living lives condemned by the laws of the Universe. If things took the contrary course, if all the modes of folly and wickedness brought no trouble in life— then indeed we might complain of the indifference of a Providence leaving the victory to evil.

Bad men rule by the feebleness of the ruled: and this is just; the triumph of weaklings would not be just.

9. It would not be just, because Providence cannot be a something reducing us to nothingness: to think of Providence as everything, with no other thing in existence, is to annihilate Providence itself, since it could have no field of action; nothing would exist except the Divine. As things are, the Divine, of course, exists, but has reached forth to something other—not to reduce that to nothingness but to preside over it; thus in the case of Man, for instance, the Divine presides as the Providence, preserving the character of human nature, that is the character of a being under the providential law, which, again, implies subjection to what that law may enjoin.

And that law enjoins that those who have made themselves good shall know the best of life, here and later, the bad the reverse. But the law does not warrant the wicked in expecting that their prayers should bring others to sacrifice themselves for their sakes; or that the gods should lay aside the divine life in order to direct their daily concerns; or that good men, who have chosen a path nobler than all earthly rule, should become their rulers. I The perverse have never given a single thought to how they might be good rulers of others; intent upon their own well-being,[6] they I are all spite against anyone that becomes good of his own motion, though if good men were placed in authority the total of goodness would be increased.

In sum: Man has come into existence, a living being but not a member of the noblest order; he occupies by choice an intermediate rank; still, in that place in which he exists, Providence does not allow him to be reduced to nothing; on the contrary he is ever being led upwards by all those varied devices which the Divine employs in its labour to increase the dominance of moral value. The human race, therefore, is not deprived by Providence of its rational being; it retains its share, though necessarily limited, in wisdom, intelligence, executive power, and right-doing, the right-doing, at least, of individuals to each other—and even in wronging others people think they are doing right and only paying what is due.

Man is, therefore, a noble creation, as perfect as the scheme allows; a part, no doubt, in the fabric of the All, he yet holds a lot higher than that of all the other living things of earth.

Now, no one of any intelligence complains of these others, man's inferiors, which serve to the adornment of the world; it would be feeble indeed to complain of animals biting man, as if we were to pass our days asleep. No: the animal, too, exists of necessity, and is serviceable in many ways, some obvious and many progressively discovered—so that not one lives without profit even to humanity. It is ridiculous, also, to complain that many of them are dangerous—there are dangerous men abroad as well—and if they distrust us, and in their distrust attack, is that anything to wonder at?

10. But: if the evil in men is involuntary, if their own will has not made them what they are, how can we either blame wrongdoers or even reproach their victims with suffering through their own fault?

If there is a Necessity, bringing about human wickedness either by force of the celestial movement or by a rigorous sequence set up by the First Cause, is not the evil a thing rooted in Nature? And if thus the Reason-Principle of the universe is the creator of evil, surely all is injustice?

No: men are no doubt involuntary sinners in the sense that they do not actually desire to sin; but this does not alter the fact that wrongdoers, of their own choice, are, themselves, the agents; it is because they themselves act that the sin is their own; if they were not agents they could not sin.

The Necessity (held to underlie human wickedness) is not an outer force (actually compelling the individual), but exists only in the sense of a universal relationship.

Nor is the force of the celestial Movement such as to leave us powerless: if the universe were something outside and apart from us it would stand as its makers willed so that, once the gods had done their part, no man, however impious, could introduce anything contrary to their intention. But, as things are, efficient act does come from men: given the starting Principle, the secondary line, no doubt, is inevitably completed; but each and every principle contributes towards the sequence. Now Men are Principles, or, at least, they are moved by their characteristic nature towards all that is good, and that nature is a Principle, a freely acting cause.

11. Are we, then, to conclude that particular things are determined by necessities rooted in Nature and by the sequence of causes, and that everything is as good as anything can be?

No: the Reason-Principle is the sovereign, making all: it wills things as they are and, in its reasonable act, it produces even what we know as evil: it cannot desire all to be good: an artist would not make an animal all eyes; and in the same way, the Reason-Principle would not make all divine; it makes Gods but also celestial spirits, the intermediate order, then men, then the animals; all is graded succession, and this in no spirit of grudging but in the expression of a Reason teeming with intellectual variety.

We are like people ignorant of painting who complain that the colours are not beautiful everywhere in the picture: but the Artist has laid on the appropriate tint to every spot. Note also that cities, however well governed, are not composed of citizens who are all equal. Again, we are censuring a drama because the persons are not all heroes but include a servant and a rustic and some scurrilous clown; yet take away the low characters and the power of the drama is gone; these are part and parcel of it.

12. Suppose this Universe to be the direct creation of the Reason-Principle applying itself, quite unchanged, to Matter, retaining, that is, the differentiation of parts which it derives from its Prior, the Intellectual Principle—then, this its product, so produced, must be of supreme and unparalleled excellence. The Reason-Principle cannot be a thing of entire identity or even of closely compact diversity; and the mode in which it is here manifested is no matter of censure since its function is to be all things, each single thing in some distinctive way.

But (it will be asked) has it not, besides itself entering Matter, brought other beings down? Has it not for example brought souls into Matter and, in adapting them to its creation, twisted them against their own nature and been the ruin of many of them? And can this be right?

The answer is that the souls are, in a fair sense, members of this Reason-Principle and that it has not adapted them to the creation by perverting them, but has set them in the place here to which their quality entitles them.

13. And we must not despise the familiar observation that there is something more to be considered than the present. There are the periods of the past and, again, those in the future; and these have everything to do with fixing worth of place.

Thus a man, once a ruler, will be made a slave because he abused his power and because the fall is to his future good. Those that have misused money will be made poor—and to the good poverty is no hindrance. Those that have unjustly killed, are killed in turn, unjustly as regards the murderer but justly as regards the victim, and those that are to suffer are thrown into the path of those that administer the merited treatment.

It is not an accident that makes a man a slave; no one is a prisoner by chance; every bodily outrage has its due cause. The man once did what he now suffers. A man that murders his mother will become a woman and be murdered by a son; a man that wrongs a woman will become a woman, to be wronged.

Hence arises that awesome word Adrasteia (the Inevadable Retribution); for in very truth this ordinance is an Adrasteia, Justice itself and a wonderful wisdom.

We cannot but recognize from what we observe in this universe that some such principle of order prevails throughout the entire of existence—the minutest of things a tributary to the vast total; the marvellous art shown not merely in the mightiest works and sublimest members of the All, but even amid such littleness as one would think Providence must disdain: the varied workmanship of wonder in any and every animal form; the world of vegetation, too; the grace of fruits and even of leaves, the lavishness, the delicacy, the diversity of exquisite bloom: and all this not issuing once, and then to die out, but made ever and ever anew as the Transcendent Beings move variously over this earth.

In all the changing, there is no change by chance: there is no taking of new forms but to desirable ends and in ways worthy of Divine Powers. All that is Divine executes the Act of its quality; its quality is the expression of its essential Being: and this essential Being in the Divine is the Being whose activities produce as one thing the desirable and the just—for if the good and the just are not produced there, where, then, have they their being?

14. The ordinance of the Cosmos, then, is in keeping with the Intellectual

Principle. True, no reasoning went to its creation, but it so stands that the keenest reasoning must wonder—since no reasoning could be able to make it otherwise—at the spectacle before it, a product which, even in the Kinds of the partial and particular Sphere, displays the Divine Intelligence to a degree in which no arranging by reason could express it. Every one of the ceaselessly recurrent types of being manifests a creating Reason-Principle above all censure. No fault is to be found unless on the assumption that everything ought to come into being with all the perfection of those that have never known such a coming, the Eternals. In that case, things of the Intellectual realm and things of the realm of sense must remain one unbroken identity for ever.

In this demand for more good than exists, there is implied a failure to recognize that the form allotted to each entity is sufficient in itself; it is like complaining because one kind of animal lacks horns. We ought to understand both that the Reason-Principle must extend to every possible existent and, at the same time, that every greater must include lesser things, that to every whole belong its parts, and that all cannot be equality unless all part is to be absent.

This is why in the Over-World each entity is all, while here, below, the single thing is not all (is not the Universe but a 'Self'). Thus too, a man, an individual, in so far as he is a part, is not Humanity complete: but wheresoever there is associated with the parts something that is no part (but a Divine, an Intellectual, Being), this makes a whole of that in which it dwells. Man, man as partial thing, cannot be required to have attained to the very summit of goodness: if he had, he would have ceased to be of the partial order. Not that there is any grudging in the whole towards the part that grows in goodness and dignity; such an increase in value is a gain to the beauty of the whole; the lesser grows by being made over in the likeness of the greater, by being admitted, as it were, to something of that greatness, by sharing in that rank, and thus even from this place of man, from man's own self, something gleams forth, as the stars shine in the divine firmament, so that all appears one great and lovely figure—living or wrought in the furnaces of craftsmanship—with stars radiant not only in the ears and on the brow but on the breasts too, and wherever else they may be displayed in beauty.

15. These considerations apply very well to things considered as standing alone: but there is a stumbling-block, a new problem, when we think of all these forms, permanent and ceaselessly produced, in mutual relationship.

The animals devour each other: men attack each other: all is war without rest, without truce: this gives new force to the question how Reason can be author of the plan and how all can be declared well done.

This new difficulty is not met by the former answer: that all stands as well as the nature of things allows; that the blame for their inferior condition falls on Matter dragging them down; that, given the plan as we know it, evil cannot be eliminated and should not be; that the Matter making its presence felt is still not supreme but remains an element taken in from outside to contribute to a definite total, or rather to be itself brought to order by Reason.

The Divine Reason is the beginning and the end; all that comes into being must be rational and fall at its coming into an ordered scheme reasonable at every point. Where, then, is the necessity of this bandit war of man and beast?

This devouring of Kind by Kind is necessary as the means to the transmutation of living things which could not keep form for ever even though no other killed them: what grievance is it that when they must go their dispatch is so planned as to be serviceable to others?

Still more, what does it matter when they are devoured only to return in some new form? It comes to no more than the murder of one of the personages in a play; the actor alters his make-up and enters in a new role. The actor, of course, was not really killed; but if dying is but changing a body as the actor changes a costume, or even an exit from the body like the exit of the actor from the boards when he has no more to say or do—though he will still return to act on another occasion—what is there so very dreadful in this transformation of living beings one into another?

Surely it is much better so than if they had never existed: that way would mean the bleak quenching of life, precluded from passing outside itself; as the plan holds, life is poured copiously throughout a Universe, engendering the universal things and weaving variety into their being, never at rest from producing an endless sequence of comeliness and shapeliness, a living pastime.

Men directing their weapons against each other—under doom of death yet neatly lined up to fight as in the pyrrhic sword-dances of their sport—this is enough to tell us that all human intentions are but play, that death is nothing terrible, that to die in a war or in a fight is but to taste a little beforehand what old age has in store, to go away earlier and come back the sooner. So for misfortunes that may accompany life, the loss of property, for instance; the loser will see that there was a time when it was not his, that its possession is but a mock boon to the robbers, who will in their turn lose it to others, and even, that to retain property is a greater loss than to forfeit it.

Murders, death in all its guises, the reduction and sacking of cities, all must be to us just such a spectacle as the changing scenes of a play; all is but the varied incident of a plot, costume on and off, acted grief and lament. For on earth, in all the succession of life, it is not the Soul within but the Shadow outside of the authentic man, that grieves and complains and acts out the plot on this world stage which men have dotted with stages of their own constructing. All this is the doing of man knowing no more than to live the lower and outer life, and never perceiving that, in his weeping and in his graver doings alike, he is but at play; to handle austere matters austerely is reserved for the thoughtful: the other kind of man is himself a futility. Those incapable of thinking gravely read gravity into frivolities which correspond to their own frivolous nature. Anyone that joins in their trifling and so comes to look on life with their eyes must understand that by lending himself to such idleness he has laid aside his own character. If Socrates himself takes part in the trifling, he trifles in the outer Socrates.

We must remember, too, that we cannot take tears and laments as proof that anything is wrong; children cry and whimper where there is nothing amiss.

16. But if all this is true, what room is left for evil? Where are we to place wrongdoing and sin?

How explain that in a world organized in good, the efficient agents (human beings) behave unjustly, commit sin? And how comes misery if neither sin nor injustice exists?

Again, if all our action is determined by a natural process, how can the distinction be maintained between behaviour in accordance with nature and behaviour in conflict with it?

And what becomes of blasphemy against the divine? The blasphemer is made what he is: a dramatist has written a part insulting and maligning himself and given it to an actor to play.

These considerations oblige us to state the Logos (the Reason-Principle of the Universe) once again, and more clearly, and to justify its nature.

This Reason-Principle, then—let us dare the definition in the hope of conveying the truth—this Logos is not the Intellectual Principle unmingled, not the Absolute Divine Intellect; nor does it descend from the pure Soul alone; it is a dependent of that Soul while, in a sense, it is a radiation from both those divine Hypostases: the Intellectual Principle and the Soul—the Soul as conditioned by the Intellectual Principle—engender this Logos which is a Life holding restfully a certain measure of Reason.

Now all life, even the least valuable, is an activity, and not a blind activity like that of flame; even where there is not sensation the activity of life is no mere haphazard play of Movement: any object in which life is present, any object which participates in Life, is at once enreasoned in the sense that the activity peculiar to life is formative, shaping as it moves.

Life, then, aims at pattern as does the pantomimic dancer with his set movements; the mime, in himself, represents life, and, besides, his movements proceed in obedience to a pattern designed to symbolize life.

Thus far to give us some idea of the nature of Life in general.

But this Reason-Principle which emanates from the complete unity, divine Mind, and the complete unity Life (= Soul)—is neither a uniate complete Life nor a uniate complete divine Mind, nor does it give itself whole and all-including to its subject. (By an imperfect communication) it sets up a conflict of part against part: it produces imperfect things and so engenders and maintains war and attack, and thus its unity can be that only of a sum-total, not of a thing undivided. At war with itself in the parts which it now exhibits, it has the unity, or harmony, of a drama torn with struggle. The drama, of course, brings the conflicting elements to one final harmony, weaving the entire story of the clashing characters into one thing; while in the Logos the conflict of the divergent elements rises within the one element, the Reason-Principle: the comparison therefore is rather with a harmony emerging directly from the conflicting elements themselves, and the question becomes what introduces clashing elements among these Reason-Principles.

Now in the case of music, tones high and low are the product of Reason-Principles which, by the fact that they are Principles of harmony, meet in the unit of Harmony, the absolute Harmony, a more comprehensive Principle, greater than they and including them as its parts. Similarly in the Universe at large we find contraries—white and black, hot and cold, winged and wingless, footed and footless, reasoning and unreasoning—but all these elements are members of one living body, their sum-total; the Universe is a self-accordant entity, its members everywhere clashing but the total being the manifestation of a Reason-Principle. That one Reason-Principle, then, must be the unification of conflicting Reason-Principles whose very opposition is the support of its coherence and, almost, of its Being.

And indeed, if it were not multiple, it could not be a Universal Principle, it could not even be at all a Reason-Principle; in the fact of its being a Reason-Principle is contained the fact of interior difference. Now the maximum of difference is contrariety; I admitting then that the Reason-Principle creates difference, it will create it[7] in the greatest I and not in the least degree; in other words, the Reason-Principle, bringing about differentiation to the uttermost degree, will of necessity create contrarieties: it will be complete only by producing itself not in merely diverse things but in contrary things.

17. The nature of the Reason-Principle is adequately expressed in its Act and, therefore, the wider its extension the nearer will its productions approach to full contrariety: hence the world of sense is less a unity than is its Reason-Principle; it contains a wider multiplicity and contrariety: its partial members will, therefore, be urged by a closer intention towards fullness of life, a warmer desire for unification.

But desire often destroys the desired; it seeks its own good, and if the desired object is perishable, the ruin follows: and the partial thing (a human being, for example) straining towards its completing principle draws towards itself all it possibly can.

Thus, with the good we have the bad: we have the opposed movements of a dancer guided by one artistic plan; we recognize in his steps the good as against the bad, and see that in the opposition lies the merit of the design.

But, thus, the wicked disappear?

No: their wickedness remains; simply, their role is not of their own planning.

But, surely, this excuses them?

No; excuse lies with the Reason-Principle—and the Reason-Principle does not excuse them.

No doubt all are members of this Principle, but one is a good man, another is bad—the larger class, this—and it goes as in a play; the poet while he gives each actor a part is also using them as they are in their own persons: I he does not himself create[8] leading actor, I second, third; he simply gives suitable words to each, and by that assignment fixes each man's standing.

Thus, every man has his place, a place that fits the good man, a place that fits the bad: each within the two orders of men makes his way, naturally, reasonably, to the place, good or bad, that suits him, and takes the position he has made his own. There he talks and acts, in blasphemy and crime or in all goodness: for the actors bring to this play what they were before it was ever staged.

In the dramas of human art the poet provides the words but the actors add their own quality, good or bad—for they have more to do than merely repeat the author's words: in the truer drama which dramatic genius imitates in its degree, the Soul displays itself in a part assigned by the creator of the piece.

As the actors of our stages get their masks and their costume, robes of state or rags, so a Soul is allotted its fortunes, and not at haphazard but always under a Reason: it adapts itself to the fortunes assigned to it, attunes itself, ranges itself rightly to the drama, to the whole Principle of the piece: then it speaks out its business, exhibiting at the same time all that a Soul can express of its own quality, as a singer in a song. A voice, a bearing, naturally fine or vulgar, may increase the charm of a piece; on the other hand, an actor with his ugly voice may make a sorry exhibition of himself, yet the drama stands as good a work as ever: the dramatist taking the action which a sound criticism suggests, disgraces one, taking his part from him, with perfect justice: another man he promotes to more serious roles or to any more important play he may have, while the first is cast for whatever minor work there may be.

Just so the Soul, entering this drama of the Universe, making itself a part of the Play, bringing to its acting its personal excellence or defect, set in a definite place at the entry and accepting from the author its entire role—superimposed upon its own character and conduct—just so, it receives in the end its punishment and reward.

But these actors, souls, hold a peculiar dignity: they act in a vaster place than any stage: the Author has made them masters of all this world; they have a wide choice of place; they themselves determine the honour or discredit in which they are agents since their place and part are in keeping with their quality: they therefore fit into the Reason-Principle of the Universe, each adjusted, most legitimately, to the appropriate environment, as every string of the lyre is set in the precisely right position, determined by the Principle directing musical utterance, for the due production of the tones within its capacity. All is just and good in the Universe in which every actor is set in his own quite appropriate place, though it be to utter in the Darkness and in Tartarus the dreadful sounds whose utterance there is well.

This Universe is good not when the individual is a stone, but when everyone throws in his own voice towards a total harmony, singing out a life—thin, harsh, imperfect, though it be. The Syrinx does not utter merely one pure note; there is a thin obscure sound which blends in to make the harmony of Syrinx music: the harmony is made up from tones of various grades, all the tones differing, but the resultant of all forming one sound.

Similarly the Reason-Principle entire is one, but it is broken into unequal parts: hence the difference of place found in the Universe, better spots and worse; and hence the inequality of souls, finding their appropriate surroundings amid this local inequality. The diverse places of this sphere, the souls of unequal grade and unlike conduct, are well exemplified by the distinction of parts in the Syrinx or any other instrument: there is local difference, but from every position every string gives forth its own tone, the sound appropriate, at once, to its particular place and to the entire plan.

What is evil in the single soul will stand a good thing in the universal system; what in the unit offends nature will serve nature in the total event—and still remains the weak and wrong tone it is, though its sounding takes nothing from the worth of the whole, just as, in another order of image, the executioner's ugly office does not mar the well-governed state: such an officer is a civic necessity; and the corresponding moral type is often serviceable; thus, even as things are, all is well.

18. Souls vary in worth; and the difference is due, among other causes, to an almost initial inequality; it is in reason that, standing to the Reason-Principle as parts, they should be unequal by the fact of becoming separate.

We must also remember that every soul has its second grade and its third, and that, therefore, its expression may take any one of three main forms. But this point must be dealt with here again: the matter requires all possible elucidation.

❚ We ought not perhaps to think of actors having the right to add something to the poet's words—which would mean that the drama as it stood was not perfectly filled in and that they were to supply where the Author had left blank spaces here and there. The actor would then be something else as well; he would be a part of the poet, with a fore-knowledge of the words which the other actors would use, and would so be able to bind together all the strands of the story in their proper order.[9] ❚

For, in the All, the sequences, including what follows upon wickedness, become Reason-Principles, and therefore in right reason. Thus: from adultery and the violation of prisoners the process of nature will produce fine children, to grow, perhaps, into fine men; and where wicked violence has destroyed cities, other and nobler cities may rise in their place.

But does not this make it absurd to introduce souls as responsible causes, some acting for good and some for evil? If we thus exonerate the Reason-Principle from any part in wickedness do we not also cancel its credit for the good? Why not simply take the doings of these actors (in the universal drama) for representative parts of the Reason-Principle as the doings of stage-actors are representative parts of the stage-drama? Why not admit that the Reason-Principle itself includes evil action as much as good action, and inspires the precise conduct of all its representatives? Would not this be all the more plausible in that the universal drama is the completer creation and that the Reason-Principle is the source of all that exists?

But this raises the question, What motive could lead the Logos to produce evil?

The explanation, also, would take away all power in the Universe from souls, even those nearest to the divine; they would be all mere parts of a Reason-Principle.

And, further—unless all Reason-Principles are souls—why should some be souls and others exclusively Reason-Principles ❚ when every one of them belongs to[10] a Soul? ❚

NOTES TO ENNEAD III.2

1. FIRST EDITION: "Authentic *Kosmos* . . . lower *kosmos* . . ."

2. FIRST EDITION: "It was the *First* and . . ."

    TAYLOR: ". . . it is indeed the first of beings . . ."

    GUTHRIE: "It occupied the first rank . . ."

    ARMSTRONG: "For it was the first . . ."

3. FIRST EDITION: "... I came *perfect above all forms* of life ..."

ARMSTRONG: "... I came from him perfect above all living things ..."

TAYLOR: "... from whence I am formed perfect, composed from all animals ..."

GUTHRIE: "... I issued complete, including all animated beings ..."

4. FIRST EDITION: "... and dwell with the *one Soul of all. For the embodied lives by virtue of a Form or Idea: individual or partial things exist by virtue of Universals; from these priors they derive their life and maintenance,* for life here ..."

TAYLOR: "... with universal soul. But bodies are changed according to form, and particulars according to the whole, since animals are produced and nourished by their interposition; for life ..."

GUTHRIE: "... the universal Soul. The bodies are alive by their form, and by the whole that each of them constitutes (by its union with a soul), since they are animals, and since they nourish themselves; for in the sense-world life ..."

ARMSTRONG: "... with the universal soul. Bodies live by species, and individual bodies as far as they are wholes, if living things both come from them and are to be nourished by them; for life ..."

5. FIRST EDITION: "... the earth is but a *central* point, and *may be considered as simply* one among the stars."

ARMSTRONG: "... but the earth is like a central point even in comparison with only one of the stars."

GUTHRIE: "The earth occupies the centre and seems to be one of the stars."

TAYLOR: "... but earth is, as it were, the centre of the universe, and ranks among the number of stars."

6. FIRST EDITION: "The perverse have never *made a single effort to bring the good into authority, nor do they take any steps to improve themselves;* they ..."

ARMSTRONG: "... for they themselves have never taken any trouble to see that there should be good rulers of the rest of mankind, who would care that it should be well with them, but they are envious ..."

GUTHRIE: "The latter never busy themselves with promoting the good to the governing of other men, and themselves to be good ..."

7. FIRST EDITION: "... admitting that *this differentiation exists and creates,* it will create *difference* in the greatest ..."

ARMSTRONG: "... if in general it ['rational formative pattern'—ed.] makes one thing different from another, it will also make them different in the extreme ..."

TAYLOR: "If reason then is something different, and that which is different is productive of something, that which it produces must certainly be more different than itself;"

GUTHRIE: "Now if Reason contain a difference, and produce different things, the difference that exists in these things is greater than that which exists in Reason."

JOHN DECK's comment in *Nature, Contemplation, and the One* (p. 75, Larson 1991 edition) is helpful: "Yet logos, reason, the expression of the primitive through-and-through duality of the Nous, is 'different in relation to itself' (i.e., composed of the same and the other), and so produces maximum otherness, contrariety (III.2.16, 45-58). This contrariety is resolved and at peace in the Nous and in the soul, but in the sensible All it finds expression as a war of logoi, as a development with collisions and mutual impedances."

8. FIRST EDITION: ". . . he does not himself *rank the men as* leading actor . . ."

TAYLOR: ". . . the poet is not the cause that one is first in ability in the play, another second . . ."

ARMSTRONG: "He does not himself rank them as leading actor . . ."

GUTHRIE: "The obtaining of the first, second or third rank by an actor does not depend on the poet."

9. FIRST EDITION has this paragraph as: "We *may* perhaps think of actors having the right to add something to the poet's words: *the drama as it stands is* not perfectly filled in, and they *are* to supply where the Author *has* left blank spaces here and there; the *actors are to* be something else as well; *they become parts* of the poet, *who on his side has* a fore-knowledge of the *word they will add, and so is* able to bind *into one story what the actors bring in and what is to follow.*"

GUTHRIE and TAYLOR support MacKenna's first-edition interpretation; ARMSTRONG supports Page's changes.

10. FIRST EDITION: ". . . when *the All is itself* a Soul?"

TAYLOR: ". . . when at the same time universal reason is a certain soul?"

GUTHRIE: "Otherwise if the Reason of the universe be a Soul, why should certain 'reasons' be souls, and others only ('seminal') reasons'?"

ARMSTRONG: "And are all rational principles souls, or why are some souls and some only rational principles, when every one of them belongs to some soul?"

THIRD TRACTATE

Providence: Second Treatise

1. What is our answer?

All events and things, good and evil alike, are included under the Universal Reason-Principle of which they are parts—strictly 'included', for this Universal Idea does not engender them but encompasses them.

The Reason-Principles are acts or expressions of a Universal Soul; its parts (i.e., events good and evil) are expressions of these Soul-parts.

This unity, Soul, has different parts; the Reason-Principles, correspondingly, will also have their parts, and so, too, will the ultimates of the system, all that they bring into being.

The Souls are in harmony with each other and so, too, are their acts and effects; but it is harmony in the sense of a resultant unity built out of contraries. All things, as they rise from a unity, come back to unity by a sheer need of nature; differences unfold themselves, contraries are produced, but all is drawn into one organized system by the unity at the source.

The principle may be illustrated from the different classes of animal life: there is one genus, horse, though horses among themselves fight and bite and show malice and angry envy: so all the others within the unity of their Kind; and so humanity.

All these types, again, can be ranged under the one Kind, that of living things; objects without life can be thought of under their specific types and then be resumed under the one Kind of the 'non-living'; if we choose to go further yet, living and non-living may be included under the one Kind, 'Beings', and, further still, under the Source of Being.

Having attached all to this source, we turn to move down again in continuous division: we see the Unity fissuring, as it reaches out into Universality, and yet embracing all in one system so that with all its differentiation it is one multiple living thing—an organism in which each member executes the function of its own nature while it still has its being in that One Whole; fire burns; horse does horse work; men give each the appropriate act of the peculiar personal quality—and upon the several particular Kinds to which each belongs follow the acts, and the good or evil of the life.

2. Circumstances are not sovereign over the good of life, for they themselves follow harmoniously upon their priors and come in as members of a sequence. The Leading-Principle holds all the threads while the minor agents, the individuals, serve according to their own capacities, as in a war the generalissimo lays down the plan and his subordinates do their best to its furtherance. The Universe has been ordered by a Providence that may be compared to a general; he has considered operations, conditions, and such practical needs as food and drink, arms and engines of war; all the problem of reconciling these complex elements has been worked out beforehand so as to make it probable that the final event may be success. The entire scheme emerges from the general's mind with a certain plausible promise, though it cannot cover the enemy's operations, and there is no power over the disposition of the enemy's forces: but where 'the mighty leader' is in question whose power extends over all that is, what can pass unordered, what can fail to fit into the plan?

3. For, even though the I is sovereign in choosing, yet by the fact of the choice the thing done takes its place in the ordered total. Your personality does not come from outside into the universal scheme; you are a part of it, you and your personal disposition.

But what is the cause of this initial personality?

This question resolves itself into two: are we to make the Creator, if Creator there is, the cause of the moral quality of the individual or does the responsibility lie with the creature?

Or is there, perhaps, no responsibility? After all, none is charged in the case of plants brought into being without the perceptive faculties; no one is blamed because animals are not all that men are—which would be like complaining that men are not all that gods are. Reason acquits plant and animal and their maker; how can it complain because men do not stand above humanity?

If the reproach simply means that Man might improve by bringing from his own stock something towards his betterment we must allow that the man failing in this is answerable for his own inferiority: but if the betterment must come not from within the man but from without, from his Author, it is folly to ask more than has been given, as foolish in the case of man as in plant and animal.

The question is not whether a thing is inferior to something else but whether in its own Kind it suffices to its own part; universal equality there cannot be.

Then the Reason-Principle has measured things out with the set purpose of inequality?

Certainly not: the inequality is inevitable by the nature of things: the Reason-Principle of this Universe follows upon a phase of the Soul; the Soul itself follows upon an Intellectual Principle, and this Intellectual Principle is not one among the things of the Universe but is all things; in all things, there is implied variety of things; where there is variety and not identity there must be primals, secondaries, tertiaries, and every grade downward. Forms of life, then, there must be that are not pure Soul but the dwindling of souls enfeebled stage by stage of the process. There is, of course, a Soul in the Reason-Principle constituting a living being, but it is another Soul (a lesser phase), not that (the Supreme Soul) from which the Reason-Principle (of the World) itself derives; and this Universal Reason-Principle weakens as it proceeds towards matter, and what it engenders is still more deficient. Consider how far the engendered stands from its origin and yet, what a marvel!

In sum, nothing can secure to a thing of process the quality of the prior order, loftier than all that is product and amenable to no charge in regard to it: the wonder is, only, that it reaches and gives to the lower at all, and that the traces of its presence should be so noble. And if its out-giving is greater than the lower can appropriate, the debt is the heavier; all the blame must fall upon the unreceptive creature, and Providence be the more exalted.

4. If man were all of one piece—I mean, if he were nothing more than a made thing, acting and acted upon according to a fixed nature—he could be no more subject to reproach and punishment than the mere animals. But as the scheme holds, man is singled out for condemnation when he does evil; and this with justice. For he is no mere thing made to rigid plan; his nature contains a Principle apart and free.

This does not, however, stand outside of Providence or of the Reason of the All; the Over-World cannot be cut off from the World of Sense. The higher shines down upon the lower, and this illumination is Providence in its highest aspect. The Reason-Principle has two phases, one which creates the things of process and another which links them with the higher I beings: the creative phase constitutes[1] the I over-providence on which depends that lower providence which is the secondary Reason-Principle inseparably united with its primal: the two—the Major and Minor Providence—acting together produce the universal woof, the one all-comprehensive Providence.

Men possess, then, a distinctive Principle: but not all men turn to account all that is in their Nature; there are men that live by one Principle and men that live by another or, rather, by several others, the least noble. For all these Principles are present even when not acting upon the man—though we cannot think of them as lying idle; everything performs its function.

'But,' it will be said, 'what reason can there be for their not acting upon the man once they are present; inaction must mean absence?'

We maintain their presence always, nothing void of them.

But surely not where they exercise no action? If they necessarily reside in all men, surely they must be operative in all—this Principle of free action, especially.

First of all, this free Principle is not an absolute possession of the animal Kinds and is not even an absolute possession to all men.

So this Principle is not the only effective force in all men?

There is no reason why it should not be. There are men in whom it alone acts, giving its character to the life, while all else is but Necessity (and therefore outside of blame).

For (in the case of an evil life) whether it is that the constitution of the man is such as to drive him down the troubled paths or whether (the fault is mental or spiritual in that) the desires have gained control, we are compelled to attribute the guilt to the substratum (something inferior to the highest principle in Man). We would be naturally inclined to say that this substratum (the responsible source of evil) must be Matter and not, as our argument implies, the Reason-Principle; it would appear that not the Reason-Principle but Matter were the dominant, crude Matter at the extreme and then Matter as shaped in the realized man: but we must remember that to this free Principle in man (which is a phase of the All Soul) the Substratum (the direct inferior to be moulded) is (not Matter but) the Reason-Principle itself with whatever that produces and moulds to its own form, so that neither crude Matter nor Matter organized in our human total is sovereign within us.

The quality now manifested may be probably referred to the conduct of a former life; we may suppose that previous actions have made the Reason-Principle now governing within us inferior in radiance to that which ruled before; the Soul which later will shine out again is for the present at a feebler power.

And any Reason-Principle may be said to include within itself the Reason-Principle of Matter which therefore it is able to elaborate to its own purposes, either finding it consonant with itself or bestowing upon it the quality which makes it so. The Reason-Principle of an ox does not occur except in connexion with the Matter appropriate to the ox-kind. It must be by such a process that the transmigration, of which we read (in Plato) takes place; the Soul must lose its nature, the Reason-Principle be transformed; thus there comes the ox-soul which once was Man.

The degradation, then, is just.

Still, how did the inferior Principle ever come into being, and how does the higher fall to it?

Once more—not all things are Firsts; there are Secondaries and Tertiaries, of a nature inferior to that of their Priors; and a slight tilt is enough to determine the departure from the straight course. Further, the linking of any one being with any other amounts to a blending such as to produce a distinct entity, a compound of the two; it is not that the greater and prior suffers any diminution of its own nature; the lesser and secondary is such from its very beginning; it is in its own nature the lesser thing it becomes, and if it suffers the consequences, such suffering is merited: all our reasonings on these questions must take account of previous living as the source from which the present takes its rise.

5. There is, then, a Providence, which permeates the Cosmos from first to last, not everywhere equal, as in a numerical distribution, but proportioned, differing, according to the grades of place—just as in some one animal, linked from first to last, each member has its own function, the nobler organ the higher activity while others successively concern the lower degrees of the life, each part acting of itself, and experiencing what belongs to its own nature and what comes from its relation with every other. Strike, and what is designed for utterance gives forth the appropriate volume of sound while other parts take the blow in silence but react in their own especial movement; the total of all the utterance and action and receptivity constitutes what we may call the personal voice, life, and history of the living form. The parts, distinct in kind, have distinct functions: the feet have their work and the eyes theirs; the understanding serves to one end, the Intellectual Principle to another.

But all sums to a unity, a comprehensive Providence. From the inferior grade downwards is Fate: the upper is Providence alone: for in the Intellectual Cosmos all is Reason-Principle or its Priors—Divine Mind and unmingled Soul—and immediately upon these follows Providence which rises from Divine Mind, is the content of the Unmingled Soul and, through this Soul, is communicated to the Sphere of living things.

This Reason-Principle comes as a thing of unequal parts, and therefore its creations are unequal, as, for example, the several members of one living being. But after this allotment of rank and function, all act consonant with the will of the gods keeps the sequence and is included under the providential government, for the Reason-Principle of Providence is god-serving.

I Activity of a different kind is linked to Providence but not[2] performed by it: I men or other agents, living or lifeless, are causes of certain things happening, and any good that may result is taken up again by Providence. In the total, then, the right rules and what has happened amiss is transformed and corrected. Thus, to take an example from a single body, the Providence of a living organism implies its health; let it be gashed or otherwise wounded, and that Reason-Principle which governs it sets to work to draw it together, knit it anew, heal it, and put the affected part to rights.

In sum, evil belongs to the sequence of things, but it comes (not from Providence but) from Necessity. It originates in ourselves; it has its causes no doubt, but we are not, therefore, forced to it by Providence: some of these causes we adapt to the operation of Providence and of its subordinates, but with others we fail to make the connexion; the act instead of being ranged under the will of Providence consults the desire of the agent alone or of some other element in the Universe, something which is either itself at variance with Providence or has set up some such state of variance in ourselves.

The one circumstance does not produce the same result wherever it acts; the normal operation will be modified from case to case: Helen's beauty told very differently on Paris and on Idomeneus; bring together two handsome people of loose character and two living honourably and the resulting conduct is very different; a good man meeting a libertine exhibits a distinct phase of his nature and, similarly, the dissolute answer to the society of their betters.

The act of the libertine is not done by Providence or in accordance with Providence; neither is the action of the good done by Providence—it is done by the man—but it is done in accordance with Providence, for it is an act consonant with the Reason-Principle. Thus a patient following his treatment is himself an agent and yet is acting in accordance with the doctor's method inspired by the art concerned with the causes of health and sickness: what one does against the laws of health is one's act, but an act conflicting with the Providence of medicine.

6. But, if all this be true, how can evil fall within the scope of seership? The

predictions of the seers are based on observation of the Universal Circuit: how can this indicate the evil with the good?

Clearly the reason is that all contraries coalesce. Take, for example, Shape and (its contrary) Matter: the living being (of the lower order) is a coalescence of these two; so that to be aware of the Shape and the Reason-Principle is to be aware of the Matter on which the Shape has been imposed.

The living-being of the compound order is not present (as pure and simple Idea) like the living being of the Intellectual order: in the compound entity we are aware, at once, of the Reason-Principle and of the inferior element brought under form. Now the Universe is such a compound living thing: to observe, therefore, its content is to be aware not less of its lower elements than of the Providence which operates within it.

This Providence reaches to all things, even those that come into being; its scope therefore includes living things with their actions and states—mixed states through the joint action of Reason-Principle and Necessity.

These, then, are presented as mingled both by their initial nature and by the continuous process of their existence; and the Seer is not able to make a perfect discrimination setting on the one side Providence with all that happens under Providence and on the other side what the substrate communicates to its product. Such discrimination is not for a man, not for a wise man or a divine man: one may say it is the prerogative of a god. Not causes but facts lie in the Seer's province; his art is the reading of the scriptures of Nature which tell of the ordered and never condescend to the disorderly; the movement of the Universe utters its testimony to him and, before men and things reveal themselves, brings to light what severally and collectively they are.

Here conspires with There and There with Here, elaborating together the consistency and eternity of a Cosmos and by their correspondences revealing the sequence of things to the trained observer—for every form of divination turns upon correspondences. ❙ Universal disparity there could not be; there must be some measure of assimilation.[3] ❙ This probably is the meaning of the saying that Correspondences maintain the Universe.

This is a correspondence of inferior with inferior, of superior with superior, eye with eye, foot with foot, everything with its fellow and, in another order, virtue with right action and vice with unrighteousness. Admit such correspondence in the All and we have the possibility of prediction. If the one order acts on the other, the relation is not that of maker to thing made—the two are coeval—it is the interplay of members of one living being; each in its own place and way moves as its own nature demands, to every organ its grade and task, and to every grade and task its effective organ. A single Reason-Principle is at work.

7. And since the higher exists, there must be the lower as well. The Universe is a thing of variety, and how could there be an inferior without a superior or a superior without an inferior? We cannot complain about the lower in the higher; rather, we must be grateful to the higher for giving something of itself to the lower.

In a word, those that would like evil driven out from the All would drive out Providence itself.

What would Providence have to provide for? Certainly not for itself or for the Good: when we speak of a Providence above, we mean an act upon something below.

That which resumes all under a unity is a Principle in which all things exist together and the single thing is All. From this Principle, which remains internally unmoved, particular things push forth as from a single root which never itself emerges. They are a branching into part, into multiplicity, each single outgrowth bearing its trace of the common source. Thus, phase by phase, there is finally the production into this world; some things close still to the root, others widely separate in the continuous progression until we have, in our metaphor, bough and crest, foliage and fruit. At the one side all is one point of unbroken rest, on the other is the ceaseless process, leaf and fruit, all the things of process carrying ever within themselves the Reason-Principles of the Upper Sphere, and striving to become trees in their own minor order and producing, if at all, only what is in strict gradation from themselves.

As for the abandoned spaces in what corresponds to the branches‖ these too draw upon other parts which, despite all their variance, grow from the root itself;[4] and the branches‖ again operate upon their own furthest extremities: operation is to be traced only from point to next point, but, in the fact, there has been both inflow and outgo (of creative or modifying force) at the very root which, itself again, has its priors.

The things that act upon each other are branchings from a far-off beginning and so stand distinct; but they derive initially from the one source: all interaction is like that of brothers, resemblant as drawing life from the same parents.

NOTES TO ENNEAD III.3

1. FIRST EDITION: "... beings: *these higher beings constitute* the ..."

 ARMSTRONG: "... those higher principles are providence which acts from above ..."

2. FIRST EDITION begins sentence as: "*All such right doing, then,* is linked to Providence; but *it is not therefore* performed by it:"

GUTHRIE: "All such actions are related (to the plan of Providence); they are not done by Providence;"

ARMSTRONG: "Then, too, these kind of actions [the kind which cause our difficulties about providence, i.e. evil actions] are linked up with the good ones, but they are not done by providence . . ." Brackets are Armstrong's.

3. FIRST EDITION has this sentence as: "Universal *interdependence, there could not be, but universal resemblance there must.*"

GUTHRIE: ". . . for things were not to depend on each other, but to have relations founded on their resemblance." Guthrie also cross-references III.2.6.

ARMSTRONG: "For it would not have been right for all things to be cut off from each other but they had to be made like each other, in some way at least."

4. FIRST EDITION: ". . . these too draw upon *the root, from* which, despite all their variance, *they also derive;* and the branches . . ."

ARMSTRONG: " . . . what are like empty spaces between the branches are filled with shoots which also grow from the root, these, too, in a different way;"

GUTHRIE: "As to the parts . . . which are hollow, such as the branches, they receive from the root the sap which is to fill them;"

FOURTH TRACTATE

Our Tutelary Spirit

1. Some Existents (Absolute Unity and Intellectual-Principle) remain at rest while their Hypostases, or Expressed-Ideas, come into being; but, in our view, the Soul generates by its motion—generates the sensitive faculty considered as Expression-Form and the faculty of growth in which Soul extends to the vegetable order. Even as it is present in human beings the Soul carries this faculty of growth with it, but it is not the dominant since it is not the whole man: in the vegetable order it is the highest since there is nothing to rival it; but at this phase it is no longer reproductive, or, at least, what it produces is of quite another order; here life ceases; all later production is lifeless.

What does this imply?

Everything engendered down to this point (of sheer lifelessness) comes into being shapeless, and takes form by orientation towards its author and supporter: therefore (and even more certainly) the thing engendered on the further side can be no image of the Soul, since it is not even alive; it must be an utter Indetermination. No doubt even in things of the nearer order there was indetermination, but within a form; they were undetermined not utterly but only in contrast with their perfect state: at this extreme point we have the utter lack of determination. Let it be raised to its highest degree and it becomes body by taking such shape as serves its scope; then it becomes the recipient of its author and sustainer: this presence in body is the only example of the boundaries of Higher Existents running into the boundary of the Lower.

2. It is of this Soul especially that we read 'All Soul has care for the Soulless'—though the several souls thus care in their own degree and way. The passage continues—'Soul passes through the entire heavens in forms varying with the variety of place'—the sensitive form, the reasoning form, even the vegetative form—and this means that the phase of the Soul which is dominant carries out its own ends while the rest, not present, is idle.

Now, in humanity the lower is not supreme; it is an accompaniment; but neither does the better rule unfailingly; the lower element also has a footing, and Man, therefore, lives in part under sensation, for he has the organs of sensation, and in large part even by the merely vegetative principle for the body grows and propagates: all the graded phases are in a collaboration, but the entire form, man, takes rank by the dominant, and when the life-principle leaves the body it is what it is, what it most intensely lived.

This is why we must break away towards the High: we dare not keep ourselves set towards the sensuous principle, following the images of sense, or towards the merely vegetative, intent upon the gratifications of eating and procreation; our life must be pointed towards the Intellective, towards the Intellectual-Principle, towards God.

Those that have maintained the human level are men once more. Those that have lived wholly to sense become animals—corresponding in species to the particular temper of the life—ferocious animals where the sensuality has been accompanied by a certain measure of spirit, gluttonous and lascivious animals where all has been appetite and satiation of appetite. Those who in their pleasures have not even lived by sensation, but have gone their way in a torpid grossness, become mere growing things, for only or mainly the vegetative principle was active in them, and such men have been busy be-treeing themselves. Those, we read, that, otherwise untainted, have loved song become vocal animals; kings ruling unreasonably but with no other vice are eagles; futile and flighty visionaries ever soaring skyward, become high-flying birds; observance of civic and secular virtue makes man again, or where the merit is less marked, one of the animals of communal tendency, a bee or the like.

3. What, then, is the spirit (guiding the present life and determining the future?)
The Spirit of here and now.

And the God?

The God of here and now.

Spirit, God—this in act within us conducts every life; for, even here and now, it is the dominant of our nature.

That is to say that the dominant is the spirit which takes possession of the human being at birth?

No: the dominant is the Prior of the individual spirit; it presides inoperative while its secondary acts: so that if the acting force is that of men of the sense-life, the tutelary spirit is the Rational Being, while if we live by that Rational Being, our tutelary spirit is the still higher Being, not directly operative but assenting to the working principle. The words 'You shall yourselves choose (your presiding spirit)' are true, then; for by our life we elect our own loftier.

But how does this spirit come to be the determinant of our fate?

It is not when the life is ended that it conducts us here or there; it operates during the lifetime; when we cease to live, our death hands over to another principle this energy of our own personal career.

That principle (of the new birth) strives to gain control, and if it succeeds it also lives and itself, in turn, possesses a guiding spirit (its next higher): if on the contrary it is weighed down by the developed evil in the character, this burden is the penalty which it pays: the evil-liver loses grade because during his life the active principle of his being took the tilt towards the brute by force of affinity. If, on the contrary, the Man is able to follow the leading of his higher spirit, he rises: he lives that spirit; that noblest part of himself to which he is being led becomes sovereign in his life; this made his own, he works for the next above until he has attained the height.

For the Soul is many things, is all, is the Above and the Beneath to the totality of life: and each of us is an Intellectual Cosmos, linked to this world by what is lowest in us, but, by what is the highest, to the Divine Intellect: by all that is intellective we are permanently in that higher realm, but at the fringe of the Intellectual we are fettered to the lower; it is as if we gave forth from it some emanation towards that lower, or rather some Act, which however leaves our diviner part not in itself diminished.

4. But is this lower extremity of our intellective phase fettered to body for ever?

No: if we turn, this turns by the same act.

And the Soul of the All—are we to think that when it turns from this sphere its lower phase similarly withdraws?

No: for it never accompanied that lower phase of itself; it never knew any coming, and therefore never came down; it remains unmoved above, and the material frame of the Universe draws close to it, and, as it were, takes light from it, no hindrance to it, in no way troubling it, simply lying unmoved before it.

But has the Universe, then, no sensation? 'It has no sight', we read, since it has no eyes, and obviously it has not ears, nostrils, nor tongue. Then has it perhaps such a consciousness as we have of our own inner conditions?

No: where all is the working out of one nature, there is nothing but still rest; there is not even enjoyment. Sensibility is present as the quality of growth is, unrecognized. But the Nature of the World will be found treated elsewhere; what stands here is all that the question of the moment demands.

5. But if the presiding Spirit and the conditions of life are chosen by the Soul in the over-world, how can anything be left to our independent action here?

The answer is that that very choice in the over-world is merely an allegorical statement of the Soul's tendency and temperament, a total character which it must express wherever it operates.

But if the tendency of the Soul is the master-force and, in the Soul, the dominant is that phase which has been brought to the fore by a previous history, then the body stands acquitted of any bad influence upon it? The Soul's quality exists before any bodily life; it has exactly what it chose to have; and, we read, it never changes its chosen spirit; therefore neither the good man nor the bad is the product of this life?

Is the solution, perhaps, that man is potentially both good and bad but becomes the one or the other by force of act?

But what if a man temperamentally good happens to enter a disordered body, or if a perfect body falls to a man naturally vicious?

The answer is that the Soul, to whichever side it inclines, has in some varying degree the power of working the forms of body over to its own temper, since outlying and accidental circumstances cannot overrule the entire decision of a soul. Where we read that, after the casting of lots, the sample lives are exhibited with the casual circumstances attending them and that the choice is made upon vision, in accordance with the individual temperament, we are given to understand that the real determination lies with the Souls, who adapt the allotted conditions to their own particular quality.

The Timaeus indicates the relation of this guiding spirit to ourselves: it is not entirely outside of ourselves; is not bound up with our nature; is not the agent of our action; it belongs to us as belonging to our Soul, but not in so far as we are particular human beings living a life to which it is superior: take the passage in this sense and it is consistent; understand this spirit otherwise and there is contradiction. And the description of the spirit, moreover, as 'the power which consummates the chosen life', is, also, in agreement with this interpretation; for while its presidency saves us from falling much deeper into evil, the only direct agent within us is some thing neither above it nor equal to it but under it: Man cannot cease to be characteristically Man.

6. What, then, is the achieved Sage?

One whose Act is determined by the higher phase of the Soul.

It does not suffice to perfect virtue to have only this spirit (equivalent in all men) as co-operator in the life: the acting force in the Sage is the Intellective Principle which therefore is itself his presiding spirit or is guided by a presiding spirit of its own, no other than the very divinity.

But this exalts the Sage above the Intellectual Principle as possessing for presiding spirit the Prior to the Intellectual Principle: how then does it come about that he was not, from the very beginning, all that he now is?

The failure is due to the disturbance caused by birth—though, before all reasoning, there exists the instinctive movement reaching out towards its own.

An instinct which the Sage finally rectifies in every respect?

Not in every respect: the Soul is so constituted that its life-history and its general tendency will answer not merely to its own nature but also to the conditions among which it acts.

The presiding spirit, as we read, conducting a soul to the Underworld ceases to be its guardian—except when the soul resumes (in its later choice) the former state of life.

But, meanwhile, what happens to it?

From the passage (in the Phaedo) which tells how it presents the soul to judgement we gather that after the death it resumes the form it had before the birth, but that then, beginning again, it is present to the souls in their punishment in the period before their renewed life—a time not so much of living as of expiation.

But the souls that enter into brute bodies, are they controlled by some thing less than this presiding spirit? No: theirs is still a spirit, but an evil or a foolish one.

And the souls that attain to the highest?

Of these higher souls some live in the world of Sense, some above it: and those in the world of Sense inhabit the sun or another of the planetary bodies; the others occupy the fixed sphere (above the planetary) holding the place they have merited through having lived here the superior life of reason.

We must understand that, while our souls do contain an Intellectual Cosmos, they also contain a subordination of various forms like that of the Cosmic Soul. The World Soul is distributed so as to produce the fixed sphere and the planetary circuits corresponding to its graded powers: so with our souls; they must have their provinces according to their different powers, parallel to those of the World Soul: each must give out its own special act; released, each will inhabit there a star consonant with the temperament and faculty in act within and constituting the principle of the life; and this star or the next highest power will stand to them as God or more exactly as tutelary spirit.

But here some further precision is needed.

Emancipated souls, for the whole period of their sojourn there above, have transcended the Spirit-nature and the entire fatality of birth and all that belongs to this visible world, for they have taken up with them that phase of the Soul's existence in which the desire of earthly life is vested. This phase may be described as 'that which becomes divisible among bodies', for it is what enters bodily forms and multiplies itself by this division among them. But its distribution is not (arithmetical, not) a matter of magnitudes; wherever it is present, there is the same thing present entire; its unity can always be reconstructed: when living things—animal or vegetal—(distribute themselves and) produce their constant succession of new forms, they do so in virtue of the self-distribution of this phase of the Soul, for it must be as much distributed among the new forms as the propagating originals are. In some cases it communicates its force by permanent presence—the life principle in plants for instance; in other cases it withdraws after imparting its virtue—for instance where from the putridity of dead animal or vegetable matter a multitudinous birth is produced from one organism.

A power corresponding to this in the All must reach down and co-operate in the life of our world—in fact the very same power.

If the Soul returns to this Sphere it finds itself under the same spirit or a new, according to the life it is to live. With this spirit it embarks in the skiff of the universe: the 'spindle of Necessity' then takes control and appoints the seat for the voyage, the seat of the lot in life.

The Universal circuit is like a breeze, and the voyager, still or stirring, is carried forward by it. He has a hundred varied experiences, fresh sights, changing circumstances, all sorts of events. The vessel itself furnishes incident, tossing as it drives on. And the voyager also acts of himself in virtue of that individuality which he retains because he is on the vessel in his own person and character. Under identical circumstances individuals answer very differently in their movements and desires and acts: hence it comes about that, be the occurrences and conditions of life similar or dissimilar, the result may differ from man to man, as on the other hand a similar result may be produced by dissimilar conditions: this (force of circumstance)[1] it is that constitutes destiny.

NOTE TO ENNEAD III.4

1. FIRST EDITION: ". . . conditions: this *(personal answer to incident)* it is that constitutes destiny."

ARMSTRONG: ". . . for that is what destiny is like."

FIFTH TRACTATE

Love

1. What is Love? A God, a Celestial Spirit, a state of mind? Or is it, perhaps, sometimes to be thought of as a God or Spirit and sometimes merely as an experience? And what is it essentially in each of these respects?

These important questions make it desirable to review prevailing opinions on the matter, the philosophical treatment it has received and, especially, the theories of the great Plato who has many passages dealing with Love, from a point of view entirely his own.

Plato does not treat of it as simply a state observed in souls; he also makes it a Spirit-being; so that we read of the birth of Eros, under definite circumstances and by a certain parentage.

Now everyone recognizes that the emotional state for which we make this 'Love' responsible rises in souls aspiring to be knit in the closest union with some beautiful object, and that this aspiration takes two forms, that of the good whose devotion is for beauty itself, and that other which seeks its consummation in some vile act. But this generally admitted distinction opens a new question: we need a philosophical investigation into the origin of the two phases.

It is sound, I think, to find the primal source of Love in a tendency of the Soul towards pure beauty, in a recognition, in a kinship, in an unreasoned consciousness of friendly relation. The vile and ugly is in clash, at once, with Nature and with God: Nature produces by looking to the Good, for it looks towards Order—which has its being in the consistent total of the good, while the unordered is ugly, a member of the system of evil—and besides, Nature itself, clearly, springs from the divine realm, from Good and Beauty; and when anything brings delight and the sense of kinship, its very image attracts.

Reject this explanation, and no one can tell how the mental state rises and what are its causes: it is the explanation of even copulative love, which is the will to beget in beauty; Nature seeks to produce the beautiful and therefore by all reason cannot desire to procreate in the ugly.

Those that desire earthly procreation are satisfied with the beauty found on earth, the beauty of image and of body; it is because they are strangers to the Archetype, the source of even the attraction they feel towards what is lovely here. There are souls to whom earthly beauty is a leading to the memory of that in the higher realm and these love the earthly as an image; those that have not attained to this memory do not understand what is happening within them, and take the image for the reality. Once there is perfect self-control, it is no fault to enjoy the beauty of earth; where appreciation degenerates into carnality, there is sin.

Pure Love seeks the beauty alone, whether there is Reminiscence or not; but there are those that feel, also, a desire of such immortality as lies within mortal reach; and these are seeking Beauty in their demand for perpetuity, the desire of the eternal; Nature teaches them to sow the seed and to beget in beauty, to sow towards eternity, but in beauty through their own kinship with the beautiful. And indeed the eternal is of the one stock with the beautiful, the Eternal-Nature is the first shaping of beauty and makes beautiful all that rises from it.

The less the desire for procreation, the greater is the contentment with beauty alone, yet procreation aims at the engendering of beauty; it is the expression of a lack; the subject is conscious of insufficiency and, wishing to produce beauty, feels that the way is to beget in a beautiful form. Where the procreative desire is lawless or against the purposes of nature, the first inspiration has been natural, but they have diverged from the way, they have slipped and fallen, and they grovel; they neither understand whither Love sought to lead them nor have they any instinct to production; they have not mastered the right use of the images of beauty; they do not know what the Authentic Beauty is.

Those that love beauty of person without carnal desire love for beauty's sake; those that have—for women, of course—the copulative love, have the further purpose of self-perpetuation: as long as they are led by these motives, both are on the right path, though the first have taken the nobler way. But, even in the right, there is the difference that the one set, worshipping the beauty of earth, look no further, while the others, those of recollection, venerate also the beauty of the other world while they, still, have no contempt for this in which they recognize, as it were, a last outgrowth, an attenuation of the higher. These, in sum, are innocent frequenters of beauty, not to be confused with the class to whom it becomes an occasion of fall into the ugly—for the aspiration towards a good degenerates into an evil often.

So much for love, the state.

Now we have to consider Love, the God.

2. The existence of such a being is no demand of the ordinary man, merely; it is supported by Theologians (Orphic teachers) and, over and over again, by Plato to whom Eros is child of Aphrodite, minister of beautiful children, inciter of human souls towards the supernal beauty or quickener of an already existing impulse thither. All this requires philosophical examination. A cardinal passage is that in the Symposium where we are told Eros was not a child of Aphrodite but born on the day of Aphrodite's birth, Penia, Poverty, being the mother, and Poros, Possession, the father.

The matter seems to demand some discussion of Aphrodite since in any case Eros is described as being either her son or in some association with her. Who then is Aphrodite, and in what sense is Love either her child or born with her or in some way both her child and her birth-fellow?

To us Aphrodite is twofold; there is the heavenly Aphrodite, daughter of Ouranos or Heaven: and there is the other the daughter of Zeus and Dione, this is the Aphrodite who presides over earthly unions; the higher was not born of a mother and has no part in marriages, for in Heaven there is no marrying.

The Heavenly Aphrodite, daughter of Kronos—who is no other than the Intellectual Principle—must be the Soul at it divinest: unmingled as the immediate emanation of the unmingled; remaining ever Above, as neither desirous nor capable of descending to this sphere, never having developed the downward tendency, a divine Hypostasis essentially aloof, so unreservedly an Authentic Being as to have no part with Matter—and therefore mythically 'the unmothered'—justly called not Celestial Spirit but God, as knowing no admixture, gathered cleanly within itself.

Any nature springing directly from the Intellectual Principle must be itself also a clean thing: it will derive a resistance of its own from its nearness to the Highest, for all its tendency, no less than its fixity, centres upon its author whose power is certainly sufficient to maintain it Above.

Soul then could never fall from its sphere; it is closer held to the divine Mind than the very sun could hold the light it gives forth to radiate about it, an outpouring from itself held firmly to it, still.

But following upon Kronos—or, if you will, upon Heaven (Ouranos), the father of Kronos—the Soul directs its Act towards him and holds closely to him and in that love brings forth the Eros through whom it continues to look towards him. This Act of the Soul has produced an Hypostasis, a Real-Being; and the mother and this Hypostasis—her offspring, noble Love—gaze together upon Divine Mind. Love, thus, is ever intent upon that other loveliness, and exists to be the medium between desire and that object of desire. It is the eye of the desirer; by its power what loves is enabled to see the loved thing. But it is first;

before it becomes the vehicle of vision, it is itself filled with the sight; it is first, therefore, and not even in the same order—for desire attains to vision only through the efficacy of Love, while Love, in its own Act, harvests the spectacle of beauty playing immediately above it.

3. That Love is a Hypostasis (a 'Person'), a Real-Being sprung from a Real-Being—lower than the parent but authentically existent—is beyond doubt.

For the parent-Soul was a Real-Being sprung directly I from the Act (of the Hypostasis) that ranks before it and from the Real-Being of all that authentically is; and it looks, rapt, towards the Principle which is Primary Being (the Intellectual Principle).[1] That was the first object I of its vision; it looked towards it as towards its good, and it rejoiced in the looking; and the quality of what it saw was such that the contemplation was the overmastering preoccupation of the seer; in virtue of that rapture, of its position in regard to its object, of the intensity of its gaze, the Soul conceived and brought forth an offspring worthy of itself and of the vision. Thus; there is a strenuous activity of contemplation in the Soul; there is an emanation towards it from the object contemplated; and Eros is born, the Love which is an eye filled with its vision, a seeing that bears its image with it; Eros taking its name, probably, from the fact that its essential being is due to this *horasis*, this seeing. Of course Love, as an emotion, will take its name from Love, the Person, since a Real-Being cannot but be prior to what lacks this reality. The mental state will be designated as Love, like the Hypostasis, though it is no more than a particular act directed towards a particular object; but it must not be confused with the Absolute Love, the Divine Being. The Eros that belongs to the supernal Soul must be of one temper with it; it must itself look aloft as being of the household of that Soul, dependent upon that Soul, its very offspring; and therefore caring for nothing but the contemplation of the Gods.

Once that Soul which is the primal source of light to the heavens is recognized as an Hypostasis standing distinct and aloof, it must be admitted that Love too is distinct I and aloof. To describe the Soul as 'celestial' is not to question its separateness (or immateriality); our[2] own best I we conceive as inside ourselves and yet something apart. So, we must think of this Love—as essentially resident where the unmingling Soul inhabits.

But besides this purest Soul, there must be also a Soul of the All: at once there is another Love—the eye with which this second Soul looks upwards—like the supernal Eros engendered by force of desire. This Aphrodite, the secondary Soul, is of this Universe—not Soul unmingled alone, not Soul the Absolute—giving birth, therefore, to the Love concerned with the universal life; no, this is the Love presiding over marriages; but it, also, has its touch of the upward desire; and, in the degree of that striving, it stirs and leads upwards the souls of the young and every soul with which it is incorporated in so far as there is a natural tendency to remembrance of the divine. For every soul is striving towards The Good, even the mingling Soul and that of particular beings, for each holds directly from the divine Soul, and is its offspring.

4. Does each individual Soul, then, contain within itself such a Love in essence and substantial reality?

Since not only the pure All-Soul but also that of the Universe contains such a Love, it would be difficult to explain why our personal Soul should not. It must be so, even, with all that has life.

This indwelling love is no other than the Spirit which, as we are told, walks with every being, the affection dominant in each several nature. It implants the characteristic desire; the particular Soul, strained towards its own natural objects, brings forth its own Eros, the guiding spirit realizing its worth and the quality of its Being.

As the All-Soul contains the Universal Love, so must the single Soul be allowed its own single Love: and as closely as the single Soul holds to the All-Soul, never cut off but embraced within it, the two together constituting one principle of life, so the single separate Love holds to the All-Love. Similarly, the individual Love keeps with the individual Soul as that other, the great Love, goes with the All-Soul; and the Love within the All permeates it throughout so that the one Love becomes many, showing itself where it chooses at any moment of the Universe, taking definite shape in these its partial phases and revealing itself at its will.

In the same way we must conceive many Aphrodites in the All, Spirits entering it together with Love, all emanating from an Aphrodite of the All, a train of particular Aphrodites dependent upon the first, and each with the particular Love in attendance: this multiplicity cannot be denied, if Soul be the mother of Love, and Aphrodite mean Soul, and Love be an act of a Soul seeking good.

This Love, then, leader of particular souls to The Good, is twofold: the Love in the loftier Soul would be a god ever linking the Soul to the divine; the Love in the mingling Soul will be a celestial spirit.

5. But what is the nature of this Spirit—of the Celestials (Daimones) in general?

The Spirit-Kind is treated in the Symposium where, with much about the others, we learn of Eros—Love—born to Penia—Poverty—and Poros—Possession—who is son of Metis—Resource—at Aphrodite's birth feast.

But (the passage has been misunderstood for) to take Plato as meaning, by

Eros, this Universe—and not simply the Love native within it—involves much that is self-contradictory.

For one thing, the universe is described as a blissful god and as self-sufficing,while this 'Love' is confessedly neither divine nor self-sufficing but in ceaseless need.

Again, this Cosmos is a compound of body and soul; but Aphrodite to Plato is the world-soul itself, therefore Aphrodite would necessarily be a constituent part of Eros, (not mother but) dominant member! A man is the man's Soul; if the world is, similarly, the world's Soul, then Aphrodite, the Soul, is identical with Love, the Cosmos! And why should this one spirit, Love, be the Universe to the exclusion of all the others, which certainly are sprung from the same Essential-Being? Our only escape would be to make the Cosmos a complex of Celestials.

Love, again, is called the Dispenser of beautiful children: does this apply to the Universe? Love is represented as homeless, bedless, and bare-footed: would not that be a shabby description of the Cosmos and quite out of the truth?

6. What then, in sum, is to be thought of Love and of his 'birth' as we are told of it?

Clearly we have to establish the significance, here, of Poverty and Possession, and show in what way the parentage is appropriate: we have also to bring these two into line with the other Celestials, since one spirit nature, one spirit essence, must characterize all unless they are to have merely a name in common.

We must, therefore, lay down the grounds on which we distinguish the Gods from the Celestials—that is, when we emphasize the separate nature of the two orders and are not, as often in practice, including these Spirits under the common name of Gods.

It is our teaching and conviction that the Gods are immune to all passion, while we attribute experience and emotion to the Celestials which, though eternal Beings and directly next to the Gods, are already a step towards ourselves and stand between the divine and the human.

But by what process (of degeneration) was the immunity lost? What in their nature led them downwards to the inferior?

And other questions present themselves.

Does the Intellectual Realm include no member of this spirit order, not even one? And does the Cosmos contain only these spirits, God being confined to the Intellectual? Or are there Gods in the sub-celestial too, the Cosmos itself being a God, the third, as is commonly said, and the Powers down to the Moon being all Gods as well?

It is best not to use the word 'Celestial' of any Being of that Realm; the word

'God' may be applied to the Essential-Celestial—the auto-daimon, if he exists—and even to the Visible Powers of the Universe of Sense down to the Moon; Gods, these too, visible, secondary, sequent upon the Gods of the Intellectual Realm, consonant with Them, held about Them, as the radiance about the star.

What, then, are these spirits?

A Celestial is the representative generated by each Soul when it enters the Cosmos.

And why, by a Soul entering the Cosmos?

Because Soul pure of the Cosmos generates not a Celestial Spirit but a God; hence it is that we have spoken of Love, offspring of Aphrodite the Pure Soul, as a God.

But, first, what prevents every one of the Celestials from being an Eros, a Love? And why are they not untouched by Matter like the Gods?

On the first question: every Celestial born in the striving of the Soul towards the good and beautiful is an Eros; and all the souls within the Cosmos do engender this Celestial; but other Spirit-Beings, equally born from the Soul of the All, but by other faculties of that Soul, have other functions: they are for the direct service of the All, and administer particular things to the purpose of the Universe entire. The Soul of the All must be adequate to all that is and therefore must bring into being spirit powers serviceable not merely in one function but to its entire charge.

But what participation can the Celestials have in Matter, and in what Matter?

Certainly none in bodily Matter; that would make them simply living things of the order of sense. And if, even, they are to invest themselves in bodies of air or of fire, their nature must have already been altered before they could have any contact with the corporeal. The Pure does not mix, unmediated, with body—though many think that the Celestial-Kind, of its very essence, comports a body aerial or of fire.

But (since this is not so) why should one order of Celestial descend to body and another not? The difference implies the existence of some cause or medium working upon such as thus descend. What would constitute such a medium?

We are forced to assume that there is a Matter of the Intellectual Order, and that Beings partaking of it are thereby enabled to enter into the lower Matter, the corporeal.

7. This is the significance of Plato's account of the birth of Love.

The drunkenness of the father Poros or Possession is caused by Nectar, 'wine yet not existing'; Love is born before the realm of sense has come into being: Penia (Poverty) had participation in the Intellectual before the lower image of that divine Realm had appeared; she dwelt in that Sphere, but as a mingled being consisting partly of Form but partly also of that indetermination which belongs to the Soul before she attains the Good and when all her knowledge of Reality is a fore-intimation veiled by the indeterminate and unordered: in this state (of fore-feeling and desiring The Good) Poverty brings forth the Hypostasis, Love.

This, then, is a union of Reason with something that is not Reason but a mere indeterminate striving in a being not yet illuminated: the offspring Love, therefore, is not perfect, not self-sufficient, but unfinished, bearing the signs of its parentage, the undirected striving and the self-sufficient Reason. This offspring is a Reason-Principle but not purely so; for it includes within itself an aspiration ill-defined, unreasoned, unlimited—it can never be sated as long as it contains within itself that element of the Indeterminate. Love, then, clings to the Soul, from which it sprang as from the principle of its Being, but it is lessened by including an element of the Reason-Principle which did not remain self-concentrated but blended with the indeterminate, not, it is true, by immediate contact but through its emanation. Love, therefore, is like a goad; it is without resource in itself; even winning its end, it is poor again.

It cannot be satisfied because a thing of mixture never can be so: true satisfaction is only for what has its plenitude in its own being; where craving is due to an inborn deficiency, there may be satisfaction at some given moment but it does not last. Love, then, has on the one side the powerlessness of its native inadequacy, on the other the resource inherited from the Reason-Kind.

Such must be the nature and such the origin of the entire Spirit Order: each—like its fellow, Love—has its appointed sphere, is powerful there, and wholly devoted to it, and, like Love, none is ever complete of itself but always straining towards some good which it sees in things of the partial sphere.

❙ We understand, now, why good men have no other Love than that for the Absolute and Authentic Good, and never follow the random attraction.

To be ranged under other Spirits is to be directed to one or other among them: such men abandon the Love (of the Good) which they possessed without exercising it[3] and live by some other spirit ❙ adopted by them as more closely attuned to the operative part of the Soul in them. Those that go after evil are natures that have merged all the Love-Principles within them in the evil desires springing in their hearts and allowed the right reason, which belongs to our kind, to fall under the spell of false ideas from another source.

All the natural Loves, all that serve the ends of Nature, are good; in a lesser Soul, inferior in rank and in scope; in the greater Soul, superior; but all belong to the order of Being. Those forms of Love that do not serve the purposes of Nature are merely accidents attending on perversion: in no sense are they Real-Beings or even manifestations of any Reality; for they are no true issue of Soul;

they are merely accompaniments of a spiritual flaw which the Soul auto-matically exhibits in the total of disposition and conduct.

In a word; all that is truly good in a Soul acting to the purposes of nature and within its appointed order, all this is Real-Being: anything else is alien, no act of the Soul, but merely something that happens to it: a parallel may be found in false mentation, notions behind which there is no reality as there is in the case of authentic ideas, the eternal, the strictly defined, in which there is at once an act of true knowing, a truly knowable object and authentic existence—and this not merely in the Absolute, but also in the particular being that is occupied by the authentically knowable and by the Intellectual-Principle manifest in every several form. In each particular human being we must admit the existence of the authentic Intellective Act and of the authentically knowable object—though not as wholly merged into our being, since we are not these in the absolute I and not exclusively these.

It follows that Love, like our intellectual activities, is concerned with abso-lute things:[4] if we sometimes care I for the partial, that affection is not direct but accidental, like our knowledge that a given triangular figure is made up of two right angles because the absolute triangle is so.

8. But what are we to understand by this Zeus with the garden into which, we are told, Poros or Wealth entered? And what is the garden?

We have seen that the Aphrodite of the Myth is the Soul and that Poros, Wealth, is the Reason-Principle of the Universe: we have still to explain Zeus and his garden.

We cannot take Zeus to be the Soul, which we have agreed is represented by Aphrodite.

Plato, who must be our guide in this question, speaks in the Phaedrus of this God, Zeus, as the Great Leader—though elsewhere he seems to rank him as one of three—but in the Philebus he speaks more plainly when he says that there is in Zeus not only a royal Soul, but also a royal Intellect.

As a mighty Intellect and Soul, he must be a principle of Cause; he must be the highest for several reasons but especially because to be King and Leader is to be the chief cause: Zeus then is the Intellectual Principle. Aphrodite, his daughter, issue of him, dwelling with him, will be Soul, her very name Aphro-dite (= the *habra*, delicate) indicating the beauty and gleam and innocence and delicate grace of the Soul.

And if we take the male gods to represent the Intellectual Powers and the female gods to be their souls—to every Intellectual Principle its companion Soul—we are forced, thus also, to make Aphrodite the Soul of Zeus; and the identification is confirmed by Priests and Theologians who consider Aphrodite and Hera one and the same and call Aphrodite's star ('Venus') the star of Hera.

9. This Poros, Possession, then, is the Reason-Principle of all that exists in the Intellectual Realm and in the supreme Intellect; but being more diffused, kneaded out as it were, it must touch Soul, be in Soul (as the next lower principle).

For, all that lies gathered in the Intellect is native to it: nothing enters from without; but 'Poros intoxicated' is some Power deriving satisfaction outside itself: what, then, can we understand by this member of the Supreme filled with Nectar but a Reason-Principle falling from a loftier essence to a lower? This means that the Reason-Principle upon 'the birth of Aphrodite' left the Intellectual for the Soul, breaking into the garden of Zeus.

A garden is a place of beauty and a glory of wealth: all the loveliness that Zeus maintains takes its splendour from the Reason-Principle within him; for all this beauty is the radiation of the Divine Intellect upon the Divine Soul, which it has penetrated. What could the Garden of Zeus indicate but the images of his Being and the splendours of his glory? And what could these divine splendours and beauties be but the Reason-Principles streaming from him?

These Reason-Principles—this Poros who is the lavishness, the abundance of Beauty—are at one and are made manifest; this is the Nectar-drunkenness. For the Nectar of the gods can be no other than what the god-nature receives from outside itself, and that whose place is after the divine Mind (namely, Soul) receives a Reason-Principle.

The Intellectual Principle possesses itself to satiety, but there is no 'drunken' abandonment in this possession which brings nothing alien to it. But the Reason-Principle—as its offspring, a later hypostasis—is already a separate Being and established in another Realm, and so is said to lie in the garden of this Zeus who is divine Mind; and this lying in the garden takes place at the moment when, in our way of speaking, Aphrodite enters the realm of Being.

'Our way of speaking'—for myths, if they are to serve their purpose, must necessarily import time-distinctions into their subject and will often present as separate, Powers which exist in unity but differ in rank and faculty; and does not philosophy itself relate the births of the unbegotten and discriminate where all is one substance? The truth is conveyed in the only manner possible; it is left to our good sense to bring all together again.

On this principle we have, here, Soul (successively) dwelling with the divine Intelligence, breaking away from it, and yet again being filled to satiety with Reason-Principles—the beautiful abounding in all plenty, so that every

splendour become manifest in it with the images of whatever is lovely—
Soul which, taken as one all, is Aphrodite, while in it may be distinguished the
Reason-Principles summed under the names of Plenty and Possession, produced by the downflow of the Nectar of the over realm. The splendours
contained in Soul are thought of as the garden of Zeus with reference to their
existing within Life; and Poros sleeps in this garden in the sense of being sated
and heavy with its produce. Life is eternally manifest, an eternal existent among
the existences, and the banqueting of the gods means no more than that they
have their Being in that vital blessedness. And Love—'born at the banquet of
the gods'—has of necessity been eternally in existence, for it springs from the
intention of the Soul towards its Best, towards the Good; as long as Soul has
been, Love has been.

Still this Love is of mixed quality. On the one hand there is in it the lack which
keeps it craving: on the other, it is not entirely destitute; the deficient seeks more
of what it has, and certainly nothing absolutely void of good would ever go
seeking the Good.

It is said then to spring from Poverty and Possession in the sense that Lack and
Aspiration and the Memory of the Reason-Principles, all present together in the
Soul, produce that Act towards The Good which is Love. Its Mother is Poverty,
since striving is for the needy; and this Poverty is Matter, for Matter is the wholly
poor: the very ambition towards the Good is a sign of existing indetermination;
there is a lack of shape and of Reason in that which must aspire towards the
Good, I and the greater degree of indetermination implies the lower depth of
materiality. To the thing aspiring the Good is an Ideal-Principle distinct and
unchanging, and aspiration prepares that which would receive the Good to
offer itself as Matter to the incoming power.

Thus Love is, at once, in some degree a thing of Matter and at the same time
a Celestial sprung of the Soul's unsatisfied longing for The Good.[5] I

NOTES TO ENNEAD III.5

1. FIRST EDITION: ". . . from the Act of the Hypostasis that ranks before it: *it had life; it was a constituent in* the Real-Being of all that authentically is—*in the Real-Being which* looks, rapt, towards the *very Highest*. That was the first object . . ."

ARMSTRONG: ". . . which came into being from the activity which existed before it, and from the substance of the world of real beings, which also looks towards that which was the first substance, and looks towards it with great intensity."

GUTHRIE: ". . . born of the activity which is superior to her (the primary Being), a living Being, emanating from the primary Being, and attached to the contemplation thereof."

2. FIRST EDITION: "... and aloof, *though not, perhaps, so loftily celestial a being as the Soul. Our own best* ..."

GUTHRIE handles the whole thought as: "Now as we consider the Soul which first radiates its light on heaven as separate from matter, we must admit that the love which is connected with her, is likewise separate from matter. If we say that this pure Soul really resides in heaven, it is in the sense in which we say that that which is most precious in us (the reasonable soul) resides in our body, and, nevertheless, is separate from matter. This love must, therefore, reside only there where resides this pure Soul."

ARMSTRONG: "But since we say that that higher soul which primarily illuminates heaven is separate, we shall also make this Love separate—however much we call this soul 'heavenly': for, though we say, too, that the best in us men is 'in' us, all the same we give it a separate existence."

3. FIRST EDITION: "We understand, now, why good men have no other Love—*no other Eros of life*—than that for the Absolute and Authentic Good, and never follow the random *attractions known to those ranged under the lower Spirit Kind.*
    "*Each human being is set under his own Spirit-Guides, but this is mere blank possession when they ignore their own* and live by some other spirit ..."

GUTHRIE and ARMSTRONG both support Page's change.

4. FIRST EDITION: "... and not exclusively these—*and hence our longing for* absolute things: *it is the expression of our intellective activities:* if we sometimes care ..."

ARMSTRONG: "... hence our love is of simple realities, for so are our thoughts;"

GUTHRIE: "... and hence comes our love for generalities. Our conceptions, indeed, usually trend toward the general."

5. FIRST EDITION: "... and the greater degree of *effort* implies the lower depth of materiality. A thing aspiring *towards* the Good is an Ideal-principle *only when the striving (with attainment) will leave it still unchanged in Kind: when it must take in something other than itself, its aspiration is the presentment of* Matter to the incoming power.
    "Thus Love is at once, in some degree a thing of Matter and at the same time a Celestial, sprung of the *Soul; for Love lacks its Good but, from its very birth, strives towards It.*"

GUTHRIE: "Even indetermination, which characterizes the desire of the good, makes the being which desires the Good play the part of matter—since such a being would have neither form nor reason, considered only from its desiring. It is a form only inasmuch as it remains within itself. As soon as it desires to attain a new perfection, it is matter relatively to the being from whom it desires to receive somewhat.
    "That is why Love is both a being which participates in matter, and is also a Guardian born of the soul; it is the former, inasmuch as it does not completely possess the good; it is the latter, inasmuch as it desires the Good from the very moment of its birth."

ARMSTRONG: "... because the indefiniteness of the desire for the good—for there is no shape or rational forming principle in that which desires it—makes the aspiring thing more like matter in so far as it aspires. But the good, in relation to that which aspires to it, is form only, remaining in itself; and that which aspires to receive it prepares its receptive capacity as matter for the form which is to come upon it. So Love is a material kind of being, and he is a spirit produced from soul in so far as soul falls short of the good but aspires to it."

SIXTH TRACTATE

The Impassivity of the Unembodied

1. In our theory, feelings are not states; they are action upon experience, action accompanied by judgement: the states, we hold, are seated elsewhere; they may be referred to the vitalized body; the judgement resides in the Soul, and is distinct from the state—for, if it is not distinct, another judgement is demanded, one that is distinct, and, so, we may be sent back for ever.

Still, this leaves it undecided whether in the act of judgement the judging faculty does or does not take to itself something of its object.

If (as is sometimes asserted) the judging faculty does actually receive an imprint, then it partakes of the state—though what are called the Impressions may be of quite another nature than is supposed; they may be like Thought, that is to say they may be acts rather than states; there may be, here too, awareness without participation.

For ourselves, it could never be in our system—or in our liking—to bring the Soul down to participation in such modes and modifications as the warmth and cold of material frames.

What is known as I the affective[1] faculty I of the Soul—*to pathêtikon*—would need to be identified: we must satisfy ourselves as to whether this too, like the Soul as a unity, is to be classed as immune or, on the contrary, as precisely the only part susceptible of being affected; this question, however, may be held over; we proceed to examine its preliminaries.

Even in the superior phase of the Soul—that which precedes I the affective[1] faculty I and any sensation—how can we reconcile immunity with the indwelling of vice, false notions, ignorance? Inviolability; and yet likings and dislikings, the Soul enjoying, grieving, angry, grudging, envying, desiring, never at peace but stirring and shifting with everything that confronts it!

If the Soul were material and had magnitude, it would be difficult, indeed quite impossible, to make it appear to be immune, unchangeable, when any of such emotions lodge in it. But let us consider it as an Authentic Being, devoid of magnitude and necessarily indestructible; we must be very careful then how we attribute any such experiences to it or we will find ourselves unconsciously making it subject to dissolution. If its essence is a Number or as we hold a Reason-Principle, under neither head could it be susceptible of feeling. We can think, only, that it entertains unreasoned reasons and experiences unexperienced, all transmuted from the material frames, foreign and recognized only by parallel, so that it possesses in a kind of non-possession and knows affection without being affected. How this can be demands inquiry.

2. Let us begin with virtue and vice in the Soul. What has really occurred when, as we say, vice is present? In speaking of extirpating evil and implanting goodness, of introducing order and beauty to replace a former ugliness, we talk in terms of real things in the Soul.

Now when we make virtue a harmony, and vice a breach of harmony, we accept an opinion approved by the ancients; and the theory helps us decidedly to our solution. For if virtue is simply a natural concordance among the phases of the Soul, and vice simply a discord, then there is no further question of any foreign presence; harmony would be the result of every distinct phase or faculty joining in, true to itself; discord would mean that not all chimed in at their best and truest. Consider, for example, the performers in a choral dance; they sing together though each one has his particular part, and sometimes one voice is heard while the others are silent; and each brings to the chorus something of his own; it is not enough that all lift their voices together; each must sing, choicely, his own part to the music set for him. Exactly so in the case of the Soul; there will be harmony when each faculty performs its appropriate part.

Yes: but this very harmony constituting the virtue of the Soul must depend upon a previous virtue, that of each several faculty within itself; and before there can be the vice of discord there must be the vice of the single parts, and these can be bad only by the actual presence of vice as they can be good only by the presence of virtue. It is true that no presence is affirmed when vice is identified with ignorance in the reasoning faculty of the Soul; ignorance is not a positive thing; but in the presence of false judgements—the main cause of vice—must it not be admitted that something positive has entered into the Soul, something perverting the reasoning faculty? So, the initiative faculty; is it not, itself, altered as one varies between timidity and boldness? And the desiring faculty, similarly, as it runs wild or accepts control?

Our teaching is that when the particular faculty is sound it performs the reasonable act of its essential nature, obeying the reasoning faculty in it which derives from the Intellectual Principle and communicates to the rest. And this following of reason is not the acceptance of an imposed shape; it is like using the eyes; the Soul sees by its act, that of looking towards reason. The faculty of sight in the performance of its act is essentially what it was when it lay latent; its act is not a change in it, but simply its entering into the relation that belongs to its essential character; it knows—that is, sees—without suffering any change: so, precisely, the reasoning phase of the Soul stands towards the Intellectual Principle; this it sees by its very essence; this vision is its knowing faculty; it takes in no stamp, no impression; all that enters it is the object of vision—possessed, once more, without possession; it possesses by the fact of knowing but 'without possession' in the sense that there is no incorporation of anything left behind by the object of vision, like the impression of the seal on sealing-wax.

And note that we do not appeal to stored-up impressions to account for memory: we think of the mind awakening its powers in such a way as to possess something not present to it.

Very good: but is it not different before and after acquiring the memory?

Be it so; but it has suffered no change—unless we are to think of the mere progress from latency to actuality as change—nothing has been introduced into the mind; it has simply achieved the Act dictated by its nature.

It is universally true that the characteristic Act of immaterial entities is performed without any change in them—otherwise they would at last be worn away—theirs is the Act of the unmoving; where act means suffering change, there is Matter: an immaterial Being would have no ground of permanence if its very Act changed it.

Thus in the case of Sight, the seeing faculty is in act but the material organ alone suffers change: judgements (true or false, are not changes within the Soul; they) are similar to visual experiences.

But how explain the alternation of timidity and daring in the initiative faculty?

Timidity would come by the failure to look towards the Reason-Principle[1] or by finding it corrupted[2] or I by some defect in the organs of action—some lack or flaw in the bodily equipment—or by outside prevention of the natural act or by the mere absence of adequate stimulus: boldness would arise from the reverse conditions: neither implies any change, or even any experience, in the Soul.

So with the faculty of desire: what we call loose living is caused by its acting unaccompanied; it has done all of itself; the other faculties, whose business it is to make their presence felt in control and to point the right way, have lain I in abeyance: it could have looked away from itself, no longer acting alone; it could have found leisure to contemplate those other faculties so far as was in its power.[3]I

Often, moreover, the vice of the desiring faculty will be merely some ill condition of the body, and its virtue, bodily soundness; thus there would again be no question of anything imported into the Soul.

3. But how do we explain likings and aversions? Sorrow, too, and anger and pleasure, desire and fear—are these not changes, affectings, present and stirring within the Soul?

This question cannot be ignored. To deny that changes take place and are intensely felt is in sharp contradiction to obvious facts. But, while we recognize this, we must make very sure what it is that changes. To represent the Soul or Mind as being the seat of these emotions is not far removed from making it blush or turn pale; it is to forget that while the Soul or Mind is the means, the effect takes place in the distinct organism, the animated body.

At the idea of disgrace, the shame is in the Soul; but the body is occupied by the Soul—not to trouble about words—is, at any rate, close to it and very different from soulless matter; and so, is affected in the blood, mobile in its nature. Fear begins in the mind; the pallor is simply the withdrawal of the blood inwards. So in pleasure, I the elation is in the body and makes itself felt; the purely mental phase entails no modification:[4] I the same is true of pain. So desire is ignored in the Soul where the impulse takes its rise; what comes outward thence, the sensibility knows.

When we speak of the Soul or Mind being moved—as in desire, reasoning, judging—we do not mean that it is driven into its act; these movements are its own acts.

In the same way when we call Life a movement we have no idea of a changing substance; the naturally appropriate act of each member of the living thing makes up the Life, which is, therefore, not a shifting thing.

To bring the matter to the point: put it that act, life, tendency, are no changements; that memories are not forms stamped upon the mind, that notions are not of the nature of impressions on sealing-wax; we thence draw the general conclusion that in all such states and movements the Soul, or Mind, is unchanged in substance and in essence, that virtue and vice are not something imported into the Soul—as heat and cold, blackness or whiteness are importations into body—but that, in all this relation, matter and spirit are exactly and comprehensively contraries.

4. We have, however, still to examine what is called the affective phase of the Soul. This has, no doubt, been touched upon above where we dealt with the nature of the various passions as grouped about the initiative phase of the Soul and the desiring faculty: but more is required; we must begin by forming a clear idea of what is meant by this affective faculty of the Soul.

In general terms it means the centre about which we recognize the affections to be grouped; and by affections we mean those states upon which follow pleasure and pain.

Now among these affections we must distinguish. Some are pivoted upon judgements; thus, a Man judging his death to be at hand may feel fear; foreseeing some fortunate turn of events, he is happy: the opinion lies in one sphere; the affection is stirred in another. Sometimes the affections take the lead and automatically bring in the notion which thus becomes present to the appropriate faculty: but as we have explained, an act of opinion does not introduce any change into the Soul or Mind: what happens is that from the notion of some impending evil is produced the quite separate thing, fear, and this fear, in turn, becomes known in that part of the Mind which is said under such circumstances to harbour fear.

But what is the action of this fear upon the Mind?

The general answer is that it sets up trouble and confusion before an evil anticipated. It should, however, be quite clear that the Soul or Mind is the seat of all imaginative representation—both the higher representation known as opinion or judgement and the lower representation which is not so much a judgement as a vague notion unattended by discrimination, something resembling the action by which, as is believed, the 'Nature' of common speech produces, unconsciously, the objects of the partial sphere. It is equally certain that in all that follows upon the mental act or state, the disturbance, confined to the body, belongs to the sense-order; trembling, pallor, inability to speak, have obviously nothing to do with the spiritual portion of the being. The Soul, in fact, would have to be described as corporeal if it were the seat of such symptoms: besides, in that case the trouble would not even reach the body since the only transmitting principle, oppressed by sensation, jarred out of itself, would be inhibited.

None the less, there is an affective phase of the Soul or Mind and this is not corporeal; it can be, only, some kind of Ideal-form.

Now Matter is the one field of the desiring faculty, as of the principles of nutrition, growth, and engendering, which are root and spring to desire and to every other affection known to this Ideal-form. No Ideal-form can be the victim of disturbance or be in any way affected: it remains in tranquillity; only the Matter associated with it can be affected by any state or experience induced by the movement which its mere presence suffices to set up. Thus the vegetal principle induces vegetal life but it does not, itself, pass through the processes of vegetation; it gives growth but it does not grow; in no movement which it originates is it moved with the motion it induces; it is in perfect repose, or, at least, its movement, really its act, is utterly different from what it causes elsewhere.

The nature of an Ideal-form is to be, of itself, an activity; it operates by its mere presence: it is as if Melody itself plucked the strings. The affective phase of the Soul or Mind will be the operative cause of all affection; it originates the movement either under the stimulus of some sense-presentment or independently—and it is a question to be examined whether the judgement leading to the movement operates from above or not—but the affective phase itself remains unmoved like Melody dictating music. The causes originating the movement may be likened to the musician; what is moved is like the strings of his instrument, and, once more, the Melodic Principle itself is not affected, but only the strings, though, however much the musician desired it, he could not pluck the strings except under dictation from the principle of Melody.

5. But why have we to call in Philosophy to make the Soul immune if it is thus (like the Melodic Principle of our illustration) immune from the beginning?

Because representations attack it at what we call the affective phase and cause a resulting experience, a disturbance, to which disturbance is joined the image of threatened evil: this amounts to an affection and Reason seeks to extinguish it, to ban it as destructive to the well-being of the Soul which by the mere absence of such a condition is immune, the one possible cause of affection—the representation in the Soul—not being present.

Take it that some such affections have engendered appearances presented before the Soul or Mind from without but taken (for practical purposes) to be actual experiences within it—then Philosophy's task is like that of a man who wishes to throw off the shapes presented in dreams, and to this end recalls to waking condition the mind that is breeding them.

But what can be meant by the purification of a Soul that has never been stained and by the separation of the Soul from a body to which it is essentially a stranger?

The purification of the Soul is simply to allow it to be alone; it is pure when it keeps no company; when it looks to nothing without itself; when it entertains no alien thoughts—be the mode or origin of such notions or affections what they may, a subject on which we have already touched—when it no longer sees in the world of image, much less elaborates images into veritable affections. Is it not a true purification to turn away towards the exact contrary of earthly things?

Separation, in the same way, is the condition of a soul no longer entering into the body to lie at its mercy; it is to stand as a light, set in the midst of trouble but unperturbed through all.

In the particular case of the affective phase of the Soul, purification is its awakening from the baseless visions which beset it, the refusal to see them; its separation consists in limiting its descent towards the lower and accepting no picture thence, ▎ and of course in the banning of all that it ignores when the pneuma (finer-body or spirit) on which it is poised is not turbid from gluttony and surfeit of impure flesh, but is a vehicle so slender that the Soul may ride upon it in tranquillity.[5] ▎

6. That the Intellectual Essence, wholly of the order of Ideal-form, must be taken as impassive has been already established.

But Matter also is an incorporeal, though after a mode of its own; we must examine, therefore, how this stands, whether it is passive, as is commonly held, a thing that can be twisted to every shape and kind, or whether it too must be considered impassive and in what sense and fashion so. But in engaging this question and defining the nature of matter we must correct certain prevailing errors about the nature of the Authentic Existent, about Essence, about Being.

The Existent—rightly so called—is that which has authentic existence, that, therefore, which is existent completely, and therefore again, that which at no point fails in existence. Having existence perfectly, it needs nothing to preserve it in being; it is, on the contrary, the source and cause from which all that appears to exist derives that appearance. This admitted, it must of necessity be in life, in a perfect life: if it failed it would be as much the non-existent as the existent. But: the Being thus indicated is Intellect, is wisdom unalloyed. It is, therefore, determined and I rounded off. In power all-embracing, no measure can place it[6] in default. I

Hence its eternity, its identity, its utter irreceptivity and impermeability. If it took in anything, it must be taking in something outside itself, that is to say, Existence would at last include non-existence. But it must be Authentic Existence all through; it must, therefore, present itself equipped from its own stores with all that makes up Existence so that all stands together and all is one thing. The Existent (Real Being) must have thus much of determination: if it had not, then it could not be the source of the Intellectual Principle and of Life which would be importations into it originating in the sphere of non-Being; and Real Being would be lifeless and mindless; but mindlessness and lifelessness are the characteristics of non-being and must belong to the lower order, to the outer borders of the existent; for Intellect and Life rise from the Beyond-Existence (the Indefinable Supreme)—though Itself has no need of them—and are conveyed from It into the Authentic Existent.

If we have thus rightly described the Authentic Existent, we see that it cannot be any kind of body nor the under-stuff of body: in such entities the Being is simply the existing of things outside of Being.

But body, a non-existence? Matter, on which all this universe rises, a non-existence? Mountain and rock, the wide solid earth, all that resists, all that can be struck and driven, surely all proclaims the real existence of the corporeal? And how, it will be asked, can we, on the contrary, attribute Being, and the only Authentic Being, to entities like Soul and Intellect, things having no weight or pressure, yielding to no force, offering no resistance, things not even visible?

Yet even the corporeal realm witnesses for us; the resting earth has certainly a scantier share in Being than belongs to what has more motion and less solidity—and less than belongs to its own most upward element, for fire begins, already, to flit up and away outside of the body-kind.

In fact, it appears to be precisely the most self-sufficing that bear least hardly, least painfully, on other things, while the heaviest and earthiest bodies—deficient, falling, unable to bear themselves upward—these, by the very down-thrust due to their feebleness, offer the resistance which belongs to the falling habit and to the lack of buoyancy. It is lifeless objects that deal the severest blows; they hit hardest and hurt most; where there is life—that is to say participation in Being—there is beneficence towards the environment, all the greater as the measure of Being is fuller.

Again, Movement, which is a sort of life within bodies, an imitation of true Life, is the more decided where there is the least of body—a sign that the waning of Being makes the object affected more distinctly corporeal.

The changes known as affections show even more clearly that where the bodily quality is most pronounced, susceptibility is at its intensest—earth more susceptible than other elements, and these others again more or less so in the degree of their corporeality: sever the other elements and, failing some preventive force, they join again; but earthy matter divided remains apart indefinitely. Things whose nature represents a diminishment have no power of recuperation after even a slight disturbance and they perish; thus what has most definitely become body, having most closely approximated to non-being, lacks the strength to reknit its unity: the heavy and violent crash of body against body works destruction, and weak is powerful against weak, non-being against its like.

Thus far we have been meeting those who, on the evidence of thrust and resistance, identify body with real being and find assurance of truth in the phantasms that reach us through the senses, those, in a word, who, like dreamers, take for actualities the figments of their sleeping vision. The sphere of sense, the Soul in its slumber; for all of the Soul that is in body is asleep and the true getting-up is not bodily but from the body: in any movement that takes the body with it there is no more than a passage from sleep to sleep, from bed to bed; the veritable waking or rising is from corporeal things; for these, belonging to the Kind directly opposed to Soul, present to it what is directly opposed to its essential existence: their origin, their flux, and their perishing are the warning of their exclusion from the Kind whose Being is Authentic.

7. We are thus brought back to the nature of that underlying matter and the things believed to be based upon it; investigation will show us that Matter has no reality and is not capable of being affected.

Matter must be bodiless—for body is a later production, a compound made by Matter in conjunction with some other entity. Thus it is included among incorporeal things in the sense that body is something that is neither Real-Being nor Matter.

Matter is not Soul; it is not Intellect, is not Life, is no Ideal-Principle, no Reason-Principle; it is no limit or bound, for it is mere indetermination; it is not a power, for what does it produce?

It lives on the farther side of all these categories and so has no title to the name of Being. It will be more plausibly called a non-being, **|** and this not in the sense that movement and station are Not-Being (i.e., as merely different from Being) but in the sense[7] of veritable Not-Being, **|** so that it is no more than the image and phantasm of Mass, a bare aspiration towards substantial existence; it is stationary but not in the sense of having position, it is in itself invisible, eluding all effort to observe it, present where no one can look, unseen for all our gazing, ceaselessly presenting contraries in the things based upon it, it is large and small, more and less, deficient and excessive; a phantasm unabiding and yet unable to withdraw—not even strong enough to withdraw, so utterly has it failed to accept strength from the Intellectual Principle, so absolute its lack of all Being.

Its every utterance, therefore, is a lie; it pretends to be great and it is little, to be more and it is less; and the Existence with which it masks itself is no Existence, but a passing trick making trickery of all that seems to be present in it, phantasms within a phantasm; it is like a mirror showing things as in itself when they are really elsewhere, filled in appearance but actually empty, containing nothing, pretending everything. Into it and out of it move mimicries of the Authentic Existents, images playing upon an image devoid of Form, visible against it by its very formlessness; they seem to modify it but in reality effect nothing, for they are ghostly and feeble, have no thrust and meet none in Matter either; they pass through it leaving no cleavage, as through water; or they might be compared to shapes projected so as to make some appearance upon what we can know only as the Void.

Further: if visible objects were of the rank of the originals from which they have entered into Matter we might believe Matter to be really affected by them, for we might credit them with some share of the power inherent in their senders: but the objects of our experiences are of very different virtue than the realities they represent, and we deduce that the seeming modification of matter by visible things is unreal since the visible thing itself is unreal, having at no point any similarity with its source and cause. Feeble in itself, a false thing and projected upon a falsity, like an image in dream or against water or on a mirror, it can but leave Matter unaffected; and even this is saying too little, for water and mirror do give back a faithful image of what presents itself before them.

8. It is a general principle that, to be modified, an object must be opposed in faculty and in quality to the forces that enter and act upon it.

Thus where heat is present, the change comes by something that chills, where damp by some drying agency: we say a subject is modified when from warm it becomes cold, from dry wet.

A further evidence is in our speaking of a fire being burned out, when it has passed over into another element; we do not say that the Matter has been burned out: in other words, modification affects what is subject to dissolution; the acceptance of modification is the path towards dissolution; susceptibility to modification and susceptibility to dissolution go necessarily together. But Matter can never be dissolved. What into? By what process?

Still: Matter harbours heat, cold, qualities beyond all count; by these it is differentiated; it holds them as if they were of its very substance and they blend within it—since no quality is found isolated to itself—Matter lies there as the meeting ground of all these qualities with their changes as they act and react in the blend: how, then, can it fail to be modified in keeping? The only escape would be to declare Matter utterly and for ever apart from the qualities it exhibits; but the very I notion of a substratum[8] implies I that any and every thing present in it has some action upon it.

9. In answer: it must, first, be noted that there are a variety of modes in which an object may be said to be present to another or to exist in another. There is a 'presence' which acts by changing the object—for good or for ill—as we see in the case of bodies, especially where there is life. But there is also a 'presence' which acts, towards good or ill, with no modification of the object, as we have indicated in the case of the Soul. Then there is the case represented by the stamping of a design upon wax, where the 'presence' of the added pattern causes no modification in the substance nor does its obliteration diminish it. And there is the example of Light whose presence does not even bring change of pattern to the object illuminated. A stone becoming cold does not change its nature in the process; it remains the stone it was. A line does not cease to be a line for being coloured; nor, we may take it, does a surface cease to be a surface; but might there not be a modification of I the underlying mass?[9] I No: it is impossible to think of I mass[9] I being modified by colour—for, of course, we must not talk of modification when there is no more than a presence, or at most a presenting of shape.

Mirrors and transparent objects, even more, offer a close parallel; they are quite unaffected by what is seen in or through them: material things are re-flections, and the Matter on which they appear is further from being affected than is a mirror. Heat and cold are present in Matter, but the Matter itself suffers no change of temperature: growing hot and growing cold have to do only with quality; a quality enters and brings the impassible Substance under a new state—though, by the way, research into nature may show that cold is nothing positive but an absence, a mere negation. The qualities come together into Matter, but only those which are contraries can act upon each other: what effect, for example, could fragrance have on sweetness or the colour-quality on the quality of form, any quality on another of some unrelated order? **I** Therefore, it is entirely reasonable to suppose that qualities can co-exist in a medium (or sub-stratum) without being affected by each other's presence or by the presence of the medium.[10] **I**

A thing can be hurt only by something related to it, and similarly things are not changed or modified by any chance presence: modification comes by contrary acting upon contrary; things merely different leave each other as they were. Such modification by a direct contrary can obviously not occur in an order of things to which there is no contrary: Matter, therefore (the mere absence of Reality), cannot be modified: any modification that takes place can occur only in some compound of Matter and reality, or, speaking generally, in some agglomeration of actual things. The Matter itself—isolated, quite apart from all else, utterly simplex—must remain immune, untouched in the midst of all the interacting agencies; just as when people fight within their four walls, the house and the air in it remain without part in the turmoil.

We may take it, then, that while the qualities that appear upon Matter group to produce each the effect belonging to its nature, yet Matter itself remains immune, even more definitely immune than any of those qualities entering into it which, not being contraries, are not affected by each other.

10. Further: if Matter were susceptible of modification, it must acquire some-thing by the incoming of the new state; it will either adopt that state, or, at least, it will be in some way different from what it was. Now upon this first incoming quality suppose a second to supervene; the recipient is no longer Matter but a modification of Matter: this second quality, perhaps, departs but it has acted and therefore leaves something of itself after it; the substratum is still further altered. This process proceeding, the substratum ends by becoming something quite different from Matter; it becomes a thing settled in many modes and many shapes; at once it is debarred from being the all-recipient; it will have closed the entry against many incomers. In other words, the Matter is no longer there: Matter is destructible.

No: if there is to be a Matter at all, it must be always identically as it has been from the beginning: to speak of Matter as changing is to speak of it as not being Matter.

Another consideration: it is a general principle that a thing changing must remain within its constitutive Ideal-Form so that the alteration is only in the accidents and not in the essential thing; the changing object must retain this fundamental permanence, and the permanent substance cannot be the member of it which accepts modification.

Therefore there are only two possibilities: the first, that Matter itself changes and so ceases to be itself, the second that it never ceases to be itself and therefore never changes.

We may be answered that it does not change in its character as Matter: but no one could tell us in what other character it changes; and we have the admission that the Matter in itself is not subject to change.

Just as the Ideal Principles stand immutably in their essence—which consists precisely in their permanence—so, since the essence of Matter consists in its being Matter (the substratum to all material things) it must be permanent in this character; because it is Matter, it is immutable. In the Intellectual realm we have the immutable Idea; here we have Matter, itself similarly immutable.

11. I think, in fact, that Plato had this in mind where he justly speaks of the Images of Real Existents 'entering and passing out': these particular words are not used idly: he wishes us to grasp the precise nature of Matter's participation in the Ideal-Forms.

The difficulty on this point is not really that which presented itself to most of our predecessors—how the Forms enter into Matter—it is rather the mode of their presence in it.

It is in fact strange at sight that Matter should remain itself intact, unaffected by Ideal-Forms present within it, especially seeing that these are affected by each other. It is surprising, too, that the entrant Forms should regularly expel preceding shapes and qualities, and that the modification (which cannot touch Matter) should affect what is a compound (of Ideal-Form with Matter) and this, again, not at haphazard but precisely where there is need of the incoming or outgoing of some certain Ideal-form, the compound being deficient through the absence of a particular principle whose presence will complete it.

But the reason is that the fundamental nature of Matter can take no increase by anything entering it, and no decrease by any withdrawal: what from the beginning it was, it remains. It is not like those things whose lack is merely that of arrangement and order which can be supplied without change of substance as when we dress or decorate something bare or ugly.

But where the bringing to order must cut through to the very nature, the base original must be transmuted: it can leave ugliness for beauty only by a change of substance. Matter, then, thus brought to order must lose its own nature in the supreme degree unless its baseness is an accidental: if it is base in the sense of being Baseness the Absolute, it could never participate in order, and if evil in the sense of being Evil the Absolute, it could never participate in good.

We conclude that Matter's participation in Form is not by way of modification within itself: the process is very different; it is a bare seeming. Perhaps we have here the solution of the difficulty as to how Matter, essentially evil, can be reaching towards The Good: there would be (in this 'seeming') no such participation as would destroy its essential nature. Given this mode of pseudo-participation—in which Matter would, as we say, retain its nature, unchanged, always being what it has essentially been—there is no longer any reason to wonder as to how, while essentially evil, it yet participates in Ideal-Form: for, by this mode, it does not abandon its own character: participation is the law, but it participates only just so far as its essence allows. Under a mode of participation which allows it to remain on its own footing, I its essential nature stands none the less, unaffected by the Ideal-Form which merely passes through[11] it: I it is by no means the less evil for remaining immutably in its own order. If it had authentic participation in The Good and were veritably changed, it would not be essentially evil.

In a word, when we call Matter evil we are right only if we mean that it is not amenable to modification by The Good; but that means simply that it is subject to no modification whatever.

12. This is Plato's conception: to him participation does not, in the case of Matter, comport any such presence of an Ideal-Form in a substance to be shaped by it as would produce one compound thing made up of the two elements changing at the same moment, merging into one another, modified each by the other.

In his haste to his purpose he raises many difficult questions, but he is determined to disown that view; he labours to indicate in what mode Matter can receive the Ideal-forms without being, itself, modified. The direct way is debarred since it is not easy to point to things actually present in a base and yet leaving that base unaffected: he therefore devises a metaphor for participation without modification (a plastic material, gold, moulded into various patterns), one which supports, also, his thesis that all appearing to the senses is void of substantial existence and that the region of mere seeming is vast.

Holding, as he does, that it is the patterns displayed upon Matter that cause all experience in material bodies while the Matter itself remains unaffected, he chooses this way of stating its immutability, leaving us to make out for ourselves that those very patterns impressed upon it do not comport any experience, any modification, in itself.

In the case, no doubt, of the bodies that take one pattern or shape after having borne another, it might be said that there was a change, the variation of shape being made verbally equivalent to a real change: but since Matter is essentially without shape or magnitude, the appearing of shape upon it can by no freedom of phrase be described as a change within it. On this point if one accepts that 'colour' and other sensible qualities 'exist by convention' (i.e., only in our belief and not objectively), one may safely say that the underlying Kind contains nothing whatever in the mode commonly supposed.

But if we reject even the idea of its really containing at least the patterns upon it, how is it, in any sense, a recipient?

The answer is that in the metaphor cited we have some reasonably adequate indication of the impassibility of I Matter coupled with the seeming presence of images[12] not present. I

But we cannot leave the point of its impassibility without a warning against allowing ourselves to be deluded by sheer custom of speech.

Plato speaks of Matter as becoming wet and inflamed, but we must remember the words that follow: 'and taking the shape of air and of water': this blunts the expressions 'becoming wet, becoming inflamed'; once we have Matter thus admitting these shapes, we learn that it has not itself become a shaped thing but that the shapes remain distinct as they entered. We see, further, that the expression 'becoming inflamed' is not to be taken strictly: it is rather a case of becoming fire. Becoming fire is very different from becoming inflamed which implies an outside agency and, therefore, susceptibility to modification. Matter, being itself a portion of fire, cannot be said to catch fire. To suggest that the fire not merely permeates the matter, but actually sets in on fire is like saying that a statue permeates its bronze (and 'statufies' it).

Further, if what enters must be an Ideal-Principle how could it set Matter aflame? But what if it is a pattern or condition? No: the object set aflame is so in virtue of the combination of Matter and condition.

But how can this follow on the conjunction when no unity has been produced by the two?

Even if such a unity had been produced, it would be a unity of things not mutually sharing experiences but acting upon the external. And the question would then arise whether both were active or whether the sole action was not that of one (the form) preventing the other (the Matter) from slipping away?

But (another difficulty) when any material thing is severed, must not the Matter be divided with it? Surely the bodily modification and other experience that have accompanied the sundering, must have occurred, identically, within the Matter?

This reasoning would force the destructibility of Matter upon us: 'the body is dissolved; then the Matter is dissolved.' We would have to allow Matter to be a thing of quantity, a magnitude. But since it is not a magnitude it could not have the experiences that belong to magnitude and, on the larger scale, since it is not body it cannot know the experiences of body.

In fact those that declare Matter subject to modification may as well declare it body right out.

13. Further, they must explain in what sense they hold that Matter tends to slip away from its form (the Idea). Can we conceive it stealing out from stones and rocks or whatever else envelops it?

And of course they cannot pretend that Matter in some cases rebels and sometimes not. For if once it makes away of its own will, why should it not always escape? If it is fixed despite itself, it must be enveloped by some Ideal-form for good and all. This, however, leaves still the question why a given portion of Matter does not remain constant to any one given form: the reason lies mainly in the fact that the Ideas are constantly passing into it.

In what sense, then, is it said to elude form?

By very nature and for ever?

But does not this precisely mean that it never ceases to be itself, in other words that its one form is an invincible formlessness? In no other sense has Plato's dictum any value to those that invoke it.

Matter (we read) is 'the receptacle and nurse of all generation'.

Now if Matter is such a receptacle and nurse, all generation is distinct from it; and since all the changeable lies in the realm of generation, Matter, existing before all generation, must exist before all change.

'Receptacle' and 'nurse'; then it retains its identity; it is not subject to modification. Similarly if it is (as again we read) 'the ground on which individual things appear and disappear', and so, too, if it is 'a place', 'a base'. The description may be challenged as situating the Ideas in space; yet to Matter it attributes no condition but merely probes[13] after its distinctive manner of being.

And what is that?

This nature of which we are thinking (Matter)[14] cannot be included among Existents but must utterly rebel from the Essence of Real Beings and be therefore wholly something other than they—for they are Reason-Principles and possess Authentic Existence—it must inevitably, by virtue of that difference, retain its integrity to the point of being permanently closed against them and, more, of rejecting close participation in any image of them.

Only on these terms can it be completely different: once it took any Idea to hearth and home, it would become a new thing, for it would cease to be the thing apart, the ground of all else, the receptacle of absolutely any and every form. If there is to be a ceaseless coming into it and going out from it, itself must be unmoved and immune in all the come and go. The Entrant will enter as an image, the untrue entering the untruth.

But, at least, in a true entry?

No: how could there be a true entry into that which, by being falsity, is banned from ever touching truth?

Is this then a pseudo-entry into a pseudo-entity—something merely brought near, as faces enter the mirror, there to remain just as long as the people look into it?

Yes: if we eliminated the Authentic Existents from this Sphere, nothing of all now seen in sense would appear one moment longer.

Here the mirror itself is seen, for it is itself an Ideal-Form of a kind (has some degree of Real Being); but bare Matter, which is no Idea, is not a visible thing; if it were, it would have been visible in its own character before anything else appeared upon it. The condition of Matter may be illustrated by that of air penetrated by light and remaining, even so, unseen because it is invisible whatever happens.

The reflections in the mirror are not taken to be real, all the less since the appliance on which they appear is seen and remains while the images disappear, but Matter is not seen either with the images or without them. But suppose the reflections on the mirror remaining and the mirror itself not seen, we would never doubt the solid reality of all that appears.

If, then, there is, really, something in a mirror, we may suppose objects of sense to be in Matter in precisely that way: if in the mirror there is nothing, if there is only a seeming of something, then we may judge that in Matter there is the same delusion and that the seeming is to be traced to the Substantial-Existence of the Real-Beings, that Substantial-Existence in which the Authentic has the real participation while only an unreal participation can belong to the unauthentic since their condition must differ from that which they would know if the parts were reversed, if the Authentic-Existents were not and they were.

14. But would this mean that if there were no Matter nothing would exist?

Precisely as in the absence of a mirror, or something of similar power, there would be no reflection.

A thing whose very nature is to be lodged in something else cannot exist where the base is lacking—and it is the character of a reflection to appear in something not itself.

Of course supposing anything to desert from the Authentic Beings, this would not need an alien base: but these Beings are not subject to flux, and therefore any outside manifestation of them implies something other than themselves, something offering a base to what never enters, something which by its presence, in its insistence, by its cry for help, in its beggardom, strives as it were by violence to acquire and is always disappointed so that its Poverty is enduring, its cry unceasing.

This alien base exists and the myth represents it as a pauper to exhibit its nature, to show that Matter is destitute of The Good. The claimant does not ask for all the Giver's store, but it welcomes whatever it can get; in other words, what appears in Matter is not Reality.

The name, too (Poverty), conveys that Matter's need is never met. The union with Poros, Possession, is designed to show that I Matter does not consort with Reality, with Plenitude, but with a thing of cunning—in fact, with the illusion of the image.[15] I

It is, of course, impossible that an outside thing belonging in any degree to Real-Being—whose nature is to engender Real-Beings—should utterly fail of participation in Reality: but here we have something perplexing; we are dealing with utter Non-Being, absolutely without part in Reality; what is this participation by the non-participant, and how does mere neighbouring confer anything on that which by its own nature is precluded from any sort of attachment?

The answer is that all that impinges upon this Non-Being is flung back as from a repelling substance; we may think of an echo returned from a repercussive plane surface; it is precisely because of the lack of retention that the phenomenon is supposed to belong to that particular place and even to arise there.

If Matter were participant and received Reality to the extent I which we are asked[16] to imagine, I it would be penetrated by a Reality thus sucked into its constitution. But we know that the Entrant is not thus absorbed: Matter remains as it was, taking nothing to itself: it is the check to the forthwelling of Authentic Existence; it is a ground that repels; it is a mere receptacle to the Realities as they take their common path (of emanation) and here meet and mingle. It resembles those reflecting vessels, filled with water, which are often set against the sun to produce fire: the heat rays prevented, by their contrary within, from being absorbed are flung out as one mass.

It is in this sense and way that Matter becomes the cause of the generated realm; the combinations within it hold together only after some such reflective mode.

15. Now the objects attracting the sun-rays to themselves—illuminated by a fire of the sense-order—are necessarily of the sense-order; there is perceptibility because there has been a union of things at once external to each other and

continuous, contiguous, in direct contact, two extremes in one line. But the Reason-Principle operating upon Matter is external to it only in a very different mode and sense: exteriority in this case is amply supplied by contrariety of essence and can dispense with any opposite ends (any question of lineal position); or, rather, the difference is one that actually debars any local extremity; sheer incongruity of essence, the utter failure in relationship, inhibits admixture (between Matter and any form of Being).

The reason, then, of the immutability of Matter is that the entrant principle neither possesses it nor is possessed by it. Consider, as an example, the mode in which an opinion or representation is present in the mind; there is no admixture; the notion that came goes in its time, still integrally itself alone, taking nothing with it, leaving nothing after it, because it has not been blended with the mind; there is no 'outside' in the sense of contact broken, and the distinction between base and entrant is patent not to the senses but to the reason.

In that example, no doubt, the mental representation—though it seems to have a wide and unchecked control—is an image, while the Soul (Mind) is in its nature not an image (but a Reality): none the less the Soul or Mind certainly stands to the concept as Matter, or in some analogous relation. The representation, however, does not cover the Mind over; on the contrary it is often expelled by some activity there; however urgently it presses in, it never effects such an obliteration as to be taken for the Soul; it is confronted there by indwelling powers, by Reason-Principles, which repel all such attack.

Matter—feebler far than the Soul for any exercise of power, and possessing no phase of the Authentic Existents, not even in possession of its own falsity— lacks the very means of manifesting itself, utter void as it is; it becomes the means by which other things appear, but it cannot announce its own presence. Penetrating thought may arrive at it, discriminating it from Authentic Existence; then, it is discerned as something abandoned by all that really is, by even the dimmest semblants of being, as a thing dragged towards every shape and property and appearing to follow—yet in fact not even following.

16. An Ideal-Principle approaches and leads Matter towards some desired dimension, ⏽investing this underlie with a magnitude from itself: Matter neither has the dimension nor acquires it; all that shows upon it of dimension derives from the Ideal-Principle.[17]⏽

Eliminate this Ideal-Form and the substratum ceases to be a thing of magnitude, or to appear so: the mass produced by the Idea was, let us suppose, a man or a horse; the horse-magnitude came upon the Matter when a horse was produced upon it; when the horse ceases to exist upon the Matter, the magnitude of the horse departs also. If we are told that the horse implies a certain determined bulk and that this bulk is a permanent thing, we answer that what is permanent in this case is not the magnitude of the horse but the magnitude of mass in general. That same magnitude might be fire or earth; on their disappearance their particular magnitudes would disappear with them. Matter, then, can never take to itself either pattern or magnitude; if it did, it would no longer be able to turn from being fire, let us say, into being something else; it would become and be fire once for all.

In a word, though Matter is far extended—so vastly as to appear coextensive with all this sense-known Universe—yet if the Heavens and their content came to an end, all magnitude would simultaneously pass from Matter with, beyond a doubt, all its other properties; it would be abandoned to its own Kind, retaining nothing of all that which, in its own peculiar mode, it had hitherto exhibited.

Where an entrant force can effect modification it will inevitably leave some trace upon its withdrawal; but where there can be no modification, nothing can be retained; light comes and goes, and the air is as it always was.

That a thing essentially devoid of magnitude should come to a certain size is no more astonishing than that a thing essentially devoid of heat should become warm: Matter's essential existence is quite separate from its existing in bulk, since, of course, magnitude is an immaterial principle as pattern is. Besides, if we are not to reduce Matter to nothing, it must be all things by way of participation, and magnitude is one of those all things.

In bodies, necessarily compounds, magnitude—though not a determined magnitude—must be present as one of the constituents; it is implied in the very notion of body; but Matter—not a body—excludes even undetermined magnitude.

17. Nor can we, on the other hand, think that Matter is simply Absolute Magnitude.

Magnitude is not, like Matter, a receptacle; it is an Ideal-Principle: it is a thing standing apart to itself, not some definite mass. ▎ When it desires to abandon its station in the Intellectual-Principle or in the Soul and assume (physical) magnitude, it gives to its images (the material forms)—aspiring and moving towards it and eagerly imitating its act—a power of reproducing their states in their own derivatives. The Magnitude which has gone forth to the image-making stage has recourse to the Absolute Magnitude and carries with it the littleness of Matter, and so by extending Matter enables it, devoid though it be of all content,[18] to exhibit the appearance of Magnitude. ▎ It must be understood that spurious Magnitude consists in the fact that a thing (Matter) not possessing actual Magnitude strains towards it and has the extension of that straining.

All that is Real Being gives forth a reflection of itself upon all else; every Reality, therefore, has Magnitude which by this process is communicated to the Universe.

The Magnitude inherent in each Ideal-Principle—that of a horse or of anything else—combines with Magnitude the Absolute with the result that, irradiated by that Absolute, Matter entire takes Magnitude and every particle of it becomes a mass; in this way, by virtue at once of the totality of Idea with its inherent magnitude and of each several specific Idea, all things appear under mass; Matter takes on what we conceive as extension; it is compelled to assume a relation to the All and, gathered under this Idea and under Mass, to be all things—in the degree in which the operating power can lead the really nothing to become all.

By the conditions of Manifestation, colour rises from non-colour (= from the colourless prototype of colour in the Ideal Realm). Quality, known by the one name with its parallel in the sphere of Primals, rises, similarly, from non-quality: in precisely the same mode, the Magnitude appearing upon Matter rises from non-Magnitude or from that Primal which is known to us by the same name; so that material forms become visible through standing midway between bare underlie and Pure Idea. All is perceptible by virtue of this origin in the Intellectual Sphere but all is falsity since the base in which the manifestation takes place is a non-existent.

Particular entities thus attain their magnitude through being drawn out by the power of the Existents which mirror themselves and make space for themselves in them. And no violence is required to draw them into all the diversity of shapes and kinds because the phenomenal All exists by Matter (by Matter's essential all-receptivity) and because each several Idea, moreover, draws Matter its own way by the power stored within itself, the power it holds from the Intellectual Realm. Matter is manifested in this sphere as Mass by the fact that it mirrors the Absolute Magnitude; Magnitude here is the reflection in the mirror. Matter must go as one total thing wherever the image (of the Idea) calls it; it is everywhere submissive—the material of determination and not the determined thing itself: what is, in its own character, no determined thing may become determined by an outside force, though, in becoming thus determined, it does not become the definite thing in question, for thus it would lose its own characteristic indetermination.

18. I If one has the intellection of Magnitude—assuming that this intellection is of such power as not merely to subsist within itself but to be urged outward as it were by the intensity of its life—one will necessarily realize it[19] in a Kind I (= Matter) not having its being in the Intellective Principle, not previously

possessing the Idea of Magnitude or any trace of that Idea or any other.

What then will it produce (in this Matter) by virtue of that power?

Not horse or cow: these are the product of other Ideas.

No: this Principle comes from the source of Magnitude (= is primal 'Magnitude') and therefore Matter can have no extension, in which to harbour the Magnitude of the Principle, but can take in only its reflected appearance.

To the thing which does not enjoy Magnitude in the sense of having mass-extension in its own substance and parts, the only possibility is that it present some partial semblance of Magnitude, such as being continuous, not here and there and everywhere, that its parts be related within it and ungapped. I The image of Magnitude cannot appear on any basis of equality in a small mass— it is, after all, an image of Magnitude: yet it aspires to the full presentment of that Absolute Magnitude and approaches it as nearly as the company of its inseparable associate (Matter) will allow:[20] thus it confers I Magnitude upon that (= Matter) which has none and cannot even muster up the appearance of having any, and the visible resultant exhibits the Magnitude of mass.

Matter, then, wears Magnitude as a dress thrown about it I by its association with that image of Magnitude to whose movement it must answer; but it does not, for that, change its Kind; if the image[21] which I has clothed it were to withdraw, it would once again be what it permanently is, what it is by its own strength, or it would have precisely the Magnitude lent to it by any other form that happens to be present in it.

The (Universal) Soul—containing the Ideal Principles of Real-Beings, and itself an Ideal Principle—includes all in concentration within itself, just as the Ideal Principle of each particular entity is complete and self-contained: it, therefore, sees these principles of sensible things because they are turned, as it were, towards it and advancing to it: but it cannot harbour them in their plurality, for it cannot depart from its Kind; it sees them, therefore, stripped of mass. Matter, on the contrary, destitute of resisting power since it has no Act of its own and is a mere shadow, can but accept all that an active power may choose to send. In what is thus sent, from the Reason-Principle in the Intellectual Realm, there is already contained a degree of the partial object that is to be formed: in the image-making impulse within the Reason-Principle there is already a step (towards the lower manifestation) or we may put it that the downward movement from the Reason-Principle is a first form of the partial: utter absence of partition would mean no movement but (sterile) repose. Matter cannot be the home of all things in concentration as the Soul is: if it were so, it would belong to the Intellective Sphere. It must be (like the Soul) all-recipient but not in that partless mode. It is to be the Place of all things, and it must therefore extend universally, offer itself to all things, serve to all interval:

thus it will be a thing unconfined to any moment (of space or time) but laid out in submission to all that is to be.

But would we not expect that some one particularized form should occupy Matter (at once) and so exclude such others as are not able to enter into combination?

No: for there is no first Idea—except the Ideal Principle of the Universe—and, by this Idea, Matter is (the seat of) all things at once and of the particular thing in its parts—for the Matter of a living being is disparted according to the specific parts of the organism: if there were no such partition nothing would exist but the Reason-Principle.

19. The Ideal Principles entering into Matter **|** as to a Mother [22] affect it neither **|** for better nor for worse.

Their action is not upon Matter but upon each other; these powers conflict with their opponent principles, not with their substrata—unless the substrata are taken as comprised with the entrant forms—Cold (the Principle) annuls Heat, and Whiteness annuls Blackness; or, the opponents blend to form an intermediate quality. Only that is affected which enters into combinations: being affected is losing something of self-identity.

In beings of soul and body, the affection occurs in the body, modified according to the qualities and powers presiding at the act of change: in all such dissolution of constituent parts, in the new combinations, in all variation from the original structure, the affection is bodily, the Soul or Mind having no more than an accompanying knowledge of the more drastic changes, or perhaps not even that. (Body is modified: Mind knows) but the Matter concerned remains unaffected; heat enters, cold leaves it, and it is unchanged because neither Principle is associated with it as friend or enemy.

So the appellation 'Recipient and Nurse' is the better description: Matter is the mother only in the sense indicated; it has no begetting power. But probably the term 'Mother' is used by those who think of a Mother as Matter to the offspring, as a container only, giving nothing to them, the entire bodily frame of the child being formed out of food. But if the mother does give anything to the offspring she does so not in her quality as Matter but as being an Ideal-Form; for only the Idea is generative; the contrary Kind is sterile.

This, I think, is why the doctors of old, teaching through symbols and mystic representations, exhibit the ancient Hermes with the generative organ always in active posture; this is to convey that the generator of things of sense is the Intellectual Reason-Principle: the sterility of Matter, eternally unmoved, is indicated by the eunuchs surrounding it in its representation as the All-Mother.

This too exalting title is conferred upon it in order to indicate that it is the source of things in the sense of being their underlie: it is an approximate name chosen for a general conception; there is no intention of suggesting a complete parallel with motherhood to those not satisfied with a surface impression but needing a precisely true presentment; by a remote symbolism, the nearest they could find, they indicate that Matter is sterile, not female to full effect, female in receptivity only, not in pregnancy: this they accomplish by exhibiting Matter as approached by what is neither female nor effectively male, but castrated of that impregnating power which belongs only to the unchangeably masculine.

NOTES TO ENNEAD III.6

1. FIRST EDITION: "... the *Impressionable* faculty ..."

    TAYLOR: "... the passive part of the soul ..."

    GUTHRIE: "... that part of the soul, that is called the passive (or affective, or irrational)..."

    ARMSTRONG: "... the part of the soul which is said to be subject to affections ..."

2. FIRST EDITION: "... or by *looking towards some inferior phase of it* or ..."

    ARMSTRONG: "... or by looking to the reason when it is in a bad state ..."

    TAYLOR: "... or because it looks to depraved reason ..."

    GUTHRIE: "... or considers reason as having already become evil ..."

3. FIRST EDITION: "... in abeyance; *the Seer in the Soul was occupied elsewhere, for, though not always at least sometimes, it has leisure for a certain degree of contemplation of other concerns.*"

    GUTHRIE: "... the rational part, whose function it is to see (by considering the notions it receives from intelligence), is occupied with something else, for it does not do everything simultaneously, being busy with some other action; it considers other than corporeal things, so far as it can."

    TAYLOR: "... the power whose province it is to see, performs something else, and not all things; but is elsewhere at leisure, in consequence of seeing as much as possible other things."

    ARMSTRONG: "If it [the desiring part—ed.] saw the other parts it would be different, and would not do everything but might perhaps take a rest by looking, as far as it could, at the other parts."

4. FIRST EDITION: "... the elation is *mental, but* makes itself felt *in the body;* the purely mental phase *has not reached the point of sensation.*"

    ARMSTRONG: "... the happy, relaxed feeling, which penetrates to sense-perception, belongs to the body, but the part of pleasure which belongs to the soul is no longer an affection."

    TAYLOR: "... In pleasure, also, the sensible diffusion of it subsists about the body; but that which takes place about the soul is no longer passion."

5. FIRST EDITION: "... and of course in the banning *for its part too* of all *which the higher Soul ignores* when *it has arisen from the trouble storm and is no longer bound to the flesh by the chains of sensuality and of multiplicity but has subdued to itself the body and its entire surrounding so that it holds sovereignty, tranquilly, over all.*"

GUTHRIE: "... it means annihilating the things from which she thus is separated, so that she is no longer choked by the whirlwind of the spirit which breaks loose whenever the body is allowed to grow too strong; the latter must be weakened so as to govern it more easily."

TAYLOR: "It will also consist in taking away those things by the ablation of which this part likewise will be separated, when it is not permitted to lie in a spirit turbid from gluttony, lest it should be suffocated in flesh, but when that in which it dwells is attenuated, so that it may be quietly carried in it."

ARMSTRONG: "But separating it could also mean taking away the things from which it is separated when it is not standing over a vital breath turbid from gluttony and sated with impure meats, but that in which it resides is so fine that it can ride on it in peace."

6. FIRST EDITION: "... rounded off; *it is nothing potentially that is not of the same determined order, otherwise (that is if it contained even potentially the undetermined) it would be* in default."

TAYLOR: "... and nothing is there in capacity which does not also possess a mighty power; since otherwise it would be deficient."

GUTHRIE: "Nothing outside of it exists even potentially; otherwise it would not fully satisfy itself."

ARMSTRONG: "... there must be nothing to which its power does not extend, nor must its power be quantitatively limited; otherwise it would be defective."

7. FIRST EDITION: "... and this *in the sense not of movement (away from Being) or station (in Not-Being) but* of veritable Not-Being ..." ARMSTRONG, TAYLOR, and GUTHRIE all translate in the same sense as the fourth edition.

8. FIRST EDITION: "... notion of *Substance* implies ..."

TAYLOR: "But everything which is in a subject, is in such a manner present with the subject, as to impart something to it from itself."

GUTHRIE: "But every quality which is present in a subject cannot be present in it without communicating to it something of itself."

ARMSTRONG: "... but everything which is present in a substrate is present in such a way as to give something from itself to the substrate."

9. FIRST EDITION: "... the underlying *Matter?*" TAYLOR has "the subject body"; ARMSTRONG has "the body underlying it"; GUTHRIE has "corporeal substance."

10. FIRST EDITION has this sentence as: "*The illustration of the mirror may well indicate to us that a given substratum may contain something quite distinct from itself—even something standing to it as a direct contrary—and yet remain entirely unaffected by what is thus present to it or merged into it.*"

TAYLOR: "... a thing may be in that which is different from it, without injuring by its presence that with which it is present."

ARMSTRONG: "... it is possible for one thing to be in the same place as another, or in another, without troubling by its presence that with which or in which it is."

GUTHRIE: "This shows how one quality can give place to another in a same subject, or how one thing can be in another, without its presence causing any modification in the subject for which or in which it is present."

11. FIRST EDITION: "... its essential nature stands none the less, *whatsoever the Idea, within that limit, may communicate to* it:"

ARMSTRONG: ". . . it receives no damage which extends to its being from that which gives it [form] in this way, . . ." Brackets are Armstrong's.

TAYLOR: ". . . it is not injured in its essence by that which thus imparts something to it."

12. FIRST EDITION: ". . . Matter coupled with the *presence upon it of what may be described as images of things* not present."

TAYLOR, GUTHRIE, and ARMSTRONG all translate in the same sense as the fourth edition.

13. FIRST EDITION has this sentence as: "*Where Plato describes and identifies it as 'a ground to the ideas' he is not attributing any state to it; he is probing* after its distinctive manner of being."

TAYLOR, GUTHRIE, and ARMSTRONG all support MacKenna's original translation.

14. FIRST EDITION: "This *which we think of as a Nature-Kind* cannot . . ."

ARMSTRONG, TAYLOR, and GUTHRIE all support Page's fourth-edition translation.

15. FIRST EDITION: ". . . Matter does not *attain to* Reality, *to* Plenitude, but *to some bare sufficiency—in point of fact to imaging skill.*"

GUTHRIE: "When Poverty is said to unite with Abundance, we do not mean that it unites with Existence or Fulness, but with a work of wonderful skill, namely, a thing that is nothing but specious appearance." Guthrie also cross-references the myth of Pandora in IV.3.14.

ARMSTRONG: ". . . it [Poverty—ed.] is not united with real being or with plenitude but with a resourceful thing, that is, with the cleverness of the apparition."

TAYLOR: ". . . the assertion . . . does not signify that this connection was with [real] being, nor with satiety, but with a certain artificial thing, i.e. with the wisdom of a phantasm." Brackets are Taylor's.

16. FIRST EDITION: ". . . which we are *apt* to imagine . . ."

ARMSTRONG: ". . . if matter really was participant and received being in the way one thinks it does . . ."

GUTHRIE: "If matter participated in the existence of genuine beings and received them within itself, as might easily be thought . . ."

TAYLOR: "If, however, matter so participated and received, as some one may think it does. . ."

17. FIRST EDITION: ". . . investing this *non-existent* underlie with a magnitude from itself *which never becomes incorporate—for Matter, if it really incorporated magnitude, would be a mass.*"

ARMSTRONG: ". . . makes it a size by imposing the size from itself on matter, which is not the size and does not in this way become it; for [if it did] the size imposed on it would be [real] magnitude." Brackets are Armstrong's.

18. FIRST EDITION has the second and third sentences of this paragraph as: "*The fact is that the self-gathered content of the Intellectual Principle or of the All-Soul, desires expansion (and thereby engenders secondaries): in* its images—aspiring and moving towards it and eagerly imitating its act—*is vested a similar* power of reproducing their states in their own derivatives. The Magnitude *latent in the expansive tendency of the Image-making phase (of the Intellect or All-Soul) runs forth into the Absolute Magnitude of the Universe; this in turn enlists into the process the spurious magnitude of Matter: the content of the Supreme, thus, in virtue of its own prior extension enables Matter—which never possesses a content—*to exhibit the appearance of Magnitude."

GUTHRIE: "But as that which exists in intelligence or in the soul desired to acquire magnitude, it imparted to the things that desired to imitate magnitude by their aspiration or movement, the power to impress on some other object a modification analogous to their own. Thus magnitude, by developing in the procession of imagination, dragged along with itself the smallness of matter, made it seem large by extending it along with itself, without becoming filled by that extension."

TAYLOR: "Since, however, that which is placed in intellect or in soul, wishes to be great, it imparts to those things which by proceeding as it were, endeavour to imitate it, by the desire of, or motion towards it, the ability of impressing the same passion in another thing. That which is great, therefore, running in the progression of the phantasy so as to cause the smallness of matter to run in conjunction with it, occasions matter also to appear great, though it is not filled by the co-extension."

ARMSTRONG: "But since, while it is at rest in intellect or in soul, it wants to be large, it gives to the things which, in a way, want to imitate it by an aspiration for it or a movement towards it the ability to insert their affection into something else. So, then, size, running on in its image-making progression, and making the littleness of matter run with it towards this very size, has made it by extension, though it is not filled, appear to be large."

19. FIRST EDITION (ellipses indicate words identical in both editions) begins section as: "*The Ideal Principle possessing* the *Intellection (= Idea, Noesis)* of Magnitude—assuming . . . of its life—will necessarily realise *itself* in a Kind . . ."

GUTHRIE: "Let us now suppose that a conception of magnitude were possessed by some being which would have the power not only to be in itself, but also to produce itself externally; and that it should meet a nature (such as matter) that was incapable of existing within intelligence, of having a form, of revealing any trace of real magnitude, or any quality."

TAYLOR: "If some one, therefore, possessing an intellectual conception of magnitude, should have this conception attended with a power not only of subsisting in itself, but also of proceeding as it were externally, and the power should receive a nature not existing in the intellectual perceiver, nor having a certain form, nor a certain vestige of magnitude or of any other form . . ."

ARMSTRONG: "Suppose that someone had a thought of size, if his thought had power not only to exist in itself but was taken outside, so to speak, by its power, it would take hold of a nature which did not exist in the thinker, and had no form and no trace of size, or of anything else either."

20. FIRST EDITION begins this sentence as: "*An adequate reflection of a great mass cannot be produced* in a small *space—mere size prevents—but the greater, pursuing the hope of that* full *self-*presentment, *makes progress towards it and brings about a nearer approach to adequate mirroring in the parallel from which it can never withhold its radiation:* thus it confers . . ."

GUTHRIE: "Indeed, it was impossible for a small mass to contain an image of magnitude that would equal the real magnitude, since it is only an image of magnitude; but, carried away with the hope of achieving the magnitude to which it aspired, this image extended to its limit, along with matter, which shared its extension because matter could not follow it. That is how this image of magnitude magnified what was not great . . ."

TAYLOR: "For it is not possible that in a small bulk, there should still be an equal image of magnitude, since it is an image of greatness; but so far as it aspires through its hope, it accedes as far as it is possible for it to accede, and running in conjunction with that which is not able to leave it, it causes that to be great which is not great, yet not so as to appear to be the magnitude which is seen in bulk."

ARMSTRONG: "For the image of size, since it is an image of size, cannot endure to be equal still in a small mass, but in proportion as it aspires to the hope of reaching [real] size, it advances as far as it can with that which runs along with it and cannot be left behind, and gives size . . ." Brackets are Armstrong's.

21. FIRST EDITION (ellipses indicate words identical in both editions): ". . . by its association with that *Absolute* Magnitude . . . change its Kind; if the *Idea* which . . ."

COMMENT: Neither Armstrong, Guthrie, nor Taylor offers a clear resolution to the disagreement between MacKenna and Page here. Also, their words are too different from the above and from one another for a brief excerpt to be helpful. It is worthwhile, however, to look into how each of them handles this whole section (section 18).

22. FIRST EDITION: ". . . as to a Mother *(to be 'born into the Universe')* affect it neither . . ." MacKenna is alone in making this addition.

SEVENTH TRACTATE

Time and Eternity

1. Eternity and Time; two entirely separate things, we explain, 'the one having its being in the everlasting Kind, the other in the realm of Process, in our own Universe'; and, by continually using the words and assigning every phenomenon to the one or the other category, we come to think that, both by instinct and by the more detailed attack of thought, we hold an adequate experience of them in our minds without more ado.

When, perhaps, we make the effort to clarify our ideas and close into the heart of the matter we are at once unsettled: our doubts throw us back upon ancient explanations; we choose among the various theories, or among the various interpretations of some one theory, and so we come to rest, satisfied, if only we can counter a question with an approved answer, and glad to be absolved from further inquiry.

Now, we must believe that some of the venerable philosophers of old discovered the truth; but it is important to examine which of them really hit the mark and by what guiding principle we can ourselves attain to certitude.

What, then, does Eternity really mean to those who (thus casually) describe it as something different from Time? We begin with Eternity, since, when the standing Exemplar is known, its representation in image—which Time is understood to be—will be clearly apprehended—though it is of course equally true, admitting this relationship of Time as image to Eternity the original, that if we chose to begin by identifying Time we could thence proceed upwards by Recognition (the Platonic Anamnesis) and become aware of the Kind which it images.

2. What definition are we to give of Eternity?

Can it be identified with the (divine or) Intellectual Substance itself?

This would be like identifying Time with the Universe of Heavens and Earth—an opinion, it is true, which appears to have had its adherents. No doubt we conceive, we know, Eternity as something most august; most august, too, is the Intellectual Kind; and there is no possibility of saying that the one is more majestic than the other;—the Absolute One may be left out of account, since not even majesty can be predicated of it;—there is therefore a certain excuse for identifying Eternity with the Intellectual World, all the more since the Intellectual Substance and Eternity have the one scope and content.

Still; by the fact of representing the one as contained within the other, by making Eternity a predicate to the Intellectual Existents—'the Nature of the Exemplar', we read, 'is eternal'—we cancel the identification; Eternity becomes a separate thing, something surrounding that Nature or lying within it or present to it. And the majestic quality of both does not prove them identical: it might be transmitted from the one to the other. So, too, Eternity and the Divine Nature envelop the same entities, yes; but not in the same way: the Divine may be thought of as enveloping parts, Eternity as embracing its content in an unbroken whole, with no implication of part, but merely from the fact that all eternal things are so by conforming to it.

May we, perhaps identify Eternity with Repose-There as Time has been identified with Movement-Here?

This would bring on the counter-question whether Eternity is presented to us as Repose in the general sense or as the Repose that envelops the Intellectual Essence.

On the first supposition we can no more talk of Repose being eternal than of Eternity being eternal: to be eternal is to participate in an outside thing, Eternity.

Further, if Eternity is Repose, what becomes of Eternal Movement, which, by this identification, would become a thing of Repose?

Again, the conception of Repose scarcely seems to include that of perpetuity—I am speaking, of course, not of perpetuity in the time-order (which might follow on absence of movement) but of that which we have in mind when we speak of Eternity.

If, on the other hand, Eternity is identified with the Repose of the divine Essence, all the other categories of the divine are put outside of Eternity.

Besides, the conception of Eternity requires not merely Repose but also unity—and, in order to keep it distinct from Time, a unity excluding interval—but neither that unity nor that absence of interval enters into the conception of Repose as such.

Lastly, this unchangeable Repose in unity is a predicate asserted of Eternity, which, therefore, is not itself Repose, the absolute, but a participant in Repose.

3. What, then, can this be, this something in virtue of which we declare the entire divine Realm to be Eternal, everlasting? We must come to some understanding of this perpetuity with which Eternity is either identical or in conformity.

It must be at once something in the nature of unity and yet a notion compact of diversity, or (more exactly) a Kind, a Nature, that waits upon the Existents of that Other World, either associated with them or known in and upon them, they collectively being this Nature which, with all its unity, is yet diverse in power and essence. Considering this multifarious power, we declare it to be Essence or Being so far as it is in some sense a subject or substratum; where we see life we think of it as Movement; where all is unvaried self-identity we call it Repose; and we know it as, at once, Difference and Identity when we recognize that all is unity with variety.

Then we reconstruct; we sum all into a collected unity once more, a sole Life in the Supreme; we concentrate Diversity and all the endless production of act: thus we know Identity, a concept or, rather, a Life never varying, not becoming what previously it was not, the thing immutably itself, broken by no interval; and knowing this, we know Eternity.

We know it as a Life changelessly motionless and ever holding the Universal content in actual presence; not this now and now that other, but always all; not existing now in one mode and now in another, but a consummation without part or interval. All its content is in immediate concentration as at one point; nothing in it ever knows development: all remains identical within itself, knowing nothing of change, for ever in a Now, since nothing of it has passed away or will come into being, but what it is now, that it is ever.

Eternity, therefore—while not the Substratum (not the essential foundation of the Divine or Intellectual Principle)—may be considered as the radiation of this Substratum: it exists as the announcement of the Identity in the Divine, of that state—of being thus and not otherwise—which characterizes what has no futurity but eternally is.

What future, in fact, could bring to that Being anything which it now does not possess; and could it come to be anything which it is not once for all?

There exists no source or ground from which anything could make its way into that standing present; any imagined entrant will prove to be not alien but already integral. And as it can never come to be anything at present outside it, so, necessarily, it cannot include any past; what can there be that once was in it and now is gone? Futurity, similarly, is banned; nothing could be yet to come to it. Thus no ground is left for its existence but that it be what it is.

That which neither has been nor will be, but simply possesses being; that which enjoys stable existence as neither in process of change nor having ever changed—that is Eternity. Thus we come to the definition: the Life—instantaneously entire, complete, at no point broken into period or part—which belongs to the Authentic Existent by its very existence, this is the thing we were probing for—this is Eternity.

4. We must, however, avoid thinking of it as an accidental from outside grafted upon that Nature: it is native to it, integral to it.

It is discerned as present essentially in that Nature like everything else that we can predicate There—all immanent, springing from that Essence and inherent to that Essence. For whatsoever has primal Being must be immanent to the Firsts and be a First—Eternity equally with the beauty that is among them and of them and equally with the truth that is among them.

❙ Some of the predicates reside, as it were, in a partial phase of the All-Being; others are[1] inherent in the All ❙ taken as a totality, since that Authentic All is not a thing patched up out of external parts, but is authentically an all because its parts are engendered by itself. It is like the truthfulness in the Supreme which is not an agreement with some outside fact or being but is inherent in each member about which it is the truth. To an authentic All it is not enough that it be everything that exists: it must possess all-ness in the full sense that nothing whatever is absent from it. Then nothing is in store for it: if anything were to come, that thing must have been lacking to it, and it was, therefore, not All. And what, of a Nature contrary to its own, could enter into it when it is (the Supreme and therefore) immune? Since nothing can accrue to it, it cannot seek change or be changed or ever have made its way into Being.

Engendered things are in continuous process of acquisition; eliminate futurity, therefore, and at once they lose their being; if the non-engendered are made amenable to futurity they are thrown down from the seat of their existence, for, clearly, existence is not theirs by their nature if it appears only as a being about to be, a becoming, an advancing from stage to stage.

The essential existence of generated things seems to lie in their existing from the time of their generation to the ultimate of time after which they cease to be: but such an existence is compact of futurity, and the annulment of that futurity means the stopping of the life and therefore of the essential existence.

Existence for the (generated) All must similarly consist in a goal to be attained: for this reason it keeps hastening towards its future, dreading to rest, seeking to draw Being to itself by a perpetual variety of production and action and by its circling in a sort of ambition after Essential Existence.

And here we have, incidentally, lighted upon the cause of the Circuit of the All; it is a movement which seeks perpetuity by way of futurity.

The Primals, on the contrary, in their state of blessedness have no such aspiration towards anything to come: they are the whole, now; what life may be thought of as their due, they possess entire; they, therefore, seek nothing, since there is nothing future to them, nothing external to them in which any futurity could find lodgement.

Thus the perfect and all-comprehensive essence of the Authentic Existent does not consist merely in the completeness inherent in its members; its essence includes, further, its established immunity from all lack with the exclusion, also, of all that is without Being—for not only must all things be contained in the All and Whole, but it can contain nothing that is, or was ever, non-existent—and this State and Nature of the Authentic Existent is Eternity: in our very word, Eternity means Ever-Being (*aion = aiei on*).

5. This Ever-Being is realized when upon examination of an object I am able to say—or rather, to know—that in its very Nature it is incapable of increment or change; anything that fails by that test is no Ever-Existent or, at least, no Ever-All-Existent.

But is perpetuity enough in itself to constitute an Eternal?

No: the object must, further, include such a Nature-Principle as to give the assurance that the actual state excludes all future change, so that it is found at every observation as it always was.

Imagine, then, the state of a being which cannot fall away from the vision of this but is for ever caught to it, held by the spell of its grandeur, kept to it by virtue of a nature itself unfailing—or even the state of one that must labour towards Eternity by directed effort, but then to rest in it, immovable at any point, assimilated to it, co-eternal with it, contemplating Eternity and the Eternal by what is Eternal within the self.

Accepting this as a true account of an eternal, a perdurable Existent—one which never turns to any Kind outside itself, that possesses life complete once for all, that has never received any accession, that is now receiving none and will never receive any—we have, with the statement of a perduring Being, the statement also of perdurance and of Eternity: perdurance is the corresponding state arising from the (divine) substratum and inherent in it; Eternity (the Principle as distinguished from the property of everlastingness) is that substratum carrying that state in manifestation.

Eternity, thus, is of the order of the I supremely great; intuition identifies it[2] with God: I it may fitly be described as God made manifest, as God declaring what He is, as existence without jolt or change, and therefore as also the firmly living.

And it should be no shock that we find plurality in it; each of the Beings of the Supreme is multiple by virtue of unlimited force; for to be limitless implies failing at no point, and Eternity is pre-eminently the limitless since (having no past or future) it spends nothing of its own substance.

Thus a close enough definition of Eternity would be that it is a life limitless in the full sense of being all the life there is and a life which, knowing nothing of past or future to shatter its completeness, possesses itself intact I for ever.[3] I

6. Now the Principle thus stated, all good and beauty, and everlasting, is centred in The One, sprung from It, and pointed towards It, never straying from It, but ever holding about It and in It and living by Its law; and it is in this reference, as I judge, that Plato—finely, and by no means inadvertently but with profound intention—wrote those words of his, 'Eternity stable in Unity'; he wishes to convey that Eternity is not merely something circling on its traces into a final unity, but has (instantaneous) Being about The One as the unchanging Life of the Authentic-Existent. This is certainly what we have been seeking: this Principle, at rest within the One, is Eternity; possessing this stable quality, being itself at once the absolute self-identical and none the less the active manifestation of an unchanging Life set towards the Divine and dwelling within It, untrue, therefore, neither on the side of Being nor on the side of Life—this will be Eternity (the Real-Being we have sought).

Truly to be comports never lacking existence and never knowing variety in the mode of existence: Being is, therefore, self-identical throughout, and, therefore, again is one undistinguishable thing. Being can have no this and that; it cannot be treated in terms of intervals, unfoldings, progression, extension; there is no grasping any first or last in it.

If, then, there is no first or last in this Principle, if existence is its most authentic possession and its very self, and this in the sense that its existence is Essence or Life—then, once again, we meet here what we have been discussing, Eternity.

I Observe that the use of the word 'everlasting' and the reference to unbroken continuity must be taken as a mere convenience of exposition; the word is not strictly applicable to Eternity, but is at best a pointer to the imperishable and leads the mind to the thought of ever-increasing, not to say unending, expansion.[4] I We might perhaps prefer to speak of 'Being', without any attribute; but since this term is applicable to Essence and some writers have used the word Essence for things of process, we cannot convey our meaning to them without introducing some word carrying the notion of perdurance.

There is, of course, no difference between Being and Everlasting Being; just as there is none between a philosopher and a true philosopher: the attribute 'true' came into use because there arose what masqueraded as philosophy; and for similar reasons 'everlasting' was adjoined to 'Being', and 'Being' to 'everlasting', and we have (the tautology of) 'Everlasting Being'. We must take this 'Everlasting' as expressing no more than Authentic Being: it is merely a partial expression of a potency which ignores all interval or term and can look forward to nothing by way of addition to the All which it possesses. The Principle of which this is the statement will be the All-Existent, and, as being all, can have no failing or deficiency, cannot be at some one point complete and at some other lacking.

Things and beings in the Time order—even when to all appearance complete, as a body is when fit to harbour a soul—are still bound to sequence; they are deficient to the extent of that thing, Time, which they need: let them have it, present to them and running side by side with them, and they are by that very fact incomplete; completeness is attributed to them only by an accident of language.

But the conception of Eternity demands something which is in its nature complete without sequence; it is not satisfied by something measured out to any remoter time or even by something limitless, but, in its limitless reach, still having the progression of futurity: it requires something immediately possessed of the due fullness of Being, something whose Being does not depend upon any quantity (such as instalments of time) but subsists before all quantity.

Itself having no quantity, it can have no contact with anything quantitative since its Life cannot be made a thing of fragments, in contradiction to the partlessness which is its character; it must be without parts in the Life as in the essence.

The phrase 'He was good' (used by Plato of the Demiurge) **I** refers to a conception of the All (i.e., to the Intelligible Universe); the past tense is used simply to signify the absence of any origin in Time: so that also[5] this Universe **I** has had no temporal beginning; and if we speak of something 'before' it, that is only in the sense of the Cause from which it takes its Eternal Existence. Plato used the word ('was') merely for the convenience of exposition, and later corrects it as inappropriate to the order vested with the Eternity he conceives and affirms.

7. Now comes the question whether, in all this discussion, we are not merely helping to make out a case for some other order of Beings and talking of matters alien to ourselves.

But how could that be? What understanding can there be failing some point of contact? And what contact could there be with the utterly alien?

We must then have, ourselves, some part or share in Eternity.

Still, how is this possible to us who exist in Time?

The whole question turns on the distinction between being in Time and being in Eternity, and this will be best realized by probing to the nature of Time. We must, therefore, descend from Eternity to the investigation of Time, to the realm of Time: till now we have been taking the upward way; we must now take the downward—not to the lowest levels but within the degree in which Time itself is a descent from Eternity.

If the venerable sages of former days had not treated of Time, our method would be to begin by linking to (the idea of) Eternity (the idea of) its Next (its inevitable downward or outgoing subsequent in the same order), then setting forth the probable nature of such a Next and proceeding to show how the conception thus formed tallies with our own doctrine.

But, as things are, our best beginning is to range over the most noteworthy of the ancient opinions and see whether any of them accord with ours.

Existing explanations of Time seem to fall into three classes:

Time is variously identified with what we know as Movement, with a moved object, and with some phenomenon of Movement: obviously it cannot be Rest or a resting object or any phenomenon of rest, since, in its characteristic idea, it is concerned with change.

Of those that explain it as Movement, some identify it with any and every Movement, others with that of the All. Those that make it a moved object would identify it with the orb of the All. Those that conceive it as some phenomenon of Movement treat it, severally, either as a period or as a standard of measure or, more generally, as an accompaniment, whether of Movement in general or of ordered Movement.

8. Movement Time cannot be—whether movement of every kind is taken and a united total made up of all or whether only ordered movement is meant—since movement, in either sense, takes place in Time. And, of course, if there is any movement not in Time, the identification with Time becomes all the less tenable.

In a word, Movement must be distinct from the medium in which it takes place.

And, with all that has been said or is still said, one consideration is decisive: Movement can come to rest, can be intermittent; Time is continuous.

We will be told that the Movement of the All is continuous (and so may be identical with Time).

But, if the reference is to the Circuit of the heavenly system, this Circuit takes place in Time, and the time taken by the total Circuit is twice the time taken by half the Circuit; whether we count the whole or only the first half, it is nevertheless the same movement of the heavenly system.

Further, the fact that we hear of the Movement of the outermost sphere being the swiftest confirms our theory. Obviously, it is the swiftest of movements by taking the lesser time to traverse the greater space—the very greatest—all other moving things are slower by taking a longer time to traverse a mere segment of the same extension: in other words, Time is not this movement.

And, if Time is not even the movement of the Cosmic Sphere much less is it the sphere itself, though that has been identified with Time on the ground of its being in motion.

Is it, then, some phenomenon or connexion of Movement?

I Let us⁶ suppose I it to be extent, or duration, of Movement.

Now, to begin with, Movement, even continuous, has no unchanging extent (as Time the equable has), I since—to take only motion⁷ in space—it may be I faster or slower; there must, therefore, be some unit of standard outside it, by which these differences are measurable, and this outside standard would more properly be called Time. And failing such a measure, which extent would be Time, that of the fast or of the slow—or rather which of them all, since these speed-differences are limitless?

Is it the extent I of the ordered Movement?⁸I

Again, this gives us no unit since the movement is infinitely variable; we would have, thus, not Time but Times.

The extent of the Movement of the All, then?

If this means extent as inherent in the movement itself, we have Movement pure and simple (and not Time). Admittedly, Movement answers to measure—in two ways. First there is space; the movement is commensurate with the area it passes through, and this area is its extent. But this gives us, still, space only, not Time. Secondly, the circuit, considered apart from distance traversed, has the extent of its continuity, of its tendency not to stop but to proceed indefinitely: but this is merely amplitude of Movement; search it, tell its vastness, and, still, Time has no more appeared, no more enters into the matter, than when one certifies a high pitch of heat; all we have discovered is Motion in ceaseless succession, like water flowing ceaselessly, motion and extent of motion.

Succession or repetition gives us Number—dyad, triad, &c.—and the extent traversed is a matter of Magnitude; thus we have Quantity of Movement—in the form of number, dyad, triad, dekad, or in the form of extent apprehended in what we may call the amount of the Movement: but, the idea of Time we have not. That definite Quantity is (not Time but) merely something occurring within Time, for, otherwise Time is not everywhere but is something belonging to Movement which thus would be its substratum or basic-stuff: once more, then, we would be making Time identical with Movement; for the extent of Movement is not something outside it but is❙ simply its continuousness; if this continuousness is in Time, its only difference from the instantaneous (or non-continuous) is precisely that it is in Time, and therefore the[9] extended move-ment❙ and its extent are not Time; they are in Time. Those that explain Time as extent of Movement must mean not the extent of the movement itself but something which determines its extension, something with which the move-ment keeps pace in its course. But what this something is, we are not told; yet it is, clearly, Time, that in which all Movement proceeds. This is what our discussion has aimed at from the first: 'What, essentially, is Time?' It comes to this: we ask 'What is Time?' and we are answered, 'Time is the extension of Movement in Time'!

On the one hand Time is said to be an extension apart from and outside that of Movement; and we are left to guess what this extension may be: on the other hand, it is represented as the extension of Movement; and this leaves the difficulty what to make of the extension of Rest—though one thing may con-tinue as long in repose as another in motion, so that we are obliged to think of one thing, Time, that covers both Rest and Movement, and, therefore, stands distinct from either.

What then is this thing of extension? To what order of beings does it belong? It obviously is not spatial, for place, too, is something outside it.

9. 'A Number, a Measure, belonging to Movement?'

'Measure' is more plausible since Movement is a continuous thing; but let us consider.

To begin with, we have the doubt which met us when we probed its identification with extent of Movement: is Time the measure of any and every Movement?

Have we any means of calculating disconnected and lawless Movement? What number or measure would apply? What would be the principle of such a Measure?

One Measure for movement slow and fast, for any and every movement: then that number and measure would be like the dekad, by which we reckon horses and cows, or like some common standard for liquids and solids. If Time is this kind of Measure, we learn, no doubt, of what objects it is a Measure—of Movements—but we are no nearer understanding what it is in itself.

Or: we may take the dekad and think of it, apart from the horses or cows, as a pure number; this gives us a measure which, even though not actually applied, has a definite nature. Is Time, perhaps, a Measure in this sense?

No: to tell us no more of Time in itself than that it is such a number is merely to bring us back to the dekad we have already rejected, or to some similar abstract figure.

If, on the other hand, Time is (not such an abstraction but) a Measure possessing a continuous extent of its own, it must have quantity, like a foot-rule; it must have magnitude; it will, clearly, be in the nature of a line traversing the path of Movement. But, itself thus sharing in the movement, how can it be a Measure of Movement? Why should the one of the two be the measure rather than the other? Besides, an accompanying measure is more plausibly considered as a measure of the particular movement it accompanies than of Movement in general. ❙Further, what is measured must be continuous, or else our measuring line will come to a stop.[10]❙

The fact is that we are not to think of a measure outside and apart, but of a combined thing, a measured Movement, and we are to discover what measures it.

Given a Movement measured, are we to suppose the measure to be a magnitude?

If so, which of these two would be Time, the measured movement or the measuring magnitude? For Time (as measure) must be either the movement measured by magnitude, or the measuring magnitude itself, or something using the magnitude like a yard-stick to appraise the movement. In all three cases, as we have indicated, the application is scarcely plausible except where continuous movement is assumed; unless the movement proceeds smoothly, and even unintermittently and as embracing the entire content of the moving object, great difficulties arise in the identification of Time with any kind of measure.

Let us, then, suppose Time to be this 'measured Movement', measured by quantity. Now the Movement if it is to be measured requires a measure outside itself; this was the only reason for raising the question of the accompanying measure. In exactly the same way the measuring magnitude, in turn, will require a measure, because only when the standard shows such and such an extension can the degree of movement be appraised. Time then will be, not the magnitude accompanying the Movement, but that numerical value by which the magnitude accompanying the Movement is estimated. But that number can be only the abstract figure which represents the magnitude, and it is difficult to see how an abstract figure can perform the act of measuring.

And, supposing that we discover a way in which it can, we still have not Time, the measure, but a particular quantity of Time, not at all the same thing: Time means something very different from any definite period: before all question as to quantity is the question as to the thing of which a certain quantity is present.

Time, we are told, is the number outside Movement and measuring it, like the tens applied to the reckoning of the horses and cows but not inherent in them: we are not told what this Number is; yet, applied or not, it must, like that dekad, have some nature of its own.

Or 'it is that which accompanies a Movement and measures it by its successive stages'; but we are still left asking what this thing recording the stages may be.

In any case, once a thing—whether by point or standard or any other means—measures succession, it must measure according to time: this number appraising movement degree by degree must, therefore, if it is to serve as a measure at all, be something dependent upon time and in contact with it: for, either, degree is spatial, merely—the beginning and end of the Stadium, for example—or in the only alternative, it is a pure matter of Time: the succession of early and late is stage of Time, Time ending upon a certain Now or Time beginning from a Now.

Time, therefore, is something other than the mere number measuring Movement, whether Movement in general or ordered Movement.

Further: why should the mere presence of a number give us Time—a number measuring or measured; for the same number may be either—if Time is not given us by the fact of Movement itself, the movement which inevitably contains in itself a succession of stages? To make the number essential to Time is like saying that magnitude has not its full quantity unless we can estimate that quantity.

Again, if Time is, admittedly, endless, how can number apply to it?

Are we to take some portion of Time and find its numerical statement? That simply means that Time existed before number was applied to it.

We may, therefore, very well think that it existed before the Soul or Mind that estimates it—if, indeed, it is not to be thought to take its origin from the Soul—for no measurement by anything is necessary to its existence; measured or not, it has the full extent of its being.

And suppose it to be true that the Soul is the appraiser, using Magnitude as the measuring standard, how does this help us to the conception of Time?

10. Time, again, has been described as some sort of a sequence upon Movement, but we learn nothing from this, nothing is said, until we know what it is that produces this sequential thing; probably the cause and not the result would turn out to be Time.

And, admitting such a thing, there would still remain the question whether it came into being before the movement, with it, or after it; and, whether we say before or with or after, we are speaking of order in Time: and thus our definition is, 'Time is a sequence upon movement *in Time*'!

Enough. Our main purpose is to show what Time is, not to refute false definition. To traverse point by point the many opinions of our many predecessors would mean a history rather than an identification; we have treated the various theories as fully as is possible in a cursory review: and, notice, that which makes Time the Measure of the All-Movement is refuted by our entire discussion and, especially by the observations upon the Measurement of Movement in general, for all the argument—except, of course, that from irregularity—applies to the All as much as to particular Movement.

We are, thus, at the stage where we are to state what Time really is.

11. To this end we must go back to the state we affirmed of Eternity, unwavering Life, undivided totality, limitless, knowing no divagation, at rest in unity and intent upon it. Time was not yet: or at least it did not exist I for the Eternal Beings. It is we that must create Time out of the concept and nature of progressive derivation, which remained latent in the Divine Beings.

How Time emerged we can scarcely call upon the Muses to relate since they were not in existence then—perhaps not even if they had been; though the Cosmos itself, when once engendered, could no doubt tell us best how Time arose[11] and became manifest. I Something thus the story must run:

Time at first—in reality before that 'first' was produced by desire of succession I —Time lay, though not yet as Time, in the Authentic Existent together with the Cosmos itself; the Cosmos also was merged in the Authentic and motionless within it. But there was an active principle there, one set on governing itself and realizing itself (= the All-Soul), and it chose to aim at something more than its present: it stirred from its rest, and the Cosmos stirred with it. 'And we (the active principle and the Cosmos),[12] stirring to a ceaseless succession, I to a next, to the discrimination of identity and the establishment of ever new difference, traversed a portion of the outgoing path and produced an image of Eternity, produced Time.'

For the Soul contained an unquiet faculty, always desirous of translating elsewhere what it saw in the Authentic Realm, and it could not bear to retain within itself all the dense fullness of its possession.

A seed is at rest; the nature-principle within, uncoiling outwards, makes way towards what seems to it a large life; but by that partition it loses; it was a unity self-gathered, and now, in going forth from itself, it fritters its unity away; it advances into a weaker greatness. It is so with this faculty of the Soul, when it produces the Cosmos known to sense—the mimic of the Divine Sphere, moving not in the very movement of the Divine but in its similitude, in an effort to reproduce that of the Divine. To bring this Cosmos into being, the Soul first laid aside its eternity and clothed itself with Time; this world of its fashioning it then gave over to be a servant to Time, making it at every point a thing of Time, setting all its progressions within the bournes of Time. For the Cosmos moves only in Soul—the only Space open to it to move in—and therefore its Movement has always been in the Time which inheres in Soul.

Putting forth its energy in act after act, in a constant progress of novelty, the Soul produces succession as well as act; taking up new purposes added to the old it brings thus into being what had not existed in that former period when its purpose was still dormant and its life was not as it since became: the life is changed and that change carries with it a change of Time. Time, then, is contained in differentiation of Life; the ceaseless forward movement of Life brings with it unending Time; and Life as it achieves its stages constitutes past Time.

Would it, then, be sound to define Time as the Life of the Soul in movement as it passes from one stage of act or experience to another?

Yes; for Eternity, we have said, is Life in repose, unchanging, self-identical, always endlessly complete; and there is to be an image of Eternity—Time—such an image as this lower All presents of the Higher Sphere. Therefore over against that higher Life there must be another life, known by the same name as the more veritable Life of the Soul; over against that Movement of the Intellectual Soul there must be the movement of some partial phase; over against that Identity, Unchangeableness and Stability there must be that which is not constant in the one hold but puts forth multitudinous acts; over against that Oneness without extent or interval there must be an image of oneness, a unity of link and succession; over against the immediately Infinite and All-comprehending, that which tends, yes, to infinity but by tending to a perpetual futurity; over against the Whole in concentration, there must be that which is to be a whole by stages never final. The lesser must always be working towards the increase of its Being; this will be its imitation of what is immediately complete, self-realized, endless without stage: only thus can its Being reproduce that of the Higher.

Time, however, is not to be conceived as outside of Soul; Eternity is not outside of the Authentic Existent: nor is it to be taken as a sequence or succession to Soul, any more than Eternity is to the Divine. It is a thing seen upon Soul, inherent, coeval to it, as Eternity to the Intellectual Realm.

12. We are brought thus to the conception of a Natural-Principle—Time—a certain expanse (a quantitative phase) of the Life of the Soul, a principle moving forward by smooth and uniform changes following silently upon each other— a Principle, then, whose Act is (not one like that of the Supreme but) sequent.

But let us conceive this power of the Soul to turn back and withdraw from the life-course which it now maintains, from the continuous and unending activity of an ever-existent Soul not self-contained or self-intent but concerned about doing and engendering: imagine it no longer accomplishing any Act, setting a pause to this work it has inaugurated; let this outgoing phase of the Soul become once more, equally with the rest, turned to the Supreme, to Eternal Being, to the tranquilly stable.

What would then exist but Eternity?

All would remain in unity; how could there be any diversity of things? What earlier or later would there be, I what futurity?[13]I What ground would lie ready to the Soul's operation but the Supreme in which it has its Being? Or, indeed, what operative tendency could it have even to That since a prior separation is the necessary condition of tendency?

The very sphere of the Universe would not exist; for it cannot antedate Time: it, too, has its Being and its Movement in Time; and if it ceased to move, the Soul-Act (which is the essence of Time) continuing, we could measure the period of its Repose by that standard outside it.

If, then, the Soul withdrew, sinking itself again into its primal unity, Time would disappear: the origin of Time, clearly, is to be traced to the first stir of the Soul's tendency towards the production of the sensible Universe with the consecutive act ensuing. This is how 'Time'—as we read—'came into Being simultaneously with' this All: the Soul begot at once the Universe and Time; in that activity of the Soul this Universe sprang into being; the activity is Time, the Universe is a content of Time. No doubt it will be urged that we read also of 'the orbit of the Stars being Times': but do not forget what goes with these words; 'the stars exist', we are told, 'for the display and delimitation of Time', and 'that there may be a manifest Measure'. No indication of Time could be derived from (observation of) the Soul; no portion of it can be seen or handled, so it could not be measured in itself, especially when there was as yet no knowledge of counting; therefore the Demiurge (in the Timaeus) brings into being night and day; in their difference is given Duality—from which, we read, arises the concept of Number.

We observe the tract between a sunrise and its return and, as the movement is uniform, we thus obtain a Time-interval upon which to support ourselves, and we use this as a standard. We have thus a measure of Time. Time itself is not a measure. How would it set to work? And what kind of thing is there of which it could say, 'I find the extent of this equal to such and such a stretch of my own extent?' What is this 'I'? Obviously something by which measurement is known. Time, then, serves towards measurement but is not itself the Measure: the Movement of the All will be measured according to Time, but Time will not, of its own nature, be a Measure of Movement: primarily a Kind to itself, it will incidentally exhibit the magnitudes of that movement.

And the reiterated observation of Movement—the same extent found to be traversed in such and such a period—will lead to the conception of a definite quantity of Time past.

This brings us to the fact that, in a certain sense, the Movement, the orbit of the universe, may legitimately be said to measure Time—in so far as that is possible at all—since any definite stretch of that circuit occupies a certain quantity of Time, and this is the only grasp we have of Time, our only understanding of it: what that circuit measures—by indication, that is—will be Time, manifested by the Movement but not brought into being by it.

This means that the measure of the Spheric Movement has itself been measured by a definite stretch of that Movement and therefore is something different; as measure, it is one thing and, as the measured, it is another; (its being measure or) its being measured cannot be of its essence.

We are no nearer knowledge than if we said that the foot-rule measures Magnitude while we left the concept Magnitude undefined; or, again, we might as well define Movement—whose limitlessness puts it out of our reach—as the thing measured by Space; the definition would be parallel since we can mark off a certain space which the Movement has traversed and say the one is equivalent to the other.

13. The Spheral Circuit, then, performed in Time, indicates it: but when we come to Time itself there is no question of its being 'within' something else: it must be primary, a thing 'within itself'. It is that in which all the rest happens, in which all movement and rest exist smoothly and under order; something following a definite order is necessary to exhibit it and to make it a subject of knowledge—though not to produce it—it is known by order whether in rest or in motion; in motion especially, for Movement better moves Time into our ken than rest can, and it is easier to estimate distance traversed than repose maintained.

This last fact has led to Time being called a measure of Movement when it should have been described as something measured by Movement and then defined in its essential nature; it is an error to define it by a mere accidental concomitant and so to reverse the actual order of things. Possibly, however, this reversal was not intended by the authors of the explanation: but, at any rate, we do not understand them; they plainly apply the term Measure to what is in reality the measured and leave us unable to grasp their meaning: our perplexity may be due to the fact that their writings—addressed to disciples acquainted with their teaching—do not explain what this thing, measure or measured object, is in itself.

Plato does not make the essence of Time consist in its being either a measure or a thing measured by something else.

Upon the point of the means by which it is known, he remarks that the Circuit advances an infinitesimal distance for every infinitesimal segment of Time, so that from that observation it is possible to estimate what the Time is, how much it amounts to: but when his purpose is to explain its essential nature he tells us that it sprang into Being simultaneously with the Heavenly system, a reproduction of Eternity, its image in motion, Time necessarily unresting as the Life with which it must keep pace: and 'coeval with the Heavens' because it is this same Life (of the Divine Soul) which brings the Heavens also into being; Time and the Heavens are the work of the one Life.

Suppose that Life, then, to revert—an impossibility—to perfect unity: Time, whose existence is in that Life, and the Heavens, no longer maintained by that Life, would end at once.

It is the height of absurdity to fasten on the succession of earlier and later occurring in the life and movement of this sphere of ours, to declare that it must be some definite thing and to call it Time, while denying the reality of the more truly existent Movement, that of the Soul, which has also its earlier and later: it cannot be reasonable to recognize succession in the case of the Soulless Movement—and so to associate Time with that—while ignoring succession and the reality of Time in the Movement from which the other takes its imitative existence; to ignore, that is, the very Movement in which succession first appears, a self-actuated movement which, engendering its own every operation, creates the sequence by which each instant no sooner comes into existence than it passes into the next.

But: we treat the Cosmic Movement as overarched by that of the Soul and bring it under Time; yet we do not set under Time that Soul-Movement itself with all its endless progression: what is our explanation of this paradox?

Simply, that the Soul-Movement has for its Prior (not Time but) Eternity which knows neither its progression nor its extension. The descent towards Time begins with this Soul-Movement; it made Time and harbours Time as a concomitant to its Act.

And this is how Time is omnipresent: that Soul is absent from no fragment of the Cosmos just as our Soul is absent from no particle of ourselves. As for those who pronounce Time a thing of no substantial existence, of no reality, they clearly belie God Himself whenever they say 'He was' or 'He will be': for the existence indicated by the 'was' and 'will be' can have only such reality as belongs to that in which it is said to be situated: but this school demands another style of argument.

Meanwhile we have a supplementary observation to make.

Take a man walking and observe the advance he has made; that advance gives you the quantity of movement he is employing: and when you know that quantity—represented by the ground traversed by his feet, for, of course, we are supposing the bodily movement to correspond with the pace he has set within himself—you know also the movement that exists in the man himself before the feet move.

You must relate the body, carried forward during a given period of Time, to a certain quantity of Movement causing the progress and to the Time it takes, and that again to the Movement, equal in extension, within the man's soul.

But the Movement within the Soul—to what are you to refer that?

Let your choice fall where it may, from this point there is nothing but the unextended: and this is the primarily existent, the container to all else, having itself no container, brooking none.

And, as with Man's Soul, so with the Soul of the All.

Is Time, then, within ourselves as well?

Time is in every Soul of the order of the All-Soul, present in like form in all; for all the Souls are the one Soul.

And this is why Time can never be broken apart, any more than Eternity which, similarly, under diverse manifestations, has its Being as an integral constituent of all the eternal Existences.

NOTES TO ENNEAD III.7

1. FIRST EDITION begins this paragraph as: "*In one aspect, no doubt, Eternity resides* in a partial phase of the All-Being; *but in another aspect it is* inherent in the All . . ."

TAYLOR: "And in a certain degree, indeed, the whole itself is as it were in a part, and the things which are there are as parts in a whole, as if in reality this were an *all* not collected from parts, but itself generating parts, in order that through this it may be truly all."

GUTHRIE: "There the whole in a certain way exists within the part; the parts also are in the whole;"

ARMSTRONG: "And some of these [things which have primary existence—ed.] are as if in a part of the existent whole, others in the whole . . ."

2. FIRST EDITION: ". . . supremely great; *it proves on investigation to be identical* with God:"

GUTHRIE: ". . . reason dictates that eternity is something venerable, identical with the divinity. (That is, with this divinity that intelligible existence is.)"

ARMSTRONG: ". . . eternity is a majestic thing, and thought declares it identical with the god." Armstrong adds that this god is the Second Hypostasis.

TAYLOR: ". . . eternity is venerable, and as our intellectual conception of it says, is the same with deity."

3. FIRST EDITION: "... for ever. *To the notion of a Life (a Living-Principle) all-comprehensive add that it never spends itself, and we have the statement of a Life instantaneously infinite.*"

TAYLOR, GUTHRIE, and ARMSTRONG all include this last sentence, though Armstrong brackets and footnotes it as "clearly a rather unintelligent gloss on the one before it."

4. FIRST EDITION has this sentence as: "Observe that *such words as 'always, never, sometimes'* must be taken as mere *conveniences* of exposition: thus *'always'—used in the sense not of time but of incorruptibility and endlessly complete scope—might set up the false notion of stage and interval.*"

GUTHRIE: "When we say that existence exists always, and that there is not one time in which it is, and another in which it is not, we speak thus only for the sake of greater clearness; for when we use the word 'always,' we do not take it in an absolute sense; but if we use it to show that existence is incorruptible, it might well mislead the mind in leading it to issue out from the unity (characteristic of eternity) to make it run through the manifold (which is foreign to eternity). 'Always' further indicates that existence is never defective."

TAYLOR: "But when we say that it is always, and that it is not at one time being, and at another time non-being, it is requisite to think that we thus speak for the sake of perspicuity; since the term always, is perhaps not properly employed, but is assumed for the purpose of manifesting its incorruptible nature ..."

ARMSTRONG: "But when we use the word 'always' and say that it does not exist at one time but not at another, we must be thought to be putting it this way for our own sake; for the 'always' was perhaps not being used in its strict sense, but, taken as explaining the incorruptible, might mislead the soul into imagining an expansion of something becoming more, and again, of something which is never going to fail."

5. FIRST EDITION: "... refers to *the Idea of the All; and its very indefiniteness signifies the utter* absence of *relation to* Time: so that *even* this Universe ..."

TAYLOR: "... must be referred to the conception of the universe, signifying that what is beyond the universe, does not originate from a certain time; so that neither is the world allotted a certain temporal beginning ..."

GUTHRIE: "... does indeed refer to the notion of the universe, and indicates that, in the Principle superior to the universe, nothing began to exist at any particular time. Never, therefore, did the universe begin to exist within time ..."

ARMSTRONG: "... takes us back to the thought of the All [the physical universe]; he indicates that by virtue of the transcendent All it has no beginning in time; so that the universe, too, did not have a temporal beginning ..." Brackets are Armstrong's.

6. FIRST EDITION: "Let us, *tentatively,* suppose ..."

7. FIRST EDITION: "... since, *even* in space, it may be ..."

ARMSTRONG: "... quicker and slower, even movement in space."

8. FIRST EDITION: "... of the *subordinate* Movement (*= movement of things of earth*)?"

TAYLOR, GUTHRIE, and ARMSTRONG all support "ordered" movement.

9. FIRST EDITION: "... simply its continuousness, *and we need not halt upon the difference between the momentary and the continuous, which is simply one of manner and degree. The* extended movement ..."

ARMSTRONG: "... the comparison of movement which does not happen all at once with what is all at once [the instantaneous] can only be made in time. In what way will the non-instantaneous differ from the instantaneous? By being in time, so that movement which extends over a distance and the distance covered by it are not the actual thing, time, but are in time."

10. FIRST EDITION: "Further, *this entire discussion assumes continuous movement, since the accompanying principle, Time, is itself unbroken (but a full explanation implies justification of Time in repose).*"

11. FIRST EDITION: ". . . for the Eternal Beings, *though its being was implicit in the Idea and Principle* of progressive derivation.

"*But from the Divine Beings thus at rest within themselves, how did this Time first emerge?*

"*We* can scarcely call upon the Muses to *recount its origin* since they were not in existence then—perhaps not even if they had been. *The engendered thing, Time, itself, can best tell us how it rose* and became manifest . . ."

TAYLOR: "But time was not yet, at least was not in those natures; but was about to be generated by the reason and nature of that which is posterior. Intelligibles, therefore, quietly energizing in themselves, he who desires to know how time first fell, will not perhaps call upon the Muses who did not then exist, to tell him. Perhaps, however, he will, since the Muses also then had a being. Perhaps, too, he will find time itself generated, so far as it is generated and unfolded into light. But he will speak about it as follows:" Taylor also adds, in a footnote: "Time, as well as the world, is said to have been generated, not because it once was not, for it always existed, but because it depends for its subsistence on causes naturally prior to itself."

ARMSTRONG: "Time did not yet exist, not at any rate for the beings of that world; we shall produce time by means of the form and nature of what comes after. If, then, these beings were at rest in themselves, one could hardly, perhaps, call on the Muses, who did not then yet exist, to tell us 'how time first came out': but one might perhaps (even if the Muses did exist then after all) ask time when it has come into being to tell us how it did come into being and appear. It might say . . ."

12. FIRST EDITION (ellipses indicate identical words in both editions: "—Time lay, *self-concentrated, at rest within* the Authentic Existent: *it was not yet Time; it* was merged . . . it stirred from its rest, and *Time* stirred with it. And we (*i.e. human Souls as summed in the principle of developing Life, the All-Soul?*) we, stirring to a ceaseless succession . . ."

ARMSTRONG: ". . . it was at rest with eternity in real being; it was not yet time . . . this moved, and time moved with it; and so, always moving on to the 'next' and the 'after,' and what is not the same, but one thing after another, we made a long stretch of our journey and constructed time as an image of eternity."

TAYLOR and GUTHRIE also translate that "time" rather than "the Cosmos" was originally "merged" and subsequently "stirred."

13. FIRST EDITION: ". . . what *long-lasting or short-lasting?*"

TAYLOR: "And what will be prior or posterior, or more extended?"

GUTHRIE: "How could she contain priority, posteriority, or more or less duration of time?"

ARMSTRONG: "What sense would 'before' still have, and what 'after' or 'future'?"

EIGHTH TRACTATE [1]

Nature, Contemplation, and the One

1. Supposing we played a little before entering upon our serious concern and maintained that all things are striving after Contemplation, looking to Vision as their one end—and this, not merely beings endowed with reason but even the unreasoning animals, the Principle that rules in growing things, and the Earth that produces these—and that all achieve their purpose in the measure possible to their kind, each attaining Vision and possessing itself of the End in its own way and degree, some things in entire reality, others in mimicry and in image—we would scarcely find anyone to endure so strange a thesis. But in a discussion entirely among ourselves there is no risk in a light handling of our own ideas.

Well—in the play of this very moment am I engaged in the act of Contemplation?

Yes; I and all that enter this play are in Contemplation: our play aims at Vision; and there is every reason to believe that child or man, in sport or earnest, is playing or working only towards Vision, that every act is an effort towards Vision; the compulsory act, which tends rather to bring the Vision down to outward things, and the act thought of as voluntary, less concerned with the outer, originate alike in the effort towards Vision.

The case of Man will be treated later on: let us speak, first, of the earth and of the trees and vegetation in general, asking ourselves what is the nature of Contemplation in them, how we relate to any Contemplative activity the labour and productiveness of the earth, how Nature, held to be devoid of reason and even of conscious representation, can either harbour Contemplation or produce by means of the Contemplation which it does not possess.

2. There is, obviously, no question here of hands or feet, of any implement borrowed or inherent: Nature needs simply the Matter which it is to work upon and bring under Form; its productivity cannot depend upon mechanical operation. What driving or hoisting goes to produce all that variety of colour and pattern?

The wax-workers, whose methods have been cited as parallel to the creative act of Nature, are unable to make colours; all they can do is to impose upon their handicraft colours taken from elsewhere. None the less there is a parallel which demands attention: in the case of workers in such arts there must be something locked up within themselves, an efficacy not going out from them and yet guiding their hands in all their creation; and this observation should have indicated a similar phenomenon in Nature; it should be clear that this indwelling efficacy, which makes without hands, must exist in Nature, no less than in the craftsman—but, there, as a thing completely inbound. Nature need possess no outgoing force as against that remaining within; the only moved thing is Matter; there can be no moved phase in this Nature-Principle; any such moved phase could not be the primal mover; this Nature-Principle is no such moved entity; it is the unmoved Principle operating in the Cosmos.

We may be answered that the Reason-Principle is, no doubt, unmoved, but that the Nature-Principle, another being, operates by motion.

But, if Nature entire is in question here, it is identical with the Reason-Principle; and any part of it that is unmoved is the Reason-Principle. The Nature-Principle must be an Ideal-Form, not a compound of Form and Matter; there is no need for it to possess (such a changeable element as) Matter, hot and cold: the Matter that underlies it, on which it exercises its creative act, brings all that with it, or, natively without quality, becomes hot and cold, and all the rest, when brought under Reason: Matter, to become fire, demands the approach not of fire but of a Reason-Principle.

This is no slight evidence that in the animal and vegetable realms the Reason-Principles are the makers and that Nature is a Reason-Principle producing a second Reason-Principle, its offspring, which, in turn, while itself, still, remaining intact, communicates something to the underlie, Matter.

The Reason-Principle presiding over visible Shape is the very ultimate of its order, a dead thing unable to produce further: that which produces in the created realm is the living Reason-Principle—brother, no doubt, to that which gives mere shape, but having life-giving power.

3. But if this Reason-Principle (Nature) is in act—and produces by the process indicated—how can it have any part in Contemplation?

To begin with, since in all its production it is stationary and intact, a Reason-Principle self-indwelling, it is in its own nature a Contemplative act. All doing must be guided by a Reason-Principle, and will therefore be distinct from that Principle: the Reason-Principle then, as accompanying and guiding the work, will be distinct from the work; not being action but Reason-Principle it is, necessarily, Contemplation. Taking the Reason-Principle, the Logos, in all its phases, the lowest and last springs from a mental act (in the higher Logos) and is itself a contemplation, though only in the sense of being contemplated I (i.e., of being object and not subject),[2]I but above it stands the total Logos with its two distinguishable phases, first, that identified not as Nature but as All-Soul and, next, that operating in Nature and being itself the Nature-Principle.

And does this Reason-Principle, Nature, spring from a contemplation?

Wholly and solely.

From self-contemplation, then? Or what are we to think? It derives from a Contemplation and some contemplating Being; how are we to suppose it to have Contemplation itself?

The Contemplation springing from the reasoning faculty—that, I mean, of planning its own content—it does not possess.

But why not, since it is a phase of Life, a Reason-Principle, and a creative Power?

Because to plan for a thing is to lack it: Nature does not lack; it creates because it possesses. Its creative act is simply its possession of its own characteristic Essence; now its Essence, since it is a Reason-Principle, is to be at once an act of contemplation and an object of contemplation. In other words, the Nature-Principle produces by virtue of being an act of contemplation, an object of contemplation, and a Reason-Principle; on this triple character depends its creative efficacy.

Thus the act of production is seen to be in Nature an act of contemplation, for creation is the outcome of a contemplation which never becomes anything else, which never does anything else, but creates by simply being a contemplation.

4. And Nature, asked why it brings forth its works, might answer if it cared to listen and to speak:

'It would have been more becoming to put no question but to learn in silence just as I myself am silent and make no habit of talking. And what is your lesson? This; that whatsoever comes into being is my vision, seen in my silence, the vision that belongs to my character who, sprung from vision, am vision-loving and create vision by the vision-seeing faculty within me. The mathematicians from their vision draw their figures: but I draw nothing: I gaze and the figures of the material would take being as if they fell from my contemplation. As with my mother (the All-Soul) and the Beings that begot me so it is with me: they are born of a Contemplation and my birth is from them, not by their Act but by their Being; they are the loftier Reason-Principles, they contemplate themselves and I am born.'

Now what does this tell us?

It tells: that what we know as Nature is a Soul, offspring of a yet earlier Soul of more powerful life; that it possesses, therefore, in its repose, a vision within itself; that it has no tendency upward nor even downward but is at peace, steadfast, in its own Essence; that, in this immutability accompanied by what may be called Self-Consciousness, it possesses—within the measure of its possibility—a knowledge of the realm of subsequent things perceived in virtue of that understanding and consciousness; and, achieving thus a resplendent and delicious spectacle, has no further aim.

Of course, while it may be convenient to speak of 'understanding' or 'perception' in the Nature-Principle, this is not in the full sense applicable to other beings; we are applying to sleep a word borrowed from the wake.

For the Vision on which Nature broods, inactive, is a self-intuition, a spectacle laid before it by virtue of its unaccompanied self-concentration and by the fact that in itself it belongs to the order of intuition. It is a Vision silent but somewhat blurred, for there exists another, a clearer, of which Nature is the image: hence all that Nature produces is weak; the weaker act of intuition produces the weaker object.

In the same way, human beings, when weak on the side of contemplation, find in action their trace of vision and of reason: their spiritual feebleness unfits them for contemplation; they are left with a void, because they cannot adequately seize the vision; yet they long for it; they are hurried into action as their way to the vision which they cannot attain by intellection. They act from the desire of seeing their action, and of making it visible and sensible to others when the result shall prove fairly well equal to the plan. Everywhere, doing and making will be found to be either an attenuation or a complement of vision—attenuation if the doer was aiming only at the thing done; complement if he is to possess something nobler to gaze upon than the mere work produced.

Given the power to contemplate the Authentic, who would run, of choice, after its image?

The relation of action to contemplation is indicated in the way duller children, inapt to study and speculation, take to crafts and manual labour.

5. This discussion of Nature has shown us how the origin of things is a Contemplation: we may now take the matter up to the higher Soul; we find that the Contemplation pursued by this, its instinct towards knowing and inquiring, the birth pangs set up by the knowledge it attains, its teeming fullness, have caused it—in itself all one object of Vision—to produce another Vision (that of the Cosmos): it is just as a given science, complete in itself, becomes the source and cause of what might be called a minor science in the student who attains to some partial knowledge of all its divisions. But the visible objects and the objects of intellectual contemplation of this later creation are dim and helpless by the side of the content of the Soul.

The primal phase of the Soul—inhabitant of the Supreme and, by its participation in the Supreme, filled and illuminated—remains unchangeably There; but in virtue of that first participation, that of the primal participant, a secondary phase also participates in the Supreme, and this secondary goes forth ceaselessly as Life streaming from Life; for energy runs through the Universe and there is no extremity at which it dwindles out. But, travel as far as it may, it never draws that first part of itself from the place whence the outgoing began: for if it abandoned its prior (the Intellectual-Principle), it would no longer be everywhere (its continuous Being would be broken and) it would be present at the end, only, of its course.

None the less that which goes forth cannot be equal to that which remains.

In sum, then:

The Soul is to extend throughout the Universe, no spot void of its energy: but, a prior is always different from its secondary, and energy is a secondary, rising as it must from contemplation or act; act, however, is not at this stage existent since it depends upon contemplation: therefore the Soul while its phases differ must, in all of them, remain a contemplation, and what seems to be an act done under contemplation must be in reality that weakened contemplation of which we have spoken: the engendered must respect the Kind, but in weaker form, dwindled in the descent.

All goes softly since nothing here demands the parade of thought or act upon external things: it is a Soul in vision and, by this vision, creating its own subsequent—this Principle (of Nature), itself also contemplative but in the feebler degree since it lies further away and cannot reproduce the quality or experiences of its prior—a Vision creates the Vision.

(Such creative contemplation is not inexplicable) for no limit exists either to contemplation or to its possible objects, I and this explains how the Soul's creation is everywhere:³I where can this thing fail to be, which is one identical thing in every soul? Vision is not cabined within the bournes of magnitude.

This, of course, does not mean that the Soul is present at the same strength in each and every place and thing—any more than that it is at the same strength in each of its own phases.

The Charioteer (the Leading Principle of the Soul, in the Phaedrus Myth) gives the two horses (its two dissonant faculties) what he has seen and they, taking that gift, showed that they were hungry for what made that vision; there was something lacking to them: if in their desire they acted, their action aimed at what they craved for—and that was vision, and an object of vision.

6. Action, thus, is set towards contemplation and an object of contemplation, so that even those whose life is in doing have seeing as their object; what they have not been able to achieve by the direct path, they hope to come at by the circuit.

Further: suppose they succeed; they desired a certain thing to come about, not in order to be unaware of it but to know it, to see it present before the mind:

their success is the laying up of a vision. We act for the sake of some good; this means not for something to remain outside ourselves, not in order that we may possess nothing but that we may hold the good of the action. And hold it, where? Where but in the mind?

Thus once more, action is brought back to contemplation: for (mind or) Soul is a Reason-Principle and anything that one lays up in the Soul can be no other than a Reason-Principle, a silent thing, the more certainly such a principle as the impression made is the deeper.

This vision achieved, the acting instinct pauses; the mind is satisfied and seeks nothing further; the contemplation, in one so conditioned, remains absorbed within as having acquired certainty to rest upon. The brighter the certainty, the more tranquil is the contemplation as having acquired the more perfect unity; and—for now we come to the serious treatment of the subject—

In proportion to the truth with which the knowing faculty knows, it comes to identification with the object of its knowledge.

As long as duality persists, the two lie apart, parallel as it were to each other; there is a pair in which the two elements remain strange to one another, as when Reason-Principles laid up in the mind or Soul remain idle.

Hence the Reason-Principle[4] must not be left to lie outside but must be made one identical thing with the Soul of the novice so that he finds it really his own.

The Soul, once domiciled within that Principle[5] and brought to likeness with it, becomes productive, active; what it failed to hold[6] by its primary nature it now grasps with knowledge and applies in deed, so becoming, as it were, a new thing and, informed as it now is by the purely intellectual, it sees (in its outgoing act) as a stranger looking upon a strange world. It was, no doubt, essentially a Reason-Principle, even an Intellectual Principle; but its function is to see a (lower) realm which these do not see.

For, it is not a complete thing: it has a lack; it is incomplete in regard to its Prior; yet it, also, has a tranquil vision of what it produces. What it has once effectively brought into being it produces no more, for all its productiveness is determined by its lack: it produces for the purpose of scrutiny,[7] in the desire of knowing all its content: when there is question of practical things it adapts its content to the outside order.

The Soul has a greater content than Nature has and therefore it is more tranquil; it is more nearly complete and therefore more contemplative. It is, however, not perfect, and is all the more eager to penetrate the object of contemplation, and it seeks the vision that comes by observation. It leaves its native realm and busies itself elsewhere; then it returns, and it possesses its vision by means of that phase of itself from which it had parted. The self-indwelling Soul inclines less to such experiences.

❚ The Sage, then, has gone through a process of reasoning when he expounds his act to others; but in relation to[8] himself he is Vision: ❚ such a man is already set, not merely in regard to exterior things but also within himself, towards what is one and at rest: all his faculty and life are inward-bent.

7. Certain principles, then, we may take to be established—some self-evident, others brought out by our treatment above:

All the forms of Authentic Existence spring from vision and are a vision. Everything that springs from these Authentic Existences in their vision is an object of vision—manifest to sensation or to true knowledge or to surface-awareness. All act aims at this knowing; all impulse is towards knowledge, all that springs from vision exists to produce Ideal-Form, that is a fresh object of vision, so that universally, as images of their engendering principles, they all produce objects of vision, Ideal-Forms. In the engendering of these existences, imitations of the Authentic, it is made manifest that the creating powers operate not for the sake of creation and action but in order to produce an object of vision. This same vision is the ultimate purpose of all the acts of the mind and, even further downward, of all sensation, since sensation also is an effort towards knowledge; lower still, Nature, producing similarly its subsequent principle, brings into being the vision and Reason-Principle that we know in it. It is certain, also, that as the Firsts exist in vision all other things must be straining towards the same condition; the starting-point is, universally, the goal.

When living things reproduce their kind, it is that the Reason-Principles within stir them; the procreative act is the expression of a contemplation, a travail towards the creation of many forms, many objects of contemplation, so that the universe may be filled full with Reason-Principles and that contemplation may be, as nearly as possible endless: to bring anything into being is to produce an Idea-Form and that again is to enrich the universe with contemplation: all the failures, alike in being and in doing, are but the swerving of visionaries from the object of vision: in the end the sorriest craftsman is still a maker of forms, ungracefully. So Love, too, is vision with the pursuit of Ideal-Form.

8. From this basis we proceed:

In the advancing stages of Contemplation rising from that in Nature, to that in the Soul and thence again to that in the Intellectual-Principle itself, the object contemplated becomes progressively a more and more intimate possession of the Contemplating Beings, more and more one thing with them; and in the advanced Soul the objects of knowledge, well on the way towards the Intellectual-Principle, are close to identity with their container.

Hence we may conclude that, in the Intellectual-Principle itself, there is complete identity of Knower and Known, and this not by way of domiciliation, as in the case of even the highest soul, but by Essence, by the fact that, there, 'Being and Knowing are identical'; we cannot stop at a principle containing separate parts; there must always be a yet higher, a principle above all such diversity.

The Supreme must be an entity in which the two are one; it will, therefore, be a Seeing that lives, not an object of vision like things existing in something other than themselves: what exists in an outside element owes its life to that element; it is not self-living.

I If, therefore, the pure object of Intellection or Contemplation is to have life, it must be Life Absolute and[9] distinct from I the vegetative or sensitive life or any other life determined by Soul.

In a certain sense no doubt all lives are thoughts—but qualified as thought vegetative, thought sensitive, and thought psychic.

What, then, makes them thoughts?

The fact that they are Reason-Principles. Every life is some form of thought, but of a dwindling clearness like the degrees of life itself. The first and clearest Life and the first Intelligence are one Being. The First Life, then, is an Intellection and the next form of Life is the next Intellection and the last form of Life is the last form of Intellection. Thus every Life is of this order; it is an Intellection.

But while men may recognize grades in life they reject grades in thought; to them there are thoughts (full and perfect) and anything else is no thought.

This is simply because they do not seek to establish what Life is.

The essential is to observe that, here again, all reasoning shows that whatever exists is a bye-work of visioning: if, then, the truest Life is such by virtue of an Intellection and is identical with the truest Intellection, then the truest Intellection is a living being; Contemplation and its object constitute a living thing, a Life, two inextricably one.

The duality, thus, is a unity; but how is this unity also a plurality?

The explanation is that the object of Contemplation is not a unity: even when that object is the One itself, it is not seen as a unity; if it were, the Intellectual-Principle cannot exist. The Highest began as a unity but did not remain as it began; all unknown to itself, it became manifold; it grew, as it were, pregnant: desiring universal possession, it flung itself outward, though it were better had it never known the desire by which a Secondary came into being: it is like a Circle (in the Idea) which in projection becomes a figure, a surface, a circumference, a centre, a system of radii, of upper and lower segments. The Whence is the better; the Whither is less good: the Whither is not of the quality of the Whence-and-Whither, and the Whence-and-Whither is not of the quality of the Whence alone.

The Intellectual-Principle on the other hand was never merely the Principle of an inviolable unity; it was a universal as well and, being so, was the Intellectual-Principle of all things. Being, thus, all things and the principle of all, it must be such that every part of it is universal, is all things: otherwise, it contains a part which is not Intellectual-Principle: it will be a juxtaposition of non-Intellectuals, a huddled heap waiting to be made over from the mass of things into the Intellectual-Principle!

We conclude that this Being is limitless and that in all the outflow from it there is no lessening, either in its emanation, since this also is the entire universe, nor in itself, the starting point, since it is no assemblage of parts (to be diminished by any outgo).

9. Clearly a Being of this nature is not the primal existent; there must exist that which transcends it, that Being (the Absolute), to which all our discussion has been leading.

In the first place, Plurality is later than Unity. The Intellectual-Principle is a number (= the expression of a plurality); and number derives from unity: the source of a number such as this must be the authentically One. Further, it is the sum of an Intellectual-Being with the object of its Intellection, so that it is a duality; and, given this duality, we must find what exists before it.

What is this?

The Intellectual-Principle taken separately, perhaps?

No: an Intellect is always inseparable from an intelligible object; eliminate the intelligible, and the Intellectual-Principle disappears with it. If, then, what we are seeking cannot be the Intellectual-Principle but must be something that rejects the duality there present, then the Prior demanded by that duality must be something on the further side of the Intellectual-Principle.

But might it not be the Intelligible object itself

No: for the Intelligible makes an equally inseparable duality with the Intellectual-Principle.

If, then, neither the Intellectual-Principle nor the Intelligible Object can be the First Existent, what is?

Our answer can only be:

The source of both.

What will This be; under what character can we picture It?

(We will be told that) It must be either Intellective or without Intellection: if Intellective it is the Intellectual-Principle; if not, it will be without even knowledge of itself—and then, what is there so august about it?

If we define it as The Good and the wholly simplex, we will, no doubt, be telling the truth, but we will not be giving any certain and lucid account of it as long as we have in mind no entity in which to lodge the conception by which we define it.

Yet: our knowledge of everything else comes by way of our intelligence; our power of knowing the intelligence itself is[10] by means of the intelligence: but this Entity transcends all of the intellectual nature; by what direct intuition, then, can it be brought within our grasp?

To this question the answer is that we can know it only in the degree of human faculty: we indicate it by virtue of what in ourselves is like it.

For in us, also, there is something of that Being; nay, nothing, ripe for that participation, can be void of it.

Wherever you be, you have only to range over against this omnipresent Being that in you which is capable of drawing from It, and you have your share in it: imagine a voice sounding over a vast waste of land, and not only over the emptiness alone but over human beings; wherever you be in that great space you have but to listen and you take the voice entire—entire though yet with a difference.

And what do we take when we thus point the Intelligence?

The Intellectual-Principle in us must mount to its origins: essentially a thing facing two ways, it must deliver itself over to those powers within it which tend upward; if it seeks the vision of that Being, it must become something more than Intellect.

For the Intellectual-Principle is the earliest form of Life: it is the Activity presiding over the outflowing of the universal Order—the outflow, that is, of the first moment, not that of the continuous process.

In its character as Life, as emanation, as containing all things in their precise forms and not merely in the agglomerate mass—for this would be to contain them (against its specific character) imperfectly and inarticulately—it must of necessity derive from some other Being, from one that does not emanate but is the Principle of Emanation, of Life, of Intellect, and of the Universe.

For the Universe is not a Principle and Source: it springs from a source, and that source cannot be the All or anything belonging to the All since it is to generate the All, and must be not a plurality but the Source of plurality since universally a begetting power is less complex than the begotten. Thus the Being that has engendered the Intellectual-Principle must be more simplex than the Intellectual-Principle.

We may be told that this engendering Principle is the One-and-All.

But, at that, it must be either each separate entity from among all or it will be all things in the one mass.

Now if it were the massed total of all, it must be of later origin than any of the things of which it is the sum; if it precedes the total, it differs from the things that make up the total and they from it: if it and the total of things constitute a co-existence, it is not a Source. But what we are probing for must be a Source; it must exist before all, that all may be fashioned as sequel to it.

As for the notion that it may be each separate entity of the All, this would make a self-Identity into a what you like, where you like, indifferently, and would, besides, abolish all distinction in things themselves.

Once more we see that this can be no thing among things but must be prior to all things.

10. And what will such a Principle essentially be?

The potentiality of the Universe: the potentiality whose non-existence would mean the non-existence of all the Universe and even of the Intellectual-Principle which is the primal Life and all Life.

This Principle on the thither side of Life is the cause of Life—for that Manifestation of Life which is the Universe of things is not the First Activity; it is itself poured forth, so to speak, like water from a spring.

Imagine a spring that has no source outside itself; it gives itself to all the rivers, yet is never exhausted by what they take, but remains always integrally as it was; the tides that proceed from it are at one within it before they run their several ways, yet all, in some sense, know beforehand down what channels they will pour their streams.

Or: think of the Life coursing throughout some mighty tree while yet it is the stationary Principle of the whole, in no sense scattered over all that extent but, as it were, vested in the root: it is the giver of the entire and manifold life of the tree, but remains unmoved itself, not manifold but the Principle of that manifold life.

And this surprises no one: though it is in fact astonishing how all that varied vitality springs from the unvarying, and how that very manifoldness could not be unless before the multiplicity there were something all singleness; for, the Principle is not broken into parts to make the total; on the contrary, such partition would destroy both; nothing would come into being if its cause, thus broken up, changed character.

Thus we are always brought back to The One.

Every particular thing has a One of its own to which it may be traced; the All has its One, its Prior but not yet the Absolute One; through this we reach that Absolute One, where all such reference comes to an end.

Now when we reach a One—the stationary Principle—in the tree, in the animal, in Soul, in the All—we have in every case the most powerful, the precious element: when we come to the One in the Authentically Existent Beings—their Principle and source and potentiality—shall we lose confidence and suspect it of being—nothing?

Certainly this Absolute is none of the things of which it is the source—its nature is that nothing can be affirmed of it—not existence, not essence, not life—since it is That which transcends all these. But possess yourself of it by the very elimination of Being and you hold a marvel. Thrusting forward to This, attaining, I and resting in yourself,[11] seek I to grasp it more and more—understanding it by that intuitive thrust alone, but knowing its greatness by the Beings that follow upon it and exist by its power.

11. Another approach:

The Intellectual-Principle is a Seeing, and a Seeing which itself sees; therefore it is a potentiality which has become effective.

This implies the distinction of Matter and Form in it—as there must be in all actual seeing—the Matter in this case being the Intelligibles which the Intellectual-Principle contains and sees. All actual seeing implies duality; before the seeing takes place there is the pure unity (of the power of seeing). That unity (of principle) acquires duality (in the act of seeing), and the duality is (always to be traced back to) a unity.

Now as our sight requires the world of sense for its satisfaction and realization, so the vision in the Intellectual-Principle demands, for its completion, The Good.

It cannot be, itself, The Good, since then it would not need to see or to perform any other Act; for The Good is the centre of all else, and it is by means of The Good that every thing has Act, while The Good is in need of nothing and therefore possesses nothing beyond itself.

Once you have uttered 'The Good', add no further thought: by any addition, and in proportion to that addition, you introduce a deficiency.

Do not even say that it has Intellection; you would be dividing it; it would become a duality, Intellect and The Good. The Good has no need of the Intellectual-Principle which, on the contrary, needs it, and attaining it, is shaped into Goodness and becomes perfect by it: the Form thus received, sprung from The Good, brings it to likeness with The Good.

Thus the traces of The Good discerned upon it must be taken as indication of the nature of that Archetype: we form I a conception of its true character[12] I from its image playing upon the Intellectual-Principle. This image of itself it has communicated to the Intellect that contemplates it: thus all the striving is on the side of the Intellect, which is the eternal striver and eternally the attainer. The Being beyond neither strives, since it feels no lack, nor attains, since it has no striving. And this marks it off from the Intellectual-Principle, to which characteristically belongs the striving, the concentrated strain towards its Form.

Yet: The Intellectual-Principle; beautiful; the most beautiful of all; lying lapped in pure light and in 'clear radiance'; circumscribing the Nature of the Authentic Existents; the original of which this beautiful world is a shadow and an image; tranquil in the fullness of glory since in it there is nothing devoid of intellect, nothing dark or out of rule; a living thing in a life of blessedness: this, too, must overwhelm with awe any that has seen it, and penetrated it, to become a unit of its Being.

But: as one that looks up to the heavens and sees the splendour of the stars thinks of the Maker and searches, so whoever has contemplated the Intellectual Universe and known it and wondered for it must search after its Maker too. What Being has raised so noble a fabric? And how? Who has begotten such a child, this Intellectual-Principle, this lovely abundance so abundantly endowed?

The Source of all this cannot be an Intellect; nor can it be an abundant power: it must have been before Intellect and abundance were; these are later and things of lack; abundance had to be made abundant and Intellection needed to know.

These are very near to the un-needing, to that which has no need of knowing, they have abundance and intellection authentically, as being the first to possess. But, there is That before them which neither needs nor possesses anything, since, needing or possessing anything else, it would not be what it is—The Good.

NOTES TO ENNEAD III.8

1. This tractate is the first part of a major work comprising III.8 (30), V.8 (31), V.5 (32), and II.9 (33). See first footnote to II.9.

2. FIRST EDITION: "(i.e. of being *the conscious product of a Contemplation?*) . . ."

TAYLOR gives the thought as: ". . . that which is the last proceeds from contemplation, and is called contemplation, because by this it is generated and received;"

GUTHRIE: ". . . the reason which holds the last rank itself proceeds from contemplation, and in this sense still deserves the name of contemplation because it is produced by the contemplation (of the soul)."

ARMSTRONG: ". . . in every rational principle its last and lowest manifestation springs from contemplation, and is contemplation in the sense of being contemplated;"

3. FIRST EDITION: ". . . and this explains how the *Soul is universal*:"

ARMSTRONG: "This is why soul makes everywhere . . ."

TAYLOR: ". . . and on this account they proceed through all things."

GUTHRIE: ". . . that is why it extends to everything ."

4. FIRST EDITION: ". . . as when *Ideal*-Principles laid up in the mind or soul remain idle. "Hence the *Idea* must not . . ."

ARMSTRONG uses "rational principles/rational principle"; TAYLOR and GUTHRIE both use "reasons/reason." GUTHRIE footnotes his usage with: "That is, the essence of the known object, a pun on 'reason,' as in II.6.2."

5. FIRST EDITION: ". . . within that *Idea* and . . ." See previous footnote.

6. FIRST EDITION: ". . . what it *always held* by its . . ."

TAYLOR: ". . . she perceives what she previously possessed . . ."

GUTHRIE: "Thus she observes the thing that she (unconsciously) possessed . . ."

ARMSTRONG gives this whole sentence as: "The soul, then, when it has become akin to and disposed according to the rational principle, still, all the same, utters and propounds it—for it did not possess it primarily—and learns it thoroughly and by its proposition becomes other than it, and looks at it, considering it, like one thing looking at another;"

7. FIRST EDITION: ". . . for the purpose of *Contemplation* . . ."

TAYLOR: ". . . perceiving what she possesses:"

ARMSTRONG: ". . . with a view to examining it . . ."

8. FIRST EDITION begins the sentence as: "The Sage, then, *is the man made over into a Reason-Principle: to others he shows his act but in* himself he is Vision:"

TAYLOR: "Hence the worthy soul becomes reason itself, and what it is in itself it demonstrates to others; but with respect to itself it is sight;"

GUTHRIE: "Consequently the wise mind is identical with reason, and in itself possesses what it manifests to others."

ARMSTRONG: "The truly good and wise man, therefore, has already finished reasoning when he declares what he has in himself to another; but in relation to himself he is vision."

9. FIRST EDITION begins the sentence: "*Now admitting the existence of a living thing that is at once a Thought and its object, it must be a Life* distinct from . . ."

DECK: "If, then, a certain theorema and noema is to live, it must be self-life, not vegetative, or sensitive, or the other kinds of soul-life." GUTHRIE and ARMSTRONG support Page.

10. FIRST EDITION: ". . . our power *is that* of knowing the *intelligible* by means of the intelligence . . ."

TAYLOR gives the whole thought as: ". . . since it is *through* and *with* intellect that intelligent natures derive their knowledge of other things, by what collected intuition can we perceive a nature exalted above intellect itself?"

GUTHRIE: ". . . since the knowledge of the other objects in all beings who can know something intelligent, occurs through Intelligence and lies in Intelligence, by what rapid intellection (or intuition) could we grasp this Principle that is superior to Intelligence?"

ARMSTRONG: ". . . since knowledge of other things comes to us from intellect, and we are able to know intellect by intellect, by what sort of simple intuition could one grasp this which transcends the nature of intellect?"

11. FIRST EDITION: "... and resting in *its content*, seek ..."

ARMSTRONG: "And, throwing yourself upon it and coming to rest within it ..."

GUTHRIE: "By directing your glance towards it, by reaching it, and resting in it, you will get a unitary and simple intuition thereof;"

TAYLOR: "... directing yourself towards him, and pursuing his latent retreats till you repose in his solitary deity, you will now behold him by a vision perfectly simple and one;"

12. FIRST EDITION: "... a conception of its *Authentic Being*..."

TAYLOR: "... we ought to estimate the dignity of its exemplar, considering its reality ..."

ARMSTRONG: "... conceive its true archetype, forming an idea of it in oneself ..."

GUTHRIE: "... conceiving of its true character ..."

NINTH TRACTATE

Detached Considerations

1. 'The Intellectual-Principle' (= the Divine Mind)—we read (in the Timaeus)—'looks upon the Ideas indwelling in that Being which is the Essentially Living' (= according to Plotinus, the Intellectual Realm), and then—the text proceeds—the Creator 'planned that what the Intellectual-Principle saw existing in that essentially Living Being should find place in this lower universe also.'

Are we meant to gather that the Ideas came into being before the Intellectual-Principle so that it 'sees them' as previously existent?

The first step is to make sure whether the 'Living Being' of the text is to be distinguished from the Intellectual-Principle as another thing than it.

It might be argued that the Intellectual-Principle is the Contemplator and therefore that the Living-Being contemplated is not the Intellectual-Principle but must be described as the Intellectual Object, so that the Intellectual-Principle must possess the Ideal realm as something outside of itself.

But this would mean that it possesses images and not the realities, since the realities are in the Intellectual Realm which it contemplates: Reality—we read—is in the Authentic Existent which contains the essential form of particular things.

No: even though the Intellectual-Principle and the Intellectual Object are distinct, they are not apart except for just that distinction.

Nothing in the statement cited is inconsistent with the conception that these two constitute one substance—though in a unity admitting that distinction, of the intellectual act (as against passivity), without which there can be no question of an Intellectual-Principle and an Intellectual Object: what is meant is not that the contemplatory Being possesses its vision as in some other principle, but that it contains the Intellectual Realm within itself.

The Intelligible Object is the Intellectual-Principle itself in its repose, unity, immobility: the Intellectual-Principle, contemplator of that object—of the Intellectual-Principle thus in repose—is an active manifestation of the same Being, an Act which contemplates its unmoved phase and, as thus contemplating, stands as Intellectual-Principle to that of which it has the intellection: it is Intellectual-Principle in virtue of having that intellection, and at the same time is Intellectual Object, by assimilation.

This, then, is the Being which planned to create in the lower Universe what it saw existing in the Supreme, the four orders of living beings.

No doubt the passage (of the Timaeus) seems to imply tacitly that this planning Principle is distinct from the other two: but the three—the Essentially-Living, the Intellectual-Principle, and this planning Principle—will, to others, be manifestly one: the truth is that, by a common accident, a particular trend of thought has occasioned the discrimination.

We have dealt with the first two; but the third—this Principle which decides to work upon the objects (the Ideas) contemplated by the Intellectual-Principle within the Essentially-Living, to create them, to establish them in their partial existence—what is this third?

It is possible that in one aspect the Intellectual-Principle is the principle of partial existence, while in another aspect it is not.

The entities thus particularized from the unity are products of the Intellectual-Principle which thus would be, to that extent, the separating agent. On the other hand it remains in itself, indivisible; division begins with its offspring, which, of course, means with Souls: and thus a Soul—with its particular Souls—may be the separative principle.

This is what is conveyed where we are told that the separation is the work of the third Principle and begins within the Third: for to this Third belongs the discursive reasoning which is no function of the Intellectual-Principle but characteristic of its secondary, of Soul, to which precisely, divided by its own Kind, belongs the Act of division.

2. . . . For in any one science the reduction of the total of knowledge into its separate propositions does not shatter its unity, chipping it into unrelated fragments; in each distinct item is latent the entire body of the science, an integral thing in its highest Principle and its last detail: and similarly a man must so discipline himself that the first Principles of his Being are also his completions, are totals, that all be pointed towards the loftiest phase of the

Nature: when a man has become this unity in the best, he is in that other realm; for it is by this highest within himself, made his own, that he holds to the Supreme.

3. At no point did the All-Soul come into Being: it never arrived, for it never knew place; what happens is that body, neighbouring with it, participates in it: hence Plato does not place Soul in body but body in Soul. The others, the secondary Souls, have a point of departure—they come from the All-Soul—and they have a place into which to descend and in which to change to and fro, a place, therefore, from which to ascend: but this All-Soul is for ever Above, resting in that Being in which it holds its existence as Soul and followed, as next, by the Universe or, at least, by all beneath the sun.

The partial Soul is illuminated by moving towards the Soul above it; for on that path it meets Authentic Existence. Movement towards the lower is towards non-Being: and this is the step it takes when it is set on self; for by willing towards itself it produces its lower, an image of itself—a non-Being—and so is wandering, as it were, into the void, stripping itself of its own determined form. And this image, this undetermined thing, is blank darkness, for it is utterly without reason, untouched by the Intellectual-Principle, far removed from Authentic Being.

As long as it remains at the mid-stage it is in its own peculiar region; but when, by a sort of inferior orientation, it looks downward, it shapes that lower image and flings itself joyfully thither.

4. . . . How, then, does Unity give rise to Multiplicity?

By its omnipresence: there is nowhere where it is not; it occupies, therefore, all that is; at once, it is manifold—or, rather, it is all things.

If it were simply and solely everywhere, all would be this one thing alone: but it is, also, in no place, and this gives in the final result that while all exists by means of it, in virtue of its omnipresence, all is distinct from it in virtue of its being nowhere.

But why is it not merely present everywhere but in addition nowhere-present?

Because universality demands a previous unity. It must, therefore, pervade all things and make all, but not be the universe which it makes.

5. The Soul itself must exist as Seeing—with the Intellectual-Principle as the object of its vision—it is undetermined before it sees but is **I** naturally apt for intellection:[1]**I** in other words, Soul is Matter to (its determinant) the Intellectual-Principle.

6. When we exercise intellection upon ourselves, we are, obviously, observing an intellective nature, for otherwise we would not be able to have that intellection.

We know, and it is ourselves that we know; therefore we know the reality of a knowing nature: therefore, before that intellection in Act, there is another intellection, one at rest, so to speak.

Similarly, that self-intellection is an act upon a reality and upon a life; therefore, before the Life and Real-Being concerned in the intellection there must be another Being and Life. In a word, intellection is vested in the activities themselves: since, then, the activities of self-intellection are intellective-forms, We, the Authentic We, are the Intelligibles and self-intellection conveys the Image of the Intellectual Sphere.

7. The Primal is a potentiality of Movement and of Repose—and so is above and beyond both—its next subsequent has rest and movement about the Primal. Now this subsequent is the Intellectual-Principle—so characterized by having intellection of something not identical with itself whereas the Primal is without intellection. A knowing principle I has duality, even in self-knowledge;[2] and, I moreover, it knows itself as deficient since its virtue consists in this knowing and not in its own bare Being.

8. In the case of everything which has developed from possibility to actuality the actual is that which remains self-identical for its entire duration—and this it is which makes perfection possible even in things of the corporeal order, as for instance in fire—but the actual of this kind cannot be everlasting since (by the fact of their having once existed only in potentiality) Matter has its place in them. In anything, on the contrary, not composite (= never touched by Matter or potentiality) and possessing actuality, that actual existence is eternal. There is, however, the case, also, in which a thing, itself existing in actuality, stands as potentiality to some other form of Being.

9. ... I But the First dwells beyond Being;[3] the Authentic Existents I constitute the Intellectual-Principle with which Motion and Rest begin. The Primal touches nothing, but is the centre round which those other Beings lie in repose and in movement. For Movement is aiming, and the Primal aims at nothing; what could the Summit aspire to?

Has It, even, no Intellection of Itself? I Or can It, as possessing Itself be said in general terms to know Itself?

But intellection (or knowledge)[4] does not mean I self-ownership; it means turning the gaze towards the Primal: now the act of intellection is itself the Primal Act, and there is therefore no place for any earlier one. The Being projecting this Act transcends the Act so that Intellection is secondary to the Being in which it resides. Intellection is not the transcendently venerable thing—neither Intellection in general nor even the Intellection of The Good. Apart from and over any Intellection stands The Good itself.

The Good therefore needs no consciousness.

What sort of consciousness can be conceived in it?

Consciousness of the Good as existent or non-existent?

If of existent Good, that Good exists before and without any such consciousness: if the act of consciousness produces that Good, then The Good was not previously in existence—and, at once, the very consciousness falls to the ground since it is no longer consciousness of The Good.

But would not all this mean that the First does not even live?

The First cannot be said to live, except only as the source of Life.

All that has self-consciousness and self-intellection is derivative; it observes itself in order, by that activity, to become master of its Being: and if it study itself this can mean only that ignorance inheres in it and that it is of its own nature lacking and to be made perfect by Intellection.

All thinking and knowing must, here, be eliminated: the addition introduces deprivation and deficiency.

NOTES TO ENNEAD III.9

1. FIRST EDITION: "... naturally apt *to see:*"

   GUTHRIE: "... disposed to see and think;"

   ARMSTRONG: "... naturally adapted to intellection:"

2. FIRST EDITION: "... has duality *(that entailed by being the knower of something)* and ..."

   ARMSTRONG: "So that which thinks is double, even if it thinks itself, and defective ..."

3. FIRST EDITION: "... But the First *is not to be envisaged as made up from Gods of a transcendent order: no;* the Authentic Existents ..."

   GUTHRIE: "The divinities which occupy the highest rank are nevertheless not the First;"

   ARMSTRONG: "But the First beyond being does not think:"

4. FIRST EDITION: "*It possesses itself and therefore is* said in general terms to know itself. ... [preceding ellipses are MacKenna's—ed.] But intellection does not mean ..."

   ARMSTRONG: "Is it not said in a general way to think in that it possesses itself? It is not by possessing itself that anything is said to think, but by looking at the First."

   GUTHRIE: "... they who say that He thinks Himself mean by it only that He possesses Himself. But when one says that a thing thinks, it is not because it possesses itself, it is because it contemplates the First;"

THE FOURTH ENNEAD

FIRST TRACTATE

On the Essence of the Soul (I)

1. IN THE Intellectual Cosmos dwells Authentic Essence, with the Intellectual-Principle (Divine Mind) as the noblest of its content, but containing also souls, since every soul in this lower sphere has come thence: that is the world of unembodied souls while to our world belong those that have entered body and undergone bodily division.

There the Intellectual-Principle is a concentrated all—nothing of it distinguished or divided—and in that Cosmos of unity all souls are concentrated also, with no spatial discrimination.

But there is a difference:

The Intellectual-Principle is for ever repugnant to distinction and to partition. Soul, there without distinction and partition, has yet a nature lending itself to divisional existence: its division is secession, entry into body.

In view of this seceding and the ensuing partition we may legitimately speak of it as 'divided among bodies'.

But if so, how can it still be described as indivisible?

In that the secession is not of the Soul entire; something of it holds its ground, that in it which recoils from separate existence.

'Formed from the undivided essence and the essence divided among bodies': this description of Soul must therefore mean that it has phases above and below, that it is attached to the Supreme and yet reaches down to this sphere, like a radius from a centre.

Thus it is that, entering this realm, it possesses still the vision inherent to that superior phase in virtue of which it unchangingly maintains its integral nature. Even here it is not exclusively the partible soul: it is still the impartible as well: what in it knows partition is parted without partibility; undivided as giving itself to the entire body, a whole to a whole, it is divided as being effective in every part.

SECOND TRACTATE

On the Essence of the Soul (II)

1. In our attempt to elucidate the Essence of the Soul, we show it to be neither a material fabric nor, among immaterial things, a harmony. The theory that it is some final development, some entelechy, we pass by, holding this to be neither true as presented nor practically definitive.

No doubt we make a very positive statement about it when we declare it to belong to the Intellectual Kind, to be of the divine order; but a deeper penetration of its nature is demanded.

In that allocation we were distinguishing things as they fall under the Intellectual or the sensible, and we placed the Soul in the former class; now, taking its membership of the Intellectual for granted, we must investigate by another path the more specific characteristics of its nature.

There are, we hold, things primarily apt to partition, tending by sheer nature towards separate existence: they are things in which no part is identical either with another part or with the whole, while, also, their part is necessarily less than the total and whole: these are magnitudes of the realm of sense, masses, each of which has a station of its own so that none can be identically present in entirety at more than one point at one time.

But to that order is opposed Essence (Real-Being); this is in no degree susceptible of partition; it is unparted and impartible; interval is foreign to it, cannot enter into our idea of it: it has no need of place and is not, in diffusion or as an entirety, situated within any other being: it is poised over all beings at once, and this is not in the sense of using them as a base but in their being neither capable nor desirous of existing independently of it; it is an essence eternally unvaried: it is common to all that follows upon it: it is like the circle's centre to which all the radii are attached while leaving it unbrokenly in possession of itself, the starting-point of their course and of their essential being, the ground in which they all participate: thus the indivisible is the principle of these divided existences and in their very outgoing they remain enduringly in contact with that stationary essence.

So far we have the primarily indivisible—supreme among the Intellectual and Authentically Existent—and we have its contrary, the Kind definitely divisible in things of sense; but there is also another Kind, of earlier rank than the sensible yet near to it and resident within it—an order, not, like body, primarily a thing of part, but becoming so upon incorporation. The bodies are separate, and the Ideal-Form which enters them is correspondingly sundered while, still, it is present as one whole in each of its severed parts, since amid that multiplicity in which complete individuality has entailed complete partition, there is a permanent identity; we may think of colour, qualities of all kinds, some particular shape, which can be present in many unrelated objects at the one moment, each entire and yet with no community of experience among the various manifestations. In the case of such Ideal-Forms we may affirm complete partibility.

But, on the other hand, that first utterly indivisible Kind must be accompanied by a subsequent Essence, engendered by it and holding indivisibility from it but, in virtue of the necessary outgo from source, tending firmly towards the contrary, the wholly partible; this secondary Essence will take an intermediate place between the first substance, the undivided, and that which is divisible in material things and resides in them. Its presence, however, will differ in one respect from that of colour and quantity; these, no doubt, are present identically and entire throughout diverse material masses, but each several manifestation of them is as distinct from every other as the mass is from the mass.

The magnitude present in any mass is definitely one thing, yet its identity from part to part does not imply any such community as would entail common experience; within that identity there is diversity, for it is a condition only, not (as in the case of soul) the actual Essence.

❙ The Essence, which we place above this Kind and assert to come very near to the impartible,[1] is at once ❙ an Essence and an entrant into body; upon embodiment, it experiences a partition unknown before it thus bestowed itself.

In whatsoever bodies it occupies—even the vastest of all, that in which the entire universe is included—it gives itself to the whole without abdicating its unity.

This unity of an Essence is not like that of body, which is a unit by the mode of continuous extension, the mode of distinct parts each occupying its own space. Nor is it such a unity as we have dealt with in the case of quality.

The nature, at once divisible and indivisible, which we affirm to be soul, has not the unity of an extended thing: it does not consist of separate sections; its divisibility lies in its presence at every point of the recipient, but it is indivisible as dwelling entire in the total and entire in any part.

To have penetrated this idea is to know the greatness of the Soul and its power, the divinity and wonder of its being, as a nature transcending the sphere of Things.

Itself devoid of mass, it is present to all mass: it exists here and yet is there, and this not in distinct phases but with unsundered identity: thus it is 'parted and not parted', or, better, it has never known partition, never become a parted thing, but remains a self-gathered integral, and is 'parted among bodies' merely in the sense that bodies, in virtue of their own sundered existence, cannot receive it unless in some partitive mode; the partition, in other words, is an occurrence in body, not in soul.

2. It can be demonstrated that soul must necessarily be of just this nature, and that there can be no other soul than such a being, one neither wholly impartible nor wholly partible but both at once.

If it had the nature of body it would consist of isolated members each unaware of the conditions of every other; there would be a particular soul—say a soul of the finger—answering as a distinct and independent entity to every local experience; in general terms, there would be a multiplicity of souls administering each individual; and, moreover, the universe would be governed not by one soul but by an incalculable number, each standing apart to itself. But without a dominant unity, continuity is meaningless.

The theory that impressions reach the leading-principle by progressive stages must be dismissed as mere illusion.

In the first place, it affirms without investigation a 'leading' phase of the Soul.

What can justify this assigning of parts to the Soul, and distinguishing one part from another? What quantity, or what difference of quality, can apply to a thing defined as a self-consistent whole of unbroken unity?

Again, would perception be vested in that leading principle alone, or in the other phases as well?

If a given experience bears only I on that 'leading principle', the principle must be lodged in some part of the organism—but what part?—in order to exercise the perception;[2] if, on the other hand, I it fastens on some other phase of the Soul—one not constituted for sensation—that phase cannot transmit any experience to the leading principle, and there can be no sensation.

Again, suppose sensation vested in the 'leading-principle' itself: then, a first alternative, it will be felt in some one part of that (some specifically sensitive phase), the other part excluding a perception which could serve no purpose; or, in the second alternative, there will be many distinct sensitive phases, an infinite number, with difference from one to another. In that second case, one sensitive phase will declare 'I had this sensation primarily'; others will have to say 'I felt the sensation that rose elsewhere'; but either the site of the experience will be a matter of doubt to every phase except the first, or each of the parts of the Soul will be deceived into allocating the occurrence within its own particular sphere.

If, on the contrary, the sensation is vested not merely in the 'leading principle', but in any and every part of the Soul, what special function raises the one rather than the other into that leading rank, or why is the sensation to be referred to it rather than elsewhere? And how, at this, account for the unity of the knowledge brought in by diverse senses, by eyes, by ears?

On the other hand, if the Soul is a perfect unity—utterly strange to part, a self-gathered whole—if it continuously eludes all touch of multiplicity and divisibility—then, no whole taken up into it can ever be ensouled; soul will stand as circle-centre to every object (remote on the circumference), and the entire mass of a living being is soulless still.

There is, therefore, no escape: soul is, in the degree indicated, one and many, parted and impartible. We cannot question the possibility of a thing being at once a unity and multi-present, since to deny this would be to abolish the principle which sustains and administers the universe: there must be a Kind which encircles and supports all and conducts all with wisdom, a principle which is multiple since existence is multiple, and yet is one soul always since a container must be a unity: by the multiple unity of its nature, it will furnish life to the multiplicity of the series of an all; by its impartible unity, it will conduct a total to wise ends.

In the case of things not endowed with intelligence, the 'leading principle' is their mere unity—a lower reproduction of the Soul's efficiency.

This is the deeper meaning of the profound passage (in the Timaeus), where we read: 'By blending the impartible, eternally unchanging essence with that in division among bodies, he produced a third form of essence partaking of both qualities.'

Soul, therefore, is, in this definite sense, one and many; the Ideal-Form resident in body is many and one; bodies themselves are exclusively many; the Supreme is exclusively one.

NOTES TO ENNEAD IV.2

1. FIRST EDITION: "The Essence, *very near to the impartible, which we assert to belong to the Kind we are now dealing with*, is at once . . ."

GUTHRIE: ". . . the nature that approaches the absolutely indivisible 'Being' is a genuine 'being' (such as is the soul)."

ARMSTRONG: ". . . the reality which we affirm to be immediately above this nature [of the forms in body], and bordering on the indivisible reality, is . . ." Brackets are Armstrong's.

TAYLOR: "That, however, in this middle nature which accedes to an impartible essence, is . . ."

2. FIRST EDITION: "... on that 'leading principle,' *it would not be felt as lodged in any particular members of the organism;* if, on the other hand ..."

> GUTHRIE: "If that ['predominating'—ed.] part exclusively, it will feel only so long as the received impression will have been transmitted to itself, in its particular residence; but if ..."

> TAYLOR: "if ... the ruling part alone [is sentient—ed.], it will then perceive, when the sensible passion falls on this part established in a certain place; but if ..."

> ARMSTRONG: "And if only the ruling principle perceives, and the object of perception comes into contact with the ruling principle itself, in what place will it perceive the object of perception as situated? But if ..."

THIRD TRACTATE

Problems of the Soul (I)

1. The Soul: what dubious questions concerning it admit of solution, or where we must abide our doubt—with, at least, the gain of recognizing the problem that confronts us—this is matter well worth attention. On what subject can we more reasonably expend the time required by minute discussion and investigation? Apart from much else, it is enough that such an inquiry illuminates two grave questions: of what sphere the Soul is the principle and whence the Soul itself springs. Moreover, we will be only obeying the ordinance of the God who bade us know ourselves.

❙ Our general instinct to seek and learn will, in all reason, set us inquiring into the nature of the instrument with which we search; so, equally, will our longing to possess ourselves of the adorable vision of the Intellectual-Principle. Even in the universe Soul has this double tendency (towards Intellect and towards body), so that we would expect differences of emphasis in things of part. How souls are described as[1] receptacles of the divine being ❙ will need to be examined; but this we may leave aside until we are considering the mode in which soul comes to occupy body. For the moment we return to our argument against those who maintain our souls to be offshoots from the Soul of the universe (parts and not an identity modally parted).

Our opponents will probably deny the validity of our arguments against the theory that the human soul is a mere segment of the All-Soul—the considerations, namely, that it is of identical scope, and that it is intellective in the same degree, supposing them, even, to admit that equality of intellection.

They will object that parts must necessarily fall under one Ideal-Form with their wholes. And they will adduce Plato as expressing their view where, in demonstrating that the All is ensouled, he says that as our body is a portion of the body of the All, so our soul is a portion of the Soul of the All. It is admitted on clear evidence that we are borne along by the Circuit of the All; we will be told that—taking character and destiny from it, strictly inbound with it—we must derive our souls, also, from what thus bears us up, and that as within ourselves every part absorbs from our soul, so, analogically, we, standing parts to the universe, absorb from the Soul of the All as parts of it. They will urge also that the dictum 'The collective soul cares for all the unensouled', carries the same implication and could be uttered only in the belief that nothing whatever of later origin stands outside the Soul of the universe, the only soul there can be there to concern itself with the unensouled.

2. To this our first answer is that to place certain things under one identical class—by admitting an identical range of operation—is to make them of one common species, and puts an end to all mention of part; the reasonable conclusion would be, on the contrary, that there is one identical soul, every separate manifestation being that soul complete.

❙ Let our opponents once admit the unity: they will go on to make it dependent on a principle (Soul Absolute) in which we have no longer the soul of this or that, but a soul of nowhere, a soul belonging neither to the Cosmos, nor to anything else, and yet vested with the creation of whatever serves as soul to the Cosmos and to[2] every ensouled thing. ❙

The Soul considered as an entirety cannot be a soul of any one given thing—since it is an Essence (a divine Real-Being)—or, at least, there must be a soul which is not exclusively the soul of any particular thing, and those attached to particulars must so belong merely temporally and in some mode of accident.

In such questions as this it is important to clarify the significance of 'part'.

Part, as understood of body—uniform or varied—need not detain us; it is enough to indicate that, when part is mentioned in respect of things whose members are alike, it refers to mass and not to Ideal-Form (specific idea): take for example, whiteness: the whiteness in a portion of milk is not a part of the whiteness of milk in general: we have the whiteness of a portion, not a portion of whiteness; for whiteness is utterly without magnitude; has nothing whatever to do with quantity.

That is all we need say with regard to part in material things; but part in the unembodied may be taken in various ways. We may think of it in the sense familiar in numbers, 'two' a part of 'ten'—in abstract numbers of course—or as we think of a segment of a circle or line (abstractly considered), or, again, of a section or branch of knowledge.

In the case of the units of reckoning and of geometrical figure, exactly as in that of corporeal masses, partition must diminish the total; the part must be less than the whole; for these are things of quantity, and have their being as things of quantity; and—since they are not the Ideal-Form Quantity—they are subject to increase and decrease.

Now in such a sense as this, part cannot be affirmed of the Soul.

The Soul is not a thing of quantity; we are not to conceive of the All-Soul as some standard ten with particular souls as its constituent units.

Such a conception would entail many absurdities:

The Ten could not be (essentially) a unity (the Soul would be an aggregation, not a self-standing Real-Being) and, further—unless every one of the single constituents were itself an All-Soul—the All-Soul would be formed of non-souls.

Again, it is admitted that the particular soul—this 'part of the All-Soul'—is of one Ideal-Form with it, but this does not entail the relation of part to whole, since in objects formed of continuous parts there is nothing inevitably making any portion uniform with the total: take, for example, the parts of a circle or square; we may divide it in different ways so as to get our part; a triangle need not be divided into triangles; all sorts of different figures are possible: yet an absolute uniformity is admitted to reign throughout soul.

In a line, no doubt, the part is inevitably a line; but even here there is a necessary difference in size; and if in the case of the Soul we similarly called upon magnitude as the distinction between constituents and collective soul, then soul, thus classed by magnitude, becomes quantitative, and is simply body.

But it is admitted that all souls are alike, and are entireties; clearly, soul is not subject to part in the sense in which magnitudes are: our opponents themselves would not consent to the notion of the All-Soul being whittled down into fragments, yet this is what they would be doing, annulling the All-Soul—if any collective soul existed at all—making it a mere piece of terminology, thinking of it like wine separated into many portions, each portion, in its jar, being described as a portion of the total thing, wine.

Next there is the conception of the individual soul as a part in the sense in which we speak of some single proposition as a part of the science entire.

The theorem is separate, but the science stands as one undivided thing, the separation into theorems being simply the act of making each constituent notion explicit and efficient: this is partition without severance; each item potentially includes the whole science, which itself remains an unbroken total.

❙ Is this the appropriate parallel?

Yes; in such a relationship the All-Soul, of which the particular souls are to be a part, will not be the Soul of any definite thing, but an entity standing aloof;

that means that it will not even be the Soul of the Cosmos, since this will be, itself, one of those partial souls; thus all alike (cosmic soul and particular souls) will be partial and of one nature.

Then why (we may be asked) does one soul belong to the Cosmos and the rest only to parts of the Cosmos?[3]

3. Is it a question of part in the sense that, taking one living being, the Soul in a finger might be called a part of the Soul entire?

This would carry the alternative that either there is no soul outside of body, or that—no soul being within body—the thing described as the Soul of the universe is, none the less, outside the body of the universe. That is a point to be investigated, but for the present we must consider what kind of soul this parallel would give us.

If the particular soul is a part of the All-Soul only in the sense that this bestows itself upon all living things of the partial sphere, such a self-bestowal does not imply division; on the contrary, it is the identical soul that is present everywhere, the one complete thing, multi-present at the one moment: there is no longer question of a soul that is a part against a soul that is an all—especially where an identical power is present. Even difference of function, as in eyes and ears, cannot warrant the assertion of distinct parts concerned in each separate act—such allotment we may leave to others—all is met by the notion of one identical thing, but a thing in which a distinct power operates in each separate function. All the powers are present either in seeing or in hearing; the difference in impression received is due to the difference in the organs concerned; all the varying impressions are our various responses to Ideal-Forms that can be taken in a variety of modes.

A further proof (of the unity of soul) is that perception demands a common gathering place; every organ has its distinct function, and is competent only upon its own material, and must interpret each several experience in its own fashion; the judgement upon these impressions must, then, be vested in some one principle, a judge informed upon all that is said and done.

But again: 'Everywhere unity' applies both to Soul itself and to its various functions. To identify the relation of All-Soul to particular souls with the relation between a soul and its sensations would entail that no particular soul but only the All-Soul could have thought or knowledge; to localize thought is to recognize the separate existence of the individual soul. But since the soul is a rational soul, by the very same title by which the All-Soul is called rational,[4] then what is thought of as a part must in reality be no part but the identity of an unparted thing.

4. But if this is the true account of the unity of soul, we must be able to meet the problems that ensue: firstly, the difficulty of one thing being present at the same moment in all things; and, secondly, the difficulty of soul in body as against soul not embodied.

We might be led to think that all soul must always inhabit body; this would seem especially plausible in the case of the Soul of the universe, not thought of as ever leaving its body as the human soul does: there exists, no doubt, an opinion that even the human soul, while it must leave the body, can not become an utterly disembodied thing; but, assuming its complete disembodiment, how comes it that the human soul can go free of the body but the All-Soul not, though they are one and the same?

There is no such difficulty in the case of the Intellectual-Principle; by the primal differentiation, this separates, no doubt, into partial things but things unsundered from each other, and eternal unity is secured by virtue of the indivisible nature of that Essence: it is not so easy to explain how, in the case of the Soul described as 'divisible among bodies', such differentiated souls can still remain one thing.

A possible solution may be offered:

The unit, Soul, (it may be conceived) holds aloof, not actually falling into body; the differentiated souls—the All-Soul, with the others—issue from the unity while still constituting, within certain limits, an association. They are one soul by the fact that they do not belong unreservedly to any particular being; they meet, so to speak, fringe to fringe; they strike out here and there, but are held together at the source much as light is a divided thing upon earth, shining in this house and that, and yet remains uninterruptedly one identical substance.

The All-Soul would always remain above, since essentially it has, even in its lower phase, nothing to do with descent or with attending to this sensible sphere: our human souls do not similarly remain for ever above, because their lot is cast for this sphere, and because they give attention to a thing (the body) which requires their care.

The one—the lowest soul in the total of the All-Soul—would correspond to that in some great growth, silently, unlaboriously conducting the whole; our own lowest soul might be compared to the insect life in some rotted part of the growth—for this is the ratio of the animated body to the universe—while the other soul in us, of one ideal nature with the higher parts of the All-Soul, may be imaged as the gardener concerned about the insects lodged in the tree and anxiously working to amend what is wrong; or we may contrast a healthy man living with the healthy and, by his thought or by his act, lending himself to the service of those about him, with, on the other side, a sick man intent upon his own care and cure, and so not only living in the body but body-bound.

5. But what place is left for the particular souls, yours and mine and another's?

May we suppose the Soul to be appropriated on the lower ranges to some individual, but to belong on the higher to that other sphere?

At this there would be a Socrates as long as Socrates' soul remained in body; but Socrates ceases to exist, precisely on attainment of the highest.

Now nothing of Real Being is ever annulled.

In the Supreme, the Intellectual-Principles are not annulled, for in their differentiation there is no bodily partition; each separate phase possesses identical being within the diversity. It is exactly so with the souls.

By their succession they are linked to the several Intellectual-Principles, for they are the expressions, the Logoi, of the Intellectual-Principles, of which they are the unfolding; brevity has opened out to multiplicity; by that point of their being which least belongs to the partial order, they are attached each to its own Intellectual original: they have already chosen the way of division; but to the extreme they cannot go; thus they keep, at once, identification and difference; each soul is permanently a unity (a self) and yet all are, in their total, one being.

Thus the gist of the matter is established: one soul the source of all; the many founded in that one, on the analogy of the Intellectual-Principle; those many are at once divided and undivided; that Soul which abides in the Supreme is the one expression or Logos of the Intellectual-Principle, and from it spring other Reason-Principles, partial but immaterial, exactly as in the differentiation of the Supreme.

6. But how comes it that while the All-Soul has produced a Cosmos, the Soul of the particular has not, though it is of the one ideal Kind and contains, it too, all things in itself?

We have indicated that a thing may enter and dwell at the same time in various places; this ought to be explained, and the inquiry would show how an identity resident simultaneously here and there may, in its separate appearances, act or react—or both—after distinct modes; but the matter deserves to be examined in a special discussion.

To return, then: how and why has the All-Soul produced a Cosmos, while the particular souls simply administer some one part of it?

In the first place, we are not surprised when men of identical knowledge differ greatly in effective power.

But the reason, we will be asked.

The answer might be that there is a similar difference of degree among souls, the one never having fallen away from the All-Soul, but dwelling within it and assuming body therein, while the others received their allotted spheres when the body was already in existence, when their sister soul was already in rule and, as it were, had already prepared habitations for them. Again, the reason may be that the one (the creative All-Soul) looks towards the universal Intellectual-Principle (the exemplar of all that can be) while the others are more occupied with the Intellectual within themselves, that which is already of the sphere of part; perhaps, too, these also could have created, but that they were anticipated by that originator—the work accomplished before them—an impediment inevitable whichsoever of the souls were first to operate.

But it is safer to account for the creative act by nearer connexion with the over-world; the souls whose tendency is exercised within the Supreme have the greater power; immune in that pure seat they create securely; for the greater power takes the least hurt from the material within which it operates; I and the power of these souls derives from their remaining[5] enduringly attached I to the over-world: it creates, therefore, self-gathered and the created things gather round it; the other souls, on the contrary, themselves go forth; that can mean only that they have deserted towards the abyss; a main phase in them is drawn downward and pulls them with it in the desire towards the lower.

The 'secondary and tertiary souls', of which we hear, must be understood in the sense of closer or remoter position: it is much as in ourselves the relation to the Supreme is not identical from soul to soul; some of us are capable of becoming Uniate, others of striving and almost attaining, while a third rank is much less apt; it is a matter of the degree or powers of the Soul by which our expression is determined—the first degree dominant in the one person, the second, the third (the merely animal life) in others while, still, all of us contain all the powers.

7. So far, so good: but what of the passage in the Philebus taken to imply that the other souls are parts of the All-Soul?

The statement there made does not bear the meaning read into it; it expresses only, what the author was then concerned with, that the world is ensouled—a teaching which he maintains in the observation that it is preposterous to make the world soulless when we, who contain a part of the body of the All, have a soul; how, he asks, could there be soul in the part and none in the total?

He makes his teaching quite clear in the Timaeus, where he shows us the other souls brought into existence after the All-Soul, but 'compounded from the same mixing bowl'; secondary and tertiary are duly marked off from the primal, but every form of soul is presented as being of identical ideal-nature with the All-Soul.

As for the saying of the Phaedrus, 'The collective soul cares for all the un-ensouled', this simply tells us that the corporeal kind cannot be controlled—fashioned, set in place, or brought into being—by anything but the Soul. And we cannot think that there is one soul whose nature includes this power and another without it. 'The perfect soul', we read, that of the All, 'going its lofty journey', operates upon the Cosmos not by sinking into it, but, as it were, by brooding over it; and 'every perfect soul exercises this governance'; he distinguishes the other, the Soul in this sphere (not as a part, or as a different being, but) as 'the soul when its wing is broken'.

As for our souls being entrained in the Cosmic Circuit, and taking character and condition thence; this is no indication that they are parts: soul-nature may very well take some tincture from even the qualities of place, from water and from air; residence in this city or in that, and the varying make-up of the body may have their influence (upon our human souls which, yet, are no parts of place or of body).

We have always admitted that as members of the universe we take over something from the All-Soul; we do not deny the influence of the Cosmic Circuit; but against all this we oppose another soul in us (the Intellectual as distinguished from the merely vitalizing) proven to be distinct by that power of opposition.

As for our being begotten children of the Cosmos, we answer that in motherhood the entrant soul is distinct, is not the mother's.

8. These considerations, amounting to the settlement of the question, are not countered by the phenomenon of sympathy; the response between soul and soul is due to the mere fact that all spring from that self-same soul (the hypostasis Soul) from which springs the Soul of the All.

We have already stated that the one soul is also multiple; and we have dealt with the different forms of relationship between part and whole: we have investigated the different degrees existing within soul; we may now add, briefly, that differences might be induced, also, by the bodies with which the Soul has to do, and, even more, by the character and mental operations carried over from the conduct of the previous lives. 'The life-choice made by a soul has a correspondence'—we read—'with its former lives.'

As regards the nature of soul in general, the differences have been defined in the passage in which we mentioned the secondary and tertiary orders and laid down that, while all souls are all-comprehensive, each ranks according to its operative phase—one becoming Uniate in the achieved act, another in knowledge, another in desire, according to the distinct orientation by which each is, or tends to become, what it looks upon. The very fulfilment and perfectionment attainable by souls cannot but be different.

But, if in the total the organization in which they have their being is compact of variety—as it must be since every Reason-Principle is a unity of multiplicity and variety—and may be thought of as a psychic animated organism having many shapes at its command: if this is so and all constitutes a system in which being is not cut adrift from being, if there is nothing chance-borne among beings as there is none even in bodily organisms, then it follows that Soul must be a determined number; for, once again, Being must be stable; the members of the Intellectual must possess identity, each numerically one; this is the condition of individuality. Where, as in bodily masses, the Ideal-Form is not essentially native, and the individuality is therefore in flux, existence is specific and can rise only out of imitation of the Authentic Existences; these last, on the contrary, not rising out of any such conjunction (as the duality of Form and dead Matter) have their being in that which is numerically one, that which was from the beginning, and neither becomes what it has not been nor can cease to be what it is.

Even supposing Real-Beings (such as soul) to be produced by some other principle, they are certainly not made from Matter; or, if they were, the creating principle must infuse into them, from within itself, something of the nature of Real-Being; but, at this, it would itself suffer change, as it created more or less. And, after all, why should it thus produce at any given moment? Why is it not always producing?

Moreover, the produced total, variable from more to less, could not be an eternal: yet the Soul, it stands agreed, is eternal.

But what becomes of the Soul's infinity if it is thus fixed?

The infinity is a matter of power: there is question, not of the Soul's being divisible into an infinite number of parts, but of an infinite possible effectiveness: it is infinity in the sense in which the Supreme God, also, is free of all bound.

This means that it is no external limit that defines the individual being or the extension of souls any more than of God; on the contrary each in right of its own power is all that it chooses to be: and we are not to think of it as going forth from itself (losing its unity by any partition): the fact is simply that the element within it, which is apt to entrance into body, has the power of immediate projection any whither: the Soul is certainly not wrenched asunder by its presence at once in foot and in finger. Its presence in the All is similarly unbroken; over its entire range it exists in every several part of everything having even vegetal life, even in a part cut off from the main; in any possible segment it is as it is at its source. For the body of the All is a unit, and soul is everywhere present to it as to one thing.

When some animal rots and a multitude of others spring from it, the Life-Principle now present is not the particular soul that was in the larger body; that body has ceased to be receptive of soul, or there would have been no death; what happens is that whatsoever in the product of the decay is apt material for animal existence of one kind or another becomes ensouled by the fact that soul is nowhere lacking, though a recipient of soul may be. This new ensouling does not mean however an increase in the number of souls: all depend from the one or, rather, all remains one: it is as with ourselves; some elements are shed, others grow in their place; the soul abandons the discarded and flows into the newcoming as long as the one soul of the man holds its ground; in the All the one soul holds its ground for ever; its distinct contents now retain soul and now reject it, but the total of spiritual beings is unaffected.

9. But we must examine how soul comes to inhabit the body—the manner and the process—a question certainly of no minor interest.

The entry of soul into body takes place under two forms.

Firstly, there is the entry—metensomatosis—of a soul present in body by change from one (wholly material) frame to another, or the entry—not known as metensomatosis, since the nature of the earlier habitacle is not certainly definable—of a soul leaving an aerial or fiery body for one of earth.

Secondly, there is the entry from the wholly bodiless into any kind of body; this is the earliest form of any dealing between body and soul, and this entry especially demands investigation.

What then can be thought to have happened when soul, utterly clean from body, first comes into commerce with the bodily nature?

It is reasonable, necessary even, to begin with the Soul of the All. Notice that if we are to explain and to be clear, we are obliged to use such words as 'entry' and 'ensoulment', though never was this All unensouled, never did body subsist with soul away, never was there Matter unelaborate; we separate, the better to understand; there is nothing illegitimate in the verbal and mental sundering of things which must in fact be co-existent.

The true doctrine may be stated as follows:

In the absence of body, soul could not have gone forth, since there is no other place to which its nature would allow it to descend. Since go forth it must, it will generate a place for itself; at once body, also, exists.

While the Soul (as an eternal, a Divine Being) is at rest—in rest firmly based on Repose, the Absolute—yet, as we may put it, that huge illumination of the

Supreme pouring outwards comes at last to the extreme bourne of its light and dwindles to darkness; this darkness, now lying there beneath, the Soul sees and by seeing brings to shape; for in the law of things this ultimate depth, neighbouring with soul, may not go void of whatsoever degree of that Reason-Principle it can absorb, the dimmed reason of reality at its faintest.

Imagine that a stately and varied mansion has been built; it has never been abandoned by its architect, who, yet, is not tied down to it; he has judged it worthy in all its length and breadth of all the care that can serve to its Being— as far as it can share in Being—or to its beauty, but a care without burden to its director, who never descends, but presides over it from above: this gives the degree in which the Cosmos is ensouled, not by a soul belonging to it, but by one present to it; it is mastered, not master; not possessor, but possessed. The Soul bears it up, and it lies within, no fragment of it unsharing.

The Cosmos is like a net which takes all its life, as far as ever it stretches, from being wet in the water; it is at the mercy of the sea which spreads out, taking the net with it just so far as it will go, for no mesh of it can strain beyond its set place: the Soul is of so far-reaching a nature—a thing unbounded—as to embrace the entire body of the All in the one extension; so far as the universe extends, there soul is; ▌and if the universe had no existence, extension would be no concern of soul;[6] ▌it is eternally what it is. The universe spreads as broad as the presence of soul; the bound of its expansion is the point at which, in its downward egression from the Supreme, it still has soul to bind it in one: it is a shadow as broad as the Reason-Principle proceeding from soul; and that Reason-Principle is of scope to generate a cosmic bulk as vast as lay in the purposes of the Idea (the Divine forming power) which it conveys.

10. In view of all this we must now work back from the items to the unit, and consider the entire scheme as one enduring thing.

Just as in the groups air-light-sun and moon-light-sun the members exist simultaneously, though having degrees of primary, secondary, tertiary (i.e. having a logical or causal sequence), so we have Soul eternally unchanging, then graded series like that of fire stretching from primary to ultimate, where the ultimate is conceived as a shadow cast by fire and at once illuminated so that something of the nature of the Forming-Idea (of fire) hovers over the outcast that at first lay in blank obscurity. It is brought under the scheme of reason ▌by the efficacy of soul whose total being[7] latently holds this rationalizing power.▌ As we know, the Reason-Principles carried in animal seed fashion and shape living beings into so many universes in the small. For whatsoever touches soul is moulded to the nature of soul's own Real-Being.

We are not to think that the Soul acts upon the object by conformity to any external judgement; there is no pause for willing or planning: any such proce-dure would not be an act of sheer nature, but one of applied art: but art is of later origin than soul; it is an imitator, producing dim and feeble copies—toys, things of no great worth—and it is dependent upon all sorts of mechanism by which alone its images can be produced. The Soul, on the contrary, is sovran over material things by might of Real-Being; it gives them existence; their qual-ity is determined by its lead, and those elementary things cannot stand against its will. On the later level, things are hindered one by the other, and thus often fall short of the characteristic shape I at which their narrowly based Reason-Principle must be aiming; in the world as a whole (as distinct from its parts) the entire shape[8] comes from soul, I and all that is produced takes and keeps its appointed place in a unity, so that the engendered thing, without labour as without clash, becomes all that it should be. In the world the Soul has elaborated its creation, the images of the gods, dwellings for men, each existing to some peculiar purpose.

Soul could produce none but the things which truly represent its powers: fire produces warmth; another source produces cold; soul has a double efficacy, its act within itself, and its act from within outwards towards the new production.

In soulless entities, I the inner act remains dormant, and any efficiency they have is to bring to their own likeness whatever is amenable.[9] I All existence has this tendency to bring other things to likeness; but the Soul has the distinction of possessing at once an action of conscious attention within itself, and an action towards the outer. It has thus the function of giving life to all that does not live by prior right, and the life it gives is commensurate with its own; that is to say, living in reason, it communicates reason to the body—an image of the reason within itself, just as the life given to the body is an image of Real-Being—and it bestows, also, upon that material the appropriate shapes of which it contains the Reason-Forms.

The content of the creative soul includes the Ideal shapes of gods and of all else: and hence it is that the Cosmos contains all.

11. I think, therefore, that those ancient sages, who sought to secure the presence of divine beings by the erection of shrines and statues, showed insight into the nature of the All; they perceived that, though this Soul is everywhere tractable, its presence will be secured all the more readily when an appropriate receptacle is elaborated, a place especially capable of receiving some portion or phase of it, something reproducing it, or representing it and serving like a mirror to catch an image of it.

It belongs to the nature of the All to make its entire content reproduce, most felicitously, the Reason-Principles in which it participates; every particular thing is the image within matter of a Reason-Principle which itself images a pre-material Reason-Principle: thus every particular entity is linked to that Divine Being in whose likeness it is made, the divine principle which the Soul contemplated and contained in the act of each creation. Such mediation and representation there must have been since it was equally impossible for the created to be without share in the Supreme, and for the Supreme to descend into the created.

❙ The sun of that sphere—let us return to it as our example—is an Intellectual-Principle,[10] and immediately upon it follows ❙ the Soul depending from it, stationary Soul from stationary Intelligence. But the Soul borders also upon the sun of this sphere, and becomes the medium by which it is linked to the over-world; it plays the part of an interpreter between what emanates from that sun down to this lower, and what rises—as far as, through Soul, anything can—from the lower to the higher.

Nothing, in fact, is far away from anything; things are not remote; there is, no doubt, the aloofness of difference and of mingled natures as against the un-mingled; but selfhood has nothing to do with spatial position, and in unity itself there may still be distinction.

These Beings (the heavenly bodies) are divine in virtue of cleaving to the Supreme, because, by the medium of the Soul thought of as descending, they remain linked with the Primal Soul, and through it are veritably what they are called and possess the vision of the Intellectual-Principle, the single object of contemplation to that soul in which they have their being.

12. The souls of men, seeing their images in the mirror of Dionysus as it were, have entered into that realm in a leap downward from the Supreme: yet even they are not cut off from their origin, from the divine Intellect; it is not that they have come bringing the Intellectual-Principle down in their fall; it is that though they have descended even to earth, yet their higher part holds for ever above the heavens.

Their initial descent is deepened since that mid-part of theirs is compelled to labour in care of the care-needing thing into which they have entered. But Zeus, the father, takes pity on their toils and makes the bonds in which they labour soluble by death and gives respite in due time, freeing them from the body, that they too may come to dwell there where the Universal Soul, unconcerned with earthly needs, has ever dwelt.

For the container of the total of things must be a self-sufficing entity and remain so: in its periods it is wrought out to purpose under its Reason-Principles which are perdurably valid; by these periods it reverts unfailingly, in the measured stages of defined life-duration, to its established character; it is leading the things of this realm to be of one voice and plan with the Supreme. And thus the cosmic content is carried forward to its purpose, everything in its co-ordinate place, under one only Reason-Principle operating alike in the descent and return of souls and to every purpose of the system.

We may know this also by the concordance of the souls with the ordered scheme of the Cosmos; I they are not dependent,[11] but, I by their descent, they have put themselves in contact, and they stand henceforth in harmonious association with the cosmic circuit—to the extent that their fortunes, their life-experiences, their choosing and refusing, are announced by the patterns of the stars—and out of this concordance rises as it were one musical utterance: the music, the harmony, by which all is described (the harmony of the spheres), is the best witness to this truth.

Such a consonance can have been procured in one only way:

The All must, in every detail of act and experience, be an expression of the Supreme, which must dominate alike its periods and its stable ordering and the life-careers varying with the movement of the souls as they are sometimes absorbed in that highest, sometimes in the heavens, sometimes turned to the things and places of our earth. All that is Divine Intellect will rest eternally above, and could never fall from its sphere but, poised entire in its own high place, will communicate to things here through the channel of Soul. Soul in virtue of neighbourhood is more closely modelled upon the Idea uttered by the Divine Intellect, and thus is able to produce order in the movement of the lower realm, one phase (the World-Soul) maintaining the unvarying march (of the cosmic circuit), the other (the Soul of the Individual) adapting itself to times and seasons.

The depth of the descent, also, will differ—sometimes lower, sometimes less low—and this even in its entry into any given Kind: all that is fixed is that each several soul descends to a recipient indicated by affinity of condition; it moves towards the thing which it There resembled, and enters, accordingly, into the body of man or animal.

13. The Ineluctable, the Cosmic Law is, thus, rooted in a natural principle under which each several entity is overruled to go, duly and in order, towards that place and Kind to which it characteristically tends, that is towards the image of its primal choice and constitution.

In that archetypal world every form of soul is near to the image (the thing in the world of copy) to which its individual constitution inclines it; there is therefore no need of a sender or leader acting at the right moment to bring it at the right moment whether into body or into a definitely appropriate body: of its own motion it descends at the precisely true time and enters where it must. To every soul its own hour; when that strikes it descends and enters the body suitable to it as at the cry of a herald; thus all is set stirring and advancing as by a magician's power or by some mighty traction; it is much as, in any living thing, the Soul itself effects the fulfilment of the natural career, stirring and bringing forth, in due season, every element—beard, horn, and all the successive stages of tendency and of output—or, as it leads a tree through its normal course within set periods.

The souls go forth neither under compulsion nor of freewill; or, at least, freedom, here, is not to be regarded as action upon preference; it is more like such a leap of the nature as moves men to the instinctive desire of sexual union, or, in the case of some, to fine conduct; the motive lies elsewhere than in the reason: like is destined unfailingly to like, and each moves hither or thither at its fixed moment.

Even the Intellectual-Principle, which is before all the Cosmos, has, it also, its destiny, that of abiding intact above, and of giving downwards; what it sends down is the particular whose existence is implied in the law (or decreed system) of the universal; for the universal broods closely over the particular; it is not from without that the law derives the power by which it is executed; on the contrary the law is given in the entities upon whom it falls; these bear it about with them. Let but the moment arrive, and what it decrees will be brought to act by those beings in whom it resides; they fulfil it because they contain it; it prevails because it is within them; it becomes like a heavy burden, and sets up in them a painful longing to enter the realm to which they are bidden from within.

14. Thus it comes about that this Cosmos, lit with many lights, gleaming in its souls, receives still further graces, gifts from here and from there, from the gods of the Supreme, and from those other Intellectual-Principles whose nature it is to ensoul. This is probably the secret of the myth in which, after Prometheus had moulded woman, the other gods heaped gifts upon her, Hephaistos 'blending the clay with moisture and bestowing the human voice and the form of a goddess'; Aphrodite bringing her gifts, and the Graces theirs, and other gods other gifts, and finally calling her by the name (Pandora) which tells of gift and of all giving—for all have added something to this formation brought to being by a Promethean, a fore-thinking power. As for the rejection of Prometheus' gift by after-thought, Epimetheus, what can this signify but that the wiser choice is to remain in the Intellectual realm? Pandora's creator is fettered, to

signify that he is in some sense held by his own creation; such a fettering is external and the release by Hercules tells that there is power in Prometheus, so that he need not remain in bonds.

Take the myth as we may, it is certainly such an account of the bestowal of gifts upon the Cosmos as harmonizes with our explanation of the universal system.

15. The souls peering forth from the Intellectual Realm descend first to the heavens and there put on a body; this becomes at once the medium by which as they reach out more and more towards magnitude (physical extension) they proceed to bodies progressively more earthy. Some even plunge from heaven to the very lowest of corporeal forms; others pass, stage by stage, too feeble to lift towards the higher the burden they carry, weighed downwards by their heaviness and forgetfulness.

As for the differences among them, these are due to variation in the bodies entered, or to the accidents of life, or to upbringing, or to inherent peculiarities of temperament, or to all these influences together, or to specific combinations of them.

Then again some have fallen unreservedly into the power of the destiny ruling here: some yielding betimes are betimes too their own: there are those who, while they accept what must be borne, have the strength of self-mastery in all that is left to their own act; they have given themselves to another dispensation: they live by the code of the aggregate of beings, the code which is woven out of the Reason-Principles and all the other causes ruling in the Cosmos, out of soul movements and out of laws springing in the Supreme; a code, therefore, consonant with those higher existences, founded upon them, linking their sequents back to them, keeping unshakeably true all that is capable of holding itself set towards the divine nature, and leading round by all appropriate means whatsoever is less natively apt.

In fine all diversity of condition in the lower spheres is determined by the descendent beings themselves.

16. The punishment justly overtaking the wicked must therefore be ascribed to the cosmic order which leads all in accordance with the right.

But what of chastisements, poverty, illness, falling upon the good outside of all justice? These events, we will be told, are equally interwoven into the world order and fall under prediction, and must consequently have a cause in the general reason: are they therefore to be charged to past misdoing?

No: such misfortunes do not answer to reasons established in the nature of things; they are not laid up in the master-facts of the universe, but were merely accidental sequents: a house falls, and anyone that chances to be underneath is killed, no matter what sort of man he be: two squadrons of cavalry are moving in perfect order—or one if you like—but anything getting in the way is wounded or trampled down. Or we may reason that the undeserved stroke can be no evil to the sufferer in view of the beneficient interweaving of the All; or again, no doubt, that nothing is unjust that finds justification in a past history.

We may not think of some things being fitted into a system with others abandoned to the capricious; if things must happen by cause, by natural sequences, under one Reason-Principle and a single set scheme, we must admit that the minor equally with the major is fitted into that order and pattern.

Wrongdoing from man to man is wrong in the doer and must be imputed, but, as belonging to the established order of the universe, is not a wrong within that order or even as regards the innocent sufferer; it is a thing that had to be, and, if the sufferer is good, the issue is to his gain. For we cannot think that this ordered combination proceeds without God and justice; we must take it to be precise in the distribution of due, while, yet, the reason of things elude us, and to our ignorance the scheme presents matter of censure.

17. Various considerations explain why the souls going forth from the Intellectual proceed first to the heavenly regions. The heavens, as the noblest portion of sensible space, would border with the least exalted of the Intellectual, and will, therefore, be first ensouled, first to participate as most apt; while what is of earth is at the very extremity of progression, least endowed towards participation, remotest from the unembodied.

All the souls, then, shine down upon the heavens and spend there the main of themselves and the best; only their lower phases illuminate the lower realms; and those souls which descend deepest show their light furthest down—not themselves the better for the depth to which they have penetrated.

There is, we may put it, something that is centre; about it, a circle of light shed from it; round centre and first circle alike, another circle, light from light; outside that again, not another circle of light but one which, lacking light of its own, must borrow.

The last we may figure to ourselves as an outer ring, or rather sphere, of a nature to receive light from that third realm, its next higher, in proportion to the light which that itself receives. Thus all begins with the great light, shining self-centred; in accordance with the reigning plan (that of emanation) this gives forth its brilliance; the later (divine) existents (souls) add their radiation—some of them remaining above while there are some that are drawn further downward, attracted by the splendour of the object they illuminate. These last find that their charges need more and more care: the steersman of a storm-tossed ship is so intent on saving it that he forgets his own interest and never thinks that he is recurrently in peril of being dragged down with the vessel; similarly the souls are intent upon contriving for their charges and finally come to be pulled down by them; they are fettered in bonds of sorcery, gripped and held by their concern for the realm of Nature.

If every living being were of the character of the All—perfect, self-sufficing, in peril from no outside influence—the Soul now spoken of as indwelling would not occupy the body; it would infuse life while clinging, entire, within the Supreme.

18. There remains still something to be said on the question whether the Soul uses deliberate reason before its descent and again when it has left the body.

Reasoning is for this sphere; it is the act of the Soul fallen into perplexity, distracted with cares, diminished in strength: the need of deliberation goes with the less self-sufficing intelligence; craftsmen faced by a difficulty stop to consider; where there is no problem, their art works on by its own forthright power.

But if souls in the Supreme operate without reasoning, how can they be called reasoning souls?

One answer might be that they have the power of deliberating to happy issue, should occasion arise: but all is met by defining the particular kind of reasoning intended: we may represent to ourselves a reasoning that flows uninterruptedly from the Intellectual-Principle in them, an inherent state, I an enduring activity, a reflection, we may say, of the Principle itself;[12] I in this way they would be users of reason even when in that over-world. We certainly cannot think of them, it seems to me, as employing words when they are wholly in the Intellectual: and in the heavenly regions, where they occupy bodies, the deliberation of doubt and difficulty which they practise here (on earth) must be unknown to them; all their act must fall into place by sheer force of their nature; there can be no question of commanding or of taking counsel; they will know, each, what is to be communicated from another, by present consciousness. Even in our own case here, eyes often know what is not spoken; and there (in the heaven) the whole body is pure, and every being is, as it were, an eye, nothing is concealed or sophisticated, there is no need of speech, everything is seen and known. As for the Celestials (the Daimones) and souls in the air, they may well use speech; for all such are simply Animate-Beings.

19. Are we to think of the indivisible phase of the Soul and the divided as making one thing in a coalescence; or is the indivisible in a place of its own and under conditions of its own, the divisible being a sequent upon it, a separate part of it, as distinct as the reasoning phase is from the unreasoning?

The answer to this question will emerge when we make plain the nature and function to be attributed to each.

The indivisible phase is mentioned (in the passage of Plato) without further qualification; but not so the divisible; ▌'that existence (or essence)'[13] we read ▌ 'which becomes divisible in bodies'—and even this last is presented as becoming ▌partible,[14]▌ not as being so once for all.

'In bodies': we must, then, satisfy ourselves as to what form of soul is required to produce life in the corporeal, and what there must be of soul present throughout such a body, such a completed organism.

Now, every sensitive power—by the fact of being sensitive throughout— tends to become a thing of parts: present at every distinct point of sensitive- ness, it may be thought of as divided. In the sense, however, that it is present as a whole at every such point, it cannot be said to be wholly divided; it 'becomes divisible in body'. We may be told that no such partition is implied in any sensations but those of touch; but this is not so; where the participant is body (of itself insensitive and nontransmitting) that divisibility in the sensitive agent will be a condition of all other sensations, though in less degree than in the case of touch. Similarly the vegetative function in the Soul, with that of growth, indicates divisibility; and, admitting such locations as that of desire at the liver and emotional activity at the heart, we have the same result. ▌ It may of course be the case that Plato does not include desire and emotion in this blending of the elements of the Soul; he may regard them as rising in some special way out of one of these elements. Reasoning[15] and the act of the in- tellect ▌—these, certainly, are not vested in the body; their task is not accom- plished by means of the body which in fact is detrimental to any thinking on which it is allowed to intrude.

Thus the indivisible phase of the Soul stands distinct from the divisible; they do not form a unity, but, on the contrary, a whole consisting of parts, each part a self-standing thing having its own peculiar virtue. None the less, if that phase which becomes divisible in body holds indivisibility by communication from the superior power, then this one same thing (the Soul in body) may be at once indivisible and divisible; it will be, as it were, a blend, a thing made up of its own divisible self with, in addition, the quality that it derives from above itself.

20. Here a question rises to which we must find an answer: whether these and the other powers which we call 'parts' of the Soul are situated, all, in place; or whether some have place and standpoint, others not; or whether again none are situated in place.

The matter is difficult: if we do not allot to each of the parts of the Soul some form of place, but leave all unallocated—no more within the body than outside it—we leave the body soulless, and are at a loss to explain plausibly the origin of acts performed by means of the bodily organs: if, on the other hand, we suppose some of those phases to be (capable of situation) in place but others not so, we will be supposing that those parts to which we deny place are ineffective in us, or, in other words, that we do not possess our entire soul.

This simply shows that neither the Soul entire nor any part of it may be considered to be within the body as in a space: space is a container, a container of body; it is the home of such things as consist of isolated parts, and is never, therefore, found whole in any part; now, the Soul is not a body and is no more contained than containing.

Neither is it in body as in some vessel: whether as vessel or as place of location, the body would remain, in itself, unensouled. If we are to think of some passing-over from the Soul—that self-gathered thing—to the containing vessel, then soul is diminished by just as much as the vessel takes.

Space, again, in the strict sense is unembodied, and is not, itself, body; why, then, should it need soul?

Besides (if the Soul were contained as in space) contact would be only at the surface of the body, not throughout the entire mass.

Many other considerations equally refute the notion that the Soul is in body as (an object) in space; for example, this space would be shifted with every movement, and a thing itself would carry its own space about.

Of course if by space we understand the interval separating objects, it is still less possible that the Soul be in body as in space: such a separating interval must be a void; but body is not a void; the void must be that in which body is placed; body (not soul) will be in the void.

Nor can it be in the body as in some substratum: anything in a substratum is a condition affecting that—a colour, a form—but the Soul (is no condition of something else,) is a separate existence.

Nor is it present as a part in the whole: soul is no part of body. If we are asked to think of soul as a part in the living total we are faced with the old difficulty: how it is in that whole. It is certainly not there as the wine is in the wine jar, or as the 'jar' (liquid measure) is in the jar (vessel), or as some object is self-present.

Nor can the presence be that of a whole in its part: it would be absurd to think of the Soul as a total of which the body should represent the parts.

It is not present as Form is in Matter; for the Form as in Matter is inseparable, and, further, is something superimposed upon an already existent thing; soul, on the contrary, is that which engenders the Form residing within the Matter and therefore is not the Form. If the reference is not to the Form actually present, but to Form as a thing existing apart from all formed objects, it is hard to see how such an entity has found its way ￨ into body.[16]￨

How comes it then that everyone speaks of soul as being in body?

Because the Soul is not seen and the body is: we perceive the body, and by its movement and sensation we understand that it is ensouled, and we say that it possesses a soul; to speak of residence is a natural sequence. If the Soul were visible, an object of the senses, radiating throughout the entire life, if it were manifest in full force to the very outermost surface, we would no longer speak of soul as in body; we would say the minor was within the major, the contained within the container, the fleeting within the perdurable.

21. What does all this come to? What answer do we give to any who, with no opinion of his own to assert, asks us to explain this presence? And what do we say to the question whether there is one only mode of presence of the entire soul or different modes, phase and phase?

Of the modes currently accepted for the presence of one thing in another, none really meets the case of the Soul's relation to the body. Thus we are given as a parallel the steersman in the ship; this serves adequately to indicate that the Soul is potentially separable, but the mode of presence, which is what we are seeking, it does not exhibit.

We can imagine it within the body in some incidental way—for example, as a voyager in a ship—but scarcely as the steersman: and, of course, too, the steersman is not omnipresent to the ship as the Soul is to the body.

May we, perhaps, compare it to the science or skill that acts through its appropriate instruments—through a helm, let us say, which should happen to be a live thing—so that the soul effecting the movements dictated by seamanship is an indwelling directive force?

No: the comparison breaks down, since the science is something outside of helm and ship.

Is it any help to adopt the illustration of the steersman taking the helm, and to station the Soul within the body as the steersman may be thought to be within the material instrument through which he works? Soul, whenever and wherever it chooses to operate, does in much that way move the body.

No; even in this parallel we have no explanation of the mode of presence within the instrument; we cannot be satisfied without further search, a closer approach.

22. May we think that the mode of the Soul's presence to body is that of the presence of light to the air?

This certainly is presence with distinction: the light penetrates through and through, but nowhere coalesces; the light is the stable thing, the air flows in and out; when the air passes beyond the lit area it is dark; under the light it is lit: we have a true parallel to what we have been saying of body and soul, for the air is in the light rather than the light in the air.

Plato therefore is wise when, in treating of the All, he puts the body in its soul and not its soul in the body, and says that while there is a region of that soul which contains body, there is another region to which body does not enter—certain powers, that is, with which body has no concern. And what is true of the All-Soul is true of the others.

There are, therefore, certain soul-powers whose presence to body must be denied.

The phases present are those which the nature of body demands: they are present without being resident—either in any parts of the body or in the body as a whole.

For the purposes of sensation the sensitive phase of the Soul is present to the entire sensitive being: for the purposes of act, differentiation begins; every soul phase operates at a point peculiar to itself.

23. I explain: a living body is illuminated by soul: each organ and member participates in soul after some manner peculiar to itself; the organ is adapted to a certain function, and this fitness is the vehicle of the soul-faculty under which the function is performed; thus the seeing faculty acts through the eyes, the hearing faculty through the ears, the tasting faculty through the tongue, the faculty of smelling through the nostrils, and the faculty of sentient touch is present throughout, since in this particular form of perception the entire body is an instrument in the Soul's service.

The vehicles of touch are at the ends of the nerves—which, moreover, are vehicles of the faculty by which the movements of the living being are effected—in them the soul-faculty concerned makes itself present; the nerves start from the brain. The brain therefore has been considered as the centre and seat of the principle which determines feeling and impulse and the entire act of the organism as a living thing; where the instruments are found to be linked, there the operating faculty is assumed to be situated. But it would be wiser to say only that there is situated the first activity of the operating faculty: the power to be exercised by the operator—in keeping with the particular instrument—must be considered as concentrated at the point at which the instrument is to be first applied; or, since the Soul's faculty is of universal scope, the sounder statement is that the point of origin of the instrument is the point of origin of the act.

Now, the faculty presiding over sensation and impulse is vested in the sensitive and representative soul; it draws upon the Reason-Principle immediately above itself; downward, it is in contact with an inferior of its own: on this analogy the uppermost member of the living being was taken by the ancients to be obviously its seat; they lodged it in the brain, or not exactly in the brain but in I that sensitive part which, they tell us, has its seat within the brain. They saw that some phase of soul must be definitely allocated to body—at the point most receptive of its activity—while that phase (the reasoning) which is utterly isolated from body must be in contact with something[17] which is a form of soul I (and not merely of the vegetative or other quasi-corporeal forms but) of that soul apt to the appropriation of the perceptions originating in the Reason-Principle.

Such a linking there must be, since in perception there is some element of judging, in representation something intuitional, and since impulse and appetite derive from representation and reason. The reasoning faculty, therefore, is present where these experiences occur, present not as in a place but in the fact that what is there draws upon it. As regards perception we have already explained in what sense it is local.

But every part of the body includes the vegetal principle, that principle of growth and nourishment which maintains the organism by means of the blood; this nourishing medium is contained in the veins; the veins and blood have their origin in the liver: from observation of these facts the power concerned was assigned a place; the phase of the Soul, which has to do with desire, was allocated to the liver. Certainly what brings to birth and nourishes and gives growth must have the desire of these functions. Blood—subtle, light, swift, pure—is the vehicle most apt to animal spirit: the heart, then, its well-spring, the place where such blood is sifted into being, is taken as the fixed centre of the ebullition of the passionate nature.

24. Now comes the question of the Soul leaving the body: where does it go?

It cannot remain in this world where there is no natural recipient for it; and it cannot remain attached to anything not of a character to hold it: it can be held here when only it is less than wise, containing within itself something of that which lures it.

If it does contain any such alien element it gives itself, with increasing attachment, to the sphere to which that element naturally belongs and tends.

The space open to the Soul's resort is vast and diverse; the difference will come by the double force of the individual condition and of the justice reigning in things. No one can ever escape the suffering entailed by ill deeds done: the divine law is ineluctable, carrying bound up, as one with it, the fore-ordained execution of its doom. The sufferer, all unaware, is swept onward towards his due, hurried always by the restless driving of his errors, until at last wearied out by that against which he struggled, he falls into his fit place and, by self-chosen movement, is brought to the lot he never chose. And the law decrees, also, the intensity and the duration of the suffering while it carries with it, too, the lifting of chastisement and the faculty of rising from those places of pain— all by power of the harmony that maintains the universal scheme.

Souls, body-bound, are apt to body-punishment; clean souls no longer drawing to themselves at any point any vestige of body are, by their very being, outside the bodily sphere; body-free, containing nothing of body—there where Essence is, and Being, and the Divine within the Divinity, among Those, within That, such a soul must be.

If you still ask Where, you must ask where those Beings are—and in your seeking, seek otherwise than with the sight, and not as one seeking for body.

25. Now comes the question, equally calling for an answer, whether those souls that have quitted the places of earth retain memory of their lives—all souls or some, of all things, or of some things, and, again, for ever or merely for some period not very long after their withdrawal.

A true investigation of this matter requires us to establish first what a remembering principle must be—I do not mean what memory is, but in what order of beings it can occur. The nature of memory has been indicated, laboured even, elsewhere; we still must try to understand more clearly what characteristics are present where memory exists.

Now a memory has to do with something brought into ken from without, something learned or something experienced; the Memory-Principle, therefore, cannot belong to such beings as are immune from experience and from time.

No memory, therefore, can be ascribed to any divine being, or to the Authentic-Existent or the Intellectual-Principle: these are intangibly immune; time does not approach them; they possess eternity centred around Being; they know nothing of past and sequent; all is an unbroken state of identity, not receptive of change. Now a being rooted in unchanging identity cannot entertain memory, since it has not and never had a state differing from any previous state, or any new intellection following upon a former one, so as to be aware of contrast between a present perception and one remembered from before.

But what prevents such a being (from possessing memory in the sense of) perceiving, without variation in itself, such outside changes as, for example, the cosmic periods?

Simply the fact that following the changes of the revolving Cosmos it would have perception of earlier and later: intuition and memory are distinct.

We cannot hold its self-intellections to be acts of memory; this is no question of something entering from without, to be grasped and held in fear of an escape; if its intellections could slip away from it (as a memory might) its very Essence (as the Hypostasis of inherent Intellection) would be in peril.

For the same reason memory, in the current sense, cannot be attributed to the Soul in connexion with the ideas inherent in its essence: these it holds not as a memory but as a possession, though, by its very entrance into this sphere, they are no longer the mainstay of its Act.

The Soul-action which is to be observed seems to have induced the Ancients to ascribe memory, and 'Recollection' (the Platonic Anamnesis), to souls bringing into outward manifestation the ideas they contain: we see at once that the memory here indicated is another kind; it is a memory outside of time.

But, perhaps, this is treating too summarily a matter which demands minute investigation. It might be doubted whether that recollection, that memory, really belongs to the highest soul and not rather to another, a dimmer, or even to the Couplement, the Living-Being. And if to that dimmer soul, when and how has it come to be present; if to the Couplement, again when and how?

We are driven thus to inquire into these several points: in which of the constituents of our nature is memory vested—the question with which we started; if in the Soul, then in what power or part; if in the Animate or Couplement—which has been supposed, similarly, to be the seat of sensation— then by what mode it is present, and how we are to define the Couplement; finally whether sensation and intellectual acts may be ascribed to one and the same agent, or imply two distinct principles.

26. Now if sensations of the active order depend upon the Couplement of soul and body, sensation must be of that double nature. Hence it is classed as one of the shared acts: the Soul, in the feeling, may be compared to the workman in such operations as boring or weaving, the body to the tool employed: the body is passive and menial; the Soul is active, reading such impressions as are made upon the body or discerned by means of the body, perhaps entertaining only a judgement formed as the result of the bodily experiences.

In such a process it is at once clear that the sensation is a shared task; but the memory is not thus made over to the Couplement, since the Soul has from the first taken over the impression, either to retain or to reject.

It might be ventured that memory, no less than sensation, is a function of the Couplement, on the ground that bodily constitution determines our memories good or bad; but the answer would come that, whether the body happens or not to be a hindrance, the act of remembering would still be an act of the Soul. And in the case of matters learned (and not merely felt, as corporeal experiences), how can we think of the Couplement of soul and body as the remembering principle? Here, surely, it must be soul alone?

We may be told that the living-being is a Couplement in the sense of something entirely distinct formed from the two elements (so that it might have memory though neither soul nor body had it). But, to begin with, it is absurd to class the living-being as neither body nor soul; these two things cannot so change as to make a distinct third, nor can they blend so utterly that the Soul shall become a mere potentiality in the animate whole. And, further, supposing they could so blend, memory would still be due to the Soul just as in honey-wine all the sweetness will be due to the honey.

It may be suggested that the Soul is indeed a remembering principle, but only because, having lost its purity and acquired some degree of modification by its presence in body, it becomes capable of reproducing the imprints of sensible objects and experiences, and because, seated, as roughly speaking it is, within the body, it may reasonably be thought capable of accepting such impressions, and in such a manner as to retain them (thus in some sense possessing memory).

But, to begin with, these imprints are not magnitudes (are not of corporeal nature at all); there is no resemblance to seal impressions, no stamping of a resistant matter, for there is neither the down-thrust (as of the seal) nor (the acceptance) as in the wax: the process is entirely of the intellect, though exercised upon things of sense; and what kind of resistance (or other physical action) can be affirmed in matters of the intellectual order, or what need can there be of body or bodily quality as a means?

Further there is one order of which the memory must obviously belong to the Soul; it alone can remember its own movements, for example its desires and those frustrations of desire in which the coveted thing never came to the body: the body can have nothing to tell about things which never approached it, and the Soul cannot use the body as a means to the remembrance of what the body by its nature cannot know.

If the Soul is to have any significance—to be a definite principle with a function of its own—we are forced to recognize two orders of fact, an order in which the body is a means but all culminates in soul, and an order which is of the Soul alone. This being admitted, aspiration will belong to soul, and so, as a consequence, will that memory of the aspiration and of its attainment or frustration, without which the Soul's nature would fall into the category of the unstable (that is to say of the undivine, unreal). Deny this character of the Soul and at once we refuse it perception, consciousness, any power of comparison, almost any understanding. Yet these powers of which, embodied, it becomes the source cannot be absent from its own nature. On the contrary; it possesses certain activities to be expressed in various functions whose accomplishment demands bodily organs; at its entry it brings with it (as vested in itself alone) the powers necessary for some of these functions, while in the case of others it brings the very activities themselves.

Memory, in point of fact, is impeded by the body: even as things are, addition often brings forgetfulness; with thinning and clearing away, memory will often revive. The Soul is a stability; the shifting and fleeting thing which body is can be a cause only of its forgetting, not of its remembering—Lethe stream may be understood in this sense—and memory is a fact of the Soul.

27. But of what soul—of that which we envisage as the more divine, by which we are human beings, or that other which springs from the All?

Memory must be admitted in both of these, personal memories and shared memories; and when the two souls are together, the memories also are as one; when they stand apart, assuming that both exist and endure, each soon forgets the other's affairs, retaining for a longer time its own. Thus it is that the Shade of Hercules in the lower regions—this 'Shade', as I take it, being the characteristically human part—remembers all the action and experience of the life, since that career was mainly of the hero's personal shaping; yet the other souls (in Homer) in which the higher phase was coupled with the lower could, for all their different standing, have nothing to recount but the events of that same life: perhaps they would add also some moral judgement.

What the Hercules standing outside the Shade spoke of we are not told: what can we think that other, the freed and isolated, soul would recount?

The soul which still drags a burden[18] will tell of all the man did and felt; but upon death there will appear, as time passes, memories of the lives lived before, some of the events of the most recent life being dismissed as trivial. As it grows away from the body, it will revive things forgotten in the corporeal state, and if it passes in and out of one body after another, it will tell over the events of the discarded life, it will treat as present that which it has just left, and it will remember much from the former existence. But with lapse of time it will come to forgetfulness of any things that were mere accretion.

Then, free and alone at last, what will it have to remember?

The answer to that question depends on our discovering in what faculty of the Soul memory resides.

28. Is memory vested in the faculty by which we perceive and learn? Or do we remember objects of desire with the desiring faculty and objects of anger with the passionate faculty?

This will be maintained on the ground that there could scarcely be both a first faculty in direct action and a second to remember what that first experiences. It is certain that the desiring faculty is apt to be stirred by what it has once enjoyed; the object presents itself again; evidently, memory is at work; why else, the same object with the same attraction?

But, at that, we might reasonably ascribe to the desiring faculty the very perception of the desired objects and then the desire itself to the perceptive faculty, and so on all through, and in the end conclude that the distinctive names merely indicate the function which happens to be uppermost.

Yet the perception is very different from faculty to faculty; certainly it is sight and not desire that sees the object; desire is stirred merely as a result of the seeing, by a transmission; its act is not in the nature of an identification of an object seen; all is simply blind response (automatic reaction). Similarly with rage; sight reveals the offender and the passion leaps; we may think of a shepherd seeing a wolf at his flock, and a dog, seeing nothing, who springs to the scent or the sound.

In other words the desiring faculty has had the emotion, but the trace it keeps of the event is not a memory; it is a condition, something passively accepted: there is another faculty that was aware of the enjoyment and retains the memory of what has happened. This is confirmed by the fact that many satisfactions which the desiring faculty has enjoyed are not retained in the memory: if memory resided in the desiring faculty, such forgetfulness could not be.

29. Are we, then, to refer memory to the perceptive faculty and so make one principle of our nature the seat of both awareness and remembrance?

Now supposing the very Shade, as we were saying in the case of Hercules, has memory, then the perceptive faculty is twofold; and even if the faculty that remembers is not the faculty that perceives but some other thing, the remembering faculty is twofold. And, further, if the memory deals with matters learned, the perceptive faculty (in order to be identical with memory) will be concerned with thoughts (as well as with matters of observation and feeling): but these two orders certainly require two separate faculties.

Must we then suppose a common faculty of apprehension (one covering both sense-perceptions and ideas) and assign memory in both orders to this?

The solution might serve if there were one and the same percipient for objects of sense and objects of the Intellectual-Kind; but if these stand in definite duality, then, for all we can say or do, we are left with two separate principles of memory; and, supposing each of the two orders of soul to possess both principles, then we have four.

And, on general grounds, what compelling reason is there that the principle by which we perceive should be the principle by which we remember, that these two acts should be vested in the one faculty? Why must the seat of our intellectual action be also the seat of our remembrance of that action? The most powerful thought does not always go with the readiest memory; people of equal perception are not equally good at remembering; some are especially gifted in perception, others, never swift to grasp, are strong to retain.

But, once more, admitting two distinct principles. something quite separate remembering what sense-perception has first known—still this something must have felt what it is required to remember?

No; we may well conceive that where there is to be memory of a sense-perception, this perception becomes a mere presentment, and that to this image-grasping power, a distinct thing, belongs the memory, the retention of the object: for in this imaging faculty the perception culminates; the impression passes away but the vision remains present to the imagination.

By the fact of harbouring the presentment of an object that has disappeared, the imagination is, at once, a seat of memory: where the persistence of the image is brief, the memory is poor; people of powerful memory are those in whom the image-holding power is firmer, not easily allowing the record to be jostled out of its grip.

Remembrance, thus, is vested in the imaging faculty; and memory deals with images. Its differing quality or degree from man to man we would explain by difference or similarity in the strength of the individual powers, by conduct like or unlike, by bodily conditions present or absent, producing change and disorder or not—a point this, however, which need not detain us here.

30. But what of the memory of mental acts: do these also fall under the imaging faculty?

If every mental act is accompanied by an image we may well believe that this image, fixed and like a picture of the thought, would explain how we remember the object of knowledge once entertained. But if there is no such necessary image, another solution must be sought. Perhaps memory would be the reception, into the image-making faculty, of ❙ the verbal formula[19]❙ which accompanies the mental conception: this mental conception—an indivisible thing, and one that never rises to the exterior of the consciousness—lies unknown below; ❙ the verbal formula[19]❙ —the revealer, the bridge between the concept and the image-taking faculty—exhibits the concept as in a mirror; the apprehension by the image-taking faculty would thus constitute the enduring presence of the concept, would be our memory of it.

This explains, also, another fact: the Soul is unfailingly intent upon intellection; only when it acts upon this image-making faculty does its intellection become a human perception: intellection is one thing, the perception of an intellection is another: we are continuously intuitive but we are not unbrokenly aware: the reason is that the recipient in us receives from both sides, absorbing not merely intellections but also sense-perceptions.

31. But if each of the two phases of the Soul, as we have said, possesses memory, and memory is vested in the imaging faculty, there must be two such faculties. Now that is all very well as long as the two souls stand apart; but, when they are at one in us, what becomes of the two faculties, and in which of them is memory vested?

If each soul has its own imaging faculty the images must in all cases be duplicated, since we cannot think that one faculty deals only with intellectual objects, and the other with objects of sense, a distinction which inevitably implies the co-existence in man of two life-principles utterly unrelated.

And if both orders of image act upon both orders of soul, what difference is there in the souls; and how does the fact escape our knowledge?

The answer is that, when the two souls chime each with each, the two imaging faculties no longer stand apart; the union is dominated by the imaging faculty of the higher [20] soul, and thus the image perceived is as one; the less powerful is like a shadow attending upon the dominant, like a minor light merging into a greater: when they are in conflict, in discord, the one soul is distinctly apart, a self-standing thing, while the image in the other [21] is not perceived, for the simple reason that the separate being of the two souls escapes observation.

The two have run into a unity in which, yet, one is the loftier: this loftier knows all; when it breaks from the union, it retains some of the experiences of its companion, but dismisses others; thus we accept the talk of our less valued associates, but, on a change of company, we remember little from the first set and more from those in whom we recognize a higher quality.

32. But the memory of friends, children, wife? Country too, and all that the better sort of man may reasonably remember?

All these, the one (the lower man) retains with emotion, the authentic man passively: for the experience, certainly, was first felt in that lower phase from which however, the best of such impressions pass over to the graver soul in the degree in which the two are in communication.

The lower soul must be always striving to attain to memory of the activities of the higher: this will be especially so when it is itself of a fine quality, for there will always be some that are better from the beginning and bettered here by the guidance of the higher.

The loftier, on the contrary, must desire to come to a happy forgetfulness of all that has reached it through the lower: for one reason, there is always the possibility that the excellence of the higher goes with a baseness in the lower, which is only kept down by sheer force. In any case the more urgent the intention towards the Supreme, the more extensive will be the Soul's forgetfulness, unless indeed when the entire living has, even here, been such that memory has nothing but the noblest to deal with: in this world itself, all is best when human interests have been held aloof; so, therefore, it must be with the memory of them. In this sense we may truly say that the good soul is the forgetful. It flees multiplicity; it seeks to escape the unbounded by drawing all to unity, for only thus is it free from entanglement, light-footed, self-conducted. Thus it is that even in this world the soul which has the desire of the other is putting away, amid its actual life, all that is foreign to that order. I While it is in the heavenly regions it puts away more again. Little of what it gathered here is taken with it to the Intellectual Realm.

The Hercules of whom we spoke (the Shade)[22] would still tell I of his feats: but there is the other man to whom all of that is trivial; he has been translated to a holier place; he has won his way to the Intellectual Realm; he is more than Hercules, proven in the combats in which the combatants are the wise.

NOTES TO ENNEAD IV.3

1. FIRST EDITION: "Our general instinct to seek and learn, *our longing to possess ourselves of whatsoever is lovely in the vision,* will, in all reason, set us enquiring into the nature of the instrument with which we search.

"*Now even in the universal Intellect (Divine Mind) there was duality,* so that we would expect differences of *condition* in things of part: *how some things rather than others came to be receptacles of the divine beings . . .*"

ARMSTRONG and TAYLOR both favor the first-edition sense. GUTHRIE's translation is unique: "... it is no more than right first to apply ourselves to finding out the nature of the principle that embarks in these researches; and as we are seeking what is lovable, we will do well to contemplate the most beautiful of spectacles (that of our own intellectual nature); for if there be a duality, in the universal (Soul), so much more likely will there be a duality in individual intelligences. We should also examine the sense in which it may be said that souls are sanctuaries of the divinity;"

2. FIRST EDITION: "*Our opponents after first admitting* the unity go on to make *our soul* dependent on *something else, something* in which we have no longer the soul of this or that, *even of the universe,* but a soul of nowhere, a soul belonging neither to the kosmos, nor to anything else, and yet vested with *all the function inherent to the kosmic soul and to that of* every ensouled thing."

ARMSTRONG: "But if they make it one they attach it to something else, which is no longer the soul of this or that but is not itself the soul of anything, either of the universe or of anything else, but makes that which is soul both of the universe and of anything ensouled."

GUTHRIE: "Now, assertion of the unity of the universal Soul defines her as being something different (from individual souls); namely, a principle which, specially belonging neither to one nor the other, neither to an individual, nor to a world, nor to anything else, itself carries out what is carried out by the world and every living being."

TAYLOR: "But making one soul, they will also suspend it from something else, which no longer being something pertaining to this thing or that, but neither belonging to the world, or to any other thing, will effect the very same thing, as is effected by [the life] of the world, and of any animated being whatever." Brackets are Taylor's.

3. FIRST EDITION (ellipses indicate same words in both editions): "Is this the appropriate parallel?

"No; in such a relationship the All-Soul . . . would not be the soul of any definite thing . . . would not even be the soul of the Kosmos; it would, in fact, be itself, one of those partial souls; thus all alike . . . would be partial and of one nature; and, at that, there would be no reason for making any such distinction."

TAYLOR, GUTHRIE, and ARMSTRONG all avoid a yes/no structure and translate in the sense here expressed by Armstrong: "If this is how it is with the whole soul and the others, the whole, of which the parts are parts of this kind, will not be the soul of anything, but an independent reality: so it will not even be the soul of the universe, but this too will be one of the partial souls. So all [both individual souls and the soul of the universe] will be parts of one, since they have the same form. But how then does one come to be the soul of the universe, and the others of parts of the universe?" Brackets are Armstrong's.

4. FIRST EDITION: "But again: 'Everywhere, Unity': in the variety of functions if each 'part of the soul' were as distinct as are the entrant sensations, none of those parts could have knowledge; awareness would belong only to that judging faculty—or, if local, every such act of awareness would stand quite unrelated to any other. But since the soul is a rational soul, by the very same title by which it is an All-Soul, and is called the rational soul, in the sense of being a whole (and so not merely 'reasoning locally'), then what is thought of as a part must in reality be no part but the identity of an unparted thing."

GUTHRIE and TAYLOR translate the entire passage in the first-edition sense. ARMSTRONG has it as follows: "But we have already said that the soul is one thing everywhere, also in its different functions. And if our souls were like sense-perceptions, it is not possible for each one of us to think himself, but the soul of the All [would have to do the thinking]; but if our thinking was our own, each soul would be independent. But since the soul is also rational, and rational in the sense in which the universal soul is called rational, that which is called a part will be the same as the whole, not a part of the whole." Brackets are Armstrong's.

5. FIRST EDITION: ". . . and this power remains enduringly attached . . ."

TAYLOR and GUTHRIE clearly support this rendering. ARMSTRONG has: ". . . and power comes from abiding above."

6. FIRST EDITION: ". . . and if the universe had no existence, the extent of soul would be the same;"

TAYLOR and GUTHRIE clearly support Page's change, although they say "body" instead of "universe."

ARMSTRONG: "If body did not exist, it would make no difference to soul as regards size;"

7. FIRST EDITION: ". . . by the efficacy of soul whose *entire extension* latently holds this rationalising power."

ARMSTRONG: ". . . since soul has potentially in it, and throughout the whole of it, the power to set in order according to rational principles;"

TAYLOR: ". . . by the power of soul, which possesses in itself wholly a power of adorning by reasons [or productive principles];" Brackets are Taylor's.

GUTHRIE: ". . . in virtue of the entire universal Soul's independent power of embellishing matter by means of reasons . . ."

8. FIRST EDITION: ". . . at which their *unextended* Reason-Principle must be aiming; *in that other world (under the soul but above the material)* the entire shape *(as well as the idea)* comes from soul . . ."

GUTHRIE supports the first edition, ARMSTRONG supports the fourth.

TAYLOR has an interesting variant on the whole sentence and to the end of the paragraph: "For in things of a posterior nature which impede each other, matter is frequently deprived of the attainment of the appropriate form which the productive principle [latent] in the seed wished it to have. There, however, [i.e., in the universe], the whole form being generated by soul, and the generated natures having at the same time an arrangement, that which is produced becomes beautiful without labour, and without impediment. But in the universe are fabricated, some things indeed which are statues of the Gods, others which are the habitations of men, and others which are adapted to other things." Brackets are Taylor's.

9. FIRST EDITION: ". . . the *outgo (natural to everything)* remains dormant, and any efficiency they have is to bring to their own likeness whatever is amenable *to their act.*"

ARMSTRONG: "In soulless things the one power, so to speak, lies asleep in them; and the power from them which goes out to something else consists in making like themselves that which is capable of being affected." TAYLOR also translates in this sense. GUTHRIE handles the first part the same but ends with: "and that which they exert on others consists in assimilating to themselves that which is capable of an experience."

10. FIRST EDITION: "*The Intellectual-Principle in the Supreme has ever been the sun of that sphere—let us accept that as the type of the creative Logos—*and immediately upon it follows . . ."

TAYLOR and GUTHRIE both clearly support the first edition.

ARMSTRONG: "So that sun in the divine realm is Intellect—let this serve as an example for our discourse—and next after it is . . ."

11. FIRST EDITION: ". . . they are not *independent,* but . . ."

TAYLOR: ". . . souls . . . are not suspended from the universe, but co-adapt themselves . . ."

GUTHRIE: ". . . souls . . . conform to this order without depending on it; and perfectly harmonize with . . ."

ARMSTRONG has the whole thought as: "The harmonious adjustment of the souls to the order of this All of ours witnesses to this; they are not cut off from it, but fit themselves in . . ."

12. FIRST EDITION: ". . . an enduring activity, *an assertion that is real;*"

TAYLOR: ". . . a stable energy which is as it were an evolution of intellectual light . . ."

GUTHRIE: ". . . an immanent act, a reflection of this power in souls . . ."

ARMSTRONG: ". . . a static activity and a kind of reflection of Intellect . . ."

13. FIRST EDITION: ". . . 'that *soul*' we read . . ."

ARMSTRONG: "Plato says that soul 'becomes divisible . . ."

GUTHRIE: "When Plato . . . insists that she [soul—ed.] is divisible . . ."

14. We have restored "partible," as in the first three editions, in place of the fourth-edition "particle," which we take as a typographical error.

15. FIRST EDITION: "It *is to be noted, however, as regards these (the less corporeal) sensations, that the body may possibly not experience them as a fact of the conjoint thing but in another mode, as rising within some one of the elements of which it has been participant (as inherent, purely, in some phase of the associated soul): reasoning* and the act of the intellect . . ."

GUTHRIE and TAYLOR incline toward the first-edition sense.

ARMSTRONG has: "But perhaps Plato does not admit that these sensations occur in the mixture of which we have been speaking: perhaps he considers that they arise in another way and as a result of some one of the things which have been already received." Armstrong footnotes this sentence with: "I take the subject of *paralambanei* here to be 'Plato,' not, as most editors (including Henry-Schwyzer), 'the body.'"

16. FIRST EDITION: ". . . into body, *and at any rate this makes the soul separable.*"

TAYLOR and GUTHRIE include the additional clause; ARMSTRONG omits it.

17. FIRST EDITION: ". . . that sensitive part which *is the medium through which the Reason-Principle impinges* upon the brain. They saw that *something* must be definitely allocated to body—at the point most receptive of *the act of reason*—while *something*, utterly isolated from body must be in contact with *that superior thing* which is a form of soul . . ."

TAYLOR: ". . . reason was placed by the ancients in the summit of the whole animal, viz. in the head; not as being [immediately] situated in the brain, but in this sensitive power, through which [as a medium] reason is established in the brain. For it is requisite to assign the sensitive power to the body, and to that which is especially the recipient of the energy of the body. But it is necessary that the form of the soul which is able to receive apprehensions from reason, should communicate with reason which has no communication with the body." Brackets are Taylor's.

ARMSTRONG: ". . . the ancients thus put reason at the highest point of the whole living creature at the head, supposing it to be not in the brain but in this perceptive faculty which in the way described above was situated in the brain. For one part of the soul had to give itself to body, and to the part of body most receptive of its activity, but the other part, which had no communication with body, was under the absolute necessity of communicating with the first part, which was a form of soul, and of soul capable of apprehending what came from reason."

GUTHRIE: ". . . the ancients localized reason . . . in the head; not that reason is in the brain, but because reason is seated in the sense-power, by the intermediation of which, only, reason may be said to reside in the brain. The sense-power, surely, had to be attributed to the body, and, within the body, to organs most capable of lending themselves to its action. Reason, which has no (direct) dealing with the body, had however to be in relation with the sense-power, which is a form of the soul, and can participate in reason."

18. FIRST EDITION: "The soul, *still a dragged captive,* will tell . . ." MACKENNA alone makes this interpretation.

19. FIRST EDITION: ". . . the *Reason-Principle* . . ."

GUTHRIE and TAYLOR both use "reason," whereas ARMSTRONG has "verbal expression." GUTHRIE's treatment of the whole passage is outstanding (corresponding in MacKenna's translation with "Perhaps memory" and running to the end of the section): "Perhaps reason, whose actualization always accompanies thought, has the function of receiving it and transmitting it to imagination. Indeed, thought is indivisible, and so long as it is not evoked from the depths of intelligence, it remains as it were hidden within it. Reason develops it, and making it pass from the state of thought to that of image, spreads it out as it were in a mirror, for our imagination. That is why we grasp (the thought) only when the soul, which always desires rational thought, has achieved a thought. There is a difference between thought and the perception of thought. We are always thinking, but we do not always perceive our thought. That comes from the fact that the principle that perceives the thoughts also perceives the sensations, and occupies itself with both in turn." Guthrie also cross-references to Ennead I.4.10.

20. FIRST EDITION: ". . . by the *more powerful of the faculties of the* soul . . ."

TAYLOR and ARMSTRONG clearly support the fourth edition; GUTHRIE has "the most powerful dominates . . ."

21. FIRST EDITION: ". . . the *minor* is distinctly apart, a self-standing thing—*though its isolation* is not perceived . . ."

GUTHRIE: ". . . then only one of them manifests, and the other is entirely ignored, just as we always ignore that we have two souls;"

TAYLOR: ". . . then the one shines forth through itself; but it is concealed in the other, because in short that there are two souls is concealed from us."

ARMSTRONG: ". . . the other image becomes manifest by itself, but we do not notice what is in the other power, and we do not notice in general the duality of the souls."

22. FIRST EDITION: "*It brings there very little of what it has gathered here; as long as it is in the heavenly regions only, it will have more than it can retain.*
"The Hercules of *the heavenly regions* would still tell . . ."

TAYLOR: "Hence, when it is there, it remembers but a few things of a terrestrial nature; but it remembers more of them when it is in the heavens. And Hercules, indeed, [when in Hades] may speak . . ." Brackets are Taylor's.

GUTHRIE: "She therefore retains but few earthly things when she has arrived to the intelligible world; she has more of them when she inhabits the heavens. Hercules (in heaven) may well vaunt . . ."

ARMSTRONG: ". . . and there are few things here that are also there; and when it is in heaven it will abandon still more. And Homer's Heracles might talk . . ."

FOURTH TRACTATE

Problems of the Soul (II)

1. What, then, will be the Soul's discourse, what its memories in the Intellectual Realm, when at last it has won its way to that Essence?

Obviously from what we have been saying, it will be in contemplation of that order, and have its Act upon the things among which it now is; failing such Contemplation and Act, its being is not there. Of things of earth it will know nothing; it will not, for example, remember an act of philosophic virtue, or even that in its earthly career it had contemplation of the Supreme.

When we seize anything in the direct intellectual act there is room for nothing else than to know and to contemplate the object; the subject is not included in the act of knowing, but asserts itself, if at all, later and is a sign of the altered; this means that, once purely in the Intellectual, no one of us can have any memory of our experience here. Further; if all intellection is timeless—as appears from the fact that the Intellectual beings are of eternity, not of time—there can be no memory in the intellectual world, not merely none of earthly things but none whatever: all is presence There; **I** for there is no discursive thought, no passing from one point to another.[1]**I**

I No division, then, of genera into species? no progression from lower to higher, to wider generality? For the higher principle (the Intellectual) evidently not, since it is fully realized as a self-contained unity; but why not for the Soul which has attained to the Intellectual Realm? Yet even the Soul[2] may have the intuition,**I** not by stages and parts, of that Being which is without stage and part.

But that would be in the nature of grasping a pure unity?

No: in the nature of grasping all the intellectual facts of a many that constitutes a unity. For since the object of vision has variety (distinction within its essential oneness) the intuition must be multiple and the intuitions various, just as in a face we see at the one glance eyes and nose and all the rest.

But is not this impossible when the object to be thus divided and treated as a thing of grades is a pure unity?

No: there has already been discrimination within the Intellectual-Principle; the Act of the Soul is little more than a reading of this.

First and last is in the Ideas not a matter of time, and so does not bring time into the Soul's intuition of earlier and later among them. There is a grading by order as well: the ordered disposition of some growing thing begins with root and reaches to topmost point, but, to one seeing the plant as a whole, there is no other first and last than simply that of the order.

Still, the Soul (in this intuition within the divine) looks to what is a unity; next it entertains multiplicity, all that is: how explain this grasping first of the unity and later of the rest?

❙ The explanation is that the unity of the Soul's faculty (of intuition) is not incompatible with multiplicity in the object; it does not possess all its content in a single act of thought; each act is incomplete in itself, but all are being constantly exercised; the faculty is permanently there and its effects are external. The object itself is no unity and can therefore harbour a multiplicity which previously it did not contain.[3]❙

2. Enough on that point: we come now to the question of memory of the personality.

There will not even be memory of the personality; no thought that the contemplator is the self—Socrates, for example—or that it is Intellect or Soul. In this connexion it should be borne in mind that, in contemplative vision, especially when it is vivid, we are not at the time aware of our own personality; we are in possession of ourselves, but the activity is towards the object of vision with which the thinker becomes identified; he has made himself over as matter to be shaped; he takes ideal form under the action of the vision while remaining, potentially, himself. This means that he is actively himself when he has intellection of nothing.

Or, if he is himself (pure and simple), he is empty of all: if, on the contrary, he is himself (by the self-possession of contemplation) in such a way as to be identified with what is all, then by the act of self-intellection he has the simultaneous intellection of all: in such a case self-intuition by personal activity brings the intellection, not merely of the self, but also of the total therein embraced; and similarly the intuition of the total of things brings that of the personal self as included among all.

But such a process would appear to introduce into the Intellectual that element of change against which we ourselves have only now been protesting?

The answer is that, while unchangeable identity is essential to the Intellectual-Principle, the Soul, lying so to speak on the borders of the Intellectual Realm, is amenable to change; it has, for example, its inward advance, and obviously anything that attains position near to something motionless does so by a change directed towards that unchanging goal and is not itself motionless in the same degree. Nor is it really change to turn from the self to the constituents of self or from those constituents to the self; and in this case the contemplator is the total; the duality has become unity.

None the less the Soul, even in the Intellectual Realm, is under the dispensation of a variety confronting it and a content of its own?

No: once pure in the Intellectual, it too possesses that same unchangeableness: for it possesses identity of essence; when it is in that region it must of necessity enter into oneness with the Intellectual-Principle by the sheer fact of its self-orientation, for by that intention all interval disappears; the Soul advances and is taken into unison, and in that association becomes one with the Intellectual-Principle—but not to its own destruction: the two are one, and two. In such a state there is no question of stage and change: the Soul, without motion (but by right of its essential being) would be intent upon its intellectual act, and in possession, simultaneously, of its self-awareness; for it has become one simultaneous existence with the Supreme.

3. But it leaves that conjunction; it cannot suffer that unity; it falls in love with its own powers and possessions, and desires to stand apart; it leans outward, so to speak: then, it appears to acquire a memory of itself.

In this self-memory a distinction is to be made: the memory dealing with the Intellectual Realm upbears the Soul, not to fall; the memory of things here bears it downwards to this universe; the intermediate memory dealing with the heavenly sphere holds it there too; and, in all its memory, the thing it has in mind it is and grows to; for this bearing-in-mind must be either intuition (i.e. knowledge with identity) or representation by image: and the imaging in the case of the Soul is not a taking in of something (as of an impression) but is vision and condition—so much so, that, in its very sense-sight, it is the lower in the degree in which it penetrates the object. Since its possession of the total of things is not primal but secondary, it does not become all things perfectly (in becoming identical with the All in the Intellectual); it is of the boundary order, situated between two regions, and has tendency to both.

4. In that realm it has also vision, through the Intellectual-Principle, of The Good which does not so hold to itself as not to reach the Soul; what intervenes between them is not body and therefore is no hindrance—and, indeed, where bodily forms do intervene there is still access in many ways from the primal to the tertiaries.

If, on the contrary, the Soul gives itself to the inferior, the same principle of penetration comes into play, and it possesses itself, by memory and imagination, of the thing it desired: and hence the memory, even dealing with the highest, is not the highest. Memory, of course, must be understood not merely of what might be called the sense of remembrance, but so as to include a condition induced by the past experience or vision. There is such a thing as possessing more powerfully without consciousness than in full knowledge; with full awareness the possession is of something quite distinct from the self; unconscious possession runs very close to identity, and any such approach to identification with the lower means the deeper fall of the Soul.

If the Soul, on abandoning its place in the Supreme, revives its memories of the lower, it must have in some form possessed them even there, though the activity of the beings in that realm kept them in abeyance: they could not be in the nature of impressions permanently adopted—a notion which would entail absurdities—but were no more than a potentiality realized after return. When that energy of the Intellectual world ceases to tell upon the Soul, it sees what it saw in the earlier state before it revisited the Supreme.

5. But this power which determines memory, is it also the principle by which the Supreme becomes effective in us?

At any time when we have not been in direct vision of that sphere, memory is the source of its activity within us; when we have possessed that vision, its presence is due to the principle by which we enjoyed it: this principle awakens where it wakens; and it alone has vision in that order; for this is no matter to be brought to us by way of analogy, or by the syllogistic reasoning whose grounds lie elsewhere; the power which we possess of discoursing upon the Intellectual Beings, so far as such discourse is here possible, is vested in that principle which alone is capable of their contemplation. That we must awaken, so to speak, and thus attain the vision of the Supreme, as one, standing on some lofty height and lifting his eyes, sees what to those that have not mounted with him is invisible.

Memory, by this account, commences after the Soul has left the higher spheres; it is first known in the celestial period.

A soul that has descended from the Intellectual region to the celestial and there comes to rest, may very well be understood to recognize many other souls known in its former state—supposing that, as we have said, it retains recollection of much that it knew here. This recognition would be natural if the bodies with which those souls are vested in the celestial must reproduce the former appearance; supposing the spherical form (of the stars inhabited by souls in the mid-realm) means a change of appearance, recognition would go by character, by the distinctive quality of personality: this is not fantastic; conditions changing need not mean a change of character. If the souls have mutual conversation, this too would mean recognition.

But those whose descent from the Intellectual is complete, how is it with them?

They will recall their memories, of the same things, but with less force than those still in the celestial, since they have had other experiences to remember, and the lapse of time will have utterly obliterated much of what was formerly present to them.

But what way of remembering the Supreme is left if the souls have turned to the sense-known Cosmos, and are to fall into this sphere of process?

They need not fall to the ultimate depth: their downward movement may be checked at some one moment of the way; and as long as they have not touched the lowest of the region of process (the point at which non-being begins) there is nothing to prevent them rising once more.

6. Souls that descend, souls that change their state—these, then, may be said to have memory, which deals with what has come and gone; but what subjects of remembrance can there be for souls whose lot is to remain unchanged?

The question touches memory in the stars in general, and also in the sun and moon and ends by dealing with the Soul of the All, even by audaciously busying itself with the memories of Zeus himself. The inquiry entails the examination and identification of acts of understanding and of reasoning in these beings, if such acts take place.

Now if, immune from all lack, they neither seek nor doubt, and never learn, nothing being absent at any time from their knowledge—what reasonings, what processes of rational investigation, can take place in them, what acts of the understanding?

Even as regards human concerns they have no need for observation or method; their administration of our affairs and of earth's in general does not go so; the right ordering, which is their gift to the universe, is effected by methods very different.

7. In other words, they have seen God and they do not remember?

Ah, no: it is that they see God still and always, and that as long as they see, they cannot tell themselves they have had the vision; such reminiscence is for souls that have lost it.

Well, but can they not tell themselves that yesterday, or last year, they moved round the earth, that they lived yesterday or at any given moment in their lives?

Their living is eternal, and eternity is an unchanging unity. To identify a yesterday or a last year in their movement would be like dividing the forward movement of the feet into a number of separate movements, and finding a this or a that and an entire series in what is a single act. The movement of the celestial beings is one movement: it is our measuring that presents us with many movements, and with distinct days determined by intervening nights: There all is one day; series has no place; no yesterday, no last year.

Still: the space traversed is different; there are the various sections of the

Zodiac: why, then, should not the Soul say, 'I have traversed that section and now I am in this other?' If, also, it looks down over the concerns of men, must it not see the changes that befall them, that they are not as they were, and, by that observation, that the beings and the things concerned were otherwise formerly? And does not that mean memory?

8. But, we need not record in memory all we see; mere incidental concomitants need not occupy the imagination; when things vividly present to intuition, or knowledge, happen to occur in concrete form, it is not necessary—unless for purposes of a strictly practical administration—to pass over that direct acquaintance, and fasten upon the partial sense-presentation, which is already known in the larger knowledge.

I will take this point by point:

First: it is not essential that everything seen should be laid up in the mind; for when the object is of no importance, or of no personal concern, the sensitive faculty, stimulated by the differences in the objects present to vision, acts without accompaniment of the will, and is alone in entertaining the impression. The Soul does not take into its deeper recesses such differences as do not meet any of its needs, or serve any of its purposes. Above all, when the Soul's act is directed towards another order, it must utterly reject the memory of such things, things over and done with now, and not even taken into knowledge when they were present.

On the second point: circumstances, purely accidental, need not be present to the imaging faculty, and if they do so appear they need not be retained or even observed, and in fact the impression of any such circumstance does not entail awareness. Thus in local movement, if there is no particular importance to us in the fact that we pass through first this and then that portion of air, or that we proceed from some particular point, we do not take notice, or even know it as we walk. Similarly, if it were of no importance to us to accomplish any given journey, mere movement in the air being the main concern, we would not trouble to ask at what particular point of place we were, or what distance we had traversed; if we have to observe only the act of movement and not its duration, nothing to do which obliges us to think of time, the minutes are not recorded in our minds.

And finally, it is of common knowledge that, when the understanding is possessed of the entire act undertaken and has no reason to foresee any departure from the normal, it will no longer observe the detail; in a process unfailingly repeated without variation, attention to the unvarying detail is idleness.

So it is with the stars. They pass from point to point, but they move on their own affairs and not for the sake of traversing the space they actually cover; the vision of the things that appear on the way, the journey by, nothing of this is their concern; their passing this or that is of accident not of essence, and their intention is to greater objects: moreover each of them journeys, unchangeably, the same unchanging way; and again, there is no question to them of the time they spend in any given section of the journey, even supposing time-division to be possible in the case. All this granted, nothing makes it necessary that they should have any memory of places or times traversed. Besides, this life of the ensouled stars is one identical thing, since even their spatial movement is pivoted upon identity and resolves itself into a movement not spatial but vital, the movement of a single living being whose act is directed to itself, a being which to anything outside is at rest, but is in movement by dint of the inner life it possesses, the eternal life. Or we may take the comparison of the movement of the heavenly bodies to a choral dance; if we think of it as a dance which comes to rest at some given period, the entire dance, accomplished from beginning to end, will be perfect while at each partial stage it was imperfect: but if the dance is a thing of eternity, it is in eternal perfection. And if it is in eternal perfection, it has no points of time and place at which it will achieve perfection; it will, therefore, have no concern about attaining to any such points: it will, therefore, make no measurements of time or place; it will have, therefore, no memory of time and place.

If the stars live a blessed life in their vision of the life inherent in their souls, and if, by force of their souls' tendency to become one, and by the light they cast from themselves upon the entire heavens, they are like the strings of a lyre which, being struck in tune, sing a melody in some natural scale: if this is the way the heavens, as one, are moved, and the component parts in their relation to the whole—the sidereal system moving as one, and each part in its own way, to the same purpose, though each too hold its own place—then our doctrine is all the more surely established; the life of the heavenly bodies is the more clearly an unbroken unity.

9. But Zeus—ordering all, governor, guardian, and disposer, possessor for ever of the 'kingly soul' and the 'kingly intellect', bringing all into being by his providence, and presiding over all things as they come, administering all under plan and system, unfolding the periods of the Cosmos, many of which stand already accomplished—would it not seem inevitable that, in this multiplicity of concern, Zeus should have memory of all the periods, their number, and their differing qualities? Contriving the future, co-ordinating, calculating for what is to be, must he not surely be the chief of all in remembering, as he is the most resourceful in producing?

Even this matter of Zeus' memory of the cosmic periods is difficult; it is a question of their being numbered, and of his knowledge of their number. A determined number would mean that the All had a beginning in time (which is not so); if the periods are unlimited, Zeus cannot know the number of his works.

The answer is that I he will know himself to be a unity existing in virtue of one life for ever and in this sense unlimited; and his knowledge of this unity[4] will not be as of something seen from outside but as of something embraced in true knowledge, I for this unlimited is an eternal indweller within himself— or, to be more accurate, eternally follows upon him—and is seen by an indwelling knowledge; Zeus knows his own unlimited life, and, in that knowledge, knows the activity that flows from him to the Cosmos; but he knows it in its unity not in its process.

10. The ordering principle is twofold; there is the principle known to us as the Demiurge and there is the Soul of the All; we apply the appellation Zeus sometimes to the Demiurge and sometimes to the principle conducting the universe.

When under the name of Zeus we are considering the Demiurge we must leave out all notions of stage and progress, and recognize one unchanging and timeless life.

But the life in the Cosmos, the life which carries the leading principle of the universe, still needs elucidation; does it operate without calculation, without searching into what ought to be done?

Yes: for what must be stands shaped before the Cosmos, and is ordered without any setting in order: the ordered things are merely the things that come to be; and the principle that brings them into being is Order itself; this production is an act of a soul linked with an unchangeably established wisdom whose reflection in that soul is Order. It is an unchanging wisdom, and there can therefore be no changing in the soul which mirrors it, not sometimes turned towards it and sometimes away from it—and in doubt because it has turned away—but an unremitting soul performing an unvarying task.

The leading principle of the universe is a unity—and one that is sovran without break, not sometimes dominant and sometimes dominated. What source is there for any such multiplicity of leading principles as might result in contest and hesitation? And this governing unity must always desire the one thing: what could bring it to wish now for this and now for that, to its own greater perplexing? But observe: no perplexity need follow upon any development of this Soul, essentially a unity. The All stands a multiple thing no doubt, having parts, and parts clashing with parts, but that does not imply that it need be in doubt as to its conduct: that Soul does not take its essence from its ultimates or from its parts, but from the Primals; it has its source in the First and thence, along an unhindered path, it flows into a total of things, conferring grace, and, because it remains one same thing occupied in one task, dominating. To suppose it pursuing one new object after another is to raise the question whence that novelty comes into being: the Soul, besides, would be in doubt as to its action; its very work, the Cosmos, would be the less well done by reason of the hesitancy which such calculations would entail.

11. The administration of the Cosmos is to be thought of as that of a living unit: there is the action determined by what is external, and has to do with the parts, and there is that determined by the internal and by the principle: thus a doctor basing his treatment on externals and on the parts directly affected will often be baffled and obliged to all sorts of calculation, while Nature will act on the basis of principle and need no deliberation. And in so far as the Cosmos is a conducted thing, its administration and its administrator will follow not the way of the doctor but the way of Nature.

And in the case of the universe, the administration is all the less complicated from the fact that the Soul actually circumscribes, as parts of a living unity, all the members which it conducts. For all the Kinds included in the universe are dominated by one Kind, upon which they follow, fitted into it, developing from it, growing out of it, just as the Kind manifested in the bough is related to the Kind in the tree as a whole.

What place, then, is there for reasoning, for calculation, what place for memory, where wisdom and knowledge are eternal, unfailingly present, effective, dominant, administering in an identical process?

The fact that the product contains diversity and difference does not warrant the notion that the producer must be subject to corresponding variations. On the contrary, the more varied the product, the more certain the unchanging identity of the producer: even in the single animal the events produced by Nature are many and not simultaneous; there are the age periods, the developments at fixed epochs—horns, beard, maturing breasts, the acme of life, procreation—but the principles which initially determined the nature of the being are not thereby annulled; there is process of growth, but no diversity in the initial principle. The identity underlying all the multiplicity is confirmed by the fact that the principle constituting the parent is exhibited unchanged, undiminished, in the offspring. We have reason, then, for thinking that one and the same wisdom envelops both, and that this is the unalterable wisdom of the Cosmos taken as a whole; it is manifold, diverse and yet simplex, presiding over the most comprehensive of living beings, and in no wise altered within itself by this multiplicity, but stably one Reason-Principle, the concentrated totality of things: if it were not thus all things, it would be a wisdom of the later and partial, not the wisdom of the total, universal living being (the physical Cosmos).

12. It may be urged that all the multiplicity and development are the work of Nature, but that, since there is wisdom within the All, there must be also, by the side of such natural operation, acts of reasoning and of memory.

But this is simply a human error which assumes wisdom to be what in fact is unwisdom, taking the search for wisdom to be wisdom itself. For what can reasoning be but a struggle, the effort to discover the wise course, to attain the principle which is true and derives from real-being? To reason is like playing the cithara for the sake of achieving the art, like practising with a view to mastery, like any learning that aims at knowing. What reasoners seek, the wise hold: wisdom, in a word, is a condition in a being that possesses repose. Think what happens when one has accomplished the reasoning process: as soon as we have discovered the right course, we cease to reason: we rest because we have come to wisdom. If then we are to range the leading principle of the All among learners, we must allow it reasonings, perplexities, and those acts of memory which link the past with the present and the future: if it is to be considered as a knower, then the wisdom within it consists in a rest possessing the object (absolved, therefore, from search and from remembrance).

Again, if the leading principle of the universe knows the future—as it must— then obviously it will know by what means that future is to come about; given this knowledge, what further need is there of its reasoning towards it, or confronting past with present? And, of course, this knowledge of things to come—admitting it to exist—is not like that of the diviners; it is that of the actual causing principles holding the certainty that the thing will exist, the certainty inherent in the all-disposers, above perplexity and hesitancy; the notion is constituent and therefore unvarying. The knowledge of future things is, in a word, identical with that of the present; it is a knowledge in repose and thus a knowledge transcending the processes of cogitation.

If the leading principle of the universe does not know the future which it is of itself to produce, it cannot produce with knowledge or to purpose; it will produce just what happens to come, that is to say by haphazard. As this cannot be, it must create by some stable principle; its creations, therefore, will be shaped in the model stored up in itself; there can be no varying, for, if there were, there could also be failure.

The produced universe will contain difference, but its diversities spring not from its own action but from its obedience to superior principles which, again, spring from the creating power, so that all is guided by Reason-Principles in their series; thus the creating power is in no sense subjected to experimenting, to perplexity, to that preoccupation which to some minds makes the administration of the All seem a task of difficulty. Preoccupation would obviously imply the undertaking of alien tasks, some business—that would mean—not completely within the powers; but where the power is sovran and sole, it need take thought of nothing but itself and its own will, which means its own wisdom, since in such a being the will is wisdom. Here, then, creating makes no demand, since the wisdom that goes to it is not sought elsewhere, but is the creator's very self, drawing on nothing outside—not, therefore, on reasoning or on memory, which are handlings of the external.

13. But what is the difference between the Wisdom thus conducting the universe and the principle known as Nature?

This Wisdom is a first (within the All-Soul) while Nature is a last: for Nature is an image of that Wisdom, and, as a last in the Soul, possesses only the last reflection of the Reason-Principle: we may imagine a thick waxen seal, in which the imprint has penetrated to the very uttermost film so as to show on both sides, sharp cut on the upper surface, faint on the under. Nature, thus, does not know, it merely produces: what it holds it passes, automatically, to its next; and this transmission to the corporeal and material constitutes its making power: it acts as a thing warmed communicating to what lies in next contact to it the principle of which it is the vehicle so as to make that also warm in some less degree.

Nature, being thus a mere communicator, does not possess even the imaging act. There is (within the Soul) intellection, superior to imagination; and there is imagination standing midway between that intellection and the impression of which alone Nature is capable. For Nature has no perception or consciousness of anything; imagination (the imaging faculty) has consciousness of the external, for it enables that which entertains the image to have knowledge of the experience encountered, ∎ while intellection also engenders—of itself and by an act derived from its own active principle.[5]∎

Thus the Intellectual-Principle possesses: the Soul of the All eternally receives from it; this is the Soul's life; its consciousness is its intellection of what is thus eternally present to it; what proceeds from it into Matter and is manifested there is Nature, with which—or even a little before it—the series of real being comes to an end, for all in this order are the ultimates of the intellectual order and the beginnings of the imitative.

There is also the decided difference that Nature operates towards Matter, and receives from it: soul, near to Nature but superior, operates towards Matter but without receiving in turn; and there is the still higher phase (the purely

Intellectual) with no action whatever upon body or upon Matter.

14. Of the corporeal thus brought into being by Nature the elemental materials of things are its very produce, but how do animal and vegetable forms stand to it?

Are we to think of them as containers of Nature present within them?

Light goes away and the air contains no trace of it, for light and air remain each itself, never coalescing: is this the relation of Nature to the formed object?

It is rather that existing between fire and the object it has warmed: the fire withdrawn, there remains a certain warmth, distinct from that in the fire, a property, so to speak, of the object warmed. For the shape which Nature imparts to what it has moulded must be recognized as a form quite distinct from Nature itself, though it remains a question to be examined whether besides this (specific) form there is also an intermediary, a link connecting it with Nature, the general principle.

The difference between Nature and the Wisdom described as dwelling in the All has been sufficiently dealt with.

15. But there is a difficulty affecting this entire settlement: Eternity is characteristic of the Intellectual-Principle, time of the Soul—for we hold that time has its substantial being in the activity of the Soul, and springs from soul—and, since time is a thing of division and (unlike eternity) comports a past, it would seem that the activity producing it must also be a thing of division, and that its attention to that past must imply that even the All-Soul has memory? We repeat, identity belongs to the eternal, time must be the medium of diversity; otherwise there is nothing to distinguish them, especially since we deny that the activities of the Soul can themselves experience change.

Can we escape by the theory that, while human souls—receptive of change, even to the change of imperfection and lack—are in time, yet the Soul of the All, as the author of time, is itself timeless? But if it is not in time, what causes it to engender time rather than eternity?

The answer must be that the realm it engenders is not that of eternal things but a realm of things enveloped in time: it is just as the (human) souls are not in time, but some of their experiences and productions are. For a soul is eternal, and is before time; and what is in time is of a lower order than time itself: I time is folded around what is in time exactly as—we read—place and number are[6] folded about what is in place and in number. I

16. But if in the Soul thing follows thing, if there is earlier and later in its productions, if it engenders or creates in time, then it must be looking towards

the future; and if towards the future, then towards the past as well?

No: prior and past are in the things it produces; in itself nothing is past; all, as we have said, is one simultaneous grouping of Reason-Principles. In the engendered simultaneity has gone, and with it identity of place: hands and feet, spatially undifferentiated in the Reason-Principles, are apart in the realm of sense. Of course, even in that ideal realm there is apartness, but in a characteristic mode, just as in a mode there is priority.

Now, apartness may be explained as simply differentiation: but how account for priority unless on the assumption of some ordering principle arranging from above, and in that disposal necessarily affirming a serial order?

There must be such a principle, or all would exist simultaneously; but the indicated conclusion does not follow unless order and ordering principle are distinct; if the ordering principle is Primal Order, there is no such affirmation of series; there is simply making, the making of this thing after that thing. The affirmation would imply that the ordering principle looks away towards Order and therefore is not, itself, Order.

But how are Order and this orderer one and the same?

Because the ordering principle is no conjoint of matter and idea but is soul, pure idea, the power and energy second only to the Intellectual-Principle: and because the succession is a fact of the things themselves, inhibited as they are from this comprehensive unity. The ordering soul remains august, a circle, as we may figure it, in complete adaptation to its centre, widening outward, but fast upon it still, an outspreading without interval.

The total scheme may be summarized in the illustration of The Good as a centre, the Intellectual-Principle as an unmoving circle, the Soul as a circle in motion, its moving being its aspiration: the Intellectual-Principle possesses and has ever embraced that which is beyond being; the Soul must seek it still: the sphere of the universe, by its possession of the Soul thus aspirant, is moved to the aspiration which falls within its own nature; this is no more than such power as body may have, the mode of pursuit possible where the object pursued is debarred from entrance; it is the motion of coiling about, with ceaseless return upon the same path—in other words, it is circuit.

17. But how comes it that the intuitions and the Reason-Principles of the Soul are not in the same timeless fashion within ourselves, but that here the later of order is converted into a later of time—bringing in all these doubts?

Is it because in us the governing and the answering principles are many and there is no sovran unity?

That condition; and, further, the fact that our mental acts fall into a series according to the succession of our needs, being not self-determined but guided by the variations of the external: thus the will changes to meet every incident as each fresh need arises and as the external impinges in its successive things and events.

A variety of governing principles must mean variety in the images formed upon the representative faculty, images not issuing from one internal centre, but, by difference of origin and of acting-point, strange to each other, and so bringing compulsion to bear upon the movements and efficiencies of the self.

When the desiring faculty is stirred, there is a presentment of the object—a sort of sensation, in announcement and in picture, of the experience—calling us to follow and to attain: the personality, whether it resists or follows and procures, is necessarily thrown out of equilibrium. The same disturbance is caused by passion urging revenge and by the needs of the body; every other sensation or experience effects its own change upon our mental attitude; then there is the ignorance of what is good and the indecision of a soul (a human soul) thus pulled in every direction; and, again, the interaction of all these perplexities gives rise to yet others.

But do variations of judgement affect that very highest in us?

No: the doubt and the change of standard are of the Conjoint (of the soul-phase in contact with body); still, the right reason of that highest is weaker by being given over to inhabit this mingled mass: not that it sinks in its own nature: it is much as amid the tumult of a public meeting the best adviser speaks but fails to dominate; assent goes to the roughest of the brawlers and roarers, while the man of good counsel sits silent, ineffectual, overwhelmed by the uproar of his inferiors.

The lowest human type exhibits the baser nature; the man is a compost calling to mind some inferior political organization: in the mid-type we have a citizenship in which some better section sways a democratic constitution not out of control: in the superior type the life is aristocratic; it is the career of one emancipated from what is base in humanity and tractable to the better; in the finest type, where the man has brought himself to detachment, the ruler is one only, and from this master principle order is imposed upon the rest, so that we may think of a municipality in two sections, the superior city and, kept in hand by it, the city of the lower elements.

That the All-Soul is a single unchanging identity, whereas the individual souls admit variation, has now been sufficiently demonstrated.

18. There remains the question whether the body possesses any force of its own—so that, with the incoming of the Soul, it lives in some individuality—or

whether all it has is this Nature we have been speaking of, the superior principle which enters into relations with it.

Certainly the body, container of soul and of nature, cannot even in itself be as a soulless form would be: it cannot even be like air traversed by light; it must be like air storing heat: the body holding animal or vegetative life must hold also some shadow of soul; and it is body thus modified that is the seat of corporeal pains and pleasures which appear before us, the true human being, in such a way as to produce knowledge without emotion. By 'us, the true human being' I mean the higher soul, for, in spite of all, the modified body is not alien but attached to our nature and is a concern to us for that reason: 'attached', for this is not ourselves nor yet are we free of it; it is an accessory and dependent of the human being; 'we' means the master-principle; the conjoint, similarly, is in its own way an 'ours'; and it is because of this that we care for its pain and pleasure, in proportion as we are weak rather than strong, gripped rather than working towards detachment, regarding the body as the most honourable phase of our being, as the true man, and into this penetrating.

Pleasure and pain and the like must not be attributed to the Soul alone, but to the modified body and to something intermediary between soul and body and made up of both. A unity is independent: thus body alone, a lifeless thing, can suffer no hurt—in its dissolution there is no damage to the body, but merely to its unity—and soul in similar isolation cannot even suffer dissolution, and by its very nature is immune from evil.

But when two distinct things become one in an artificial unity, there is a probable source of pain to them in the mere fact that they were inapt to partnership. This does not, of course, refer to two bodies; that is a question of one nature; and I am speaking of two natures. When one distinct nature seeks to associate itself with another, a different, order of being—the lower participating in the higher, but unable to take more than a faint trace of it—then the essential duality becomes also a unity, but a unity standing midway between what the lower was and what it cannot absorb, and therefore a troubled unity; the association is artificial and uncertain, inclining now to this side and now to that in ceaseless vacillation; and the total hovers between high and low, telling, downward bent, of misery but, directed to the above, of longing for unison.

19. Thus what we know as pleasure and pain may be identified: pain is our perception of a body despoiled, deprived of the image of the Soul; pleasure our perception of the living frame in which the image of the Soul is brought back to harmonious bodily operation. The painful experience takes place in that living frame; but the perception of it belongs to the sensitive phase of the Soul, which,

as neighbouring the living body, feels the change and makes it known to the principle (the imaging faculty) into which the sensations finally merge; then the body feels the pain, or at least the body is affected: thus in an amputation, when the flesh is cut the cutting is an event within the material mass; but the pain felt in that mass is there felt because it is not a mass pure and simple, but a mass under certain (non-material) conditions; it is to that modified substance that the sting of the pain is present, and the Soul feels it by an adoption due to what we think of as proximity.

And, itself unaffected, it feels the corporeal conditions at every point of its being, and is thereby enabled to assign every condition to the exact spot at which the wound or pain occurs. Being present as a whole at every point of the body, if it were itself affected the pain would take it at every point, and it would suffer as one entire being, so that it could not know, or make known, the spot affected; it could say only that at the place of its presence there existed pain—and the place of its presence is the entire human being. As things are, when the finger pains the man is in pain because one of his members is in pain; we class him as suffering, from his finger being painful, just as we class him as fair from his eyes being blue.

But the pain itself is in the part affected unless we include in the notion of pain the sensation following upon it, in which case we are saying only that distress implies the perception of distress. But (this does not mean that the Soul is affected:) we cannot describe the perception itself as distress; it is the knowledge of the distress and, being knowledge, is not itself affected, or it could not know and convey a true message: a messenger, affected, overwhelmed by the event, would either not convey the message or not convey it faithfully.

20. As with bodily pain and pleasure so with the bodily desires; their origin, also, must be attributed to what thus stands midway, to that modified corporeal nature.

Body undetermined cannot be imagined to give rise to appetite and purpose, nor can pure soul be occupied about sweet and bitter: all this must belong to what is specifically body but chooses to be something else as well, and so has acquired a restless movement unknown to the Soul and by that acquisition is forced to aim at a variety of objects, to seek, as its changing states demand, sweet or bitter, water or warmth, with none of which it could have any concern if it remained untouched by life.

In the case of pleasure and pain we showed how upon distress follows the knowledge of it, and that the Soul, seeking to alienate what is causing the condition, inspires a withdrawal which the member primarily affected has itself indicated, in its own mode, by its contraction. Similarly in the case of desire: there is the knowledge in the sensation (the sensitive phase of the Soul) and in the next lower phase, that described as the 'Nature' which carries the imprint of the Soul to the body; that Nature knows the fully formed desire which is the culmination of the less formed desire in body; sensation knows the image thence imprinted upon the Nature; and from the moment of the sensation the Soul, which alone is competent, acts upon it, sometimes procuring, sometimes on the contrary resisting, taking control and paying heed neither to that which originated the desire nor to that which subsequently entertained it.

But why, thus, two phases of desire; why should not the body as a determined entity (the living total) be the sole desirer?

Because there are (in man) two distinct things, this Nature and the body, which through it, becomes a living being: the Nature precedes the determined body which is its creation, made and shaped by it; it cannot originate the desires; they must belong to the living body meeting the experiences of this life and seeking in its distress to alter its state, to substitute pleasure for pain, sufficiency for want: this Nature must be like a mother reading the wishes of a suffering child, and seeking to set it right and to bring it back to herself; in her search for the remedy she attaches herself by that very concern to the sufferer's desire and makes the child's experience her own.

In sum, the living body may be said to desire of its own motion in a fore-desiring with, perhaps, impulse as well; Nature desires for, and because of, that living body; granting or withholding belongs to another again, the higher soul.

21. That this is the phase of the human being in which desire takes its origin is shown by observation of the different stages of life: in childhood, youth, maturity, the bodily desires differ; health or sickness also may change them, while the (psychic) faculty is of course the same through all: the evidence is clear that the variety of desire in the human being results from the fact that he is a corporeal entity, a living body subject to every sort of vicissitude.

The total movement of desire is not always stirred simultaneously with what we call the impulses to the satisfaction even of the lasting bodily demands; it may refuse assent to the idea of eating or drinking until reason gives the word: this shows us desire—the degree of it existing in the living body—advancing towards some object, with Nature (the lower soul-phase) refusing its co-operation and approval, and as sole arbiter between what is naturally fit and unfit, rejecting what does not accord with the natural need.

We may be told that the changing state of the body is sufficient explanation of the changing desires in the faculty; but that would require the demonstration that the changing condition of a given entity could effect a change of desire in another, in one which cannot itself gain by the gratification; for it is not the desiring faculty that profits by food, liquid, warmth, movement, or by any relief from over-plenty or any filling of a void; all such services touch the body only.

22. And as regards vegetal forms? Are we to distinguish between a sort of corporeal echo and the principle which gives rise to it—a principle that would be tendency or desire in us and is growth in them? Or are we to think that, while the earth (which nourishes them) contains the principle of desire by virtue of containing soul, the vegetal realm possesses only this latter reflection of desire?

The first point to be decided is what soul is present in the earth.

Is it one coming from the sphere of the All, a radiation upon earth from that which Plato seems to represent as the only thing possessing soul primarily? Or are we to go by that other passage where he describes earth as 'the first and oldest of all the gods within the scope of the heavens', and assigns to it, as to the other stars, a soul peculiar to itself?

It is difficult to see how earth could be a god if it did not possess a soul thus distinct: but the whole matter is obscure since Plato's statements increase or at least do not lessen the perplexity. It is best to begin by facing the question as a matter of reasoned investigation.

That earth possesses the vegetal soul may be taken as certain from the vegetation upon it. But we see also that it produces animals; why then should we not argue that it is itself animated? And, animated, no small part of the All, must it not be plausible to assert that it possesses an Intellectual-Principle by which it holds its rank as a god? If this is true of every one of the stars, why should it not be so of the earth, a living part of the living All? We cannot think of it as sustained from without by an alien soul and incapable of containing one appropriate to itself.

Why should those fiery globes be receptive of soul and the earthly globe not? The stars are equally corporeal, and they lack the flesh, blood, muscle, and pliant material of earth, which besides is of more varied content and includes every form of body. If the earth's immobility is urged in objection, the answer is that this refers only to spatial movement.

But how can perception and sensation (implied in ensoulment) be supposed to occur in the earth?

How (we return) do they occur in the stars? Feeling does not belong to fleshy matter: soul to have perception does not require body; body, on the contrary, requires soul to maintain its being and its efficiency: judgement (the foundation of perception) belongs to the soul which overlooks the body, and, from what is experienced there, forms its decisions.

But, we will be asked to say what are the experiences, within the earth, upon which the earth-soul is thus to form its decisions: certainly vegetal forms, in so far as they belong to earth, have no sensation or perception: in what then, and through what, does such sensation take place, for (we will be told) sensation without organs is too rash a notion. Besides, what would this sense-perception profit the Soul? It could not be necessary to knowledge: surely the consciousness of wisdom suffices to beings which have nothing to gain from sensation?

This argument is not to be accepted: it ignores the consideration that, apart from all question of practical utility, objects of sense provide occasion for a knowing which brings pleasure: thus we ourselves take delight in looking upon sun, stars, sky, landscape, for their own sake. But we will deal with this point later: for the present I we ask, presuming that the earth has perceptions and sensations and is a living being, what objects it would perceive[7] and by what method: I this requires us to examine certain difficulties, and above all to decide whether earth could have sensation without organs, and whether this would be directed to some necessary purpose even when incidentally it might bring other results as well.

23. A first principle is that the knowing of sensible objects is an act of the Soul, or of the living conjoint, becoming aware of the quality of certain corporeal entities, and appropriating the Ideal-Forms present in them.

This apprehension must belong either to the Soul isolated, self-acting, or to Soul in conjunction with some other entity?

Isolated, self-acting, how is it possible? Self-acting, it has knowledge of its own content, and this is not perception but intellection: if it is also to know things outside itself it can grasp them only in one of two ways: either it must assimilate itself to the external objects, or it must enter into relations with something that has been so assimilated.

Now as long as it remains self-centred it cannot assimilate: a single point cannot assimilate itself to an external line: even line cannot adapt itself to line in another order, line of the intellectual to line of the sensible, just as fire of the intellectual and man of the intellectual remain distinct from fire and man of the sensible. Even Nature, the soul-phase which brings man into being, does not come to identity with the man it shapes and informs: it has the faculty of dealing with the sensible, but it remains isolated, and, its task done, ignores all but the intellectual as it is itself ignored by the sensible and utterly without means of grasping it.

Suppose something visible lying at a distance: the Soul sees it; now, admitting to the full that at first only the pure Form of the thing is seized—a total without discerned part—yet in the end it becomes to the seeing soul an object whose complete detail of colour and form is known: this shows that there is something more here than the outlying thing and the Soul; for the Soul is immune from experience; there must be a third, something not thus exempt; and it is this intermediate that accepts the impressions of shape and the like.

This intermediate must be able to assume the modifications of the material object so as to be an exact reproduction of its states, and it must be of the one elemental-stuff: it, thus, will exhibit the condition which the higher principle is to perceive; and the condition must be such as to preserve something of the originating object, and yet not be identical with it: the essential vehicle of knowledge is an intermediary which, as it stands between the Soul and the originating object, will, similarly, present a condition midway between the two spheres, of sense and the intellectual—linking the extremes, receiving from one side to exhibit to the other, in virtue of being able to assimilate itself to each. As an instrument by which something is to receive knowledge, it cannot be identical with either the knower or the known: but it must be apt to likeness with both—akin to the external object by its power of being affected, and to the internal, the knower, by the fact that the modification it takes becomes a Form.

If this theory of ours is sound, bodily organs are necessary to sense-perception, as is further indicated by the reflection that the Soul entirely freed of body can apprehend nothing in the order of sense.

The organ must be either the body entire or some member set apart for a particular function; thus touch for one, vision for another. The tools of craftsmanship will be seen to be intermediaries between the judging worker and the judged object, disclosing to the experimenter the particular character of the matter under investigation: thus a ruler, representing at once the straightness which is in the mind and the straightness of a plank, is used as an intermediary by which the operator proves his work.

Some questions of detail remain for consideration elsewhere: is it necessary that the object upon which judgement or perception is to take place should be in contact with the organ of perception, or can the process occur across space upon an object at a distance? Thus, is the heat of a fire really at a distance from the flesh it warms, the intermediate space remaining unmodified; is it possible to see colour over a sheer blank intervening between the colour and the eye, the organ of vision reaching to its object by its own power?

For the moment we have one certainty, that perception of things of sense belongs to the embodied soul and takes place through the body.

24. The next question is whether perception is concerned only with need.

The Soul, isolated, has no sense-perception; sensations go with the body;

sensation itself therefore must occur by means of the body to which the sensations are due; it must be something brought about by association with the body.

Thus either sensation occurs in a soul compelled to follow upon bodily states—since every graver bodily experience reaches at last to soul—or sensation is a device by which a cause is dealt with before it becomes so great as actually to injure us or even before it has begun to make contact.

At this, sense-impressions would aim at utility. They may serve also to knowledge, but that could be service only to some being not living in knowledge but stupefied as the result of a disaster, and the victim of a Lethe calling for constant reminding: they would be useless to any being free from either need or forgetfulness. This reflection enlarges the inquiry: it is no longer a question of earth alone, but of the whole star-system, all the heavens, the Cosmos entire. For it would follow that, in the sphere of things not exempt from modification, sense-perception would occur in every part having relation to any other part: in a whole, however—having relation only to itself, immune, universally self-directed and self-possessing—what perception could there be?

Granted that the percipient must act through an organ and that this organ must be different from the object perceived, then the universe, as an All, can have (no sensation since it has) no organ distinct from object: it can have self-awareness, as we have; but sense-perception, the constant attendant of another order, it cannot have.

Our own apprehension of any bodily condition apart from the normal is the sense of something intruding from without: but besides this, we have the apprehension of one member by another; why then should not the All use the sphere of the fixed stars to perceive the sphere of the planets and the latter to perceive the earth and the earth's content?

Things of earth are certainly affected by what passes in other regions of the All; what, then, need prevent the All from having, in some appropriate way, the perception of those changes? In addition to that self-contemplating vision vested in the sphere of the fixed stars, may it not have a seeing power like that of an eye able to announce to the All-Soul what has passed before it? Even granted that it is entirely unaffected I by other experiences,[8] I why, still, should it not see like an eye, ensouled as it is, all lightsome?

Still: 'eyes were not necessary to it', we read. If this meant simply that nothing is left to be seen outside of the All, still there is the inner content, and there can be nothing to prevent it seeing what constitutes itself: if the meaning is that such self-vision could serve to no use, we may think that it has vision not as a main intention for vision's sake but as a necessary concomitant of its characteristic nature: it is difficult to conceive why such a body should be incapable of seeing.

25. But the organ is not the only requisite to vision or to perception of any kind: there must be a state of the Soul inclining it towards the sphere of sense.

Now it is the Soul's character to be ever in the Intellectual sphere, and even though it were apt to sense-perception, I this could be prevented by[9] that I intention towards the highest; to ourselves when absorbed in the Intellectual, vision and the other acts of sense are in abeyance for the time; and, in general, any special attention blurs every other. The desire of apprehension from part to part—a subject examining itself—is merely curiosity even in beings of our own standing, and, unless for some definite purpose, is waste of energy: and the desire to apprehend something external—for the sake of a pleasant sight—is the sign of suffering or deficiency.

Smelling, tasting flavours (and such animal perceptions) may perhaps be described as mere accessories, distractions of the Soul, while seeing and hearing would belong to the sun and the other heavenly bodies as incidentals to their being. This would not be unreasonable if seeing and hearing are means by which they apply themselves to their function.

But if they so apply themselves, they must have memory; it is impossible that they should have no remembrance if they are to be benefactors; their service could not exist without memory.

26. Their knowledge of our prayers is due to what we may call an enlinking, a determined relation of things fitted into a system; so, too, the fulfilment of the petitions; in the art of magic all looks to this enlinkment: prayer and its answer, magic and its success, depend upon the sympathy of enchained forces.

This seems to oblige us to accord sense-perception to the earth.

But what perception?

Why not, to begin with, that of contact-feeling, the apprehension of part by part, the apprehension of fire and the other elements by its entire mass in a sensation transmitted upwards to the earth's leading principle? A corporeal mass (such as that of the earth) may be sluggish but is not utterly inert. Such perceptions, of course, would not be of trifles, but of the graver movement of things.

But why even of them?

Because those gravest movements could not possibly remain unknown where there is an immanent soul.

And there is nothing against the idea that sensation in the earth exists for the sake of the human interests furthered by the earth. They would be served by means of the sympathy that has been mentioned; petitioners would be heard and their prayers met, though in a way not ours. And the earth, both in its own interest and in that of beings distinct from itself, might have the experiences of the other senses also—for example, smell and taste where, perhaps, the scent of juices or sap might enter into its care for animal life as in the constructing or restoring of their bodily part.

But we need not demand for earth the organs by which we, ourselves, act: not even all the animals have these; some, without ears, perceive sound.

For sight it would not need eyes—though if light is indispensable how can it see?

That the earth contains the principle of growth must be admitted; it is difficult not to allow in consequence that, since this vegetal principle is either spirit (pneuma) or contained in spirit, the earth is primarily of the spiritual order; and how can we doubt that in spirit all is lucid? This becomes all the more evident when we reflect that, besides being as spirit lightsome, it is physically illuminated moving in the light of the cosmic revolution.

There is, thus, no longer any absurdity or impossibility in the notion that the soul in the earth has vision: we must, further, consider that it is the soul of no mean body; that in fact it is a god since certainly this soul must be for ever good.

27. If the earth transmits the generative soul to growing things—or retains it while allowing a vestige of it to constitute the vegetal principle in them—at once the earth is ensouled, as our flesh is, and any generative power possessed by the plant world is of its bestowing: this phase of the Soul is immanent in the body of the growing thing, and transmits to it that better element by which it differs from the broken-off part, no longer a thing of growth but a mere lump of material.

But does the entire body of the earth similarly receive anything from the Soul?

Yes: for we must recognize that earthly material broken off from the main body differs from the same remaining continuously attached; thus stones increase as long as they are embedded, and, from the moment they are separated, stop at the size attained.

We must conclude, then, that every part and member of the earth carries its vestige of this principle of growth, an under-phase of that entire principle which belongs not to this or that member but to the earth as a whole: next in order is the nature (the soul-phase) concerned with sensation, this not interfused (like the vegetal principle) but in contact from above: then the higher soul and the Intellectual-Principle constituting together the being known as Hestia (Earth-Mind) and Demeter (Earth-Soul)—a nomenclature indicating the human intuition of these truths, asserted in the attribution of a divine name and nature.

28. Thus much established, we may return on our path: we have to discuss the seat of the passionate element in the human being.

Pleasures and pains—the conditions, that is, not the perception of them—and the nascent stage of desire, we assigned to the body as a determined thing, the body brought, in some sense, to life: are we entitled to say the same of the nascent stage of passion? Are we to consider passion in all its forms as vested in the determined body or in something belonging to it, for instance in the heart or the bile necessarily taking condition within a body not dead? ❙ And are we to think that that which bestows the vestige of the soul is again a distinct entity, or is the vestige in the case of passion an independent thing, and not derived from a vegetal[10] or percipient faculty? ❙

Now in the first case the soul-principle involved, the vegetal, pervades the entire body, and the vestigial phase which it bestows is bestowed upon the entire body, so that pain and pleasure and nascent desire for the satisfaction of need are present all over it—there is possibly some doubt as to the sexual impulse, which, however, it may suffice to assign to the organs by which it is executed—but in general the region about the liver may be taken to be the starting-point of desire, since it is the main acting point of the vegetal principle which transmits the vestige phase of the soul to the liver and body—the seat, because the spring.

But in this other case, of passion, we have to settle what it is, what form of soul it represents: does it act by communicating a lower phase of itself to the regions round the heart, or is it set in motion by the higher soul-phase impinging upon the Conjoint (the animate-total), or is there in such conditions no question of soul-phase, but simply passion itself producing the act or state of (for example) anger?

Evidently the first point for inquiry is what passion is.

Now we all know that we feel anger not only over our own bodily suffering, but also over that of our friends, and indeed over any victim of unseemly conduct. It is at once evident that anger implies some subject capable of sensation and of judgement: and this consideration suffices to show that the vegetal nature is not its source, that we must look for its origin elsewhere.

On the other hand, anger follows closely upon bodily states; people in whom the blood and the bile are intensely active are as quick to anger as those of cool blood and no bile are slow; animals grow angry through some bodily condition in themselves rather than from any clear recognition of physical danger; all this forces us again to place the seat of anger in the strictly corporeal element, the principle by which the animal organism is held together. Similarly, that anger or its first stirring depends upon the condition of the body follows from the consideration that the same people are more irritable ill than well, fasting than after food: it would seem that the bile and the blood, acting as vehicles of life, produce these emotions.

Our conclusion (reconciling with these corporeal facts the psychic or mental element indicated) will identify, first, some suffering in the body answered by a movement in the blood or in the bile: I sensation ensues and the representative faculty, which brings the Soul to partake in the condition of the affected body, is directed towards the cause of the pain. Again, the reasoning soul may from its place above act in its own mode when a breach of order has become manifest to it—a breach which may not involve the body: it will then call[11] in the alliance I of that ready passionate faculty which is the natural combatant of the evil disclosed.

Thus anger has two phases; there is firstly that which, rising apart from all process of reasoning, draws reason to itself by the medium of the imaging faculty, and secondly that which, rising in reason, touches finally upon the specific principle of the emotion. Both these depend upon the existence of that principle of vegetal life and generation by which the body becomes an organism aware of pleasure and pain: this principle it was that made the body a thing of bile and bitterness, and thus it leads the indwelling soul-phase to corresponding states—churlish and angry under stress of environment—so that being wronged itself, it tries, as we may put it, to return the wrong upon its surroundings, and bring them to the same condition.

That this soul-vestige, which determines the movements of passion, is of one essence (consubstantial) with the other is evident from the consideration that those of us less avid of corporeal pleasures, especially those that wholly repudiate the body, are the least prone to anger and to all experiences not rising from reason.

That this vegetal principle, underlying anger, should be present in trees and yet passion be lacking in them cannot surprise us since they are not subject to the movements of blood and bile. If the occasions of anger presented themselves where there is no power of sensation there could be no more than a physical ebullition with something approaching to resentment (an unconscious reaction); where sensation exists there is at once something more; the recognition of wrong and of the necessary defence carries with it the intentional act.

But the division of the unreasoning phase of the Soul into a desiring faculty and a passionate faculty—the first identical with the vegetal principle, the second being a lower phase of it acting upon the blood or bile or upon the entire living organism—such a division would not give us a true opposition, for the two would stand in the relation of earlier phase to derivative.

This difficulty is reasonably met by considering that both faculties are derivatives and making the division apply to them in so far as they are new productions from a common source; for the division applies to movements of desire as such, not to the essence from which they rise.

That essence is not, of its own nature, desire; it is, however, the force which by consolidating itself with the active manifestation proceeding from it makes the desire a completed thing. And that derivative which culminates in passion may not unreasonably be thought of as a vestige-phase lodged about the heart, since the heart is not the seat of the Soul, but merely the centre to that portion of the blood which is concerned in the movements of passion.

29. But—keeping to our illustration, by which the body is warmed by soul and not merely illuminated by it—how is it that when the higher soul withdraws there is no further trace of the vital principle?

For a brief space there is; and, precisely, it begins to fade away immediately upon the withdrawal of the other, as in the case of warmed objects when the fire is no longer near them: similarly hair and nails still grow on the dead; animals cut to pieces wriggle for a good time after; these are signs of a life-force still indwelling.

Besides, simultaneous withdrawal would not prove the identity of the higher and lower phases: when the sun withdraws there goes with it not merely the light emanating from it, guided by it, attached to it, but also at once that light seen upon obliquely situated objects, a light secondary to the sun's and cast upon things outside of its path (reflected light showing as colour); the two are not identical and yet they disappear together.

But is this simultaneous withdrawal or frank obliteration?

The question applies equally to this secondary light and to the corporeal life, that life which we think of as being completely sunk into body.

No light whatever remains in the objects once illuminated; that much is certain: but we have to ask whether it has sunk back into its source or is simply no longer in existence.

How could it pass out of being, a thing that once has been?

But what really was it? We must remember that what we know as colour belongs to bodies by the fact that they throw off light, yet when corruptible bodies are transformed the colour disappears and we no more ask where the colour of a burned-out fire is than where its shape is.

Still: the shape is merely a configuration, like the lie of the hands clenched or spread; the colour is no such accidental but is more like, for example, sweetness: when a material substance breaks up, the sweetness of what was sweet in it, and the fragrance of what was fragrant may very well not be annihilated, but enter into some other substance, passing unobserved there because the new habitat is not such that the entrant qualities now offer anything solid to perception.

May we not think that, similarly, the light belonging to bodies that have been dissolved remains in being while the solid total, made up of all that is characteristic, disappears?

It might be said that the seeing is I merely 'convention-bound' (or subjective),[12] so I that what we call qualities do not actually exist in the substances.

But this is to make the qualities indestructible and not dependent upon the composition of the body; it would no longer be the Reason-Principles within the sperm that produce, for instance, the colours of a bird's variegated plumage; these principles would merely blend and place them, or if they produced them would draw also on the full store of colours in the sky, producing in the sense, mainly, of showing in the formed bodies something very different from what appears in the heavens.

But whatever we may think on this doubtful point, if, as long as the bodies remain unaltered, the light is constant and unsevered, then it would seem natural that, on the dissolution of the body, the light—both that in immediate contact and any other attached to that—should pass away at the same moment, unseen in the going as in the coming.

But in the case of the Soul it is a question whether the secondary phases follow their priors—the derivatives their sources—or whether every phase is self-governing, isolated from its predecessors and able to stand alone; in a word, whether no part of the Soul is sundered from the total, but all the souls are simultaneously one soul and many, and, if so, by what mode; this question, however, is treated elsewhere.

Here we have to inquire into the nature and being of that vestige of the soul actually present in the living body: if there is truly a soul, then, as a thing never cut off from its total, it will go with soul as soul must: if it is rather to be thought of as belonging to the body, as the life of the body, we have the same question that rose in the case of the vestige of light; we must examine whether life can exist without the presence of soul, except of course in the sense of soul living above and acting upon the remote object.

30. We have declared acts of memory unnecessary to the stars, but we allow them perceptions, hearing as well as seeing; for we said that prayers to them were heard—our supplications to the sun, and those, even, of certain other men to

the stars. It has, moreover, been the belief that in answer to prayer they accomplish many human wishes, and this so light-heartedly that they become not merely helpers towards good but even accomplices in evil. Since this matter lies in our way it must be considered, for it carries with it grave difficulties that very much trouble those who cannot think of divine beings as, thus, authors or auxiliaries in unseemliness even including the connexions of loose carnality.

In view of all this it is especially necessary to study the question with which we began, that of memory in the heavenly bodies.

It is obvious that, if they act on our prayers and if this action is not immediate, but with delay and after long periods of time, they remember the prayers men address to them. This is something that our former argument did not concede; though it appeared plausible that, for their better service of mankind, they might have been endowed with such a faculty as we ascribed to Demeter and Hestia—unless only the earth is to be thought of as beneficent to man.

We have, then, to attempt to show: firstly, how acts implying memory in the heavenly bodies are to be reconciled with our system as distinguished from those others which allow them memory as a matter of course; secondly, what vindication of those gods of the heavenly spheres is possible in the matter of seemingly anomalous acts—a question which philosophy cannot ignore; then too, since the charge goes so far, we must ask whether credence is to be given to those who hold that the entire heavenly system can be put under spell by man's skill and audacity: our discussion will also deal with the spirit-beings and how they may be thought to minister to these ends—unless indeed the part played by the Celestials prove to be settled by the decision upon the first questions.

31. Our problem embraces all act and all experience throughout the entire Cosmos—whether due to nature, in the current phrase, or effected by art. The natural proceeds, we must hold, from the All towards its members and from the members to the All, or from member to other member: the artificial either remains, as it began, within the limit of the art—attaining finality in the artificial product alone—or is the expression of an art which calls to its aid natural forces and agencies, and so sets up act and experience within the sphere of the natural.

When I speak of the act and experience of the All I mean the total effect of the entire cosmic circuit upon itself and upon its members: for by its motion it sets up certain states both within itself and upon its parts, upon the bodies that move within it, and upon all that it communicates to those other parts of it, the things of our earth.

The action of part upon part is manifest; there are the relations and operations of the sun, both towards the other spheres and towards the things of earth;

360 PLOTINUS: THE ENNEADS

and again relations among elements of the sun itself, of other heavenly bodies, of earthly things, and of things in the other stars, demand investigation.

As for the arts: such as look to house building and the like are exhausted when the object is achieved; there are again those—medicine, farming, and other serviceable pursuits—which deal helpfully with natural products, seeking to bring them to natural efficiency; and there is a class—rhetoric, music, and every other method of swaying mind or soul, with their power of modifying for better or for worse—and we have to ascertain what these arts come to and what kind of power lies in them.

On all these points, in so far as they bear on our present purpose, we must do what we can to work out some approximate explanation.

It is abundantly evident that the Circuit is a cause; it modifies, firstly, itself and its own content, and undoubtedly also it tells on the terrestrial, not merely in accordance with bodily conditions but also by the states of the soul it sets up; and each of its members has an operation upon the terrestrial and in general upon all the lower.

Whether there is a return action of the lower upon the higher need not trouble us now: for the moment we are to seek, as far as discussion can exhibit it, the method by which action takes place; and we do not challenge the opinions universally or very generally entertained.

We take the question back to the initial act of causation. It cannot be admitted that either heat or cold and the like—what are known as the primal qualities of the elements—or any admixture of these qualities, should be the first causes we are seeking; equally inacceptable, that while the sun's action is all by heat, there is another member of the Circuit operating wholly by cold—incongruous in the heavens and in a fiery body—nor can we think of some other star operating by liquid fire.

Such explanations do not account for the differences of things, and there are many phenomena which cannot be referred to any of these causes. Suppose we allow them to be the occasion of moral differences—determined, thus, by bodily composition and constitution under a reigning heat or cold—does that give us a reasonable explanation of envy, jealousy, acts of violence? Or, if it does, what, at any rate, are we to think of good and bad fortune, rich men and poor, gentle blood, treasure trove?

An immensity of such examples might be adduced, all leading far from any corporeal quality that could enter the body and soul of a living thing from the elements: and it is equally impossible that the will of the stars, a doom from the All, any deliberation among them, should be held responsible for the fate of each and all of their inferiors. It is not to be thought that such beings engage themselves in human affairs in the sense of making men thieves, slave-dealers, burglars, temple-strippers, or debased effeminates practising and lending themselves to disgusting actions: that is not merely unlike gods; it is unlike mediocre men; it is, perhaps, beneath the level of any existing being where there is not the least personal advantage to be gained.

32. If we can trace neither to material agencies (blind elements) nor to any deliberate intention the influences from without which reach to us and to the other forms of life and to the terrestrial in general, what cause satisfactory to reason remains?

The secret is: firstly, that this All is one universally comprehensive living being, encircling all the living beings within it, and having a soul, one soul, which extends to all its members in the degree of participant membership held by each, secondly, that every separate thing is an integral part of this All by belonging to the total material fabric—unrestrictedly a part by bodily membership, while, in so far as it has also some participation in the All-Soul, it possesses in that degree spiritual membership as well, perfect where participation is in the All-Soul alone, partial where there is also a union with a lower soul.

But, with all this gradation, each several thing is affected by all else in virtue of the common participation in the All, and to the degree of its own participation.

This One-All, therefore, is a sympathetic total and stands as one living being; the far is near; it happens as in one animal with its separate parts: talon, horn, finger, and any other member are not continuous and yet are effectively near; intermediate parts feel nothing, but at a distant point the local experience is known. Correspondent things not side by side but separated by others placed between, the sharing of experience by dint of like condition—this is enough to ensure that the action of any distant member be transmitted to its distant fellow. Where all is a living thing summing to a unity there is nothing so remote in point of place as not to be near by virtue of a nature which makes of the one living being a sympathetic organism.

Where there is similarity between a thing affected and the thing affecting it, the affection is not alien; where the affecting cause is dissimilar the affection is alien and unpleasant.

Such hurtful action of member upon member within one living being need not seem surprising: within ourselves, in our own activities, one constituent can be harmed by another; bile and animal spirit seem to press and goad other members of the human total: in the vegetal realm one part hurts another by sucking the moisture from it. And in the All there is something analogous to bile and animal spirit, as to other such constituents. For visibly it is not merely one living organism; it is also a manifold. In virtue of the unity the individual is preserved by the All: in virtue of the multiplicity of things having various contacts, difference often brings about mutual hurt; one thing, seeking its own need, is detrimental to another; what is at once related and different is seized as food; each thing, following its own natural path, wrenches from something else what is serviceable to itself, and destroys or checks in its own interest whatever is becoming a menace to it: each, occupied with its peculiar function, assists no doubt anything able to profit by that, but harms or destroys what is too weak to withstand the onslaught of its action, like fire withering things round it or greater animals in their march thrusting aside or trampling under foot the smaller.

The rise of all these forms of being, their destruction, and their modification, whether to their loss or gain, all goes to the fulfilment of the natural unhindered life of that one living being: for it was not possible for the single thing to be as if it stood alone; the final purpose could not serve to that only end, intent upon the partial: the concern must be for the whole to which each item is member: things are different both from each other and in their own stages, therefore cannot be complete in one unchanging form of life; nor could anything remain utterly without modification if the All is to be durable; for the permanence of an All demands varying forms.

33. The Circuit does not go by chance but under the Reason-Principle of the living whole; therefore there must be a harmony between cause and caused; there must be some order ranging things to each other's purpose, or in due relation to each other: every several configuration within the Circuit must be accompanied by a change in the position and condition of things subordinate to it, which thus by their varied rhythmic movement make up one total dance-play.

In our dance-plays there are outside elements contributing to the total effect—fluting, singing, and other linked accessories—and each of these changes in each new movement: there is no need to dwell on these; their significance is obvious. But besides this there is the fact that the limbs of the dancer cannot possibly keep the same positions in every figure; they adapt themselves to the plan, bending as it dictates, one lowered, another raised, one active, another resting as the set pattern changes. The dancer's mind is on his own purpose; his limbs are submissive to the dance-movement which they accomplish to the end, so that the connoisseur can explain that this or that figure is the motive for the lifting, bending, concealment, effacing, of the various members of the body; and in all this the executant does not choose the particular motions for their own sake; the whole play of the entire person dictates the necessary position to each limb and member as it serves to the plan.

Now this is the mode in which the heavenly beings (the diviner members of the All) must be held to be causes wherever they have any action, and, when they do not act, to indicate.

Or, a better statement: the entire Cosmos puts its entire life into act, moving its major members with its own action and unceasingly setting them in new positions; by the relations thus established, of these members to each other and to the whole, and by the different figures they make together, the minor members in turn are brought under the system as in the movements of some one living being, so that they vary according to the relations, positions, configurations: the beings thus co-ordinated are not the causes; the cause is the co-ordinating All; at the same time it is not to be thought of I as acting upon a material distinct from itself,[13] for I there is nothing external to it since it is the cause by actually being all: on the one side the configurations, on the other the inevitable effects of those configurations upon a living being moving as a unit and, again, upon a living being (an All) thus by its nature conjoined and concomitant and, of necessity, at once subject and object to its own activities.

34. For ourselves, while whatever in us belongs to the body of the All should be yielded to its action, we ought to make sure that we submit only within limits, realizing that the entire man is not thus bound to it: intelligent servitors yield a part of themselves to their masters but in part retain their personality, and are thus less absolutely at beck and call, as not being slaves, not utterly chattels.

The changing configurations within the All could not fail to be produced as they are, since the moving bodies are not of equal speed.

Now the movement is guided by a Reason-Principle; the relations of the living whole are altered in consequence; here in our own realm all that happens reacts in sympathy to the events of that higher sphere: it becomes, therefore, advisable to ask whether we are to think of this realm as following upon the higher by agreement, or to attribute to the configurations the powers underlying the events, and whether such powers would be vested in the configurations simply or in the relations of the particular items.

It will be said that one position of one given thing has by no means an identical effect—whether of indication or of causation—in its relation to another and still less to any group of others, since each several being seems to have a natural tendency (or receptivity) of its own.

The truth is that the configuration of any given group entails both the members and their relationship, and, changing the members, though the relationship remain the same, the effect will be different.

But, this being so, the power will belong, not to the positions but to the beings holding those positions?

To both taken together. For as things change their relations, and as any one thing changes place, there is a change of power.

But what power? That of causation or of indication?

To this double thing—the particular configuration of particular beings— there accrues often the twofold power, that of causation and that of indication, but sometimes only that of indication. Thus we are obliged to attribute powers both to the configuration and to the beings entering into them. In mime dancers each of the hands has its own power, and so with all the limbs; the relative positions have much power; and, for a third power, there is that of the accessories and concomitants; underlying the action of the performers' limbs, there are such items as the clutched fingers and the muscles and veins following suit.

35. But we must give some explanation of these powers. The matter requires a more definite handling. How can there be a difference of power between one triangular configuration and another?

How can there be the exercise of power from star to star; under what law, and within what limits?

The difficulty is that we are unable to attribute causation either to the bodies of the heavenly beings or to their wills: their bodies are excluded because the product transcends the causative power of body, their will because it would be unseemly to suppose divine beings to produce unseemliness.

Let us keep in mind what we have laid down:

The being we are considering is a living unity, and therefore necessarily self-sympathetic: it is under a law of reason and therefore the unfolding process of its life must be self-accordant: that life has no haphazard, but knows only harmony and ordinance: all the groupings follow reason: all single beings within it, all the members of this living whole in their choral dance are under a rule of Number.

Holding this in mind we are forced to certain conclusions: in the expressive act of the All are comprised equally the configurations of its members and these members themselves, minor as well as major entering into the configurations. This is the mode of life of the All; and its powers work together to this end under the Nature in which the producing agency within the Reason-Principles has brought them into being. The groupings (within the All) are themselves in the nature of Reason-Principles since they are the out-spacing of a living-being, its reason-determined rhythms and conditions, and the entities thus spaced-out and grouped to pattern are its various members: then again there are the powers of the living being—distinct these, too—which may be considered as parts of it, always excluding deliberate will which is external to it, not contributory to the nature of the living All.

The will of any organic thing is one; but the distinct powers which go to constitute it are far from being one: yet all the several wills look to the object aimed at by the one will of the whole: for the desire which the one member entertains for another is a desire within the All: a part seeks to acquire something outside itself, but that external is another part of which it feels the need: the anger of a moment of annoyance is directed to something alien, growth draws on something outside, all birth and becoming has to do with the external; but all this external is inevitably something included among fellow members of the system: through these its limbs and members, the All is bringing this activity into being while in itself it seeks—or better, contemplates—The Good. Right will, then, the will which stands above accidental experience, seeks The Good and thus acts to the same end with it. When men serve another, many of their acts are done under order, but the good servant is the one whose purpose is in union with his master's.

In all the efficacy of the sun and other stars upon earthly matters we can but believe that though the heavenly body is intent upon the Supreme, yet—to keep to the sun—its warming of terrestrial things, and every service following upon that, all springs from itself, its own act transmitted in virtue of soul, the vastly efficacious soul of Nature. Each of the heavenly bodies, similarly, gives forth a power, involuntary, by its mere radiation: all things become one entity, grouped by this diffusion of power, and so bring about wide changes of condition; thus the very groupings have power since their diversity produces diverse conditions; that the grouped beings themselves have also their efficiency is clear since they produce differently according to the different membership of the groups.

That configuration has power in itself is within our own observation here. Why else do certain groupments, in contradistinction to others, terrify at sight though there has been no previous experience of evil from them? If some men are alarmed by a particular groupment and others by quite a different one, the reason can be only that the configurations themselves have efficacy, each upon a certain type—an efficacy which cannot fail to reach anything naturally disposed to be impressed by it, so that in one groupment things attract observation which in another pass without effect, even for the same observer.

If we are told that beauty is the motive of attraction, does not this mean simply that the power of appeal to this or that mind depends upon pattern, configuration? How can we allow power to colour and none to configuration?

It is surely untenable that an entity should have existence and yet have no power to effect: existence carries with it either acting or answering to action, some things having action alone, others both.

At the same time there are powers apart from pattern: and, in things of our realm, there are many powers dependent not upon heat and cold but upon forces due to differing properties, forces which have been shaped to ideal-quality by the action of Reason-Principles and communicate in the power of Nature: thus the natural properties of stones and the efficacy of plants produce many astonishing results.

36. The Universe is immensely varied, the container of all the Reason-Principles and of infinite and diverse efficacies. In man, we are told, the eye has its power, and the bones have their varied powers, and so with each separate part of hand and of foot; and there is no member or organ without its own definite function, some separate power of its own—a diversity of which we can have no notion unless our studies take that direction. What is true of man must be true of the universe, and much more, since all this order is but a representation of the higher: it must contain an untellably wonderful variety of powers, with which, of course, the bodies moving through the heavens will be most richly endowed.

We cannot think of the universe as a soulless habitation, however vast and varied, a thing of materials easily told off, kind by kind—wood and stone and whatever else there be, all blending into a cosmos: it must be alert throughout, every member living by its own life, nothing that can have existence failing to exist within it.

And here we have the solution of the problem, How an ensouled living form can include the soulless: for this account allows grades of living within the whole, grades to some of which we deny life only because they are not perceptibly self-moved: in the truth, all of these have a hidden life; and the thing whose life is patent to sense is made up of things which do not live to sense, but, none the less, confer upon their resultant total wonderful powers towards living. Man would never have reached to his actual height if the powers by which he acts were the completely soulless elements of his being; similarly the All could not have its huge life unless its every member had a life of its own; this however does not necessarily imply a deliberate intention; the All has no need of intention to bring about its acts: it is older than intention, I and therefore many things exercise their powers in its service.[14] I

37. We must not rob the universe of any factor in its being. If any of our theorists of today seek to explain the action of fire—or of any other such form, thought of as an agent—they will find themselves in difficulties unless they recognize

the act to be the object's function in the All, and give a like explanation of other natural forces in common use.

We do not habitually examine or in any way question the normal: we set to doubting and working out identifications when we are confronted by any display of power outside everyday experience: we wonder at a novelty, and yet the customary is as wonderful if anyone brings forward each single object and explains to our ignorance the efficacy vested in it.

Some such power, not necessarily accompanied by reason, every single item possesses; for each has been brought into being and into shape within a universe; each in its kind has partaken of soul through the medium of the ensouled All, as being embraced by that definitely constituted thing: each then is a member of an animate being which can include nothing that is less than a full member (and therefore a sharer in the total of power)—though one thing is of mightier efficacy than another, and, especially, members of the heavenly system than the objects of earth, since they draw upon a purer nature—and these powers are widely productive. But productivity does not comport intention in what appears to be the source of the thing accomplished: there is efficacy, too, where there is no will: even attention is not necessary to the communication of power; the very transmission of soul may proceed without either.

A living being, we know, may spring from another without any intention, and as without loss so without consciousness in the begetter: in fact any intention the animal exercised could be in abeyance, or at least not the cause of propagation.

And, if intention is unnecessary to the propagation of life, much more so is attention.

38. Whatever springs automatically from the All out of that distinctive life of its own, and, in addition to that self-moving activity, whatever is due to some specific agency—for example, to prayers, simple or taking the form of magic incantations—this entire range of production is to be referred, not to some one of the heavenly bodies, but to the nature of the thing produced (i.e., to a certain natural tendency in the product to exist with its own quality).

All that forwards life or some other useful purpose is to be ascribed to the transmission characteristic of the All; it is something flowing from the major of an integral to its minor. Where we think we see the transmission of some force unfavourable to the production of living beings, the flaw must be found in the inability of the subject to take in what would serve it: for what happens does not happen upon a void; there is always specific form and quality; anything that could be affected must have an underlying nature definite and characterized. The inevitable blendings, further, have their constructive effect, every element adding something contributory to the life. Then again some influence may come into play at the time when the forces of a beneficent nature are not acting: the co-ordination of the entire system of things does not always allow to each several entity everything that it needs: and further we ourselves add a great deal to what is transmitted to us.

None the less all entwines into a unity: and there is something wonderful in the agreement holding among these various things of varied source, even of sources frankly opposite; the secret lies in a variety within a unity. When by the standard of the better kind among things of process anything falls short—the reluctance of its material substratum having prevented its perfect shaping under Idea—it may be thought of as being deficient in that noble element whose absence brings to shame: the thing is a blend, something due to the high beings, an alloy from the underlying nature, something added by the self.

39. Because all is ever being knit, all brought to culmination in unity, therefore all events are indicated; but 'virtue is not a matter of compulsion'; its spontaneity is equally inwoven into the ordered system by the general law that the things of this sphere are pendant from the higher, that the content of our universe lies in the hands of the diviner beings in whom our world is participant.

We cannot, then, refer all that exists to Reason-Principles inherent in the seed of things (Spermatic Reasons); the universe is to be traced further back, to principles whose content is more primal than that of the principles in the seed. Such spermatic principles cannot be the containers of things which arise independently of them, such as what enters from Matter (the reasonless) into membership of the All, or what is due to the mere interaction of existences.

No: the Reason-Principle of the universe would be better envisaged as a wisdom uttering order and law to a state, in full knowledge of what the citizens will do and why, and in perfect adaptation of law to custom; thus the code is made to thread its way in and out through all their conditions and actions with the honour or infamy earned by their conduct; and all coalesces by a kind of automatism.

The signification which exists is not a first intention; it arises incidentally by the fact that in a given collocation the members will tell something of each other: all is unity sprung of unity and therefore one thing is known by way of another, a cause in the light of the caused, the sequent as rising from its precedent, the compound from the constituents which must make themselves known in the linked total.

If all this is sound, at once our doubts fall and we need no longer ask whether the transmission of any evil is due to the gods (the stars).

For, in sum: firstly, intentions are not to be considered as the operative causes; necessities inherent in the nature of things account for all that comes from above; it is a matter of the inevitable relation of parts, and, besides, all is the sequence to the living existence of a unity. Secondly, there is the large contribution made by the individual. Thirdly, each several communication, good in itself, takes another quality in the resultant combination. Fourthly, the life in the Cosmos does not look to the individual but to the whole. Finally, there is Matter, the underlie, which being given one thing receives it as something else, and is unable to make the best of what it takes.

40. But magic spells; how can their efficacy be explained?

By the reigning sympathy and by the fact in Nature that there is an agreement of like forces and an opposition of unlike, and by the diversity of those multitudinous powers which converge in the one living universe.

There is much drawing and spell-binding dependent on no interfering machination; I the true magic is the 'Friendship' and the 'Strife' which exist within the All.[15] I Here is the primal mage and sorcerer—discovered by men who thenceforth turn those same ensorcellations and magic arts upon one another.

Love is given in Nature; the qualities inducing love induce mutual approach: hence there has arisen an art of magic love-drawing I whose practitioners apply by contact certain substances adapted to diverse temperaments and so informed with love as to effect a bond of union;[16] they knit I soul to soul as they might train two separate trees towards each other. The magician, too, draws on these patterns of power, and by ranging himself also into the pattern is able tranquilly to possess himself of these forces with whose nature and purpose he has become identified. Supposing the mage to stand outside the All, his evocations and invocations would no longer avail to draw up or to call down; but as things are he operates from no outside standground, he pulls knowing the pull of everything towards any other thing in the living system.

The tune of an incantation, a significant cry, the mien of the operator, these too have a natural leading power over the Soul upon which they are directed, drawing it with the force of mournful patterns or tragic sounds; for it is the reasonless soul, not the will or wisdom, that is beguiled by music, a form of sorcery which raises no question, whose enchantment, indeed, is welcomed, though not demanded, from the performers. Similarly with regard to prayers; there is no question of a will that grants; the powers that answer to incantations do not act by will; a human being fascinated by a snake has neither perception nor sensation of what is happening; he knows only after he has been caught, and his highest mind is never caught. In other words, some influence falls from the being addressed upon the petitioner—or upon someone else—but that being itself, sun or star, perceives nothing of it all.

41. The prayer is answered by the mere fact that part and other part are wrought to one tone like a musical string which, plucked at one end, vibrates at the other also. Often, too, the sounding of one string awakens what might pass for a perception in another, the result of their being in harmony and tuned to one musical scale; now, if the vibration in a lyre affects another by virtue of the sympathy existing between them, then certainly in the All—even though it is constituted in contraries—there must be one melodic system; for it contains its unisons as well, and its entire content, even to those contraries, is a kinship.

Thus, too, whatever is hurtful to man—the passionate spirit, for example, drawn by the medium of the gall into the principle seated in the liver—comes with no intention of hurt; it is simply as one transferring fire to another might innocently burn him: no doubt, since he actually set the other on fire he is a cause, but only as the attacking fire itself is a cause, that is by the merely accidental fact that the person to whom the fire was being brought blundered in taking it.

42. It follows that, for the purposes which have induced this discussion, the stars have no need of memory or of any sense of petitions addressed to them; they give no such voluntary attention to prayers as some have thought: it is sufficient that, in virtue simply of the nature of parts and of parts within a whole, something proceeds from them whether in answer to prayer or without prayer. We have the analogy of many powers—as in some one living organism—which, independently of plan or as the result of applied method, act without any collaboration of the will: one member or function is helped or hurt by another in the mere play of natural forces; and the art of doctor or magic healer will compel some one centre to purvey something of its own power to another centre. Just so the All: I it purveys spontaneously, but it purveys also under spell; a petition brings to some one part the power laid up for each: the All gives to its members by a natural act, and the petitioner is no alien.[17] I Even though the suppliant be a sinner, the answering need not shock us; sinners draw from the brooks; and the giver does not know of the gift but simply gives—though we must remember that all is one woof and the giving is always consonant with the order of the universe. I A man may therefore help himself to what lies open to all, but if he does so beyond what is right, punishment follows by ineluctable law.[18] I

In sum, we must hold that the All cannot be affected; its leading principle remains for ever immune whatsoever happens to its members; the affection is really present to them, but since nothing existent can be at strife with the total of existence, no such affection conflicts with its impassivity.

Thus the stars, in so far as they are parts, can be affected and yet are immune on various counts; their will, like that of the All, is untouched, just as their bodies and their characteristic natures are beyond all reach of harm; if they give by means of their souls, their souls lose nothing; their bodies remain unchanged or, if there is ebb or inflow, it is of something going unfelt and coming unawares.

43. And the Proficient (the Sage), how does he stand with regard to magic and philtre-spells?

In the Soul he is immune from magic; his reasoning part cannot be touched by it, he cannot be perverted. But there is in him the unreasoning element which comes from the (material) All, and in this he can be affected, or rather this can be affected in him. Philtre-love, however, he will not know, for that would require the consent of the higher soul to the trouble stirred in the lower. And, just as the unreasoning element responds to the call of incantation, so the adept himself will dissolve those horrible powers by counter-incantations. Death, disease, any experience within the material sphere, these may result, yes; for anything that has membership in the All may be affected by another member, or by the universe of members; but the essential man is beyond harm.

That the effects of magic should be not instantaneous but developed is only in accord with Nature's way.

Even the Celestials, the Daimones, are not on their unreasoning side immune: there is nothing against ascribing acts of memory and experiences of sense to them, in supposing them to accept the traction of methods laid up in the natural order, and to give hearing to petitioners; this is especially true of those of them that are closest to this sphere, and in the degree of their concern about it.

For everything that looks to another is under spell to that: what we look to, draws us magically. Only the self-intent go free of magic. Hence every action has magic as its source, and the entire life of the practical man is a bewitchment: we move to that only which has wrought a fascination upon us. This is indicated where we read: 'for the burgher of great-hearted Erechtheus has a pleasant face' (but you should see him naked; then you would be cautious). For what conceivably turns a man to the external? He is drawn, drawn by the arts not of magicians but of the natural order which administers the deceiving draught and links this to that, not in local contact but in the fellowship of the philtre.

44. Contemplation alone stands untouched by magic; no man self-gathered falls to a spell; for he is one, and that unity is all he perceives, so that his reason is not beguiled but holds the due course, fashioning its own career and accomplishing its task.

In the other way of life, it is not the essential man that gives the impulse; it is not the reason; the unreasoning also acts as a principle, and finds its premises in emotion. Caring for children, planning marriage—everything that works as bait, taking value by dint of desire—these all tug obviously: so it is with our action, sometimes stirred, not reasonably, by a certain spirited temperament, sometimes as foolishly by greed; political interests, the siege of office, all betray a forth-summoning lust of power; action for security springs from fear; action for gain, from desire; action undertaken for the sake of sheer necessities—that is, for supplying the insufficiency of nature—indicates, manifestly, the cajoling force of nature to the safeguarding of life.

We may be told that no such magic underlies good action, since, at that, Contemplation itself, certainly a good action, implies a magic attraction.

The answer is that there is no magic when actions recognized as good are performed upon sheer necessity with the recollection that the veritable good is elsewhere; this is simply knowledge of need; it is not a bewitchment binding the life to this sphere or to any thing alien; all is permissible under duress of human nature, and in the spirit of adaptation to the needs of existence in general— or even to the needs of the individual existence, since it certainly seems reasonable to fit oneself into life rather than to withdraw from it.

When, on the contrary, the agent falls in love with what is good in those actions, and, cheated by the mere track and trace of the Authentic Good, makes them his own, then, in his pursuit of a lower good, he is the victim of magic. For all dalliance with what wears the mask of the authentic, all attraction towards that mere semblance, tells of a mind misled by the spell of forces pulling towards unreality.

The sorcery of Nature is at work in this; to pursue the non-good as a good, drawn in unreasoning impulse by its specious appearance: it is to be led unknowing down paths unchosen; and what can we call that but magic?

Alone in immunity from magic is he who, though drawn by the alien parts of his total being, withholds his assent to their standards of worth, recognizing the good only where his authentic self sees and knows it, neither drawn nor pursuing, but tranquilly possessing and so never charmed away.

45. From this discussion it becomes perfectly clear that the individual member of the All contributes to that All in the degree of its kind and condition; thus it acts and is acted upon. In any particular animal each of the limbs and organs, in the measure of its kind and purpose, aids the entire being by service performed and counts in rank and utility: it gives what is in its gift and takes from its fellows in the degree of receptive power belonging to its kind; there is something like a common sensitiveness linking the parts, and in the orders in which each of the

parts is also animate, each will have, in addition to its rank as part, the very particular functions of a living being.

We have learned, further, something of our human standing; we know that we too accomplish within the All a work not confined to the activity and receptivity of body in relation to body; we know that we bring to it that higher nature of ours, linked as we are by affinities within us towards the answering affinities outside us; becoming by our soul and the conditions of our kind thus linked—or, better, being linked by Nature—with our next highest in the celestial or daemonic realm, and thence onwards with those above the Celestials, we cannot fail to manifest our quality. Still, we are not all able to offer the same gifts or to accept identically: if we do not possess good, we cannot bestow it; nor can we ever purvey any good thing to one that has no power of receiving good. Anyone that adds his evil to the total of things is known for what he is and, in accordance with his kind, is pressed down into the evil which he has made his own, and hence, upon death, goes to whatever region fits his quality—and all this happens under the pull of natural forces.

For the good man, the giving and the taking and the changes of state go quite the other way; the particular tendencies of the nature, we may put it, transpose the cords (so that we are moved by that only which, in Plato's metaphor of the puppets, draws towards the best).

Thus this universe of ours is a wonder of power and wisdom, everything 'by a noiseless road' coming to pass 'according to a law' which none may elude—which the base man never conceives though it is leading him, all unknowingly, to that place in the All where his lot must be cast—which the just man knows, and, knowing, sets out to the place he must, understanding, even as he begins the journey, where he is to be housed at the end, and having the good hope that he will be with gods.

In a living being of small scope the parts vary but slightly, and have but a faint individual consciousness, and, unless possibly in a few and for a short time, are not themselves alive. But in a living universe, of high expanse, where every entity has vast scope and many of the members have life, there must be wider movement and greater changes. We see the sun and the moon and the other stars shifting place and course in an ordered progression. It is therefore within reason that the souls, also, should have their changes, not retaining unbrokenly the same quality, but ranged in some analogy with their action and experience—some taking rank as head and some as foot in a disposition consonant with the Universal Being which has its degrees in better and less good. A soul, which neither chooses the highest that is here, nor has lent itself to the lowest, is one which has abandoned another, a purer, place, taking this sphere in free election.

The punishments of wrongdoing are like the treatment of diseased parts of the body—here, medicines to knit sundered flesh; there, amputations; elsewhere, change of environment and condition—and the penalties are planned to bring health to the All by settling every member in the fitting place: and this health of the All requires that one man be made over anew and another, sick here, be taken hence to where he shall be weakly no longer.

NOTES TO ENNEAD IV.4

1. FIRST EDITION: ". . . for *nothing passes away, there is no change from old to new*."

ARMSTRONG supports the fourth edition. GUTHRIE: ". . . for each (of the essences of the intelligible world) are always present to the intelligence which is not obliged to go through them successively, passing from one to the other."

2. FIRST EDITION begins the paragraph as: "*This, however, does not alter the fact that distinction exists in that realm—downwards from the Supreme to the Ideas, upward from the Ideas to the Universal and to the Supreme. Admitting that the Highest, as a self-contained unity, has no outgoing effect, that does not prevent the soul which has attained to the Supreme from exerting its own characteristic Act: it certainly* may have the intuition . . ." MacKenna is alone in this interpretation.

3. FIRST EDITION has this paragraph as: "The explanation is that the unity of *this power (the Supreme) is such as to allow of its being multiple to another principle (the soul), to which it is all things and therefore does not present itself as one indivisible object of intuition: its activities do not (like its essence) fall under the rule of unity; they are for ever multiple in virtue of that abiding power, and in their outgoing they actually become all things.*

"*For with the Intellectual or Supreme—considered as distinct from the One—there is already the power of harbouring that Principle of Multiplicity, the source of things not previously existent in its superior.*"

ARMSTRONG: "The one power is one in such a way that it becomes many in something else, and does not comprehend all things by one act of intelligence. For its acts are individual, but always together in a power which remains unchanged, but is divided in other things. For that intelligible object is able in virtue of its not being one to receive in itself the nature of the many which did not previously exist."

GUTHRIE: "The potentiality which is One is one in such a manner that it is multiple when it is contemplated by another principle (Intelligence), because then it is not simultaneously all things in one single thought. Indeed, the actualizations (of Intelligence) are not a unity; but they are all produced by an ever permanent potentiality; they therefore become multiple in the other principles (the intelligibles); for Intelligence, not being unity itself, can receive within its breast the nature of the multiple which did not formerly exist (in the One)."

4. FIRST EDITION: ". . . he will know *all* to be *one thing* existing in virtue of one life for ever: *it is* in this sense *that the All is* unlimited, and *thus* Zeus' knowledge of *it* will not be as of something seen from outside but as of something embraced in true knowledge . . ."

GUTHRIE supports the first edition. ARMSTRONG: "Now he will know that his work is one and a single life for ever—this is how the number is unlimited—and will know the unity not externally, but in his work;"

5. FIRST EDITION: "... while *Nature's function is to engender*—of itself *though in* an act derived from *the* active principle *(of the soul)*."

GUTHRIE supports the first edition. ARMSTRONG: "but intellect itself is origin and activity which comes from the active principle itself."

6. FIRST EDITION: "... time is folded around what is in time exactly as—we read—*it is* folded about what is in place and in number."

GUTHRIE supports the first edition and also attributes, as MacKenna does, the "we read" to Plato. ARMSTRONG has "for time must encompass what is in time, as is the case, Aristotle says, with what is in place and number." Armstrong credits the reference to *Physics* Delta, 12, 221a18 and 28–30.

7. FIRST EDITION: "... we ask *whether* the earth has perceptions and sensations, and *if so through what vital members these would take place* and by what method:"

ARMSTRONG: "... we must go back to the question whether the earth has perceptions, and of what it has perceptions, and how long it has them."

GUTHRIE: "We must therefore first investigate if the earth possess senses, to what animals sensation naturally belongs, and how sensation operates."

8. FIRST EDITION: "... by *its lower* ..."

GUTHRIE: "other passions."

ARMSTRONG: "other affections."

9. FIRST EDITION: "... this could *not accompany* that ..."

ARMSTRONG supports the fourth edition. GUTHRIE interprets the thought as: "... mere possession of the faculty of sensation would not necessarily imply its exercise, because it would be entirely devoted to objects of a higher nature."

10. FIRST EDITION has this sentence as: "*Or* are we to think that *just as* that which bestows the vestige of the soul is [omits "again"—ed.] a distinct entity, *so we may reason in this case—the passionate element being one distinct thing, itself,* and not *deriving* from *any passionate* or percipient faculty?"

ARMSTRONG: "... and also [enquire—ed.] whether, if it is something else which gives it, the passionate power is the trace of soul, or whether here the passionate spirit is this one particular thing, no longer derived from a power of growth or perception."

GUTHRIE: "Is anger different from the principle which gives the body a trace of the soul, or is it an individual power, which depends on no other power, whether irascible or sensitive?"

11. FIRST EDITION: "... sensation ensues and the *soul, brought by means of the representative faculty* to partake in the condition of the affected body, is directed towards the cause of the pain: the reasoning soul, *in turn*, from its place above—*the phase not inbound with body*—acts in its own mode when *the* breach of order has become manifest to it: it calls in the alliance ..."

ARMSTRONG: "... a perception occurs, and the mental image puts the soul in touch with the state of the qualified body, and the soul launches itself against what has caused the pain; but on the other hand, the process can start from above: the reasoning soul, when a wrong appears, even if it is not a wrong which concerns the body, has that impassioned thing just described ready to hand and makes an ally of it ..."

GUTHRIE: "... there arises a sensation which arouses the imagination; the latter then instructs the soul of the state of the organism, and disposes the soul to attack what causes this suffering. On the other hand, when the reasonable soul judges that we have been injured, she grows excited, even if there were no disposition to anger in the body."

12. FIRST EDITION: "... merely *the sequel to some law (of our own nature)*, so ..."

ARMSTRONG: "One might of course say that one sees by convention, and that the so-called qualities are not in their substrates." In a footnote, Armstrong attributes this reference to the teaching of Democritus the Atomist, for whom "secondary qualities" exist only "by convention."

13. FIRST EDITION: "... as *seeking to do one thing and actually doing another*, for ..."

ARMSTRONG supports the fourth edition.

GUTHRIE : "He who plans the figures does not do one thing while busying Himself with another, because He is not acting on something different from Himself;"

14. FIRST EDITION: "... and therefore *its powers have many servitors.*"

GUTHRIE supports the first edition. ARMSTRONG supports the fourth.

15. FIRST EDITION: "... the true magic is *internal to the All, its attractions and, not less, its repulsions.*"

GUTHRIE: "The real magic is the Love that reigns in the universe, with its contrary of Hate."

ARMSTRONG: "... the true magic is the 'Love' and also the 'Strife' in the All."

16. FIRST EDITION: "... whose practitioners, *by the force of contact implant in others a new temperament, one favouring union as being informed with love; they knit ...*"

GUTHRIE: "By this art, magicians bring together the natures which have an innate love for each other; they unite one soul to another as one cross-fertilizes distant plants;"

ARMSTRONG: "... a magical art of love, used by those who apply by contact to different people different magical substances designed to draw them together and with a love-force implanted in them; they join ..."

17. FIRST EDITION: "... it purveys spontaneously, but it purveys also under spell; *some entity (acting like the healer) is concerned for a member situated within itself and summons the All which, then, pours in its gift; it gives to its own part by the natural law we have cited since* the petitioner is no alien *to it.*"

ARMSTRONG: "... the All gives to its parts, both spontaneously and if someone else magically attracts [its power] to a part of it; for it lies at the disposal of its parts by its own natural disposition, and so the one who makes the prayer is no alien." Brackets are Armstrong's.

GUTHRIE: "... the universe communicates to its parts something of its own power, either automatically, or as a result of the attraction exercised by the individual. This is a natural process, since he who asks is not foreign to it."

18. FIRST EDITION has this sentence as: "*There is, therefore, no necessity by ineluctable law that one who has helped himself to what lies open to all should receive his deserts then and there.*"

GUTHRIE: "Consequently, if an evil individual asks and obtains what is within reach of all, there is no reason why he should be punished."

ARMSTRONG: "... if someone takes what he ought not from what lies at the disposal of all, justice pursues him by an inevitable law."

FIFTH TRACTATE

Problems of the Soul (III); or, on Sight

1. We undertook to discuss the question whether sight is possible in the absence of any intervening medium, such as air or some other form of what is known as transparent body: this is the time and place.

It has been explained that seeing and all sense-perception can occur only through the medium of some bodily substance, since in the absence of body the Soul is utterly absorbed in the Intellectual Sphere. Sense-perception being the gripping not of the Intellectual but of the sensible alone, the Soul, if it is to form any relationship of knowledge, or of impression, with objects of sense, must be brought in some kind of contact with them by means of whatever may bridge the gap.

The knowledge, then, is realized by means of bodily organs: through these, which (in the embodied soul) are almost of one growth with it, being at least its continuations, it comes into something like unity with the sensible object, since this mutual approach brings about a certain degree of identity (which is the basis of knowledge).

Admitting, then, that some contact with an object is necessary for knowing it, the question of a medium falls to the ground in the case of things identified by any form of touch; but in the case of sight—we leave hearing over for the present—we are still in doubt; is there need of some bodily substance between the eye and the illumined object?

No: such an intervening material may accidentally impinge upon the vision, but essentially it adds nothing to seeing power.

Dense bodies, such as clay, actually prevent sight; the less material the intervening substance is the more clearly we see; the intervening substance, then, is a hindrance, or, if not that, at least not a help.

It will be objected that vision implies that whatever intervenes between seen and seer must first (and progressively) experience the object and be, as it were, shaped to it; we will be reminded that anyone standing in front of us and facing to the object sees it equally; we will be asked to deduce that if all the space intervening between seen and seer did not carry the impression of the object we could not receive it.

But all the need is met when the impression reaches that which is adapted to receive it; there is no need for the intervening space to be impressed. If it is, the impression will be of quite another order: the rod between the fisher's hand and the torpedo fish is not affected in the same way as the hand that feels the shock.

And yet there too, if rod and line did not intervene, the hand would not be affected—though even that may be questioned, since after all the fisherman, we are told, is numbed if the torpedo merely lies in his net.

The whole matter seems to bring us back to that sympathy of which we have treated. If a certain thing is of a nature to be sympathetically affected by another in virtue of some similitude between them, then anything intervening, not sharing in that similitude, will not be affected, or at least not similarly. If this be so, anything naturally disposed to be affected will take the impression more vividly in the absence of intervening substance, even of some substance capable, itself, of being affected.

2. If sight depends upon the linking of the light of vision with the light leading progressively to the illumined object, then by the very hypothesis one intervening substance, the light, is indispensable: but if the illuminated body, which is the object of vision, serves as an agent operating certain changes, some such change might very well impinge immediately upon the eye, requiring no medium; this all the more, since, as things are, the intervening substance, which actually does exist, is in some degree changed at the point of contact with the eye (and so cannot be in itself a requisite to vision).

Those who have made vision a forthgoing act (and not an incoming from the object) need not postulate an intervening substance—unless, indeed, to provide against the ray from the eye failing on its path—but this is a ray of light and light flies straight. Those who make vision depend upon resistance are obliged to postulate an intervening substance

The champions of the image, with its transit through a void, are seeking the way of least resistance; but since the entire absence of intervenient gives a still easier path they will not oppose that hypothesis.

So, too, those that explain vision by sympathy must recognize that an intervening substance will be a hindrance as tending to check or block or enfeeble that sympathy; this theory, especially, requires the admission that any intervenient, and particularly one of kindred nature, must blunt the perception by itself absorbing part of the activity. Apply fire to a body continuous through and through, and no doubt the core will be less affected than the surface: but where we are dealing with the sympathetic parts of one living being, there will scarcely be less sensation because of the intervening substance, or, if there should be, the degree of sensation will still be proportionate to the nature of the separate part, with the intervenient acting merely as a certain limitation; this, though, will not be the case where the element introduced is of a kind to overleap the bridge.

But this is saying that the sympathetic quality of the universe depends upon its being one living thing, and that our amenability to experience depends upon our belonging integrally to that unity; would it not follow that continuity is a condition of any perception of a remote object?

The explanation is that continuity and its concomitant, the bridging substance, come into play because a living being must be a continuous thing, but that, none the less, the receiving of impression is not an essentially necessary result of continuity; if it were, everything would receive such impression from everything else, and if thing is affected by thing in various separate orders, there can be no further question of any universal need of intervening substance.

Why it should be specially requisite in the act of seeing would have to be explained: in general, an object passing through the air does not affect it beyond dividing it; when a stone falls, the air simply yields; nor is it reasonable to explain the natural direction of movement by resistance; to do so would bring us to the absurdity that resistance accounts for the upward movement of fire, which, on the contrary, overcomes the resistance of the air by its own essentially quick energy. If we are told that the resistance is brought more swiftly into play by the very swiftness of the ascending body, that would be a mere accidental circumstance, not a cause of the upward motion: in trees the upthrust from the root depends on no such external propulsion; we, too, in our movements cleave the air and are in no wise forwarded by its resistance; it simply flows in from behind to fill the void we make.

If the severance of the air by such bodies leaves it unaffected, why must there be any severance before the images of sight can reach us?

And, further, once we reject the theory that these images reach us by way of some outstreaming from the objects seen, there is no reason to think of the air being affected and passing on to us, in a progression of impression, what has been impressed upon itself.

If our perception is to depend upon previous impressions made upon the air, then we have no direct knowledge of the object of vision, but know it only as through an intermediary, in the same way as we are aware of warmth where it is not the distant fire itself that warms us, but the warmed intervening air. That is a matter of contact; but sight is not produced by contact: the application of an object to the eye would not produce sight; what is required is the illumination of the intervening medium; for the air in itself is a dark substance. If it were not for this dark substance there would probably be no reason for the existence of light: the dark intervening matter is a barrier, and vision requires that it be overcome by light. Perhaps also the reason why an object brought close to the eye cannot be seen is that it confronts us with a double obscuration, its own and that of the air.

3. For the most convincing proof that vision does not depend upon the

transmission of impressions of any kind made upon the air, we have only to consider that in the darkness of night we can see a fire and the stars and their very shapes.

No one will pretend that these forms are reproduced upon the darkness and come to us in linked progression; if the fire thus rayed out its own form, there would be an end to the darkness. In the blackest night, when the very stars are hidden and show no gleam of their light, we can see the fire of the beacon-stations and of maritime signal-towers.

Now if, in defiance of all that the senses tell us, we are to believe that in these examples the fire (as light) traverses the air, then what the eye sees must be that dimmed reproduction in the air, not the clearness of the fire itself. But if an object can be seen on the other side of some intervening darkness, much more would it be visible with nothing intervening.

One point may no doubt be made: the impossibility of vision without an intervening substance does not depend upon that absence in itself: the sole reason is that, with that absence, there would be an end to the sympathy reigning in the living whole and relating the parts to each other in an existent unity.

Perception of every kind seems to depend on the fact that our universe is a living whole sympathetic to itself: that it is so, appears from the universal participation in power from member to member, and especially in remote power.

No doubt it would be worth inquiry—though we pass it for the present—what would take place if there were another cosmos, another living whole having no contact with this one, and 'the far ridges of our heavens' had sight: would our sphere see that other as from a mutually present distance, or could there be no dealing at all from this to that?

To return; there is a further consideration showing that sight is not brought about by this alleged modification of the intervenient.

Any modification of the air substance would necessarily be corporeal: there must be such an impression as is made upon sealing wax. But this would require that each part of the object of vision be impressed on some corresponding portion of the intervenient: the intervenient, however, in actual contact with the eye would be just that portion whose dimensions the pupil is capable of receiving. But as a matter of fact the entire object appears before the pupil; and it is seen entire by all within that air space for a great extent, in front, sideways, close at hand, from the back, as long as the line of vision is not blocked. This shows that any given portion of the air contains the object of vision, in face view so to speak, and, at once, we are confronted by no merely corporeal phenomena; the facts are explicable only as depending upon the greater laws, the spiritual, of a living being one and self-sensitive.

4. But there is the question of the linked light that must relate the visual organ to its object.

Now, firstly: since the intervening air is not necessary—unless in the purely accidental sense that air may be necessary to light—the light that acts as intermediate in vision will be unmodified: vision depends upon no modification whatever. This one intermediate, light, would seem to be necessary, but, unless light is corporeal, no intervening body is requisite: and we must remember that intervenient and borrowed light is essential not to seeing in general but to distant vision; the question whether light absolutely requires the presence of air we will discuss later. For the present one matter must occupy us:

If in the act of vision that linked light becomes ensouled, I if the Soul (or mind) permeates it and enters into union with it, as happens with the eye's interior light, then in the apprehending of the external object[1]—which is what vision really is I —the intervening light is not a necessity: the process of seeing will be like that of touch; the visual faculty of the Soul will perceive by the fact of having entered into the light; all that intervenes remains unaffected, serving simply as the field over which the vision ranges.

This brings up the question whether the sight is made active over its field by the sheer presence of a distance spread before it, or by the presence of a body of some kind within that distance.

If by the presence of such a body, then there will be vision though there be no intervenient; if the distance is the sole attractive agent, then we are forced to think of the visible object as being a kind utterly without energy, performing no act. But so inactive a body cannot be: touch tells us that, for it does not merely announce that something is by and is touched: it is acted upon by the object so that it reports distinguishing qualities in it, qualities so effective that even at a distance touch itself would register them but for the accidental that it demands proximity.

We catch the heat of a fire just as soon as the intervening air does; no need to wait for it to be warmed: the denser body, in fact, takes in more warmth than the air has to give; in other words, the air transmits the heat but is not the source of our warmth.

When on the one side, that of the object, there is the power in any degree of an outgoing act, and on the other, that of the sight, the capability of being acted upon, surely the object needs no medium through which to be effective upon what it is fully equipped to affect: this would be needing not a help but a hindrance.

Or, again, consider the Dawn: there is no need that the light first flood the air and then come to us; the event is simultaneous to both: often, in fact, we see (in the distance) when the light is not as yet round our eyes at all but very far off, before, that is, the air has been acted upon: here we have vision without any modified intervenient, vision before the organ has received the light with which it is to be linked.

It is difficult to reconcile with this theory the fact of seeing stars or any fire by night.

If (as by the theory of an intervenient) the percipient mind or soul remains within itself and needs the light only as one might need a stick in the hand to touch something at a distance, then the perception will be a sort of tussle: the light must be conceived as something thrusting, something aimed at a mark, and similarly, the object, considered as an illuminated thing, must be conceived to be resistant; for this is the normal process in the case of contact by the agency of an intervenient.

Besides, even on this explanation, the mind must have previously been in contact with the object in the entire absence of intervenient; only if that has happened could contact through an intervenient bring knowledge, a knowledge by way of memory, and, even more emphatically, by way of reasoned comparison (ending in identification): but this process of memory and comparison is excluded by the theory of first knowledge through the agency of a medium.

Finally, we may be told that the impinging light is modified by the thing to be seen and so becomes able to present something perceptible before the visual organ; but this simply brings us back to the theory of an intervenient changed midway by the object, an explanation whose difficulties we have already indicated.

5. But some doubt arises when we consider the phenomena of hearing.

Perhaps we are to understand the process thus: the air is modified by the first movement; layer by layer it is successively acted upon by the object causing the sound; it finally impinges in that modified form upon the sense, the entire progression being governed by the fact that all the air from starting point to hearing point is similarly affected.

Perhaps, on the other hand, the intervenient is modified only by the accident of its midway position, so that, failing any intervenient, whatsoever sound two bodies in clash might make would impinge without medium upon our sense?

Still, air is necessary; there could be no sound in the absence of the air set vibrating in the first movement, however different be the case with the intervenient from that onwards to the perception point.

The air would thus appear to be the dominant in the production of sound: two bodies would clash without even an incipient sound, but that the air, struck in their rapid meeting and hurled outward, passes on the movement successively till it reaches the ears and the sense of hearing.

But if the determinant is the air, and the impression is simply of air-movements, what accounts for the differences among voices and other sounds? The sound of bronze against bronze is different from that of bronze against some other substance: and so on; the air and its vibration remain the one thing, yet the difference in sounds is much more than a matter of greater or less intensity.

If we decide that sound is caused by a percussion upon the air, then obviously nothing turning upon the distinctive nature of air is in question: it sounds at a moment in which it is simply a solid body, until (by its distinctive character) it is sent pulsing outwards: thus air in itself is not essential to the production of sound; all is done by clashing solids as they meet and that percussion, reaching the sense, is the sound. This is shown also by the sounds formed within living beings not in air but by the friction of parts; for example, the grinding of teeth and the crunching of bones against each other in the bending of the body, cases in which the air does not intervene.

But all this may now be left over; we are brought to the same conclusion as in the case of sight; the phenomena of hearing arise similarly in a certain co-sensitiveness inherent in a living whole.

6. We return, then, to the question whether there could be light if there were no air, the sun illuminating corporeal surfaces across an intermediate void which, as things are, takes the light accidentally by the mere fact of being in the path. Supposing air to be the cause of the rest of things being thus affected, the substantial existence of light is due to the air; light becomes a modification of the air, and of course if the thing to be modified did not exist neither could the modification.

The fact is that primarily light is no appanage of air, and does not depend upon the existence of air: it belongs to every fiery and shining body, it constitutes even the gleaming surface of certain stones.

Now if, thus, it enters into other substances from something gleaming, could it exist in the absence of its container?

There is a distinction to be made: if it is a quality, some quality of some substance, then light, equally with other qualities, will need a body in which to lodge: if, on the contrary, it is an activity rising from something else, we can surely conceive it existing, though there be no neighbouring body but, if that is possible, a blank void which it will overleap and so appear on the farther side: it is powerful, and may very well pass over unhelped. If it were of a nature to fall, nothing would keep it up, certainly not the air or anything that takes its light; there is no reason why they should draw the light from its source and speed it onwards.

Light is not an accidental to something else, requiring therefore to be lodged in a base; nor is it a modification, demanding a base in which the modification occurs: if this were so, it would have to remain with whatever object might fall within its path; but it does not; it must come, therefore, as easily as it vanishes.

But where can it be?

Space, pure and simple, is all that it needs.

With unchecked motion of the light outward, the material sun will be losing its energy, for the light is its expression.

Perhaps; but then no other object can possess it. The expressive Act proceeds from a base but does not seek to enter into a base, though having some operation upon any base that may be present.

Life is also an Act, the Act of the Soul, and it remains so when anything—the human body, for instance—comes in its path to be affected by it; and it is equally an Act though there be nothing for it to modify: surely this may be true of light, if we may regard it as the characteristic Act of the luminary source. Certainly light is not brought into being by the dark thing, air, which on the contrary tends to gloom it over with some touch of earth so that it is no longer the brilliant reality: as reasonable to talk of some substance being sweet because it is mixed with something bitter.

If we are told that light is a mode of the air, we answer that this would necessarily imply that the air itself is changed to produce the new mode; in other words, its characteristic darkness must change into non-darkness; but we know that the air maintains its character, in no wise affected: the modification of a thing is an experience within that thing itself: light therefore is not a modification of the air, but a self-existent in whose path the air happens to be present.

On this point we need dwell no longer; but there remains still a question.

7. Our investigation may be furthered by inquiring: Whether light finally perishes or simply returns to its source.

If it be a thing requiring to be caught and kept, domiciled within a recipient, we might think of it finally passing out of existence: if it be an Act not flowing out and away—but in a circuit, with more of it within than is in outward progress from the luminary of which it is the Act—then it will not cease to exist as long as that centre is in being. And as the luminary moves, the light will reach new points—not in virtue of any change of course in or out or around, but simply because the Act of the luminary exists and where there is no impediment is effective. Even if the distance of the sun from us were far greater than it is, the light would be continuous all that further way, as long as nothing checked or blocked it in the interval.

We distinguish two forms of activity; one is gathered within the luminary and is comparable to the life of the shining body; this is the vaster and is, as it were, the foundation or wellspring of all the act; the other lies next to the surface, the outer image of the inner content, a secondary activity though inseparable from the former. For every existent has an Act which is in its likeness: as long as the one exists, so does the other; yet while the original is stationary the activity reaches forth, in some things over a wide range, in others less far. There are weak and faint activities, and there are some, even, that do not appear; but there are also things whose activities are great and far-going; in the case of these the activity must be thought of as being lodged, both in the active and powerful source and in the point at which it settles. This may be observed in the case of an animal's eyes where the pupils gleam: they have a light which shows outside the orbs. Again there are living things which have an inner fire that in darkness shines out when they expand themselves and ceases to ray outward when they contract: the fire has not perished; it is a mere matter of it being rayed out or not.

But has the light gone inward?

No: it is simply no longer on the outside because the fire (of which it is the activity) is no longer outward-going but has withdrawn towards the centre.

But surely the light has gone inward too?

No: only the fire, and when that goes inward the surface consists only of the non-luminous body; the fire can no longer act towards the outer.

The light, then, raying from bodies is an outgoing activity of a luminous body; the light within luminous bodies—understand, such as are primarily luminous—is the essential being embraced under the Form of that body. When such a body is brought into association with Matter, its activity produces colour: when there is no such association it does not give colour—it gives merely an incipient on which colour might be formed—for it belongs to another being (primal light) with which it retains its link, unable to desert from it, or from its (inner) activity.

And light is incorporeal even when it is the light of a body; there is therefore no question, strictly speaking, of its withdrawal or of its being present—these terms do not apply to its modes—and its essential existence is to be an activity. As an example: the image upon a mirror may be described as an activity exercised by the reflected object upon the potential recipient: there is no outgoing from the object (or ingoing into the reflecting body); it is simply that, as long as the object stands there, the image also is visible, in the form of colour shaped to a certain pattern, and when the object is not there, the reflecting surface no longer holds what it held when the conditions were favourable.

So it is with the soul considered as the activity of another and prior soul: as long as that prior retains its place, its next, which is its activity, abides.

But what of a soul which is not an activity but the derivative of an activity—

as we maintained the life-principle domiciled in the body to be—is its presence similar to that of the light caught and held in material things?

No; for in those things the colour is due to an actual intermixture of the active element (the light being alloyed with Matter); whereas the life-principle of the body is something that holds from another soul closely present to it.

But when the body perishes—by the fact that nothing without part in soul can continue in being—when the body is perishing, no longer supported by that primal life-giving soul, or by the presence of any secondary phase of it, it is clear that the life-principle can no longer remain; but does this mean that the life perishes?

No: not even it; for it, too, is an image of that first out-shining; it is merely no longer where it was.

8. Imagine that beyond the heavenly system there existed some solid mass, and that from this sphere there was directed to it a vision utterly unimpeded and unrestricted: it is a question whether that solid form could be perceived by what has no sympathetic relation with it, since we have held that sympathetic relation comes about in virtue of the nature inherent in some one living being.

Obviously, if the sympathetic relationship depends upon the fact that percipients and things perceived are all members of one living being, no acts of perception could take place: that far body could be known only if it were a member of this living universe of ours—which condition being met, it certainly would be. But what if, without being thus in membership, it were a corporeal entity, exhibiting light and colour and the qualities by which we perceive things, and belonging to the same ideal category (having the same specific character) as the organ of vision?

If our supposition (of perception by sympathy) is true, there would still be no perception—though we may be told that the hypothesis is clearly untenable since there is absurdity in supposing that sight can fail in grasping an illuminated object lying before it, and that the other senses in the presence of their particular objects remain unresponsive. **|** [2] **|**

But why does such a failing appear impossible to us? We answer: because here and now in all the act and experience of our senses, we are within a unity, and members of it. What the conditions would be otherwise, remains to be considered: if living sympathy suffices the theory is established; if not, there are other considerations to support it.

That every living being is self-sensitive allows of no doubt; if we are concerned with a living being, no more need be said; and what is true of the total must be true of the members, as inbound in that one life.

But what if we are invited to accept the theory of knowledge by likeness (rejecting knowledge by the self-sensitiveness of a living unity)?

Awareness must be determined by the nature and character of the living being in which it occurs; perception, then, means that the likeness demanded by the hypothesis is within this self-identical living being—for the organ by which the perception takes place is in the likeness of the object perceived: thus perception is reduced to a mental awareness by means of organs akin to the object.

If, then, something that is a living whole perceives not its own content but things like to its content, it must perceive them under the conditions of that living whole; this means that, in so far as it has perception, the objects appear not as its content but as related to its content.

And the objects are thus perceived as related because the mind itself has related them in order to make them amenable to its handling: in other words, the causative soul or mind in that other sphere is utterly alien, and the things there, supposed to be related to the content of this living whole, can be nothing to our minds.

This absurdity shows that the hypothesis contains a contradiction which naturally leads to untenable results. In fact, under one and the same heading, it presents mind and no mind, it makes things kin and no kin, it confuses similar and dissimilar: containing these irreconcilable elements, it amounts to no hypothesis at all. It even supposes that the mind is in that external object, and therefore tells of an All which is not all, of a something which is at once distinct and not distinct, of a nothingness which is no nothingness, of a complete thing that is incomplete: the hypothesis therefore must be dismissed; no deduction is possible where a thesis cancels its own propositions.

NOTES TO ENNEAD IV.5

1. FIRST EDITION: "... if the *soul or mind* permeates it and enters into union with it, as *it does in its more inward acts such as understanding*—which is what vision really is ..."

   ARMSTRONG: "... and the soul moves through it and is present in it, as it is also the case with the light within the eye, then of course in the apprehension of the object, which is what seeing is ..."

   GUTHRIE: "... if the soul should, so to speak, interpenetrate it, uniting with it as she unites with the interior light, there would be no need of intermediary light for the perception of the visible object."

   COMMENT: Note that neither Armstrong nor Guthrie characterizes the object (as Page does in the fourth edition) as "external."

2. FIRST EDITION introduces the next six paragraphs, there in brackets, with the following parenthetical remark: "The following passage, to nearly the end, is offered tentatively as a possible help to the interpretation of an obscure and corrupt place." Armstrong's long footnote (page 315 of volume IV of the Loeb Classical Library edition) is interesting.

SIXTH TRACTATE

Perception and Memory

1. Perceptions are no imprints, we have said, are not to be thought of as seal-impressions on soul or mind: accepting this statement, there is one theory of memory which must be definitely rejected.

Memory is not to be explained as the retaining of information in virtue of the lingering of an impression which in fact was never made; the two things stand or fall together; either an impression is made upon the mind and lingers when there is remembrance, or, denying the impression, we cannot hold that memory is its lingering. Since we reject equally the impression and the retention we are obliged to seek for another explanation of perception and memory, one excluding the notions that the sensible object striking upon soul or mind makes a mark upon it, and that the retention of this mark is memory.

If we study what occurs in the case of the most vivid form of perception, we can transfer our results to the other cases, and so solve our problem.

In any perception we attain by sight, the object is grasped there where it lies in the direct line of vision; it is there that we attack it; there, then, the perception is formed; the mind looks outward; this is ample proof that it has taken and takes no inner imprint, and does not see in virtue of some mark made upon it like that of the ring on the wax; it need not look outward at all if, even as it looked, it already held the image of the object, seeing by virtue of an impression made upon itself. It includes with the object the interval, for it tells at what distance the vision takes place: how could it see as outlying an impression within itself, separated by no interval from itself? Then, the point of magnitude: how could the mind, on this hypothesis, define the external size of the object or perceive that it has any—the magnitude of the sky, for instance, whose stamped imprint would be too vast for it to contain? And, most convincing of all, if to see is to accept imprints of the objects of our vision, we can never see these objects themselves; we see only vestiges they leave within us, shadows: the things themselves would be very different from our vision of them. And, for a conclusive consideration, we cannot see if the living object is in contact with the eye; we must look from a certain distance; this must be more applicable to the mind; supposing the mind to be stamped with an imprint of the object, it could not grasp as an object of vision what is stamped upon itself. For vision demands a duality, of seen and seeing: the seeing agent must be distinct and act upon an impression outside it, not upon one occupying the same point with it: sight can deal only with an object not inset but outlying.

2. But if perception does not go by impression, what is the process?

The mind affirms something not contained within it: this is precisely the characteristic of a power—not to accept impression but, within its allotted sphere, to act.

Besides, the very condition of the mind being able to exercise discrimination upon what it is to see and hear is not, of course, that these objects be equally impressions made upon it; on the contrary, there must be no impressions, nothing to which the mind is passive; there can be only acts of that in which the objects become known.

Our tendency is to think of any of the faculties as unable to know its appropriate object by its own uncompelled act; to us it seems to submit to its environment rather than simply to perceive it, though in reality it is the master, not the victim.

As with sight, so with hearing. It is the air which takes the impression, a kind of articulated stroke which may be compared to letters traced upon it by the object causing the sound; but it belongs to the faculty, and the soul-essence, to read the imprints thus appearing before it, as they reach the point at which they become matter of its knowledge.

In taste and smell also we distinguish between the impressions received and the sensations and judgements; these last are mental acts, and belong to an order apart from the experiences upon which they are exercised.

The knowing of the things belonging to the Intellectual is not in any such degree attended by impact or impression: they come forward, on the contrary, as from within, unlike the sense-objects known as from without: they have more emphatically the character of Acts; they are Acts in the stricter sense, for their origin is in the Soul, and every concept of this Intellectual order is the Soul about its Act.

Whether, in this self-vision, the Soul is a duality and ❙ views itself as from the outside, whereas the Intellectual-Principle is a unity, or whether, in the first case as in the second, the duality of subject and object is resolved in[1] a unity— this question is investigated elsewhere. ❙

3. With this prologue we come to our discussion of Memory.

That the Soul, or mind, having taken no imprint, yet achieves perception of what it in no way contains need not surprise us; or rather, surprising though it is, we cannot refuse to believe in this remarkable power.

The Soul is in its essential nature the Reason-Principle of all things; it is ❙ ultimate[2] ❙ among Intellectual Beings and the ❙ ultimate[2] ❙ Reason-Principle of the Beings of the Intellectual Realm, and it is the primal Reason-Principle of the entire realm of sense.

Thus it has dealings with both orders—benefited and quickened by the one, but by the other beguiled, falling before resemblances, and so led downwards as under spell. Poised midway, it is aware of both spheres.

Of the Intellectual it is said to have intuition by memory upon approach, for it knows them by a certain natural identity with them; its knowledge is not attained by besetting them, so to speak, but by in a definite degree possessing them; they are its natural vision; they are itself in a more radiant mode, and it rises from its duller pitch to that greater brilliance in a sort of awakening, a progress from its latency to its Act.

To the sense-order it stands in a similar nearness and to such things it gives a radiance out of its own store and, as it were, elaborates them to visibility: the power is always ripe and, so to say, in travail towards them, so that, whenever it puts out its strength in the direction of what has once been present in it, it sees that object as present still; and the more intent its effort the more durable is the presence. This is why, it is agreed, children are better at remembering; the things presented to them are not constantly withdrawn but remain in sight; in their case the attention is still limited and not scattered: those whose faculty and mental activity are busied upon a multitude of subjects pass quickly over all, lingering on none.

Now, if memory were a matter of seal-impressions retained, the multiplicity of objects would have no weakening effect on the memory. Further, on the same hypothesis, we would have no need of thinking back to revive remembrance; nor would we be subject to forgetting and recalling; all would lie engraved within.

The very fact that we train ourselves to remember shows that what we get by the process is a strengthening of the mind: just so, exercises for feet and hands enable us to do easily acts which are in no sense contained or laid up in those members, but to which they may be fitted by persevering effort.

How else can it be explained that we forget a thing heard once or twice but remember what is often repeated, and that we recall a long time afterwards what at first hearing we failed to hold?

It is no answer to say that the parts present themselves sooner than the entire imprint—why should they too be forgotten?—(there is no question of parts, for) the last hearing, or our effort to remember, brings the thing back to us in a flash.

All these considerations testify to an evocation of that faculty of the Soul, or mind, in which remembrance is vested: the mind is strengthened, either generally or to this particular purpose.

Observe these facts: memory follows upon attention; those who have memorized much, by dint of their training in the use of leading indications (suggestive words and the like), reach the point of being easily able to retain without such aid: must we not conclude that the basis of memory is the soul-power brought to full strength?

The lingering imprints of the other explanation would tell of weakness rather than power; for to take imprint easily is to be yielding. An impression is something received passively; the strongest memory, then, would go with the least active nature. But what happens is the very reverse: in no pursuit do technical exercises tend to make a man less the master of his acts and states. It is as with sense-perception; the advantage is not to the weak, the weak eye for example, but to that which has the fullest power towards its exercise. In the old, it is significant, the senses are dulled and so is the memory.

Sensation and memory, then, are not passivity but power.

And, once it is admitted that sensations are not impressions, the memory of a sensation cannot consist in the retention of an impression that was never made.

Yes: but if it is an active power of the mind, a fitness towards its particular purpose, why does it not come at once—and not with delay—to the recollection of its unchanging objects?

Simply because the power needs to be poised and prepared: in this it is only like all the others, which have to be readied for the task to which their power reaches, some operating very swiftly, others only after a certain self-concentration.

Quick memory does not in general go with quick wit: the two do not fall under the same mental faculty; runner and boxer are not often united in one person; the dominant Idea differs from man to man.

Yet there could be nothing to prevent men of superior faculty from reading impressions on the mind; why should one thus gifted be incapable of what would be no more than a passive taking and holding?

❙ In general Soul is faculty (and not receptivity), as is evident from its lack of extension (its immateriality).[3]❙

And—one general reflection—it is not extraordinary that everything concerning soul should proceed in quite other ways than appears to people who either have never inquired, or have hastily adopted delusive analogies from the phenomena of sense, and persist in thinking of perception and remembrance in terms of characters inscribed on plates or tablets; the impossibilities that beset this theory escape those that make the Soul incorporeal equally with those to whom it is corporeal.

NOTES TO ENNEAD IV.6

1. FIRST EDITION: "... views itself as from the outside—*while seeing the Intellectual-Principle as a unity, and itself with the Intellectual-Principle* as a unity—this question is investigated elsewhere."

ARMSTRONG: "But we discuss elsewhere whether the soul sees itself as two and as another, but Intellect is one, or whether both the dualities are one."

GUTHRIE: "We shall however have to relegate to another place the question whether the soul sees herself as double, contemplating herself as another object, so to speak, and whether she sees intelligence as single in a manner such that both herself and intelligence seem but one."

COMMENT: Armstrong says that the "elsewhere" is probably V.6.1–2; Guthrie suggests V.3.

2. Reference to other translations shows that "ultimate" in this context clearly means "last" and/or "lowest."

3. FIRST EDITION has sentence as: "*That memory is a power of the Soul (not a capacity for taking imprint) is established at a stroke by the consideration that the soul is without magnitude.*"

GUTHRIE supports the first edition; ARMSTRONG supports the fourth.

SEVENTH TRACTATE

The Immortality of the Soul

1. Whether every human being is immortal or we are wholly destroyed, or whether something of us passes over to dissolution and destruction, while something else, that which is the true man, endures for ever—this question will be answered here for those willing to investigate our nature.

We know that man is not a thing of one only element; he has a Soul and he has, whether instrument or adjunct in some other mode, a body: this is the first distinction; it remains to investigate the nature and essential being of these two constituents.

Reason tells us that the body as, itself too, a composite, cannot for ever hold together; and our senses show us it breaking up, wearing out, the victim of destructive agents of many kinds, each of its constituents going its own way, one part working against another, perverting, wrecking, and this especially when the material masses are no longer presided over by the reconciling Soul.

And when each single constituent is taken as a thing apart, it is still not a unity; for it is divisible into shape and matter, the duality without which bodies at their very simplest cannot cohere.

The mere fact that, as material forms, they have bulk means that they can be lopped and crushed and so come to destruction.

If this body, then, is really a part of us, we are not wholly immortal; if it is an instrument of ours, then, as a thing put at our service for a certain time, it must be in its nature passing.

The sovran principle, the authentic man, will be as Form to this Matter or as agent to this instrument, and thus, whatever that relation be, the Soul is the man.

2. But of what nature is this sovran principle?

If material, then definitely it must fall apart; for every material entity, at least, is something put together.

If it is not material but belongs to some other Kind, that new substance must be investigated in the same way or by some more suitable method.

But our first need is to discover into what this material form, since such the Soul is to be, can dissolve.

Now: of necessity life is inherent to soul: this material entity, then, which we call soul must have life ingrained within it; but (being a composite, as by hypothesis material) it must be made up of two or more bodies; that life, then, will be vested, either in each and all of those bodies or in one of them to the exclusion of the other or others; if this be not so, then there is no life present anywhere.

If any one of them contains this ingrained life, that one is the Soul. But what sort of an entity have we there; what is this body which of its own nature possesses soul?

Fire, air, water, earth, are in themselves soulless—whenever soul is in any of them, that life is borrowed—and there are no other forms of body than these four: even the school that believes there are has always held them to be bodies, not souls, and to be without life.

None of these, then, having life, it would be extraordinary if life came about by bringing them together; it is impossible, in fact, that the collocation of material entities should produce life, or mindless entities mind.

No one, moreover, would pretend that a mere chance mixing could give such results: some regulating principle would be necessary, some cause directing the admixture: that guiding principle would be—soul.

Body—not merely because it is a composite, but even were it simplex—could not exist unless there were soul in the universe, for body owes its being to the entrance of a Reason-Principle into Matter, and only from soul can a Reason-Principle come.

3. Anyone who rejects this view, and holds that either atoms or some entities void of part coming together produce soul, is refuted by the very unity of soul and by the prevailing sympathy as much as by the very coherence of the

constituents. Bodily materials, in nature repugnant to unification and to sensation, could never produce unity or self-sensitiveness, and soul is self-sensitive. And, again, constituents void of part could never produce body or bulk.

Perhaps we will be asked to consider body as a simple entity (disregarding the question of any constituent elements): they will tell us, then, that no doubt, as purely material, it cannot have a self-springing life—since matter is without quality—but that life is introduced by the fact that the Matter is brought to order under Forming-Idea. But if by this Forming-Idea they mean an essential, a real being, then it is not the conjoint of body and Idea that constitutes soul: it must be one of the two items and that one, being (by hypothesis) outside of the Matter, cannot be body: to make it body would simply force us to repeat our former analysis.

If on the contrary they do not mean by this Forming-Idea a real being, but some condition or modification of the Matter, they must tell us how and whence this modification, with resultant life, can have found the way into the Matter: for very certainly Matter does not mould itself to pattern or bring itself to life.

It becomes clear that since neither Matter nor body in any mode has this power, life must be brought upon the stage by some directing principle external and transcendent to all that is corporeal.

In fact, body itself could not exist in any form if soul-power did not: body passes; dissolution is in its very nature; all would disappear in a twinkling if all were body. It is no help to erect some one mode of body into soul; made of the same Matter as the rest, this soul-body would fall under the same fate: of course it could never really exist: the universe of things would halt at the material, failing something to bring Matter to shape.

Nay more: Matter itself could not exist: the totality of things in this sphere is dissolved if it be made to depend upon the coherence of a body which, though elevated to the nominal rank of 'soul', remains air, fleeting breath (the Stoic pneuma, rarefied matter, 'spirit' in the lower sense), whose very unity is not drawn from itself.

All bodies are in ceaseless process of dissolution; how can the Cosmos be made over to any one of them without being turned into a senseless haphazard drift? This pneuma—orderless except under soul—how can it contain order, reason, intelligence? But: given soul, all these material things become its collaborators towards the coherence of the Cosmos and of every living being, all the qualities of all the separate objects converging to the purposes of the universe: failing soul in the things of the universe, they could not even exist, much less play their ordered parts.

4. Our opponents themselves are driven by stress of fact to admit the necessity

of a prior to body, a higher thing, some phase or form of soul; their 'pneuma' (finer-body or spirit) is intelligent, and they speak of an 'intellectual fire'; this 'fire' and 'spirit' they imagine to be necessary to the existence of the higher order which they conceive as demanding some base, though the real difficulty, under their theory, is to find a base for material things whose only possible base is, precisely, the powers of soul.

Besides, if they make life and soul no more than this 'pneuma', what is the import of that repeated qualification of theirs 'in a certain state', their refuge when they are compelled to recognize some acting principle apart from body? If not every pneuma is a soul, but thousands of them soulless, and only the pneuma in this 'certain state' is soul, what follows? Either this 'certain state', this shaping or configuration of things, is a real being or it is nothing.

If it is nothing, only the pneuma exists, the 'certain state' being no more than a word; this leads imperatively to the assertion that Matter alone exists, Soul and God I and everything else without exception[1] I mere words, the lowest alone is.

If on the contrary this 'configuration' is really existent—something distinct from the underlie or Matter, something residing in Matter but itself immaterial as not constructed out of Matter, then it must be a Reason-Principle, incorporeal, a separate nature.

There are other equally cogent proofs that the soul cannot be any form of body.

Body is either warm or cold, hard or soft, liquid or solid, black or white, and so on through all the qualities by which one is different from another; and again if a body is warm it diffuses only warmth, if cold it can only chill, if light its presence tells against the total weight which if heavy it increases; black, it darkens; white, it lightens; fire has not the property of chilling or a cold body that of warming.

Soul, on the contrary, operates diversely in different living beings, and has quite contrary effects in any one: its productions contain the solid and the soft, the dense and the sparse, bright and dark, heavy and light. If it were material, its quality—and the colour it must have—would produce one invariable effect and not the variety actually observed.

5. Again, there is movement: all bodily movement is uniform; failing an incorporeal soul, how account for diversity of movement? Predilections, reasons, they will say; that is all very well, but these already contain that variety and therefore cannot belong to body which is one and simplex, and, besides, is not participant in reason—that is, not in the sense here meant, but only as it is influenced by some principle which confers upon it the qualities of, for instance, being warm or cold.

Then there is growth under a time-law, and within a definite limit: how can this belong strictly to body? Body can indeed be brought to growth, but cannot induce growth except in the sense that the material mass may include a capacity to serve the principle whose action upon the body causes growth.

Supposing the soul to be at once a body and the cause of growth, then, if it is to keep pace with the substance it augments, it too must grow; that means it must add to itself a similar bodily material. For the added material must be either soul or soulless body: if soul, whence and how does it enter, and by what process is it adjoined (to the soul which by hypothesis is body); if soulless, how does such an addition become soul, falling into accord with its precedent, making one thing with it, sharing the stored impressions and notions of that initial soul instead, rather, of remaining an alien ignoring all the knowledge laid up before?

Would not such a soulless addition be subject to just such loss and gain of substance, in fact to the non-identity, which marks the rest of our material mass?

And if this were so, how explain our memories of our recognition of familiar things when we have no stably identical soul?

Assume soul to be a body: now in the nature of body, characteristically divisible, no one of the parts can be identical with the entire being; soul, then, is a thing of defined size, and if curtailed must cease to be what it is; in the nature of a quantitative entity this must be so, for if a thing of magnitude on diminution retains its identity in virtue of its quality, this is only saying that bodily and quantitatively it is different even if its identity consists in a quality quite independent of quantity.

What answer can be made by those declaring soul to be corporeal? Is every part of the soul, in any one body, soul entire, soul perfectly true to its essential being? and may the same be said of every part of the part? If so, the magnitude makes no contribution to the soul's essential nature, as it must if soul (as corporeal) were a definite magnitude: it is, as body cannot be, present as a whole in many places, a complete identity at each and every point, the part all that the whole is.

To deny that every part is soul is to make soul a compound from soulless elements. Further, if a definite magnitude, the double limit of larger or smaller, is to be imposed upon each separate soul, then anything outside those limits is no soul.

Now, a single coition and a single sperm suffice to a twin birth or in the animal order to a litter; there is a splitting and diverging of the seed, every diverging part being obviously a whole: surely no honest mind can fail to gather that a thing in which part is identical with whole has a nature which transcends quantity, and must of necessity be without quantity: only so could it remain identical when quantity is filched from it, only by being indifferent to amount or extension, by being in essence something apart. Thus the Soul and the Reason-Principles are without quantity.

6. It is easy to show that if the Soul were a corporeal entity, there could be no sense-perception, no mental act, no knowledge, no moral excellence, nothing of all that is noble.

There can be no perception without a unitary percipient whose identity enables it to grasp an object as an entirety.

The several senses will each be the entrance point of many diverse perceptions; in any one object there may be many characteristics; any one organ may be the channel of a group of objects, as for instance a face is known not by a special sense for separate features, nose, eyes, &c., but by one sense observing all in one act.

When sight and hearing gather their varying information, there must be some central unity to which both report. How could there be any statement of difference unless all sense-impressions appeared before a common identity able to take the sum of all?

This there must be, as there is a centre to a circle; the sense-impressions converging from every point of occurrence will be as lines striking from a circumference to what will be a true centre of perception as being a veritable unity.

If this centre were to break into separate points—so that the sense-impressions fell upon the two ends of a line—then, either it must reknit itself to unity and identity, perhaps at the mid-point of the line, or all remains unrelated, every end receiving the report of its particular field exactly as you and I have our distinct sense-experiences.

Suppose the sense-object be such a unity as a face: all the points of observation must be brought together in one visual total, as is obvious since there could be no panorama of great expanses unless the detail were compressed to the capacity of the pupils. I Much more must this be true when the sense-objects impinge upon the centre of consciousness in the guise of indivisible thoughts. Either the object is unified or—supposing it to have quantity and extension—the centre of consciousness must² coincide with it I point by point of their co-expansion so that any given point in the faculty will perceive solely what coincides with it in the object: and thus nothing in us could perceive any thing as a whole.

This cannot be: the faculty entire must be a unity; no such dividing is possible; this is no matter in which we can think of equal sections coinciding; the centre of consciousness has no such relation of equality with any sensible object. The only possible ratio of divisibility would be that of the number of diverse elements in the impinging sensation: are we then to suppose that each part of the soul, and every part of each part, will have perception? Or will the part of the parts have none? That is impossible: every part, then, has perception; the (hypothetical) magnitude, of soul and each part of soul, is infinitely divisible; there will therefore be in each part an infinite number of perceptions of the object, and therefore an infinitude of representations of it at our centre of consciousness.

If the sentient be a material entity (as we are invited to believe), sensation could only be of the order of seal-impressions struck by a ring on wax, in this case by sensible objects on the blood or on the air.

If, at this, the impression is like one made in liquids—as would be reasonable—it will be confused and wavering as upon water, and there can be no memory. If the impressions are permanent, then either no fresh ones can be stamped upon the occupied ground—and there can be no change of sensations—or, others being made, the former will be obliterated; and all record of the past is done away with.

If memory implies fresh sensations imposed upon former ones, the earlier not barring their way, the Soul cannot be a material entity.

7. We come to the same result by examining the sense of pain. We say there is pain in the finger: the trouble is doubtless in the finger, but our opponents must admit that the sensation of the pain is in the centre of consciousness. The suffering member is one thing, the sense of suffering is another: the entire soul is involved: how does this happen?

By transmission, they will say: the psychic pneuma (= the semi-material principle of life) stationed at the finger suffers first; and stage by stage the trouble is passed on until at last it reaches the centre of consciousness.

But on this theory, there must be a sensation in the spot first suffering pain, and another sensation at a second point of the line of transmission, another in the third, and so on; many sensations, in fact an unlimited series, to deal with one pain; and at the last moment the centre of consciousness has the sensation of all these sensations and of its own sensation to boot. Or to be exact, these serial sensations will not be of the pain in the finger: the sensation next in succession to the suffering finger will be of pain at the joint, a third will tell of a pain still higher up: there will be a series of separate pains. The centre of consciousness will not feel the pain seated at the finger, but only that impinging upon itself: it will know this alone, ignore the rest, and so have no notion that the finger is in pain.

Thus: transmission would not give sensation of the actual condition at the affected spot: it is not in the nature of body that where one part suffers there should be knowledge in another part—for body is a magnitude, and the parts of every magnitude are distinct parts—; therefore we need, as the sentient, something of a nature to be identical to itself at any and every spot; this property can belong only to some other form of being than body.

8. It can be shown also that the intellectual act would similarly be impossible if the Soul were any form of body.

If sensation is apprehension by means of the Soul's employment of the body, intellection cannot be a similar use of the body or it would be identical with sensation. If then intellection is apprehension apart from body, much more must there be a distinction between the body and the intellective principle: sensation for objects of sense, intellection for the intellectual object. And even if this be rejected, it must still be admitted that there do exist intellections of intellectual objects and perceptions of objects not possessing magnitude: how, we may then ask, can a thing of magnitude know a thing that has no magnitude, or how can the partless be known by means of what has parts? We will be told, 'By some partless part'. But, at this, the intellective will not be body: for contact does not need a whole; one point suffices. If then it be conceded—and it cannot be denied—that the primal intellections deal with objects completely incorporeal, absolute ideal forms, the principle of intellection itself must know by virtue of being, or becoming, free from body. Even if they hold that intellection deals with the ideal forms in Matter, still it always takes place by abstraction from the bodies (in which these forms appear) and the separating agent is the Intellectual-Principle. For assuredly the process by which we abstract circle, triangle, line, or point, is not carried through by the aid of flesh or Matter of any kind; in all such acts the Soul or mind must separate itself from the material: at once we see that it cannot be itself material. Similarly it will be agreed that, as beauty and justice are things without magnitude, so must be the intellective act that grasps them.

When such non-magnitudes come before the Soul, it receives them by means of its partless phase and they will take position there in partless wise.

Again: if the Soul is a body, how can we account for its virtues—moral excellence (Sophrosyne), justice, courage, and so forth? All these could be only some kind of rarefied body (pneuma), or blood in some form; or we might see courage as a certain resisting power in that pneuma; moral quality would be its happy blending; beauty would lie wholly in the agreeable form of impressions received, such comeliness as leads us to describe people as attractive and beautiful from their bodily appearance. No doubt strength and grace of form go well enough with impressions on rarefied body; but what can this rarefied body want with moral excellence? On the contrary its interest would lie in being comfortable in its environments and contacts, in being warmed or pleasantly cool, in bringing everything smooth and caressing and soft around it: what could it care about a just distribution?

Then consider the objects of the Soul's contemplation, virtue, and the other Intellectual forms with which it is occupied; are these eternal or are we to think that virtue rises here or there, helps, then perishes? These things must have an author and a source and there, again, we are confronted by something perdurable: the Soul's contemplation, then, must be of the eternal and unchanging, like the concepts of geometry: if eternal and unchanging, these objects are not bodies: and that which is to receive them must be of equivalent nature: it cannot therefore be body, since all body-nature lacks permanence, is a thing of flux.

8[1]. There are those who insist on the activities observed in bodies—warming, chilling, thrusting, pressing—and class soul with body, as it were to assure its efficacy. This ignores the double fact that the very bodies themselves exercise such efficiency by means of the incorporeal powers operating in them, and that these are not the powers we attribute to soul: intellection, perception, reasoning, desire, wise and effective action in all regards, these point to a very different form of being.

In transferring to bodies the powers of the unembodied, this school leaves nothing to that higher order. And yet that it is precisely in virtue of bodiless powers that bodies possess their efficiency is clear from certain reflections:

It will be admitted that quality and quantity are two different things, that body is always a thing of quantity but not always a thing of quality: matter is not qualified. This admitted, it will not be denied that quality, being a different thing from quantity, is a different thing from body. Obviously quality could not be body when it has not quantity as (by the admission) all body must; and, again, as we have said, body, any thing of mass, on being reduced to fragments ceases to be what it was, but the quality it possessed remains intact in every particle— for instance the sweetness of honey is still sweetness in each speck—this shows that sweetness and all other qualities are not body.

Further: if the powers in question were bodies, then necessarily the stronger powers would be large masses and those less efficient small masses: but if there are large masses with small powers while not a few of the smaller masses manifest great powers, then the efficiency must be vested in something other than magnitude; efficacy, thus, belongs to non-magnitude.

Again; Matter, they tell us, remains unchanged as long as it is body, but produces variety upon accepting qualities; is not this proof enough that the entrants (with whose arrival the changes happen) are Reason-Principles not of the material or bodily order?

They must not remind us that when pneuma and blood are no longer present, animals die: these are necessary no doubt to life, but so are many other things of which none could possibly be soul: and neither pneuma nor blood is present throughout the entire being; but soul is.

8². If the Soul is body and permeates the entire body-mass, still even in this entire permeation the blending must be in accord with what occurs in all cases of bodily admixing.

Now: if in the admixing of bodies neither constituent can retain its efficacy, the Soul too could no longer be effective within the bodies; it could but be latent; it will have lost that by which it is soul, just as in an admixture of sweet and bitter the sweet disappears: we have, thus, no soul.

Two bodies (i.e. by hypothesis, the Soul and the human body) are blended, each entire through the entirety of the other; where the one is, the other is also; each occupies an equal extension and each the whole extension; no increase of size has been caused by the juncture: the one body thus inblended can have left in the other nothing undivided. This is no case of mixing in the sense of considerable portions alternating; that would be described as collocation: no; the incoming entity goes through the other to the very minutest point—an impossibility, of course; the less becoming equal to the greater; still, all is traversed throughout and divided throughout. Now if, thus, the inblending is to occur point by point, leaving no undivided material anywhere, the division of the body concerned must have been a division into (geometrical) points: an impossibility. The division is an infinite series—any material particle may be cut in two—and the infinities are not merely potential, they are actual.

Therefore body cannot traverse anything as a whole traversing a whole. But soul does this. It is therefore incorporeal.

8³. We come to the theory that this pneuma is in an earlier form the nature-principle, but on entering the cold and being tempered by it develops into soul by growing finer under that new condition. This is absurd at the start, since many living beings rise in warmth and have a soul that has not been tempered by cold: still that is the theory—the Soul has an earlier form, and develops its true nature by force of external accidents. Thus these teachers make the inferior precede the higher, and before that inferior they put something still lower, their 'Habitude'. It is obvious that the Intellectual-Principle is last and has sprung from the Soul, for if it were first of all, the order of the series must be, second the Soul, then the nature-principle, and always the later inferior, as the system actually stands.

I If they identify God with the Intellectual-Principle and treat him as later[3] engendered and I deriving intellection from without, soul and intellect and God may prove to have no existence: this would follow if a potentiality could not come to existence, or does not become actual, unless the corresponding actuality exists. And what could lead it onward if there were no separate being in previous actuality? Even on the absurd supposition that the potentially existent brings itself to actuality, it must be looking to some Term, and that must be no potentiality but actual.

I No doubt we may conceive a potentiality which retains eternal self-identity and of itself imparts actuality: it is still of a lower order than the actuality which is its[4] desired Term.I

Thus the higher is the earlier, and it has a nature other than body, and it exists always in actuality: Intellectual-Principle and Soul precede Nature: thus, Soul does not stand at the level of pneuma or of body.

These arguments are sufficient in themselves, though many others have been framed, to show that the Soul is not to be thought of as a body.

8[4]. Soul belongs, then, to another nature. What is this? Is it something which, while distinct from body, still belongs to it, for example a harmony or accord?

This view, which the Pythagorean school holds with some difference, envisages the Soul as comparable to the accord in the strings of a lyre. When the lyre is strung a certain condition is produced upon the strings, and this is known as accord: in the same way our body is formed of distinct constituents brought together, and the blend produces at once life and that soul which is the condition existing upon the bodily total.

That this opinion is untenable has already been shown at length. The Soul is a prior (to body), the accord is a secondary to the lyre. Soul rules, guides, and often combats the body; as an accord of body it could not do these things. Soul is a real being, accord is not. That due blending (or accord) of the corporeal materials which constitute our frame would be simply health. Each separate part of the body, entering as a distinct entity into the total, would require a distinct soul (its own accord or note), so that there would be many souls to each person. Weightiest of all: before this soul there would have to be another soul to bring about the accord as, in the case of the musical instrument, there is the musician who produces the accord upon the strings by his own possession of the principle on which he tunes them: neither musical strings nor human bodies could put themselves in tune.

Briefly, the soulless is treated as ensouled, the unordered becomes orderly by accident, and instead of order being due to soul, soul itself owes its substantial existence to order—which is self-caused. Neither in the sphere of the partial, nor in that of wholes could this be true. The Soul, therefore, is not a harmony or accord.

8⁵. We come to the doctrine of the Entelechy, and must inquire how it is applied to soul.

It is thought that in the Conjoint of body and soul the Soul holds the rank of Form to the Matter I which is the body—not, be it noted,⁵ every example I of body or body as merely such, but 'a natural organic body having the potentiality of life'.

Now; if the Soul has been so injected as to be assimilated into the body as the design of a statue is worked into the bronze, it will follow that, upon any dividing of the body, the Soul is divided with it, and if any part of the body is cut away a fragment of soul must go with it. Since an Entelechy must be inseparable from the being of which it is the accomplished actuality, the withdrawal of the Soul in sleep cannot occur; in fact sleep itself cannot occur. Moreover, if the Soul is an Entelechy, there is an end to the resistance offered by reason to the desires; the total (of body and Entelechy-Soul) must have one uniform experience throughout, and be aware of no internal contradiction. Sense-perception might occur; but intellection would be impossible. The very upholders of the Entelechy are thus compelled to introduce another soul, the Intellect, to which they ascribe immortality. The reasoning soul, then, must be an Entelechy—if the word is to be used at all—in some other mode.

Even the sense-perceiving soul, in its possession of the impressions of absent objects, must hold these without aid from the body; for otherwise the impression must be present in it like shape and images, and that would mean that it could not take in fresh impressions: the perceptive soul, then, cannot be described as this Entelechy inseparable from the body. Similarly the desiring principle, dealing not only with food and drink but with things quite apart from body; this also is no inseparable Entelechy.

There remains the vegetal principle which might seem to suggest the possibility that, in this phase, the Soul may be the inseparable Entelechy of the doctrine. But it is not so. The principle of every growth lies at the root; in many plants the rest of the body withers at the root or just above it: it is clear that the life-principle, the vegetal soul, has concentrated itself at that one spot and deserted the rest: it was therefore not present in the whole as an inseparable Entelechy. Again, before the plant's development the life-principle is situated in that small beginning: if, thus, it passes from large growth to small and from the small to the entire growth, why should it not pass outside altogether?

An Entelechy is not a thing of parts; how then could it be present partwise in the partible body?

An identical soul is now the soul of one living being, now of another: how could the soul of the first become the soul of the latter if soul were the Entelechy of one particular being? Yet that this transference does occur is evident from the facts of animal metensomatosis.

The substantial existence of the Soul, then, does not depend upon serving as Form to anything: it is an Essence which does not come into being by finding a seat in body; it exists before it becomes also **I** the soul of some particular living being.[6]**I**

What, then, is the Soul's Being? If it is neither body nor a state or experience of body, but is act and creation: if it holds much and gives much, and is an existence outside of body; of what order and character must it be? Clearly it is what we describe as Veritable Essence. The other order, the entire corporeal Kind, is process; it appears and it perishes; in reality it never possesses Being, but is merely protected, in so far as it has the capacity, by participating in what authentically is.

9. Over against that body stands the order of Being which is self-caused, which comprises all that truly is and neither enters into being nor passes away, whose dissolution would mean the end of all things never to be restored if once this had ceased to be, the sustaining principle of things individually, and of this Cosmos, which owes its maintenance and its ordered system to the Soul.

Soul is the starting-point of motion and becomes the leader and provider of motion to all else: it moves by its own quality and every living material form owes life to the Soul, which of itself lives in a life that, being essentially innate, can never fail.

Not all things can have a life merely at second hand; this would give an infinite series: there must be some nature which, having life primally, shall be of necessity indestructible, immortal, as the source of life to all else that lives. This is the region in which all that is divine and blessed must be situated, living and having being of itself, possessing primal being and primal life, and in its own essence rejecting all change, neither coming to be nor passing away.

Whence could such Being arise or into what could it disappear?—the very word, strictly used, means that the thing is perdurable. Similarly white, the colour, cannot be now white and now not white: if this 'white' were a real being it would be eternal as well as being white: the colour is merely white but whatsoever possesses being, indwelling by nature and primal, will possess also eternal duration. In such an entity this primal and eternal Being cannot be dead like stone or plank: it must be alive, and that with a life unalloyed as long as it remains self-gathered: when the primal Being blends with an inferior principle, it is hampered in its relation to the highest, but without suffering the loss of its own nature since it can always recover its earliest state by turning its tendency back to its own.

10. That the Soul is of the family of the diviner nature, the eternal, is clear from our demonstration that it is not material: besides it has neither shape or colour nor is it tangible. But there are other proofs.

Assuming that the divine and the authentically existent possesses a life beneficent and wise, we take the next step and begin with working out the nature of our own soul.

Let us consider a soul, not one that has appropriated the unreasoned desires and impulses of the bodily life, or any other such emotion and experience, but one that has cast all this aside, and as far as possible has no commerce with the bodily. Such a soul demonstrates that all evil is accretion, alien, and that in the purged soul the noble things are immanent, wisdom and all else that is good, as its native store.

If this is the soul once it has returned to its self, how deny that it is of the nature we have identified with all the divine and eternal? Wisdom and authentic virtue are divine, and could not be found in the chattel mean and mortal: what possesses these must be divine by its very capacity of the divine, the token of kinship and of identical substance.

Hence, too, any one of us that exhibits these qualities will differ but little as far as soul is concerned from the Supernals; he will be less than they only to the extent in which the soul is, in him, associated with body.

This is so true that, if every human being were at that stage, or if a great number lived by a soul of that degree, no one would be so incredulous as to doubt that the Soul in man is immortal. It is because we see everywhere the spoiled souls of the great mass that it becomes difficult to recognize their divinity and immortality.

To know the nature of a thing we must observe it in its unalloyed state, since any addition obscures the reality. Clear, then look: or, rather, let a man first purify himself and then observe: he will not doubt his immortality when he sees himself thus entered into the pure, the Intellectual. For, what he sees is an Intellectual-Principle looking on nothing of sense, nothing of this mortality, but by its own eternity having intellection of the eternal: he will see all things in this Intellectual substance, himself having become an Intellectual Cosmos and all lightsome, illuminated by the truth streaming from The Good, which radiates truth upon all that stands within that realm of the divine.

Thus he will often feel the beauty of that word, 'Farewell: I am to you an immortal God', for he has ascended to the Supreme, and is all one strain to enter into likeness with it.

If the purification puts the human into knowledge of the highest, then, too, the science latent within becomes manifest, the only authentic knowing. For it is not by running hither and thither outside of itself❙ that the Soul discerns Moral Wisdom and Justice: it learns them of its own nature, in its intellectual grasp of itself and of its primal state, seeing their images deeply impressed upon itself—images which,[7] one mass of rust from long neglect, it has restored to purity.❙

Imagine living gold: it files away all that is earthy about it, all that kept it in self-ignorance preventing it from knowing itself as gold; seen now unalloyed it is at once filled with admiration of its worth and knows that it has no need of any other glory than its own, triumphant if only it be allowed to remain purely to itself.

11. What intelligent mind can doubt the immortality of such a value, one in which there is a life self-springing and therefore not to be destroyed?

This is at any rate a life not imported from without, not present in the mode of the heat in fire—for if heat is characteristic of the fire proper, it certainly is adventitious to the Matter underlying the fire; or fire, too, would be everlasting—it is not in any such mode that the Soul has life: this is no case of a Matter underlying and a life brought into that Matter and making it into soul (as heat comes into matter and makes it fire).

Either life is Essential Reality, and therefore self-living—the very thing we have been seeking—and undeniably immortal: or it, too, is a compound and must be traced back through all the constituents until an immortal substance is reached, something deriving movement from itself, and therefore debarred from accepting death.

Even supposing life could be described as a condition imposed upon Matter, still the source from which this condition entered the Matter must necessarily be admitted to be immortal simply by being unable to take into itself the opposite of the life which it conveys.

Of course, life is no such mere condition, but an independent principle, effectively living.

12. A further consideration is that if every soul is to be held dissoluble the universe must long since have ceased to be: if it is pretended that one kind of soul, our own for example, is mortal, and another, that of the All, let us suppose, is immortal, we demand to know the reason of the difference alleged.

Each is a principle of motion, each is self-living, each touches the same sphere by the same tentacles, each has intellection of the celestial order and of the super-celestial, each is seeking to win to what has essential being, each is moving upwards to the primal source.

Again: the Soul's understanding of the Absolute Forms by means of the visions stored up in it is effected within itself; such perception is reminiscence; the Soul then must have its being before embodiment, and drawing on an eternal science, must itself be eternal.

Every dissoluble entity, that has come to be by way of groupment, must in the nature of things be broken apart by that very mode which brought it together: but the Soul is one and simplex, living not in the sense of potential reception of life but by its own energy; and this can be no cause of dissolution.

But, we will be told, it tends to destruction by having been divided (in the body) and so becoming fragmentary.

No, the Soul, as we have shown, is not a mass, not a quantity.

May not it change and so come to destruction?

No: the change that destroys annuls the form but leaves the underlying substance: and that could not happen to anything except a compound.

If it can be destroyed in no such ways it is necessarily indestructible.

13. But how does the Soul enter into body from the aloofness of the Intellectual?

There is the Intellectual-Principle which remains among the intellectual beings, living the purely intellective life; and this, knowing no impulse or appetite, is for ever stationary in that Realm. But immediately following upon it, there is that which has acquired appetite and, by this accruement, has already taken a great step outward; it has the desire of elaborating order on the model of what it has seen in the Intellectual-Principle: pregnant by those Beings, and in pain to the birth, it is eager to make, to create. In this new zest it strains towards the realm of sense: while in union with the Soul of the All, it transcends the sphere administered and joins in the governance of the universe; but when it chooses to administer the partial, it exiles itself to enter the place in which it finds its appropriate task: still it is not wholly and exclusively held by body; some part of it is unembodied, and, especially, the Intellectual-Principle in it remains immune. As a whole it is partly in body, partly outside: it has plunged from among the primals and entered this sphere of tertiaries: the process has been an activity of the Intellectual-Principle, which thus, while itself remaining in its identity, operates throughout the Soul to flood the universe with beauty and penetrant order—immortal mind, eternal in its unfailing energy, acting through immortal soul.

14. As for the souls of the other living beings, fallen to the degree of entering

brute bodies, these too must be immortal. And if there is in the animal world any other phase of soul, its only possible origin, since it is the life-giver, is, still, that one principle of life: so too with the soul in the vegetal order.

All have sprung from one source, all have life as their own, all are incorporeal, indivisible, all are real-beings.

If we are told that man's soul being tripartite must as a compound entity be dissolved, our answer shall be that pure souls upon their emancipation will put away all that has fastened to them at birth, all that increment which the others will long retain.

But even that inferior phase thus laid aside will not be destroyed as long as its source continues to exist, for nothing from the realm of Real Being shall pass away.

15. Thus far we have offered the considerations appropriate to those asking for demonstration: those whose need is conviction by evidence of the more material order are best met from the abundant records relevant to the subject: there are the oracles of the Gods ordering the appeasing of wronged souls and the honouring of the dead as still sentient, a practice common to all mankind: and also, not a few souls, once among men, have continued to serve them after quitting the body and by revelations, practically helpful, make clear, as well, that the other souls, too, have not ceased to be.

NOTES TO ENNEAD IV.7

1. FIRST EDITION and ARMSTRONG both omit "and everything else without exception".

GUTHRIE: "and all other things"; TAYLOR: "and every thing [except matter] . . ."

2. FIRST EDITION: "Much more must this be true *in the case of thoughts, partless entities as they are, impinging* upon the centre of consciousness *which (to receive them) must itself be void of part.*

"Either *this* or—supposing *the centre of consciousness* to *be a thing of* quantity and extension *the sensible object* will coincide with it . . ."

ARMSTRONG: "So still more when they reach the ruling principle they will become like partless thoughts—and this ruling principle will be partless; or if this is a size the sense-objects would be divided up along with it . . ."

TAYLOR: "Hence, in a still greater degree the forms which arrive at the ruling part of the soul, become as it were conceptions; and therefore this part also must be impartible. For if it had magnitude, it would be co-divided with the object of sensible perception . . ."

GUTHRIE handles the whole thought as: "So much the more, therefore, must the sensations that centre in the (Stoic) 'directing principle' [Guthrie here references IV.2.2—ed.] resemble indivisible intuitions and be perceived by an indivisible principle. If the latter possessed extension, it could, like the sense-object, be divided; each of its parts would thus perceive one of the parts of the sense-object, and nothing within us would grasp the object in its totality."

3. FIRST EDITION: "If they *treat* God *as they do* the Intellectual-Principle—as later, engendered and . . ." Note comma after "later" in first but not in fourth.

GUTHRIE: "In this [Stoic—ed.] system the divinity, by the mere fact of his possessing intelligence, is posterior and begotten, possessing only an incidental intelligence."

ARMSTRONG supports the fourth edition. TAYLOR doesn't translate this passage.

4. FIRST EDITION has sentence as: "No doubt *the eternally self-identical may have potentiality and be self-led to self-realisation, but even in this case the being considered as actualised is of higher order than the being considered as merely capable of actualisation and moving towards a desired Term.*"

GUTHRIE: ". . . on the hypothesis that what is potential can permanently remain identical, it will of itself pass into actualization, and will be superior to the being which is potential only because it will be the object of the aspiration of such a being."

ARMSTRONG: ". . . if the potential is to have the property of always remaining the same, it will bring itself to an actuality corresponding to itself, and this will be better than that which is potential, as it is the potential's desired objective."

TAYLOR doesn't translate this passage.

5. FIRST EDITION: ". . . which *here* is the *ensouled* body—not, then, *Form to* every example . . ."

ARMSTRONG and GUTHRIE clearly support the first edition. TAYLOR doesn't translate the passage.

6. FIRST EDITION: ". . . the soul of some particular, *for example, of a* living being, *whose body would by this doctrine be the author of its soul.*" GUTHRIE also adds the clarifying clause at the end; ARMSTRONG does not. TAYLOR has none of this passage at all.

7. FIRST EDITION: ". . . that the *soul understands morality and right conduct*: it learns them of its own nature, in its *contact with itself*, in its intellectual grasp of itself, seeing deeply impressed upon *it the images of its primal state; what was* one mass of rust from long neglect it has restored to purity."

ARMSTRONG has the whole passage as: "For it is certainly not by running around outside that the soul 'sees self-control and justice', but itself by itself in its understanding of itself and what it formerly was, seeing them standing in itself like splendid statues all rusted with time which it has cleaned:"

GUTHRIE: "Indeed, it is not by an excursion among external objects that the soul attains the intuition of wisdom and virtue, but by re-entering into herself, in thinking herself in her primitive condition. Then she clears up and recognizes in herself the divine statues, soiled by the rust of time."

TAYLOR: "For the soul does not by running to externals behold temperance and justice, but perceives them herself by herself, in the intellection of herself, and of that which she formerly was, and views them like statues established in herself, which through time have become covered with rust. These she then purifies, just as if gold were animated . . ."

EIGHTH TRACTATE

The Soul's Descent into Body

1. Many times it has happened: lifted out of the body into myself; becoming external to all other things and self-encentred; beholding a marvellous beauty; then, more than ever, assured of community with the loftiest order; enacting the noblest life, acquiring identity with the divine; stationing within It by having attained that activity; poised above whatsoever within the Intellectual is less than the Supreme: yet, there comes the moment of descent from intellection to reasoning, and after that sojourn in the divine, I ask myself how it happens that I can now be descending, and how did the Soul ever enter into my body, the Soul which, even within the body, is the high thing it has shown itself to be.

Heraclitus, who urges the examination of this matter, tells of 'compulsory alternation from contrary to contrary', speaks of ascent and descent, says that 'change reposes', and that 'it is weariness to keep toiling at the same things and to be always overcome by them'; but he seems to teach by metaphor, not concerning himself about making his doctrine clear to us, probably with the idea that it is for us to seek within ourselves as he sought for himself and found.

Empedocles—where he says that it is law for faulty souls to descend to this sphere, and that he himself was here because he turned 'a deserter, wandered from God, in slavery to a raving discord'—reveals neither more nor less than Pythagoras and his school seem to me to convey on this as on many other matters; but in his case, versification has some part in the obscurity.

We have to fall back on the illustrious Plato, who uttered many noble sayings about the Soul, and has in many places dwelt upon its entry into body, so that we may well hope to get some light from him.

What do we learn from this philosopher?

We will not find him so consistent throughout that it is easy to discover his mind.

Everywhere, no doubt, he expresses contempt for all that is of sense, blames the commerce of soul with body as an enchainment, an entombment, and upholds as a great truth the saying of the Mysteries that the Soul is here a prisoner. In the Cavern of Plato and in the Cave of Empedocles, I discern this universe, where the 'breaking of the fetters' and the 'ascent' from the depths are figures of the wayfaring towards the Intellectual Realm.

In the Phaedrus he makes a failing of the wings the cause of the entry to this realm: and there are periods which send back the Soul after it has risen; there are judgements and lots and fates and necessities driving other souls down to this order.

In all these explanations he finds guilt in the arrival of the Soul at body. But treating, in the Timaeus, of our universe he exalts the Cosmos and entitles it 'a blessed god', and holds that the Soul was given by the goodness of the Creator to the end that the total of things might be possessed of intellect, for thus intellectual it was planned to be, and thus it cannot be except through soul. There is a reason, then, why the Soul of this All should be sent into it from God: in the same way the Soul of each single one of us is sent, that the universe may be complete; it was necessary that all beings of the Intellectual should be tallied by just so many forms of living creatures here in the realm of sense.

2. Inquiring, then, of Plato as to our own soul, we find ourselves forced to inquire into the nature of soul in general—to discover what there can be in its character to bring it into partnership with body, and, again, what this Cosmos must be in which, willing unwilling or in any way at all, soul has its activity.

We have to face also the question as to whether the Creator has planned well, or whether the World-Soul, it may be, resembles our human souls which, in governing their inferior, the body, must sink deeper and deeper into it if they are to control it.

No doubt the individual body—though in all cases appropriately placed within the universe—is of itself in a state of dissolution, always on the way to its natural terminus, demanding much irksome forethought to save it from every kind of outside assailant, always gripped by need, requiring every help against constant difficulty: but the body inhabited by the World-Soul— complete, competent, self-sufficing, exposed to nothing contrary to its nature—this needs no more than a brief word of command, while the governing soul is undeviatingly what its nature makes it wish to be, and, amenable neither to loss nor to addition, knows neither desire nor distress.

This is how we come to read that our soul, entering into association with that complete soul and itself thus made perfect, 'walks the lofty ranges, administering the entire Cosmos', and that as long as it does not secede and is neither inbound to body nor held in any sort of servitude, so long it tranquilly bears its part in the governance of the All, exactly like the World-Soul itself; for in fact it suffers no hurt whatever by furnishing body with the power to well-being and to existence, since not every form of care for the inferior need wrest the providing soul from its own sure standing in the highest.

The Soul's care for the universe takes two forms: there is the supervising of the entire system, brought to order by deedless command in a kingly presidence, and there is that over the individual, implying direct action, the hand to the task, one might say, in immediate contact: in the second kind of care the agent absorbs much of the nature of its object.

Now in its comprehensive government of the heavenly system, the Soul's method is that of an unbroken transcendence in its highest phases, with penetration by its lower power: at this, God can no longer be charged with lowering the All-Soul, which has not been deprived of its natural standing and from eternity possesses and will unchangeably possess that rank and habit which could never have been intruded upon it against the course of nature but must be its characteristic quality, neither failing ever nor ever beginning.

Where we read that the souls of stars stand to their bodily forms as the All-Soul to the body of the All—for these starry bodies are declared to be members of the Soul's circuit—we are given to understand that the star-souls also enjoy the blissful condition of transcendence and immunity that becomes them.

And so we might expect: commerce with the body is repudiated for two only reasons, as hindering the Soul's intellective act and as filling it with pleasure, desire, pain; but neither of these misfortunes can befall a soul which has never deeply penetrated into the body, is not a slave but a sovereign ruling a body of such an order as to have no need and no shortcoming and therefore to give ground for neither desire nor fear.

There is no reason why it should be expectant of evil with regard to such a body nor is there any such preoccupied concern, bringing about a veritable descent, as to withdraw it from its noblest and most blessed vision; it remains always intent upon the Supreme, and its governance of this universe is effected by a power not calling upon act.

3. The Human Soul, next:

Everywhere we hear of it as in bitter and miserable durance in body, a victim to troubles and desires and fears and all forms of evil, the body its prison or its tomb, the Cosmos its cave or cavern.

Now this does not clash with the first theory (that of the impassivity of soul as in the All); for the descent of the human Soul has not been due to the same causes (as that of the All-Soul).

All that is Intellectual-Principle has its being—whole and all—in the place of Intellection, what we call the Intellectual Cosmos: but there exist, too, the intellective powers included in its being, and the separate intelligences—for the Intellectual-Principle is not merely one; it is one and many. In the same way there must be both many souls and one, the one being the source of the differing many just as from one genus there rise various species, better and worse, some of the more intellectual order, others less effectively so.

In the Intellectual-Principle a distinction is to be made: there is the Intellectual-

Principle itself, which like some huge living organism contains potentially all the other forms; and there are the forms thus potentially included now realized as individuals. We may think of it as a city which itself has soul and life, and includes, also, other forms of life; the living city is the more perfect and powerful, but those lesser forms, in spite of all, share in the one same living quality: or, another illustration, from fire, the universal, proceed both the great fire and the minor fires; yet all have the one common essence, that of fire the universal, or, more exactly, participate in that from which the essence of the universal fire proceeds.

No doubt the task of the Soul, in its more emphatically reasoning phase, is intellection: but it must have another as well, or it would be undistinguishable from the Intellectual-Principle. To its quality of being intellective it adds the quality by which it attains its particular manner of being: it ceases to be an Intellectual-Principle, and has thenceforth its own task, as everything must that exists in the Intellectual Realm.

It looks towards its higher and has intellection; **|** towards itself and orders, administers, governs its lower.[1]**|**

The total of things could not have remained stationary in the Intellectual Cosmos, once there was the possibility of continuous variety, of beings inferior but as necessarily existent as their superiors.

4. So it is with the individual souls; the appetite for the divine Intellect urges them to return to their source, but they have, too, a power apt to administration in this lower sphere; they may be compared to the light attached upwards to the sun, but not grudging its bounty to what lies beneath it. In the Intellectual, then, they remain with the All-Soul, and are immune from care and trouble; in the heavenly sphere, inseparable from the All-Soul, they are administrators with it, just as kings, associated with the supreme ruler and governing with him, do not descend from their kingly stations: the Souls indeed are thus far in the one place; but there comes a stage at which they descend from the universal to become partial and self-centred; in a weary desire of standing apart they find their way, each to a place of its very own. This state long maintained, the Soul is a deserter from **|** the totality;[2]**|** its differentiation has severed it; its vision is no longer set in the Intellectual; it is a partial thing, isolated, weakened, full of care, intent upon the fragment; severed from the whole, it nestles in one form of being; for this it abandons all else, entering into and caring for only the one, for a thing buffeted about by a worldful of things: thus it has drifted away from the universal and, by an actual presence, it administers the particular; it is caught into contact now, and tends to the outer to which it has become present and into whose inner depths it henceforth sinks far.

With this comes what is known as the casting of the wings, the enchaining in body: the Soul has lost that innocency of conducting the higher which it knew when it stood with the All-Soul, that earlier state to which all its interest would bid it hasten back.

It has fallen: it is at the chain: debarred from expressing itself now through its intellectual phase, it operates through sense; it is a captive; this is the burial, the encavernment, of the Soul.

But in spite of all it has, for ever, something transcendent: by a conversion towards the intellective act, it is loosed from the shackles and soars—when only it makes its memories the starting-point of a new vision of essential being. Souls that take this way have place in both spheres, living of necessity the life there and the life here by turns, the upper life reigning in those able to consort more continuously with the divine Intellect, the lower dominant where character or circumstances are less favourable.

All this is indicated by Plato, without emphasis, where he distinguishes those of the second mixing-bowl, describes them as 'parts', and goes on to say that, having in this way become partial, they must of necessity experience birth.

Of course, where he speaks of God sowing them, he is to be understood as when he tells of God speaking and delivering orations; what is rooted in the nature of the All is figuratively treated as coming into being by generation and creation: stage and sequence are transferred, for clarity of exposition, to things whose being and becoming are everlasting.

5. It is possible to reconcile all these apparent contradictions—the divine sowing to birth, as opposed to a descent aiming at the completion of the universe; the judgement and the cave; necessity and free choice—in fact the necessity includes the choice; embodiment as an evil; the Empedoclean teaching of a flight from God, a wandering away, a sin bringing its punishment; the 'solace by flight' of Heraclitus; in a word, a voluntary descent which is also involuntary.

All degeneration is no doubt involuntary, yet when it has been brought about by an inherent tendency, that submission to the inferior may be described as the penalty of an act.

On the other hand these experiences and actions are determined by an eternal law of nature, and they are due to the movement of a being which in abandoning its superior is running out to serve the needs of another: hence there is no inconsistency or untruth in saying that the Soul is sent down by God; final results are always to be referred to the starting-point even across many intervening stages.

Still there is a twofold flaw: the first lies in the motive of the Soul's descent (its audacity, its Tolma), and the second in the evil it does when actually here: the first is punished by what the Soul has suffered by its descent: for the faults committed here, the lesser penalty is to enter into body after body—and soon to return—by judgement according to desert, the word judgement indicating a divine ordinance; but any outrageous form of ill-doing incurs a proportionately greater punishment administered under the surveillance of chastising daimons.

Thus, in sum, the Soul, a divine being and a dweller in the loftier realms, has entered body: it is a god, a later phase of the divine: but, under stress of its powers and of its tendency to bring order to its next lower, it penetrates to this sphere in a voluntary plunge: if it turns back quickly all is well; it will have taken no hurt by acquiring the knowledge of evil and coming to understand what sin is, by bringing its forces into manifest play, by exhibiting those activities and productions which, remaining merely potential in the unembodied, might as well never have been even there, if destined never to come into actuality, so that the Soul itself would never have known that suppressed and inhibited total.

The act reveals the power, a power hidden, and we might almost say obliterated or non-existent, unless at some moment it became effective: in the world as it is, the richness of the outer stirs us all to the wonder of the inner whose greatness is displayed in acts so splendid.

6. Something besides a unity there must be or all would be indiscernibly buried, shapeless within that unbroken whole: none of the real beings (of the Intellectual Cosmos) would exist if that unity remained at halt within itself: the plurality of these beings, offspring of the unity, could not exist without their own nexts taking the outward path; these are the beings holding the rank of souls.

In the same way the outgoing process could not end with the souls, their issue stifled: every Kind must produce its next; it must unfold from some concentrated central principle as from a seed, and so advance to its term in the varied forms of sense. The prior will remain unalterably in the native seat; and the next lower will be begotten to it by all the ineffable power of its being.

To this power we cannot impute any halt, any limit of jealous grudging; it must move for ever outward until the universe stands accomplished to the ultimate possibility. All, thus, is produced by an inexhaustible power giving its gift to the universe, no part of which it can endure to see without some share in its being.

There is, besides, no principle that can prevent anything from partaking, to the extent of its own individual receptivity, in the nature of Good. If, therefore, Matter has always existed, that existence is enough to ensure its participation in the being which, according to each receptivity, communicates the supreme Good universally: if, on the contrary, Matter has come into being as a necessary sequence of the causes preceding it, that origin would similarly prevent it standing apart from the scheme as though it were out of reach of the principle to whose grace it owes its existence.

In sum: the loveliness that is in the sense-realm is an index of the nobleness of the Intellectual sphere, displaying its power and its goodness alike: and all things are for ever linked; the one order Intellectual in its being, the other of sense; one self-existent, the other eternally taking its being by participation in that first, and to the full of its power reproducing the Intellectual nature.

7. The Kind, then, with which we are dealing is twofold, the Intellectual against the sensible: better for the Soul to dwell in the Intellectual, but, given its proper nature, it is under compulsion to participate in the sense-realm also. There is no grievance in its not being, through and through, the highest; it holds mid-rank among the authentic existences, being of divine station but at the lowest extreme of the Intellectual and skirting the sense-known nature; thus, while it communicates to this realm something of its own store, it absorbs in turn whenever—instead of employing in its government only its safeguarded phase—it plunges in an excessive zeal to the very midst of its chosen sphere; then it abandons its status as whole soul with whole soul, though even thus it is always able to recover itself by turning to account the experience of what it has seen and suffered here, learning, so, the greatness of rest in the Supreme, and more clearly discerning the finer things by comparison with what is almost their direct antithesis. Where the faculty is incapable of knowing without contact, the experience of evil brings the clearer perception of Good.

The outgoing that takes place in the Intellectual-Principle is a descent to its own downward ultimate: it cannot be a movement to the transcendent; operating necessarily outwards from itself, wherein it may not stay inclosed, the need and law of Nature bring it to its extreme term, to soul—to which it entrusts all the later stages of being while itself turns back on its course.

The Soul's operation is similar: its next lower act is this universe: its immediate higher is the contemplation of the Authentic Existences. To individual souls such divine operation takes place only at one of their phases and by a temporal process when from the lower in which they reside they turn towards the noblest; but that soul, which we know as the All-Soul, has never entered the lower activity, but, immune from evil, has the property of knowing its lower by inspection, while it still cleaves continuously to the beings above itself; thus its double task becomes possible; it takes hence and, since as soul it cannot escape touching this sphere, it gives hither.

8. And—if it is desirable to venture the more definite statement of a personal

conviction clashing with the general view—even our human Soul has not sunk entire; something of it is continuously in the Intellectual Realm, though if that part, which is in this sphere of sense, hold the mastery, or rather be mastered here and troubled, it keeps us blind to what the upper phase holds in contemplation.

The object of the Intellectual Act comes within our ken only when it reaches downward to the level of sensation: for not all that occurs at any part of the Soul is immediately known to us; a thing must, for that knowledge, be present to the total soul; thus desire locked up within the desiring faculty ❙ remains unknown except when we make it fully ours by the central faculty of perception, or by deliberate[3] choice, or by both at once.❙ Once more, every soul has something of the lower on the body side and something of the higher on the side of the Intellectual-Principle.

The Soul of the All, as an entirety, governs the universe through that part of it which leans to the body side, but since it does not exercise a will based on calculation as we do—but proceeds by purely intellectual act as in the execution of an artistic conception—its ministrance is that of a labourless overpoising, only its lowest phase being active upon the universe it embellishes.

The souls that have gone into division and become appropriated to some thing partial have also their transcendent phase, but are preoccupied by sensation, and in the mere fact of exercising perception they take in much that clashes with their nature and brings distress and trouble since the object of their concern is partial, deficient, exposed to many alien influences, filled with desires of its own and taking its pleasure, that pleasure which is its lure.

But there is always the other (the transcendent phase of soul), that which finds no savour in passing pleasure, but holds its own even way.

NOTES TO ENNEAD IV.8

1. FIRST EDITION: ". . . towards itself *and conserves its peculiar being; towards its lower* and orders, administers, governs."

GUTHRIE and TAYLOR both support the first edition; ARMSTRONG supports the fourth.

2. FIRST EDITION: ". . . the *All;*"

ARMSTRONG : "the All"; TAYLOR: "the whole"; GUTHRIE : "the universal Soul."

3. FIRST EDITION: ". . . remains unknown except when we make it fully ours by the central faculty of perception, or by *the individual* choice or by both at once."

GUTHRIE: ". . . is by us cognized only when we perceive it by the interior sense or by discursive reason, or by both simultaneously." TAYLOR and ARMSTRONG agree with Guthrie.

NINTH TRACTATE

Are All Souls One?

1. That the Soul of every individual is one thing we deduce from the fact that it is present entire at every point of the body—the sign of veritable unity—not some part of it here and another part there. In all sensitive beings the sensitive soul is an omnipresent unity, and so in the forms of vegetal life the vegetal soul is entire at each several point throughout the organism.

Now are we to hold similarly that your soul and mine and all are one, and that the same thing is true of the universe, the soul in all the several forms of life being one soul, not parcelled out in separate items, but an omnipresent identity?

If the soul in me is a unity, why need that in the universe be otherwise, seeing that there is no longer any question of bulk or body? And if that, too, is one soul, and yours and mine belong to it, then yours and mine must also be one: and if, again, the soul of the universe and mine depend from one soul, once more all must be one.

What then in itself is this one soul?

First we must assure ourselves of the possibility of all souls being one as that of any given individual is.

It must, no doubt, seem strange that my soul and that of any and everybody else should be one thing only: it might mean my feelings being felt by someone else, my goodness another's too, my desire his desire, all our experience shared with each other and with the (one-souled) universe, so that the very universe itself would feel whatever I felt.

Besides how are we to reconcile this unity with the distinction of reasoning soul and unreasoning, animal soul and vegetal?

Yet if we reject that unity, the universe itself ceases to be one thing and souls can no longer be included under any one principle.

2. Now to begin with, the unity of soul, mine and another's, is not enough to make the two totals of soul and body identical. An identical thing in different recipients will have different experiences; the identity Man, in me as I move and you at rest, moves in me and is stationary in you: there is nothing stranger, nothing impossible, in any other form of identity between you and me; nor would it entail the transference of my emotion to any outside point: when in any one body a hand is in pain, the distress is felt not in the other but by the soul in the total body.

In order that my feelings should of necessity be yours, the unity would have to be corporeal: only if the two recipient bodies made one, would the souls feel as one.

We must keep in mind, moreover, that many things that happen even in one same body escape the notice of the entire being, especially when the bulk is large: thus in huge sea-beasts, it is said, the animal as a whole will be quite unaffected by some membral accident too slight to traverse the organism.

Thus unity in the subject of any experience does not imply that the resultant sensation will be necessarily felt with any force upon the entire being and at every point of it: some transmission of the experience may be expected, and is indeed undeniable, but a full impression on the sense there need not be.

That one identical soul should be virtuous in me and vicious in someone else is not strange: it is no more than saying that an identical thing may be active here and inactive there.

We are not asserting the unity of soul in the sense of a complete negation of multiplicity—only of the Supreme can that be affirmed—we are thinking of soul as simultaneously one and many, participant in the nature 'which becomes divided among bodies', but at the same time a unity by virtue of belonging to that order which 'suffers no division'.

In myself some experience occurring in a part of the body may take no effect upon the entire man, but anything occurring in the higher reaches would tell upon the partial: in the same way any influx from the All upon the individual will have manifest effect since the points of sympathetic contact are numerous, but as to any operation from ourselves upon the All there can be no certainty.

3. Yet, looking at another set of facts, reflection tells us that we are in sympathetic relation to each other, suffering at the sight of pain, caught up in pleasure, naturally drawn to forming attachments; and all this can be due only to some unity among us.

Again, if spells and other forms of magic are efficient even at a distance to attract us into sympathetic relations, the agency can be no other than the one soul.

A quiet word induces changes in a remote object, and makes itself heard at vast distances—proof of the oneness of all things within the one soul.

But how reconcile this unity with the existence of a reasoning soul, an unreasoning, even a vegetal soul?

(It is a question of powers): the indivisible phase is classed as reasoning because it is not in division among bodies, but there is the later phase, divided among bodies, but still one thing and distinct only so as to secure sense-perception throughout; this is to be classed as another power; and there is the forming and making phase which again is a power. But a variety of powers does not conflict with unity; seed contains many powers and yet it is one thing, and from that unity rises, again, a variety which is also a unity.

But why are not all the powers of this unity present everywhere?

The answer is that even in the case of the individual soul described, similarly, as permeating its body, sensation is not equally present in all the parts, reason does not operate at every point, the principle of growth is at work where there is no sensation—and yet all these powers join in the one soul when the body is laid aside.

The nourishing faculty as dependent from the All belongs also to the All-Soul: why then does it not come equally from ours?

Because what is nourished by the action of this power is a member of the All, which itself has sensation passively; ▌ but the perception which judges its object with the help of an Intellectual-Principle belongs to the individual, and soul does not need it to create what has already taken shape in the All: certainly it would itself have created it,[1] had the power not been previously included, of necessity, in the nature of the All. ▌

4. These reflections should show that there is nothing strange in that reduction of all souls to one. But it is still necessary to inquire into the mode and conditions of the unity.

Is it the unity of origin in a unity? And if so, is the one divided or does it remain entire and yet produce variety? and how can an essential being, while remaining its one self, bring forth others?

Invoking God to become our helper, let us assert that the very existence of many souls makes certain that there is first one from which the many rise.

Let us suppose, even, the first soul to be corporeal.

Then (by the nature of body) the many souls could result only from the splitting up of that entity, each an entirely different substance: if this body-soul be uniform in kind, each of the resultant souls must be of the one kind; they will all carry the one Form undividedly and will differ only in their volumes. Now, if their being souls depended upon their volumes they would be distinct; but if it is Ideal-Form that makes them souls, then all are, in virtue of this Idea, one.

But this is simply saying that there is one identical soul dispersed among many bodies, and that, preceding this, there is yet another not thus dispersed, the source of the soul in dispersion which may be thought of as a widely repeated image of the soul in unity—much as a multitude of seals bear the impression of one ring. By that first mode the one soul is expended in a multiplicity of souls: in the second mode it is incorporeal. Similarly if the soul were a condition or modification of body, we could not wonder that this quality (the condition or modification)—this one thing from one source—should be present in many objects. The same reasoning would apply if soul were an effect (or manifestation) of the Conjoint.

We, of course, hold it to be bodiless, an essential existence.

5. How then can a multitude of essential beings be really one?

Obviously either the one essence will be entire in all, or the many will rise from a one which remains unaltered and yet includes the one-many in virtue of giving itself, without self-abandonment, to its own multiplication.

It is competent thus to give and remain, because while it penetrates all things it can never itself be sundered: this is an identity in variety.

There is no reason for dismissing this explanation: we may think of a science with its constituents standing as one total, the source of all those various elements: again, there is the seed, a whole, producing those new parts in which it comes to its division; each of the new growths is a whole while the whole remains undiminished: only the material element is under the mode of part, and all the multiplicity remains an entire identity still.

It may be objected that in the case of science the constituents are not each the whole.

But even in the science, while the constituent selected for handling to meet a particular need is present actually and takes the lead, still all the other constituents accompany it in a potential presence, so that the whole is in every part: only in this sense (of particular attention) is the whole science distinguished from the part: all, we may say, is here simultaneously effected: each part is at your disposal as you choose to take it; the part invites the immediate interest, but its value consists in its approach to the whole.

The detail cannot be considered as something separate from the entire body of speculation: so treated it would have no technical or scientific value; it would be childish divagation. The one detail, when it is matter of science, potentially includes all. Grasping one such constituent of his science, the expert deduces the rest by force of sequence.

(As a further illustration of unity in plurality) the geometrician, in his analysis, shows that the single proposition includes all the items that go to constitute it and all the propositions which can be developed from it.

It is our feebleness that leads to doubt in these matters; the body obscures the truth, but There all stands out clear and separate.

NOTE TO ENNEAD IV.9

1. FIRST EDITION: "... but the perception, which *is an intellectual judgement, is individual and has no need to create what already exists, though it would have done so* had the power not been previously included, of necessity, in the nature of the All."

ARMSTRONG: "... but the perception which judges with intelligence belongs to the individual, and there was no need for this to shape that which had its shaping from the All. It would also have made this shaping, if it had not been necessary for it to be in this All."

GUTHRIE: "As to the sense-power which rises as far as the judgement, and which is united to every intelligence, there was no need for it to form what had already been formed by the Whole, but it could have given its forms if these forms were not parts of the Whole which produces them."

THE FIFTH ENNEAD

FIRST TRACTATE

The Three Initial Hypostases

1. WHAT CAN it be that has brought the souls to forget the father, God, and, though members of the Divine and entirely of that world, to ignore at once themselves and It?

The evil that has overtaken them has its source in self-will, in the entry into the sphere of process, and in the primal differentiation with the desire for self-ownership. They conceived a pleasure in this freedom and largely indulged their own motion; thus they were hurried down the wrong path, and in the end, drifting further and further, they came to lose even the thought of their origin in the Divine. A child wrenched young from home and brought up during many years at a distance will fail in knowledge of its father and of itself: the souls, in the same way, no longer discern either the divinity or their own nature; ignorance of their rank brings self-depreciation; they misplace their respect, honouring everything more than themselves; all their awe and admiration is for the alien, and, clinging to this, they have broken apart, as far as a soul may, and they make light of what they have deserted; their regard for the mundane and their disregard of themselves bring about their utter ignoring of the Divine.

Admiring pursuit of the external is a confession of inferiority; and nothing thus holding itself inferior to things that rise and perish, nothing counting itself less honourable and less enduring than all else it admires could ever form any notion of either the nature or the power of God.

A double discipline must be applied if human beings in this pass are to be reclaimed, and brought back to their origins, lifted once more towards the Supreme and One and First.

There is the method, which we amply exhibit elsewhere, declaring the dishonour of the objects which the Soul holds here in honour; the second teaches or recalls to the Soul its race and worth; this latter is the leading truth, and, clearly brought out, is the evidence of the other.

It must occupy us now, for it bears closely upon our inquiry and is its natural preliminary: the seeker is soul and it must start from a true notion of the nature and quality by which soul may undertake the search; it must study itself in order to learn whether it has the faculty for the inquiry, the eye for the object proposed, whether in fact we ought to seek; for if the object is alien the search must be futile, while if there is relationship the solution of our problem is at once desirable and possible.

2. Let every soul recall, then, at the outset the truth that soul is the author of all living things, that it has breathed the life into them all, whatever is nourished by earth and sea, all the creatures of the air, the divine stars in the sky; it is the maker of the sun; itself formed and ordered this vast heaven and conducts all that rhythmic motion: and it is a principle distinct from all these to which it gives law and movement and life, and it must of necessity be more honourable than they, for they gather or dissolve as soul brings them life or abandons them, but soul, since it never can abandon itself, is of eternal being.

How life was purveyed to the universe of things and to the separate beings in it may be thus conceived:

That great soul must stand pictured before another soul, one not mean, a soul that has become worthy to look, emancipate from the lure, from all that binds its fellows in bewitchment, holding itself in quietude. Let not merely the enveloping body be at peace, body's turmoil stilled, but all that lies around, earth at peace, and sea at peace, and air and the very heavens. Into that heaven, all at rest, let the great soul be conceived to roll inward at every point, penetrating, permeating, from all sides pouring in its light. As the rays of the sun throwing their brilliance upon a louring cloud make it gleam all gold, so the soul entering the material expanse of the heavens has given life, has given immortality: what was abject it has lifted up; and the heavenly system, moved now in endless motion by the soul that leads it in wisdom, has become a living and a blessed thing; the soul domiciled within, it takes worth where, before the soul, it was stark body—clay and water—or, rather, the blankness of Matter, the absence of Being, and, as an author says, 'the execration of the Gods'.

The Soul's nature and power will be brought out more clearly, more brilliantly, if we consider next how it envelops the heavenly system and guides all to its purposes: for it has bestowed itself upon all that huge expanse so that every interval, small and great alike, all has been ensouled.

The material body is made up of parts, each holding its own place, some in mutual opposition and others I variously separated;'I the Soul is in no such condition; it is not whittled down so that life tells of a part of the Soul and springs where some such separate portion impinges; each separate life lives by the Soul entire, omnipresent in the likeness of the engendering father, entire in unity and entire in diffused variety. By the power of the Soul the manifold and diverse heavenly system is a unit: through soul this universe is a God: and the sun is a God because it is ensouled; so too the stars: and whatsoever we ourselves may be, it is all in virtue of soul; for 'dead is viler than dung'.

This, by which the gods are divine, must be the oldest God of them all: and our own soul is of that same nature, so that to consider it, purified, freed from all accruement, is to recognize in ourselves that same value which we have found soul to be, honourable above all that is bodily. For what is body but earth, and even if it be fire (as Stoics think), what (but soul) is its burning power? So it is with all the compounds of earth and fire, even with water and air added to them.

If, then, it is the presence of soul that brings worth, how can a man slight himself and run after other things? You honour the Soul elsewhere; honour then yourself.

3. The Soul once seen to be thus precious, thus divine, you may hold the faith that by its possession you are already nearing God: in the strength of this power make upwards towards Him: at no great distance you must attain: there is not much between.

But over this divine, there is a still diviner: grasp the upward neighbour of the Soul, its prior and source.

Soul, for all the worth we have shown to belong to it, is yet a secondary, an image of the Intellectual-Principle: reason uttered is an image of the reason stored within the Soul, and in the same way soul is an utterance of the Intellectual-Principle: it is even the total of its activity, the entire stream of life sent forth by that Principle to the production of further being; it is the forthgoing heat of a fire which has also heat essentially inherent. But within the Supreme we must see energy not as an overflow but in the double aspect of integral inherence with the establishment of a new being. Sprung, in other words, from the Intellectual-Principle, soul is intellective, but with an intellection operating by the method of reasonings: for its perfecting it must look to that Divine Mind, which may be thought of as a father watching over the development of his child born imperfect in comparison with himself.

Thus its substantial existence comes from the Intellectual-Principle; and the Reason within it becomes Act in virtue of its contemplation of that prior; for its thought and act are its own intimate possession when it looks to the Supreme Intelligence; those only are soul-acts which are of this intellective nature and are determined by its own character; all that is less noble is foreign (traceable to Matter) and is accidental to the Soul in the course of its peculiar task.

In two ways, then, the Intellectual-Principle enhances the divine quality of the Soul, as father and as immanent presence; nothing separates them but the fact that they are not one and the same, that there is succession, that over against a recipient there stands the Ideal-Form received; but this recipient, Matter to the Supreme Intelligence, is also noble as being at once informed by divine intellect and uncompounded.

What the Intellectual-Principle must be is carried in the single word that Soul, itself so great, is still inferior.

4. But there is yet another way to this knowledge:

Admiring the world of sense as we look out upon its vastness and beauty and the order of its eternal march, thinking of the gods within it, seen and hidden, and the celestial spirits and all the life of animal and plant, let us mount to its archetype, to the yet more authentic sphere: there we are to contemplate all things as members of the Intellectual—eternal in their own right, vested with a self-springing consciousness and life—and, presiding over all these, the unsoiled Intelligence and the unapproachable wisdom.

That archetypal world is the true Golden Age, I age of Kronos, whose very name suggests (in Greek) Abundance (*koros*) and Intellect (*nous*).[2] I For here is contained all that is immortal: nothing here but is Divine Mind; all is God; this is the place of every soul. Here is rest unbroken: for how can that seek change, in which all is well; what need that reach to, which holds all within itself; what increase can that desire, which stands utterly achieved? All its content, thus, is perfect, that itself may be perfect throughout, as holding nothing that is less than the divine, nothing that is less than intellective. Its knowing is not by search but by possession, its blessedness inherent, not acquired; for all belongs to it eternally and it holds the authentic Eternity imitated by Time which, circling round the Soul, makes towards the new thing and passes by the old. Soul deals with thing after thing—now Socrates; now a horse: always some one entity from among beings—but the Intellectual-Principle is all and therefore its entire content is simultaneously present in that identity: this is pure being in eternal actuality; nowhere is there any future, for every then is a now; nor is there any past, for nothing there has ever ceased to be; everything has taken its stand for ever, an identity well pleased, we might say, to be as it is; and everything, in that entire content, is Intellectual-Principle and Authentic-Existence; and the total of all is Intellectual-Principle entire and Being entire. Intellectual-Principle by its intellective act establishes Being, which in turn, as the object of intellection, becomes the cause of intellection and of existence to the Intellectual-Principle—though, of course, there is another cause of intellection which is also a cause to Being, both rising in a source distinct from either.

Now while these two are coalescents, having their existence in common, and are never apart, still the unity they form is two-sided; there is Intellectual-Principle as against Being, the intellectual agent as against the object of intellection; we consider the intellective act and we have the Intellectual-Principle; we think of the object of that act and we have Being

Such difference there must be if there is to be any intellection; but similarly there must also be identity (since, in perfect knowing, subject and object are identical).

Thus the Primals (the first 'Categories') are seen to be: Intellectual-Principle; Existence; Difference; Identity: we must include also Motion and Rest: Motion provides for the intellectual act, Rest preserves identity as Difference gives at once a Knower and a Known, for, failing this, all is one, and silent.

▌There must be Difference also among the objects of intellection compared one with another; and Identity in the self-identity of each, and, again, in the common ground of their diversity—the diversity which[3] constitutes Difference.▌

The Intellectual Cosmos thus a manifold, Number and Quantity arise: Quality is the specific character of each of these Ideas which stand as the principles from which all else derives.

5. As a manifold, then, this God, the Intellectual-Principle, ▌exists above[4] the Soul here, ▌the Soul which once for all stands linked a member of the divine, unless by a deliberate apostasy.

Bringing itself close to the divine Intellect, becoming, as it were, one with this, it seeks still further: what Being, now, has engendered this God, what is the Simplex preceding this multiple; what the cause at once of its existence and of its existing as a manifold; what the source of this Number, this Quantity?

Number, Quantity, is not primal: obviously before even duality, there must stand the unity.

The Dyad is a secondary; deriving from unity, it finds in unity the determinant needed by its native indetermination: once there is any determination, there is Number, in the sense, of course, of the real (the archetypal) Number. And the Soul is such a number. For the Primals are not masses or magnitudes; all of that gross order is later, real only to the sense-thought; even in seed the effective reality is not the moist substance but the unseen—that is to say Number (as the determinant of individual being) and the Reason-Principle (of the product to be).

Thus by what we call the Number and the Dyad of that higher realm, we mean Reason Principles and the Intellectual-Principle: but ▌while the Dyad is undetermined—representing, as it were, the underlie (or Matter) of the Intellectual World—the number which rises from the Dyad and The One is always a Form-Idea: thus the Intellectual-Principle is, so to speak, shaped by the Ideas rising within it—or rather, it is shaped in a certain sense by The One and in another sense by itself, since its potential vision becomes actual and intellection is, precisely, an act of vision in which subject and object are identical.[5] ▌

6. But how and what does the Intellectual-Principle see and, especially, how

has it sprung from that which is to become the object of its vision?

The mind demands the existence of these Beings, but it is still in trouble over the problem endlessly debated by the most ancient philosophers: from such a unity as we have declared The One to be, how does anything at all come into substantial existence, any multiplicity, dyad, or number? Why has the Primal not remained self-gathered so that there be none of this profusion of the manifold which we observe in existence and yet are compelled to trace to that absolute unity?

In venturing an answer, we first invoke God Himself, not in loud word but in that way of prayer which is always within our power, leaning in soul towards Him by aspiration, alone towards the alone. But if we seek the vision of that great Being within the Inner Sanctuary—self-gathered, tranquilly remote above all else—we begin by considering the images stationed at the outer precincts, or, more exactly to the moment, the first image that appears. How the Divine Mind comes into being must be explained:

Everything moving has necessarily an object towards which it advances; but since the Supreme can have no such object, we may not ascribe motion to it: anything that comes into being after it can be produced only as a consequence of its unfailing self-intention; and, of course, we dare not talk of generation in time, dealing as we are with eternal Beings: where we speak of origin in such reference, it is in the sense, merely, of cause and subordination: origin from the Supreme must not be taken to imply any movement in it: that would make the Being resulting from the movement not a second principle but a third: the Movement would be the second hypostasis.

Given this immobility in the Supreme, it can neither have yielded assent nor uttered decree nor stirred in any way towards the existence of a secondary.

What happened, then? What are we to conceive as rising in the neighbourhood of that immobility?

It must be a circumradiation—produced from the Supreme but from the Supreme unaltering—and may be compared to the brilliant light encircling the sun and ceaselessly generated from that unchanging substance.

All existences, as long as they retain their character, produce—about themselves, from their essence, in virtue of the power which must be in them—some necessary, outward-facing hypostasis continuously attached to them and representing in image the engendering archetypes: thus fire gives out its heat; snow is cold not merely to itself; fragrant substances are a notable instance; for, as long as they last, something is diffused from them and perceived wherever they are present.

Again, all that is fully achieved engenders: therefore the eternally achieved engenders eternally an eternal being. At the same time, the offspring is always minor: what then are we to think of the All-Perfect but that it can produce nothing less than the very greatest that is later than itself? This greatest, later than the divine unity, must be the Divine Mind, and it must be the second of all existence, for it is that which sees The One on which alone it leans while the First has no need whatever of it. The offspring of the prior to Divine Mind can be no other than that Mind itself and thus is the loftiest being in the universe, all else following upon it—the Soul, for example, being an utterance and act of the Intellectual-Principle as that is an utterance and act of The One. But in soul the utterance is obscured, for soul is an image and must look to its own original: that Principle, on the contrary, looks to the First without mediation—thus becoming what it is—and has that vision not as from a distance but as the immediate next with nothing intervening, close to the One as Soul to it.

The offspring must seek and love the begetter; and especially so when begetter and begotten are alone in their sphere; when, in addition, the begetter is the highest Good, the offspring (inevitably seeking its good) is attached by a bond of sheer necessity, separated only in being distinct.

7. We must be more explicit:
The Intellectual-Principle stands as the image of The One, firstly because there is a certain necessity that the first should have its offspring, carrying onward much of its quality, in other words that there be something in its likeness as the sun's rays tell of the sun. Yet The One is not an Intellectual-Principle; how then does it engender an Intellectual-Principle?

Simply by the fact that in its self-quest it has vision: this very seeing is the Intellectual-Principle. Any perception of the external indicates either sensation or intellection, sensation symbolized by a line, intellection by a circle... [corrupt passage].

Of course the divisibility belonging to the circle I does not apply to The One; here, to be sure, is a unity, but there the Unity[6] which is the potentiality of all existence. I

The items of this potentiality the divine intellection brings out, so to speak, from the unity and knows them in detail, as it must if it is to be an Intellectual-Principle.

I The One has already[7] a consciousness, I as it were, within itself of this same potentiality; it knows that it can beget an hypostasis. The Intellectual-Principle acts on its own account, determining its Being by the virtue emanating from its prior, and aware that its essence is in some sense a definite part of what belongs to that First and issues from it, that its strength lies there, and that its Being takes perfection as a derivative and a recipient from the First. It sees that, as a member in some sense of the realm of division and part, it receives life and intellection and all else it has and is, from the undivided and partless, since that First is no member of existence, but can be the source of all on condition only of being held down by no one distinctive shape but remaining the undeflected unity.

To be all in itself would place it in the realm of Being. And so the First is not a thing among the things contained by the Intellectual-Principle though the source of all. In virtue of this source things of the later order are essential beings; for from that fact there is determination; each has its form: what has being cannot be envisaged as outside of limit; the nature must be held fast by boundary and fixity; though to the Intellectual Beings this fixity is no more than determination and form, the foundations of their substantial existence.

'Of this lineage' is the Intellectual-Principle as we have described it—Intellectual-Principle in its purest form and worthy therefore to be descended from no other than the first principle of all; as it comes into existence, all other beings must be simultaneously engendered by it—all the beauty of the Ideas, all the Gods of the Intellectual realm. And it still remains pregnant with this offspring; for it has, so to speak, drawn all within itself again, holding them lest they fall away towards Matter to be brought up in the House of Rhea (in the realm of flux). This is the meaning hidden in the Mysteries, and in the Myths of the gods: Kronos, as the wisest of the gods before the birth of Zeus, absorbs his offspring and, full within himself, is the Intellectual-Principle (*nous*) in its plenty (*koros*); afterwards, the myth proceeds, Kronos engenders Zeus, outcome of his plenty: in other words the offspring of the Divine Intellect, perfect within itself, is Soul (the life-principle carrying forward the Ideas in the Divine Mind). The perfection entails the offspring; a power so vast could not remain unfruitful.

Now, with Soul as with Intellect, the engendered could not be higher than its progenitor; it must be a lesser, an image; it will be undetermined, as its progenitor was, but will receive determination, and, so to speak, its shaping idea, from the progenitor.

Yet the offspring of the Intellectual-Principle must be a Reason-Principle, that is to say, a substantial existence (hypostasis) identified with the principle of deliberative thought (in the Timaeus): such then is that (higher Soul) which circles about the Divine Mind, its light, its image inseparably attached to it: on the upper level united with it, filled from it, enjoying it, participant in its nature, intellective with it, but on the lower level in contact with the realm beneath itself, or, rather, generating in turn an offspring which must lie beneath; of this lower we will treat later; so far we deal still with the Divine.

8. This is the explanation of Plato's Triplicity, in the passage where he names as the Primals the Beings gathered about the King of All and establishes a Secondary containing the Secondaries and a Third containing the Tertiaries.

He teaches, also, that there is an author of the Cause, that is of the Intellectual-Principle, which to him is the Creator who made the Soul, as he tells us, in the famous mixing bowl. This author of the causing principle, of the divine mind, is to him the Good, that which transcends the Intellectual-Principle and transcends Being: often too he uses the term 'The Idea' to indicate Being and the Divine Mind. Thus Plato knows the order of generation—from the Good, the Intellectual-Principle; from the Intellectual-Principle, the Soul. These teachings are, therefore, no novelties, no inventions of today, but long since stated, if not stressed; our doctrine here is the explanation of an earlier and can show the antiquity of these opinions on the testimony of Plato himself.

Earlier, Parmenides made some approach to the doctrine in identifying Being with Intellectual-Principle while separating Real Being from the realm of sense.

'Knowing and Being are one thing', he says, and this unity is to him motionless in spite of the intellection he attributes to it: to preserve its unchanging identity he excludes all bodily movement from it; and he compares it to a huge sphere in that it holds and envelops all existence and that its intellection is not an outgoing act but internal. Still, with all his affirmation of unity, his own writings lay him open to the reproach that his unity turns out to be a multiplicity.

The Platonic Parmenides is more exact; the distinction is made between the Primal One, a strictly pure Unity, and a secondary One which is a One-Many and a third which is a One-and-Many; thus he too is in accordance with our thesis of the Three Kinds.

9. Anaxagoras, again, in his assertion of a Mind pure and unmixed, affirms a simplex First and a sundered One, though writing long ago he failed in precision.

Heraclitus, with his sense of bodily forms as things of ceaseless process and passage, knows the One as eternal and intellectual.

In Empedocles, similarly, we have a dividing principle, 'Strife', set against 'Friendship'—which is The One and is to him bodiless, while the elements represent Matter.

Later there is Aristotle; he begins by making the First transcendent and intellective but cancels that primacy by supposing it to have self-intellection. Further, he affirms a multitude of other intellective beings—as many indeed as there are orbs in the heavens; one such principle as mover to every orb—and thus his account of the Intellectual Realm differs from Plato's and, I failing necessity, he brings in probability; though it is doubtful whether he has even probability on his side, since it would be more probable[8] that all the spheres, I as contributory to one system, should look to a unity, to the First.

We are obliged also to ask whether to Aristotle's mind all these Intellectual

Beings spring from one, and that one their First; or whether the Principles in the Intellectual are many.

If from one, then clearly the Intellectual system will be analogous to that of the universe of sense—sphere encircling sphere, with one, the outermost, dominating all: the First (in the Intellectual) will envelop the entire scheme and will be an Intellectual (or Archetypal) Cosmos; and as in our universe the spheres are not empty but the first sphere is thick with stars and none without them, so, in the Intellectual Cosmos, those principles of Movement will envelope a multitude of Beings, and that world will be the realm of the greater reality.

If on the contrary each is a principle, then the effective powers become a matter of chance; under what compulsion are they to hold together and act with one mind towards that work of unity, the harmony of the entire heavenly system? Again what can make it necessary that the material bodies of the heavenly system be equal in number to the Intellectual moving principles, and how can these incorporeal Beings be numerically many when there is no Matter to serve as the basis of difference?

For these reasons the ancient philosophers that ranged themselves most closely to the school of Pythagoras and of his later I followers[9] have I insisted upon this Nature, some developing the subject in their writings while others treated of it merely in unwritten discourses, some no doubt ignoring it entirely.

10. We have shown the inevitability of certain convictions as to the scheme of things:

There exists a Principle which transcends Being; this is The One, whose nature we have sought to establish in so far as such matters lend themselves to proof. Upon The One follows immediately the Principle which is at once Being and the Intellectual-Principle. Third comes the Principle, Soul.

Now just as these three exist for the system of Nature, so, we must hold, they exist for ourselves. I am not speaking of the material order—all that is separable—but of what lies beyond the sense realm in the same way as the Primals are beyond all the heavens; I mean the corresponding aspect of man, what Plato calls the Interior Man.

Thus our soul, too, is a divine thing, belonging to another order than sense; such is all that holds the rank of soul, but (above the life-principle) there is the Soul perfected as containing Intellectual-Principle with its double phase, reasoning and giving the power to reason. The reasoning phase of the Soul, needing no bodily organ for its thinking but maintaining, in purity, its distinctive Act that its thought may be uncontaminated—this we cannot err in placing, separate and not mingled into body, within the first Intellectual. We may not seek any point of space in which to seat it; it must be set outside of all space: its distinct quality, its separateness, its immateriality, demand that it be a thing alone, untouched by all of the bodily order. That is why we read of the universe, that the Demiurge cast the Soul around it from without—understand that phase of soul which is permanently seated in the Intellectual—and of ourselves that the charioteer's head reaches upwards towards the heights.

The admonition to sever soul from body is not, of course, to be understood spatially—that separation stands made in Nature—the reference is to holding our rank, to use of our thinking, to an attitude of alienation from the body in the effort to lead up and attach to the over-world, equally with the other, that phase of soul seated here and, alone, having to do with body, creating, moulding, spending its care upon it.

11. Since there is a Soul which reasons upon the right and good—for reasoning is an inquiry into the rightness and goodness of this rather than that—there must exist some permanent Right, the source and foundation of this reasoning in our soul; how, else, could any such discussion be held? Further, since the Soul's attention to these matters is intermittent, there must be within us an Intellectual-Principle acquainted with that Right not by momentary act but in permanent possession. Similarly there must be also the principle of this principle, its cause, God. This Highest cannot be divided and allotted, must remain intangible but not bound to space, it may be present at many points, wheresoever there is anything capable of accepting one of its manifestations: thus a centre is an independent unity; everything within the circle has its term at the centre; and to the centre the radii bring each their own. Within our nature is such a centre by which we grasp and are linked and held; and those of us are firmly in the Supreme whose being is concentrated There.

12. Possessed of such powers, how does it happen that we do not lay hold of them, but for the most part, let these high activities go idle—some, even, of us never bringing them in any degree to effect?

The answer is that all the Divine Beings are unceasingly about their own act, the Intellectual-Principle and its Prior always self-intent; and so, too, the Soul maintains its unfailing movement; for not all that passes in the Soul is, by that fact, perceptible; we know just as much as impinges upon the faculty of sense. Any activity not transmitted to the sensitive faculty has not traversed the entire Soul: we remain unaware because the human being includes sense-perception; man is not merely a part (the higher part) of the Soul but the total.

None the less every being of the order of soul is in continuous activity as long as life holds, continuously executing to itself its characteristic act: knowledge of the act depends upon transmission and perception. If there is to be perception of what is thus present, we must turn the perceptive faculty inward and hold it to attention there. Hoping to hear a desired voice we let all others pass and are alert for the coming at last of that most welcome of sounds: so here, we must let the hearings of sense go by, save for sheer necessity, and keep the Soul's perception bright and quick to the sounds from above.

NOTES TO ENNEAD V.1

1. FIRST EDITION: "... variously *interdependent;*"

ARMSTRONG supports the fourth edition.

TAYLOR: "... one body indeed, being situated differently from another, and some bodies being opposite, but others being suspended from each other."

GUTHRIE: "Though these may be located in different parts ..."

2. FIRST EDITION: "... age of Kronos, *who is the Intellectual-Principle as being the offspring or exuberance of God.*"

GUTHRIE: "... the real Saturnian realm, which is nothing else than pure intelligence."

TAYLOR: "... a life which is in reality under Saturn, flourishes there; Saturn being a God, and a pure intellect."

ARMSTRONG: "... the true life of Kronos, a god who is fulness and intellect." Armstrong adds, in a footnote: "For Plotinus, here and elsewhere, the word *koros* is applied to Intellect or Soul in its two meanings of 'satiety' (signifying the plenitude of intelligible being) and 'boy' (the son of the Father, the One): cp. ch. 7 below and III.8.11; V.8.12–13."

3. FIRST EDITION has this sentence as: "*So too* the objects of intellection (*the ideal content of the Divine Mind*)—identical in virtue of the self-concentration of the principle which is their common ground—*must still be distinct each from another; this distinction* constitutes Difference."

TAYLOR: "It is necessary, however, that intellective natures should be different from each other; and that they should also be the same with each other, since they subsist in the same thing, and there is something common in all of them. Diversity, likewise, is *otherness.*"

ARMSTRONG: "... and the objects of thought, also, must have otherness in relation to each other. But one must include sameness, because it is one with itself, and all have some common unity; and the distinctive quality of each is otherness."

GUTHRIE: "The elements of thought (subject and object) must thus stand in the relation of differences, but also in that of unity, because they form a consubstantial unity, and because there is a common element in all that is derived therefrom. Besides, here difference is nothing else than distinction."

4. FIRST EDITION: "... exists *within* the Soul here ..."

TAYLOR: "... exists in the soul which is here ..."

GUTHRIE: "Thus the human soul is full of this divinity (of intelligence);"

ARMSTRONG: "... which is over the soul ..."

5. FIRST EDITION: ". . . while the Dyad is, *as regards that sphere*, undetermined—representing, as it were, the underly (or Matter) of *The One*—the *later* Number *(or Quantity)*—*that* which rises from the Dyad *(Intellectual-Principle)* and The One—is *not Matter to the later existents but is their forming-Idea, for all of them take shape*, so to speak, *from the ideas* rising within *this. The determination of the Dyad is brought about partly from its object—The One—and partly from itself, as is the case with all vision in the act of sight: intellection (the Act of the Dyad) is vision occupied upon The One.*"

GUTHRIE: "The 'pair' is indeterminate so far as it plays the part of substrate (in respect to unity). The number that is derived from the pair, and the one, constitute every kind of form, so that Intelligence has a shape which is determined by the ideas begotten within it. Its shape is derived in one respect from the one, and in another respect, from itself, just like actualized sight. Thought, indeed, is actualized sight, and both these entities (the faculty and the actualization) form but one."

TAYLOR: "But the duad indeed is indefinite, when it is assumed as analogous to a subject. Number, however, which proceeds from it and *the one*, is each form of things; intellect being as it were formed by the species of things which are generated in it. But it is formed in one manner from *the one*, and in another from itself, in the same manner as sight which is in energy. For intelligence is sight perceiving, both being one."

ARMSTRONG: ". . . the dyad is indefinite when one forms an idea of it by what may be called the substrate, but each and every number which comes from it and the One is a form, as if Intellect was shaped by the numbers which came to exist in it; but it is shaped in one way by the One and in another by itself, like sight in its actuality; for intellection is seeing sight, and both are one."

6. FIRST EDITION: ". . . does not apply to *the Intellectual-Principle; all, there too,* is a unity, *though a unity* which is the potentiality of all existence."

GUTHRIE and TAYLOR support the first edition completely.

ARMSTRONG: ". . . the circle is of a kind which can be divided; but this [intellectual apprehension] is not so. There is One here also, but the One is the productive power of all things." Brackets are Armstrong's.

7. FIRST EDITION: "*It* [Intellectual-Principle—ed.] has *besides* a consciousness . . ."

ARMSTRONG, GUTHRIE, and TAYLOR all translate this thought in terms of Intellectual-Principle.

8. FIRST EDITION: ". . . failing *reason*, he brings in *necessity; though whatever reasons he had alleged there would always have been the objection that* it would be more *reasonable* that all the spheres . . ."

GUTHRIE and TAYLOR support the first edition.

ARMSTRONG: ". . . making a probable assumption which has no philosophical necessity. But one might doubt whether it is even probable: for it would be more probable that all the spheres . . ."

9. FIRST EDITION: ". . . followers *and to that of Pherekudes,* have . . ."

ARMSTRONG, GUTHRIE, and TAYLOR all match the first edition, though using the spelling "Pherecydes."

SECOND TRACTATE

The Origin and Order of the Beings following on the First

1. 'The One is all things and no one of them'; the source of all things is not all things; and yet it is all things in a transcendental sense—all things, so to speak, having run back to it: or, more correctly, not all as yet are within it, they will be.

But a universe from an unbroken unity, in which there appears no diversity, I no joins of any kind?[1]I

It is precisely because there is nothing within the One that all things are from it: in order that Being may be brought about, the source must be no Being but Being's generator, in what is to be thought of as the primal act of generation. Seeking nothing, possessing nothing, lacking nothing, the One is perfect and, in our metaphor, has overflowed, and its exuberance has produced the new: this product has turned again to its begetter and been filled and has become its contemplator and so an Intellectual-Principle.

That station towards the One (the fact that something exists in presence of the One) establishes Being; that vision directed upon the One establishes the Intellectual-Principle; standing towards the One to the end of vision, it is simultaneously Intellectual-Principle and Being; and, attaining resemblance in virtue of this vision, it repeats the act of the One in pouring forth a vast power.

This second outflow is an image or representation of the Divine Intellect as the Divine Intellect represented its own prior, The One.

This active power sprung from essence (from the Intellectual-Principle considered as Being) is Soul.

ISoul arises out[2] of the motionless Intellectual-PrincipleI—which itself sprang from its own motionless prior—but the Soul's operation is not similarly motionless; its image is generated from its movement. It takes fullness by looking to its source; but it generates its image by adopting another, a downward, movement.

This image of Soul is Sense and Nature, the vegetal principle.

Nothing, however, is completely severed from its prior. I Thus the higher[3] Soul I appears to reach away as far down as to the vegetal order: in some sense it does, since the life of growing things is within its province; but it is not present entire; when it has reached the vegetal order it is there in the sense that having moved thus far downwards it produces—by its outgoing and its tendency towards the less good—another hypostasis or form of being, just as its prior (the loftier phase of the Soul) is produced from the Intellectual-Principle which yet remains in untroubled self-possession.

2. There is, accordingly, from the first principle to ultimate an outgoing in which unfailingly each principle retains its own seat while its offshoot takes another rank, a lower, though on the other hand every being is in identity with its prior as long as it holds that contact.

In the case of soul entering some vegetal form, what is there is one phase, the more rebellious and less intellectual, outgone to that extreme; in a soul entering an animal, the faculty of sensation has been dominant and brought it there; I in soul entering man or any other rational being the movement outward has[4] come from the Intellectual-Principle I in the sense that the soul, possessing that principle as immanent to its being, has an inborn desire of intellectual activity and of movement in general.

But, looking more minutely into the matter, when shoots or topmost boughs are lopped from some growing thing, where goes the soul that was present in them? Simply, whence it came: soul never knew spatial separation and therefore is always within the source. If you cut the root to pieces, or burn it, where is the life that was present there? In the soul, which never went outside of itself.

No doubt, despite this permanence, the soul must have been in something if it re-ascends; and if it does not, it is still somewhere; it is in some other vegetal soul: but all this means merely that it is not crushed into some one spot; if a soul-power re-ascends, it is within the soul-power preceding it; that in turn can be only in the soul-power prior again, the phase reaching upwards to the Intellec-tual-Principle. Of course nothing here must be understood spatially: soul never was in space; and the Divine Intellect, again, is distinguished from soul as being still more free.

Soul thus is nowhere but in the Principle which has that characteristic existence at once nowhere and everywhere.

If the soul on its upward path has halted midway before wholly achieving the supreme heights, it has a mid-rank life and has centred itself upon the mid-phase of its being.

I All in that region is the One and not the One—nothing else because deriving thence, yet not that because the One[5] in giving it forth is not merged into it. I

There exists, thus, a life, as it were, of huge extension, a total in which each several part differs from its next, all making a self-continuous whole under a law of discrimination by which the various forms of things arise with no effacement of any prior in its secondary.

The soul which has reached the vegetal order—does it produce nothing? It engenders precisely the Kind in which it is thus present: how, is a question to be handled from another starting point.

NOTES TO ENNEAD V.2

1. FIRST EDITION: "*. . . not even duality?*"

GUTHRIE: "duality,"

ARMSTRONG: "doubleness,"

TAYLOR: "nor any duplicity."

2. FIRST EDITION: "Soul arises *as the idea and act* of the motionless Intellectual-Principle . . ." Taylor, Guthrie, and Armstrong do not include the specification here, but instead begin the thought parallel with the previous sentence as:

TAYLOR: "And this energy from essence is soul, which was generated from intellect permanently abiding."

GUTHRIE: "The actualization that proceeds from Essence (and Intelligence) is the universal Soul. She is born of Intelligence, and determines herself without Intelligence issuing from itself . . ."

ARMSTRONG: "This activity springing from the substance of Intellect is Soul, which comes to be this while Intellect abides unchanged:"

3. FIRST EDITION: "Thus the *human* Soul . . ."

GUTHRIE: "human soul,"

TAYLOR: "the soul of man,"

ARMSTRONG: "the higher soul."

4. FIRST EDITION: ". . . in soul entering man, [omits "or any other rational being"] the movement outward has *either been wholly of its reasoning part or has* come from the Intellectual-Principle . . ."

ARMSTRONG and TAYLOR clearly support the first edition.

GUTHRIE: "When she passes into man, it is because she is led to do so by the exercise of discursive reason, either by the movement by which she proceeds from Intelligence . . ."

5. FIRST EDITION: "All in that *mid*-region is *Intellectual-Principle not wholly itself*—nothing else because deriving thence *(and therefore of that name and rank)* yet not that because the *Intellectual-Principle* in giving it forth is not merged into it."

GUTHRIE and TAYLOR support the first edition; ARMSTRONG supports the fourth.

THIRD TRACTATE

The Knowing Hypostases and the Transcendent

1. Are we to think that a being knowing itself must contain diversity, that self-knowledge can be affirmed only when some one phase of the self perceives other phases, and that therefore an absolutely simplex entity would be equally incapable of introversion and of self-awareness?

No: a being that has no parts or phases may have this consciousness; in fact there would be no real self-knowing in an entity presented as knowing itself in virtue of being a compound—some single element in it perceiving other elements—as we may know our own form and entire bodily organism by sense-perception: such knowing does not cover the whole field; the knowing element has not had the required cognizance at once of its associates and of itself; this is not the self-knower asked for; it is merely something that knows something else.

Either we must exhibit the self-knowing of an uncompounded being—and show how that is possible—or abandon the belief that any being can possess veritable self-cognition.

To abandon the belief is not possible in view of the many absurdities thus entailed.

It would be already absurd enough to deny this power to the Soul (or mind), but the very height of absurdity to deny it to the nature of the Intellectual-Principle, presented thus as knowing the rest of things but not attaining to knowledge, or even awareness, of itself.

It is the province of sense and in some degree of understanding and judgement, but not of the Intellectual-Principle, to handle the external, though whether the Intellectual-Principle holds the knowledge of these things is a question to be examined, but it is obvious that the Intellectual-Principle must have knowledge of the Intellectual objects. Now, can it know those objects alone or must it not simultaneously know itself, the being whose function it is to know just those things? Can it have self-knowledge in the sense (dismissed above as inadequate) of knowing its content while it ignores itself? Can it be aware of knowing its members and yet remain in ignorance of its own knowing self? Self and content must be simultaneously present: the method and degree of this knowledge we must now consider.

2. We begin with the Soul, asking whether it is to be allowed self-knowledge and what the knowing principle in it would be and how operating.

The sense-principle in it, we may at once decide, takes cognizance only of the external; even in any awareness of events within the body it occupies, this is still the perception of something external to a principle dealing with those bodily conditions not as within but as beneath itself.

The reasoning-principle in the Soul acts upon the representations standing before it as the result of sense-perception; these it judges, combining, distinguishing: or it may also observe the impressions, so to speak, rising from the Intellectual-Principle, and has the same power of handling these; and reasoning will develop to wisdom where it recognizes the new and late-coming impressions (those of sense) and adapts them, so to speak, to those it holds from long before—the act which may be described as the Soul's Reminiscence.

So far as this, the efficacy of the Intellectual-Principle in the Soul certainly reaches; but is there also introversion and self-cognition or is that power to be reserved strictly for the Divine Mind?

If we accord self-knowing to this phase of the Soul we make it an Intellectual-Principle and will have to show what distinguishes it from its prior; if we refuse it self-knowing, all our thought brings us step by step to some principle which has this power, and we must discover what such self-knowing consists in. If, again, we do allow self-knowledge in the lower we must examine the question of degree; for if there is no difference of degree, then the reasoning principle in Soul is the Intellectual-Principle unalloyed.

We ask, then, whether the understanding principle in the Soul has equally the power of turning inwards upon itself or whether it has no more than that of comprehending the impressions, superior and inferior, which it receives.

The first stage is to discover what this comprehension is.

3. Sense sees a man and transmits the impression to the understanding. What does the understanding say? It has nothing to say as yet; it accepts and waits; unless, rather, it questions within itself, 'Who is this?'—someone it has met before—and then, drawing on memory, says, 'Socrates'.

If it should go on to develop the impression received, it distinguishes various elements in what the representative faculty has set before it; supposing it to say 'Socrates, if the man is good', then, while it has spoken upon information from the senses, its total pronouncement is its own; it contains within itself a standard of good.

But how does it thus contain the good within itself?

It is, itself, of the nature of the good and it has been strengthened still towards the perception of all that is good by the irradiation of the Intellectual-Principle upon it; for this pure phase of the Soul welcomes to itself the images implanted from its prior.

But why may we not distinguish this understanding phase as Intellectual-

Principle and take Soul to consist of the later phases from the sensitive downwards?

Because all the activities mentioned are within the scope of a reasoning faculty, and reasoning is characteristically the function of Soul.

Why not, however, absolve the question by assigning self-cognizance to this phase?

Because we have allotted to Soul the function of dealing—in thought and in multiform action—with the external, and we hold that observation of self and of the content of self must belong to Intellectual-Principle.

If any one says, 'Still; what precludes the reasoning Soul from observing its own content by some special faculty?' he is no longer positing a principle of understanding or of reasoning but, simply, bringing in the Intellectual-Principle unalloyed.

But what precludes the Intellectual-Principle from being present, unalloyed, within the Soul? Nothing, we admit; but are we entitled therefore to think of it as a phase of Soul?

We cannot describe it as belonging to the Soul though we do describe it as our Intellectual-Principle, something distinct from the understanding, advanced above it, and yet ours even though we cannot include it among soul-phases: it is ours and not ours; and therefore we use it sometimes and sometimes not, whereas we always have use of the understanding; the Intellectual-Principle is ours when we act by it, not ours when we neglect it.

But what is this acting by it? Does it mean that we become the Intellectual-Principle so that our utterance is the utterance of the Intellectual-Principle, or that (at best) we represent it?

We are not the Intellectual-Principle; we represent it in virtue of that highest reasoning faculty which draws upon it.

Again; we perceive by means of the perceptive faculty and are not, ourselves, the percipients: may we then say the same of the understanding (the principle of reasoning and discursive thought)?[1]

No: our reasoning is our own; we ourselves think the thoughts that occupy the understanding—for this is actually the We—but the operation of the Intellectual-Principle enters from above us as that of the sensitive faculty from below; the We is the Soul at its highest, the mid-point between two powers, between the sensitive principle, inferior to us, and the intellectual principle superior. We think of the perceptive act as integral to ourselves because our sense-perception is uninterrupted; we hesitate as to the Intellectual-Principle both because we are not always occupied with it and because it exists apart, not a principle inclining to us but one to which we incline when we choose to look upwards.

The sensitive principle is our scout; the Intellectual-Principle our King.

4. But we, too, are king when we are moulded to the Intellectual Principle.

That correspondence may be brought about in two ways: either through laws of conduct engraved upon our souls as tablets or else by our being, as it were, filled full of the Divine Mind, which again may have become to us a thing seen and felt as a presence.

Hence our self-knowing ensues because it is in virtue of this thing present that we know all other things; or because we know the faculty which discerns this principle of knowledge by means of the faculty itself; or because we become actually identical with the principle.

Thus the self-knower is a double person: there is the one that takes cognizance of the principle in virtue of which understanding occurs in the Soul or mind; and there is the higher, knowing himself by the Intellectual-Principle with which he becomes identical: this latter knows the self as no longer man but as a being that has become something other through and through: he has thrown himself as one thing over into the superior order, taking with him only that better part of the Soul which alone is winged for the Intellectual Act and gives the man, once established There, the power to appropriate what he has seen.

We can scarcely suppose this understanding faculty to be unaware that it has understanding; that it takes cognizance of things external; that in its judgements it decides by the rules and standards within itself held directly from the Intellectual-Principle; that there is something higher than itself, something which, moreover, it has no need to seek but fully possesses. Can knowledge of its own essence elude a principle which admittedly knows the place it holds and the work it has to do? It affirms that it springs from Intellectual-Principle whose second and image it is, that it holds all within itself, the universe of things, engraved, so to say, upon it as all is held There by the eternal engraver. Aware so far of itself, can it be supposed to halt at that? Are we to suppose that all we can do is to apply a distinct power of our nature and come thus to awareness of that Intellectual-Principle as aware of itself? Or may we not appropriate that principle—which belongs to us as we to it—and thus attain to awareness, at once, of it and of ourselves? Yes: this is the necessary way if we are to experience the self-knowledge vested in the Intellectual-Principle. And a man becomes Intellectual-Principle when, ignoring all other phases of his being, he sees through that only and sees only that and so knows himself by means of the self—in other words attains the self-knowledge which the Intellectual-Principle possesses.

5. Does it all come down, then, to one phase of the self knowing another phase?

That would be a case of knower distinguished from known, and would not be self-knowing.

What, then, if the total combination were supposed to be of one piece, knower quite undistinguished from known, so that, seeing any given part of itself as identical with itself, it sees itself by means of itself, knower and known thus being entirely without differentiation?

To begin with, the distinction in one self thus suggested is a strange phenomenon. How is the self to make the partition? The thing cannot happen of itself. And, again, which phase makes it? The phase that decides to be the knower or that which is to be the known? Then how can the knowing phase know itself in the known when it has chosen to be the knower and put itself apart from the known? In such self-knowledge by sundering it can be aware only of the object, not of the agent; it will not know its entire content, or itself as an integral whole; it knows the phase seen but not the seeing phase and thus has knowledge of something else, not self-knowledge.

In order to perfect self-knowing it must bring over from itself the knowing phase as well: seeing subject and seen objects must be present as one thing. Now if in this coalescence of seeing subject with seen objects the objects were merely representations of the reality, the subject would not possess the realities: if it is to possess them it must do so not by seeing them as the result of any self-division but by knowing them, containing them, before any self-division occurs.

At that, the object known must be identical with the knowing act (or agent), the Intellectual-Principle, therefore, identical with the Intellectual Realm. And in fact, if this identity does not exist, neither does truth; the Principle that should contain realities is found to contain a transcript, something different from the realities; that constitutes non-truth; Truth cannot apply to something conflicting with itself; what it affirms it must also be.

Thus we find that the Intellectual-Principle, the Intellectual Realm, and Real Being constitute one thing, which is the Primal Being; the primal Intellectual-Principle is that which contains the realities or, rather, which is identical with them.

But taking Primal Intellection and its intellectual object to be a unity, how does that give an Intellective Being knowing itself? An intellection enveloping its object or identical with it is far from exhibiting the Intellectual-Principle as self-knowing.

All turns on the identity. The intellectual object is itself an activity, not a mere potentiality, since then it would not be intellectual; it is not lifeless; nor are the life and intellection brought into it as into something naturally devoid of them, some stone or other dead matter; no, the intellectual object is essentially existent, the primal reality. As an active force, the first activity, it must be, also itself, the noblest intellection, intellection possessing real being since it is entirely true; and such an intellection, primal and primally existent, can be no other than the primal principle of Intellection: for that primal principle is no potentiality and cannot be an agent distinct from its act and thus, once more, possessing its essential being as a mere potentiality. As an act—and one whose very being is an act—it must be undistinguishably identical with its act: but Being and the Intellectual object are also identical with that act; therefore the Intellectual-Principle, its exercise of intellection, and the object of intellection all are identical. Given its intellection identical with intellectual object and the object identical with the Principle itself, it cannot but have self-knowledge: its intellection operates by the intellectual act, which is itself, upon the intellectual object, which similarly is itself. It possesses self-knowing, thus, on every count; the act is itself; and the object, seen in that act-self, is itself.

6. Thus we have shown that there exists that which in the strictest sense possesses self-knowing.

This self-knowing agent, perfect in the Intellectual-Principle, is modified in the Soul.

The difference is that, while the Soul knows itself as within something else, the Intellectual-Principle knows itself as self-depending, knows all its nature and character, and knows by right of its own being and by simple introversion. When it looks upon the authentic existences it is looking upon itself; its vision is its effective existence, and this efficacy is itself since the Intellectual-Principle and the Intellectual Act are one: this is an integral seeing itself by its entire being, not a part seeing by a part.

But has our discussion issued in an Intellectual-Principle having a persuasive activity (furnishing us with probability)?

No: it brings compulsion, not persuasion; compulsion belongs to the Intellectual-Principle, persuasion to the Soul or mind, and we seem to desire to be persuaded rather than to see the truth in the pure intellect.

As long as we were Above, collected within the Intellectual nature, we were satisfied; we were held in the intellectual act; we had vision because we drew all into unity—for the thinker in us was the Intellectual Principle telling us of itself—and the Soul or mind was motionless, assenting to that act of its prior. But now that we are once more here—living in the secondary, the Soul—we seek for persuasive probabilities: it is through the image we desire to know the archetype.

Our way is to teach our Soul how the Intellectual-Principle exercises self-vision; the phase thus to be taught is that which already touches the intellective order, that which we call the understanding or intelligent Soul, indicating by the very name (*dia-noia*) that it is already of itself in some degree an Intellectual-Principle or that it holds its peculiar power through and from that Principle. This phase must be brought to understand by what means it has knowledge of the thing it sees and warrant for what it affirms: if it became what it affirms, it would by that fact possess self-knowing. All its vision and affirmation being in the Supreme or deriving from it—There where itself also is—it will possess self-knowledge by its right as a Reason-Principle, claiming its kin and bringing all into accord with the divine imprint upon it.

The Soul therefore (to attain self-knowledge) has only to set this image (that is to say, its highest phase) alongside the veritable Intellectual-Principle which we have found to be identical with the truths constituting the objects of intellection, the world of Primals and Reality: for this Intellectual-Principle, by very definition, cannot be outside of itself, the Intellectual Reality: self-gathered and unalloyed, it is Intellectual-Principle through all the range of its being—for unintelligent intelligence is not possible—and thus it possesses of necessity self-knowing, as a being immanent to itself and one having for function and essence to be purely and solely Intellectual-Principle. This is no doer; the doer, not self-intent but looking outward, will have knowledge, in some kind, of the external, but, if wholly of this practical order, need have no self-knowledge; where, on the contrary, there is no action—and of course the pure Intellectual-Principle cannot be straining after any absent good—the intention can be only towards the self; at once self-knowing becomes not merely plausible but inevitable; what else could living signify in a being immune from action and existing in Intellect?

7. The contemplating of God, we might answer.

But to admit its knowing God is to be compelled to admit its self-knowing. It will know what it holds from God, what God has given forth or may; with this knowledge, it knows itself at the stroke, for it is itself one of those given things—in fact is all of them. Knowing God and His power, then, it knows itself, since it comes from Him and carries His power upon it; if, because here the act of vision is identical with the object, it is unable to see God clearly, then all the more, by the equation of seeing and seen, we are driven back upon that self-seeing and self-knowing in which seeing and thing seen are undistinguishably one thing.

And what else is there to attribute to it?

Repose, no doubt; but to an Intellectual-Principle Repose is not an abdication from intellect; its Repose is an Act, the act of abstention from the alien: in all forms of existence repose from the alien leaves the characteristic activity intact, especially where the Being is not merely potential but fully realized.

In the Intellectual-Principle, the Being is an Act and in the absence of any other object it must be self-directed; by this self-intellection it holds its Act within itself and upon itself; all that can emanate from it is produced by this self-centring and self-intention; first self-gathered, it then gives itself or gives something in its likeness; fire must first be self-centred and be fire, true to fire's natural Act; then it may reproduce itself elsewhere.

Once more, then: the Intellectual-Principle is a self-intent activity, but Soul has the double phase, one inner, intent upon the Intellectual-Principle, the other outside it and facing to the external; by the one it holds the likeness to its source; by the other, even in its unlikeness, it still comes to likeness in this sphere, too, by virtue of action and production; in its action it still contemplates, and its production produces forms **I**—detached intellections, so to speak—with the result[2] that all **I** its creations are representations of the divine Intellection and of the divine Intellect, moulded upon the archetype, of which all are emanations and images, the nearer more true, the very latest preserving some faint likeness of the source.

8. Now comes the question: what sort of thing does the Intellectual-Principle see in seeing the Intellectual Realm and what in seeing itself?

We are not to look for an Intellectual realm reminding us of the colour or shape to be seen on material objects: the intellectual antedates all such things; and even in our sphere the production is very different from the Reason-Principle in the seeds from which it is produced. The seed principles are invisible and the beings of the Intellectual still more characteristically so; the Intellectuals are of one same nature with the Intellectual Realm which contains them, just as the Reason-Principle in the seed is identical with the Soul, or life-principle, containing it.

But the Soul (considered as apart from the Intellectual-Principle) has no vision of what it thus contains, for it is not the producer but, like the Reason-Principles also, an image of its source: that source is the brilliant, the authentic, the primarily existent, the thing self-sprung and self-intent; but its image, Soul, is a thing which can have no permanence except by attachment, by living in that other; the very nature of an image is that as a dependent it shall have its being in something else, if at all it exist apart from its original. Hence this image (Soul) has not vision, for it has not the necessary light, and if it should see, then, as finding its completion elsewhere, it sees another, not itself.

In the pure Intellectual there is nothing of this: the vision and the envisioned are a unity; the seen is as the seeing and seeing as seen.

What, then, is there that can pronounce upon the nature of this all-unity?

That which sees: and to see is the function of the Intellectual-Principle. Even in our own sphere (we have a parallel to this self-vision of a unity), our vision is light or rather becomes one with the light, and it sees light for it sees colours.

In the intellectual, the vision sees not through some medium but by and through itself alone, for its object is not external: by one light it sees another, not through any intermediate agency; a light sees a light, that is to say a thing sees itself. This light shining within the Soul enlightens it; that is, it makes the Soul intellective, working it into likeness with itself, the light above.

Think of the traces of this light upon the Soul, then say to yourself that such, and more beautiful and broader and more radiant, is the light itself; thus you will approach to the nature of the Intellectual-Principle and the Intellectual Realm, for it is this light, itself lit from above, which gives the Soul its brighter life.

It is not the source of the generative life of the Soul which, on the contrary, it draws inward, preserving it from such diffusion, holding it to the love of the splendour of its Prior.

Nor does it give the life of perception and sensation, for that looks to the external and to what acts most vigorously upon the senses, whereas one accepting that light of truth may be said no longer to see the visible, but the very contrary.

This means in sum that the life the Soul takes thence is an intellective life, a trace of the life in the (divine) Intellect, in which alone the authentic exists.

The life in the Divine Intellect is also an Act: it is the primal light outlamping to itself primarily, its own torch; light-giver and lit at once; the authentic intellectual object, knowing at once and known, seen to itself and needing no other than itself to see by, self-sufficing to the vision, since what it sees it is; known to us by that very same light, our knowledge of it attained through itself, for from nowhere else could we find the means of telling of it. By its nature, its self-vision is the clearer but, using it as our medium, we too may come to see by it.

In the strength of such considerations we lead up our own Soul to the Divine, so that it poses itself as an image of that Being, its life becoming an imprint and a likeness of that Higher, its every act of thought making it over into the Divine and the Intellectual.

If the Soul is questioned as to the nature of that Intellectual-Principle—the perfect and all-embracing, the primal self-knower—it has but to enter into that Principle, or to sink all its activity into that, and at once it shows itself to be in effective possession of those priors whose memory it never lost: thus, as an image of the Intellectual-Principle, it can make itself the medium by which to attain some vision of it; it draws upon that within itself which is most closely resemblant, as far as resemblance is possible between divine Intellect and any phase of Soul.

9. In order, then, to know what the Divine Mind is we must observe Soul and especially its most God-like phase.

One certain way to this knowledge is to separate first, the man from the body—yourself, that is, from your body; next to put aside that Soul which moulded the body, and, very earnestly, the system of sense with desires and impulses and every such futility, all setting definitely towards the mortal: what is left is the phase of the Soul which we have declared to be an image of the Divine Intellect, ❙ retaining some light from that source, like the light of the sun which goes beyond its spherical mass, issues from it and plays about it.[3] ❙

Of course we do not pretend that the sun's light (as the analogy might imply) remains a self-gathered and sun-centred thing: it is at once outrushing and indwelling; it strikes outward continuously, lap after lap, until it reaches us upon our earth: we must take it that all the light, including that which plays about the sun's orb, has travelled; otherwise we would have next to the orb a void expanse. The Soul, on the contrary—a light springing from the Divine Mind and shining about it—is in closest touch with that source; it is not in transit but remains centred there, and, in likeness to that principle, it has no place: the light of the sun is actually in the air, but the Soul is clean of all such contact so that its immunity is patent to itself and to any other of the same order.

And by its own characteristic act, though not without reasoning process, it knows the nature of the Intellectual-Principle which, on its side, knows itself without need of reasoning, for it is ever self-present whereas we become so by directing our Soul towards it; our life is broken and there are many lives, but that principle needs no changings of life or of things; the lives it brings to being are for others, not for itself: it cannot need the inferior; nor does it for itself produce the less when it possesses or is the all, nor the images when it possesses or is the prototype.

Anyone not of the strength to lay hold of the first Soul, that possessing pure intellection, must grasp that which has to do with our ordinary thinking and thence ascend: if even this prove too hard, let him turn to account the sensitive phase which carries the ideal forms of the less fine degree, that phase which, too, with its powers, is immaterial and lies just within the realm of Ideal-principles.

One may even, if it seem desirable, begin as low as the reproductive Soul and its very production and thence make the ascent, mounting from those ultimate ideal principles to the ultimates in the higher sense, that is to the primals.

10. This matter need not be elaborated at present: it suffices to say that ❙ if the created were all, it would not be ultimate: but the Supreme does include primals, the primals because the producers. In other words there must be, with the made, the making source and these must be identical; otherwise there will be need of a Transcendent. But will not this Transcendent demand in turn a further transcendent? No: the demand comes from the Intellectual-Principle.[4] ❙ If we

are asked why this Transcendent also should not have self-vision **|** (a duality to be transcended),[5]**|** our answer is that it has no need of vision; but this we will discuss later: for the moment we go back, since the question at issue is gravely important.

We repeat that the Intellectual-Principle must have, actually has, self-vision, firstly because it has multiplicity, next because it exists for the external and therefore must be a seeing power, one seeing that external; in fact its very essence is vision. Given some external, there must be vision; and if there be nothing external the Intellectual-Principle (Divine Mind) exists in vain. Unless there is something beyond bare unity, there can be no vision: vision must converge with a visible object. And this which the seer is to see can be only a multiple, no undistinguishable unity; nor could a universal unity find anything upon which to exercise any act; all, one and desolate, would be utter stagnation; in so far as there is action, there is diversity. If there be no distinctions, what is there to do, what direction in which to move? An agent must either act upon the extern or be a multiple and so able to act upon itself: making no advance towards anything other than itself, it is motionless, and where it could know only blank fixity it can know nothing.

The intellective power, therefore, when occupied with the intellectual act, must be in a state of duality, whether one of the two elements stand actually outside or both lie within: the intellectual act will always comport diversity as well as the necessary identity, and in the same way its characteristic objects (the Ideas) must stand to the Intellectual-Principle as at once distinct and identical. This applies equally to the single object; there can be no intellection except of something containing separable detail and, since the object is a Reason-Principle (a discriminated Idea), it has the necessary element of multiplicity. The Intellectual-Principle, thus, is informed of itself by the fact of being a multiple organ of vision, an eye receptive of many illuminated objects. If it had to direct itself to a memberless unity, it would be dereasoned: what could it say or know of such an object? The self-affirmation of (even) a memberless unity implies the repudiation of all that does not enter into the character: in other words, it must be multiple as a preliminary to being itself.

Then, again, in the assertion 'I am this particular thing', either the 'particular thing' is distinct from the assertor—and there is a false statement—or it is included within it, and, at once, multiplicity is asserted: otherwise the assertion is 'I am what I am', or 'I am I'.

If it be no more than a simple duality able to say 'I and that other phase', there is already multiplicity, for there is distinction and ground of distinction, there is number with all its train of separate things.

In sum, then, a knowing principle must handle distinct items: its object must, at the moment of cognition, contain diversity; otherwise the thing remains unknown; there is mere conjunction, such a contact, without affirmation or comprehension, as would precede knowledge, the intellect not yet in being, the impinging agent not percipient.

Similarly the knowing principle itself cannot remain simplex, especially in the act of self-knowing: all silent though its self-perception be, it is dual to itself.

Of course The One has no need of minute self-handling since it has nothing to learn by an intellective act; it is in full possession of its being before Intellect exists. Knowledge implies desire, for it is, so to speak, discovery crowning a search; the utterly undifferentiated remains self-centred and makes no inquiry about that self: anything capable of analysing its content must be a manifold.

11. Thus the Intellectual-Principle, in the act of knowing the Transcendent, is a manifold. It knows the Transcendent in very essence but, with all its effort to grasp that prior as a pure unity, it goes forth amassing successive impressions, so that, to it, the object becomes multiple: thus in its outgoing to its object it is not (fully realized) Intellectual-Principle; it is an eye that has not yet seen; in its return it is an eye possessed of the multiplicity which it has itself conferred: it sought something of which it found the vague presentment within itself; it returned with something else, the manifold quality with which it has of its own act invested the simplex.

If it had not possessed a previous impression of the Transcendent it could never have grasped it, but this impression, originally of unity, becomes an impression of multiplicity; and the Intellectual-Principle in taking cognizance of that multiplicity knows the Transcendent and so is realized as an eye possessed of its vision.

It is now Intellectual-Principle since it actually holds its object, and holds it by the act of intellection: before, it was no more than a tendance, an eye blank of impression: it was in motion towards the transcendental; now that it has attained, it has become Intellectual-Principle: always self-constitutive, it now, in virtue of this intellection, holds the character of Intellectual-Principle, of Essential Existence, and of Intellectual Act where, previously, not possessing the Intellectual Object, it was not Intellectual Perception, and, not yet having exercised the Intellectual Act, it was not Intellectual-Principle.

The Principle before all these principles is no doubt the first principle of the universe, but not as immanent: immanence is not for primal sources but for engendering secondaries; that which stands as primal source of everything is not a thing but is distinct from all things: it is not, then, a member of the total but earlier than all, earlier, thus, than the Intellectual-Principle—which in fact envelops the entire train of things.

Thus we come, once more, to a Being above the Intellectual-Principle and, since the sequent amounts to no less than the All, we recognize, again, a Being above the All. This assuredly cannot be one of the things to which it is prior. We may not call it Intellect; therefore, too, we may not call it the Good, if the Good is to be taken in the sense of some one member of the universe; if we mean that which precedes the universe of things, the name may be allowed.

The Intellectual-Principle is established in multiplicity; its intellection, self-sprung though it be, is in the nature of something added to it (some accidental dualism) and makes it multiple: the utterly simplex, and therefore first of all beings, must, then, transcend the Intellectual-Principle; and, obviously, if this had intellection it would no longer transcend the Intellectual-Principle but be it, and at once be a multiple.

12. But why, after all, should it not be such a manifold as long as it remains one substantial existence, having the multiplicity not of a compound being but of a unity with a variety of activities?

Now, no doubt, if these various activities are not themselves substantial existences—but merely manifestations of latent potentiality—there is no compound; but, on the other hand, it remains incomplete until its substantial existence be expressed in act. If its substantial existence consists in its Act, and this Act constitutes multiplicity, then its substantial existence will be strictly proportioned to the extent of the multiplicity.

We allow this to be true for the Intellectual-Principle to which we have allotted (the multiplicity of) self-knowing; but for the first principle of all, never. Before the manifold, there must be The One, that from which the manifold rises: in all numerical series, the unit is the first.

But—we will be answered—for number, well and good, since the suite makes a compound; but in the real beings why must there be a unit from which the multiplicity of entities shall proceed?

Because (failing such a unity) the multiplicity would consist of disjointed items, each starting at its own distinct place and moving accidentally to serve to a total.

But, they will tell us, the Activities in question do proceed from a unity, from the Intellectual-Principle, a simplex.

By that they admit the existence of a simplex prior to the Activities; and they make the Activities perdurable and class them as substantial existences (hypostases); but as Hypostases they will be distinct from their source, which will remain simplex; while its product will in its own nature be manifold and dependent upon it.

Now if these activities arise from some unexplained first activity in that principle, then it too contains the manifold: if on the contrary they are the very earliest activities and the source and cause of any multiple product and the means by which that Principle is able, before any activity occurs, to remain self-centred, then they are allocated to the product of which they are the cause; for this principle is one thing, the activities going forth from it are another, since it is not, itself, in act. If this be not so, the first act cannot be the Intellectual-Principle: the One does not provide for the existence of an Intellectual-Principle which thereupon appears; that provision would be something (an Hypostasis) intervening between the One and the Intellectual-Principle its offspring. There could, in fact, be no such providing in The One, for it was never incomplete; and such provision could name nothing that ought to be provided. It cannot be thought to possess only some part of its content, and not the whole; nor did anything exist to which it could turn in desire. Clearly anything that comes into being after it arises without shaking to its permanence in its own habit. It is essential to the existence of any new entity that the First remain in self-gathered repose throughout: otherwise, it moved before there was motion and had intellectual act before any intellection—unless, indeed, that first act (as motionless and without intelligence) was incomplete, nothing more than a tendency. And what could be the object of such a tendency born of frustration?

The only reasonable explanation of act flowing from it lies in the analogy of light from a sun. The entire intellectual order may be figured as a kind of light with the One in repose at its summit as its King: but this manifestation is not cast out from it—that would cause us to postulate another light before the light—but the One shines eternally, resting upon the Intellectual Realm; this, not identical with its source, is yet not severed from it nor of so remote a nature as to be less than Real-Being; it is no blind thing, but is seeing, self-knowing, the primal knower.

The One, as transcending Intellect, transcends knowing: above all need, it is above the need of the knowing which pertains solely to the Secondary Nature. Knowing is a unitary thing, but defined: the first is One, but undefined: a defined One would not be the One-Absolute: the absolute is prior to the definite.

13. Thus The One is in truth beyond all statement: any affirmation is of a thing; but 'all-transcending, resting above even the most august divine Mind'—this is the only true description, since it does not make it a thing among things, I nor name it where no name could identify it:[6] I we can but try to indicate, in our own feeble way, something concerning it. When in our perplexity we object, 'Then it is without self-perception, without self-consciousness, ignorant of itself', we must remember that we have been considering it only in its opposites.

I If we assume within it the distinction of knowing and known,[7] we make it a manifold; I and if we allow intellection in it, we make it at that point indigent: supposing that in fact intellection accompanies it, intellection by it must be superfluous.

Self-intellection—which is the truest—implies the entire perception of a total self formed from a variety converging into an integral; every single unit in this variety is self-subsistent and has no need to look outside itself: if its intellectual act is, on the other hand, directed upon something outside, then the agent is deficient and the intellection faulty.

The wholly simplex and veritable self-sufficing can be lacking at no point: self-intellection begins in that principle which, secondarily self-sufficing, yet needs itself and therefore needs to know itself; this principle, by its self-presence, achieves its sufficiency in virtue of its entire content (it is the all): it becomes thus competent from the total of its being, in the act of living towards itself and looking upon itself.

Consciousness, as the very word indicates, is a conperception, an act exercised upon a manifold: and even intellection, earlier (nearer to the divine) though it is, implies that the agent turns back upon itself, upon a manifold, then. If that agent says no more than 'I am a being', it speaks (by the implied dualism) as a discoverer of the extern; and rightly so, for being is a manifold; when it faces towards the unmanifold and says, 'I am that being', it misses both itself and the being (since the simplex cannot be thus divided into knower and known): if it is to utter truth it cannot indicate by 'being' something (single) like a stone; in the one phrase multiplicity is asserted; for the being thus affirmed—the veritable, as distinguished from such a mere container of some trace of being as ought not to be called a being since it stands merely as image to archetype—this must possess multiplicity.

But will not each item in that multiplicity be an object of intellection to us?

Taken bare and single, no: but Being itself is manifold within itself, and whatever else you may name has Being.

This accepted, it follows that anything that is to be thought of as the most utterly simplex of all, cannot have self-intellection; to have that would mean being multiple. The Transcendent, thus, neither knows itself nor is known in itself.

14. How, then, do we ourselves come to be speaking of it?

No doubt we deal with it, but we do not state it; we have neither knowledge nor intellection of it.

But in what sense do we even deal with it when we have no hold upon it?

We do not, it is true, grasp it by knowledge, but that does not mean that we are utterly void of it; we hold it not so as to state it, but so as to be able to speak about it. And we can and do state what it is not, while we are silent as to what it is: we are, in fact, speaking of it in the light of its sequels; unable to state it, we may still possess it.

Those divinely possessed and inspired have at least the knowledge that they hold some greater thing within them though they cannot tell what it is; from the movements that stir them and the utterances that come from them they perceive the power, not themselves, that moves them: in the same way, it must be, we stand towards the Supreme when we hold the Intellectual-Principle pure; we know the divine Mind within, that which gives Being and all else of that order: but we know, too, that other, know that it is none of these, but a nobler principle than anything we know as Being; fuller and greater; above reason, mind, and feeling; conferring these powers, not to be confounded with them.

15. Conferring—but how? As itself possessing them or not? How can it convey what it does not possess, and yet if it does possess how is it simplex? And if, again, it does not, how is it the source of the manifold?

A single, unmanifold emanation we may very well allow—how even that can come from a pure unity may be a problem, but we may always explain it on the analogy of the irradiation from a luminary—but a multitudinous production raises question.

The explanation is, that what comes from the Supreme cannot be identical with it and assuredly cannot be better than it—what could be better than The One or could exceed it in any sense? The emanation, then, must be less good, that is to say, less self-sufficing: now what must that be which is less self-sufficing than The One? Obviously the Not-One, that is to say, multiplicity but a multiplicity striving towards unity; that is to say, a One-that-is-many.

All that is not One is conserved by virtue of the One, and from the One derives its characteristic nature: if it had not attained such unity as is consistent with being made up of multiplicity we could not affirm its existence: if we are able to affirm the nature of single things, this is in virtue of the unity, the identity even, which each of them possesses. But the all-transcendent, utterly void of multiplicity, has no mere unity of participation but is unity's self, independent of all else, as being that from which, by whatever means, all the rest take their degree of unity in their standing, near or far, towards it.

❙The second principle shows that it is next in order (after the all-transcendent One) by the fact that its multiplicity is at the same time an all-embracing unity:⁸❙ all the variety lies in the midst of a sameness, and identity cannot be separated from diversity since all stands as one; each item in that content, by the fact of participating in life, is a One-many: for the item could not make itself manifest as a One-and-all.

Only the Transcendent can be that; it is the great beginning, and the beginning must be a really existent One, wholly and truly One, while its sequent, poured down in some way from the One, is all, a total which has participation in unity and whose every member is similarly all and one.

What then is the All?

The total of which the Transcendent is the Source.

But in what way is it that source? In the sense, perhaps, of sustaining things as bestower of the unity of each single item?

That too; but also as having established them in being.

But how? As having, perhaps, contained them previously?

We have indicated that, thus, the First would be a manifold.

May we think, perhaps, that the First contained the universe as an indistinct total whose items are elaborated to distinct existence within the Second by the Reason-Principle there? That Second is certainly an Activity; the Transcendent would contain only the potentiality of the universe to come.

But the nature of this contained potentiality would have to be explained: it cannot be that of Matter, a receptivity, for thus the Source becomes passive, the very negation of production.

How then does it produce what it does not contain? Certainly not at haphazard and certainly not by selection. How then?

We have observed that anything that may spring from the One must be different from it. Differing, it is not One, since then it would be the Source. If unity has given place to duality, from that moment there is multiplicity; for there is variety side by side with identity, and this imports quality and all the rest.

We may take it as proved that the emanation of the Transcendent must be a Not-One, something other than pure unity: but that it is a multiplicity, and especially that it is such a multiplicity as is exhibited in the sequent universe, this is a statement worthy of deliberation: some further inquiry must be made, also, as to the necessity of any sequel to the First.

16. We have, of course, already seen that a secondary must follow upon the First, and that this is a power immeasurably fruitful; and we indicated that this truth is confirmed by the entire order of things since there is nothing, not even in the lowest ranks, void of the power of generating. We have now to add that, since things engendered tend downwards and not upwards and, especially, move towards multiplicity, the first principle of all must be less a manifold than any.

That which engenders the world of sense cannot itself be a sense-world; it must be the Intellect and the Intellectual world; similarly, the prior which engenders the Intellectual-Principle and the Intellectual world cannot be either, but must be something of less multiplicity. The manifold does not rise from the manifold: the intellectual multiplicity has its source in what is not mani-fold; by the mere fact of being manifold, the thing is not the first principle: we must look to something earlier.

All must be grouped under a unity which, as standing outside of all multi-plicity and outside of any ordinary simplicity, is the veritably and essentially simplex.

But how does the offspring of unity become a Reason-Principle, character-istically a manifold, a total, when the source is obviously not a Reason-Principle? Yet if it is not, how can we explain the derivation of Reason-Principle from non-Reason-Principle?

And how does the secondarily good (the imaged Good) derive from The Good, the Absolute? What does it hold from the Absolute Good to entitle it to the name?

Similarity to the prior is not enough, it does not help towards goodness; we demand similarity only to an actually existent Good: the goodness must depend upon derivation from a Prior of such a nature that the similarity is desirable because that Prior is good, just as the similarity would be undesirable if the Prior were not good.

Does the similarity with the Prior consist, then, in a voluntary resting upon it?

It is rather that, finding its condition satisfying, it seeks nothing: the similarity depends upon the all-sufficiency of what it possesses; its existence is agreeable because all is present to it, and present in such a way as not to be even different from it (Intellectual-Principle is Being).

All life belongs to it, life brilliant and perfect; thus all in it is at once life-principle and Intellectual-Principle, nothing in it aloof from either life or in-tellect: it is therefore self-sufficing and seeks nothing: and if it seeks nothing this is because it has in itself what, lacking, it must seek. It has, therefore, the Good within itself, either in the form of what we have called its life and intellect, or as shown in some other quality or character going to produce these.

If this (secondary principle) were The Good (The Absolute) nothing could transcend these things, life and intellect: but, given the existence of something higher, this Intellectual-Principle must possess a life directed towards that Transcendent, dependent upon it, deriving its being from it, living towards it as towards its source. The First, then, must transcend this principle of life and intellect which directs thither both the life in itself, a copy of the life-giving principle in the First, and the intellect in itself which is again a copy, though of what original there we cannot know.

17. But what can it be which is loftier than a life compact of wisdom, untouched

by struggle and error, or than an Intellect which holds the Universe—loftier, then, than all there is of life and all there is of intellect?

If we answer 'The Making Principle', there comes the question, 'making by what virtue'? and unless we can indicate something higher there than in the made, our reasoning has made no advance: we rest where we were.

We must go higher—if it were only for the reason that the self-sufficiency of the Intellectual-Principle is that of a totality of which each member is patently indigent, and that each has participated in The One and, as drawing on unity, is itself not unity.

What then is this in which each particular entity participates, the author of being to the universe and to each item of the total?

Since it is the author of all that exists, and since the multiplicity in each thing is converted into a self-sufficing existence by this presence of The One, so that even the particular itself becomes self-sufficing, then clearly this principle, author at once of Being and of self-sufficingness, is not itself a Being but is above Being and above even self-sufficing.

May we stop, content, with that? No: the Soul is yet, and even more, in pain. Is she ripe, perhaps, to bring forth, now that in her pangs she has come so close to what she seeks? No: we must call upon yet another spell if anywhere the assuagement is to be found. Perhaps in what has already been uttered, there lies the charm if only we tell it over often? No: we need a new, a further, incantation. All our effort may well skim over every truth, and through all the verities in which we have part, and yet the reality escape us when we hope to affirm, to understand: for the understanding, in order to its affirmation, must possess itself of item after item; only so does it traverse all the field: but how can there be any such peregrination of that in which there is no variety?

All the need is met by a contact purely intellective. At the moment of touch there is no power whatever to make any affirmation; there is no leisure; reasoning upon the vision is for afterwards. We may know we have had the vision when the Soul has suddenly taken light. This light is from the Supreme and is the Supreme; we may believe in the Presence when, like that other God on the call of a certain man, He comes bringing light: the light is the proof of the advent. Thus, the Soul unlit remains without that vision; lit, it possesses what it sought. And this is the true end set before the Soul, to take that light, to see the Supreme by the Supreme and not by the light of any other principle—to see the Supreme which is also the means to the vision; for that which illumines the Soul is that which it is to see, just as it is by the sun's own light that we see the sun.

But how is this to be accomplished?

Cut away everything.

NOTES TO ENNEAD V.3

1. FIRST EDITION: ". . . we perceive by means of the perceptive faculty and are (omits "not"), ourselves, the percipients: may we *not* say the same of the *intellective act?*"

GUTHRIE: "We feel through sensation, and it is we who feel. Is it also we who conceive and who simultaneously are conceived?"

TAYLOR: "For we are sentient through sense, and we ourselves perceive sensibly. Are we therefore thus dianoetically perceived, and do we thus dianoetically energize?" For helpful context and background about the intellect which is ours only when we act by it, see Taylor's long footnote concerning the "partial intellect of the Minerva series" on pages 261–262 of the Bohn's Philosophical Library edition.

ARMSTRONG supports the fourth edition. See his first footnote and critical note on page 80 of the Loeb Classical Library edition.

2. FIRST EDITION: "—*divine* intellections *perfectly wrought out*—*so* that all . . ."

TAYLOR: ". . . which are as it were intellections derived from first intelligibles."

GUTHRIE: ". . . which resemble distant thoughts, and are traces of thought and Intelligence . . ."

ARMSTRONG: ". . . which are like intellections carried out in practice, so that . . ."

3. FIRST EDITION: ". . . retaining some light from that *sun, while it pours downward upon the sphere of magnitudes (that is, of Matter) the light playing about itself which is generated from its own nature.*"

TAYLOR: ". . . which preserves something of its light; so as to resemble the light proximate to the sphere of the sun which emanating from, diffuses its light about the sun."

GUTHRIE: ". . . an image that radiates from Intelligence, as from the immense globe of the sun radiates the surrounding luminary sphere."

ARMSTRONG: ". . . preserving something of its light, like the light of the sun which, beyond its spherical mass, shines around it and from it."

4. FIRST EDITION: ". . . if the created were all, *these ultimates (the higher) need not exist:* but the Supreme does include primals, the primals because the producers. In other words, there must be, with the made, the making source; and, *unless these are to be identical,* there will be need of *some link between them. Similarly, this link which is the Intellectual-Principle demands yet a Transcendent.*"

GUTHRIE: "If the (forms) contained by Intelligence are not created forms—otherwise the forms contained in us would no longer, as they should, occupy the lowest rank—if these forms in intelligence really be creative and primary, then either these creative forms and the creative principle fuse into one single entity, or intelligence needs some other principle. But does the transcendent Principle, that is superior to Intelligence (the One), itself also need some further principle? No, because it is only Intelligence that stands in need of such an one."

TAYLOR: "If, however, not only forms that are produced, are in intellect, for they are not the last of things [when they are considered as having an intellectual subsistence]; but their productive forms are the first of things, whence also they are first;—if this be the case, it is necessary, that the producing cause of forms should also be there, and that both the productive cause and the forms produced should be one. For if this is not admitted, intellect will again be in want of something else. What then, will that which is beyond this be again in want? Or is not this, indeed, which is indigent intellect?" Brackets are Taylor's.

ARMSTRONG: "But if there were only the things which are made, there would be no ultimate realities. But in the intelligible world the principles which make are primary; it is because they make that they are primary. The primary principle, then, and the making principle must coincide, and both must be one: if not, there will be need of yet another. What then? Is there not a need of that which is beyond Intellect? Or is Intellect this?"

5. Neither the FIRST EDITION, TAYLOR, GUTHRIE, nor ARMSTRONG has this parenthetical remark.

6. FIRST EDITION: ". . . *we can give it* no name *because that would imply predication.*"

TAYLOR: "Properly speaking, however, there is no name of it, because nothing can be asserted of it."

GUTHRIE: ". . . really has no name . . . Nor can He be given any name, since we cannot assert anything about Him."

ARMSTRONG: ". . . it is not its name, but says that it is not one of all things and 'has no name', because we can say nothing of it:"

7. FIRST EDITION: "If we *make it knowable, an object of affirmation,* we make it a manifold;"

ARMSTRONG: "For we are making it many when we make it an object of knowledge and knowledge . . ."

TAYLOR: "For we make it to be multitudinous, when we admit that it is knowable and has knowledge:"

GUTHRIE: "When we suppose that He can be known, or that He possesses self-consciousness, we are already making Him manifold."

8. FIRST EDITION: "*In virtue of the unity manifested in its variety it exhibits, side by side, both an all-embracing identity and the existence of the secondary:*"

ARMSTRONG supports the fourth edition.

GUTHRIE: "Since the characteristic of that which is nearest to unity is identity, and is posterior to unity, evidently the manifoldness contained therein, must be the totality of things that are single."

TAYLOR: "But since that which is next to *the one* is characterized by sameness, and is posterior to *the one,* it is evident that the multitude of it is every where one."

FOURTH TRACTATE

How the Secondaries rise from The First: and on The One

1. Anything existing after The First must necessarily arise from that First, whether immediately or as tracing back to it through intervenients; there must be an order of secondaries and tertiaries, in which any second is to be referred to The First, any third to the second.

Standing before all things, there must exist a Simplex, differing from all its sequel, self-gathered not interblended with the forms that rise from it, and yet able in some mode of its own to be present to those others: it must be authentically a unity, not merely something elaborated into unity and so in reality no more than unity's counterfeit; it will debar all telling and knowing except that it may be described as transcending Being—for if there were nothing outside all alliance and compromise, nothing authentically one, there would be no Source. Untouched by multiplicity, it will be wholly self-sufficing, an absolute First, whereas any not-first demands its earlier, and any non-simplex needs the simplicities within itself as the very foundations of its composite existence.

There can be only one such being: if there were another, the two (as indiscernible) would resolve into one, for we are not dealing with two corporal entities.

Our One-First is not a body: nothing simplex can be a body and, as a thing of process cannot be a First, the Source cannot be a thing of generation: only a principle outside of body, and utterly untouched by multiplicity, could be The First.

Any unity, then, later than The First must be no longer simplex; it can be no more than a unity in diversity.

Whence must such a sequent arise?

It must be an offspring of The First; for suppose it the product of chance, that First ceases to be the Principle of All.

But how does it arise from The First?

If The First is perfect, utterly perfect above all, and is the beginning of all power, it must be the most powerful of all that is, and all other powers must act in some partial imitation of it. Now other beings, coming to perfection, are observed to generate; they are unable to remain self-closed; they produce: and this is true not merely of beings endowed with will, but of growing things where there is no will; even lifeless objects impart something of themselves, as far as they may; fire warms, snow chills, drugs have their own outgoing efficacy; all things to the utmost of their power imitate the Source in some operation tending to eternity and to service.

How then could the most perfect remain self-set—the First Good, the Power towards all, how could it grudge or be powerless to give of itself, and how at that would it still be the Source?

If things other than itself are to exist, things dependent upon it for their reality, it must produce since there is no other source. And, further, this engendering principle must be the very highest in worth; and its immediate offspring, its secondary, must be the best of all that follows.

2. If the Intellectual-Principle were the engendering Source, then the engendered secondary, while less perfect than the Intellectual-Principle, would be close to it and similar to it: but since the engendering Source is above the Intellectual-Principle, the secondary can only be that principle.

But why is the Intellectual-Principle not the generating source?

Because (it is not a self-sufficing simplex): the Act of the Intellectual-Principle is intellection, which means that, seeing the intellectual object towards which it has turned, it is consummated, so to speak, by that object, being in itself indeterminate like sight (a vague readiness for any and every vision) and determined by the intellectual object. This is why it has been said ❙ that 'out of the indeterminate Dyad and The One arise the Ideas and the numbers': for the Ideas and the numbers constitute[1] the Intellectual-Principle.❙

Thus it is not a simplex; it is manifold; it exhibits a certain composite quality—within the Intellectual or divine order, of course—as the principle that sees the manifold. It is, further, itself simultaneously object and agent of intellection and is on that count also a duality:❙ and it possesses, besides, another object of intellection in the order following upon The First.[2]❙

But how can the Intellectual-Principle be a product of the Intellectual Object?

In this way: the intellectual object is self-gathered (self-compact) and is not deficient as the seeing and knowing principle must be—deficient, I mean, as needing an object—it is therefore no unconscious thing: all its content and accompaniment are its possession; it is self-distinguishing throughout; it is the seat of life as of all things; it is, itself, that self-intellection which, stemming from an inner consciousness, takes place in eternal repose, that is to say, in a mode other than that of the Intellectual-Principle.

❙ But if something arises from an entity which in no way looks outside itself, it must arise when that entity is in the fullness of its being:[3]❙ stable in its identity, it produces; but the product is that of an unchanged being: the producer is unchangeably the intellectual object, the product is produced as the Intellectual Act, an Act taking intellection of its source—the only object that exists for it—

and so becoming Intellectual-Principle, that is to say, becoming another intellectual being, resembling its source, a reproduction and image of that.

But how from amid perfect rest can an Act arise?

There is in everything the Act of the Essence and the Act going out from the Essence: the first Act is the thing itself in its realized identity, the second Act is an inevitably following outgo from the first, an emanation distinct from the thing itself.

Thus even in fire there is the warmth comported by its essential nature and there is the warmth going instantaneously outward from that characterizing heat by the fact that the fire, remaining unchangeably fire, utters the Act native to its essential reality.

So it is in the divine also: or rather we have there the earlier form of the double act: the divine remains in its own unchanging being, but from its perfection and from the Act included in its nature there emanates the secondary or issuing Act which—as the output of a mighty power, the mightiest there is—attains to Real Being as second to that which stands above all Being. That transcendent was the potentiality of the All; this secondary is the All made actual.

And if this is all things, that must be above and outside of all, and, so, must transcend real being. And again, if that secondary is all things, and if above its multiplicity there is a unity not ranking among those things, once more this unity transcends Real Being and therefore transcends the Intellectual-Principle as well. There is thus something transcending Intellectual-Principle, for we must remember that real being is no corpse, the negation of life and of intellection, but is in fact identical with the Intellectual-Principle. The Intellectual-Principle is not something taking cognizance of things as sensation deals with sense objects existing independently of sense: on the contrary, it actually is the things it knows: ▌ it does not merely possess their images or representations: whence could it have taken them? No: it resides with its objects, identical with them, making a unity with them; knowledge of the immaterial is universally identical with its objects. ⁴▌

NOTES TO ENNEAD V.4

1. FIRST EDITION: "... that 'out of the indeterminate dyad and The One arise the Ideas and the numbers': for the *dyad is* the Intellectual-Principle."

GUTHRIE: "This is the reason of the saying, 'The ideas and numbers, that is, intelligence, are born from the indefinite doubleness, and the One.'"

ARMSTRONG: "... from the Indefinite Dyad and the One derive the Forms and Numbers: that is, Intellect." Armstrong adds a helpful footnote which speaks of the "dyad" here as "the indefinite life or sight which is the first moment in the timeless formation of Intellect by procession from and return upon the One." He also gives numerous references for a fuller exposition of this important doctrine. See pages 145 and 26–27 of the Loeb Classical Library edition.

2. FIRST EDITION: "... and it possesses besides another object of intellection in the Order following upon *itself*."

ARMSTRONG: "And it is also a different intelligible by being posterior to the One itself."

GUTHRIE: "But besides this intelligible (entity, namely, intelligence), there is another (higher) intelligible (the supreme Intelligible, the First)."

3. FIRST EDITION: "But if something *comes to being within* an entity which in no way looks outside itself—*and especially within a being which is the sum of being—that entity must be the source of the new thing*."

GUTHRIE: "If He begets something while remaining within Himself, He begets it precisely when He is at the highest point of individuality."

ARMSTRONG: "If, then, something comes into being while the Intelligible abides in itself, it comes into being from it when it is most of all what it is."

4. FIRST EDITION: "... *the ideas constituting them it has not borrowed:* whence could it have taken them? No: *it exists here together with the things of the universe,* identical with them, making a unity with them; *and the collective* knowledge *(in the divine mind)* of the immaterial is *the universe of things*."

GUTHRIE: "... since their forms are not introduced to them from without. From where indeed would intelligence receive these forms? Intelligence exists with the intelligible things; intelligence is identical with them, is one with them. Reciprocally, intelligible entities do not exist without their matter (that is, Intelligence)."

ARMSTRONG: "... granted that it does not get their forms from somewhere (for where could it get them from?). But it is here with its objects and the same as and one with them: the knowledge of things without matter is its objects."

FIFTH TRACTATE

That the Intellectual Beings are not outside the Intellectual-Principle: and on The Nature of the Good [1]

1. The Intellectual Principle, the veritably and essentially intellective, can this be conceived as ever falling into error, ever failing to think reality?

Assuredly no: it would no longer be intelligent and therefore no longer Intellectual-Principle: it must know unceasingly and never forget; and its knowledge can be no guess-work, no hesitating assent, no acceptance of an alien report. Nor can it call on demonstration or, if we are told it may at times act by this method, at least there must be something patent to it in virtue of its own nature. In actual fact reason tells us that all its knowledge is thus inherent to it, for there is no means by which to distinguish between the spontaneous knowledge and the other. But, in any case, some knowledge, it is conceded, is inherent to it. Whence are we to understand the certainty of this knowledge to come to it or how do its objects carry the conviction of their reality?

Consider sense-knowledge: its objects seem most patently certified, yet the doubt returns whether the apparent reality may not lie in the states of the percipient rather than in the material before him; the decision demands intelligence or reasoning. Besides, even granting that what the senses grasp is really contained in the objects, none the less what is thus known by the senses is an image: sense can never grasp the thing itself; this remains for ever outside.

Now, if the Intellectual-Principle in its act—that is in knowing the intelligible—is to know these its objects as alien, we have to explain how it makes contact with them: obviously it might never come upon them, and so might never know them; or it might know them only upon the meeting: its knowing, at that, would not be an enduring condition. If we are told that the Intellectual-Principle and the Intellectual Objects are linked in a standing unity, we demand the description of this unity.

Next, the intellections would be impressions, that is to say not native act but violence from without: now how is such impressing possible and what shape could the impressions bear?

Intellection, again, becomes at this a mere handling of the external, exactly like sense-perception. What then distinguishes it unless that it deals with objects of less extension? And what certitude can it have that its knowledge is true? Or what enables it to pronounce that the object is good, beautiful, or just, when each of these Ideas is to stand apart from itself? The very principles of judgement, by which it must be guided, would be excluded: with objects and canons alike outside it, so is truth.

Again; either the objects of the Intellectual-Principle are senseless and devoid of life and intellect or they are in possession of Intellect.

Now, if they are in possession of Intellect, that realm is a union of both, and is Truth. This combined Intellectual realm will be the Primal Intellect: we have only then to examine how this reality, conjoint of Intellectual-Principle and its object, is to be understood, whether as combining self-united identity with yet duality and difference, or what other relation holds between them.

If on the contrary the objects of Intellectual-Principle are without intelligence and life, what are they? They cannot be premises, axioms, or predicates: as predicates they would not have real existence; they would be affirmations linking separate entities, as when we affirm that justice is good though justice and good are distinct realities.

If we are told that they are self-standing entities—the distinct beings Justice and Good—then (supposing them to be outside) the Intellectual Realm will not be a unity nor be included in any unity: all is sundered individuality. Where, then, are they and what spatial distinction keeps them apart? How does the Intellectual-Principle come to meet with them as it travels round; what keeps each true to its character; what gives them enduring identity; what conceivable shape or character can they have? They are being presented to us as some collection of figures, in gold or some other material substance, the work of some unknown sculptor or graver: but at once the Intellectual-Principle which contemplates them becomes sense-perception; and there still remains the question how one of them comes to be Justice and another something else.

But the great argument is that if we go so far as to allow that these objects of Intellection are outside the Intellectual-Principle which therefore must see them as external, then inevitably it cannot possess the truth of them.

In all it looks upon, it sees falsely; for those objects must be the authentic things; yet it looks upon them without containing them and in such knowledge holds only their images; that is to say, not containing the authentic, adopting phantasms of the true, it holds the false; it never possesses reality. If it knows that it possesses the false, it must confess itself excluded from the truth; if it fails of this knowledge also, imagining itself to possess the truth which has eluded it, then the doubled falsity puts it the deeper into error.

It is thus, I suppose, that in sense-perception we have belief instead of truth; belief is our lief; we satisfy ourselves with something very different from the original which is the occasion of perception.

In fine, there would be on the hypothesis no truth in the Intellectual-Principle. But such an Intellectual-Principle would not be truth, nor truly an

Intellectual-Principle. There would be no Intellectual-Principle at all (no Divine Mind): yet elsewhere truth cannot be.

2. Thus we may not look for the Intellectual objects (the Ideas) outside of the Intellectual-Principle, treating them as impressions of reality upon it: we cannot strip it of truth and so make its objects unknowable and non-existent and in the end annul the Intellectual-Principle itself. We must provide for knowledge and for truth; we must secure reality; being must become knowable essentially and not merely in that knowledge of quality which could give us a mere image or vestige of the reality in lieu of possession, intimate association, absorption.

The only way to this is to leave nothing outside of the veritable Intellectual-Principle which thus has knowledge in the true knowing (that of identification with the object), cannot forget, need not go wandering in search. At once truth is there, this is the seat of the authentic Existents, it becomes living and intellective: these are the essentials of that most lofty Principle; and, failing them, where is its worth, its grandeur?

Only thus (by this inherence of the Ideas) is it dispensed from demonstration and from acts of faith in the truth of its knowledge: it is its entire self, self-perspicuous: it knows a prior by recognizing its own source; it knows a sequent to that prior by its self-identity; of the reality of this sequent, of the fact that it is present and has authentic existence, no outer entity can bring it surer conviction.

Thus veritable truth is not accordance with an external; it is self-accordance; it affirms nothing other than itself and is nothing other; it is at once existence and self-affirmation. What external, then, can call it to the question and from what source of truth could the refutation be brought? Any counter-affirmation (or truth) must fall into identity with the truth which first uttered itself; brought forward as new it has to appear before the Principle which made the earlier statement and to show itself identical with that: for there is no finding anything truer than the true.

3. Thus we have here one identical Principle, the Intellect, which is the universe of authentic beings, the Truth: as such it is a great god or, better, not a god among gods but the Godhead entire. It is a god, a secondary god manifesting before there is any vision of that other, the Supreme which rests over all, enthroned in transcendence upon that splendid pediment, the nature following close upon it.

The Supreme in its progress could never be borne forward upon some soulless vehicle nor even directly upon the Soul: it will be heralded by some ineffable beauty: before the great King in his progress there comes first the minor train, then rank by rank the greater and more exalted, closer to the King the kinglier; next his own honoured company until, last among all these grandeurs, suddenly appears the Supreme Monarch himself, and all—unless indeed for those who have contented themselves with the spectacle before his coming and gone away—prostrate themselves and hail him.

In that royal progress the King is of another order from those that go before him, but the King in the Supreme is no ruler over externs; he holds that most just of governances, rooted in nature, the veritable kingship, for he is King of Truth, holding sway by all reason over a dense offspring his own, a host that shares his divinity, King over a king and over kings and even more justly called father of Gods.

Zeus (Universal Soul) is in this a symbol of him, Zeus who is not content with the contemplation of his father (Kronos, divine Intellect) but looks to that father's father (to Ouranos, the Transcendent) as what may be called the divine energy working to the establishment of real being.

4. We have said that all must be brought back to a unity: this must be an authentic unity, not belonging to the order in which multiplicity is unified by participation in what is truly a One; we need a unity independent of participation, not a combination in which multiplicity holds an equal place: we have exhibited, also, the Intellectual Realm and the Intellectual-Principle as more closely a unity than the rest of things, so that there is nothing closer to The One. Yet even this is not The Purely One.

This purely One, essentially a unity untouched by the multiple, this we now desire to penetrate if in any way we may.

Only by a leap can we reach to this One which is to be pure of all else, halting sharp in fear of slipping ever so little aside and impinging on the dual: for if we fail of the centre, we are in a duality which does not even include The authentic One but belongs, on both sides, to the later order. The One does not bear to be numbered in with anything else, with a one or a two or any such quantity; it refuses to take number because it is measure and not the measured; it is no peer of other entities to be found among them; for thus, it and they alike would be included in some container and this would be its prior, the prior it cannot have. Not even essential (ideal or abstract) number can belong to The One and certainly not the still later number applying to quantities; **I** for essential number first appears as the unfailing provider of Substance[2] to the divine Intellection, **I** while quantitative number is that (still later and lower) which furnishes the Quantity found in conjunction with other things or which provides for Quantity independent of things, if this is to be thought of as number at all. The Principle which in objects having quantitative number looks to the unity from which they spring is a copy (or lower phase) of the Principle which in the earlier order of number (in essential or ideal number) looks to the veritable One; and it attains its existence without in the least degree dissipating or shattering that prior unity: the dyad has come into being, but the precedent monad still stands; and this monad is quite distinct within the dyad from either of the two constituent unities, since there is nothing to make it one rather than the other: being neither, but simply that thing apart, it is present without being inherent.

But how are the two unities distinct and how is the dyad a unity, and is this unity the same as the unity by which each of the constituents is one thing?

Our answer must be that the unity is that of a participation in the primal unity with the participants remaining distinct from that in which they partake; the dyad, in so far as it is one thing, has this participation, but in a certain degree only; the unity of an army is not that of a single building; I and even the building,³I as a thing of extension, is not strictly a unit either quantitatively or in manner of being.

Are we then to take it that the monads in the pentad and decad differ while the unity in the pentad is the same as that in the decad?

Yes, in the sense in which, big and little, ship is one with ship, army with army, city with city; otherwise, no. But certain difficulties in this matter will be dealt with later.

5. We return to our statement that The First remains intact even when other entities spring from it.

In the case of numbers the unit remains intact while something else produces, and thus number arises in dependence on the unit: much more then does the unit, The One, remain intact in the principle which is before all beings; especially since the entities produced in its likeness, while it thus remains intact, owe their existence to no other, but to its own all-sufficient power.

And just as there is, primarily or secondarily, some form or idea from the monad in each of the successive numbers—the later still participating, though unequally, in the unit—so the series of Beings following upon The First bear, each, some form or idea derived from that source. In Number the participation establishes Quantity; in the realm of Being, the trace of The One establishes reality: existence is a trace of The One—our word for entity may probably be connected with that for unity.

What we know as Being, the first sequent upon The One, advanced a little outward, so to speak, then chose to go no further, turned inward again and comes to rest and is now the reality and hearth (*ousia* and *hestia*) of the universe. Pressing (with the rough breathing) on the word for Being (*on*) we have the word for One (*hen*), an indication that in our very form of speech we tell, as far as may be, that Being (the weaker) is that which proceeds from (the stronger,) The One. Thus both the thing that comes to be and Being itself are carriers of a copy, since they are outflows from the power of The Primal One: I the Soul[4] sees I and in its emotion tries to represent what it sees and breaks into speech 'on—einai—ousia—hestia' (Existent; Existence; Essence; Hestia or Hearth), sounds which labour to express the essential nature of I the being[5] produced by I the travail of the utterer and so to represent, as far as sounds may, the origin of reality.

6. All this, however, we may leave to the individual judgement; to proceed:

This produced reality is an Ideal-form—for certainly nothing springing from the Supreme can be less—and it is not a particular form but the form of all, beside which there is no other; it follows that The First must be without form, and, if without form, then it is no Being; Being must have some definition and therefore be limited; but the First cannot be thought of as having definition and limit, for thus it would be not the Source but the particular item indicated by the definition assigned to it. If all things belong to the produced, which of them can be thought of as the Supreme? Not included among them, this can be described only as transcending them: but they are Being and the Beings; it therefore transcends Being.

Note that the phrase 'transcending Being' assigns no character, makes no assertion, allots no name, carries only the denial of particular being; and in this there is no attempt to circumscribe it: to seek to throw a line about that illimitable Nature would be folly, and anyone thinking to do so cuts himself off from any slightest and most momentary approach to its least vestige.

As one wishing to contemplate the Intellectual Nature will lay aside all the representations of sense and so may see what transcends the sense-realm, in the same way one wishing to contemplate what transcends the Intellectual attains by putting away all that is of the intellect, taught by the intellect, no doubt, that the Transcendent exists but never seeking to define it.

Its definition, in fact, could be only 'the indefinable': what is not a thing is not some definite thing. We are in agony for a true expression; we are talking of the untellable; we name, only to indicate for our own use as best we may. And this name, The One, contains really no more than the negation of plurality: under the same pressure the Pythagoreans found their indication in the symbol 'Apollo' (a = not; pollôn = of many) with its repudiation of the multiple. If we are led to think positively of The One, name and thing, there would be more truth in silence: the designation, a mere aid to inquiry, was never intended for more than a preliminary affirmation of absolute simplicity to be followed by the rejection of even that statement: it was the best that offered, but remains inadequate to express the nature indicated. For this is a principle not to be conveyed by any sound; it cannot be known on any hearing but, if at all, by vision; and to hope in that vision to see a form is to fail of even that.

7. Consider the act of ocular vision:

There are two elements here; there is the form perceptible to the sense and there is the medium by which the eye sees that form. This medium is itself perceptible to the eye, distinct from the form to be seen, but the cause of the seeing; it is perceived at the one stroke in that form and on it and hence is not distinguished from it, the eye being held entirely by the illuminated object. When on the contrary this medium presents itself alone it is seen directly—though even then actual sight demands some solid base; there must be something besides the medium which unless embracing some object eludes perception; thus the light inherent to the sun would not be perceived but for the solidity of the mass. If it is objected that the sun is light entire, this would only be a proof of our assertion: no other visible form will contain light which must, then, have no other property than that of visibility, and in fact all other visible objects are something more than light alone.

So it is with the act of vision in the Intellectual Principle.

This vision sees, by another light, the objects illuminated by the First Principle: I so long as the light is within them, it sees;⁶I declining towards the lower nature, that upon which the light from above rests, it has less of that vision. Passing over the visible and looking to the medium by which it sees, then it holds the Light and the source of Light.

But since the Intellectual-Principle is not to see this light as something external we return to our analogy: the eye is not wholly dependent upon an outside and alien light; there is an earlier light within itself, a more brilliant, which it sees sometimes in a momentary flash. At night in the darkness a gleam leaps from within the eye: or again we make no effort to see anything; the eyelids close; yet a light flashes before us; or we rub the eye and it sees the light it contains. This is sight without the act, but it is the truest seeing, for it sees light whereas its other objects were the lit, not the light.

It is certainly thus that the Intellectual-Principle, hiding itself from all the outer, withdrawing to the inmost, seeing nothing, must have its vision—not of some other light in some other thing but of the light within itself, unmingled, pure, suddenly gleaming before it; so that we are left wondering whence it came, from within or without; and when it has gone, we say, 'It was here. Yet no; it was beyond!'

8. But we ought not to question whence; there is no whence, no coming or going in place; now it is seen and now not seen. We must not run after it, but

fit ourselves for the vision and then wait tranquilly for its appearance, as the eye waits on the rising of the sun, which in its own time appears above the horizon—out of the ocean, as the poets say—and gives itself to our sight.

This Principle, of which the sun is an image, where has it its dawning, what horizon does it surmount to appear?

It stands immediately above the contemplating Intellect which has held itself at rest towards the vision, looking to nothing else than the good and beautiful, setting its entire being to that in a perfect surrender, and now tranquilly filled with power and taking a new beauty to itself, gleaming in the light of that presence.

This advent, still, is not by expectation: it is coming without approach; the vision is not of something that must enter but of something present before all else, before the Intellect itself made any movement. Yet it is the Intellect that must move, to come and to go—going because it has not known where it should stay and where that presence stays, the nowhere contained.

And if the Intellect, too, could hold itself in that nowhere—not that it is ever in place; it too is uncontained, utterly unplaced—it would remain for ever in the vision of its prior, or, indeed, not in vision but in identity, all duality annulled. But it is Intellect (having a sphere of its own) and when it is to see it must see by that in it which is not Intellect (by its divinest power).

No doubt it is wonderful that The First should thus be present without any coming, and that, while it is nowhere, nowhere is it not: but wonderful though this be in itself, the contrary would be more wonderful to those who know. Of course neither this contrary nor the wonder at it can be entertained. But we must explain:

9. Everything brought into being under some principle not itself is contained either within its maker or, if there is any intermediate, within that: having a prior essential to its being, it needs that prior always, otherwise it would not be contained at all. It is the order of nature: the last in the immediately preceding lasts, these in their priors, and so thing within thing up to the very pinnacle of source.

That Source, having no prior, cannot be contained: uncontained by any of those other forms of being, each held within the series of priors, it is orbed round all, but so as not to be pointed off to hold them part for part; it possesses but is not possessed. Holding all—though itself nowhere held—it is omnipresent, for where its presence failed something would elude its hold. At the same time, in the sense that it is nowhere held it is not present: thus it is both present and not present; not present as not being circumscribed by anything; yet, as being utterly unattached, not inhibited from presence at any point. That inhibition would mean that the First was determined by some other being; the later series, then, would be without part in the Supreme; God has His limit and is no longer self-governed but mastered by inferiors.

While the contained must be where its container is, what is uncontained by place is not debarred from any: for, imagine a place where it is not and evidently some other place retains it; at once it is contained and there is an end of its placelessness.

But if the 'nowhere' is to stand and the ascription of a 'where', implying station in the extern, is to fall, then nothing can be left void; and at once— nothing void, yet no point containing—God is sovranly present through all. We cannot think of something of God here and something else there, nor of all God gathered at some one spot: there is an instantaneous presence everywhere, nothing containing and nothing left void, everything therefore fully held by the divine.

Consider our universe. There is none before it and therefore it is not, itself, in a universe or in any place—what place was there before the universe came to be?—its linked members form and occupy the whole. But Soul is not in the universe, on the contrary the universe is in the Soul; bodily substance is not a place to the Soul; Soul is contained in Intellectual-Principle and is the container of body. The Intellectual-Principle in turn is contained in something else; but that prior principle has nothing in which to be: the First is therefore in nothing, and, therefore, nowhere. But all the rest must be somewhere; and where but in the First?

This can mean only that the First is neither remote from things nor directly within them; there is nothing containing it; it contains all. It is The Good to the universe if only in this way, that towards it all things have their being, all dependent upon it, each in its mode, so that thing rises above thing in goodness according to its fuller possession of authentic being.

10. Still, do not, I urge you, look for The Good through any of these other things; if you do, you will see not itself but its trace: you must form the idea of that which is to be grasped, cleanly standing to itself, not in any combination, the unheld in which all have hold: for no other is such, yet one such there must be.

Now it is clear that we cannot possess ourselves of the power of this principle in its concentrated fullness: so to do one must be identical with it: but some partial attainment is within our reach.

You who make the venture will throw forward all your being but you will never tell it entire—for that, you must yourself be the divine Intellect in Act— and at your utmost success it will still pass from you or, rather, you from it.

❙ When you see The Good, see it entire: later you may think of it and identify with The Good whatever you can remember.[7]❙

It is The Good since, being a power (being effective outwardly), it is the cause of the intelligent and intellective life as of life and intellect: for these grow from it as from the source of essence and of existence, the Source as being One (where all else has duality), simplex and first because before it was nothing. All derives from this: it is the origin of the primal movement which it does not possess and of the repose which is but its absence of need; for neither rest nor movement can belong to that which has no place in which either could occur; centre, object, ground, all are alike unknown to it, for it is before all. Yet its being is not limited; what is there to set bounds to it? Nor, on the other hand, is it infinite in the sense of magnitude; what place can there be to which it must extend, or why should there be movement where there is no lacking? All its infinitude resides in its power: it does not change and will not fail; and in it all that is unfailing finds duration.

11. It is infinite also by right of being a pure unity with nothing towards which to direct any partial content. Absolutely One, it has never known measure and stands outside of number, and so is under no limit either in regard to any extern or within itself; for any such determination would bring something of the dual into it. And having no constituent parts it accepts no pattern, forms no shape.

Reason recognizing it as such a nature, you may not hope to see it with mortal eyes, nor in any way that would be imagined by those who make sense the test of reality and so annul the supremely real. For what passes for the most truly existent is most truly ❙ non-existent,[8] while ❙ this unseen First is the source and principle of Being and sovran over Reality.

You must turn appearances about or you will be left void of God. You will be like those at the festivals who in their gluttony cram themselves with things which none going to the gods may touch; they hold these goods to be more real than the vision of the God who is to be honoured and they go away having had no share in the sanctities of the shrine.

In these rites of philosophy, the unseen god leaves those in doubt of his existence who think nothing patent but what may be known to the flesh: it happens as if a man slept a life through and took the dream world in perfect trust; wake him, and he would refuse belief to the report of his open eyes and settle down to sleep again.

12. Knowing demands the organ fitted to the object; eyes for one kind, ears for another: similarly some things, we must believe, are to be known by the

Intellectual-Principle in us. We must not confuse intellection with hearing or seeing; this would be trying to look with the ears or denying sound because it is not seen. Certain people, we must keep in mind, have forgotten that to which from the beginning onwards their longing and effort are pointed: for all that exists desires and aspires towards the Supreme by a compulsion of nature, as if all had received the oracle that without it they cannot be.

The perception of Beauty and the awe and the stirring of passion towards it are for those already in some degree knowing and awakened: but the Good, as possessed long since and setting up a natural tendency, is inherently present to even those asleep and brings them no wonder when some day they see it, since it is no occasional reminiscence but is always with them though in their drowse they are not aware of it: the love of Beauty on the contrary sets up pain when it appears, for those that have seen it must pursue. This love of Beauty then is later than the love of Good and comes with a more sophisticated understanding; hence we know that Beauty is a secondary: the more primal appetition, not patent to sense, our movement towards our good, gives witness that The Good is the earlier, the prior.

Again; all that have possessed themselves of The Good feel it sufficient; they have attained the end: but Beauty not all have known and those that have judge it to exist for itself and not for them, as in the charm of this world the beauty belongs only to its possessor.

Then, too, it is thought enough to appear loveable whether one is so or not: but no one wants his Good in semblance only. All are seeking The First as something ranking before aught else, but they struggle venomously for Beauty as something secondary like themselves: thus some minor personage may perhaps challenge equal honour with the King's right-hand man on pretext of similar dependence, forgetting that, while both owe their standing to the monarch, the other holds the higher rank.

The source of the error is that while both the good and the beautiful participate in the common source, The One precedes both; and that, in the Supreme also, The Good has no need of The Beautiful, while The Beautiful does need The Good.

The Good is gentle and friendly and tender, and we have it present when we but will. Beauty is all violence and stupefaction; its pleasure is spoiled with pain, and it even draws the thoughtless away from The Good as some attraction will lure the child from the father's side: these things tell of youth. The Good is the older—not in time but by degree of reality—and it has the higher and earlier power, all power in fact, for the sequent holds only a power subordinate and delegated of which the prior remains sovereign.

Not that God has any need of His derivatives: He ignores all that produced realm, never necessary to Him, and remains identically what He was before He brought it into being. So too, had the secondary never existed, He would have been unconcerned, exactly as He would not have grudged existence to any other universe that might spring into being from Him, were any such possible; of course no other such could be since there is nothing that has not existence once the All exists.

But God never was the All; that would make Him dependent upon the universe: transcending all, He was able at once to make all things and to leave them to their own being, He above.

13. The Supreme, as the Absolute Good and not merely a good being or thing, can contain nothing—not even the good.

Anything it could contain must be either good to it or not good; but in the supremely and primally Good there can be nothing not good; nor can the Absolute Good be a container to the Good: containing, then, neither the good nor the not-good it contains nothing and, containing nothing, it is alone: it is void of all but itself.

If the rest of being either is good—without being the Absolute Good—or is not good, while on the other hand the Supreme contains neither what is good nor what is not good, then, containing nothing, it is The Good by that very absence of content.

Thus we rob it of its very being as The Absolute Good if we ascribe anything to it, existence or intellect or goodness. The only way is to make every denial and no assertion, to feign no quality or content there but to permit only the 'It is' in which we pretend to no affirmation of non-existent attribute: there is an ignorant praise which, missing the true description, drags in qualities beneath the real worth and so abases; philosophy must guard against attaching to the Supreme what is later and lower: moving above all that order, it is the cause and source of all these, and is none of them.

For, once more, the nature of the Good is not such as to make it all things or a thing among all: that would range it under the same classification with them all and it would differ, thus, only by its individual quality, some speciality, some addition. At once it becomes not a unity but a duality; there is one common element not good and another element that is good; but a combination so made up of good and not good cannot be the purely good, the primarily good; the primarily good must be that principle in which the better element has more effectively participated and so attained its goodness. Any good thing has become so by communion; but that in which it has communion is not a thing among the things of the All; therefore the Good is not a thing of the All.

Since there is this good in any good thing—the specific difference by which the combination becomes good—it must enter from elsewhere than the world of things: it must be simplex, good alone: and therefore—and much more—must that source be a Good absolute and isolated.

Thus is revealed to us the Primarily existent, the Good, above all that has being, good unalloyed, containing nothing in itself, utterly unmingling, all-transcending, cause of all.

Certainly neither Being nor Beauty springs from evil or from the neutral; the maker, as the more consummate, must surpass the made.

NOTES TO ENNEAD V.5

1. This treatise is the third part of the originally continuous work comprised (in chronological order) of III.8 (30), V.8 (31), V.5 (32), and II.9 (33). Armstrong suggests that it is best read after V.8, as the last sentence of V.8 directly introduces the discussion in the first three sections of V.5.

2. FIRST EDITION: ". . . for essential number first appears as *providing duration* to the divine Intellection . . ."

ARMSTRONG: ". . . substantial number is that which continually gives existence . . ."

GUTHRIE: ". . . neither the essential intelligible Number, whose essence is identical with thought . . ."

3. FIRST EDITION: ". . . *the dyad* . . ."

GUTHRIE supports the first edition; ARMSTRONG supports the fourth.

4. FIRST EDITION: ". . . *this power* sees . . ."

ARMSTRONG: "and the [soul] which sees . . ."; GUTHRIE: "The human mind, observing . . ."

5. FIRST EDITION: ". . . the *universe* produced by . . ."

GUTHRIE: "what has been begotten by . . ."; ARMSTRONG: "that produced by . . ."

6. FIRST EDITION: ". . . *setting itself among* them, it sees *veritably*;"

ARMSTRONG: ". . . and sees the light in them;"

GUTHRIE: ". . . and the Intelligence, while seeing these objects, really sees intelligible light."

7. FIRST EDITION: "*In ordinary vision you may think to see the object entire: in this intellective act, all, less or more, that you can take to mind you may set down as The Good.*"

ARMSTRONG: "But when you see him, look at him as a whole; but when you think him, think whatever you remember about him, that he is the Good—"

GUTHRIE: "When you consider the divinity, consider Him in His totality. When you think Him, know that what you remember of Him is the Good;"

8. FIRST EDITION: ". . . non-existent—*the thing of extension least real of all*—while . . ."

ARMSTRONG and GUTHRIE both include the additional thought that the fourth edition omits here.

SIXTH TRACTATE

That the Principle transcending Being has no Intellectual Act. What being has intellection primally and what being has it secondarily

1. There is a principle having intellection of the external and another having self-intellection and thus further removed from duality.

Even the first mentioned is not without an effort towards the pure unity of which it is not so capable: it does actually contain its object, though as something other than itself.

In the self-intellective there is not even this distinction of being: self-conversing, the subject is its own object, and thus takes the double form while remaining essentially a unity. The intellection is the more profound for this internal possession of the object.

This principle is the primally intellective since there can be no intellection without duality in unity. If there is no unity, perceiving principle and perceived object will be different, and the intellection, therefore, not primal: a principle concerned with something external cannot be the primally intellective since it does not possess the object as integrally its own or as itself; if it does possess the object as itself—the condition of true intellection—the two are one. Thus (in order to primal intellection) there must be a unity in duality, while a pure unity with no counterbalancing duality can have no object for its intellection and ceases to be intellective: in other words the primally intellective must be at once simplex and something else.

But the surest way of realizing that its nature demands this combination of unity and duality is to proceed upwards from the Soul where the distinction can be made more clearly since the duality is exhibited more obviously.

I We can imagine a double light, a lesser corresponding to the soul, a purer representing its intelligible object; if now we suppose the seeing light made equal to the light which is[1] its object, I we no longer distinguish between them; the two are recognized as one: we know, indeed, that there are two, but as we see them they have become one: this gives us the relation between the intellective subject and the object of intellection (in the duality and unity required by that primal intellection): in our thought we have made the two into one; but on the other hand the one thing has become two, making itself into a duality at the moment of intellection, or to be more exact, being dual by the fact of intellection and single by the fact that its intellectual object is itself.

2. Thus there is the primally intellective and there is that in which intellection has taken another mode; but this indicates that what transcends the primarily intellective has no intellection; for, to have intellection, it must become an Intellectual-Principle, and, if it is to become that, it must possess an intellectual object and, as primarily intellective, it must possess that intellectual object as something within itself.

But it is not inevitable that every intellectual object should both possess the intellective principle in itself and exercise intellection: at that, it would be not merely object but subject as well and, besides, being thus dual, could not be primal: further, the intellectual principle that is to possess the intellectual object could not cohere unless there existed an essence purely intellectual, something which, while standing as intellectual object to the intellectual principle, is in its own essence neither an agent nor an object of intellection. The intellectual object points to something beyond itself (to a percipient); and the intellectual agent has its intellection in vain unless by seizing and holding an object—since, failing that, it can have no intellection but is consummated only when it possesses itself of its natural term.

There must have been something standing consummate independently of any intellectual act, something perfect in its own essence: thus that in which this completion is inherent must exist before intellection; in other words it has no need of intellection, having been always self-sufficing: this, then, will have no intellectual act.

Thus we arrive at: a principle having no intellection, a principle having intellection primarily, a principle having it secondarily.

It may be added that, supposing The First to be intellective, it thereby possesses something (some object, some attribute): at once it ceases to be a first; it is a secondary, and not even a unity; it is a many; it is all of which it takes intellectual possession; even though its intellection fell solely upon its own content, it must still be a manifold.

3. We may be told that nothing prevents an identity being thus multiple. But there must be a unity underlying the aggregate: a manifold is impossible without a unity for its source or ground, or at least failing some unity related or unrelated. This unity must be numbered as first before all and can be apprehended only as solitary and self-existent.

When we recognize it, resident among the mass of things, our business is to see it for what it is—present to the items but essentially distinguished from them—and, while not denying it there, to seek this underlie of all no longer as it appears in those other things but as it stands in its pure identity by itself. The identity resident in the rest of things is no doubt close to authentic identity but cannot be it; and if the identity of unity is to be displayed beyond itself it must also exist within itself alone.

It may be suggested that its existence takes substantial form only by its being resident among outside things: but, at this, it is itself no longer simplex nor could any coherence of manifolds occur. On the one hand things could take substantial existence only if they were in their own virtue simplex. On the other hand, failing a simplex, the aggregate of multiples is itself impossible: for the simplex individual thing could not exist if there were no simplex unity independent of the individual (a principle of identity), and, not existing, much less could it enter into composition with any other such: it becomes impossible then for the compound universe, the aggregate of all, to exist; it would be the coming together of things that are not, things not merely lacking an identity of their own but utterly non-existent.

Once there is any manifold, there must be a precedent unity: since any intellection implies multiplicity in the intellective subject, the non-multiple must be without intellection; that non-multiple will be the First: intellection and the Intellectual-Principle must be characteristic of beings coming later.

4. Another consideration is that if The Good (and First) is simplex and without need, it can neither need the intellective act nor possess what it does not need: in fact, it possesses nothing: it will therefore not have intellection. It is without intellection because, also, it needs no object.

Again; an Intellectual-Principle is distinct from The Good and takes a certain goodness only by its intellection of The Good.

Yet again: in any dual object there is the unity (the principle of identity) side by side with the rest of the thing; an associated member cannot be the unity of the two and there must be a self-standing unity (within the duality) before this unity of members can exist: I by the same reasoning a simplex which is found in association must exist in its own right, utterly devoid of all that belongs to it by this[2] association. I

How could anything be present in anything else unless in virtue of a source existing independently of association? The simplex (or absolute) requires no derivation; but any manifold, or any dual, must be dependent.

We may use the figure of, first, light; then, following it, the sun; as a third, the orb of the moon taking its light from the sun: Soul carries the Intellectual-Principle as something imparted and lending the light which makes it essentially intellective; Intellectual-Principle carries the light as its own though it is not purely the light but is the being into whose very essence the light has been received; highest is That which, giving forth the light to its sequent, is no other than the pure light itself by whose power the Intellectual-Principle takes character.

How can this highest have need of any other? It is not to be identified with any of the things that enter into association; the self-standing is of a very different order.

5. And again: the multiple must be always seeking its identity, desiring self-accord and self-awareness: but what scope is there within what is an absolute unity in which to move towards its identity, or at what term may it hope for self-knowing? Being above consciousness, it is above all intellective act. Intellection is not a primal either in the fact of being or in the value of being; it is secondary and derived: for The Good gives it being and moves it back towards itself, while its sequent by that movement has its characteristic vision. The intellective act may be defined as a movement towards The Good in some being that aspires towards it; the effort produces the fact; the two are coincident; to see is to have desired to see: hence again the Authentic Good has no need of intellection since itself and nothing else is its good.

❙ Intellection in all things—save the Absolute Good (to which it does not apply)—is the working of the imaged Good within them: the Intellectual-Principle recognizes the likeness, sees the Good as a good to itself, an object of attraction: it grasps at that manifestation of The Good, and if the state is constant, the vision persists. Self-intellection is incidental: it sees itself[3] in its contemplation of The Good; ❙ for it sees itself in virtue of its Act; and in all that exists the Act is towards The Good.

6. If this reasoning is valid, The Good has no scope whatever for intellection, which demands that the Good be outside it. The Good, then, is without Act. What Act, indeed, could be vested in Activity's self? No activity has yet again an activity; and whatever we may add to such activities as depend from something else, at least we must leave the first Activity of them all, that from which all depend, as an uncontaminated identity, one to which no such addition can be made.

That primal Activity, then, is not an intellection, for there is nothing upon which it could exercise intellection since it is The First; besides intellection itself does not exercise the intellective act; this belongs to some principle in which intellection is vested. There is, we repeat, duality in any thinking being; and the First is wholly above the dual.

But all this may be made more evident by a clearer recognition of the twofold principle at work wherever there is intellection:

When we affirm the reality of the Real Beings and their individual identity of being and declare that these Real Beings exist in the Intellectual Realm, we do not mean merely that they remain unchangeably self-identical by their very essence as contrasted with the fluidity and instability of the sense-realm; the sense-realm itself may contain the enduring. No; we mean rather that these principles possess, as by their own virtue, the consummate fullness of being. The Essence described as the primally existent cannot be a shadow cast by Being, but must possess Being entire; and Being is entire when it holds the form and idea of intellection and of life. In a Being, then, the existence, the intellection, the life are present as an aggregate. When a thing is a Being, it is also an Intellectual-Principle; when it is an Intellectual-Principle, it is a Being; intellection and Being are co-existents. Therefore intellection is a multiple not a unitary, and that which (like the Good) does not belong to this order can have no intellection. And if we turn to the partial and particular, there is the Intellectual form of man, and there is man, there is the Intellectual form of horse and there is horse, the Intellectual form of justice, and justice.

Thus all is dual: the unit is a duality and yet again the dual reverts to unity.

That, however, which stands outside all this category can be neither an individual unity nor an aggregate of all the duals or in any way a duality. How the duals rose from The One is treated elsewhere.

What stands above Being stands above intellection: it is no weakness in it not to know itself, since as pure unity it contains nothing which it needs to explore. But it need not even spend any knowing upon things outside itself: this which was always the Good of all gives them something greater and better than its knowledge of them—it gives them union with itself in the measure of their ability to cling to a principle thus lofty.

NOTES TO ENNEAD V.6

1. FIRST EDITION: "We can imagine *the Soul as* a double light, a lesser corresponding to the soul *proper*, a purer representing its *intellective phase*; if now we suppose *this intellective light* equal to the light which is *to be* its object . . ."

ARMSTRONG: "If then one were to imagine a double light, the soul as lesser and that which it thinks as purer light, and then imagine that the seeing light is equal to the seen . . ."

GUTHRIE: "We may imagine two lights of which the one, the soul herself, is less brilliant, and we may then posit as equal the light that sees and the light that is seen."

TAYLOR: "If some one, therefore, should make a twofold light, soul, indeed, according to the less pure, but the intelligible of it according to the purer light, and afterwards should cause that which sees to be a light equal to that which is seen . . ."

2. FIRST EDITION: ". . . by the same reasoning *there must be also the supreme unity entering into no association whatever, something which is unity-simplex by its very being*, utterly devoid of all that belongs to *the thing capable* of association."

GUTHRIE: "For the same reason, unity joined to something else presupposes absolutely simple Unity, which subsists in itself, and has nothing of what is found in unity joined to other things."

ARMSTRONG: ". . . in the same way it is necessary that, when a thing has immanent in it something simple along with something else, the simple thing should be simple in and by itself, having nothing in itself of all that it has in its association with other things."

TAYLOR: ". . . thus also it is necessary, that where a certain one which is in a certain respect simple subsists in conjunction with another thing, there should prior to it be *the one* which is perfectly simple, and which has nothing in itself of the things contained in that which subsists in conjunction with others."

3. FIRST EDITION: "*The intellective act is a movement towards the unmoved Good: thus the self-intellection in all* save the Absolute Good is the working of the imaged Good within them: the intellectual principle recognises the likeness, sees *itself* as a good to itself, an object of attraction: it grasps at that manifestation of The Good, *and in holding that holds self-vision:* if the sate *of goodness* is constant, *it remains constantly self-attractive and self-intellective.* The self-intellection is *not deliberate:* it sees itself *as an incident* in its contemplation of The Good . . . [same to end—ed.]"

GUTHRIE: "Besides, when something other than the Good thinks the Good, it thinks the Good because it takes the form of the Good, and resembles the Good. It thinks, because it-self becomes for itself a good and desirable object, and because it possesses an image of the Good. If this thing always remain in the same disposition, it will always retain this image of the Good. By thinking itself, Intelligence simultaneously thinks the Good; for it does not think itself as being actualized; yet every actualization has the Good as its goal."

TAYLOR: ". . . when that also which is different from *the good* intellectually perceives it, it does this in consequence of being boniform, and possessing a similitude to *the good.* It likewise intellectually perceives that which it sees, as good and desirable to itself. . . . if it is always thus affected, it is always this [i.e. it is always boniform]. For again, in the intellection of itself, it accidentally perceives *the good.* For looking to *the good,* it intellectually sees it, and also sees itself energizing . . ." Brackets are Taylor's.

ARMSTRONG: "For when what is other than the Good thinks it, it does so by being 'like the Good' and having a resemblance to the Good, and it thinks it as Good and as desired by itself, and as if it had a mental image of the Good. And if it is like this for ever, it thinks the Good for ever. And again, in thinking the Good it thinks itself incidentally: for it is in looking to the Good that it thinks itself; for it thinks itself in actual activity . . ."

SEVENTH TRACTATE

Is there an Ideal Archetype of Particular Beings?

1. We have to examine the question whether there exists an ideal archetype of individuals, in other words whether I and every other human being go back to the Intellectual, every (living) thing having origin and principle There.

If Socrates, Socrates' soul, is eternal, then the Authentic Socrates—to adopt the term—must be There; that is to say, the individual soul has an existence in the Supreme as well as in this world. If there is no such permanent endurance—and what was Socrates may with change of time become another soul and be Pythagoras or someone else—then the individual Socrates has not that existence in the Divine.

But if the Soul of the individual contains the Reason-Principles of all that it traverses, once more all men have their (archetypic) existence There: and it is our doctrine that every soul contains all the Reason-Principles that exist in the Cosmos: since then the Cosmos contains the Reason-Principles not merely of man, but also of all individual living things, so must the Soul. Its content of Reason-Principles, then, must be limitless, unless there be a periodical renovation bounding the boundlessness by the return of a former series.

But if (in virtue of this periodic return) each archetype may be reproduced by numerous existents, what need is there that there be distinct Reason-Principles and archetypes for each existent in any one period? Might not one (archetypal) man suffice for all, and similarly a limited number of souls produce a limitless number of men?

No: one Reason-Principle cannot account for distinct and differing individuals: one human being does not suffice as the exemplar for many distinct each from the other not merely in material constituents but by innumerable variations of ideal type: this is no question of various pictures or images reproducing an original Socrates; the beings produced differ so greatly as to demand distinct Reason-Principles. The entire soul-period conveys with it all the requisite Reason-Principles and so too the same existents appear once more under their action.

There is no need to baulk at this limitlessness in the Intellectual; it is an infinitude having nothing to do with number or part; what we may think of as its outgoing is no other than its characteristic Act.

2. But individuals are brought into being by the union of the Reason-Principles of the parents male and female: this seems to do away with a definite Reason-Principle for each of the offspring: one of the parents—the male let us say—is the source; and the offspring is determined not by Reason-Principles differing from child to child but by one only, the father's or that of the father's father.

No: a distinct Reason-Principle may be the determinant for the child since the parent contains all: they would become effective at different times.

And so of the differences among children of the same parents: it is a matter of varying dominance: not that the offspring—whether it so appears or not—has been mainly determined by, now the male, now the female but, while each principle has given itself entire and lies there within, yet the bodily substance may be effectively moulded by both or by one only of the two.

And how are the differences to be explained which are caused by birth in different parts of the womb?

Is the differentiating element to be found in the varying resistance of the material of the body?

No: if this were so, all men with the exception of one only would be untrue to nature.

Difference often results in beauty, and so there must be differing archetypes. Deformity alone should be explained by a power in Matter to thwart nature by overmastering the perfect Reason-Principles, hidden but given, all.

Still, admitting the diversity of the Reason-Principles, why need there be as many as there are men born in each Period, once it is granted that different beings may take external manifestation under the presence of the same principles?

Under the presence of all; agreed: but with the dominance of the very same? That is still open to question.

May we not take it that there may be identical reproduction from one Period to another but not in the same Period?

3. In the case of twin birth among human beings how can we make out the Reason-Principles to be different; and still more when we turn to the animals and especially those with litters?

Where the young are precisely alike, there is one Reason-Principle.

But this would mean that after all there are not as many Reason-Principles as separate beings?

As many as there are of differing beings, differing by something more than a mere failure in complete reproduction of their Idea.

And why may there not be different Reason-Principles even in beings untouched by differentiation, if indeed there be any such?

A craftsman even in constructing an object identical with a model must envisage that identity in a mental differentiation enabling him to make a second thing by bringing in some difference side by side with the identity: similarly in nature, where the new thing comes about not by reasoning but in sole virtue of Reason-Principles, that differentiation must be included in the archetypal idea, though it is not in our power to perceive the difference.

The consideration of Quantity brings the same result:

If production is undetermined in regard to Quantity, we need another line of approach; but if there is a measured system, the Quantity has been determined by the unrolling and unfolding of the Reason-Principles of all the existences.

Thus when the universe has reached its term, there will be a fresh beginning, since the entire Quantity which the Cosmos is to exhibit, every item that is to emerge in its course, all is laid up from the first in the Being that contains the Reason-Principles.

Are we, then, looking to the brute realm, to hold that there are as many Reason-Principles as distinct creatures born in a litter?

Why not? There is nothing alarming about such limitlessness in generative forces and in Reason-Principles, when Soul is there to sustain all.

As in Soul (principle of Life), so in Divine Mind (principle of Idea), there is this infinitude of recurring generative powers; the Beings there are unfailing.

EIGHTH TRACTATE

On the Intellectual Beauty[1]

1. It is a principle with us that one who has attained to the vision of the Intellectual Cosmos and grasped the beauty of the Authentic Intellect will be able also to come to understand the Father and Transcendent of that Divine Being. It concerns us, then, to try to see and say, for ourselves and as far as such matters may be told, how the Beauty of the divine Intellect and of the Intellectual Cosmos may be revealed to contemplation.

Let us go to the realm of magnitudes:—suppose two blocks of stone lying side by side: one is unpatterned, quite untouched by art; the other has been minutely wrought by the craftsman's hands into some statue of god or man, a Grace or a Muse, or if a human being, not a portrait but a creation in which the sculptor's art has concentrated all loveliness.

Now it must be seen that the stone thus brought under the artist's hand to the beauty of form is beautiful not as stone—for so the crude block would be as pleasant—but in virtue of the Form or Idea introduced by the art. This form is not in the material; it is in the designer before ever it enters the stone; and the artificer holds it not by his equipment of eyes and hands but by his participation in his art. The beauty, therefore, exists in a far higher state in the art; for it does not come over integrally into the work; that original beauty is not transferred; what comes over is a derivative and a minor: and even that shows itself upon the statue not integrally and with entire realization of intention but only in so far as it has subdued the resistance of the material.

Art, then, creating in the image of its own nature and content, and working by the Idea or Reason-Principle of the beautiful object it is to produce, must itself be beautiful in a far higher and purer degree since it is the seat and source of that beauty, indwelling in the art, which must naturally be more complete than any comeliness of the external. In the degree in which the beauty is diffused by entering into matter, it is so much the weaker than that concentrated in unity; everything that reaches outwards is the less for it, strength less strong, heat less hot, every power less potent, and so beauty less beautiful.

Then again every prime cause must be, within itself, more powerful than its effect can be: the musical does not derive from an unmusical source but from music; and so the art exhibited in the material work derives from an art yet higher.

Still the arts are not to be slighted on the ground that they create by imitation of natural objects; for, to begin with, these natural objects are themselves imitations; then, we must recognize that they give no bare reproduction of the thing seen but go back to the Reason-Principles from which Nature itself derives, and, furthermore, that much of their work is all their own; they are holders of beauty and add where nature is lacking. Thus Pheidias wrought the Zeus upon no model among things of sense but by apprehending what form Zeus must take if he chose to become manifest to sight.

2. But let us leave the arts and consider those works produced by Nature and admitted to be naturally beautiful which the creations of art are charged with imitating, all reasoning life and unreasoning things alike, but especially the consummate among them, where the moulder and maker has subdued the material and given the form he desired. Now what is the beauty here? It has nothing to do with the blood or the menstrual process: either there is also a colour and form apart from all this or there is nothing unless sheer ugliness or (at best) a bare recipient, as it were the mere Matter of beauty.

Whence shone forth the beauty of Helen, battle-sought; or of all those women like in loveliness to Aphrodite; or of Aphrodite herself; or of any human being that has been perfect in beauty; or of any of these gods manifest to sight, or unseen but carrying what would be beauty if we saw?

In all these is it not the Form-Idea, something of that realm but communicated to the produced from within the producer, just as in works of art, we held, it is communicated from the arts to their creations? Now we can surely not believe that, while the made thing and the Reason-Principle thus impressed upon Matter are beautiful, yet the Principle not so alloyed but resting still with the creator—the Idea primal and immaterial—is not Beauty.

If material extension were in itself the ground of beauty, then the creating principle, being without extension, could not be beautiful: but beauty cannot be made to depend upon magnitude since, whether in a large object or a small, the one Idea equally moves and forms the mind by its inherent power. A further indication is that as long as the object remains outside us we know nothing of it; it affects us by entry; but only as an Ideal-Form can it enter through the eyes which are not of scope to take an extended mass: we are, no doubt, simultaneously possessed of the magnitude which, however, we take in not as mass but by an elaboration upon the presented form.

Then again the principle producing the beauty must be, itself, ugly, neutral, or beautiful: ugly, it could not produce the opposite; neutral, why should its product be the one rather than the other? The Nature, then, which creates things so lovely must be itself of a far earlier beauty; we, undisciplined in discernment of the inward, knowing nothing of it, run after the outer, never understanding that it is the inner which stirs us; we are in the case of one who sees his own reflection but not realizing whence it comes goes in pursuit of it.

But that the thing we are pursuing is something different and that the beauty is not in the concrete object is manifest from the beauty there is in matters of study, in conduct and custom; briefly, in soul or mind. And it is precisely here that the greater beauty lies, perceived whenever you look to the wisdom in a man and delight in it, not wasting attention on the face, which may be hideous, but passing all appearance by and catching only at the inner comeliness, the truly personal; if you are still unmoved and cannot acknowledge beauty under such conditions, then looking to your own inner being you will find no beauty to delight you and it will be futile in that state to seek the greater vision, for you will be questing it through the ugly and impure.

This is why such matters are not spoken of to everyone; you, if you are conscious of beauty within, remember.

3. Thus there is in the Nature-Principle itself an Ideal archetype of the beauty that is found in material forms and, of that archetype again, the still more beautiful archetype in Soul, source of that in Nature. In the proficient soul this is brighter and of more advanced loveliness: adorning the soul and bringing to it a light from that greater light which is Beauty primally, its immediate presence sets the soul reflecting upon the quality of this prior, the archetype which has no such entries, and is present nowhere but remains in itself alone, and thus is not even to be called a Reason-Principle but is the creative source of the very first Reason-Principle which is the Beauty to which Soul serves as Matter.

This prior, then, is the Intellectual-Principle, the veritable, abiding and not fluctuant since not taking intellectual quality from outside itself. By what image, thus, can we represent it? We have nowhere to go but to what is less. Only from itself can we take an image of it; that is, there can be no representation of it, except in the sense that we represent gold by some portion of gold—purified, either actually or mentally, if it be impure—insisting at the same time that this is not the total thing gold, but merely the particular gold of a particular parcel. In the same way we learn in this matter from the purified Intellect in ourselves or, if you like, from the gods and the glory of the Intellect in them.

For assuredly all the gods are august and beautiful in a beauty beyond our speech. And what makes them so? Intellect; and especially Intellect operating within them (the divine sun and stars) to visibility. It is not through the loveliness of their corporeal forms: even those that have body are not gods by that beauty; it is in virtue of Intellect that they, too, are gods, and as gods beautiful. They do not veer between wisdom and folly: in the immunity of Intellect unmoving and pure they are wise always, all-knowing, taking cognizance not of the human but of their own being and of all that lies within the contemplation of Intellect. Those of them whose dwelling is in the heavens are ever in this meditation—what task prevents them?—and from afar they look, too, into that further heaven by a lifting of the head. The gods belonging to that higher Heaven itself, they whose station is upon it and in it, see and know in virtue of their omnipresence to it. For all There is heaven; earth is heaven, and sea heaven; and animal and plant and man; all is the heavenly content of that heaven: and the gods in it, despising neither men nor anything else that is there where all is of the heavenly order, traverse all that country and all space in peace.

4. To 'live at ease' is There; and to these divine beings verity is mother and nurse, existence and sustenance; all that is not of process but of authentic being they see, and themselves in all: for all is transparent, nothing dark, nothing resistant; every being is lucid to every other, in breadth and depth; light runs through light. And each of them contains all within itself, and at the same time sees all in every other, so that everywhere there is all, and all is all and each all, and infinite the glory. Each of them is great; the small is great; the sun, There, is all the stars; and every star, again, is all the stars and sun. While some one manner of being is dominant in each, all are mirrored in every other.

Movement There is pure (as self-caused), for the moving principle is not a separate thing to complicate it as it speeds.

So, too, Repose is not troubled, for there is no admixture of the unstable; and the Beauty is all beauty since it is not resident in what is not beautiful. Each There walks upon no alien soil; its place is its essential self; and, as each moves, so to speak, towards what is Above, it is attended by the very ground from which it starts: there is no distinguishing between the Being and the Place; all is Intellect, the Principle and the ground on which it stands, alike. Thus we might think that our visible sky (the ground or place of the stars), lit as it is, produces the light which reaches us from it (though of course this is really produced by the stars—as it were, by the Principles of light alone, not also by the ground as the analogy would require).

In our realm all is part rising from part and nothing can be more than partial; but There each being is an eternal product of a whole and is at once a whole and an individual manifesting as part but, to the keen vision There, known for the whole it is.

The myth of Lynceus seeing into the very deeps of the earth tells us of those eyes in the divine. No weariness overtakes this vision which yet brings no such satiety as would call for its ending; for there never was a void to be filled so that, with the fullness and the attainment of purpose, the sense of sufficiency be induced: nor is there any such incongruity within the divine that one Being There could be repulsive to another: and of course all There are unchangeable. This absence of satisfaction means only a satisfaction leading to no distaste for that which produces it; to see is to look the more, since for them to continue in the contemplation of an infinite self and of infinite objects is but to acquiesce in the bidding of their nature.

Life, pure, is never a burden; how then could there be weariness There where the living is most noble? That very life is wisdom, not a wisdom built up by reasonings but complete from the beginning, suffering no lack which could set it inquiring, a wisdom primal, unborrowed, not something added to the Being, but its very essence. No wisdom, thus, is greater; this is the authentic knowing, assessor to the divine Intellect as projected into manifestation simultaneously with it; thus, in the symbolic saying, Justice is assessor to Zeus.

(Perfect wisdom:) for all the Principles of this order, dwelling There, are as it were visible images projected from themselves, so that all becomes 'an object of contemplation to contemplators immeasurably blessed'. The greatness and power of the wisdom There we may know from this, that it embraces all the real Beings, and has made all and all follow it, and yet that it is itself those beings, which sprang into being with it, so that all is one and the essence There is wisdom. If we have failed to understand, it is that we have thought of knowledge as a mass of theorems and an accumulation of propositions, though that is false even for our sciences of the sense-realm. But in case this should be questioned, we may leave our own sciences for the present, and deal with the knowing in the Supreme at which Plato glances where he speaks of 'that knowledge which is not a stranger in something strange to it'—though in what sense, he leaves us to examine and declare, if we boast ourselves worthy of our profession. This is probably our best starting-point.

5. All that comes to be, work of nature or of craft, some wisdom has made: everywhere a wisdom presides at a making.

No doubt the wisdom of the artist may be the guide of the work; it is suffi-cient explanation of the wisdom exhibited in the arts; but the artist himself goes back, after all, to that wisdom in Nature which is embodied in himself; and this is not a wisdom built up of theorems but one totality, not a wisdom consisting of manifold detail co-ordinated into a unity but rather a unity working out into detail.

Now, if we could think of this as the primal wisdom, we need look no fur-ther, since, at that, we have discovered a principle which is neither a derivative nor a 'stranger in something strange to it'. But if we are told that, while this Reason-Principle is in Nature, yet Nature itself is its source, we ask how Nature came to possess it; and, if Nature derived it from some other source, we ask what that other source may be; if, on the contrary, the principle is self-sprung, we need look no further: but if (as we assume) we are referred to the Intellectual-Principle we must make clear whether the Intellectual-Principle engendered the wisdom: if we learn that it did, we ask whence: if from itself, then inevitably it is itself Wisdom.

The true Wisdom, then (found to be identical with the Intellectual-Prin-ciple), is Real Being; and Real Being is Wisdom; it is wisdom that gives value to Real Being; and Being is Real in virtue of its origin in wisdom. It follows that all forms of existence not possessing wisdom are, indeed, Beings in right of the wisdom which went to their forming, but, as not in themselves possessing it, are not Real Beings.

We cannot, therefore, think that the divine Beings of that sphere, or the other supremely blessed There, need look to our apparatus of science: all of that realm (the very Beings themselves), all is noble image, such images as we may conceive to lie within the soul of the wise—but There not as inscription but as authentic existence. The ancients had this in mind when they declared the Ideas (Forms) to be Beings, Essentials.

6. Similarly, as it seems to me, the wise of Egypt—whether in precise knowl-edge or by native intuition—indicated the truth where, in their effort towards philosophical statement, they left aside the writing-forms that take in the detail of words and sentences—those characters that represent sounds and convey the propositions of reasoning—and drew pictures instead, engraving in the temple-inscriptions a separate image for every separate item: **I** thus they ex-hibited the absence of discursiveness in the Intellectual Realm. [2] **I**

For each manifestation of knowledge and wisdom is a distinct image, an ob-ject in itself, an immediate unity, not an aggregate of discursive reasoning and detailed willing. Later from this wisdom in unity there appears, in another form of being, **I** a copy, already less compact, which announces the original in terms of discourse and unravels³ the causes ❙ by which things are such that the wonder rises how a generated world can be so excellent.

For, one who knows must declare his wonder that this wisdom, while not itself containing the causes by which Being exists and takes such excellence, yet imparts them to the entities produced according to its canons. This excellence, whose necessity is scarcely or not at all manifest to search, exists, if we could but find it out, before all searching and reasoning.

What I say may be considered in one chief thing, and thence applied to all the particular entities:

7. Consider the universe: we are agreed that its existence and its nature come to it from beyond itself; are we, now, to imagine that its maker first thought it out in detail—the earth, and its necessary situation in the middle; water and, again, its position as lying upon the earth; all the other elements and objects up to the sky in due place and order; living beings with their appropriate forms as we know them, their inner organs and their outer limbs—and that having thus appointed every item beforehand, he then set about the execution?

Such designing was not even possible; how could the plan for a universe come to one that had never looked outward? Nor could he work on material gathered from elsewhere as our craftsmen do, using hands and tools; feet and hands are of the later order.

One way, only, remains: all things must exist in something else; of that prior—since there is no obstacle, all being continuous within the realm of reality—there has suddenly appeared a sign, an image, whether given forth directly or through the ministry of soul or of some phase of soul matters nothing for the moment: thus the entire aggregate of existence springs from the divine world, in greater beauty There because There unmingled but mingled here.

From the beginning to end all is gripped by the Forms of the Intellectual Realm: Matter itself is held by the Forms of the elements and to these Forms are added other Forms and others again, so that it is hard to work down to crude Matter beneath all that sheathing of Form. Indeed since Matter itself is, in its degree, a Form—the lowest—all this universe is Form and there is nothing that is not Ideal Form as the archetype was. And all is made silently, since nothing had part in the making but Being and Idea—a further reason why creation went without toil. The Exemplar was the Form-Idea of an All and so an All must come into being.

Thus nothing stood in the way of the Form, and even now it dominates, despite all the clash of things: the creation is not hindered on its way even now; it stands firm in virtue of being All. To me, moreover, it seems that if we ourselves were archetypes, Ideas, veritable Being, and the Idea with which we construct here were our veritable Essence, then our creative power, too, would toillessly effect its purpose: as man now stands, he does not produce in his work a true image of himself: become man, he has ceased to be the All; ceasing to be man—we read—'he soars aloft and administers the Cosmos entire'; restored to the All he is maker of the All.

But—to our immediate purpose—it is possible to give a reason why the earth is set in the midst and why it is round and why the ecliptic runs precisely as it does, but, looking to the creating principle, we cannot say that because this was the way, therefore things were so planned: we can say only that I because the Exemplar is what it is, therefore the things of this world are[4] good; I the causing principle, we might put it reached the conclusion before all formal reasoning and not from any premises, not by sequence or plan but before either, since all of that order is later, all reason, demonstration, persuasion.

Since there is a Source, all the created must spring from it and in accordance with it; and we are rightly told not to go seeking the causes impelling a Source to produce, especially when this is the perfectly sufficient Source and identical with the Term: a Source which is Source and Term must be the All-Unity, complete in itself.

8. This then is Beauty primally: it is entire and omnipresent as an entirety; and therefore in none of its parts or members lacking in beauty; beautiful thus beyond denial. Certainly it cannot be anything (be, for example, Beauty) without being wholly that thing; it can be nothing which it is to possess partially or in which it utterly fails (and therefore it must entirely be Beauty entire).

If this principle were not beautiful, what other could be? Its prior does not deign to be beautiful; that which is the first to manifest itself—Form and object of vision to the intellect—cannot but be lovely to see. It is to indicate this that Plato, drawing on something well within our observation, represents the Creator as approving the work he has achieved: the intention is to make us feel the lovable beauty of the archetype and of the Divine Idea; for to admire a representation is to admire the original upon which it was made.

It is not surprising if we fail to recognize what is passing within us: lovers, and those in general that admire beauty here, do not stay to reflect that it is to be traced, as of course it must be, to the Beauty There. That the admiration of the Demiurge is to be referred to the Ideal Exemplar is deliberately made evident by the rest of the passage: 'He admired; and determined to bring the work into still closer likeness with the Exemplar': he makes us feel the magnificent beauty of the Exemplar by telling us that the Beauty sprung from this world is, itself, a copy from That.

And indeed if the divine did not exist, the transcendently beautiful, in a beauty beyond all thought, what could be lovelier than the things we see? Certainly no reproach can rightly be brought against this world save only that it is not That.

9. Let us, then, make a mental picture of our universe: each member shall remain what it is, distinctly apart; yet all is to form, as far as possible, a complete unity so that whatever comes into view, say the outer orb of the heavens, shall bring immediately with it the vision, on the one plane, of the sun and of all the stars with earth and sea and all living things as if exhibited upon a transparent globe.

Bring this vision actually before your sight, so that there shall be in your mind the gleaming representation of a sphere, a picture holding all the things of the universe moving or in repose or (as in reality) some at rest, some in motion. Keep this sphere before you, and from it imagine another, a sphere stripped of magnitude and of spatial differences; cast out your inborn sense of Matter, taking care not merely to attenuate it: call on God, maker of the sphere whose image you now hold, and pray Him to enter. And may He come bringing His own Universe with all the gods that dwell in it—He who is the one God and all the gods, where each is all, blending into a unity, distinct in powers but all one god in virtue of that one divine power of many facets.

More truly, this is the one God who is all the gods; for, in the coming to be of all those, this, the one, has suffered no diminishing. He and all have one existence, while each again is distinct. It is distinction by state without interval: there is no outward form to set one here and another there and to prevent any from being an entire identity; I and there is no sharing of parts between Himself and others.[5] I Nor is each of those divine wholes a power in fragment, a power totalling to the sum of the measurable segments: the divine is one all-power, reaching out to infinity, powerful to infinity: and so great is God that his very members are infinites. What place can be named to which He does not reach?

Great, too, is this firmament of ours and all the powers constellated within it, but it would be greater still, unspeakably, but that there is inbound in it something of the petty power of body; no doubt the powers of fire and other bodily substances might themselves be thought very great, but in fact, it is through their failure in the true power that we see them burning, destroying, wearing things away, and slaving towards the production of life; they destroy because they are themselves in process of destruction, and they produce because they belong to the realm of the produced.

The power in that other world has merely Being and Beauty of Being. Beauty without Being could not be, nor Being voided of Beauty: abandoned of Beauty, Being loses something of its essence. Being is desirable because it is identical with Beauty; and Beauty is loved because it is Being. How then can we debate which is the cause of the other, where the nature is one? The very figment of Being needs some imposed image of Beauty to make it passable, and even to ensure its existence; it exists to the degree in which it has taken some share in the beauty of Idea; and the more deeply it has drawn on this, the less imperfect it is, precisely because the nature which is essentially the beautiful has entered into it the more intimately.

10. This is why Zeus, although the oldest of the gods and their sovereign, advances first (in the Phaedrus myth) towards that vision, followed by gods and demigods and such souls as are of strength to see. That Being appears before them from some unseen place and rising loftily over them pours its light upon all things, so that all gleams in its radiance; it upholds some beings, and they see; the lower are dazzled and turn away, unfit to gaze upon that sun, the trouble falling the more heavily on those most remote.

Of those looking upon that Being and its content, and able to see, all take something but not all the same vision always: intently gazing, one sees the fount and principle of Justice, I another is filled with the sight of Moral Wisdom, the original of that quality as found, sometimes at least, among men and copied by them in their degree; last attainment of all is the vision of that radiance (Beauty) which, covering all the expanse, so to speak, of the Intellectual Realm, is seen[6] by those who have known already many splendid visions. I

The gods see, each singly and all as one. So, too, the souls; they see all There in right of being sprung, themselves, of that universe and therefore including all from beginning to end and having their existence There if only by that phase which belongs inherently to the Divine, though often too they are There entire, those of them that have not incurred separation.

This vision Zeus takes and it is for such of us, also, as share his love and appropriate our part in the Beauty There, the final object of all seeing, the entire beauty upon all things; for all There sheds radiance, and floods those that have found their way thither so that they too become beautiful; thus it will often happen that men climbing heights where the soil has taken a yellow glow will themselves appear so, borrowing colour from the place on which they move. The colour flowering on that other height we speak of is Beauty; or rather all There is light and beauty, through and through, for the beauty is no mere bloom upon the surface.

To those that do not see entire, the immediate impression is alone received; but those drunken with this wine, filled with the nectar, all their soul penetrated by this beauty, cannot remain mere gazers: no longer is there a spectator outside gazing on an outside spectacle; the clear-eyed hold the vision within themselves, though, for the most part, they have no idea that it is within but look towards it as to something beyond them and see it as an object of vision caught by a direction of the will.

All that one sees as a spectacle is still external; one must bring the vision within and see no longer in that mode of separation but as we know ourselves; thus a man filled with a god—possessed by Apollo or by one of the Muses—need no longer look outside for his vision of the divine being; it is but finding the strength to see divinity within.

11. Similarly any one, unable to see himself, but possessed by that God, has but to bring that divine-within before his consciousness and at once he sees an image of himself, himself lifted to a better beauty: now let him ignore that image, lovely though it is, and sink into a perfect self-identity, no such separation remaining; at once he forms a multiple unity with the God silently present; in the degree of his power and will, the two become one; should he turn back to the former duality, still he is pure and remains very near to the God; he has but to look again and the same presence is there.

This conversion brings gain: at the first stage, that of separation, a man is aware of self; but retreating inwards, he becomes possessor of all; he puts sense away behind him in dread of the separated life and becomes one in the Divine; if he plans to see in separation, he sets himself outside.

The novice must hold himself constantly under some image of the Divine Being and seek in the light of a clear conception; knowing thus, in a deep conviction, whither he is going—into what a sublimity he penetrates—he must give himself forthwith to the inner and, radiant with the Divine Intellections (with which he is now one), be no longer the seer, but, as that place has made him, the seen.

Still, we will be told, one cannot be in beauty and yet fail to see it. The very contrary: to see the divine as something external is to be outside of it; to become it is to be most truly in beauty: since sight deals with the external, there can here be no vision unless in the sense of identification with the object.

And this identification amounts to a self-knowing, a self-consciousness, guarded by the fear of losing the self in the desire of a too wide awareness.

It must be remembered that sensations of the ugly and evil impress us more violently than those of what is agreeable and yet leave less knowledge as the residue of the shock: sickness makes the rougher mark, but health, tranquilly present, explains itself better; it takes the first place, it is the natural thing, it belongs to our being; illness is alien, unnatural, and thus makes itself felt by its very incongruity, while the other conditions are native and we take no notice. Such being our nature, we are most completely aware of ourselves when we are most completely identified with the object of our knowledge.

This is why in that other sphere, when we are deepest in that knowledge by intellection, we are aware of none; we are expecting some impression on sense, which has nothing to report since it has seen nothing and never could in that order see anything. The unbelieving element is sense; it is the other, the Intellectual-Principle, that sees; and if this too doubted, it could not even credit its own existence, for it can never stand away and with bodily eyes apprehend itself as a visible object.

12. We have told how this vision it to be procured, whether by the mode of separation or in identity: now, seen in either way, what does it give to report?

The vision has been of God in travail of a beautiful offspring, God engendering a universe within himself in a painless labour and—rejoiced in what he has brought into being, proud of his children—keeping all closely by Him, for the pleasure He has in his radiance and in theirs.

Of this offspring—all beautiful, but most beautiful those that have remained within—only one has become manifest without; from him (Zeus, sovran over the visible universe), the youngest born, we may gather, as from some image, the greatness of the Father and of the Brothers that remain within the Father's house.

Still the manifested God cannot think that he has come forth in vain from the father; for through him another universe has arisen, beautiful as the image of beauty, and it could not be lawful that Beauty and Being should fail of a beautiful image.

This second Cosmos at every point copies the archetype: it has life and being in copy, and has beauty as springing from that diviner world. In its character of image it holds, too, that divine perpetuity without which it would only at times be truly representative and sometimes fail like a construction of art; for every image whose existence lies in the nature of things must stand during the entire existence of the archetype.

Hence it is false to put an end to the visible sphere as long as the Intellectual endures, or to found it upon a decision taken by its maker at some given moment.

That teaching shirks the penetration of such a making as is here involved: it fails to see that as long as the Supreme is radiant there can be no failing of its sequel but, that existing, all exists. And—since the necessity of conveying our meaning compels such terms—the Supreme has existed for ever and for ever will exist.

13. The God fettered (as in the Kronos Myth) to an unchanging identity leaves the ordering of this universe to his son (to Zeus), for it could not be in his

character to neglect his rule within the divine sphere, and, as though sated with the Authentic-Beauty, seek a lordship too recent and too poor for his might. Ignoring this lower world, Kronos (Intellectual-Principle) claims for himself his own father (Ouranos, the Absolute, or One) with all the upward-tending between them: and he counts all that tends to the inferior, beginning from his son (Zeus, the All-Soul), as ranking beneath him. Thus he holds a mid-position determined on the one side by the differentiation implied in the severance from the very highest and, on the other, by that which keeps him apart from the link between himself and the lower: he stands between a greater father and an inferior son. But since that father is too lofty to be thought of under the name of Beauty, the second God remains the primally beautiful.

Soul also has beauty, but is less beautiful than Intellect as being its image and therefore, though beautiful in nature, taking increase of beauty by looking to that original. Since then the All-Soul—to use the more familiar term—since Aphrodite herself is so beautiful, what name can we give to that other? If Soul is so lovely in its own right, of what quality must that prior be? And since its being is derived, what must that power be from which the Soul takes the double beauty, the borrowed and the inherent?

We ourselves possess beauty when we are true to our own being; our ugliness is in going over to another order; our self-knowledge, that is to say, is our beauty; in self-ignorance we are ugly.

Thus beauty is of the Divine and comes Thence only.

Do these considerations suffice to a clear understanding of the Intellectual Sphere or must we make yet another attempt by another road?

NOTES TO ENNEAD V.8

1. This tractate is the second part of a major work comprising III.8 (30), V.8 (31), V.5 (32), and II.9 (33). See first footnotes to II.9 and V.5.

2. FIRST EDITION: ". . . thus they exhibited *the mode in which the Supreme goes forth.*"

GUTHRIE skips the clause. ARMSTRONG supports the fourth edition and provides (referencing E. de Keyser's *La Signification de l'art dans les Ennéades de Plotin*) a helpful footnote pointing out that "Plotinus speaks of temples, not of sacred writings, and is therefore not misunderstanding the semi-alphabetic hieroglyphics of the sacred books but speaking of the purely ideogrammatic symbols which do appear on the temple walls."

3. FIRST EDITION: ". . . *an image*, already less compact, which announces the original in *an outward stage and seeks* the causes . . ."

GUTHRIE supports the fourth edition and mentions, in a footnote, that Plotinus here "refers to the hieratic writing, which differed from both the hieroglyphic and demotic."

ARMSTRONG: ". . . a representation in something else, already unfolded and speaking it discursively and giving the reasons . . ."

4. FIRST EDITION: ". . . because the *All* is what it is, therefore *there is a total of* good;"

   GUTHRIE: ". . . these things are good only because Intelligence is what it is."

   ARMSTRONG: ". . . but because things There are disposed as they are, the things here are beautifully disposed:"

5. FIRST EDITION: ". . . *yet* there is no sharing of parts *from one to another.*"

   ARMSTRONG: ". . . nor does each god have parts different from himself belonging to other gods than himself . . ."

   GUTHRIE: "Neither have they any parts that differ in each of them, or from each other;"

6. FIRST EDITION: ". . . another is filled with the sight of Moral Wisdom, the original of that quality as found, sometimes at least, among men, copied by them in their degree *from the divine virtue* which, covering all the expanse, so to speak, of the Intellectual Realm is seen, *last attainment of all,* by those who have known already many splendid visions."

   ARMSTRONG: ". . . another is filled with the vision of moral integrity, not the kind which men have here below, when they do have it (for this is some sort of imitation of that other), but that glory over all, playing upon what we may call the whole extension of that world, is seen at the end by those who have already seen many clear visions . . ."

   GUTHRIE: ". . . another is overwhelmed by the revelation of wisdom, of which men here below scarcely possess an enfeebled image. Indeed, our vision is only an imitation of intelligible wisdom. The latter, spreading over all beings, and as it were embracing immensity, is the last to be perceived by those who have already long contemplated these brilliant lights."

NINTH TRACTATE

The Intellectual-Principle, the Ideas, and the Authentic Existence

1. All human beings from birth onward live to the realm of sense more than to the Intellectual.

Forced of necessity to attend first to the material, some of them elect to abide by that order and, their life throughout, make its concerns their first and their last; the sweet and the bitter of sense are their good and evil; they feel they have done all if they live along pursuing the one and barring the doors to the other. And those of them that pretend to reasoning have adopted this as their philosophy; they are like the heavier birds which have incorporated much from the earth and are so weighted down that they cannot fly high for all the wings Nature has given them.

Others do indeed lift themselves a little above the earth; the better in their soul urges them from the pleasant to the nobler, but they are not of power to see the highest and so, in despair of any surer ground, they fall back, in virtue's name, upon those actions and options of the lower from which they sought to escape.

But there is a third order—those godlike men who, in their mightier power, in the keeness of their sight, have clear vision of the splendour above and rise to it from among the cloud and fog of earth and hold firmly to that other world, looking beyond all here, delighted in the place of reality, their native land, like a man returning after long wanderings to the pleasant ways of his own country.

2. What is this other place and how is it accessible?

It is to be reached by those who, born with the nature of the lover, are also authentically philosophic by inherent temper; in pain of love towards beauty but not held by material loveliness, taking refuge from that in things whose beauty is of the soul—such things as virtue, knowledge, institutions, law and custom—and thence, rising still a step, reach to the source of this loveliness of the Soul, thence to whatever be above that again, until the uttermost is reached, The First, the Principle whose beauty is self-springing: this attained, there is an end to the pain inassuageable before.

But how is the ascent to be begun? Whence comes the power? In what thought is this love to find its guide?

The guiding thought is this: that the beauty perceived on material things is borrowed.

The pattern giving beauty to the corporeal rests upon it as Idea to its Matter and the substrate may change and from being pleasant become distasteful, a sign, in all reason, that the beauty comes by participation.

Now, what is this that gives grace to the corporeal?

Two causes in their degree: the participation in beauty and the power of Soul, the maker, which has imprinted that form.

We ask then: Is soul, of itself, a thing of beauty? We find it is not since differences are manifest, one soul wise and lovely, another foolish and ugly: soul-beauty is constituted by wisdom.

The question thus becomes, What principle is the giver of wisdom to the soul? and the only answer is 'The Intellectual-Principle', the veritably intellectual, wise without intermission and therefore beautiful of itself.

But does even this suffice for our First?

No; we must look still inward beyond the Intellectual, which, from our point of approach, stands before the Supreme Beginning, in whose forecourt, as it were, it announces in its own being the entire content of the Good, that prior of all, locked in unity, of which this is the expression already touched by multiplicity.

3. We will have to examine this Nature, the Intellectual, which our reasoning identifies as the authentically existent and the veritable essential: but first we must take another path and make certain that such a principle does necessarily exist.

Perhaps it is ridiculous to set out inquiring whether an Intellectual-Principle has place in the total of being: but there may be some to hesitate even as to this and certainly there will be the question whether it is as we describe it, whether it is a separate existence, whether it actually is the real beings, whether it is the seat of the Ideas; to this we now address ourselves.

All that we see, and describe as having existence, we know to be compound; hand-wrought or compacted by nature, nothing is simplex. Now the hand-wrought, with its metal or stone or wood, is not realized out of these materials until the appropriate craft has produced statue, house, or bed, by imparting the particular Idea from its own content. Similarly with natural forms of being; those including several constituents, compound bodies as we call them, may be analysed into the materials and the Idea imposed upon the total; the human being, for example, into soul and body; and the human body into the four elements. Finding each element to be a compound of Matter and shaping principle—since the Matter of the elements is of itself shapeless—you will inquire whence this forming Idea comes; and you will ask whether in the Soul we recognize a simplex or whether this also has constituents, something representing Matter and something else representing Form, namely, the Intellectual Principle within it, this corresponding both to the shape on the statue and to the artist giving the shape.

Applying the same method to the total of things, here too we discover the Intellectual-Principle and this we set down as veritably the maker and creator of the All. The underlie has adopted, we see, certain shapes by which it becomes fire, water, air, earth; and these shapes have been imposed upon it by something else. This other is Soul which, hovering over the Four (the elements), imparts the pattern of the Cosmos, the Ideas for which it has itself received from the Intellectual-Principle as the soul or mind of the craftsman draws upon his craft for the plan of his work.

The Intellectual-Principle is in one phase the Form of the Soul, its shape; in another phase it is the giver of the shape—the sculptor, possessing inherently what is given—imparting to Soul nearly the authentic reality while what body receives is but image and imitation.

4. But, Soul reached, why need we look higher; why not make this The First?

A main reason is that the Intellectual-Principle is at once something other and something more powerful than Soul and that the more powerful is in the nature of things the prior. For it is certainly not true, as people imagine, that the Soul, brought to perfection, produces Intellect. How could that potentiality come to actuality unless there be, first, an effective principle to induce the actualization which, left to chance, might never occur?

The Firsts must be supposed to exist in actuality, looking to nothing else, self-complete. Anything incomplete must be sequent upon these, and take its completion from the principles engendering it which, like fathers, labour in the improvement of an offspring born imperfect: the produced is as Matter to the producing principle and is worked over by it into a shapely perfection.

And if, further, Soul is passible while something impassible there must be or by the mere passage of time all wears away, here too we are led to something above Soul.

Again there must be something prior to Soul because Soul is in the world and there must be something outside a world in which, all being corporeal and material, nothing has enduring reality: failing such a prior, neither man nor the Ideas would be eternal or have true identity.

These and many other considerations establish the necessary existence of an Intellectual-Principle prior to Soul.

5. This Intellectual-Principle, if the term is to convey the truth, must be understood to be not a principle merely potential and not one maturing from unintelligence to intelligence—that would simply send us seeking, once more, a necessary prior—but a principle which is intelligence in actuality and in eternity.

Now a principle whose wisdom is not borrowed must derive from itself any intellection it may make; and anything it may possess within itself it can hold only from itself: it follows that, intellective by its own resource and upon its own content, it is itself the very things on which its intellection acts.

For supposing its essence to be separable from its intellection and the objects of its intellection to be not-itself, then its essence would be unintellectual; and it would be intellectual not actually but potentially. The intellection and its object must then be inseparable—however the habit induced by our conditions may tempt us to distinguish, There too, the thinker from the thought.

What then is its characteristic Act and what the intellection which makes knower and known here identical?

Clearly, as authentic Intellection, it has authentic intellection of the authentically existent, and establishes their existence. Therefore it is the Authentic Beings.

Consider: it must perceive them either somewhere else or within itself as its very self: the somewhere else is impossible—where could that be?—they are therefore itself and the content of itself.

Its objects certainly cannot be the things of sense, as people think: no First could be of the sense-known order; for in things of sense the Idea (Form) is but an image of the authentic, an image thrown upon Matter, and every Idea thus derivative and exiled traces back to that original and is no more than an image of it.

Further, if the Intellectual-Principle is to be the maker of this All, it cannot make by looking outside itself to what does not yet exist. The Authentic Beings must, then, exist before this All, no copies made on a model but themselves archetypes, primals, and the essence of the Intellectual-Principle.

We may be told that Reason-Principles suffice (to the subsistence of the All): but then these, clearly, must be eternal; and if eternal, if immune, then they must exist in an Intellectual-Principle such as we have indicated, a principle earlier than condition, than nature, than soul, than anything whose existence is potential (or contingent).

The Intellectual-Principle, therefore, is itself the authentic existences, not a knower knowing them in some sphere foreign to it. The Authentic Beings, thus, exist neither before nor after it: it is the primal legislator to Being or, rather, is itself the law of Being. Thus it is true that 'Intellection and Being are identical'; in the immaterial the knowledge of the thing is the thing. And this is the meaning of the dictum 'I sought myself', namely, as one of the Beings: it also bears on reminiscence.

For none of the Beings is outside the Intellectual-Principle or in space; they remain for ever in themselves, accepting no change, no decay, and by that are the authentically existent. Things that arise and fall away draw on real being as something to borrow from; they are not of the real; the true being is that on which they draw.

It is by participation that the sense-known has the being we ascribe to it; the underlying nature has taken its shape from elsewhere; thus bronze and wood are shaped into what we see by means of an image introduced by sculpture or carpentry; the craft permeates the materials while remaining integrally apart from the material and containing in itself the reality of statue or couch. And it is so, of course, with all corporeal things.

This universe, characteristically participant in images, shows how the image differs from the authentic beings: against the variability of the one order, there stands the unchanging quality of the other, self-situate, not needing space because having no magnitude, holding an existence intellective and self-sufficing. The body-kind seeks its endurance in another kind; the Intellectual-Principle, sustaining by its marvellous being the things which of themselves must fall, does not itself need to look for a staying ground.

6. We take it, then, that the Intellectual-Principle is the authentic existences and contains them all—not as in a place but as possessing itself and being one thing with this its content. All are one There and yet are distinct: similarly the mind holds many branches and items of knowledge simultaneously, yet none of them merged into any other, each acting its own part at call quite independently, every conception coming out from the inner total and working singly. It is after this way, though in a closer unity, that the Intellectual-Principle is all Being in one total—and yet not in one, since each of these beings is a distinct power which, however, the total Intellectual-Principle includes as the species in a genus, as the parts in a whole. This relation may be illustrated by the powers in seed; all lies undistinguished in the unit, the formative ideas gathered as in one kernel; yet in that unit there is eye principle, and there is hand-principle, each of which is revealed as a separate power by its distinct material product. Thus each of the powers in the seed is a Reason-Principle one and complete yet including all the parts over which it presides: there will be something bodily, the liquid for example, carrying mere Matter; but the principle itself is Form and nothing else, Form identical with the generative Form belonging to the lower soul, image of a higher. This power is sometimes designated as Nature in the seed-life; its origin is in the divine; and, outgoing from its priors as light from fire, it converts and shapes the matter of things, not by push and pull and the lever work of which we hear so much, but by bestowal of the Reason-Principles.

7. Knowledge in the reasoning soul is on the one side concerned with objects of sense, though indeed this can scarcely be called knowledge and is better indicated as opinion or surface-knowing; it is of later origin than the objects since it is a reflection from them: but on the other hand there is the knowledge handling the intellectual objects and this is the authentic knowledge; it enters the reasoning soul from the Intellectual-Principle and has no dealing with anything in sense. Being true knowledge it actually is everything of which it takes cognizance; it carries as its own content the intellectual act and the intellectual object since it carries the Intellectual-Principle which actually is the primals and is always self-present and is in its nature an Act, never by any want forced to seek, never acquiring or traversing the remote—for all such experience belongs to soul—but always self-gathered, the very Being of the collective total, not an extern creating things by the act of knowing them.

Not by its thinking God does God come to be; not by its thinking Movement does Movement arise. Hence it is an error to call the Ideas intellections in the sense that, upon an intellectual act in this Principle, one such Idea or another is made to exist or exists. No: the object of this intellection must exist before the intellective act (must be the very content not the creation of the Intellectual-Principle). How else could that Principle come to know it? Certainly not (as an external) by luck or by haphazard search.

8. ❙ If, then, the Intellection is an act upon the inner content (of the Intellectual-Principle), that content is the Form, and the Form is the Idea.[1]❙

What, then, is that content?

An Intellectual-Principle and an Intellective Essence, no Idea distinguishable from the Intellectual-Principle, each actually being that Principle. The Intellectual-Principle entire is the total of the Ideas, and each of them is the (entire) Intellectual-Principle in a special form. Thus a science entire is the total of the relevant considerations each of which, again, is a member of the entire science, a member not distinct in space yet having its individual efficacy in a total.

This Intellectual-Principle, therefore, is a unity while by that possession of itself it is, tranquilly, the eternal abundance.

If the Intellectual-Principle were envisaged as preceding Being, it would at once become a principle whose expression, its intellectual Act, achieves and engenders the Beings: but, since we are compelled to think of existence as preceding that which knows it, we can but think that the Beings are the actual content of the knowing principle and that the very act, the intellection, is inherent to the Beings, as fire stands equipped from the beginning with fire-act; in this conception, the Beings contain the Intellectual-Principle as one and the same with themselves, as their own activity. ❙ But[2] Being is ❙ itself an activity: there is one activity, then, in both or, rather, both are one thing.

Being, therefore, and the Intellectual-Principle are one Nature: the Beings, and the Act of that which is, and the Intellectual-Principle thus constituted, all are one: and the resultant Intellections are the Idea of Being and its shape and its act.

It is our separating habit that sets the one order before the other: for there is a separating intellect, of another order than the true, distinct from the Intellect, inseparable and unseparating, which is Being and the universe of things.

9. What, then, is the content—inevitably separated by our minds—of this one Intellectual-Principle? For there is no resource but to represent the items in accessible form just as we study the various articles constituting one science.

This universe is a living thing capable of including every form of life; but its Being and its modes are derived from elsewhere; that source is traced back to the Intellectual-Principle: it follows that the all-embracing archetype is in the

Intellectual Principle, which, therefore, must be an intellectual Cosmos, that indicated by Plato in the phrase I 'The Idea of living being'.[3]I

Given the Reason-Principle (the outgoing divine Idea) of a certain living thing and the Matter to harbour this seed-principle, the living thing must come into being: in the same way once there exists an intellective Nature, all powerful, and with nothing to check it—since nothing intervenes between it and that which is of a nature to receive it—inevitably the higher imprints the Cosmic form and the lower accepts it. The recipient holds the Idea in division, here man, there sun, while in the giver all remains in unity.

10. All, then, that is present in the sense realm as Form comes from the Supreme. But what is not present as Form, does not. Thus of things conflicting with nature, none is There: the inartistic is not contained in the arts; lameness is not in the seed; for a lame leg is either inborn through some thwarting of the Reason-Principle or is a marring of the achieved form by accident. To that Intellectual Cosmos belong qualities, accordant with Nature, and quantities; number and mass I and relations;[4] I all actions and experiences not against nature; movement and repose, both the universals and the particulars: but There time is replaced by eternity and space by its intellectual equivalent, mutual inclusiveness.

In that Intellectual Cosmos, where all is one total, every entity that can be singled out is an intellective essence and a participant in life: it is identity and difference, movement and rest, the object moving and the object at rest, essence and quality. All There is pure essence; for every real being must be in actuality, not merely in potentiality, and therefore quality is never separated from essence.

This suggests the question whether the Intellectual Cosmos contains the form only of the things of sense or of other existents as well. But first we will consider how it stands with artistic creations. There is, by the way, no question of an ideal archetype of evil: the evil of this world is begotten of need, privation, deficiency, and is a condition peculiar to Matter distressed and to what has come into likeness with Matter.

11. Now as to the arts and crafts and their productions:

The imitative arts—painting, sculpture, dancing, pantomimic gesturing—are, largely, earth-based; they follow models found in sense, since they copy forms and movements and reproduce seen symmetries; they cannot therefore be referred to that higher sphere except indirectly, through the Reason-Principle in humanity.

On the other hand any skill which, beginning with the observation of the symmetry of living things, grows to the symmetry of all life, will be a portion of the power There which observes and mediates the symmetry reigning among all beings in the Intellectual Cosmos. Thus all music—since its thought is upon melody and rhythm—must be the earthly representation of the music there is in the rhythm of the Ideal Realm.

The crafts such as building and carpentry which give us Matter in wrought forms, may be said, in that they draw on pattern, to take their principles from that realm and from the thinking There: but in that they bring these down into contact with the sense-order, I they are not wholly in the Intellectual, except as contained in the Idea of [5] man. I So agriculture, dealing with material growths; so medicine, watching over physical health; so the art which aims at corporeal strength and well-being: power and health mean something else There, the fearlessness and self-sufficing quality of all that lives.

Oratory and generalship, administration and sovereignty—under any forms in which their activities are associated with Good and when they look to that— possess something derived thence and building up their knowledge from the knowledge There.

Geometry, as a science of the Intellectual entities, holds place There: so, too, philosophy, whose high concern is Being.

For the arts and products of art, these observations may suffice.

12. It should, however, be added that if the Idea of man exists in the Supreme, there must exist the Idea of reasoning man and of man with his arts and crafts; such arts as are the offspring of intellect must be There.

It must be observed that the Ideas will be of universals; not of Socrates but of Man: though as to man we may inquire whether the individual may not also have place There. I Ideas of individual men may be justified by the fact that the same feature varies[6] from man to man, I the simian type, for example, and the aquiline: the aquiline and the simian must be taken to be differences in the Idea of Man as there are different types of the animal: but Matter also has its effect in bringing about the degree of aquilinity. Similarly with difference of complexion, determined partly by the Reason-Principle, partly by Matter and by diversity of place.

13. It remains to decide whether only what is known in sense exists There or whether on the contrary, as Absolute-Man differs from individual man, so there is in the Supreme an Absolute-Soul differing from Soul and an Absolute-Intellect differing from Intellectual-Principle.

It must be stated at the outset that we cannot take all that is here to be image of archetype, or Soul to be an image of Absolute-Soul: one soul, doubtless, ranks higher than another, but here too, though perhaps not as identified with this realm, is the Absolute-Soul.

Every soul, authentically a soul, has some form of rightness and moral wisdom; in the souls within ourselves there is true knowing: and these attributes are no images or copies from the Supreme, as in the sense-world, but actually are those very originals in a mode peculiar to this sphere. For those Beings are not set apart in some defined place; wherever there is a soul that has risen from body, there too these are: the world of sense is one-where, the Intellectual Cosmos is everywhere. Whatever the freed soul attains to here, that it is There.

Thus, if by the content of the sense-world we mean simply the visible objects, then the Supreme contains not only what is in the realm of sense but more: if in the content of the Cosmos we mean to include Soul and the Soul-things, then all is here that is There.

14. There is, thus, a Nature comprehending in the Intellectual all that exists, and this Principle must be the source of all. But how, seeing that the veritable source must be a unity, simplex utterly?

The mode by which from the unity arises the multiple, how all this universe comes to be, why the Intellectual-Principle is all and whence it springs, these matters demand another approach.

But on the question as to whether the repulsive and the products of putridity have also their Idea—whether there is an Idea of filth and mud—it is to be observed that all that the Intellectual-Principle derived from The First is of the noblest; in those Ideas the base is not included: these repulsive things point not to the Intellectual-Principle but to the Soul which, drawing upon the Intellectual-Principle, takes from Matter certain other things, and among them these.

But all this will be more clearly brought out when we turn to the problem of the production of multiplicity from unity. Compounds, we shall see—as owing existence to hazard and not to the Intellectual-Principle, having been fused into objects of sense by their own impulse—are not to be included under Ideas.

The products of putrefaction are to be traced to the Soul's inability to bring some other thing to being—something in the order of nature, which, else, it would—but producing where it may.

In the matter of the arts and crafts, all that are to be traced to the needs of human nature are laid up in the Absolute Man.

And before the particular Soul there is another Soul, a universal, and, before that, an Absolute-Soul, which is the Life existing in the Intellectual-Principle before Soul came to be and therefore rightly called (as the Life in the Divine) the Absolute-Soul.

NOTES TO ENNEAD V.9

1. FIRST EDITION: "If, then, the Intellection is an act upon the inner content (of *a perfect unity*), that content is *at once the Idea (as object: eidos) and the Idea itself (as concept: idéa)*."

GUTHRIE: "Since the thought is something essentially one (?), the form, which is the object of thought, and the idea are one and the same thing." In a footnote, he adds: "In Greek a pun on 'eidos' and 'idea.'"

ARMSTRONG: "If, then, the thought [of Intellect] is of what is within it, that which is within it is its immanent form, and this is the Idea." Brackets are Armstrong's.

TAYLOR: "If, therefore, intelligence is truly one, that form which is the object of its perception and idea itself are one."

2. FIRST EDITION: "*Thus*, Being is . . ."

TAYLOR: "Being, likewise, is energy;"

GUTHRIE: "Now essence is . . ."

ARMSTRONG: "But being is . . ."

3. FIRST EDITION: "The *living existent*."

ARMSTRONG: ". . . the absolute living being."

GUTHRIE: ". . . the existing animal."

TAYLOR: ". . . animal itself."

4. FIRST EDITION: ". . . *origins and conditions*;"

TAYLOR: "habitudes,"

GUTHRIE: "states,"

ARMSTRONG: "relations."

5. FIRST EDITION: ". . . they are not wholly in the Intellectual: *they are founded in man*."

TAYLOR: ". . . the whole of them will not be in intelligibles, except so far as they subsist in man [i.e. in the human soul]. Brackets are Taylor's.

GUTHRIE: ". . . they cannot wholly be referred to the intelligible world, unless in so far as they are contained within human reason."

ARMSTRONG: ". . . they would not be altogether in the intelligible world, except in the [Form of] man."

6. FIRST EDITION: "*Under the heading of individuality there is to be considered the repetition of the same feature from man to man* . . ."

TAYLOR: ". . . not because he is the same with another man . . ."

ARMSTRONG: ". . . there is individuality, because the same [individual feature] is different in different people:" Brackets are Armstrong's.

GUTHRIE: ". . . the idea of the individual man, that is, of the man considered with the things that differ in each individual;"

THE SIXTH ENNEAD

FIRST TRACTATE

On the Kinds of Being: First Treatise

1. Philosophy at a very early stage investigated the number and character of the Existents. Various theories resulted: some declared for one Existent, others for a finite number, others again for an infinite number, while as regards the nature of the Existents—one, numerically finite, or numerically infinite—there was a similar disagreement. These theories, in so far as they have been adequately examined by later workers, may be passed over here; our attention must be directed upon the results of those whose examination has led them to posit on their own account certain well-defined genera.

These thinkers rejected pure unity on the ground of the plurality observed even in the Intellectual world; they rejected an infinite number as not reconcilable with the facts and as defying knowledge: considering the foundations of being to be 'genera' rather than elements strictly so called, they concluded for a finite number. Of these 'genera' some found ten, others less, others no doubt more.

But here again there is a divergence of views. To some the genera are first-principles; to others they indicate only a generic classification of the Existents themselves.

Let us begin with the well-known tenfold division of the Existents, and consider whether we are to understand ten genera ranged under the common name of Being, or ten categories. That the term Being has not the same sense in all ten is rightly maintained.

But a graver problem confronts us at the outset: Are the ten found alike in the Intellectual and in the Sensible realms? Or are all found in the Sensible and some only in the Intellectual? All in the Intellectual and some in the Sensible is manifestly impossible.

At this point it would be natural to investigate which of the ten belong to both spheres, and whether the Existents of the Intellectual are to be ranged under one and the same genus with the Existents in the Sensible, or whether the term 'Existence' (or Substance) is equivocal as applied to both realms. If the equivocation exists, the number of genera will be increased: if there is no equivocation, it is strange to find the one same 'Existence' applying to the primary and to the derivative Existents when there is no common genus embracing both primal and secondary.

These thinkers are, however, not considering the Intellectual realm in their division, which was not intended to cover all the Existents; the Supreme they overlooked.

2. But are we really obliged to consider the ten categories as genera?

Take Substance—for Substance must certainly be our starting-point: what are the grounds for regarding Substance as one single genus?

It has been remarked that Substance cannot be a single entity common to both the Intellectual and the Sensible worlds. We may add that such community would entail the existence of something prior to Intellectual and Sensible Substance alike, something distinct from both as predicated of both; and this prior would be neither body nor unembodied; for if it were one or the other, body would be unembodied, or the unembodied would be body.

This conclusion must not, however, prevent our seeking in the actual substances of the Sensible world an element held in common by Matter, by Form, and by their Composite, all of which are designated as substances, though it is not maintained that they are Substance in an equal degree; Form is held to be Substance in a higher degree than Matter, and rightly so, in spite of those who would have Matter to be the more truly real.

There is further the distinction drawn between what are known as First and Second Substances. But what is their common basis, seeing that the First are the source from which the Second derive their right to be called substances?

But, in sum, it is impossible to define Substance: determine its property, and still you have not attained to its essence. Even the definition, 'That which, numerically one and the same, is receptive of contraries', will hardly be applicable to all substances alike.

3. But perhaps we should rather speak of some single category (as distinct from a genus), embracing Intellectual Substance, Matter, Form, and the Composite of Matter and Form. One might refer to the family of the Heraclids as a unity in the sense, not of a common element in all its members, but of a common origin: similarly, Intellectual Substance would be Substance in the first degree, the others being substances by derivation and in a lower degree.

But (pursuing this principle) what is the objection to including everything in a single category, all else of which existence is predicated being derived from that one thing, Existence or Substance? Because, granted that things be no more than modifications of Substance, there is a distinct grading of substances themselves. Moreover, the single category does not put us in a position to build on Substance, or to grasp it in its very truth as the plausible source of the other substances.

Supposing we grant that all things known as substances are homogeneous as possessing something denied to the other genera, what precisely is this something, this individuality, this subject which is never a predicate, never present in any other thing as in a subject, taking its essential character from no outside source, as a quality takes character from a body and a quantity from a substance, as time is related to motion and motion to the moved?

The Second Substance is, it is true, a predicate. But predication in this case signifies a different relation from that just considered; it reveals the genus inherent in the subject and the subject's essential character, whereas whiteness is predicated of a thing in the sense of being present (as an attribute) in the thing.

The properties adduced may indeed be allowed to distinguish Substance from the other Existents. They afford a means of grouping substances together and calling them by a common name. They do not however establish the unity of a genus, and they do not bring to light the concept and the nature of Substance.

These considerations are sufficient for our purpose: let us now proceed to investigate the nature of Quantity.

4. We are told that number is Quantity in the primary sense, number together with all continuous magnitude, space, and time: these are the standards to which all else that is considered as Quantity is referred, including motion which is Quantity because its time is quantitative—though perhaps, conversely, the time takes its continuity from the motion.

If it is maintained that the continuous is a Quantity by the fact of its continuity, then the discrete will not be a Quantity. If, on the contrary, the continuous possesses Quantity as an accident, what is there common to both continuous and discrete to make them quantities?

Suppose we concede that numbers are quantities: we are merely allowing them the name of quantity; the principle which gives them this name remains obscure.

On the other hand, line and surface and body are not called quantities; they are called magnitudes: they become known as quantities only when they are rated by number—two yards, three yards. Even the natural body becomes a quantity when measured, as does the space which it occupies; but this is quantity accidental, not quantity essential; what we seek to grasp is not accidental quantity but Quantity independent and essential, Quantity-Absolute. Three oxen is not a quantity; it is their number, the three, that is Quantity; for in three oxen we are dealing with two categories. So too with a line of a stated length, a surface of a given area; the area will be a quantity but not the surface, which only comes under that category when it constitutes a definite geometric figure.

Are we then to consider numbers, and numbers only, as constituting the category of Quantity? If we mean numbers in themselves, they are (not quantities but) substances, for the very good reason that they exist independently. If we mean numbers displayed in the objects participant in number, the numbers which give the count of the objects—ten horses or ten oxen, and not ten units—then we have a paradoxical result: first, the numbers in themselves, it would appear, are substances but the numbers in objects are not; and secondly, the numbers inhere in the objects as measures (of extension or weight), yet as standing outside the objects they have no measuring power, as do rulers and scales. If, however, their existence is independent, and they do not inhere in the objects, but are simply called in for the purpose of measurement, the objects will be quantities only to the extent of participating in Quantity.

So with the numbers themselves: how can they (in these circumstances) constitute the category of Quantity? They are measures; but how do measures come to be quantities or Quantity? Doubtless in that, existing as they do among the Existents and not being adapted to any of the other categories, they find their place under the influence of verbal suggestion and so are referred to the so-called category of Quantity. We see the unit mark off one measurement and then proceed to another; and number thus reveals the amount of a thing, and the mind uses the number to measure the total.

It follows that in measuring it is not measuring essence; it pronounces its 'one' or 'two', whatever the character of the objects, even summing contraries. It does not take count of condition—hot, handsome; it simply notes how many.

Number then, whether regarded in itself or in the participant objects, goes into the category of Quantity, but the participant objects do not; 'three yards long' does not, but only the 'three'.

Why then are magnitudes classed as quantities? Not because they are so in the strict sense, but because they approximate to Quantity, and because objects in which magnitudes inhere are themselves designated as quantities. We call a thing great or small from its participation in a high number or a low. True, greatness and smallness are not claimed to be quantities, but relations: but it is by their apparent possession of quantity that they are thought of as relations. All this, however, needs more careful examination.

In sum, we hold that there is no single genus of Quantity. Only number is Quantity, the rest (magnitudes, space, time, motion) quantities only in a secondary degree. We have therefore not strictly one genus, but one category grouping the approximate with the primary and the secondary.

We have, however, to inquire in what sense the abstract numbers are substances. Can it be that they are also in a manner quantitative? Into whatever category they fall, the other numbers (those inherent in objects) can have nothing in common with them but the name.

5. Speech, time, motion—in what sense are these quantities?

Let us begin with speech. It is subject to measurement, but only in so far as it is sound; it is not a quantity in its essential nature, which nature is that it be significant, as noun and verb are significant. The air is (not its essence but) its Matter, as it is Matter to verb and noun, the components of speech.

To be more precise, we may define speech as an impact (made upon the outer air by the breath), though it is not so much the impact as the impression which the impact produces and which as it were imposes Form (upon the air). Speech, thus, is rather an action than a quantity—an action with a significance. Though perhaps it would be truer to say that while this motion, this impact, is an action, the counter-motion is an experience (or Passion); or each may be from different points of view either an action or an experience: or we may think of speech as action upon a substrate (air) and experience within that substrate.

If, however, voice is characterized not only by the impact itself but also by the air which receives it, two categories will be involved, one to represent significant impact, the other to bring out the full meaning of the first (by representing the material, air).

With regard to time, if it is to be thought of as a measure, we must determine what it is that applies this measure. It must clearly be either Soul or the Present Moment. If on the contrary we take time to be something measured and regard it as being of such and such extension—a year, for example—then we may consider it as a quantity: essentially, however, time is of a different nature; the very fact that we can attribute this or that length to it shows us that it is not length: in other words, time is not Quantity. Quantity in the strict sense is the Quantity not inbound with things; if things became quantities by mere participation in Quantity, then (not only time but) Substance itself would be identical with Quantity.

Equality and inequality must be regarded as properties of Quantity-Absolute, not of the participants, or of them not essentially but only accidentally: such participants as 'three yards' length', which becomes a quantity, not as belonging to a single genus of Quantity, but by being subsumed under the one head, the one category.

6. In considering Relation we must inquire whether it possesses the community of a genus, or whether it may on other grounds be treated as a unity.

Above all, has Relation—for example, that of right and left, double and half—

any actuality? Has it, perhaps, actuality in some cases only, as for instance in the second pair but not the first? Or is its actuality in no case conceivable?

What meaning, then, are we to attach to double and half and all other cases of less and more; to habit and disposition, reclining, sitting, standing; to father, son, master, slave; to like, unlike, equal, unequal; to active and passive, measure and measured; or again to knowledge and sensation, as related respectively to the knowable and the sensible?

Knowledge, indeed, may be supposed to possess some single activating character in relation to the known object, and similarly with sensation as related to the sense-object. The active will perform some constant function in relation to the passive, as will the measure in relation to the measured.

But what will emerge from the relation of like to like? Nothing will emerge. Likeness is the inherence of qualitative identity; its entire content is the quality present in the two objects.

From equality, similarly, nothing emerges. The relation merely presupposes the existence of a quantitative identity; it is nothing but our judgement comparing objects essentially independent and concluding, 'This and that have the same magnitude, the same quality; this has produced that; this is superior to that'.

Again, what meaning can sitting and standing have apart from sitter and stander? The term 'habit' either implies a having, in which case it signifies Possession, or else it arises from something had, and so denotes Quality; and similarly with disposition.

What then in these instances can be the meaning of correlatives apart from our conception of their juxtaposition? 'Greater' may refer to very different magnitudes; 'different' to all sorts of objects: the comparison is ours; it does not lie in the things themselves.

Right and left, before and behind, would seem to belong less to the category of Relation than to that of Situation. Right means 'situated at one point', left means 'situated at another'. But the right and left are in our conception, nothing of them in the things themselves.

Before and after are merely two times; the relation is again of our making.

7. Now if we do not mean anything by Relation but are victims of words, none of the relations mentioned can exist: Relation will be a notion void of content.

Suppose, however, that we do possess ourselves of objective truth when in comparing two points of time we pronounce one prior, or posterior, to the other, that priority and posteriority do entail something distinct from the objects to which they refer; admit an objective truth behind the relation of left and right; let it apply also to magnitudes, with their relation of excess and deficiency as something distinct from the quantities involved.

One thing, we are supposing, is double of another quite apart from our speech or thought; one thing possesses and another is possessed before we notice the fact; equals do not await our comparison but—and this applies to Quality as well as Quantity—rest upon an identity existing between the objects compared: in all the conditions in which we assert Relation the mutual relation exists over and above the objects we perceive it as already existent; our knowledge is directed upon a thing, there to be known—a clear testimony to the reality of Relation.

In these circumstances we can no longer put the question of its existence. We have simply to distinguish: sometimes the relation subsists while the objects remain unaltered and even apart; sometimes it depends upon their combination; sometimes, while they remain unchanged, the relation utterly ceases, or, as happens with right and near, becomes different. These are the facts which chiefly account for the notion that Relation has no reality in such circumstances.

Our task, thus, is to give full value to this elusive character of Relation, and then to inquire what there is that is constant in all these particular cases and whether this constant is generic or accidental; and having found this constant, we must discover what sort of actuality it possesses.

It need hardly be said that we are not to affirm Relation where one thing is simply an attribute of another, as a habit is an attribute of a soul or of a body; it is not Relation when a soul belongs to this individual or dwells in that body. Relation enters only when the actuality of the correlatives is derived from no other source than the relation itself; the actuality must be, not that which is characteristic of the substances in question, but that which is specifically called relative. Thus double with its correlative half gives actuality neither to two yards' length or the number two, nor to one yard's length or the number one; what happens is that when these quantities are viewed in their relation, they are found to be not merely two and one respectively, but to produce the assertion and to exhibit the fact of standing one to the other in the condition of double and half. Out of the objects in a certain conjunction this condition of being double and half has issued as something distinct from either; double and half have emerged as correlatives, and their being is precisely this of mutual dependence; the double exists by its superiority over the half, and the half by its inferiority; there is no priority to distinguish double from half; they arise simultaneously.

It is another question whether they endure simultaneously. Take the case of father and son, and such relationships; the father dies, but the other is still his son, and so with brothers. Moreover, we see likeness where one of the like people is dead.

8. But we are digressing: we have noted a discrepancy and suggested the way to an explanation. We must now be informed what reality, common to all cases, is possessed by this Existence derived from mutual conditions.

The common principle cannot be a body. The only alternative is that, if it does exist, it be something bodiless, either in the objects thus brought together or outside of them.

Further, if Relation always takes the same form, the term is univocal (and specific differentiation is impossible); if not, that is if it differs from case to case, the term is equivocal, and the same reality will not necessarily be implied by the mere use of the term Relation.

How then shall we distinguish relations? We may observe that some things have an inactive or dormant relation, which is only real in so far as they are entirely simultaneous; others, combining power and function with their relation, either have the relation in some mode always even though the mode be merely that of potentiality, though it becomes actual when the correlatives are brought into contact; or else they simply resolve themselves into producer and product, where the product merely gives a name to the producer of its actuality: an example of this is the relation of father to son, though here both producer and product have a sort of actuality, which we call life.

Are we thus, then, to divide Relation, and thereby reject the notion of an identical common element in the different kinds of Relation, recognizing instead two types utterly different in character? There will thus be nothing but the name in common between the active relationship which produces both activity and passivity as though these two were one, and the relationship which, though itself inactive, presupposes a separate active principle above the two correlatives. Take the case of equality, producing equals: nothing is equal without equality, nothing identical without identity. Greatness and smallness both entail a presence—the presence of greatness and smallness respectively. When we come to greater and smaller, the participants in these relations are greater and smaller only when greatness and smallness are actually observed in them.

9. It follows that in the cases specified above—agent, knowledge, and the rest—the relation must be considered as in actual operation, and the Act and the Reason-Principle in the Act must be assumed to be real: in all other cases there will be simply participation in an Ideal-Form, in a Reason-Principle.

If Reality implied embodiment, we should indeed be forced to deny Reality to these conditions called relative; if, however, we accord the pre-eminent place to the unembodied and to the Reason-Principles, and at the same time maintain that relations are Reason-Principles and participate in Ideal-Forms, we are bound to seek their causes in that higher sphere. Doubleness, it is clear, is the cause of a thing being double, and from it is derived halfness.

Some correlatives owe their designations to the same Form, others to opposite Forms; it is thus that two objects are simultaneously double and half, and one great and the other small. It may happen that both correlatives exist in one object—likeness and unlikeness, and, in general, identity and difference, so that the same thing will be at once like and unlike, identical and different.

The question arises here whether sharing in the same Form could make one man depraved and another more depraved. In the case of total depravity, clearly the two are made equal by the absence of a Form. Where there is a difference of degree, the one has participated in a Form which has failed to predominate, the other in a Form which has failed still more: or we may compare them in respect of their privation of Form, treating the privation as though it were a Form itself.

Sensation may be regarded as a Form of double origin (determined both by the sense-organ and by the sensible object); and similarly with knowledge.

Habit is an Act directed upon something had (some experience produced by habit) and binding it, as it were, with the subject having (experiencing); it has an element of creativeness.

Measurement is an Act of the measurer upon the measured object: it too is therefore a kind of Reason-Principle.

Now if the condition of being related is regarded as a Form having a generic unity, Relation must be allowed to be a single genus with an actuality represented by a Reason-Principle involved in all instances. If, however, the Reason-Principles (governing the correlatives) stand opposed and have the differences to which we have referred, there may perhaps not be a single genus, but this will not prevent all relatives being expressed in terms of a certain likeness, and falling under a single category.

But even if the cases of which we have spoken can be subsumed under a single head, it is nevertheless impossible to include in a single genus all that goes with them in the one common category: for the category is made to include negations and derivatives—not only, for example, doubleness but its negative and the object possessing doubleness. But we cannot include in one genus both the thing and its negative—double and not-double, relative and not-relative—any more than in dealing with the genus animal we can insert in it the non-animal. Moreover, doubleness and the double object have no more identity than whiteness has with what is white.

10. As regards Quality, the source of what we call a 'quale', we must in the first place consider what nature it possesses in accordance with which it produces the 'qualia', and whether, remaining one and the same in virtue of that common

ground, it has also differences whereby it produces the variety of species. If there is no common ground and the term Quality involves many connotations, there cannot be a single genus of Quality.

What then will be the common ground in habit, disposition, passive quality, figure, shape? In light, thick, and lean?

If we hold this common ground to be a power adapting itself to the forms of habits, dispositions, and physical capacities, a power which gives the possessor whatever capacities he has, we have no plausible explanation of incapacities. Besides, how are figure and the shape of a given thing to be regarded as a power?

Moreover, at this, Being will have no power *qua* Being but only when Quality has been added to it; and the activities of those substances which are activities in the highest degree, will be traceable to Quality, although they are autonomous and owe their essential character to powers wholly their own!

Perhaps, however, qualities are to be identified with powers which are posterior to the substances as such (and thus no part of their essential activities). Boxing is not a power of man *qua* man; reasoning is: in other words, reasoning, as so understood—the term is ambiguous—is not a quality, but rather what a man possesses by being a complete human being. Thus, Quality is a power which adds the property of being qualia to substances already existent.

The differences distinguishing substances from each other are called qualities only by analogy; they are, more strictly, Acts and Reason-Principles, or parts of Reason-Principles, and though they may appear merely to qualify the substance, they in fact indicate its essence.

Qualities in the true sense—those, that is, which determine qualia—being in accordance with our definition powers (but powers forming no part of the substance or essence), will in virtue of this common ground be a kind of Reason-Principle; they will also be in a sense Forms, that is, excellences and imperfections whether of soul or of body.

But how can they all be powers? Beauty or health of soul or body, very well: but surely not ugliness, disease, weakness, incapacity. In a word, is powerlessness a power?

It may be urged that these are qualities in so far as qualia are also named after them: but may not the qualia be so called by analogy, and not in the strict sense of the single principle? Not only may the term be understood in the four ways (of Aristotle), but each of the four may have at least a twofold significance.

In the first place, Quality is not merely a question of activity and passivity, involving a simple distinction between the potentially active (quality) and the passive; health, disposition and habit, disease, strength and weakness are also classed as qualities. It follows that the common ground is not power, but something we have still to seek.

Again, not all qualities can be regarded as Reason-Principles: chronic disease cannot be a Reason-Principle. Perhaps, however, we must speak in such cases of privations, restricting the term Quantities to Ideal-Forms and powers. Thus we shall have, not a single genus, but reference only to the unity of a category. Knowledge will be regarded as a Form and a power, ignorance as a privation and powerlessness.

On the other hand, powerlessness and disease are a kind of Form; disease and vice have many powers though looking to evil.

But how can a mere failure be a power? Doubtless the truth is that every quality performs its own function independently of a standard; for in no case could it produce an effect outside of its power.

Even beauty would seem to have a power of its own. Does this apply to triangularity?

Perhaps, after all, it is not a power we must consider, but a making over to Form. Thus, qualities will be determined by the forms and characteristics of the object qualified: their common element, then, will be Form and ideal type, imposed upon Substance and posterior to it.

But then, how do we account for the powers? We may doubtless remark that even the natural boxer is so by being constituted in a particular way; similarly, with the man unable to box: to generalize, the quality is a characteristic non-essential. Whatever is seen to apply alike to Being and to non-Being, as do heat and whiteness and colours generally, is one thing when associated with Being— is, for example, an Act of Being—but in the other case it is but a secondary, derived from the first, its image and likeness, and calls for a substrate to contain it.

But if Quality is determined by formation and characteristic and Reason-Principle, how explain the various cases of powerlessness and deformity? Doubtless we must think of Principles imperfectly present, as in the case of deformity. And disease—how does that imply a Reason-Principle? Here, no doubt, we must think of a principle disturbed, the Principle of health.

But it is not necessary that all qualities involve a Reason-Principle; a sufficient common ground may be found in some kind of disposition distinct from Substance, and it is what comes after the substance that constitutes Quality in an object.

But triangularity is a quality of that in which it is present; it is however no longer triangularity as such, but the triangularity present in that definite object and modified in proportion to its success in shaping that object.

Does that imply that humanity shapes the human Being? No: it constitutes his substance or essence.

11. But if these considerations are sound, why has Quality more than one species?

What is the ground for distinguishing between habit and disposition, seeing that no differentia of Quality is involved in permanence and non-permanence? A disposition of any kind is sufficient to constitute a quality; permanence is a mere external addition. It might, however, be urged that dispositions are but incomplete 'forms'—if the term may pass—habits being complete ones. But incomplete, they are not qualities; if already qualities, the permanence is an external addition.

How do physical powers form a distinct species? If they are classed as qualities in virtue of being powers, power, we have seen, is not a necessary concomitant of qualities. If, however, we hold that the natural boxer owes his quality to a particular disposition, power is something added and does not contribute to the quality, since power is found in habits also.

Another point: why is natural ability to be distinguished from that acquired by learning? Surely, if both are qualities, they cannot be differentiae of Quality: gained by practice or given in nature, it is the same ability; the differentia will be external to Quality; it cannot be deduced from the Ideal Form of (say) boxing. Whether some qualities as distinguished from others are derived from experience is immaterial; the source of the quality makes no difference—none, I mean, pointing to variations and differences of Quality.

A further question would seem to be involved: if certain qualities are derived from experience but there is a discrepancy in the manner and source of the experience, how are they to be included in the same species? And again, if some create the experience, others are created by it, the term Quality as applied to both classes will be equivocal.

And what part is played by the individual form? If it constitutes the individual's specific character, it is not a quality; if, however, it is what makes an object beautiful or ugly after the specific form has been determined, then it could claim to be a quality.

Rough and smooth, tenuous and dense may rightly be classed as qualities. It is true that they are not determined by distances and approximations, or in general by even or uneven dispositions, of parts; though, were they so determined, they might well even then be qualities.

Knowledge of the meaning of light and heavy will reveal their place in the classification. An ambiguity will however be latent in the term 'light', unless it be determined by comparative weight: it would then implicate leanness and fineness, and involve another species distinct from the four (of Aristotle).

12. If then we do not propose to divide Quality in this (fourfold) manner, what basis of division have we?

We must examine whether qualities may not prove to be divisible on the principle that some belong to the body and others to the soul. Those of the body would be subdivided according to the senses, some being attributed to sight, others to hearing and taste, others to smell and touch. Those of the soul would presumably be allotted to appetite, emotion, reason; though, again, they may be distinguished by the differences of the activities they condition, inasmuch as activities are engendered by these qualities; or according as they are beneficial or injurious, the benefits and injuries being duly classified. This last is applicable also to the classification of bodily qualities, which also produce differences of benefit and injury: these differences must be regarded as distinctively qualitative; for either the benefit and injury are held to be derived from Quality and the quale, or else some other explanation must be found for them.

A point for consideration is how the quale, as conditioned by Quality, can belong to the same category: obviously there can be no single genus embracing both.

Further, if 'boxer' is in the category of Quality, why not 'agent' as well? And with agent goes 'active'. Thus 'active' need not go into the category of Relation; nor again need 'passive', if 'patient' is a quale. Moreover, 'agent' is perhaps better assigned to the category of Quality for the reason that the term implies power and power is Quality. Alternatively, power or a particular power may be regarded as Substance; in which case the agent ceases to be a quale, without becoming a relative. 'Active' is not like 'greater': the greater, to be the greater, demands a less, whereas 'active' stands complete by the mere possession of its specific character.

It may, however, be urged that while the possession of that character makes it a quale, it is a relative in so far as it directs upon an external object the power indicated by its name. Why, then, is not 'boxer' a relative, and 'boxing' as well? Boxing is entirely related to an external object; its whole theory presupposes this external. And in the case of the other arts—or most of them—investigation would probably warrant the assertion that in so far as they affect (dispose) the Soul they are qualities, while in so far as they look outward they are active and as being directed to an external object are relatives. They are relatives in the other sense also that they are thought of as habits.

Can it then be held that there is any distinct reality implied in activity, when the active is identified with the quale? It may perhaps be held that the tendency towards action of living beings, and especially of those having free-will, implies a reality of activity (as well as a reality of Quality).

But what is the function of the active in connexion with those nonliving powers which we have classed as qualities? Doubtless to recruit any object it encounters, making the object a participant in its content.

But if one same object both acts and is acted upon, how do we then explain the active? Observe also that the greater—in itself perhaps a fixed three yards' length—will present itself as both greater and less according to its external contacts.

It will be objected that greater and less are due to participation in greatness and smallness; and it might be conceded that a thing is active or passive by participation in activity or passivity.

This is the place for inquiring also whether the qualities of the Sensible and Intellectual realms can be included under one head—a question intended only for those who ascribe qualities to the higher realm as well as the lower. And even if Ideal Forms of qualities are not posited, yet once the term 'habit' is used in reference to Intellect, the question arises whether there is anything common to that habit and the habit we know in the lower.

Wisdom too is generally admitted to exist There. Obviously, if it shares only its name with our wisdom, it is not to be reckoned among things of this sphere; if, however, the import is in both cases the same, then Quality is common to both realms—unless, of course, it be maintained that everything There, including even intellection, is Substance.

This question, however, applies to all the categories: are the two spheres irreconcilable, or can they be co-ordinated within a unity?

13. With regard to Date:

If 'yesterday', 'tomorrow', 'last year', and similar terms denote parts of time, why should they not be included in the same genus as time? It would seem only reasonable to range under time the past, present, and future, which are its species. But time is referred to Quantity; what then is the need for a separate category of Date?

If we are told that past and future—including under past such definite dates as yesterday and last year which must clearly be subordinate to past time—are not merely time, to be identified with the present moment (time-now), but are time-when, we reply, in the first place, that the notion of time-when involves time; that, further, if 'yesterday' is time-gone-by, it will be a composite, since time and gone-by are distinct notions: we have two categories instead of the single one required.

But suppose that Date is defined not as time but as that which is in time; if by that which is in time is meant the subject—Socrates in the proposition 'Socrates existed last year'—that subject is external to the notion of time, and we have again a duality.

Consider, however, the proposition 'Socrates—or some action—exists at this time'; what can be the meaning here other than 'in a part of time'? But if, admitted that Date is 'a part of time', it be felt that the part requires definition

and involves something more than mere time, that we must say (for example)
the part of time gone by, several notions are massed in the proposition: we have
the part which *qua* part is a relative; and we have 'gone-by' which, if it is to have
any import at all, must mean the past: but this 'past', we have shown, is a species
of time.

It may be urged that 'the past' is in its nature indefinite, while 'yesterday' and
'last year' are definite. We reply, first, that we demand some place in our
classification for the past: secondly, that 'yesterday', as definite past, is necessarily definite time. But definite time implies a certain quantity of time: therefore,
if time is quantitative, each of the terms in question must signify a definite
quantity.

Again, if by 'yesterday' we are expected to understand that this or that event
has taken place at a definite time gone by, we have more notions than ever.
Besides, if we must introduce fresh categories because one thing acts in another—as in this case something acts in time—we have more again from its
acting upon another in another. This point will be made plain by what follows
in our discussion of Location.

14. The category of Location; for example, 'in the Lyceum', 'in the Academy':
The Academy and the Lyceum are places, and parts of place, just as 'above',
'below', 'here' are species or parts of place; the difference is of minuter delimitation.

If then 'above', 'below', 'the middle' are places—Delphi, for example, is the
middle (of the earth)—and 'near-the-middle' is also a place—Athens, and of
course the Lyceum and the other places usually cited, are near the middle—what
need have we to go further and seek beyond place, admitting as we do that we
refer in every instance to a place?

If, however, we have in mind the presence of one thing in another, we are not
speaking of a single entity, we are not expressing a single notion.

Another consideration: when we say that a man is here, we present a relation
of the man to that in which he is, a relation of the container to the contained.
Why then do we not class as a relative whatever may be produced from this
relation?

Besides, how does 'here' differ from 'at Athens'? The demonstrative 'here'
admittedly signifies place; so, then, does 'at Athens': 'at Athens' therefore refers
to place.

Again, if 'at Athens' means 'is at Athens', then the 'is' as well as the place
belongs to the predicate; but this cannot be right: we do not regard 'is a quality'
as predicate, but 'a quality'.

Furthermore, if 'in time', 'in place' are to be ranged under a category other than that applying to time and place, why not a separate category for 'in a vessel'? Why not distinct categories for 'in Matter', 'in a subject', 'a part in a whole', 'a whole in its parts', 'a genus in its species', 'a species in a genus'? We are certainly on the way to a goodly number of categories.

15. The 'category of Action':

The quantum has been regarded as a single genus on the ground that Quantity and Number are attributes of Substance and posterior to it; the quale has been regarded as another genus because Quality is an attribute of Substance: on the same principle it is maintained that since activity is an attribute of Substance, Action constitutes yet another genus.

Does then the action constitute the category, or the activity from which the action springs, in the same way as Quality is the category, with the quale derived? Perhaps activity, action, and agent should all be embraced under a single head? But, on the one hand, the action—unlike activity—tends to comport the agent; and on the other, it signifies being in some activity and therefore Being-in-Act (actual as distinct from potential Being). Consequently the category will be one of Act rather than of Action.

Act moreover incontestably manifests itself in Substance, as was found to be the case with Quality: it is connected with Substance as being a form of motion. Thus Motion emerges as a separate genus: for, seeing that Quality is a distinct attribute of Substance, and Quantity a distinct attribute, and Relative takes its being from the relation of one substance to another, there can be no reason why Motion, also an attribute of Substance, should not also constitute a distinct genus.

16. If it be urged that Motion is but imperfect Act, there would be no objection to giving priority to Act and subordinating to it Motion, with its imperfection, as a species: Act would thus be predicated of Motion, but with the qualification 'imperfect'.

Motion is thought of as imperfect, not because it is not an Act, but because, entirely an Act, it yet entails repetition (lacks finality). It repeats, not in order that it may achieve actuality—it is already actual—but that it may attain a goal distinct from itself and posterior: it is not the motion itself that is then consummated but the result at which it aims. Walking is walking from the outset; if one were required to travel a mile and had not yet covered the ground, the deficiency would lie not in the walking—not in the motion—but in the amount of walking accomplished; no matter what the amount, it is walking and motion already: a moving man has motion and a cutter cuts before there is any question of Quantity. And just as we can speak of Act without implying time, so we can of Motion, except in the sense of motion over a defined area; Act is timeless, and so is Motion pure and simple.

Are we told that Motion is necessarily in time, inasmuch as it involves continuity? But, at this, sight, never ceasing to see, will also be continuous and in time. Our critic, it is true, may find support in that principle of proportion which states that you may make a division of no matter what motion, and find that neither the motion nor its duration has any beginning but that the division may be continued indefinitely in the direction of the motion's origin: this would mean that a motion just begun has been in progress from an infinity of time, that it is infinite as regards its beginning.

Such then is the result of separating Act from Motion: Act, we aver, is timeless; yet we are forced to maintain not only that time is necessary to quantitative motion, but, unreservedly, that Motion is quantitative in its very nature; though indeed, if it were a case of motion occupying a day or some other quantity of time, the exponents of this view would be the first to admit that Quantity is present to Motion only by way of accident.

In sum, just as Act is timeless, so there is no reason why Motion also should not primarily be timeless, time attaching to it only in so far as it happens to have such and such an extension.

Timeless change is sanctioned in the expression, 'as if change could not take place all at once'; if then change is timeless, why not Motion also?—Change, be it noted, is here distinguished from the result of change, the result being unnecessary to establish the change itself.

17. We may be told that neither Act nor Motion requires a genus for itself, but that both revert to Relation, Act belonging to the potentially active, Motion to the potentially motive. Our reply is that Relation produces relatives and is more than the mere reference to an external standard; given the existence of a thing, whether attributive or relative, it holds its essential character prior to any relationship: so then must Act and Motion, and even such an attribute as habit; they are not prevented from being prior to any relationship they may occupy, or from being conceivable in themselves. Otherwise, everything will be relative; for anything you think of—even Soul—bears some relationship to something else.

But, to return to activity proper and the action, is there any reason why these should not be referred to Relation? They must in every instance be either Motion or Act.

If, however, activity is referred to Relation and the action made a distinct genus, why is not Motion referred to Relation and the movement made a distinct genus? Why not bisect the unity, Motion, and so make activity and passivity two species of the one thing, abandoning the division into two separate genera?

18. There are other questions calling for consideration:

First: Are both Acts and motions to be included in the category of Action, with the distinction that Acts are momentary while motions, such as cutting, are in time? Or will both be regarded as motions or (at least) as involving Motion?

Secondly: Will all activities be related to passivity, or will some—for example, walking and speaking—be considered as independent of it?

Thirdly: Will all those related to passivity be classed as motions and the independent as Acts, or will the two classes overlap? Walking, for instance, which is an independent, would, one gathers, be a motion; thinking, which also does not essentially involve passivity, an Act: otherwise we must hold that thinking and walking are not even actions. But if they are not in the category of Action, where then in our classification must they fall?

It may perhaps be urged that the act of thinking, together with the faculty of thought, should be regarded as relative to the thought object; for is not the faculty of sensation treated as relative to the sensible object? If then, we may ask, in the analogue the faculty of sensation is treated as relative to the sensible object, why not the sensory act as well? The fact is that even sensation, though related to an external object, has something besides that relation: it has, namely, its own status of being either an Act or a Passion. Now the Passion is separable from the condition of being attached to some object and caused by some object: so, then, is the Act a distinct entity. Walking is similarly attached and caused, and yet has besides the status of being a motion. It follows that thought, in addition to its relationship, will have the status of being either a motion or an Act.

19. We have to ask ourselves whether there are not certain Acts which without the addition of a time-element will be thought of as imperfect and therefore classed with motions. Take for instance living and life. The life of a definite person implies a certain adequate period, just as his happiness is no merely instantaneous thing. Life and happiness are, in other words, of the nature ascribed to Motion: both therefore must be treated as motions, and Motion must be regarded as a unity, a single genus; besides the quantity and quality belonging to Substance we must take count of the motion manifested in it.

We may further find it desirable to distinguish bodily from psychic motions, or spontaneous motions from those induced by external forces, or the original from the derivative, the original motions being activities whether externally related or independent, while the derivative will be Passions.

But surely the motions having external tendency are actually identical with those of external derivation: the cutting issuing from the cutter and that effected in the object are one, though to cut is not the same as to be cut.

Perhaps, however, the cutting issuing from the cutter and that which takes place in the cut object are in fact not one, but 'to cut' implies that from a particular Act and motion there results a different motion in the object cut. Or perhaps the difference (between Action and Passion) lies not in the fact of being cut, but in the distinct emotion supervening, pain for example: passivity has also this connotation.

But when there is no pain, what occurs? Nothing, surely, but the Act of the agent upon the patient object: this is all that is meant in such cases by Action. Action, thus, becomes twofold: there is that which is accomplished in the external, and that which is not. The duality of Action and Passion, suggested by the notion that Action (always) takes place in an external, is abandoned.

Even writing, for example, though taking place upon an external object, does not call for passivity, since no effect is produced upon the tablet beyond the Act of the writer, nothing like pain; we may be told that the tablet has been inscribed, but this does not suffice for passivity.

Again, in the case of walking there is the earth trodden upon, but no one thinks of it as having experienced Passion (or suffering). Treading on a living body, we think of suffering, because we reflect not upon the walking but upon the ensuing pain: otherwise we should think of suffering in the case of the earth as well.

It is so in every case of Action: we cannot but think of it as knit into a unity with its opposite, Passion; though what we normally call Passion in the sense of suffering is an added effect and not the opposite of Action in the way in which being burned is the opposite of burning: by Passion in this sense we mean the effect supervening upon the combined facts of the burning and the being burned, whether this effect be pain or some such process as withering.

Suppose that an agent acts with the express purpose of causing pain: have we not still the duality of agent and patient, two results from the one Act? The Act may not retain the will to cause pain; but it produces something distinct from itself, a pain-causing medium which enters into the object about to experience pain: this medium, while preserving its individuality, produces something yet different, the feeling of pain.

What does this suggest? Surely that the very medium—the act of hearing, for instance—is, even before it produces pain or without producing pain at all, a Passion of that into which it enters.

But hearing, with sensation in general, is in fact not a Passion. Yet to feel pain is to experience a Passion—a Passion, however, which is not opposed to Action.

20. But though not opposed, it is still different from Action and cannot belong

to the same genus as activity; though if they are both Motion, it will so belong, on the principle that alteration must be regarded as qualitative motion.

Does it follow that whenever alteration proceeds from the agent, it will be activity and Action, the agent remaining impassive? It may be that if the agent remains impassive, the alteration will be in the category of Action; whereas if, while its energy is directed outwards, it also suffers—as in beating—it will cease to belong to that category: or perhaps there is nothing to prevent its being in both categories at one and the same moment.

If then Passivity arises in the course of Action, as is the case with rubbing, on what ground is it assigned to Action rather than to Passivity? Perhaps the Passivity arises from the fact that a counter-rubbing is involved. But are we, in view of this counter-motion, to recognize the presence of two distinct motions? No: one only.

How then can this one motion be both Action and Passion? We must suppose it to be Action in proceeding from an object, and Passion in being directed upon another—though it remains the same motion throughout.

Suppose, however, Passion to be a different motion from Action: how then does its modification of the patient object change that patient's character without the agent being affected by the patient? For obviously an agent cannot be passive to the operation it performs upon another. Can it be that the fact of motion existing elsewhere creates the Passion, which was not Passion for the agent?

If the whiteness of the swan, produced by its Reason-Principle, is given at its birth, are we to affirm Passion of the swan on its passing into being? And if the swan becomes white after birth? Suppose a cause of growth and the corresponding result: are we to say that the growth is a Passion or must we confine Passion to purely qualitative change?

One thing confers beauty and another takes it: is that which takes beauty to be regarded as patient? If then the source of beauty—tin, suppose—should deteriorate or actually disappear, while the recipient—copper—improves, are we to think of the copper as passive and the tin active?

Take the learner: how can he be regarded as passive, seeing that the Act of the agent passes into him (and becomes his Act)? How can the Act, necessarily a simple entity, be both Act and Passion? No doubt the Act is not in itself a Passion; nonetheless, the learner coming to possess it will be a patient so long as Passion is not taken to imply that he has not been active on his own account; learning—like seeing—is not analogous to being struck, since it involves the acts of apprehension and recognition.

21. How then are we to distinguish Passivity, since clearly it is not to be identified

with the Act from outside which the recipient in turn makes his own? We must look for it in cases where the patient remains without Act, the passivity pure.

Imagine, then, a case where a patient improves, though the Act tends towards deterioration. Or, say, a man's activity is guided by evil and is allowed to dominate another's without restraint. In these cases the Act is clearly wrong, the Passion blameless.

What then is the real distinction between Action and Passion? Is it that Action starts from within and is directed upon an outside object, while Passion is derived from without and fulfilled within? What, then, are we to say of such cases as thought and opinion which originate within but are not directed outwards? Again, the Passion 'being heated' rises within the self, when that self is provoked by an opinion to reflection or to anger, without the intervention of any external. Still, it remains true that Action, whether self-centred or with external tendency, is a motion rising in the self.

How then do we explain desire and other forms of aspiration? Aspiration must be a motion having its origin in the object aspired to—though some might disallow 'origin' and be content with saying that the motion aroused is subsequent to the object; in what respect, then, does aspiring differ from taking a blow or being borne down by a thrust?

Perhaps, however, we should divide aspirations into two classes, those which follow intellect being described as Actions, the merely impulsive being Passions. Passivity now will not turn on origin, without or within—'within' meaning that passivity may occur, as in decomposition, apart from external cause; but whenever a thing, without itself assisting in the process, undergoes an alteration not directed to the creation of Being but changing the thing for the worse or not for the better, such an alteration will be regarded as a Passion and as entailing passivity.

If, however, 'being heated' means acquiring heat, and is sometimes found to contribute to the production of Being and sometimes not, passivity will be identical with impassivity: besides, 'being heated' must then have a double significance (according as it does or does not contribute to Being).

The fact is, however, that 'being heated', even when it contributes to Being, involves the presence of a patient distinct from the being produced. Take the case of the bronze which has to be heated and so is a patient; the being is a statue, which is not heated except accidentally (by the accident of being contained in the bronze). If then the bronze becomes more beautiful as a result of being heated and in the same proportion, it certainly becomes so by passivity; for passivity must, clearly, take two forms: there is the passivity which tends to alteration for the worse, and there is the passivity which tends to alteration for the better or has neither tendency.

22. Passivity, thus, implies the existence within of a motion functioning somehow or other in the direction of alteration. Action too implies motion within, whether the motion be self-centred or whether it be driven by internal impulse to find its goal in an external object. There is Motion in both Action and Passion, but the difference which divides Action from Passion keeps Action as such impassive, while Passion is recognized by the fact that a new state replaces the old, though nothing is added to the essential character of the patient; whenever a new being or substance is produced, the patient remains distinct.

Thus, what is Action in one relation may be Passion in another. One same motion will be Action from the point of view of A, Passion from that of B; for the two are so disposed that they might well be consigned to the category of Relation—at any rate in the cases where the Action entails a corresponding Passion: neither correlative is found in isolation; each involves both Action and Passion, though A acts as mover and B is moved: each then involves two categories.

Again, A gives motion to B, B receives it, so that we have a giving and a receiving—in a word, a relation.

But a recipient must possess what it has received. A thing is admitted to possess its natural colour: why not its motion also (which would put motion into the category of Possession)? Besides, independent motions such as walking and thought do, in fact, involve the possession of the powers respectively to walk and to think.

We are reminded to inquire whether (thought in the form of) providence constitutes Action; to be subject to providence is apparently Passion, for such thought is directed to an external, the object of the providential arrangement. But it may well be that neither is the exercise of providence an action, even though the thought is concerned with an external, nor subjection to it a Passion. Thought itself need not be an action, for it does not go outward towards its object but merely attends to it. It is not always an activity; all Acts need not be definable as activities, for they need not produce an effect; an Act has activity only accidentally.

Does it follow (conversely) that if a man as he walks produces footprints, he cannot be considered to have performed an action? Certainly as a result of his existing something distinct from himself has come into being. Yet perhaps we should regard both action and Act as merely accidental, because he did not aim at this result: it would be as we speak of Action even in things inanimate—'fire heats', 'the drug worked'.

So much for Action and Passion.

23. As for Possession, if the term is used comprehensively, why are not all its

modes to be brought under one category? Possession, thus, would include the quantum as possessing magnitude, the quale as possessing colour; it would include fatherhood and the complementary relationships, since the father possesses the son and the son possesses the father: in short, it would include all belongings.

If, on the contrary, the category of Possession comprises only the things of the body, such as weapons and shoes, we first ask why this should be so, and why their possession produces a distinct category, while burning, cutting, burying, or casting them out do not give another or others. If it is because these things are carried on the person, then one's mantle lying on a couch will come under a different category from that of the mantle covering the person. If the ownership of possession suffices, then clearly one must refer to the one category of Possession all objects identified by being possessed, every case in which possession can be established; the character of the possessed object will make no difference.

If, however, Possession is not to be predicated of Quality because Quality stands recognized as a category, nor of Quantity because the category of Quantity has been received, nor of parts because they have been assigned to the category of Substance, why should we predicate Possession of weapons, when they too are comprised in the accepted category of Substance? Shoes and weapons are clearly substances.

How, further, is 'He possesses weapons', signifying as it does that the action of arming has been performed by a subject, to be regarded as an entirely simple notion, assignable to a single category?

Again, is Possession to be restricted to an animate possessor, or does it hold good even of a statue as possessing the objects above mentioned? The animate and inanimate seem to possess in different ways, and the term is perhaps equivocal. Similarly, 'standing' has not the same connotation as applied to the animate and the inanimate.

Besides, how can it be reasonable for what is found only in a limited number of cases to form a distinct generic category?

24. There remains Situation, which like Possession is confined to a few instances such as reclining and sitting.

Even so, the term is not used without qualification: we say 'they are placed in such and such a manner', 'he is situated in such and such a position'. The position is added from outside the genus.

In short, Situation signifies 'being in a place'; there are two things involved, the position and the place: why then must two categories be combined into one?

Moreover, if sitting signifies an Act, it must be classed among Acts; if a

Passion, it goes under the category to which belong Passions complete and incomplete.

Reclining is surely nothing but 'lying up', and tallies with 'lying down' and 'lying midway'. But if the reclining belongs thus to the category of Relation, why does not the recliner also? For as 'on the right' goes with relations, so does 'the thing on the right'; and similarly with 'the thing on the left'.

25. There are those who lay down four categories and make a fourfold division into Substrates, Qualities, States, and Relative States, and find in these a common Something, and so include everything in one genus.

Against this theory there is much to be urged, but particularly against this posing of a common Something and a single all-embracing genus. This Something, it may be submitted, is unintelligible to themselves, is indefinable, and accounts neither for bodies nor for the unembodied. Moreover, no room is left for a differentia by which this Something may be divided (to form species). Besides, this common Something is either existent or non-existent: if existent, it must be one or other of its (four) species; if non-existent, the existent is classed under the nonexistent. But the objections are countless; we must leave them for the present and consider the several heads of the division.

To the first genus are assigned Substrates, including Matter, to which is given a priority over the others; so that what is ranked as the first principle comes under the same head with things which must be posterior to it since it is their principle.

First, then: the prior is made homogeneous with the subsequent. Now this is impossible: in this relation the subsequent owes its existence to the prior, whereas among things belonging to one same genus each must have, essentially, the equality implied by the genus; for the very meaning of genus is to be predicated of the species in respect of their essential character. And that Matter is the basic source of all the rest of things, this school, we may suppose, would hardly deny.

Secondly: since they treat the Substrate as one thing, they do not enumerate the Existents; they look instead for principles of the Existents. There is, however, a difference between speaking of the actual Existents and of their principles.

If Matter is taken to be the only Existent, and all other things as modifications of Matter, it is not legitimate to set up a single genus to embrace both the Existent and the other things; consistency requires that Being (Substance) be distinguished from its modifications and that the modifications be classified.

Even the distinction which this theory makes between Substrates and the rest of things is questionable. The Substrate is (necessarily) one thing and admits of no differentia—except perhaps in so far as it is split up like one mass into its various parts; and yet not even so, since the notion of Being implies continuity:

it would be better, therefore, to speak of the Substrate in the singular.

26. But the error in this theory is fundamental. To set the potential above everything else, instead of recognizing the primacy of actuality, is in the highest degree perverse. If the potential holds the primacy among the Existents, its actualization becomes impossible; it certainly cannot bring itself into actuality: either the actual exists previously, and so the potential is not the first-principle, or, if the two are to be regarded as existing simultaneously, the first principles must be exposed to hazard. Besides, if they are simultaneous, why is not actuality given the primacy? Why is the potential more truly real than the actual?

Supposing, however, that the actual does come later than the potential, how must the theory proceed? Obviously Matter does not produce Form: the unqualified does not produce Quality, nor does actuality take its origin in the potential; for that would mean that the actual was inherent in the potential, which at once becomes a dual thing.

Furthermore, God becomes a secondary to Matter, inasmuch as even he is regarded as a body composed of Matter and Form—though how he acquires the Form is not revealed. If, however, he be admitted to exist apart from Matter in virtue of his character as a principle and a rational law, God must be unembodied, the Creative Power unembodied. If we are told that he is without Matter but is composite in essence by the fact of being a body, this amounts to introducing another Matter, the Matter of God.

Again, how can Matter be a first-principle, seeing that (according to this doctrine) it is body? Body must necessarily be a plurality, since all bodies are composite of Matter and Quality. If, however, body in this case is to be understood in some different way, then Matter is identified with body only by an equivocation.

If the possession of three dimensions is given as the characteristic of body, then we are dealing simply with mathematical body. If resistance is added, we are no longer considering a unity: besides, resistance is a quality or at least derived from Quality.

And whence is this resistance supposed to come? Whence the three dimensions? What is the source of their existence? Matter is not comprised in the concept of the three-dimensional, nor the three-dimensional in the concept of Matter; if Matter partakes thus of extension, it can no longer be a simplex.

Again, whence does Matter derive its unifying power? It is assuredly not a unifying force in itself, but only through participation in Unity.

We inevitably conclude that Mass or Extension cannot be ranked as the first of things; Non-Extension and Unity must be prior. We must begin with the One and conclude with the Many, proceed to magnitude from that which is free from magnitude: a One is necessary to the existence of a Many, Non-Magnitude to that of Magnitude. Magnitude is a unity not by being Unity-Absolute, but by participation and in an accidental mode: there must be a primary and absolute preceding the accidental, or the accidental relation is left unexplained.

The manner of this relation demands investigation. Had this been undertaken, the thinkers of this school would probably have lighted upon that Unity which is not accidental but essential and underived.

27. On other grounds also it is indefensible not to have reserved the high place for the true first-principle of things but to have set up in its stead the formless, passive and lifeless, the irrational, dark and indeterminate, and to have made this the source of Being. In this theory God is introduced merely for the sake of appearance: deriving existence from Matter he is a composite, a derivative, or worse, a mere state of Matter.

Another consideration is that if Matter is a substrate, there must be something outside it, which, acting on it and distinct from it, makes it the substrate of what it pours into it. But if God is lodged in Matter and by being involved in Matter is himself no more than a substrate, he will no longer make Matter a substrate nor be himself a substrate in conjunction with Matter. For of what will they be substrates, when that which could make them substrates is eliminated? This so-called substrate turns out to have swallowed up all that is; but a substrate must be relative, and relative not to its content but to something which acts upon it as upon a datum.

Again, the substrate comports a relation to that which is not substrate; hence, to something external to it: there must, then, be something apart from the substrate. If nothing distinct and external is considered necessary, but the substrate itself can become everything and adopt every character like the versatile dancer in the pantomime, it ceases to be a substrate: it is, in itself, everything. The mime is not a substrate of the characters he puts on; these are in fact the realization of his own personality: similarly, if the Matter with which this theory presents us comports in its own being all the realities, it is no longer the substrate of all: on the contrary, the other things can have no reality whatever, if they are no more than states of Matter in the sense that the poses of the mime are states through which he passes.

Then, those other things not existing, Matter will not be a substrate, nor will it be the matter for the Existents; it will be Matter bare, and for that reason not even Matter, since Matter is a relative. The relative is relative to something else: it must, further, be homogeneous with that something else: double is relative to half, but not Substance to double.

How then can an Existent be relative to a Non-existent, except accidentally?

But (by this theory) the True-Existent and Matter are related to each other as Existent to Existent. For if potentiality is that which holds the promise of existence and that promise does not constitute Complete Reality, the potentiality cannot be a Reality. In sum, these very teachers who deprecate the production of Realities from Non-realities, themselves produce Non-reality from Reality; for to them the universe as such is not a Reality.

But is it not a paradox that while Matter, the Substrate, is to them an existence, bodies should not have more claim to existence, the universe yet more, and not merely a claim grounded on the reality of one of its parts?

It is no less paradoxical that the living form should owe existence not to its soul but to its Matter only, the soul being but an affection of Matter and posterior to it. From what source then did Matter receive ensoulment? Whence, in short, is soul's entity derived? How does it occur that Matter sometimes turns into bodies, while another part of it turns into Soul? Even supposing that Form might come to it from elsewhere, that accession of Quality to Matter would account not for Soul, but simply for organized body soulless. If, on the contrary, there is something which moulds Matter and produces Soul, then prior to Soul the produced there must be Soul the producer.

28. Many as are the objections to this theory, we pass on for fear of the ridicule we might incur by arguing against a position itself so manifestly ridiculous. We may be content with pointing out that it assigns the primacy to the Non-existent and treats it as the very summit of Existence: in short, it places the last thing first. The reason for this procedure lies in the acceptance of sense-perception as a trustworthy guide in distinguishing the Primal from other entities.

This philosophy began by identifying the Real with body; then, viewing with apprehension the transmutations of bodies, decided that Reality was that which is permanent beneath the superficial changes—which is much as if one regarded space as having more title to Reality than the bodies within it, on the principle that the space does not perish with them. Space is as permanent as their Substrate: but it was a fault to take mere permanence as in itself a sufficient definition of the Real; the right method would have been to consider what properties must characterize Reality, by the presence of which properties it has also that of unfailing permanence. Thus if a shadow had permanence, accompanying an object through every change, that would not make it more real than the object itself. The sensible universe, as including the Substrate and a multitude of attributes, will by that multiplicity have more claim to be Reality entire than has any one of its component entities (such as the Substrate): but if the sensible universe is itself unreal, how can the Substrate support it?

Most surprising of all is that, while they make sense-perception their guarantee of everything, they hold that the Real cannot be grasped by sensation; for they have no right to assign to Matter even so much as resistance, since resistance is a quality. If, however, they profess to grasp Reality by Intellect, is it not a strange Intellect which ranks Matter above itself, giving Reality to Matter and not to itself? And as their 'Intellect' has, thus, no Real-Existence, how can it be trustworthy when it speaks of things higher than itself, things to which it has no affinity whatever?

But an adequate treatment of this entity (Matter) and of substrates will be found elsewhere.

29. Qualities must be for this school distinct from Substrates. This in fact they acknowledge by counting them as the second category. If then they form a distinct category, they must be simplex; that is to say, not composite; that is to say that as qualities, pure and simple, they must be devoid of Matter: hence, unembodied and active, since Matter is their substrate—a relation of passivity.

If nevertheless they hold Qualities to be composite, that is a strange classification which first contrasts simple and composite things, then proceeds to include them in one genus, and finally admits one of the two species (simple) into the other (composite); it is like dividing knowledge into two species, the first comprising grammatical knowledge, the second made up of grammatical and other knowledge.

Again, if they identify Qualities with qualifications of Matter, then in the first place even their Seminal Principles (Logoi) will be material, and will not have to reside in Matter to produce a composite, but prior to the composite thus produced they will themselves be composed of Matter and Form: in other words, they will not be Forms or Principles. Further, if they maintain that the Seminal Principles are nothing but Matter in a certain state, they evidently identify Qualities with States, and should accordingly classify them in their third genus. If this is a state of some peculiar kind, what precisely is its differentia? Clearly the state by its association with Quality receives (on this supposition) an accession of Reality: yet if that means that when divorced from Quality it is not a Reality, how can State be treated as a single genus or species? Certainly one genus cannot embrace the Existent and the Non-Existent.

And what is this state implanted in Matter? It is either real, or unreal: if real, it is at all events bodiless: if unreal, it is introduced to no purpose; Matter is all there is; Quality therefore is nothing. The same is true of State, for that is even more unreal; the alleged Fourth Category more so.

Matter then is the sole Reality. But how do we come to know this? Certainly not from Matter itself. Or is it from Matter itself, since Intellect is (in their view) merely a state of Matter, and even the 'state' is an empty qualification? We are left after all with Matter alone competent to make these assertions, to fathom these problems. And if its assertions were intelligent, we must wonder how it thinks and performs the functions of Soul without possessing either Intellect or Soul. If, then, it were to make foolish assertions, affirming itself to be what it is not and cannot be, to what should we ascribe this folly? Doubtless to Matter, if it was in truth Matter that spoke. But Matter does not speak; anyone who says that it does proclaims the predominance of Matter in himself; he may have a soul, but to Matter he is resigned, and lives in ignorance of himself and of the faculty alone capable of uttering the truth in these things.

30. With regard to States:

It may seem strange that States should be set up as a third class—or whatever class it is—since all States are referable to Matter. We shall be told that there is a difference among States, and that a State as in Matter has definite character-istics distinguishing it from States proper and further that, whereas Qualities are States of Matter, States properly so called belong to Qualities. But if Qual-ities are nothing but States of Matter, States (in the strict sense of the term) are ultimately reducible to Matter, and belong to Matter.

Further, how can States constitute a single genus, when there is such manifold diversity among them? How can we group together 'three yards long' and 'white'—Quantity and Quality respectively? Or again Time and Place? How can 'yesterday', 'last year', 'in the Lyceum', 'in the Academy', be States at all? How can Time be in any sense a State? Neither is Time a State nor the events in Time, neither the objects in Space nor Space itself.

And how can Action be a State? One acting is not in a state of being but in a state of Action, or rather in Action simply: no state is involved. Similarly, what is predicated of the patient is not a state of being but a state of Passion, or, strictly, Passion unqualified by state.

But it would seem that State was the right category at least for cases of Situation and Possession: yet Possession does not imply possession of some particular state, but is Possession absolute.

As for the Relative State, if the theory did not include it in the same class as the other States, another question would arise: we should have to inquire whether any actuality is attributed to this particular type of relation, for to many types actuality is denied.

It is moreover, absurd that an entity which depends upon the prior existence of other entities should be classed in the same genus with those priors: one and two must, clearly, exist before half and double can.

· · ·

The various other speculations on the subject of the Existents and the principles of the Existents, whether they have entailed an infinite or a finite number, bodily or bodiless, or even supposed the Composite to be the Authentic Existent, may well be considered severally with the help of the criticisms made by the ancients upon them.

On the Kinds of Being: Second Treatise

1. We have examined the proposed 'ten genera': we have discussed also the theory which gathers the total of things into one genus and to this subordinates what may be thought of as its four species. The next step is, naturally, to expound our own views and to try to show the agreement of our conclusions with those of Plato.

Now if we were obliged to consider Being as a unity, the following questions would be unnecessary:

Is there one genus embracing everything, or are there genera which cannot be subsumed under such a unity? Are there first-principles? Are first-principles to be identified with genera, or genera with first-principles? Or is it perhaps rather the case that while not all genera are first-principles, all first-principles are at the same time genera? Or is the converse true? Or is it the fact that in both cases only some principles are genera and only some genera principles; or that in one case all that belongs to the one class belongs to the other, whereas in the other case there is only a partial overlap?

Since, however, we affirm that Being is not a unity—the reason for this affirmation is stated by Plato and others—these questions become imperative, once we are satisfied as to the number of genera to be posited and the grounds for our choice.

The subject of our inquiry, then, is the Existent or Existents, and it presents immediately two problems demanding separate analysis:

What do we mean by the Existent?—This is naturally the first question to be examined.

What is that which, often taken for Being (or the Existent), is in our view Becoming and never really Being?—Note, however, that these concepts are not to be taken as distinguished from each other in the sense of belonging to a genus, Something, divided into Being and Becoming; and we must not suppose that Plato took this view. It would be absurd to assign Being to the same genus as non-Being: this would be to make one genus of Socrates and his portrait. The division here (between what has Being and what is in Becoming) means a definite marking-off, a setting asunder, leading to the assertion that what takes the ap-pearance of Being is not Being and implying that the nature of True Being has been quite misapprehended. Being, we are taught, must have the attribute of eternity, must be so constituted as never to belie its own nature.

This, then, is the Being of which we shall treat, and in our investigation we shall assume that it is not a unity: subsequently we ask leave to say something on the nature of Becoming and on what it is that comes to be, that is, on the nature of the world of Sense.

2. In asserting that Being is not a unity, do we imply a definite number of existences or an infinite number? What precisely do we mean by 'not a unity'? Simply that it is many as well as one, that it is, in some way, a diversified unity, a plurality in unity.

It follows that either the unity so regarded is a unity of genus under which the Existents, involving as they do plurality as well as unity, stand as species; or that while there are more genera than one, yet all are subordinate to a unity; or there may be more genera than one, though no one genus is subordinate to any other, but all with their own subordinates—whether these be lesser genera, or species with individuals for their subordinates—all are elements in one reality, and from their total the Intellectual realm—that which we know as Being—derives its constitution.

If this last is the truth, we have here not merely genera, but genera which are at the same time principles of Being. They are genera because they have sub-ordinates—other genera, and successively species and individuals; they are also principles, since from this plurality Being takes its rise, constituted in its entirety from these its elements.

Suppose, however, a number of origins which by their mere totality comprised, without possessing any subordinates, the whole of Being; these would be first-principles but not genera: it would be as if one constructed the sensible world from the four elements—fire and the others; these elements would be first-principles, but they would not be genera, unless the term 'genus' is to be used equivocally.

But does this assertion of certain genera which are at the same time first-principles imply that by combining the genera, each with its subordinates, we find the whole of Being in the resultant combination? But then, taken separately, their existence will not be actual but only potential, and they will not be found in isolation.

Suppose, on the other hand, we ignore the genera and combine the particulars: what then becomes of the ignored genera? They will, surely, exist in the purity of their own isolation, and the mixtures will not destroy them. The question of how this result is achieved may be postponed.

For the moment we take it as agreed that there are genera which are also principles of Being and that, on another plane, principles (elements) are to be opposed to compounds. We are, thus, obliged to show how many genera we recognize and why we distinguish them instead of summing them under a unity; for otherwise we imply that their coalescence into a unity is fortuitous, whereas it would be more plausible to dispense with their separate existence.

If all the genera could be species of Being, all individuals without exception being immediately subordinate to these species, then such a unification becomes feasible. But that supposition bespeaks annihilation for the genera: the species will no longer be species; plurality will no longer be subordinated to unity; everything must be the unity, unless there exist some thing or things outside the unity. The One never becomes many—as the existence of species demands—unless there is something distinct from it: it cannot of itself assume plurality, unless we are to think of it as being broken into pieces like some extended body: but even so, the force which breaks it up must be distinct from it: if it is itself to effect the breaking up—or whatever form the division may take—then it is itself previously divided.

For these and many other reasons we must abstain from positing a single genus, and especially because neither Being nor Substance can be the predicate of any given thing. If we do predicate Being, it is only as an accidental attribute; just as when we predicate whiteness of a substance, we are not predicating the Absolute Whiteness.

3. We assert, then, a plurality of Existents, but a plurality not fortuitous and so deriving from a unity.

But even admitting this derivation from a unity—a unity, however, not predicated of them in respect of their essential being—there is, surely, no reason why each of these Existents, distinct in character from every other, should not in itself stand as a separate genus.

Is, then, this unity external to the genera thus produced, this unity which is their source though it cannot be predicated of them in respect of their essence? It is indeed external; the One is beyond; it cannot, therefore, be included among the genera: it is the (transcendent) source, while they stand side by side as genera. Yet surely the One must somehow be included (among the genera)? No: it is the Existents we are investigating, not that which is beyond Existence.

We pass on, then, to consider that unity which is included, and find to our surprise the cause included with the things it causes: is it not strange that causes and effects should be brought into the same genus?

But if the unity of which we speak is included with its effects in the sense that generic and all such determinations are posterior, that these effects have nothing in common with it, that it is never predicated of them whether as their genus or in any other relation, the effects are obviously themselves genera with subordinates of their own: you may, for example, be the cause of the operation of walking, but the walking is not subordinate to you in the relation of species to genus; and if walking had nothing prior to it as its genus, but had posteriors, then it would be a (primary) genus and rank among the Existents.

Perhaps, however, we must not even suppose this unity (of Being) to be in any sense the cause of other things, these being rather its parts or elements—if the term may be allowed—and their totality constituting a single entity which our thinking divides. All unity though it be, it goes by a wonderful power out into everything; it appears as many and becomes many, when, for example, there is motion; the fecundity of its nature causes the one to be no longer one, and we, displaying what we call its parts, consider them each as a unity and make them into 'genera', unaware of our failure to see the whole at once. We display it, then, in parts, though, unable to restrain for long their natural tendency to coalesce, we bring these parts together again, resign them to the whole, and allow them to become a unity, or rather to be a unity.

All this will become clearer in the light of further consideration—when, that is to say, we have ascertained the number of the genera; for thus we shall also discover their causes. It is not enough to assert; we must advance by dint of thought and comprehension. The way is clear:

4. If we had to ascertain the nature of body and the place it holds in the universe, surely we should take some sample of body, say stone, and examine into what constituents it may be divided. There would be what we think of as the substrate of stone; its quantity—in this case, a magnitude; its quality—for example, the colour of stone. As with stone, so with every other body: we should see that in this thing, body, there are three distinguishable characteristics—the pseudo-substance, the quantity, the quality—though they all make one and are only logically trisected, the three being found to constitute the unit thing, body. If motion were equally inherent in its constitution, we should include this as well, and the four would form a unity, the single body depending upon them all for its unity and characteristic nature.

The same method must be applied in examining the Intellectual Substance and the genera and first-principles of the Intellectual sphere.

But we must begin by subtracting what is peculiar to body, its coming-to-be, its sensible nature, its magnitude—that is to say, the characteristics which produce isolation and mutual separation. It is an Intellectual Being we have to consider, an Authentic Existent, possessed of a unity surpassing that of any sensible thing.

Now the wonder comes how a unity of this type can be many as well as one. In the case of body it was easy to concede unity-with-plurality; the one body is divisible to infinity; its colour is a different thing from its shape, since in fact they are separable. But if we take Soul, single, continuous, without extension, of the highest simplicity—as the first effort of the mind makes manifest—how can we expect to find multiplicity here too? We believed that the division of the living being into body and soul was final: body indeed was manifold, composite, diversified; but in soul we imagined we had found a simplex, and boldly made a halt, supposing that we had come to the limit of our course.

Let us examine this soul, presented to us from the Intellectual realm as body from the Sensible. How is its unity a plurality? How is its plurality a unity? Clearly its unity is not that of a composite formed from diverse elements, but that of a single nature comprising a plurality.

This problem attacked and solved, the truth about the genera comprised in Being will thereby, as we asserted, be elucidated also.

5. A first point demanding consideration:

Bodies—those, for example, of animals and plants—are each a multiplicity founded on colour and shape and magnitude, and on the forms and arrangement of parts: yet all these elements spring from a unity—a unity which, if not thorough-going and complete, is at least more complete than the bodily unity which emerges from it; it has more claim also to reality, for divergence from unity involves a corresponding divergence from Reality. Since, thus, bodies take their rise from unity, but not 'unity' in the sense of the complete unity or Unity-Absolute—for this could never yield discrete plurality—it remains that they be derived from a unity pluralized. But the creative principle (in bodies) is Soul: Soul therefore is a pluralized unity.

We then ask whether the plurality here consists of the Reason-Principles of the things of process. Or is this unity not something different from the mere sum of these Principles? Certainly Soul itself is one Reason-Principle, the chief of the Reason-Principles, and these are its Act as it functions in accordance with its essential being; this essential being, on the other hand, is the potentiality of the Reason-Principles. Such is the mode in which this unity is a plurality, its plurality being revealed by the effect it has upon the external.

But, to leave the region of its effect, suppose we take it at the higher non-effecting part of Soul; is not plurality of powers to be found in this part also?

The existence of Soul will, we may presume, be at once conceded. But is this existence to be taken as identical with that of the stone? Surely not. Being in the case of the stone is not Being pure and simple, but stone-being: so here; Soul's being denotes not merely Being but Soul-being.

Is then that 'being' distinct from what else goes to complete the essence (or substance) of Soul? Is it to be identified with Being (as such), while to some differentia of Being is ascribed the production of Soul? No doubt Soul is in a sense Being, and this not as a man 'is' white, but from the fact of its being purely an essence: in other words, the being it possesses it holds from no source external to its own essence.

6. But must it not draw on some source external to its essence, if it is to be conditioned, not only by Being, but by being an entity of a particular character? But if it is conditioned by a particular character, and this character is external to its essence, its essence does not comprise all that makes it Soul; its individuality will determine it; a part of Soul will be essence, but not Soul entire.

Furthermore, what being will it have when we separate it from its other components? The being appropriate to 'a source and first-principle', or rather to all that the soul comprises in its own nature; and therefore to life, with the life and the being forming a unity.

Unity, in the sense of being one Reason-Principle? No; it is the substrate of Soul that is one, though one in such a way as to be also two or more—as many as are the Primaries which constitute Soul. Either, then, it is life as well as being, or else it possesses life.

But if life is a thing possessed, the being of the possessor is not inextricably bound up with life. If, on the contrary, this is not possession, the two, life and being, must be one.

Soul, then, is one and many—as many as are manifested in that oneness— one in its nature, many in those other things. A single Existent, it makes itself many by what we may call its motion: it is one entire, but by its striving, so to speak, to contemplate itself, it is a plurality; for we may imagine that it cannot bear to be a single Existent, when it has the power to be all that it in fact is. The cause of its appearing as many is this contemplation, and its purpose is the Act of the Intellect; if it were manifested as a bare unity, it could have no intellection, since in that simplicity it would already be identical with the object of its thought.

7. What, then, are the several entities observable in this plurality?

We have found Being (Substance) and life simultaneously present in Soul. Now, this Being is a common property of Soul, but life, likewise common to all souls, is furthermore a property of Intellect.

Having thus introduced Intellect and its life we make a single genus of what is common to all life, namely, Motion. Being and the Motion which constitutes the primary life we must consider as two genera; for even though they form a unity, they are separable to thought which finds their unity not a unity; otherwise, it could not distinguish them.

Observe also how in other things Motion or life is clearly separated from Being—a separation impossible, doubtless, in True Being, but possible in its shadow and namesake. In the portrait of a man much is left out, and above all the essential thing, life: the 'Being' of sensible things is just such a shadow of True Being, an abstraction from that Being complete which was life in the Archetype. At all events we have found the way to separate Being from life and life from Being.

Being, then, containing many species, is but one genus. Motion, however, is to be classed as neither a subordinate nor a superordinate of Being but as its concomitant; for we have not found Being serving as substrate to Motion. Motion is Being's Act; neither is separated from the other except in thought; the two natures are one; for Being is inevitably actual, not potential.

No doubt we observe Motion and Being separately, Motion as contained in Being and Being as involved in Motion, and in the One-Being (the Intellectual world) either taken separately may contain the other; but the dualism is an affirmation of our thought, and that thought sees either form as a duality within a unity.

Now Motion, thus manifested in conjunction with Being, does not alter Being's nature—unless to complete its essential character—and this nature remains for ever unchanged by the Motion so conceived: at once, then, we are forced to introduce Stability. To reject Stability would be more unreasonable than to reject Motion; for Stability is associated in our thought and conception with Being more than Motion; unalterable condition, unchanging mode, a single rational plan—these are characteristics of the higher sphere.

Stability, then, may also be taken as a single genus. Obviously distinct from Motion and perhaps even its contrary, that it is also distinct from Being may be shown by many considerations. We may especially observe that if Stability were identical with Being, so also would Motion be, with equal right. Why identity in the case of Stability and not in that of Motion, when Motion is virtually the life of Being, the Act of its Essence and of its Reality? However, on the very same principle on which we separated Motion from Being with the understanding that it is the same and not the same—that they are two and yet one—we also separate Stability from Being, holding it, yet, inseparable; it is only a logical separation entailing the inclusion among the Existents of this other genus. To identify Stability with Being, with no difference between them, and to identify Being with Motion, would be to identify Stability with Motion through the mediation of Being, and so to make Motion and Stability one and the same thing.

8. We cannot indeed escape positing these three, Being, Motion, Stability, once it is the fact that the Intellect discerns them as separates; and if it thinks of them at all, it posits them by that very thinking; if they are thought, they exist. Things whose existence is bound up with Matter have no being in the Intellect: these three principles are, however, free of Matter; and in that which goes free of Matter to be thought is to be.

We are in the presence of Intellect undefiled. Fix it firmly, but not with the eyes of the body. You are looking upon the hearth of Reality, within it a sleepless light: you see how it holds to itself, and how it puts apart things that were together, how it lives a life that endures and keeps a thought acting not upon any future but upon that which already is, upon an eternal present—a thought self-centred, bearing on nothing outside of itself.

Now in the act of Intellect there are activity and motion; in its self-intellection Substance and Being. In virtue of its Being it thinks, and it thinks of itself as Being, and of that as Being upon which it is, so to speak, pivoted. Not that its Act self-directed ranks as Substance, but Being stands as the goal and origin of that Act, the object of its contemplation though not the contemplation itself: and yet this Act too involves Being, which is its motive and its term. By the fact that its Being is actual and not merely potential, Intellect bridges the dualism (of agent and patient) and abjures separation: it identifies itself with Being and Being with itself.

The most firmly set of all things, that around which all other things revolve, Intellect creates Stability, and holds it not as from without but as springing within, as inherent. Stability is the goal of intellection, a Stability which had no beginning, and the state from which intellection was impelled was Stability, though Stability gave it no impulsion; for Motion neither starts from Motion nor ends in Motion. Again, the Form-Idea has Stability, since it is the goal of Intellect: intellection is the Idea in motion.

Thus all Existents are Being, Motion, and Stability; these are genera all-pervading, and every subsequent is a particular being, a particular stability, and a particular motion.

We have caught the radiance of Being, and beheld it in its three manifestations: Being, revealed by the Being within ourselves; the Motion of Being, revealed by the motion within ourselves; and its Stability revealed by ours. We accommodate our being, motion, stability to those (of the Intelligible world), unable however to draw any distinction but finding ourselves in the presence of entities inseparable and, as it were, interfused. We have, however, in a sense, set them a little apart, holding them down and viewing them in isolation; and thus we have observed Being, Stability, Motion—these three, of which each is a unity to itself; in so doing, have we not regarded them as being different from each other? By this posing of three entities, each a unity, we have, surely, found Being to contain Difference.

Again, inasmuch as we restore them to an all-embracing unity, identifying all with unity, do we not see in this amalgamation Identity emerging as a Real Existent?

Thus, in addition to the other three (Being, Motion, Stability), we are obliged to posit the further two, Identity and Difference, so that we have in all five genera. In so doing, we bestow Identity and Difference upon their subsequents, each of which exhibits a particular identity and a particular difference. Thus, Identity and Difference, considered apart from particulars, have the generic status.

They will, moreover, be primary genera, because nothing can be predicated of them as denoting their essential nature. Nothing, of course we mean, but Being; but this Being is not their genus, since they cannot be identified with any particular kind of being. Similarly Being will not stand as genus to Motion or Stability, for these also are not its species. Beings (or Existents) comprise not merely what are to be regarded as species of the genus Being, but also participants in Being. On the other hand, Being does not participate in the other four principles as its genera: they are not prior to Being; they do not transcend it.

9. The above considerations—to which others, doubtless, might be added—suffice to show that these are primary genera. But that they are the only primary genera, that there are no others, how can we be confident of this? Why do we not add unity to them? Quantity? Quality? Relation? and all else included by our various forerunners?

As for unity: If the term is to mean that Absolute Unity in which nothing else is present, neither Soul nor Intellect nor anything else, this can be predicated of nothing, and therefore cannot be a genus. If it denotes the unity present in Being, in which case we speak of the One-Being, this unity is not primal.

Besides, unity, containing no differences, cannot produce species, and not producing species, cannot be a genus. You cannot so much as divide unity: to divide it would be to make it many. Unity, aspiring to be a genus, becomes a plurality and annuls itself.

Again, you must add to it to divide it into species; for there can be no differentiae in unity as there are in Being. The mind accepts differences of Being, but differences within unity there cannot be. Every differentia introduces a duality destroying the unity; for the addition of a unit always does away with the previous quantity.

It may be contended that the unity which is implicit in Being and in Motion and the other genera is common to all, and that therefore Being and unity are identical. But we rejected the idea that Being is a genus over and above all the other genera, on the ground that these others are not species of Being, but beings in another mode: in the same way, we assert, unity is not a genus, the Primary Unity having a character distinct from all other unities.

Suppose that we are asked to treat Unity not as an all-comprehending genus but as having a distinctive place beside the other primary genera. We reply that if Being and unity are identified, then since Being has already been included among the genera, it is but a name that is introduced in unity: if, however, they are different, some principle is implied: if there is anything in addition (to this principle), unity is predicated of this added thing; if there is nothing added, the reference is again to that unity predicated of nothing. If, however, the unity referred to is that which accompanies Being, we have already decided that it is not unity in the primary sense.

But is there any reason why this unity should not be Primary Unity if once we exclude Unity Absolute? Do we not rank the posterior of Absolute Unity as Being, and 'Being' in the sense of the Primary Being? The reason is that the prior of this Being cannot itself be Being—or else, if the prior is Being, this is not Primary Being: but the prior of the unity is a unity.

Furthermore, unity, abstracted from Being, has no differentiae.

Again, even taking it as bound up with Being: If it is a consequent of Being, then it is a consequent of everything, and therefore the latest of things: but the genus takes priority. If it is simultaneous with Being, it is simultaneous with everything: but a genus is not thus simultaneous. If it is prior to Being, it is of the nature of a Principle, and therefore will belong only to Being; but if it serves as Principle to Being, it is not its genus: if it is not genus to Being, it is equally not a genus of anything else; for that would make Being the principle of all other things.

In sum, the unity exhibited in Being on the one hand approximates to Unity-Absolute and on the other tends to identify itself with Being: Being is a unity in relation to the Absolute, but by virtue of its sequence upon that Absolute is potentially also a plurality, whereas the Absolute Unity remains a unity and rejecting division refuses thereby to become a genus.

10. In what sense is the particular manifestation of Being a unity? Clearly, in so far as it is one thing, it forfeits its unity; with 'one' and 'thing' we have already plurality. No species can be a unity in more than an equivocal sense: a species is

a plurality, so that the 'unity' here is that of an army or a chorus. The unity of the higher order does not belong to species; unity is, thus, ambiguous, not taking the same form in Being and in particular beings.

It follows that unity is not a genus. For a genus is such that wherever it is affirmed its opposites cannot also be affirmed; anything of which unity and its opposites are alike affirmed is debarred from having unity as a genus. Consequently unity can be affirmed as a genus neither of the primary genera—since the One-Being is as much a plurality as a unity, and none of the other (primary) genera is a unity to the entire exclusion of plurality—nor of things posterior to Being, for these most certainly are a plurality. In sum, no genus can be a unity; so that unity to become a genus must forfeit its unity. The unit is prior to number yet number it must be, if it is to be a genus.

Again, the unit is a unit from the point of view of number: if it is a unit generically, it will not be a unit in the strict sense.

Again, just as the unit, as appearing in numbers, is not regarded as a genus predicated of them, but is thought of as inherent in them, so also unity, though present in Being, cannot stand as genus to Being or to the other genera or to anything whatever.

Further, as the simplex must be the principle of the non-simplex, though not its genus—for then the non-simplex too would be simplex—so it stands with unity; if unity is a Principle, it cannot be a genus to its subsequents, and therefore cannot be a genus of Being or of other things. If it is nevertheless to be a genus, everything of which it is a genus must be taken as a unit—a notion which implies the separation of unity from substance: it will not, therefore, be all-embracing. Just as Being is not a genus of everything but only of species each of which is a being, so too unity will be a genus of species each of which is a unity. But that raises the question of what difference there is between one thing and another in so far as they are both units, corresponding to the difference between one being and another.

Unity, it may be suggested, is divided in its conjunction with Being and Substance; Being because it is so divided is considered a genus—the one genus manifested in many particulars; why then should not unity be similarly a genus, inasmuch as its manifestations are as many as those of Substance and it is divided into as many particulars?

In the first place, the mere fact that an entity inheres in many things is not enough to make it a genus of those things or of anything else: in a word, a common property need not be a genus. The point inherent in a line is not a genus of lines, or a genus at all; nor again, as we have observed, is the unity latent in numbers a genus either of the numbers or of anything else: genus demands that the common property of diverse objects involve also differences arising out of its own character, that it form species, and that it belong to the essence of the objects. But what differences can there be in unity? What species does it engender? If it produces the same species as we find in connexion with Being, it must be identical with Being: only the name will differ, and the term Being may well suffice.

11. We are bound, however, to inquire under what mode unity is contained in Being. How is what is termed the 'dividing' effected? What is generic division, and does it apply to this unity? Or is its division different from the division of genera?

First then: In what sense, precisely, is any given particular called and known to be a unity? Secondly: Does 'unity' as used of the One-Being carry the same connotation as in reference to the Absolute?

Unity is not identical in all things; it has a different significance according as it is applied to the Sensible and the Intellectual realms—Being too, of course, comports such a difference—and there is a difference in the unity affirmed among sensible things as compared with each other; the unity is not the same in the cases of chorus, camp, ship, house; there is a difference again as between such discrete things and the continuous. Nevertheless, all are representations of the one exemplar, some quite remote, others more effective: the truer likeness is in the Intellectual; Soul is a unity, and still more is Intellect a unity and Being a unity.

When we predicate Being of a particular, do we thereby predicate unity, and does the degree of its unity tally with that of its being? Such correspondence is accidental: unity is not proportionate to Being; less unity need not mean less Being. An army or a choir has no less being than a house, though less unity.

It would appear, then, that the unity of a particular is related not so much to Being as to the Good: in so far as the particular attains goodness, so far is it a unity; and the degree of unity depends on this attainment. The particular aspires not simply to Being, but to a Being combined with Goodness: it is in this strain towards their good that such beings as do not possess unity strive their utmost to achieve it.

Things of nature tend by their very nature to coalesce with each other and also to unify each within itself; their movement is not away from but towards each other and inwards upon themselves. Souls, moreover, seem to desire always to pass into a unity appropriate to their substance (or reality). Unity in fact confronts them on two sides: their origin and their goal alike are unity; from unity they have arisen, and towards unity they strive. Unity is thus identical with Goodness; for no being ever came into existence without possessing, from that very moment, an irresistible tendency towards unity.

From natural things we turn to the artificial. Every art in all its operation aims at whatsoever unity its capacity and its products permit.

Most of all, Being achieves unity since it is closer at the start. That is why in speaking of other entities we assert the name only, for example man; when we say 'one man', we have in mind more than one; and if we affirm unity of him in any other connexion, we regard it as supplementary (to his essence): but when we speak of Being we use the compound expression 'One-Being' and imply in the reference to unity its close association with Goodness.

Thus for Being, as for the others, unity turns out to be, in some sense, Principle and Term, not however in the same sense as for things of the physical order—a discrepancy leading us to infer that even in unity there are degrees of priority.

How, then, do we characterize the unity (thus diverse) in Being? Are we to think of it as a common property seen alike in all its parts? In the first place (we observe) the point is common to lines and yet is not their genus, and this unity we are considering may also be common to numbers and not be their genus—though, we need hardly say, the unity of Unity-Absolute is not that of the numbers, one, two, and the rest. Secondly, in Being there is nothing to prevent the existence of prior and posterior, simple and composite: but unity, even if it be identical in all the manifestations of Being, having no differentiae can produce no species; but producing no species it cannot be a genus.

12. Enough upon that side of the question. But how does the good of numbers, lifeless things, depend upon their particular unity? Just as all other inanimates find their good in their unity.

If it should be objected that numbers are simply non-existent, we should point out that our discussion is concerned (not with units as such, but) with beings considered from the aspect of their unity.

We may again be asked how the point participates in goodness. Suppose its independent existence granted: then presumably it is chosen as an inanimate object and the question applies to all such objects. If, on the other hand, it is regarded as incorporated in such figures as the circle, then the good of the point will be merged in that of the circle: it will aspire to this good and strive to attain it, as far as it can, through the circle.

But (a different question:) how do the genera form the particulars? Is it by being broken up into parts? No; the genus exists as a whole in each of the things whose genus it is.

But how, at that, can it remain a unity? The unity of a genus must be considered as a whole-in-many.

Does it exist then only in the things participating in it? No; it has an independent existence of its own as well.—But this will, no doubt, become clearer as we proceed.

13. We turn to ask why Quantity is not included among the primary genera, and Quality also.

Quantity is not among the primaries, because these are perpetually associated with Being. Motion is bound up with Actual Being (Being-in-Act), since it is its life; with Motion Stability too gained its foothold in Reality; with these are associated even more closely Difference and Identity, so that they also are seen in conjunction with Being. But number (the basis of Quantity) is a posterior. It is posterior not only with regard to these genera but also within itself; in number the posterior is derived from the prior; this is a sequence in which the posteriors are latent in the priors (and do not appear simultaneously). Number therefore cannot be included among the primary genera; whether it constitutes a genus at all remains to be examined.

Magnitude (extended quantity) is in a still higher degree posterior and composite, for it contains within itself number, line, and surface. Now if continuous magnitude derives its quantity from number, and number is not a genus, how can magnitude hold that status? Besides, magnitudes, like numbers, admit of priority and posteriority.

If, then, Quantity be constituted by a common element in both number and magnitude, we must ascertain the nature of this common element, and consider it, once discovered, as a posterior genus, not as one of the Primaries: thus failing of primary status, it must be related, directly or indirectly, to one of the Primaries.

We may take it as clear that it is the nature of Quantity to indicate a certain quantum, and to measure the quantum of the particular; Quantity is moreover, in a sense, itself a quantum. But if the quantum is the common element in number and magnitude, either we have number as a primary with magnitude derived from it, or else number must consist of a blending of Motion and Stability, while magnitude will be a form of Motion or will originate in Motion, Motion going forth to infinity and Stability creating the unit by checking that advance.

But the problem of the origin of number and magnitude, or rather of how they subsist and are conceived, must be held over. It may, thus, be found that number is among the primary genera, while magnitude is posterior and composite; or that number belongs to the genus Stability, while magnitude must be consigned to Motion. But we propose to discuss all this at a later stage.

14. Why is Quality not included among the Primaries? Because like Quantity it

is a posterior, subsequent to Substance. Primary Substance must necessarily contain Quantity and Quality as its consequents; it cannot owe its subsistence to them, or require them for its completion: that would make it posterior to Quality and Quantity.

Now in the case of composite substances—those constituted from diverse elements—number and quantity provides a means of differentiation: their qualities also may be detached from the common core around which they are found to group themselves. But in the primary genera there is no distinction to be drawn between simples and composites; the difference is between simples (the primary genera as separate) and those same entities when completing not a particular substance but Substance as such. A particular substance may very well receive completion from Quality, for though it already has Substance before the accession of Quality, its particular character is external to Substance. But in Substance itself (the Authentic or Intelligible) all the elements are substantial.

Nevertheless, we ventured to assert elsewhere that while the complements of Substance are only by analogy called qualities, yet accessions of external origin and subsequent to Substance are really qualities; that, further, the properties which inhere in substances are their activities (Acts), while those which are subsequent are merely modifications (or Passions): we now affirm that the attributes of the particular substance are never complementary to Substance (as such); an accession of Substance does not come to the substance of man *qua* man; he is, on the contrary, Substance in a higher degree before he arrives at differentiation, just as he is already 'living being' before he passes into the rational species.

15. How then do the four genera (we have posited) complete Substance (or Reality) without qualifying it or even particularizing it?

It has been observed that Being is primary, and it is clear that none of the four—Motion, Stability, Difference, Identity—is distinct from it. That this Motion does not produce quality is doubtless also clear, but a word or two will make it clearer still.

If Motion is the Act of Substance (Reality), and Being and the Primaries in general are in Act (or actual), then Motion is not an accidental attribute: as the Act of what is necessarily actual (what necessarily involves Act), it is no longer to be considered as the complement of Substance but as Substance itself. For this reason, then, it has not been assigned to a posterior class, or referred to Quality, but has been made contemporary with Being.

The truth is not that Being first is and then takes Motion, first is and then acquires Stability: neither Stability nor Motion is a mere modification of Being.

Similarly, Identity and Difference are not later additions: Being did not grow into plurality; its very unity was a plurality; but plurality implies difference, and unity-in-plurality involves Identity.

Substance (Real Being) requires no more than these four constituents; but when we have to turn to the lower sphere, we find other principles giving rise no longer to Substance (as such) but to quantitative Substance and qualitative: these other principles may be regarded as genera but not primary genera.

16. As for Relation, manifestly an offshoot, how can it be included among primaries? Relation is of thing ranged against thing; it is not self-pivoted, but looks outward.

Location and Date are still more remote from Being. Location denotes the presence of one entity within another, so that it involves a duality; but a genus must be a unity, not a composite. Besides, place does not exist in the higher sphere, and the present discussion is concerned with the realm of True Being.

Whether time is There, remains to be considered. Presumably not. If it is a measurement, and that a measurement of Motion, we have two entities; the whole is a composite and posterior to Motion; therefore it is not on an equal footing with Motion in our classification.

Action and Passivity presuppose Motion; if, then, they exist in the higher sphere, they each involve a duality; neither is a simplex.

Possession is a duality, while Situation, as signifying one thing situated in another, is a threefold conception.

17. Why are not beauty, goodness, and the virtues, together with knowledge and intelligence, included among the primary genera?

If by goodness we mean The First—what we call the Principle of Goodness, the Principle of which we can predicate nothing, giving it this name only because we have no other means of indicating it—then goodness can be the genus of nothing: this principle is not affirmed of other things; if it were, each of these would be Goodness itself. The truth is that it is prior to Substance, not contained in it. If, on the contrary, we mean goodness as a quality, no quality can be ranked among the primaries.

Does this imply that the nature of Being is not good? Not good, to begin with, in the sense in which The First is good, but in another sense of the word: moreover, Being does not possess its goodness as a quality but as a constituent.

But the other genera too, we said, are constituents of Being, and are regarded as genera because each is a common property found in many things. If then goodness is similarly observed in every part of Substance or Being, or in most parts, why is goodness not a genus, and a primary genus? Because it is not found identical in all the parts of Being, but appears in degrees, first, second, and subsequent, whether it be because one part is derived from another—posterior from prior—or because all are posterior to the transcendent Unity, different parts of Being participating in it in diverse degrees corresponding to their characteristic natures.

If, however, we must make goodness a genus as well (as a constituent), it will be a posterior genus, for goodness is posterior to Substance and posterior to what constitutes the generic notion of Being, however unfailingly it be found associated with Being: but the Primaries, we decided, belong to Being as such, and go to form Substance.

This indeed is why we posit that which transcends Being, since Being and Substance cannot but be a plurality, necessarily comprising the genera enumerated and therefore forming a one-and-many.

It is true that we do not hesitate to speak of 'the goodness inherent in Being' when we are thinking of that Act by which Being tends, of its nature, towards the One: thus, we affirm goodness of it in the sense that it is thereby moulded into the likeness of The Good. But if this 'goodness inherent in Being' is an Act directed towards The Good, it is the life of Being: this life is Motion, and Motion is already one of the genera.

18. To pass to the consideration of beauty:

If we identify the primary Beauty with the Supreme, the same or similar arguments will apply here as applied to goodness: and if we mean the effulgence, as it were, which shines on the Form-Idea, we may observe that it is not identical in all ideas and that an effulgence is necessarily a posterior.

If we mean the beauty which identifies itself with Substance, this has been covered in our treatment of Substance.

If, again, we mean beauty in relation to ourselves as spectators in whom it produces a certain experience, this Act (of production) is Motion—and none the less Motion by being directed towards Absolute Beauty.

Knowledge, again, is Motion originating in the self; it is the observation of Being—an Act, not a State: hence it too falls under Motion, or perhaps more suitably under Stability, or even under both; if under both, knowledge must be thought of as a complex, and if a complex, is posterior.

Intelligence, since it connotes intelligent Being and comprises the total of existence, cannot be one of the genera: the true Intelligence (or Intellect) is Being taken with all its concomitants (with the other four genera); it is actually the sum of all the Existents: Being on the contrary, stripped of its concomitants, may be counted as a genus and held to be an element in Intelligence.

Justice and self-control (sophrosyny), and virtue in general—these are all various Acts of Intelligence: they are consequently not primary genera; they are posterior to a genus, that is to say, they are species.

19. Having established our four primary genera, it remains for us to inquire whether each of them of itself alone produces species. And especially, can Being be divided independently, that is without drawing upon the other genera? Surely not: the differentiae must come from outside the genus differentiated: they must be differentiae of Being proper, but cannot be identical with it.

Where then is it to find them? Obviously not in non-beings. If then in beings, and the three genera are all that is left, clearly it must find them in these, by conjunction and couplement with these, which will come into existence simultaneously with itself.

But if all come into existence simultaneously, what else is produced but that complex of all the Existents which we have just considered (Intellect)? How can other things exist over and above this all-including complex? And if all the constituents of this complex are genera, how do they produce species? How does Motion produce species of Motion? Similarly with Stability and the other genera.

A word of warning must here be given against sinking the various genera in their species; and also against reducing the genus to a mere predicate, something merely seen in the species. The genus must exist at once in itself and in its species; it blends, but it must also be pure; in contributing along with other genera to form Substance (Reality), it must not destroy itself. There are problems here that demand investigation.

But since we have identified the complex of all the Existents (or primary genera) with Intellect, and since we make Being or Substance prior to all the Existents, which may be regarded as its species or members, we may infer that the intellect, considered as fully explicit, is a subsequent.

Our treatment of this problem may serve to promote our investigation; we will take it as a kind of example, and with it embark upon our inquiry.

20. We may, then, distinguish two phases of Intellect, in one of which it may be taken as having no contact whatever with particulars and no Act upon anything; thus it is kept apart from being a particular intellect. In the same way science is prior to any of its constituent species, and the specific science is prior to any of its component parts; being none of its particulars it is the potentiality of all; each particular, on the other hand, is actually itself, but potentially the sum of all the particulars: and as with the specific science, so with science as a whole. The specific sciences lie in potentiality in science the total; even in their specific character they are potentially the whole; they have the whole predicated of them

and not merely a part of the whole. At the same time, science must exist as a thing in itself, unharmed by its divisions.

So with Intellect. Intellect as a whole must be thought of as prior to the intellects actualized as individuals; on the other hand, each particular intellect is sustained from the totality. The universal Intellect is a provider for the particular intellects, is the potentiality of them: it involves them as members of its universality, while they in turn involve the universal Intellect in their particularity, just as the particular science involves science the total.

The great Intellect, we maintain, exists in itself and the particular intellects in themselves; yet the particulars are embraced in the whole, and the whole in the particulars. The particular intellects exist by themselves and in another, the universal by itself and in those. All the particulars exist potentially in that self-existent universal, which actually is the totality, potentially each isolated member: on the other hand, each particular is actually what it is (its individual self), potentially the totality. In so far as what is predicated of them is their essence, they are actually what is predicated of them; but where the predicate is a genus, they are that only potentially. On the other hand, the universal in so far as it is a genus is the potentiality of all its subordinate species, though none of them in actuality; all are latent in it, but because its essential nature exists in actuality before the existence of the species, it does not submit to be itself particularized. If then the species are to exist in actuality, the cause must lie in the Act radiating from the universal.

21. How then by our theory does the universal Intellect produce the particulars while itself remaining a unity? In other words, how do the subordinate kinds, as we call them, arise from the four primaries? Here is this great, this infinite Intellect, not given to idle utterance but to sheer intellection, all-embracing, integral, no part, no individual: how, we ask, can it possibly be the source of all this plurality?

Number at all events it possesses in the objects of its contemplation: it is thus one and many, and the many are powers, wonderful powers, not weak but, being pure, supremely great and, so to speak, full to overflowing—powers in very truth, knowing no limit, so that they are infinite, infinity, Magnitude-Absolute.

As we survey this Magnitude with the beauty of Being within it and the glory and light around it, all contained in Intellect, we see, simultaneously, Quality already in bloom, and along with the continuity of its Act we catch a glimpse of Magnitude at rest. Then, with one, two, and three in Intellect, Magnitude appears as of three dimensions, with Quantity entire. Quantity thus given and Quality, both merging into one and, we may almost say, becoming one, there is at once shape. Difference slips in to divide both Quantity and Quality, and so we have variations in shape and differences of Quality. Identity, coming in with Difference, creates equality, Difference meanwhile introducing into Quantity inequality, whether in number or in magnitude: thus are produced circles and squares, and irregular figures, with number like and unlike, odd and even.

The life of Intellect is intelligent, and its activity (Act) has no failing-point: hence it excludes none of the constituents we have discovered within it, each one of which we now see as an intellectual function, and all of them possessed by virtue of its distinctive power and in the mode appropriate to Intellect.

But though Intellect possesses them all by way of thought, this is not discursive thought: it lacks nothing that is capable of serving as Reason-Principle, while it may itself be regarded as one great and perfect Reason-Principle, holding all the Principles as one and proceeding from its own Primaries, or rather having eternally proceeded, so that 'proceeding' is never true of it. It is a universal rule that whatever reasoning discovers to exist in Nature is to be found in Intellect apart from all ratiocination: we are apt to believe that Intellect has brought reasoning to bear on the creation of Being, and we make the same assumption in the case of the Reason-Principles which produce living beings: in fact, these Principles, prior to reasoning though they are, act invariably in the manner which the most careful reasoning would adopt in order to attain the best results.

What conditions, then, are we to think of as existing in that realm which is prior to Nature and transcends the Principles of Nature? In a sphere in which Substance (Reality) is not distinct from Intellect, and neither Being nor Intellect is of alien origin, it is obvious that Being is best served by the domination of Intellect, so that Being is what Intellect wills and is: thus alone can it be authentic and primary Being; for if Being is to be in any sense derived, its derivation must be from Intellect.

Being, thus, exhibits every shape and every quality; it is not seen as a thing determined by some one particular quality; there could not be one only, since the principle of Difference is there; and since Identity is equally there, it must be simultaneously one and many. And so Being is; such it always was: unity-with-plurality appears in all its kinds, as witness all the variations of magnitude, shape, and quality. Clearly nothing may legitimately be excluded (from Being), for the whole must be complete in the higher sphere which, otherwise, would not be the whole.

Life too burst upon Being, or rather was inseparably bound up with it; and thus it was that all living things of necessity came to be. Body too was there, since Matter and Quality were present.

Everything exists forever, unfailing, involved by very existence in eternity. Individuals have their separate entities, but are at one in the (total) unity. The complex, so to speak, of them all, thus combined, is Intellect; and Intellect, holding all existence within itself, is a complete living being, and the essential Idea of Living Being. In so far as Intellect submits to contemplation by its derivative (Soul), becoming an Intelligible, it gives that derivative the right also to be called 'intellect'.

22. We may here adduce the pregnant words of Plato: 'Inasmuch as Intellect perceives the variety and plurality of the Ideas (Forms) present in the complete Living Being...' The words apply equally to Soul; Soul is subsequent to Intellect, yet by its very nature contains the Ideas in itself, but 'perceives' more clearly in that prior. Our intellect also contains them and perceives more clearly in its prior, for while of itself it merely perceives, in the prior it also perceives its own perception.

This intellect, then, to which we ascribe 'perception', though not divorced from the prior in which it originates, evolves plurality out of unity and has bound up with it the principle of Difference: it therefore takes the form of a plurality-in-unity. A plurality-in-unity, it produces the many intellects by the dictate of its very nature.

No numerical unity, no individual thing can be found in the Intelligible; for whatever you find in that sphere is a species, since it is divorced from Matter. This may be the import of the difficult words of Plato, that 'Substance (or Being) is broken up into an infinity of parts'. So long as the division proceeds from genus to species, infinity is not reached; a limit is set by the species generated: the lowest species, however—that which is not divided into further species—may be more accurately regarded as infinite. And this is the meaning of the words: 'to relegate them once and for all to infinity and there abandon them'. As for particulars, they are, considered in themselves, infinite, but come under number by being embraced in the (total) unity. Soul has Intellect for its prior, is therefore circumscribed by number down to its ultimate extremity; at that point infinity is reached.

Such an intellect, though all-embracing and complete, is a partial thing, and its various manifestations are in actuality parts of that part. Soul too is a part of a part, though in the sense of being an Act (actuality) derived from it. When the Act of Intellect is directed upon itself, the result is the manifold (particular) intellects; when it looks outwards, Soul is produced.

If Soul acts as a genus or a species, the various (particular) souls must act as species. Their activities (Acts) will be twofold: the activity upward is Intellect; that which looks downward constitutes the other powers or faculties of Soul in due order; the lowest activity is in its contact with Matter to which it brings Form.

This lower phase of Soul does not prevent the rest from being entirely in the higher sphere: indeed what we call the lower phase is but an image of Soul: not that it is cut off from Soul; it is like the reflection in the mirror, depending upon the original which stands outside of it.

But we must keep in mind what this 'outside' means. Up to the production of the image stretches the Intellectual realm, wholly and exclusively composed of Intellectual Beings: in the same way the Sensible world, representing that in so far as it is able to retain the likeness of a Living Being, is itself a living being: the relation is like that of a portrait or reflection to the original which is regarded as prior to the water or the painting reproducing it.

The representation, notice, in the portrait or on the water is not of the dual being, but of the one element (Matter) as shaped by the other (Form). Similarly, this likeness of the Intellectual realm carries images, not of the creative element, but of the entities contained in that creator, including Man with every other living being: creator and created are alike living beings, though of a different life, and both coexist in the Intellectual realm.

THIRD TRACTATE

On the Kinds of Being: Third Treatise

1. We have now explained our conception of Reality (True Being) and considered how far it agrees with the teaching of Plato. We have still to investigate the opposed principle (the principle of Becoming).

There is the possibility that the genera posited for the Intellectual sphere will suffice for the lower also; possibly with these genera others will be required; again, the two series may differ entirely; or perhaps some of the sensible genera will be identical with their intellectual prototypes, and others different—'identical', however, being understood to mean only analogous and in possession of a common name, as our results will make clear.

We must begin on these lines:

The subject of our discussion is the Sensible realm: Sensible Existence is entirely embraced by what we know as the Universe: our duty, then, would seem to be clear enough—to take this Universe and analyse its nature, classifying its constituent parts and arranging them by genus and species. Suppose that we were making a division of speech: we should reduce its infinity to finite terms, and from the identity appearing in many instances evolve a unity, then another and another, until we arrived at some definite number; each such unit we should call a species if imposed upon individuals, a genus if imposed upon species. Thus, every species of speech—and similarly all phenomena—might be referred to a unity; speech—or element—might be predicated of them all.

This procedure, however, is, as we have already shown, impossible in dealing with the subject of our present inquiry. New genera must be sought for this Universe—genera distinct from those of the Intellectual, inasmuch as this realm is different from that, analogous indeed but never identical, a mere image of the higher. True, it involves in its composite nature the parallel existence of Body and Soul, for the Universe is a living being: essentially, however, Soul is of the Intellectual and does not enter into the structure of what is called Sensible Being.

Remembering this fact, we must—however great the difficulty—exclude Soul from the present investigation, just as in a census of citizens, taken in the interests of commerce and taxation, we should ignore the alien population. As for the experiences to which Soul is indirectly subject in its conjunction with Body and by reason of Body's presence, their classification must be attempted at a later stage, when we inquire into the details of Sensible Existence.

2. Our first observations must be directed to what passes in the Sensible realm for Substance. It is, we shall agree, only by analogy that the nature manifested in bodies is designated as Substance, and by no means because such terms as Substance or Being tally with the notion of bodies in flux; the proper term would be Becoming.

But Becoming is not a uniform nature: there are bodies comprising under the single head simples and composites, and there are accidentals or consequents, themselves capable of separate classification.

Alternatively, Becoming may be divided into Matter and the Form imposed upon Matter. These may be regarded each as a separate genus, or else both may be brought under a single category and receive alike the name of Substance.

But what, we may ask, have Matter and Form in common? In what sense can Matter be conceived as a genus, and what will be its species? What differentia is there in Matter? In which genus, Matter or Form are we to rank the composite of both? It may be this very composite which constitutes the Substance manifested in bodies, neither of the components by itself answering to the conception of Body: how, then, can we rank them in one and the same genus as the composite? How can the elements of a thing be brought within the same genus as the thing itself? Yet if we begin with bodies, our first-principles will be compounds.

Why not resort to analogy? Admitted that the classification of the Sensible cannot proceed along the identical lines marked out for the Intellectual: is there any reason why we should not for Intellectual-Being substitute Matter, and for Intellectual Motion substitute Sensible Form, which may be regarded as the life and consummation of Matter? The inertia of Matter would correspond with Stability, while the Identity and Difference of the Intellectual would find their counterparts in the ample similarity and increased diversity which obtain in the Sensible realm.

But, in the first place, Matter does not possess or acquire Form as its life or its Act; Form enters it from without, and remains foreign to its nature. Secondly, Form in the Intellectual is an Act and a motion; in the Sensible Motion is different from the Substance and accidental to it: Form in relation to Matter approximates rather to Stability than to Motion; for by determining Matter's indetermination it confers upon it a sort of rest.

In the higher realm Identity and Difference presuppose a unity at once identical and different: a thing in the lower is different only by participation in Difference and in relation to some other thing; Identity and Difference are here predicates and posterior to the subjects, as they are not in that realm.

As for Stability, how can it belong to Matter, which is distorted into every variety of mass, receiving its forms from without, and even with the aid of these forms incapable of offspring?

This mode of division must accordingly be abandoned.

3. How then do we go to work?

Let us begin by distinguishing Matter, Form, the Mixture of both, and the Attributes of the Mixture. The Attributes may be subdivided into those which are mere predicates, and those serving also as accidents. The accidents may be either inclusive or included; they, further, comprise activities, experiences, consequents.

Matter will be found common to all substances, not however as a genus, since it has no differentiae—unless indeed differentiae be ascribed to it on the ground of its taking such various forms as fire and air.

It may be held that Matter is sufficiently constituted a genus by the fact that the things in which it appears hold it in common, or in that it presents itself as a whole of parts. In this sense Matter will indeed be a genus, though not in the accepted sense of the term. Matter, we may remark, is also a single element, if the element as such is able to constitute a genus.

As to Form: the qualification 'bound up with, involved in Matter' separates a Form from other Forms: it does not, however, embrace the whole of Substantial Form (as, to be the genus of Form, it must).

We may, again, regard Form as the creator of Substance and make the

Reason-Principle of Substance dependent upon Form: yet we do not come thereby to an understanding of the nature of Substance.

We may, also, restrict Substance to the Composite. Matter and Form then cease to be substances. If they are Substance equally with the Composite, it remains to inquire what there is common to all three.

The 'mere predicates' fall under the category of Relation: such are cause and element. The accidents included in the composite substances are found to be either Quality or Quantity; those which are inclusive of the substances are of the nature of Place and Time. Activities and experiences comprise Motions; consequents Place and Time, which are consequents respectively of the Composites and of Motion.

The first three entities (Matter, Form, Composite) possess, as we have discovered, the unity of a common designation, the Sensible counterpart of Substance. Then follow in order Relation, Quantity, Quality, Time-during-which, Place-in-which, Motion, Place, Time; though we may eliminate Place and Time (as being external, mere consequents), and then Time-during-which and Place-in-which become superfluous.

Thus we have five classes, counting the first three as one. If these are not massed into a unity, the series will be Matter, Form, Composite, Relation, Quantity, Quality, Motion. The last three may, again, be included in Relation, which is capable of bearing this wider extension.

4. What, then, we have to ask, is the constant element in the first three entities? What is it that identifies them with sensible Substance?

Is it the capacity to serve as a base? But Matter, we maintain, serves as the base and seat of Form: Form, thus, will be excluded from the category of Substance. Again, the Composite is the base and seat of attributes: hence, Form combined with Matter will be the basic ground of Composites, or at any rate of all posteriors of the Composite—Quantity, Quality, Motion, and the rest.

But perhaps we may think Substance validly defined as that which is not predicated of anything else. White and black are predicated of an object having one or other of these qualities; double presupposes something distinct from itself—we refer not to the half, but to the length of wood of which doubleness is affirmed; father *qua* father is a predicate; knowledge is predicated of the subject in whom the knowledge exists; space is the limit of something, time the measure of something. Fire, on the other hand, is predicated of nothing; wood as such is predicated of nothing; and so with man, Socrates, and the composite substance in general.

Equally the Substantial Form is never a predicate, since it never acts as a modification of anything. Form is not an attribute of Matter (hence, is not predicable of Matter); it is simply a constituent of the Couplement. On the other hand, the Form of a man is not different from the man himself (and so does not 'modify' the Couplement).

Matter, similarly, is part of a whole, and belongs to something else only as to a whole and not as to a separate thing of which it is predicated. White, on the contrary, essentially belongs to something distinct from itself.

We conclude that nothing belonging to something else and predicated of it can be Substance. Substance is that which belongs essentially to itself, or, in so far as it is a part of the differentiated object, serves only to complete the Composite. Each or either part of the Composite belongs to itself, and is only affirmed of the Composite in a special sense: only *qua* part of the whole is it referred to something else; *qua* individual it is never in its essential nature predicated of an external.

It may be claimed as a common element in Matter, Form, and the Couplement that they are all substrates. But the mode in which Matter is the substrate of Form is different from that in which Form and the Couplement are substrates of their modifications.

And is it strictly true to say that Matter is the substrate of Form? Form is rather the completion which Matter's nature as pure potentiality demands.

Moreover, Form cannot be said to reside in Matter (as in a substrate). When one thing combines with another to form a unity, the one does not reside in the other; both alike are substrates of a third: thus, Man (the Form) and a man (the Composite) are substrates of their experiences, and are prior to their activities and consequents.

Substance, then, is that from which all other things proceed and to which they owe their existence; it is the centre of passivity and the source of action.

5. These are incontrovertible facts in regard to the pseudo-substance of the Sensible realm: if they apply also in some degree to the True Substance of the Intellectual, the coincidence is, doubtless, to be attributed to analogy and ambiguity of terms.

We are aware that 'the first' is so called only in relation to the things which come after it: 'first' has no absolute significance; the first of one series is subsequent to the last of another. 'Substrate', similarly, varies in meaning (as applied to the higher and to the lower), while as for passivity its very existence in the Intellectual is questionable; if it does exist there, it is not the passivity of the Sensible.

Moreover, the fact of 'not being present in a subject (or substrate)' is not universally true of Substance, unless presence in a subject be stipulated as not including the case of the part present in the whole or of one thing combining with another to form a distinct unity; a thing will not be present as in a subject in that with which it co-operates in the formation of a composite substance. Form, therefore, is not present in Matter as in a subject, nor is Man so present in Socrates, since Man is part of Socrates.

Substance, then, is that which is not present in a subject; but if we adopt the definition 'neither present in a subject nor predicated of a subject', we must add to the second 'subject' the qualification 'distinct', in order that we may not exclude the case of Man predicated of a particular man. When I predicate Man of Socrates, it is as though I affirmed, not that a piece of wood is white, but that a white object is white; for in asserting that Socrates is a man, I predicate Man (the universal) of a particular man, I affirm Man of the manhood of Socrates; I am really saying only that Socrates is Socrates, or that this particular rational animal is an animal.

It may be objected that non-presence in a subject is not peculiar to Substance, inasmuch as the differentia of a substance is no more present in a subject than the substance itself; but this objection results from taking a part of the whole substance, such as 'the two-footed' in our example, and asserting that this part is not present in a subject: if we take, not 'the two-footed' which is a particular kind of Substance, but 'two-footedness' by which we signify not Substance but Quality, we shall find that this 'two-footedness' is indeed present in a subject.

We may be told that neither Time nor Place is present in a subject. But if the definition of Time as the measure of Motion be regarded as denoting something measured, the 'measure' will be present in Motion as in a subject, while Motion will be present in the moved: if, on the contrary, it be supposed to signify a principle of measurement, the 'measure' will be present in the measurer.

Place is the limit of the surrounding space, and thus is present in that space.

The truth is, however, that the 'Substance' of our inquiry may be apprehended in directly opposite ways: it may be determined by one of the properties we have been discussing, by more than one, by all at once, according as they answer to the notions of Matter, Form, and the Couplement.

6. Granted, it may be urged, that these observations upon the nature of Substance are sound, we have not yet arrived at a statement of its essence. Our critic doubtless expects to see this 'Sensible': but its essence, its characteristic being, cannot be seen.

Do we infer that fire and water (being visible) are not Substance? They certainly are not Substance because they are visible. Why, then? Because they possess Matter? No. Or Form? No. Nor because they involve a Couplement of Matter and Form. Then why are they Substance? By existing. But does not

Quantity exist, and Quality? This anomaly is to be explained by an equivocation in the term 'existence'.

What, then, is the meaning of 'existence' as applied to fire, earth, and the other elements? What is the difference between this existence and existence in the other categories? It is the difference between being simply—that which just is—and being white. But surely the being qualified by 'white' is the same as that having no qualification? It is not the same: the latter is Being in the primary sense, the former is Being only by participation and in a secondary degree. Whiteness added to Being produces a being white; Being added to whiteness produces a white being: thus, whiteness becomes an accident of Being, and Being an accident of whiteness.

The case is not equivalent to predicating white of Socrates and Socrates of white; for Socrates remains the same, though white would appear to have a different meaning in the two propositions, since in predicating Socrates of white we include Socrates in the (whole) sphere of whiteness, whereas in the proposition 'Socrates is white' whiteness is plainly an attribute (accident) of Socrates.

'Being is white' implies, similarly, that Being possesses whiteness as an attribute, while in the proposition 'whiteness is Being (or, is a being)' whiteness is regarded as comprising Being in its own extension.

In sum, whiteness has existence because it is bound up with Being and present in it: Being is, thus, the source of its existence. Being is Being on its own account, but is white on account of whiteness—not because it is 'present in' whiteness, but because whiteness is present in it.

The Being of the Sensible resembles the white in not originating in itself. It must therefore be regarded as dependent for its being upon the Authentic Being, as white for its whiteness upon the Authentic Whiteness, which in turn possesses whiteness through participation in that Intellectual Being whose existence is underived.

7. But Matter, it may be contended, is the source of existence to the Sensible things implanted in it. From what source, then, we retort, does Matter itself derive existence and being?

That Matter is not a Primary we have established elsewhere. If it be urged that other things can have no subsistence without being implanted in Matter, we admit the claim for Sensible things. But though Matter be prior to these, it is not thereby precluded from being posterior to many things—posterior, in fact, to all the beings of the Intellectual sphere. Its existence is but a pale reflection, and less complete than that of the things implanted in it. These are Reason-Principles and more directly derived from Being: Matter has of itself no

Reason-Principle whatever; it is but a shadow of a Principle, a vain attempt to achieve a Principle.

But, our critic may pursue, Matter gives existence to the things implanted in it, just as Socrates gives existence to the whiteness implanted in himself? We reply that the higher being gives existence to the lower, the lower to the higher never.

But once concede that Form is higher in the scale of Being than Matter, and Being can no longer be regarded as a common element in both, nor Substance as a genus embracing Matter, Form, and the Couplement. True, these will have many common properties, to which we have already referred, but their being (or existence) will none the less be different. When a higher being comes into contact with a lower, the lower, though first in the natural order, is yet posterior in the scale of Reality: consequently, if Being does not belong in equal degrees to Matter, to Form, and to the Couplement, Substance can no longer be common to all three in the sense of being their genus: to their posteriors it will bear a still different relation, serving them as a common base by being bound up with all alike. Substance, thus, resembles life, dim here, clearer there, or portraits of which one is an outline, another more minutely worked. By measuring Being by its dim manifestation and neglecting a fuller revelation elsewhere, we may come to regard this dim existence as a common ground.

But this procedure is scarcely permissible. Every grade of being is a distinct whole. The dim manifestation is in no sense a common ground, just as there is no common ground in the vegetal, the sensory, and the intellectual forms of life.

We conclude that even within the Sensible world the term 'Being' must have different connotations as applied to Matter and Form, and that both derive from a single source pouring into the different streams.

We know that when a second is derived from a first and a third from the second, the one will rank higher and its successor be poorer and of lower worth; it is no less true that when two things are found to issue from the same source, one thing, subjected in a certain degree to fire, will give us an earthen jar, while another, taking less of the heat, does not produce the jar.

Perhaps we cannot even maintain that Matter and Form are derived from a single source; in the Intellectual realm itself there is a difference between them.

8. The division into elements must, in short, be abandoned, especially in regard to Sensible Substance, known necessarily by sense rather than by reason. We must no longer look for help in constituent parts, since such parts will not be substances, or at any rate not sensible substances.

Our plan must be to apprehend what is constant in stone, earth, water, and the entities which they compose—the vegetal and animal forms, considered purely as sensibles—and to confine this constant within a single genus. Neither Matter nor Form will thus be overlooked, for Sensible Substance comports them; fire and earth and the two intermediaries consist of Matter and Form, while composite things are actually many substances in one. They all, moreover, have that common property which distinguishes them from other things: serving as subjects to these others, they are never themselves present in a subject nor predicated of any other thing. Similarly, all the characteristics which we have ascribed to Substance find a place in this classification.

But Sensible Substance is never found apart from magnitude and quality: how then do we proceed to separate these accidents? If we subtract them—magnitude, figure, colour, dryness, moistness—what is there left to be regarded as Substance itself? All the substances under consideration are, of course, qualified.

There is, however, something in relation to which whatever turns Substance into qualified Substance is accidental: thus, the whole of fire is not Substance, but only a part of it—if the term 'part' be allowed.

What then can this 'part' be? Matter may be suggested. But then we must make Sensible Substance a mere conglomeration of qualities and Matter; all the qualities taken together as coagulating in a uniform Matter constitute Substance, each one separately forming a quale or a quantum or else a thing of many qualities. Everything whose absence leaves subsistence incomplete is a part of the particular substance, while all that is accidental to the substance already existent takes independent rank and is not submerged in the mixture which constitutes this so called substance.

A reservation: I do not allow that whatever combines with anything else is Substance if it helps to produce a single mass having quantity and quality, whereas taken by itself and divorced from this complementary function it is a quality: not any constituent of the amalgam is Substance, but only the amalgam as a whole.

And let no one take exception on the ground that we produce Sensible Substance from non-substances. The whole amalgam itself is not True Substance; it is merely an imitation of that True Substance which has Being apart from its concomitants, these indeed being derived from it as the possessor of True Being. In the lower realm the case is different: the underlying ground is sterile, and from its inability to produce fails to attain to the status of Being; it remains a shadow, and on this shadow is traced a sketch—the world of Appearance.

9. So much for one of the genera—the 'Substance', so called, of the Sensible realm.

But what are we to posit as its species? how divide this genus?

The genus as a whole must be identified with body. Bodies may be divided into the characteristically material and the organic: the material bodies comprise fire, earth, water, air; the organic the bodies of plants and animals, these in turn admitting of formal differentiation.

The next step is to find the species of earth and of the other elements, and in the case of organic bodies to distinguish plants and animals either according to their forms, or else by their habitations—on the earth, in the earth, and similarly for the other elements. Alternatively, bodies may be classified as light, heavy, and intermediate: some bodies in fact stand in the middle of the universe, others circumscribe it from above, others occupy a middle sphere: in each case we shall find bodies different in shape, so that the bodies of the living beings of the heavens may be differentiated from those of the other elements.

Once we have classified bodies into the four species, we are ready to combine them on a different principle, at the same time intermingling their differences of place, form, and constitution; the resultant combinations will be known as fiery or earthy on the basis of the excess or predominance of some one element.

The distinction between First and Second Substances, between fire and a given example of fire, entails a difference of a peculiar kind—the difference between universal and particular. This, however, is not a difference characteristic of Substance; there is also in Quality the distinction between what is white (in general) and a white object, between grammar and some particular grammar.

The question may here be asked: what deficiency has grammar compared with a particular grammar, and science as a whole in comparison with a science? Grammar is certainly not posterior to the particular grammar: on the contrary, the grammar as in you depends upon the prior existence of grammar as such: the grammar as in you becomes a particular by the fact of being in you; it is otherwise identical with grammar the universal.

Turn to the case of Socrates: it is not Socrates who bestows manhood upon what previously was not Man, but Man upon Socrates; the individual man exists by participation in the universal.

Besides, Socrates is merely a particular instance of Man; this particularity can have no effect whatever in adding to his essential manhood.

We may be told that Man (the universal) is Form alone, Socrates Form in Matter. But on this very ground Socrates will be less fully Man than the universal; for the Reason-Principle will be less effectual in Matter. If, on the contrary, Man is not determined by Form alone, but presupposes Matter, what deficiency has Man in comparison with the material manifestation of Man—

the Reason-Principle in isolation as compared with its embodiment in a unit of Matter?

Besides, the more general is by nature prior; hence, the Form-Idea is prior to the individual: but what is prior by nature is prior unconditionally. How then can the Form take a lower rank? The individual, it is true, is prior in the sense of being more readily accessible to our cognizance; this fact, however, entails no objective difference.

Moreover, such a difference, if established, would be incompatible with a single definition of Substance; First and Second Substances could not have the same definition, nor be brought under a single genus.

10. Another method of division is possible: substances may be classed as hot-dry, dry-cold, cold-moist, or however we choose to make the coupling. We may then proceed to the combination and blending of these couples, either halting at that point and going no further than the compound, or else subdividing by habitation—on the earth, in the earth—or by form and by the differences exhibited by living beings, not *qua* living, but in their bodies viewed as instruments of life.

Differentiation by form or shape is no more out of place than a division based on qualities—heat, cold, and the like. If it be objected that qualities go to make bodies what they are, then, we reply, so do blendings, colours, shapes. Since our discussion is concerned with Sensible Substance, it is not strange that it should turn upon distinctions related to sense-perception: this Substance is not Being pure and simple, but the Sensible Being which we call the Universe.

We have remarked that its apparent subsistence is in fact an assemblage of Sensibles, their existence guaranteed to us by sense-perception. But since their combination is unlimited, our division must be guided by the Form-Ideas of living beings, as for example the Form-Idea of Man implanted in Body; the particular Form acts as a qualification of Body, but there is nothing unreasonable in using qualities as a basis of division.

We may be told that in our division we have co-ordinated simple and composite bodies, even ranking them as opposites. But our distinction, we reply, was between material and organic bodies, and raised no question of the composite. In fact, there exists no means of opposing the composite to the simple; it is necessary to determine the simples in the first stage of division, and then, combining them on the basis of a distinct underlying principle, to differentiate the composites in virtue of their places and shapes, distinguishing for example the heavenly from the earthly.

These observations will suffice for the Being (Substance), or rather the Becoming, which obtains in the Sensible realm.

11. Passing to Quantity and the quantum, we have to consider the view which identifies them with number and magnitude on the ground that everything (in the Sensible world) is quantitatively determined—material forms numbered, their substrate spatially extended: we are here, of course, discussing not Quantity in isolation, but that which causes a piece of wood to be three yards long and gives the five in 'five horses'.

Now we have often maintained that number and magnitude are to be regarded as the only true qualities, and that Space and Time have no right to be conceived as quantitative: Time as the measure of Motion should be assigned to Relation, while Space, being that which circumscribes Body, is also a relative and falls under the same category; though continuous, it has, like Motion, not been included in Quantity.

On the other hand, why do we not find in the category of Quantity 'great' and 'small'? It is some kind of Quantity which gives greatness to the great; greatness is not a relative, though greater and smaller are relatives, since these, like doubleness, imply an external correlative.

What is it, then, which makes a mountain small and a grain of millet large? Surely, in the first place, 'small' is equivalent to 'smaller'. It is admitted that the term is applied only to things of the same kind, and from this admission we may infer that the mountain is 'smaller' rather than 'small', and that the grain of millet is not large in any absolute sense but large for a grain of millet. In other words, since the comparison is between things of the same kind, the natural predicate would be a comparative.

Again, why is not beauty classed as a relative? Beauty we regard as absolute and as a quality; 'more beautiful' is the relative. Yet even the term 'beautiful' may be attached to something which in a given relation may appear ugly: the beauty of man, for example, is ugliness when compared with that of the gods; 'the most beautiful of monkeys', we may quote, 'is ugly in comparison with any other type'. None the less, a thing is beautiful in itself; as related to something else it is either more or less beautiful.

Similarly, an object is great in itself, and its greatness is due, not to any external, but to its own participation in the Absolute Great.

Are we actually to eliminate the beautiful on the pretext that there is a more beautiful? No more then must we eliminate the great because of the greater: the greater can obviously have no existence whatever apart from the great, just as the more beautiful can have no existence without the beautiful.

12. It follows that we must allow contrariety to Quantity: whenever we speak of great and small our notions acknowledge this contrariety by evolving opposite

images, as also when we refer to many and few: indeed, 'few' and 'many' call for similar treatment to 'small' and 'great'.

'Many', predicated of the inhabitants of a house, does duty for the comparative, 'more': 'few' people are said to be in the theatre instead of 'less'.

'Many', again, necessarily involves a large numerical plurality. This plurality can scarcely be a relative; it is simply an expansion of number, its contrary being a contraction.

The same applies to the continuous (magnitude), the notion of which entails prolongation to a distant point.

Quantity, then, appears whenever there is a progression from the unit or the point: if either progression comes to a rapid halt, we have respectively 'few' and 'small'; if it goes forward and does not quickly cease, 'many' and 'great'.

What, we may be asked, is the limit of this progression? What, we retort, is the limit of beauty, or of heat? Whatever limit you impose, there is always a 'hotter'; yet 'hotter' is accounted a relative, 'hot' a pure quality.

In sum, just as there is a Reason-Principle of beauty, so there must be a Reason-Principle of greatness, participation in which makes a thing great, as the Principle of beauty makes it beautiful.

To judge from these instances, there is contrariety in Quantity. Place we may neglect as not strictly coming under the category of Quantity; if it were admitted, 'above' could only be a contrary if there were something in the universe which was 'below': as referring to the partial, the terms 'above' and 'below' are used in a purely relative sense, and must go with 'right' and 'left' into the category of Relation.

Syllable and discourse are only indirectly quantities or substrates of Quantity; it is voice that is quantitative: but voice is a kind of Motion; it must accordingly in any case (quantity or no quantity) be referred to Motion, as must activity also.

13. It has been remarked that the continuous is effectually distinguished from the discrete by their possessing the one a common, the other a separate limit.

The same principle gives rise to the numerical distinction between odd and even; and it holds good that if there are differentiae found in both contraries, they are either to be abandoned to the objects numbered, or else to be considered as differentiae of the abstract numbers, and not of the numbers manifested in the sensible objects. If the numbers are logically separable from the objects, that is no reason why we should not think of them as sharing the same differentiae.

But how are we to differentiate the continuous, comprising as it does line, surface, and solid? The line may be rated as of one dimension, the surface as of two dimensions, the solid as of three, if we are only making a calculation and do not suppose that we are dividing the continuous into its species; certainly numbers, thus grouped as prior and posterior, cannot be brought into a common genus; there is, accordingly, no common basis in first, second, and third dimensions. Yet there is a sense in which they would appear to be equal—namely, as pure measures of Quantity: of higher and lower dimensions, they are not however more or less quantitative.

Numbers have similarly a common property in their being numbers all; and the truth may well be, not that one creates two, and two creates three, but that all have a common source.

Suppose, however, that they are not derived from any source whatever, but exist independently; we at any rate conceive them as being derived, and so may be assumed to regard the smaller as taking priority over the greater: yet, even so, by the mere fact of their being numbers they are reducible to a single type.

What applies to numbers is equally true of magnitudes; though here we have to distinguish between line, surface, and solid—the last also referred to as 'body'—on the ground that, while all are magnitudes, they differ specifically.

It remains to inquire whether these species are themselves to be divided: the line into straight, circular, spiral; the surface into rectilinear and circular figures; the solid into the various solid figures—sphere and polyhedra: whether these last should be subdivided, as by the geometers, into those contained by triangular and quadrilateral planes: and whether a further division should be performed.

14. How are we to classify the straight line? Shall we deny that it is a magnitude?

The suggestion may be made that it is a qualified magnitude. May we not, then, consider straightness as a differentia of 'line', to which, and to which alone, it belongs? We at any rate draw on Quality for differentiae of Substance.

The straight line is, thus, a quantity plus a differentia; but it is not on that account a composite made up of straightness and line: if it be a composite, the composite possesses a differentia of its own.

But (if the line is a quantity) why is not the product of three lines included in Quantity? The answer is that a triangle consists not merely of three lines but of three lines in a particular disposition, a quadrilateral of four lines in a particular disposition: even the straight line involves disposition as well as quantity.

Holding that the straight line is not mere quantity, we should naturally proceed to assert that the line as limited is not mere quantity, but for the fact that the limit of a line is a point, which is in the same category, Quantity. Similarly, the limited surface will be a quantity, since lines, which have a far better right than itself to this category, constitute its limits. With the introduction of the limited surface—rectangle, hexagon, polygon—into the category of Quantity, this category will be brought to include every figure whatsoever.

If, however, by classing the triangle and the rectangle as qualia we propose to bring figures under Quality, we are not thereby precluded from assigning the same object to more categories than one: in so far as it is a magnitude—a magnitude of a particular kind—it will belong to Quantity; in so far as it presents a particular shape, to Quality.

It may be urged that the triangle is essentially a particular shape. Then what prevents our ranking the sphere also as a quality?

To proceed on these lines would lead us to the conclusion that geometry is concerned not with magnitudes but with Quality. But this conclusion is untenable; geometry is the study of magnitudes. The differences of magnitudes do not eliminate the existence of magnitudes as such, any more than the differences of substances annihilate the substances themselves.

Moreover, every surface is limited; it is impossible for any surface to be infinite in extent.

Again, when I find Quality bound up with Substance, I regard it as substantial quality: I am not less, but far more, disposed to see in figures or shapes (qualitative) varieties of Quantity. Besides, if we are not to regard them as varieties of magnitude, to what genus are we to assign them?

Suppose, then, that we allow differences of magnitude, we commit ourselves to a specific classification of the magnitudes so differentiated.

15. How far is it true that equality and inequality are characteristic of Quantity?

Triangles, it is significant, are said to be similar rather than equal. But we also refer to magnitudes as similar, and the accepted connotation of similarity does not exclude similarity or dissimilarity in Quantity. It may, of course, be the case that the term 'similarity' has a different sense here from that understood in reference to Quality.

Furthermore, if we are told that equality and inequality are characteristic of Quantity, that is not to deny that similarity also may be predicated of certain quantities. If, on the contrary, similarity and dissimilarity are to be confined to Quality, the terms as applied to Quantity must, as we have said, bear a different meaning.

But suppose similarity to be identical in both genera; Quantity and Quality must then be expected to reveal other properties held in common.

May the truth be this: that similarity is predicable of Quantity only in so far as Quantity possesses (qualitative) differences? But as a general rule differences which complete the substance (or essence) are grouped with that of which they are differences, especially when the difference is a difference of that thing alone. If in one case the difference completes the substance and not in another, we inevitably class it with that which it completes, and only consider it as independent when it is not complementary: when we say 'completes the substance', we refer not to Substance as such but to the differentiated substance; the particular object is to be thought of as receiving an accession which is non-substantial.

We must not, however, fail to observe that we predicate equality of triangles, rectangles, and figures generally, whether plane or solid: this may be given as a ground for regarding equality and inequality as characteristic of Quantity.

It remains to inquire whether similarity and dissimilarity are characteristic of Quality.

. . .

We have spoken of Quality as combining with other entities, Matter and Quantity, to form the complete Sensible Substance; this Substance, so called, may be supposed to be the resulting manifold, which is not so much an essence as a quale. Thus, for the essence of fire we must look to the Reason-Principle; the visible form which it produces is, properly speaking, a quale.

Man's essence will lie in his Reason-Principle; that which is completed in the corporeal nature is a mere image of the Reason-Principle, a quale rather than an essence.

Consider: the visible Socrates is a man, yet we give the name of Socrates to that likeness of him in a portrait, which consists of mere colours, mere pigments: similarly, it is a Reason-Principle which constitutes Socrates, but we apply the name Socrates to the Socrates we see: in truth, however, the colours and shapes which make up the visible Socrates are but reproductions of those in the Reason-Principle, while this Reason-Principle itself bears a corresponding relation to the truest Reason-Principle of Man. But we need not elaborate this point.

16. When each of the entities bound up with the pseudo-substance is taken apart from the rest, the name of Quality is given to that one among them, by which without pointing to essence or quantity or motion we signify the distinctive mark, the type or aspect of a thing—for example, the beauty or ugliness of a body. This beauty—need we say?—is identical in name only with Intellectual Beauty: it follows that the term 'Quality' as applied to the Sensible and the Intellectual is necessarily equivocal; even blackness and whiteness are different in the two spheres.

But the beauty in the germ, in the particular Reason-Principle—is this the same as the manifested beauty, or do they coincide only in name? Are we to assign this beauty—and the same question applies to deformity affecting the

Soul—to the Intellectual order, or to the Sensible?—That beauty is different in the two spheres is by now clear.—If it be embraced in Sensible Quality, then virtue must also be classed among the qualities of the lower. But surely some virtues will take rank as Sensible, others as Intellectual, qualities.

It may also be doubted whether the arts, as Reason-Principles, can fairly be classed among Sensible qualities; they are, it is true, Reason-Principles residing in Matter, but 'matter' for them means Soul. On the other hand, their being found even in company with Matter commits them in some degree to the lower sphere. Take the case of lyrical music: it is performed upon strings; melody, which may be termed a part of the art, is sensuous sound—though, perhaps, we should speak here not of parts but of manifestations (Acts): yet, called manifestations, they are none the less sensuous. The beauty inherent in body is similarly bodiless; but it is subject to sense-perception and we have therefore assigned it to the order of things bound up with body and subordinate to it.

Geometry and arithmetic are, we shall maintain, of a twofold character: in their earthly types they rank with Sensible Quality, but in so far as they are functions of pure Soul, they necessarily belong to that other world in close proximity to the Intellectual. This, too, is in Plato's view the case with music and astronomy.

The arts concerned with material objects and making use of perceptible instruments and sense-perception must be classed with Sensible Quality, even though they are dispositions of the Soul, since they are attendant upon the Soul's apostasy.

There is also every reason for consigning to this category the practical virtues whose function is directed to a social end: these do not release Soul by inclining it towards the higher; their manifestation makes for beauty in this world, a beauty regarded not as necessary but as desirable.

On this principle, the beauty in the germ, and still more the blackness and whiteness in it, will be included among Sensible Qualities.

Are we, then, to rank the individual Soul, as containing these Reason-Principles, with Sensible Substance? But we do not even identify the Principles (much less Soul) with body; we merely include them in Sensible Quality on the ground that they are connected with body and are activities of body. The constituents of Sensible Substance have already been specified; we have no intention whatever of adding to them Substance incorporeal.

As for Qualities, we hold that they are invariably incorporeal, but we have included them in the lower realm, since they are sense-orientated properties or else Reason-Principles of the individual Soul: the affections, torn between two worlds by their objects (sensible things) and their abode (the soul), we have assigned to Quality, which is indeed not bodily but manifested in body.

But we refrain from assigning Soul to Sensible Substance, on the ground that we have already referred to (Sensible) Quality those affections of Soul which are related to body. On the contrary, Soul, conceived apart from affection and Reason-Principle, we have restored to its origin, leaving in the lower realm no substance which is in any sense Intellectual.

17. This procedure, if approved, will entail a distinction between psychic and bodily qualities, the latter belonging specifically to body.

If we decide to refer all psychic qualities to the higher, we are still at liberty to perform for Sensible qualities a division founded upon the senses themselves—the eyes, the ears, touch, taste, smell; and if we are to look for further differences, colours may be subdivided according to varieties of vision, sounds according to varieties of hearing, and so with the other senses: sounds may also be classified qualitatively as sweet, harsh, soft.

Here a difficulty may be raised: we distinguish the varieties of Substance and their functions and activities, fair or foul or indeed of any kind whatsoever, on the basis of Quality, Quantity rarely, if ever, entering into the differences which produce species; Quantity, again, we divide in accordance with qualities of its own: how then are we to divide Quality itself into species? what differences are we to employ, and from what genus shall we take them? To take them from Quality itself would be no less absurd than setting up substances as differences of Substance.

How, then, are we to distinguish black from white? how differentiate colours in general from tastes and tangible qualities? By the variety of sense-organs? Then there will be no difference in the objects themselves.

But (waiving this objection) how deal with qualities perceived by the same sense-organ? We may be told that some colours integrate, others disintegrate the vision, that some tastes integrate, others disintegrate the tongue: we reply that, first, it is the actual experiences (of colour and taste, and not the sense-organs) that we are discussing and it is to these that the notions of integration and disintegration must be applied; secondly, a means of differentiating these experiences has not been offered.

It may be suggested that we divide them by their powers (or effects), and this suggestion is so far reasonable that we may well agree to divide the non-sensuous qualities, the sciences for example, on this basis; but we see no reason for resorting to their effects for the division of qualities sensuous. Even if we divide the sciences by their powers, founding our division of their processes upon the faculties of the mind, we can only grasp their differences in a rational manner if we look not only to their subject-matter but also to their Reason-Principles.

But, granted that we may divide the arts by their Reason-Principles and their theoretical content, this method will hardly apply to embodied qualities. Even in the arts themselves an explanation would be required for the differences between the Reason-Principles themselves. Besides, we have no difficulty in seeing that white differs from black; to account for this difference is the purpose of our inquiry.

18. These problems at any rate all serve to show that, while in general it is necessary to look for differences by which to separate things from each other, to hunt for differences of the differences themselves is both futile and irrational. We cannot have substances of substances, quantities of quantities, qualities of qualities, differences of differences; differences must, where possible, be found outside the genus, in creative powers and the like: but where no such criteria are present, as in distinguishing dark green from pale green, both being regarded as derived from white and black, what expedient may be suggested.

Sense-perception and intelligence may be trusted to indicate diversity but not to explain it: explanation is outside the province of sense-perception, whose function is merely to produce a variety of information; while, as for intelligence, it works exclusively with its own intuitions and never resorts to explanations to justify them in detail; there is in the movements of intelligence a diversity which separates one object from another, making further differentiation unnecessary.

Do all qualities constitute differentiae, or not? Granted that whiteness and colours in general and the qualities dependent upon touch and taste can, even while they remain species (of Quality), become differentiae of other things, how can grammar and music serve as differentiae? Perhaps in the sense that minds may be distinguished as grammatical and musical, especially if the qualities are innate, in which case they do become specific differentiae.

It remains to decide whether there can be any differentia derived from the genus to which the differentiated thing belongs, or whether it must of necessity belong to another genus. The former alternative would produce differentiae of things derived from the same genus as the differentiae themselves—for example, qualities of qualities. Virtue and vice are two states differing in quality: the states are qualities, and their differentiae qualities—unless indeed it be maintained that the state undifferentiated is not a quality, that the differentia creates the quality.

But consider the sweet as beneficial, the bitter as injurious: then bitter and sweet are distinguished, not by Quality, but by Relation. We might also be disposed to identify the sweet with the thick, and the pungent with the thin: 'thick', however, hardly reveals the essence but merely the cause of sweetness—an argument which applies equally to pungency.

We must therefore reflect whether it may be taken as an invariable rule that

Quality is never a differentia of Quality, any more than Substance is a differentia of Substance, or Quantity of Quantity.

Surely, it may be interposed, five differs from three by two. No: it exceeds it by two; we do not say that it differs: how could it differ by a 'two' in the 'three'? We may add that neither can Motion differ from Motion by Motion. There is, in short, no parallel in any of the other genera.

In the case of virtue and vice, whole must be compared with whole, and then virtue and vice will themselves be the differentiae. As for the differentiae being derived from the same genus as themselves, namely, Quality, and from no other genus, if we proceed on the principle that virtue is bound up with pleasure, vice with lust, virtue again with the acquisition of food, vice with idle extravagance, and accept these definitions as satisfactory, then clearly we may have, here too, differentiae which are not qualities.

19. With Quality we ought—so it appeared—to group the dependent qualia, in so far as Quality is bound up with them; we shall not, however, introduce into this category the qualified objects (*qua* objects), that we may not be dealing with two categories at once; we shall pass over the objects to that which gives them their (specific) name.

But how are we to classify such terms as 'not white'? If 'not white' signifies some other colour, it is a quality. But if it is merely a negation, it will be either a meaningless sound, or else a name or a definition of something actual: if a sound, it is a kind of motion; if a name or definition, it is a relative, inasmuch as names and definitions are significant. But if we are not merely concerned with an enumeration of things by genus but must take account of terms and their meanings as determining the genus in each case, then we shall assert that positive terms by merely indicating things affirm their existence whereas negative terms deny it. Perhaps, however, it would be better not to include (in the generic classification) either affirmative or negative propositions in view of their composite nature.

What view, then, shall we take of privations? If they are privations of qualities, they will themselves be qualities: 'toothless' and 'blind', for example, are qualities. 'Naked' and 'clothed', on the other hand are neither of them qualities but states: they therefore comport a relation to something else.

(With regard to passive qualities:)

Passivity, while it lasts, is not a quality but a motion; when it is a past experience remaining in one's possession, it is a quality; if one ceases to possess the experience then regarded as a finished occurrence, one is considered to have been moved—in other words, to have been in Motion. (Such is the theory.) But in none of these cases is it necessary to conceive of anything but Motion; the idea of time should be excluded; even present time has no right to be introduced.

'Well' and similar adverbial expressions are to be referred to the single generic notion (of Quality).

It remains to consider whether Quality which includes 'rubicund' must exclude 'blushing' or 'flushed'. The fact of becoming flushed is rightly not referred to Quality; for it involves passivity—in short, Motion. But if one has ceased to become flushed and is actually red, this is surely a case of Quality, which is independent of time. How indeed are we to measure the time (at which a disposition passes into a state)? We must rely on the aspect which a substance presents: by predicating of a man redness, we clearly ascribe to him a quality. Otherwise we shall maintain that states alone, and not dispositions, constitute qualities: thus, 'hot' is different from 'growing hot', 'ill' from 'turning ill'.

20. We have to ascertain whether there is not to every quality a contrary. In the case of virtue and vice even the mean appears to be contrary to the extremes.

But when we turn to colours, we do not find the intermediates so related. If we regard the intermediates as blendings of the extremes, we must not posit any contrariety other than that between black and white, but must show that all other colours are combinations of these two. Contrariety, however, demands that there be some one distinct quality in the intermediates, though this quality may be seen to arise from a combination.

It may further be suggested that contraries not only differ from each other, but also entail the greatest possible difference. But 'the greatest possible difference' would seem to presuppose that intermediates have already been established: eliminate the series, and how will you define 'the greatest possible'? Sight, we may be told, will reveal to us that grey is nearer than black to white; and taste may be our judge when we have hot, cold, and an intermediate which is neither.

That we are accustomed to act upon these assumptions is obvious enough; but the following considerations may perhaps commend themselves:

White and yellow are entirely different from each other—a statement which applies to any colour whatsoever as compared with any other; they are accordingly contrary qualities. Their contrariety is independent of the presence of intermediates: between health and disease no intermediate intrudes, and yet they are contraries.

It may be urged that the products of a contrariety exhibit the greatest diversity. But 'the greatest diversity' is clearly meaningless, unless we can point to lower degrees of diversity in the means. Thus, we cannot speak of 'the greatest diversity' in reference to health and disease. This definition of contrariety is therefore inadmissible.

Suppose that we say 'great diversity' instead of 'the greatest': if 'great' is equivalent to greater and implies a less, immediate contraries will again escape us; if, on the other hand, we mean strictly 'great' and assume that every quality shows a great divergence from every other, we must not suppose that the divergence can be measured by a comparative.

None the less, we must endeavour to find a meaning for the term 'contrary'. Can we accept the principle that when things have a certain similarity which is not generic nor in any sense due to admixture, whether in a greater or a less degree, with other 'forms', they are not contraries; contraries being rather those things which have no specific (or formal) identity? It would be necessary to stipulate that they belong to the same genus, Quality. By this definition we should cover those immediate contraries which have nothing conducing to similarity, inasmuch as there are no intermediates looking both ways, as it were, and having a mutual similarity to each other; some contraries at least have no such intermediates.

If these observations be sound, colours which have a common ground will not be contraries. But there will be nothing to prevent, not indeed every colour from being contrary to every other, but any one colour from being contrary to any other; and similarly with tastes. This will serve as a statement of the problem.

As for Degree (subsisting in Quality), it was given as our opinion that it exists in the objects participating in Quality, though whether it enters into qualities as such—into health and justice—was left open to question. If health and justice do possess some range of diversity, we must allow that habits (as a subdivision of Quality) have this range (irrespective of their participants). In the Intellectual realm, however, each unity is the whole and does not admit of degree.

21. The claim of Motion to be established as a genus will depend upon three conditions: first, that it cannot rightly be referred to any other genus; second, that nothing higher than itself can be predicated of it in respect of its essence; third, that by assuming differences it will produce species.

To what genus, then, shall we refer it? Clearly it cannot be identified with either the Substance or the Quality of the things which possess it. It cannot, further, be consigned to Action, for Passivity also comprises a variety of motions; nor again to Passivity itself, because many motions are actions: on the contrary, actions and passions are to be referred to Motion.

Furthermore, it cannot lay claim to the category of Relation on the mere ground that it has an attributive and not a self-centred existence: on this ground Quality too would find itself in that same category; for Quality is an attribute and contained in an external: and the same is true of Quantity.

If we are agreed that Quality and Quantity, though attributive, are real entities, and on the basis of this reality distinguishable as Quality and Quantity respectively: then, on the same principle, since Motion, though an attribute, has a reality prior to its attribution, it is incumbent upon us to discover the intrinsic nature of this reality. We must never be content to regard as a relative something which exists prior to its attribution, but only that which is engendered by Relation and has no existence apart from the relation to which it owes its name: the double, strictly so called, takes birth and actuality in juxtaposition with (the single measure represented by) a yard's length, and, inconceivable before, by this very process of being juxtaposed with a correlative acquires the name and exhibits the fact of being double.

What, then, is that entity, called Motion, which, though attributive, has an independent reality, which makes its attribution possible—the entity corresponding to Quality, Quantity, and Substance?

But first, perhaps, we should make sure that there is nothing prior to Motion and predicated of it as its genus.

Change may be suggested as a prior. But, in the first place, either it is identical with Motion, or else, if change be claimed as a genus, it will stand distinct from the genera so far considered: secondly, Motion will evidently take rank as a species and have some other species opposed to it—becoming, say—which will be regarded as a change but not as a motion.

What, then, is the ground for denying that becoming is a motion? The fact, perhaps, that what comes to be does not yet exist, whereas Motion has no dealings with the non-existent. But, on that ground, becoming will not be a change either. If, however, it be alleged that becoming is merely a type of alteration or growth since it takes place when things alter and grow, the antecedents of becoming are being confused with becoming itself. Yet becoming, entailing as it does these antecedents, must necessarily be a distinct species; for the event and process of becoming cannot be identified with merely passive alteration, like turning hot or white: it is possible for the antecedents to take place without becoming as such being accomplished, except in so far as the actual alteration (implied in the antecedents) has 'come to be'; birth implies animal or vegetal life, and so a Form.

The contrary might be maintained: that change is more plausibly ranked as a species than is Motion, because change signifies merely the substitution of one thing for another, whereas Motion involves also the removal of a thing from the place to which it belongs, as is shown by locomotion. Even rejecting this distinction, we must accept as types of Motion knowledge and musical performance—in short, changes of condition: thus, alteration will come to be regarded as a species of Motion—namely, motion displacing.

22. But suppose that we identify alteration with Motion on the ground that

Motion itself results in difference: how then do we proceed to define Motion?

It may roughly be characterized as the passage from the potentiality to its realization. That is potential which can either pass into a Form—for example, the potential statue—or else pass into activity—such as the ability to walk: whenever progress is made towards the statue, this progress is Motion; and when the ability to walk is actualized in walking, this walking is itself Motion: dancing is, similarly, the motion produced by the potential dancer taking his steps.

In the one type of Motion a new and distinct Form comes into existence created by the motion; the other constitutes, as it were, the pure Form of the potentiality, and leaves nothing behind it when once the motion has ceased. Accordingly, the view would not be unreasonable which, taking some Forms to be active, others inactive, regarded Motion as a dynamic Form in opposition to the other Forms which are static, and further as the cause of whatever new Form ensues upon it. To proceed to identify this motion which we are now discussing (i.e., sensible motion) with the life of bodies would not be unwarrantable; we necessarily use the same term, though the meaning is different, for the motions of Intellect and Soul.

That Motion is a genus we may be all the more confident in virtue of the difficulty—the impossibility even—of confining it within a definition.

But how can it be a Form in cases where the motion leads to deterioration, or is purely passive? Motion, we may suggest, is like the heat of the sun causing some things to grow and withering others. In so far as Motion is a common property, it is identical in both conditions; its apparent difference is due to the objects moved.

Is, then, becoming ill identical with becoming well? As motions they are identical. In what respect, then, do they differ? In their subjects? or is there some other criterion?

This question may, however, be postponed until we come to consider alteration: at present we have to discover what is the constant element in every motion, for only on this basis can we establish the claim of Motion to be a genus.

Perhaps the one term covers many meanings; its claim to generic status would then correspond to that of Being.

As a solution of the problem we may suggest that motions conducing to the natural state or functioning in natural conditions should perhaps, as we have already asserted, be regarded as being in a sense Forms, while those whose direction is contrary to nature must be supposed to be assimilated to the results towards which they lead.

But what is the constant element in alteration, in growth and birth and their opposites, in local change? What is that which makes them all motions?

Surely it is the fact that in every case the object is never in the same state before and after the motion, that it cannot remain still and in complete inactivity but, so long as the motion is present, is continually urged to take a new condition, never acquiescing in Identity but always courting Difference; deprived of Difference, Motion perishes.

Thus, Difference may be predicated of Motion, not merely in the sense that it arises and persists in a difference of conditions, but in the sense of being itself perpetual difference. It follows that Time, as being created by Motion, also entails perpetual difference: Time is the measure of unceasing Motion, accompanying its course and, as it were, carried along its stream.

In short, the common basis of all Motion is the existence of a progression and an urge from potentiality and the potential to actuality and the actual: everything which has any kind of motion whatsoever derives this motion from a pre-existent potentiality within itself of activity or passivity.

23. The Motion which acts upon Sensible objects enters from without, and so shakes, drives, rouses, and thrusts its participants that they may neither rest nor preserve their identity—and all to the end that they may be caught into that restlessness, that flustering excitability which is but an image of Life.

We must avoid identifying Motion with the objects moved: by walking we do not mean the feet but the activity springing from a potentiality in the feet. Since the potentiality is invisible, we see of necessity only the active feet—that is to say, not feet simply, as would be the case if they were at rest, but something besides feet, something invisible but indirectly seen as an accompaniment by the fact that we observe the feet to be in ever-changing positions and no longer at rest. We infer alteration, on the other hand, from the qualitative change in the thing altered.

Where, then, does Motion reside, when it moves an object, also when it passes from an inherent potentiality to actuality? In the mover? How then will the moved, the patient, participate in the motion? In the moved? Then why does not Motion remain in it, once having come? It would seem that Motion must be neither separated from the active principle nor allowed to reside in it; it must proceed from agent to patient without so inhering in the latter as to be severed from the former, passing from one to the other like a breath of wind.

Now, when the potentiality of Motion consists in an ability to walk, it may be imagined as thrusting a man forward and causing him to be continually adopting a different position; when it lies in the capacity to heat, it heats; when the potentiality takes hold of Matter and builds up the organism, we have growth; and when another potentiality demolishes the structure, the result is decay, that which has the potentiality of demolition experiencing the decay.

Where the birth-giving principle is active, we find birth; where it is impotent and the power to destroy prevails, destruction takes place—not the destruction of what already exists, but that which intervenes upon the road to existence.

Health comes about in the same way—when the power which produces health is active and predominant; sickness is the result of the opposite power working in the opposite direction.

Thus Motion is conditioned, not only by the objects in which it occurs, but also by its origins and its course, and it is a distinctive mark of Motion to be always qualified and to take its quality from circumstances.

24. With regard to locomotion: if ascending is to be held contrary to descending, and circular motion different (in kind) from motion in a straight line, we may ask how this difference is to be defined—the difference, for example, between throwing over the head and under the feet.

The driving power is one—though indeed it might be maintained that the upward drive is different from the downward, and the downward passage of a different character from the upward, especially if it be a natural motion, in which case the up-motion constitutes lightness, the down-motion heaviness.

But in all these motions alike there is the common tendency to seek an appointed place, with the result that in locomotion variety seems to depend upon externals.

As for motion in a circle and motion in a straight line, if the former is in practice indistinguishable from the latter, how can we regard them as different? The only difference lies in the shape of the course, unless the view be taken that circular motion is 'impure', as not being entirely a motion, not involving a complete surrender of identity.

However, it appears in general that locomotion is a definite unity, taking its differences from externals.

25. The nature of integration and disintegration calls for scrutiny. Are they different from the motions above mentioned, from coming-to-be and passing-away, from growth and decay, from change of place, and from alteration? or must they be referred to these? or, again, must some of these be regarded as types of integration and disintegration?

If integration implies that one element proceeds towards another, implies in short an approach, and disintegration, on the other hand, a retreat into the background, such motions may be termed local; we have clearly a case of two things moving in the direction of unity, or else making away from each other.

If, however, the things achieve a sort of fusion, mixture, blending, and if a new unity comes into being, not when the process of combination is already complete, but in the very act of combining, to which of our specified motions shall we refer this type? There will certainly be locomotion at first, but it will be succeeded by something different; just as in growth locomotion is found at the outset, though later it is supplanted by quantitative motion. The present case is similar: locomotion leads the way, but integration or disintegration does not inevitably follow; integration takes place only when the impinging elements become intertwined, disintegration only when they are rent asunder by the contact.

On the other hand, it often happens that locomotion follows disintegration, or else occurs simultaneously, though the experience of the disintegrated is not conceived in terms of locomotion: so too in integration a distinct experience, a distinct unification, accompanies the locomotion and remains separate from it.

Are we then to posit a new species for these two motions, adding to them, perhaps, alteration? A thing is altered by becoming dense—in other words, by integration; it is altered again by being rarefied—that is, by disintegration. When wine and water are mixed, something is produced different from either of the pre-existing elements: thus, integration takes place, resulting in alteration.

But perhaps we should recall a previous distinction, and while holding that integrations and disintegrations precede alterations, should maintain that alterations are none the less distinct from either; that, further, not every alteration is of this type (presupposing, that is to say, integration or disintegration), and, in particular, rarefaction and condensation are not identical with disintegration and integration, nor in any sense derived from them: to suppose that they were would involve the admission of a vacuum.

Again, can we use integration and disintegration to explain blackness and whiteness? But to doubt the independent existence of these qualities means that, beginning with colours, we may end by annihilating almost all qualities, or rather all without exception; for if we identify every alteration, or qualitative change, with integration and disintegration, we allow nothing whatever to come into existence; the same elements persist, nearer or farther apart.

Finally, how is it possible to class learning and being taught as integrations?

26. These problems call for scrutiny; but now we must return to the various specific types of Motion and inquire whether, to begin with, locomotion is not to be divided on the basis of direction, up, down, straight, circular—a question already raised; whether organic motion should be distinguished from inorganic—they are clearly not alike; whether, again, organic motions should be subdivided into walking, swimming, and flight.

Perhaps we should also distinguish in each species natural from unnatural motions: this distinction would, however, imply that motions have differences which are not external. It may indeed be the case that motions create these differences and cannot exist without them; but Nature may be supposed to be the ultimate source of these motions.

Motions may also be classed as natural, artificial, and purposive: 'natural' embracing growth and decay; 'artificial' architecture and shipbuilding; 'purposive' inquiry, learning, government, and, in general, all speech and action.

Again, with regard to growth, alteration, and becoming, the division may proceed from the natural and unnatural, or, speaking generally, from the characters of the moved objects.

27. What view are we to take of that which is opposed to Motion, whether it be Stability or Rest? Are we to consider it as a distinct genus, or to refer it to one of the genera already mentioned? We should, no doubt, be well advised to assign Stability to the Intellectual, and to look in the lower sphere for Rest alone.

First, then, we have to discover the precise nature of this Rest. If it presents itself as identical with Stability, we have no right to expect to find it in the sphere where nothing is stable and the apparently stable has merely a less strenuous motion.

Suppose the contrary: we decide that Rest is different from Stability, inasmuch as Stability belongs to the utterly immobile, Rest to the stationary which, though of a nature to move, does not move. Now, if Rest means coming to rest, it must be regarded as a motion which has not yet ceased but pauses; but if we suppose it to be incompatible with Motion, we have first to ask whether there is in the Sensible world anything without motion.

Yet nothing can experience every type of motion; certain motions must be ruled out in order that we may speak of the moving object as an object: may we not, then, say of that which has no locomotion and is at rest as far as pertains to that specific type of motion, simply that it does not move?

Rest, accordingly, is the negation of Motion: in other words, it has no generic status. It is in fact related only to one type of motion, namely, locomotion; it is therefore the negation of this motion that is meant.

But, it may be asked, why not regard Motion as the negation of Stability? We reply that Motion does not appear alone; it is accompanied by a force which actualizes its object, forcing it on, as it were, giving it a thousand forms and destroying them all: Rest, on the contrary, comports nothing but the object itself, and signifies merely that the object has no motion.

Why, then, did we not in discussing the Intellectual realm assert that Stability was the negation of Motion? Because it is not indeed possible to consider Stability as an annulling of Motion, for Stability does not exist when Motion ceases, but requires for its own existence the simultaneous existence of Motion; Stability in that realm does not arise from the fact that what is of a nature to move is not moving; what is There is stable because Stability has taken hold of it; in so far as it has Motion, it will never cease to move: thus, it is stationary under the influence of Stability, and moves under the influence of Motion. In the lower realm, too, a thing moves in virtue of Motion, but its Rest is caused by a deficiency; it has been deprived of its due motion.

What we have to observe is the essential character of this Sensible counterpart of Stability.

Consider sickness and health. A man is convalescent as he passes from sickness to health. What species of rest are we to oppose to this convalescence? If we oppose the condition from which he departs, that condition is sickness, not Stability; if that into which he passes, it is health, again not the same as Stability.

It may be declared that health or sickness is indeed some form of Stability: we are to suppose, then, that Stability is the genus of which health and sickness are species; which is absurd.

Stability may, again, be regarded as an attribute of health: according to this view health will be health before possessing Stability.

These questions may however be left to the judgement of the individual.

28. We have already indicated that Activity and Passivity are to be regarded as motions, and that it is possible to distinguish absolute motions, actions, passions.

As for the remaining so-called genera, we have shown that they are reducible to those which we have discussed.

With regard to the relative, we have maintained that Relation belongs to one object as compared with another, that the two objects enter into the relation simultaneously, and that Relation is found whenever a substance is in such a condition as to produce it; not that the substance in itself is a relative, except in so far as it constitutes part of a whole—a hand, for example, or head or cause or principle or element.

We may also adopt the ancient division of relatives into creative principles, measures, excesses and deficiencies, and those which in general separate objects on the basis of similarities and differences.

Our investigation into the kinds of Being is now complete.

FOURTH TRACTATE

On the Integral Omnipresence of the Authentic Existent (I)

1. How are we to explain the omnipresence of the Soul? Does it depend upon the definite magnitude of the material universe coupled with some native tendency in Soul to distribute itself over material mass, or is it a characteristic of Soul apart from body?

In the latter case, Soul will not appear just where body may bring it; body will meet Soul awaiting it everywhere; wheresoever body finds place, there Soul lay before ever body was; the entire material mass of the universe has been set into an existent Soul.

But if Soul spread thus wide before material extension existed, then as covering all space it would seem to be of itself a thing of magnitude, and in what mode could it exist in the All before the All was in being, before there was any All? And who can accept a Soul described as partless and massless and yet, for all that absence of extension, extending over a universe? We may perhaps be told that, though extended over the corporeal, it does not itself become so: but thus to give it magnitude as an accidental attribute leaves the problem still unsolved: precisely the same question must in all reason arise: How can the Soul take magnitude even in the mode of accident?

We cannot think of Soul being diffused as a quality is, say sweetness or colour, for while these are actual states of the masses affected so that they show that quality at every point, none of them has an independent existence; they are attributes of body and known only as in body; such quality is necessarily of a definite extension. Further, the colour at any point is independent of that at any other; no doubt the Form, White, is the same all over, but there is not arithmetical identity; in Soul there is; it is one Soul in foot and in hand, as the facts of perception show. To speak generally, in the case of qualities the one is observably distributed part for part; in the Soul the identity is undistributed; what we sometimes call distribution is simply omnipresence.

Obviously, we must take hold of the question from the very beginning in the hope of finding some clear and convincing theory as to how Soul, immaterial and without magnitude, can be thus broad-spread, whether before material masses exist or as enveloping them. Of course, should it appear that this omnipresence may occur apart from material things, there is no difficulty in accepting its occurrence within the material.

2. Side by side exist the Authentic All and its counterpart, the visible universe. The Authentic is contained in nothing, since nothing existed before it; of necessity anything coming after it must, as a first condition of existence, be contained by this All, especially since it depends upon the Authentic and without that could have neither stability nor movement.

We may be reminded that the universe cannot be contained in the Authentic as in a place, where place would mean the boundaries of some surrounding extension considered as an envelope, or some space formerly a part of the Void and still remaining unoccupied even after the emergence of the universe, that it can only support itself, as it were, upon the Authentic and rest in the embrace of its omnipresence; but this objection is merely verbal and will disappear if our meaning is grasped; we mention it for another purpose; it goes to enforce our real assertion, that the Authentic All, at once primal and veritable, needs no place and is in no way contained. The All, as being an integral, cannot fall short of itself; it must ever have fulfilled its own totality, ever reached to its own equivalence; as far as the sum of entities extends, there this is; for this is the All.

Inevitably, also, anything other than this All that may be stationed therein must have part in the All, merge into it, and hold by its strength; it is not that the thing detaches a portion of the All but that within itself it finds the All which has entered into it while still unbrokenly self-abiding, since Being cannot lodge in non-Being, but, if anything, non-Being within Being.

Being, then, is present to all Being; an identity cannot tear itself asunder; the omnipresence asserted of it must be presence within the realm of Being; that is, it must be a self-presence. And it is in no way strange that the omnipresence should be at once self-abiding and universal; this is merely saying omnipresence within a unity.

It is our way to limit Being to the sense-known and therefore to think of omnipresence in terms of the concrete; in our overestimate of the sensible, we question how that other Nature can reach over such vastness; but our great is small, and this, small to us, is great; it reaches integrally to every point of our universe—or, better, our universe, moving from every side and in all its members towards this, meets it everywhere as the omnipresent All ever stretching beyond.

The universe in all its reach can attain nothing further—that would mean overpassing the total of Being—and therefore is content to circle about it; not able to encompass or even to fill the All, it is content to accept place and subordination, for thus it preserves itself in neighbouring the higher present to it— present and yet absent; self-holding, whatever may seek its presence.

Wherever the body of the universe may touch, there it finds this All; it strives for no further advance, willing to revolve in that one circle, since to it that is the All and in that movement its every part embraces the All.

If that higher were itself in place there would be the need of seeking that precise place by a certain right path; part of seeker must touch part of sought, and there would be far and near. But since there is no far and near there must be, if presence at all, presence entire. And presence there indubitably is; this highest is present to every being of those that, free of far and near, are of power to receive.

3. But are we to think of this Authentic Being as, itself, present, or does it remain detached, omnipresent in the sense only that powers from it enter everywhere?

Under the theory of presence by powers, souls are described as rays; the source remains self-locked and these are flung forth to impinge upon particular living things.

Now, in beings whose unity does not reproduce the entire nature of that principle, any presence is presence of an emanant power: even this, however, does not mean that the principle is less than integrally present; it is not sundered from the power which it has uttered; all is offered, but the recipient is able to take only so much. But in Beings in which the plenitude of these powers is manifested, there clearly the Authentic itself is present, though still as remaining distinct; it is distinct in that, becoming the informing principle of some definite thing, it would abdicate from its standing as the total and from its uttermost self-abiding and would belong, in some mode of accident, to an- other thing as well. Still it is not the property of what may seek to join with it; it chooses where it will and enters as the participant's power may allow, but it does not become a chattel; it remains the quested and so in another sense never passes over. There is nothing disquieting in omnipresence after this mode where there is no appropriation: in the same accidental way, we may reasonably put it, Soul concurs with body, but it is Soul self-holding, not inbound with Matter, free even of the body which it has illuminated through and through.

Nor does the placelessness of Being make it surprising that it be present universally to things of place; on the contrary, the wonder would be—the more than wonder, the impossibility—if from a place of its own it were present to other things in their place, or if having place it were present at all—and, especially present, as we assert, integrally.

But set it outside of place, and reason tells us that it will be present entire where it is present at all and that, present to the total, it must be present in the same completeness to every several unity; otherwise something of it is here and something there and at once it is fragmentary, it is body.

How can we so dispart Being? We cannot break Life into parts; if the total was Life, the fragment is not. But do we not thus sunder Intelligence, one intelligence in this man, another in that? No; such a fragment would not be Intelligence. But the Being of the individual? Once more, if the total thing is Being, then a fragment could not be. Are we told that in a body, a total of parts, every member is also a body? But here we are dividing not body but a particular quantity of body, each of those divisions being described as body in virtue of possessing the Form or Idea that constitutes body; and this Idea has no magnitude, is incapable of magnitude.

4. But how explain beings by the side of Being, and the variety of intelligences and of souls, when Being has the unity of omnipresent identity and not merely that of a species, and when intellect and Soul are likewise numerically one? We certainly distinguish between the Soul of the All and the particular souls.

This seems to conflict with our view which, moreover, for all its logical necessity, scarcely carries conviction against our mental reluctance to the notion of unity identically omnipresent. It would appear more plausible to suppose a partition of the All—the original remaining undiminished—or, in a more legitimate phrase, an engendering from the All.

Thus the Authentic would be left self-gathered, while what we think of as the parts—the separate souls—would come into being to produce the multiple total of the universe.

But if the Authentic Being is to be kept unattached in order to remove the difficulty of integral omnipresence, the same considerations must apply equally to the souls; we would have to admit that they cannot be integrally omnipresent in the bodies they are described as occupying; either, Soul must be distributed, part to body's part, or it is lodged entire at some one point in the body giving forth some of its powers to the other points; and these very powers, again, present the same difficulty.

A further objection is that some one spot in the body will hold the Soul, the others no more than a power from it.

Still, how account for the many souls, many intelligences, the beings by the side of Being?

No doubt the beings proceed from the Priors in the mode only of numerical distinction and not as concrete masses, but the difficulty remains as to how they come to constitute the plenitude of the material universe.

This explanation by progression does not clear the problem.

We are agreed that diversity within the Authentic depends not upon spatial separation but sheerly upon differentiation; all Being, despite this plurality, is a unity still; 'Being neighbours Being'; 'all holds together'; and thus the Intellectual-Principle (which is Being and the Beings) remains an integral, multiple by differentiation, not by spatial distinction.

Soul too? Souls too. That principle distributed over material masses we hold to be in its own nature incapable of distribution; the magnitude belongs to the masses; when this soul-principle enters into them—or rather they into it—it is thought of as distributable only because, within the discrimination of the corporeal, the animating force is to be recognized at any and every point. For Soul is not articulated, section of Soul to section of body, there is integral omnipresence manifesting the unity of that principle, its veritable partlessness.

Now as in Soul unity does not debar variety, so with Being and the Beings; in that order multiplicity does not conflict with unity. Multiplicity. This is not due to the need of flooding the universe with life; nor is the extension of the corporeal the cause of the multiplicity of souls; before body existed, Soul was one and many; the many souls fore-existed in the All not potentially but each effectively; that one collective Soul is no bar to the variety; the variety does not abrogate the unity; the souls are apart without partition, present each to all as never having been set in opposition; they are no more hedged off by boundaries than are the multiple items of knowledge in one mind; the one Soul so exists as to include all souls; the nature of such a principle must be utterly free of boundary.

5. Herein lies its greatness, not in mass; mass is limited and may be whittled down to nothingness; in that order no such paring off is possible—nor, if it were, could there be any falling short. Where limitation is unthinkable, what fear can there be of absence at any point? Nowhere can that principle fail which is the unfailing, the everlasting, the undwindling; suppose it in flux and it must at some time flow to its end; since it is not in flux—and, besides, (as the All) it has nowhere to flow to—it lies spread over the universe; in fact it is the universe, too great to be held by body, giving, therefore, to the material universe but little of itself, the little which that participant can take.

We may not make this principle the lesser, or if in the sense of mass we do, we must not begin to mistrust the power of that less to stretch to the greater. Of course, we have in fact no right to affirm it less or to measure the thing of magnitude against that which has none; as well talk of a doctor's skill being smaller than his body. This greatness is not to be thought of in terms of quantity; the greater and less of body have nothing to do with Soul.

The nature of the greatness of Soul is indicated by the fact that as the body grows, the larger mass is held by the same Soul that sufficed to the smaller; it would be in many ways absurd to suppose a corresponding enlargement in the Soul.

6. But why does not one same soul enter more than one body?

Because any second body must approach, if it might; but the first has approached and received and keeps.

Are we to think that this second body, in keeping its soul with a like care, is keeping the same soul as the first?

Why not: what difference is there? Merely some additions (from the experiences of life, none in the Soul itself).

We ask further why one soul in foot and hand and not one soul in the distinct members of the universe.

Sensations no doubt differ from soul to soul but only as do the conditions and experiences; this is difference not in the judging principle but in the matters coming to judgement; the judge is one and the same soul pronouncing upon various events, and these not its own but belonging to a particular body; it is only as a man pronounces simultaneously upon a pleasant sensation in his finger and a pain in his head.

But why is not the soul in one man aware, then, of the judgement passed by another?

Because it is a judgement made, not a state set up; besides, the soul that has passed the judgement does not pronounce but simply judges: similarly a man's sight does not report to his hearing, though both have passed judgement; it is the reason above both that reports, and this is a principle distinct from either. Often, as it happens, reason does become aware of a verdict formed in another reason and takes to itself an alien experience: but this has been dealt with elsewhere.

7. Let us consider once more how it is possible for an identity to extend over a universe. This comes to the question how each variously placed entity in the multiplicity of the sense order can have its share in one identical Principle.

The solution is in the reasons given for refusing to distribute that principle; we are not to parcel it out among the entities of the multiple; on the contrary, we bring the distributed multiples to the unity. The unity has not gone forth to them: from their dispersion we are led to think of it as broken up to meet them, but this is to distribute the controller and container equally over the material handled.

A hand may very well control an entire mass, a long plank, or anything of that sort; the control is effective throughout and yet is not distributed, unit for unit, over the object of control: the power is felt to reach over the whole area, though the hand is only hand-long, not taking the extension of the mass it wields; lengthen the object and, provided that the total is within the strength, the power handles the new load with no need of distributing itself over the increased area. Now let us eliminate the corporeal mass of the hand, retaining the power it exerted: is not that power, the impartible, present integrally over the entire area of control?

Or imagine a small luminous mass serving as centre to a transparent sphere, so that the light from within shows upon the entire outer surface, otherwise unlit: we surely agree that the inner core of light, intact and immobile, reaches over the entire outer extension; the single light of that small centre illuminates the whole field. The diffused light is not due to any bodily magnitude of that central point which illuminates not as body but as body lit, that is by another kind of power than corporeal quality: let us then abstract the corporeal mass, retaining the light as power: we can no longer speak of the light in any particular spot; it is equally diffused within and throughout the entire sphere. We can no longer even name the spot it occupied so as to say whence it came or how it is present; we can but seek, and wonder as the search shows us the light simultaneously present at each and every point in the sphere. So with the sunlight: looking to the corporeal mass you are able to name the source of the light shining through all the air, but what you see is one identical light in integral omnipresence. Consider too the effect of bodies which intercept the sun's light (as in an eclipse): without letting the light pass through them to the side opposite to its source, they yet do not divide it. And supposing, as before, that the sun were simply an unembodied illuminant, the light would no longer be fixed to any one definite spot: having no starting-point, no centre of origin, it would be an integral unity omnipresent.

8. The light of our world can be allocated because it springs from a corporeal mass of known position, but conceive an immaterial entity, independent of body as being of earlier nature than all body, a nature firmly self-based or, better, without need of base: such a principle, incorporeal, autonomous, having no source for its rising, coming from no place, attached to no material mass, this cannot be allotted part here and part there: that would be to give it both a previous position and a present attachment. Finally, anything participating in such a principle can participate only as entirety with entirety; the principle is unaffected, undivided.

A principle attached to body might be exposed, at least by way of accident, to such partition and so be definable as passive and partible in view of its close relationship with the body of which it is so to speak a state or a Form; but that which is not inbound with body, which on the contrary body must seek, will of necessity go utterly free of every bodily modification and especially of the very possibility of partition which is entirely a phenomenon of body, belonging to its very essence. As partibility goes with body, so impartibility with the bodiless: what partition is possible where there is no magnitude? If a thing of magnitude participates to any degree in what has no magnitude, it must be by a participation without division; divisibility implies magnitude.

When we affirm unity in multiplicity we do not mean that the unity has become the multiples; we link the variety in the multiples with the unity which we discern, undivided, in them; and the unity must be understood as for ever distinct from them, from separate item and from total; that unity remains true to itself, remains itself, and so long as it remains itself cannot fail within its own scope (and therefore does reach over the multiple), yet it is not to be thought of as co-extensive with the material universe or with any member of the All; utterly outside of the quantitative, it cannot be coextensive with anything.

Extension is of body; what is not of body, but of the opposed order, must be kept free of extension; but where there is no extension there is no spatial distinction, nothing of the here and there which would end its freedom of presence. Since, then, partition goes with place—each part occupying a place of its own—how can the placeless be parted? The unity must remain self-concentrated, immune from part, however much the multiple aspire or attain to contact with it. This means that any movement towards it is movement towards its entirety, and any participation attained is participation in its entirety. Its participants, then, link with it as with something unparticipated, something never appropriated: thus only can it remain intact within itself and within the multiples in which it is manifested. And if it did not remain thus intact, it would cease to be itself; any participation, then, would not be in the object of quest but in something never quested.

9. If in such a partition of the unity, that which entered into each participant were an entire—always identical with the first—then, in the progressive severance, the firsts would become numerous, each particular becoming a first: and then what prevents these many firsts from reconstituting the collective unity? Certainly not the bodies they have entered, for those firsts cannot be present in the material masses as their Forms if they are to remain identical with the First from which they come. On the other hand, taking the part conceived as present in the multiple to be simply a power (emanating from the First), at once such a part ceases to be the unity; we have then to ask how these powers come to be cut off, to have abandoned their origin; they certainly have not moved away with no purpose in their movement.

Again, are those powers, entering the universe of sense, still within the First or not?

If they are not, we have the absurdity that the First has been lessened, disempowered, stripped of power originally possessed. Besides, how could powers thus cut off subsist apart from the foundations of their being? Suppose these powers to be at once within the First and elsewhere; then the universe of sense contains either the entire powers or parts of them; if parts of powers, the other parts are There; if entires, then either the powers There are present here also undivided—and this brings us back to an identity omnipresent in integral identity—or they are each an entire which has taken division into a multiplicity of similars so that attached to every essence there is one power only—that particularly appropriated to it—the other powers remaining powers unattached: yet power apart from Being is as impossible as Being apart from power; for There power is Being or something greater than Being.

Or, again, suppose the powers coming Thence are other than their source—lesser, fainter, as a bright light dwindles to a dim—but each attached to its essence as a power must always be: such secondary powers would be perfectly uniform and at once we are forced to admit the omnipresence of the one same power or at the least the presence—as in one and the same body—of some undivided identity integral at every point.

And if this is the case with a particular body, why not with the entire universe?

If we think of the single power as being endlessly divided, it is no longer a power entire; partition means lessening of power; and, with part of power for part of body, the conditions of consciousness cease.

Further, a vestigial cut off from its source disappears—for example, a reflected light—and in general an emanant ceases to exist once it is severed from the original which it reproduces: just so the powers derived from that source must vanish if they do not remain attached to it.

This being so, where these powers appear, their source must be present with them; thus, once more, that source must itself be omnipresent as an undivided whole.

10. We may be told that an image need not be thus closely attached to its archetype, that we know images holding in the absence of their archetype and that a warmed object may retain its heat when the fire is withdrawn.

To begin with the image and archetype: if we are reminded of an artist's picture we observe that here the image was produced by the artist, not by his subject; even in the case of a self-portrait, the picture is no 'image of archetype', since it is not produced by the painter's body, the original represented: the reproduction is due to the effective laying on of the colours.

Nor is there strictly any such making of image as we see in water or in mirrors or in a shadow; in these cases the original is the cause of the image which, at once, springs from it and cannot exist apart from it. Now, it is in this sense that we are to understand the weaker powers to be images of the Priors. As for the illustration from the fire and the warmed object, the warmth cannot be called an image of the fire unless we think of warmth as containing fire so that the two are separate things. Besides, the fire removed, the warmth does sooner or later disappear, leaving the object cold.

If we are told that these powers fade out similarly, we are left with only one imperishable: the souls, the Intellectual-Principle, become perishable; I then while Being (identical with the Intellectual-Principle) is changeless, the Beings, its productions, become transitory.[1] Yet the I sun, so long as it holds its station in the universe, will pour the same light upon the same places; to think its light may be lessened is to hold its mass perishable. But it has been abundantly stated that the emanants of the First are not perishable, that the souls, and the Intellectual-Principle with all its content, cannot perish.

11. Still, this integral omnipresence admitted, why do not all things participate in the Intellectual Order in its entirety? Why has it a first participant, a second, and so on?

We can but see that presence is determined by the fitness of the participant so that, while Being is omnipresent to the realm of Being, never falling short of itself, yet only the competent possess themselves of that presence which depends not upon situation but upon adequacy; the transparent object and the opaque answer very differently to the light. These firsts, seconds, thirds, of participance are determined by rank, by power, not by place but by differentiation; and difference is no bar to coexistence, witness soul and Intellectual-Principle: similarly our own knowledge, the trivial next the gravest; one and the same object yields colour to our sight, fragrance to smell, to every sense a particular experience, all presented simultaneously.

But would not this indicate that the Authentic is diverse, multiple?

That diversity is simplex still; that multiple is one; for it is a Reason-Principle, which is to say a unity in variety: all Being is one; the differing being is still included in Being; the differentiation is within Being, obviously not within non-Being. Being is bound up with the unity which is never apart from it; wheresoever Being appears, there appears its unity; and the unity of Being is self-standing, for presence in the sensible does not abrogate independence: things of sense are present to the Intellectual—where this occurs—otherwise than as the Intellectual is present within itself; so too body's presence to soul differs from that of knowledge to soul; two items of knowledge within the same mind are present to each other in a different manner again; a body's presence to body is, once more, another form of relation.

12. Think of a sound passing through the air and carrying a word; an ear within range catches and comprehends; and the sound and word will strike upon any

other ear you may imagine within the intervening void, upon any that attends; from a great distance many eyes look to the one object and all take it fully; all this, because eye and ear exist. In the same way what is apt for soul will possess itself of soul, while from the one identical presence ‖ another will draw, and then another.²‖

Now the sound was diffused throughout the air not in sections but as one sound, entire at every point of that space. So with sight: if the air carries a shape impressed upon it this is one undivided whole; for, wherever there be an eye, there the shape will be grasped; even to such as reject this particular theory of sight, the facts of vision still stand as an example of participation determined by an identical unity.

The sound is the clearer illustration: the form conveyed is an entirety over all the air space, for unless the spoken word were entire at every point, for every ear to catch the whole alike, the same effect could not be made upon every listener; the sound, evidently, is not strung along the air, section to section. Why, then, need we hesitate to think of Soul as a thing not extended in broken contact, part for part, but omnipresent within the range of its presence, indwelling in totality at every point throughout the All?

Entered into such bodies as are apt to it, the soul is like the spoken sound present in the air; before that entry, like the speaker about to speak—though even embodied it remains at once the speaker and the silent.

No doubt these illustrations are imperfect, but they carry a serviceable similitude: the soul belongs to that other Kind, and we must not conceive a part of it embodied and a part intact; it is at once a self-enclosed unity and a principle manifested in diversity.

Further, any newcoming entity achieving soul receives mysteriously that same principle which was equally in the previously ensouled; for it is not in the dispensation that a given part of soul situate at some given point should enter here and there; what is thought of as entering was always a self-enclosed entire and, for all the seeming entry, so remains: no real entry is conceivable. If, then, the soul never entered and yet is now seen to be present—present without waiting upon the participant—clearly it is present, here too, without breach of its self-inclusion. This can mean only that the participant came to soul; it lay outside the veritable reality but advanced towards it and so established itself in the cosmos of life. But this cosmos of life is a self-gathered entire, not divisible into constituent masses but prior to mass; whatever enters is not entering a mass; in other words, the participation is of entire in entire. Any newcomer into that cosmos of life will participate in it entire. Admitting, then, that this cosmos of life is present entire in the universe, it must be similarly entire in each several entity; an identity numerically one, it must be an undivided entire, omni-present.

13. But how account, at this, for its extension over all the heavens and all living beings?

There is no such extension. Sense-perception, by insistence upon which we doubt, tells of Here and There; but reason certifies that the Here and There do not attach to that principle; the extended has participated in that cosmos of life which itself has no extension.

Clearly no participant can participate in itself; self-participation would be merely identity. Body, then, as participant does not participate in body; body it has; its participation must be in what is not body. So too magnitude does not participate in magnitude; it has it: not even in addition of quantity does the initial magnitude participate in magnitude: the two cubits do not themselves become three cubits; what occurs is that an object totalling to a certain quantity now totals to another: for magnitude to participate in magnitude the actual two cubits must themselves become the new three (which cannot occur).

If, then, the divided and quantitatively extended is to participate in another kind, is to have any sort of participation, it can participate only in something undivided, unextended, wholly outside of quantity. Therefore, that which is to be introduced by the participation must enter as itself an omnipresent indivis-ible.

This indivisibility must, of course, not be taken in any sense of littleness: littleness would be still divisible, could not cover the extension of the partici-pant and could not maintain integral presence against that expansion. Nor is it the indivisibility of a geometric point: the participant mass is no single point but includes an infinity of points; so that on the theory this principle must be **I** an infinity of points, not a continuous whole,[3] **I** and so, again, will fail to cover the participant.

I If, then, the participant mass in its entirety is to contain that principle entire, it must hold it[4] present at its every point. **I**

14. **I** But, admitting an identical[5] soul at every point, **I** how is there a particular soul of the individual and how the good soul and the bad?

I The one principle[6] reaches **I** to the individual but none the less contains all souls and all intelligences; this, because it is at once a unity and an infinity; it holds all its content as one yet with each item distinct, though not to the point of separation. Except by thus holding all its content as one—life entire, soul entire, all intelligence—it could not be infinite; since the individualities are not fenced off from each other, it remains still one thing. It was to hold life not single but infinite and yet one life, one in the sense not of an aggregate built up but of the retention of the unity in which all rose. Strictly, of course, it is a matter not of the rising of the individuals but of their being eternally what they are; in that order, as there is no beginning, so there is no apportioning except as an interpretation by the recipient. What is of that realm is the ancient and primal; the relation to it of the thing of process must be that of approach and apparent merging with always dependence.

But we ourselves, what are We?

Are we that higher or the participant newcomer, the thing of beginnings in time?

Before we had our becoming Here we existed There, men other than now, some of us gods: we were pure souls, Intelligence inbound with the entire of reality, members of the Intellectual, not fenced off, not cut away, integral to that All. Even now, it is true, we are not put apart; but upon that primal Man there has intruded another, a man seeking to come into being and finding us there, for we were not outside of the universe. This other has wound himself about us, foisting himself upon the Man that each of us was at first. Then it was as if one voice sounded, one word was uttered, and from every side an ear attended and received and there was an effective hearing, possessed through and through of what was present and active upon it: now we have lost that first simplicity; we are become the dual thing, sometimes indeed no more than that later foisting, with the primal nature dormant and in a sense no longer present.

15. But how did this intruder find entrance?

It had a certain aptitude and it grasped at that to which it was apt. In its nature it was capable of soul: but what is unfitted to receive soul entire—present entire but not for it—takes what share it may; such are the members of the animal and vegetal order. Similarly, of a significant sound some forms of being take sound and significance together, others only the sound, the blank impact.

A living thing comes into existence containing soul, present to it from the Authentic, and by soul is inbound with Reality entire; it possesses also a body; but this body is not a husk having no part in soul, not a thing that earlier lay away in the soulless; the body had its aptitude and by this draws near: now it is not body merely, but living body. By this neighbouring it is enhanced with some impress of soul—not in the sense of a portion of soul entering into it, but that it is warmed and lit by soul entire: at once there is the ground of desire, pleasure, pain: the body of the living form that has come to be was certainly no unrelated thing.

The Soul sprung from the divine lay self-enclosed at peace, true to its own quality; but its neighbour, in uproar through weakness, instable of its own nature and beaten upon from without, I cries[7] upon the living total, I spreading the disorder at large. Thus, at an assembly the Elders may sit in tranquil meditation, but an unruly populace, crying for food and casting up a host of grievances, will bring the whole gathering into ugly turmoil; when this sort of people hold their peace so that a word from a man of sense may reach them, some passable order is restored and the baser part ceases to prevail; otherwise the silence of the better allows the rabble to rule, the distracted assembly unable to take the word from above.

This is the evil of state and of council: and this is the evil of man; man includes an inner rabble—pleasures, desires, fears—and these become masters when the man, the manifold, gives them play.

But one that has reduced his rabble and gone back to the Man he was, lives to that and is that Man again, so that what he allows to the body is allowed as to something separate.

There is the man, too, that lives partly in the one allegiance and partly in the other; he is a blend of the good that is himself with the evil that is alien.

16. But if that Principle can never fall to evil and we have given a true account of the Soul's entry or presence to body, what are we to say of the periodic Descents and Returns, the punishments, the banishment into animal forms? That teaching we have inherited from those ancient philosophers who have best probed into soul and we must try to show that our own doctrine is accordant with it, or at least not conflicting.

We have seen that the participation of things here in that higher means not that the soul has gone outside of itself to enter the corporeal, but that the corporeal has approached soul and is now participant in it; the coming affirmed by the ancients can be only that approach of the body to the higher by which it partakes of life and of soul; this has nothing to do with local entry but is some form of communion; by the 'descent' and 'embodiment' of current phrasing must be understood not that soul becomes an appanage of body but that it gives out to it something of itself; similarly, the soul's departure is the complete cessation of that communion.

The various rankings of the universe will determine various degrees of the communion; soul, ultimate of the Intellectual, will give forth freely to body as being more nearly of the one power and standing closer, as distance holds in that order.

The soul's evil will be this association, its good the release. Why? Because, even unmerged, a soul in any way to be described as attached to this universe is in some degree fallen from the All into a state of partition; essentially belonging to the All, it no longer directs its act Thither: thus, a man's knowledge is one whole, but he may guide himself by no more than some single item of it, where his good would lie in living not by some such fragment but by the total of his knowing.

That One Soul—member of the Intellectual cosmos and there merging what it has of partial into the total—has broken away, so to speak, from the All to the part and to that devotes itself, becoming partial with it; thus fire that might consume everything may be set to ply its all-power upon some trifle. So long as the soul remains utterly unattached it is soul not singled out; when it has accepted separation—not that of place but that of act determining individualities—it is a part, no longer the soul entire, or at least not entire in the first sense; when, on the contrary, it exercises no such outward control it is perfectly the All-Soul, the partial in it latent.

As for the entry into the World of the Shades, if this means into the unseen, that is its release; if into some lower place, there is nothing strange in that, since even here the soul is taken to be where the body is, in place with the body.

But on the dissolution of the body?

So long as the image-soul has not been discarded, clearly the higher will be where that is; if, on the contrary, the higher has been completely emancipated by philosophic discipline, the image-soul may very well go alone to that lower place, the authentic passing uncontaminated into the Intellectual, separated from that image but none the less the soul entire.

Let the image—offspring of the individuality—fare as it may, the true soul when it turns its light upon itself, chooses the higher and by that choice blends into the All, neither acting now nor extinct.

But it is time to return to our main theme:

NOTES TO ENNEAD VI.4

1. FIRST EDITION: ". . . then *since* Being (identical with the Intellectual-Principle) *becomes transitory, so also must* the Beings, its productions. Yet the . . ."

GUTHRIE: "Besides, it is not reasonable to admit that even the things that derive from a 'being' that wastes away also gradually exhaust themselves;"

ARMSTRONG gives the whole passage the following sense: "But if these people were going to quench these powers, first of all they will be affirming that only the One is indestructible, and will make the souls and Intellect destructible. And then they will make flow away the things which come from a substance which does not flow away."

2. FIRST EDITION: ". . . another will *derive something else.*"

ARMSTRONG supports the fourth edition. GUTHRIE has the whole thought as: "Thus the same object will impress different organs with different perceptions, because the one is an eye, and the other is an ear. Likewise, all the things that can participate in the soul do participate therein, but each receives a different power from one and the same principle."

3. FIRST EDITION: ". . . an infinity of points, not a *simultaneous entire* . . ."

ARMSTRONG: ". . . infinitely many points, and not continuous . . . "

GUTHRIE: ". . . what you might suppose was a point would include an infinity of (separate) points, and could not be continuous . . ."

4. FIRST EDITION: "If, then, the participant mass in its entirety is to contain that principle entire, *the universe* must hold *that one soul* present at its every point."

GUTHRIE: "If then every corporeal mass possess the (being) which is present everywhere, it must possess it entire in all the parts that compose it."

ARMSTRONG: "If then the whole bulk has it as a whole, it will have it in the whole of itself."

5. FIRST EDITION: "But, admitting *this one* soul at every point . . ."

GUTHRIE: "But if one and the single Soul be in each person . . ."

ARMSTRONG: "But if it is the same soul in each and every place . . ."

6. FIRST EDITION: "The one *soul* reaches . . ."

GUTHRIE: "The universal Soul communicates her life to each . . ."

ARMSTRONG: "Now, it is sufficient for each . . ."

7. FIRST EDITION: ". . . cries, *at first to itself and afterwards* upon the living total . . ."

GUTHRIE: ". . . first complained audibly by herself, and then in that part of the animal which is common to the soul and body . . ."

ARMSTRONG: ". . . first itself cried out to the community of the living thing . . ."

FIFTH TRACTATE

On the Integral Omnipresence of the Authentic Existent (II)

1. The integral omnipresence of a unity numerically identical is in fact universally received; for all men instinctively affirm the god in each of us to be one, the same in all. It would be taken as certain if no one asked how or sought to bring the conviction to the test of reasoning; with this effective in their thought, men would be at rest, finding their stay in that oneness and identity, so that nothing would wrench them from this unity. This principle, indeed, is the most solidly established of all, proclaimed by our very souls; we do not piece it up item by item, but find it within beforehand; it precedes even the principle by which we affirm unquestionably that all things seek their good; for this universal quest of good depends on the fact that all aim at unity and possess unity and that universally effort is towards unity.

Now this unity in going forth, so far as it may, towards the Other Order must become manifest as multiplicity and in some sense become multiple; but the primal nature and the appetition of the good, which is appetition of unity, lead back to what is authentically one; to this every form of Being is urged in a movement towards its own reality. For the good to every nature possessing unity is to be self-belonging, to be itself, and that means to be a unity.

In virtue of that unity the Good may be regarded as truly inherent. Hence the Good is not to be sought outside; it could not have fallen outside of what is; it cannot possibly be found in non-Being; within Being the Good must lie, since it is never a non-Being.

❚ If that Good has Being and is within the realm of Being, then it is present, self-contained, in everything: we, therefore, are not separated from Being; we are in it; nor is Being separated from us:[1] therefore all beings are one. ❚

2. Now the reasoning faculty which undertakes this problem is not a unity but a thing of parts; it brings the bodily nature into the inquiry, borrowing its principles from the corporeal: thus it thinks of the Essential Existence as corporeal and as a thing of parts; it baulks at the unity because it does not start from the appropriate principles. We, however, must be careful to ❚ bring the appropriately convincing principles to the discussion of the unity[2] of perfect Being: ❚ we must hold to the Intellectual principles which alone apply to the Intellectual Order and to Real Being.

On the one hand there is the unstable, exposed to all sorts of change, distributed in place, not so much Being as Becoming: on the other, there is that which exists eternally, not divided, subject to no change of state, neither coming into being nor falling from it, set in no region or place or support, emerging from nowhere, entering into nothing, fast within itself.

In dealing with that lower order we would reason from its own nature and the characteristics it exhibits; thus, on a plausible foundation, we achieve plausible results by a plausible system of deduction: similarly, in dealing with the Intellectual, the only way is to grasp the nature of the essence concerned and so lay the sure foundations of the argument, not forgetfully straying over into that other order but basing our treatment on what is essential to the Nature with which we deal.

In every entity the essential nature is the governing principle and, as we are told, a sound definition brings to light many even of the concomitants: where the essential nature is the entire being, we must be all the more careful to keep to that, to look to that, to refer all to that.

3. If this principle is the Authentic Existent and holds unchanging identity, does not go forth from itself, is untouched by any process of becoming or, as we

have said, by any situation in place, then it must be always self-gathered, never in separation, not partly here and partly there, not giving forth from itself: any such instability would set it in thing after thing or at least in something other than itself: then it would no longer be self-gathered; nor would it be immune, for anything within which it were lodged would affect it; immune, it is not in anything. If, then, not standing away from itself, not distributed by part, not taking the slightest change, it is to be in many things while remaining a self-concentrated entire, there is some way in which it has multi-presence; it is at once self-enclosed and not so: the only way is to recognize that while this principle itself is not lodged in anything, all other things participate in it—all that are apt and in the measure of their aptitude.

Thus, we either cancel all that we have affirmed and the principles laid down, and deny the existence of any such Nature, or, that being impossible, we return to our first position:

❙ There is a unity,[3] numerically identical, undistributed, an unbroken entire, ❙ which yet stands remote from nothing that exists by its side; but it does not, for that, need to pour itself forth: it is not necessary either that certain portions of it enter into things, or again that, while it remains wholly self-abiding, something produced and projected from it enter at various points into that other order. Either would imply something of it remaining there while the emanant is elsewhere: thus separated from what has gone forth, it would experience local division. And would those emanants be, each in itself, whole or part? ❙ If part, the unity[4] has lost its nature, ❙ that of an entire, as we have already indicated; if whole, then either the whole is broken up to coincide point for point with that in which it is become present or we are admitting that an unbroken identity can be omnipresent.

This is a reasoning, surely, founded on the thing itself and its essential nature, not introducing anything foreign, anything belonging to the other order.

4. ❙ Then consider this argument: we cannot think the god (in man)[5] to be absent at some point and present at another; all that have insight ❙ into the nature of the divine beings hold the omnipresence of this god and of all the gods, and reason assures us that so it must be.

Now all-pervasion is inconsistent with partition; that would mean no longer the god throughout but part of the god at one point and part at another; the god ceases to be one god, just as a mass cut up ceases to be a mass, the parts no longer giving the first total. Further, the god becomes corporeal.

❙ If all this is impossible, then the doctrine which all mankind disputes presents itself again: by holding the god to exist, we hold inevitably[6] the omnipresence of an integral identity. ❙

Again, if we think of the divine nature as infinite—and certainly it is confined by no bounds—this must mean that it nowhere fails; its presence must reach to everything; at the point to which it does not reach, there it has failed; something exists in which it is not.

I Now, admitting any sequent to the unity itself (the one Being), that sequent must be bound up with it; any second will be about that first and move towards it, linked to it as its offspring. In this way all participants in the later will have share in the first.[7] I The Beings of the Intellectual are thus a plurality of firsts and seconds and thirds attached like one sphere to one centre, not separated by interval but mutually present; where, therefore, the Intellectual tertiaries are present the secondaries and firsts are present too.

5. Often for the purpose of exposition—as a help towards stating the nature of the produced multiplicity—we use the example of many lines radiating from one centre; but while we provide for individualization we must carefully preserve mutual presence. Even in the case of our circle we need not think of separated radii; all may be taken as forming one surface: where there is no distinction even upon the one surface but all is power and reality undifferentiated, all the beings may be thought of as centres uniting at one central centre: we ignore the radial lines and think of their terminals at that centre, where they are at one. Restore the radii; once more we have lines, each touching a generating centre of its own, but that centre remains coincident with the one first centre; the centres all unite in that first centre and yet remain what they were, so that they are as many as are the lines to which they serve as terminals; the centres themselves appear as numerous as the lines starting from them and yet all those centres constitute a unity.

Thus we may liken the Intellectual Beings in their diversity to many centres coinciding with the one centre and themselves at one in it but appearing multiple on account of the radial lines—lines which do not generate the centres but merely lead to them. The radii, thus, afford a serviceable illustration for the mode of contact by which the Intellectual Unity manifests itself as multiple and multi-present.

6. The Intellectual Beings, thus, are multiple and one; in virtue of their infinite nature their unity is a multiplicity, many in one and one over many, a unit-plurality. They act as entire upon entire; even upon the partial thing they act as entire; but there is the difference that at first the partial accepts this working only partially though the entire enters later. Thus, when Man enters into human form there exists a particular man who, however, is still Man. From the one thing Man—man in the Idea—material man has come to constitute many individual

men: the one identical thing is present in multiplicity, in multi-impression, so to speak, from the one seal.

This does not mean that Man Absolute, or any Absolute, or the Universe in the sense of a Whole, is absorbed by multiplicity; on the contrary, the multiplicity is absorbed by the Absolute, or rather is bound up with it. There is a difference between the mode in which a colour may be absorbed by a substance entire and that in which the soul of the individual is identically present in every part of the body: it is in this latter mode that Being is omnipresent.

7. To Real Being we go back, all that we have and are; I to that we return, and to its first offshoot (Soul).[8] I Of what is There we have direct knowledge, not images or even impressions; and to know without image is to be; by our part in true knowledge we are those Beings; we do not need to bring them down into ourselves, for we are There among them. Since not only ourselves but all other things also are those Beings, we all are they; we are they while we are also one with all: therefore we and all things are one.

When we look outside of that on which we depend we ignore our unity; looking outward we see many faces; look inward and all is the one head. If a man could but be turned about—by his own motion or by the happy pull of Athene—he would see at once God and himself and the All. At first no doubt all will not be seen as one whole, but when we find no stop at which to declare a limit to our being we cease to rule ourselves out from the total of reality; we reach to the All as a unity—and this not by any stepping forward, but by the fact of being and abiding there where the All has its being.

8. For my part I am satisfied that anyone considering the mode in which Matter participates in the Ideas will be ready enough to accept this tenet of omnipresence in identity, no longer rejecting it as incredible or even difficult. This because it seems reasonable and imperative to dismiss any notion of the Ideas lying apart with Matter illumined from them as from somewhere above—a meaningless conception, for what have distance and separation to do here?

This participation cannot be thought of as elusive or very perplexing; on the contrary, it is obvious, accessible in many examples.

Note, however, that when we sometimes speak of the Ideas illuminating Matter this is not to suggest the mode in which material light pours down on a material object; we use the phrase in the sense only that, the material being image while the Ideas are archetypes, the two orders are distinguished somewhat in the manner of illuminant and illuminated. But it is time to be more exact.

We do not mean that the Idea, locally separate, shows itself in Matter like a reflection in water; the Matter touches the Idea at every point, though not in a physical contact, and, by dint of neighbourhood—nothing to keep them apart—is able to absorb thence all that lies within its capacity, the Idea itself not penetrating, not approaching, the Matter, but remaining self-locked.

We take it, then, that the Idea, say of Fire—for we had best deal with Matter as underlying the elements—is not in the Matter. The Ideal Fire, then, remaining apart, produces the form of fire throughout the entire enfired mass. Now let us suppose—and the same method will apply to all the so-called elements—that this Fire in its first material manifestation is a multiple mass. That single Fire is seen producing an image of itself in all-the sensible fires; yet it is not spatially separate; it does not, then, produce that image in the manner of our visible light: for in that case all this sensible fire, supposing that it were a whole of parts (as the analogy would necessitate), must have generated spatial positions out of itself, since the Idea or Form remains in a non-spatial world; for a principle thus pluralized must first have departed from its own character in order to be present in that many and to ensure frequent participation in the one same Form.

The Idea, impartible, gives nothing of itself to the Matter; its unbreaking unity, however, does not prevent it shaping that multiple by its own unity and being present to the entirety of the multiple, bringing it to pattern not by acting part upon part but by presence entire to the object entire. It would be absurd to introduce a multitude of Ideas of Fire, each several fire being shaped by a particular idea; the Ideas of fire would be infinite. Besides, how would these resultant fires be distinct, when fire is a continuous unity? and if we apply yet another fire to certain matter and produce a greater fire, then the same Idea must be allowed to have functioned in the same way in the new matter as in the old; obviously there is no other Idea.

9. The elements in their totality, as they stand produced, may be thought of as one spheric figure; this cannot be the piecemeal product of many makers each working from some one point on some one portion. There must be one cause; and this must operate as an entire, not by part executing part; otherwise we are brought back to a plurality of makers. The making must be referred to a partless unity, or, more precisely, the making principle must be a partless unity not permeating the sphere but holding it as one dependent thing. In this way the sphere is enveloped by one identical life in which it is inset; its entire content looks to the one life: thus all the souls are one, a one, however, which yet is infinite.

It is in this understanding that the Soul has been taken to be a numerical principle, while others think of it as in its nature a self-increasing number; this latter notion is probably designed to meet the consideration that the Soul at no point fails but, retaining its distinctive character, is ample for all, so much so that were the Cosmos vaster yet the virtue of Soul would still compass it—or rather the Cosmos still be sunk in Soul entire.

Of course, we must understand this adding of extension not as a literal increase but in the sense that the Soul, essentially a unity, becomes adequate to omnipresence; its unity sets it outside of quantitative measurement, the characteristic of that other order which has but a counterfeit unity, an appearance by participation.

The essential unity is no aggregate to be annulled upon the loss of some one of the constituents; nor is it held within any allotted limits, for so it would be the less for a set of things, more extensive than itself, outside its scope; or it must wrench itself asunder in the effort to reach to all; besides, its presence to things would be no longer as whole to all but by part to part; in vulgar phrase, it does not know where it stands; dismembered, it no longer performs any one single function.

Now if this principle is to be a true unity—where the unity is of the essence—it must in some way be able to manifest itself as including the contrary nature, that of potential multiplicity, while by the fact that this multiplicity belongs to it not as from without but as from and by itself, it remains authentically one, possessing boundlessness and multiplicity within that unity; its nature must be such that it can appear as a whole at every point; this, as encircled by a single self-embracing Reason-Principle, which holds fast about that unity, never breaking with itself but over all the universe remaining what it must be.

The unity is in this way saved from the local division of the things in which it appears; and, of course, existing before all that is in place, it could never be founded upon anything belonging to that order of which, on the contrary, it is the foundation; yet, for all that they are based upon it, it does not cease to be wholly self-gathered; if its fixed seat were shaken, all the rest would fall with the fall of their foundation and stay; nor could it be so unintelligent as to tear itself apart by such a movement and, secure within its own being, trust itself to the insecurity of place which, precisely, looks to it for safety.

10. It remains, then, poised in wisdom within itself; it could not enter into any other; those others look to it and in their longing find it where it is. This is that 'Love waiting at the door', ever coming up from without, striving towards the beautiful, happy when to the utmost of its power it attains. Even here the lover does not so much possess himself of the beauty he has loved as wait before it; that Beauty is abidingly self-enfolded but its lovers, the Many, loving it as an entire, possess it as an entire when they attain, for it was an entire that they loved. This seclusion does not prevent it sufficing to all, but is the very reason for its adequacy; because it is thus entire for all it can be The Good to all.

Similarly wisdom is entire to all, and thus 'shared by all'; it is not distributed parcelwise; it cannot without absurdity be fixed to place; it is not spread about like a colouring, for it is not corporeal; any true participation in wisdom must be participation in an identical unity wholly self-gathered. So must it be in our participation I in the Supreme;[9] I we shall not take our several portions of it, nor you some separate entire and I another. Think of what happens in Assemblies and all kinds of meetings; the road to sense is the road to unity; singly the members are far from wise; as they begin to grow together, each, in that true community of thought, generates wisdom while he recognizes it. There is nothing to prevent our intelligences meeting at one centre from their several positions; all one, they seem apart to us as when without looking we touch one object or sound one string with different fingers and think we feel several. Or take our souls in their possession of good; it is not one good for me and another for you; it is the same for both and not in the sense merely of distinct products of an identical source, the good somewhere above with something streaming from it into us; in any real receiving of good, giver is in contact with taker and gives not as to a recipient outside but to one in intimate contact.

The Intellectual giving is not an act of transmission; even in the case of corporeal objects, with their local separation, the mutual giving (and taking) is of things of one order and their communication, every effect they produce, is upon their like; what is corporeal in the All acts and is acted upon within itself, nothing external impinging upon it. Now if in body, I whose very nature is self-eluding,[10] I there is no incursion of the alien, how can there be any in the order in which no partition exists?

It is therefore by identification that we see the good and touch it, brought to it by becoming identical with what is of the Intellectual within ourselves. In that realm exists what is far more truly a cosmos of unity; otherwise there will be two sensible universes, divided into correspondent parts; the Intellectual sphere, if a unity only as this sphere is, will be undistinguishable from it—except, indeed, that it will be less worthy of respect since in the nature of things extension is appropriate in the lower while the Intellectual will have wrought out its own extension with no motive, in a departure from its very character.

And what is there to hinder this unification? There is no question of one member pushing another out as occupying too much space, any more than happens in our own minds where we take in the entire fruit of our study and observation, all uncrowded.

We may be told that this unification is not possible in Real Beings; it certainly would not be possible, if the Reals had extension.

11. But how can the unextended reach over the defined extension of the

corporeal? How can it, so, maintain itself as a unity, an identity?

This is a problem often raised and reason calls vehemently for a solution of the difficulties involved. The fact stands abundantly evident but there is still the need of intellectual satisfaction.

We have, of course, no slight aid to conviction, indeed the very strongest, in the exposition of the character of that principle. It is not like a stone, some vast block lying where it lies, covering the space of its own extension, held within its own limits, having a fixed quantity of mass and of assigned stone-power. It is a First Principle, measureless, not bounded within determined size—such measurement it gives to another order—and therefore it is all-power, nowhere under limit. Being so, it is outside of Time.

Time in its ceaseless onward sliding produces parted interval; Eternity stands in identity, pre-eminent, vaster by unending power than Time with all the vastness of its seeming progress; Time is like a radial line running out apparently to infinity but dependent upon that, its centre, which is the pivot of all its movement; as it goes it tells of that centre, but the centre itself is the unmoving principle of all the movement.

Time stands, thus, in analogy with the principle which holds fast in unchanging identity of essence: but that principle is infinite not only in duration but also in power: this infinity of power must also have its counterpart, a principle springing from that infinite power and dependent upon it; this counterpart will, after its own mode, run a course—corresponding to the course of Time—in keeping with that stationary power which is its greater as being its source: and in this too the source is present throughout the full extension of its lower correspondent.

This secondary of Power, participating as far as it may in that higher, must be identified.

Now the higher power is present integrally but, in the weakness of the recipient material, is not discerned at every point; it is present as an identity everywhere, not in the mode of the material triangle—identical though in many representations numerically multiple—but in the mode of the immaterial, ideal triangle which is the source of the material figures. If we are asked why the omnipresence of the immaterial triangle does not entail that of the material figure, we answer that not all Matter enters into the participation necessary; Matter accepts various forms and not all Matter is apt for all form; the First Matter, for example, does not lend itself to all but is for the First Kinds first and for the others in due order, though these, too, are omnipresent.

12. To return: How is that Power present to the universe?
As a One Life.

Consider the life in any living thing; it does not reach only to some fixed point, unable to permeate the entire being; it is omnipresent. If on this again we are asked, How?, we appeal to the character of this power, not subject to quantity but such that though you divide it mentally for ever you still have the same power, infinite to the core; in it there is no Matter to make it grow less and less according to the measured mass.

Conceive it as a power of an ever-fresh infinity, a principle unfailing, inexhaustible, at no point giving out, brimming over with its own vitality. If you look to some definite spot and seek to fasten on some definite thing, you will not find it. The very contrary will ensue: you will not pass on to where it is not; you will never halt at a dwindling point where it fails at last and can no longer give; you will always be able to move with it—better, to be in its entirety—and so seek no further; denying it, you have strayed away to something of another order and you fall; looking elsewhere you do not see what stands there before you.

But supposing you do thus 'seek no further', I how will you ever be convinced of attainment? [11] I

In that you have entered into the All, no longer content with the part; you cease to think of yourself as under limit but, laying all such determination aside, you become an All. No doubt you were always that, but there has been an addition and by that addition you are diminished; for the addition was not from the realm of Being—you can add nothing to Being—but from non-Being. It is not by some admixture of non-Being that one becomes an entire, but by putting non-Being away. By the lessening of the alien in you, you increase. Cast it aside and there is the All within you; engaged in the alien, you will not find the All. Not that it has to come and so be present to you; it is you that have turned from it. And turn though you may, you have not severed yourself; it is there; you are not in some far region: still there before it, you have faced to its contrary.

It is so with the lesser gods; of many standing in their presence it is often one alone that sees them; that one alone was alone in the power to see. These are the gods who 'in many guises seek our cities'; but there is That Other whom the cities seek, and all the earth I and heaven—Him who is everywhere self-abiding and from whom derives Being and the Real Beings down to Soul and Life,[12] I all bound to Him and so moving to that unity which by its very lack of extension is infinite.

NOTES TO ENNEAD VI.5

1. FIRST EDITION: "If that Good has Being and is within the realm of Being, then it is present, self-contained, in everything: we, therefore, *need not look outside of* Being; we are in it; *yet that Good is not exclusively ours:* therefore all beings are one."

GUTHRIE: "If then the Good be essence, and may be found in essence, it must be within itself in each of us. We cannot, therefore, be far from essence, but we are in it. Neither is it far from us. All (beings), therefore, constitute but a unity."

ARMSTRONG: "But if that good is being and in being, it would clearly be for each individual in himself. We have not, then, departed from being, but are in it, nor has it departed from us: so all things are one."

COMMENT: Consider this paragraph in relation to the last three paragraphs of VI.5.12.

2. FIRST EDITION: "... bring the appropriately convincing principles to the discussion of the *Unity,* of perfect Being:"

ARMSTRONG: "... take for our reasoning about the one and altogether existent principles which, being proper to it, will lead to conviction ..."

GUTHRIE: "We must, therefore, in our discussion about the one universal Essence, choose principles capable of enlisting support ..."

3. FIRST EDITION: "*The One,* numerically identical, undistributed, an unbroken entire ..."

GUTHRIE: "The Essence which is one and identical is indivisible, and exists as single everywhere."

ARMSTRONG: "... the one and the same in number which is not divided but exists as a whole ..."

4. FIRST EDITION: "If part, the *One* has lost its nature, that of an entire ..."

GUTHRIE: "If it be a part, it will not preserve the nature of the all ..."

ARMSTRONG: "... if it is a part it will not preserve the nature of the whole ..."

COMMENT: The "it" used by Guthrie and Armstrong refers to each single emanant.

5. FIRST EDITION: "Then consider this *god (in man) whom we cannot think* to be absent at some point and present in another. All that have insight ..."

GUTHRIE: "Let us, therefore, contemplate this Divinity who is not present here, and absent there, but who is everywhere. All those who have any idea of the divinities admit that they, as well as that supreme Divinity, are present everywhere."

ARMSTRONG: "But, please, look at this argument also: we deny that God is in one place but not in another. For it is accepted among all who have a notion of gods that one says, not only about that [supreme God] but about all gods, that they are present everywhere."

6. FIRST EDITION: "If all this is impossible, *the disputed doctrine* presents itself again; holding the god to *pervade the Being of man,* we hold the omnipresence of an integral identity."

ARMSTRONG: "But if all this is impossible, then again what is disbelieved in has reappeared; in every human nature believing in God goes with believing that the same thing is everywhere as a whole."

GUTHRIE: "If that be impossible, we shall have to admit that to which before we refused assent, to which all human nature testifies, namely, that the Divinity is everywhere simultaneously present, entire, and identical."

7. FIRST EDITION: "Now, admitting any sequent to the *absolute* unity, that sequent must be bound up with *the absolute*; any *third* will be about that second and move towards it, linked to it as its offspring. In this way all participants in the *Later* will have share in the *First*."

GUTHRIE: "The essences which exist beneath the One exist simultaneously with Him, are posterior to Him, refer to Him, and reattach themselves to Him as His creatures; so that to participate in what is posterior to Him is to participate in Himself."

ARMSTRONG: "For even if we may be talking about something else after the One itself, this again will be together with the One itself and what is after it will be around that One and directed to that One and like something generated from it in close touch with it, so that what participates in what comes after it has also participated in that One."

8. FIRST EDITION: ". . . to that we return *as from that we came.*"

GUTHRIE: ". . . we aspire to it, we use it as a principle, from the very beginning."

ARMSTRONG: ". . . and ascend to that and to the first which comes from it . . ."

9. FIRST EDITION: "in the *One*;"

GUTHRIE: "in this Wisdom."

ARMSTRONG: "in it," the "it" referring to "thought," which he uses throughout the passage where MacKenna uses "wisdom." (Guthrie also has "Wisdom" where Armstrong has "thought" and MacKenna has "wisdom.")

10. FIRST EDITION: ". . . whose very nature is *partition* . . ."

GUTHRIE: ". . . which by its nature as it were scatters itself (because it is in a perpetual flowing wastage) . . ."

ARMSTRONG: ". . . which by nature in a way flees from itself . . ."

11. FIRST EDITION: ". . . how *do* you *experience it?*"

ARMSTRONG: ". . . however will this happen to you?"

GUTHRIE: ". . . you will be similar to a universal Essence. How?"

12. FIRST EDITION: ". . . and heaven, *everywhere with God and in Him, possessing through Him their Being* and the Real Beings about them, down to *Soul* and *Life* . . ."

GUTHRIE: ". . . and all the heavens turn; for the universe subsists by Him, and in Him. From Him also do all real essences derive their existence; it is from Him that all depend, even the universal Soul, and the universal Life;"

ARMSTRONG: ". . . and all the sky, who everywhere abides by himself and in himself and has from himself being and the things which really are down to soul and life depending on him . . ."

SIXTH TRACTATE

On Numbers

1. It is suggested that multiplicity is a falling away from The Unity, infinity (limitlessness) being the complete departure, an innumerable multiplicity, and that this is why unlimit is an evil and we evil at the stage of multiplicity.

A thing, in fact, becomes a manifold when, unable to remain self-centred, it flows outward and by that dissipation takes extension: utterly losing unity it becomes a manifold since there is nothing to bind part to part; when, with all this outflowing, it becomes something definite, there is a magnitude.

But what is there so grievous in magnitude?

Given consciousness, there will be, since the thing must feel its exile, its sundrance from its essence. Everything seeks not the alien but itself; in that outward moving there is frustration or compulsion; a thing most exists, not when it takes multiplicity or extension, but when it holds to its own being, that is when its movement is inward. Desire towards extension is ignorance of the authentically great, a movement not on the appropriate path but towards the strange; to the possession of the self the way is inward.

Consider the thing that has taken extension; broken into so many independent items, it is now those several parts and not the thing it was; if that original is to persist, the members must stand collected to their total; in other words, a thing is itself not by being extended but by remaining, in its degree, a unity: through expansion and in the measure of the expansion, it is less itself; retaining unity, it retains its essential being.

Yet the universe has at once extension and beauty?

Yes; because it has not been allowed to slip away into the limitless but is held fast by unity; and it has beauty in virtue of Beauty, not of Magnitude; it needed Beauty to parry that magnitude; in the degree of its extension it was void of beauty and to that degree ugly. Thus extension serves as Matter to Beauty since what calls for its ordering is a multiplicity. The greater the expansion, the greater the disorder and ugliness.

2. What, then, of the 'Number of the Infinite'?

To begin with, how is Number consistent with infinity?

Objects of sense are not unlimited and therefore the Number applying to them cannot be so. Nor is an enumerator able to number to infinity; though we double, multiply over and over again, we still end with a finite number; though we range over past and future, and consider them, even, as a totality, we still end with the finite.

Are we then to dismiss absolute limitlessness and think merely that there is always something beyond?

No; that more is not in the reckoner's power to produce; the total stands already defined.

In the Intellectual the Beings are determined and with them Number, the number corresponding to their total; in this sphere of our own—as we make a man a multiple by counting up his various characteristics, his beauty and the rest—we take each image of Being and form a corresponding image of number; we multiply a non-existent in and so produce multiple numbers; if we number years we draw on the numbers in our own minds and apply them to the years; these numbers are still our possession.

3. And there is the question, How can the infinite (the limitless) have existence and remain unlimited? Whatever is in actual existence is by that very fact determined numerically.

But, first, if multiplicity holds a true place among Beings, how can it be an evil?

As existent it possesses unity; it is a unit-multiple, saved from stark multiplicity; but it is of a lessened unity and, by that inwoven multiplicity, it is evil in comparison with unity pure. No longer steadfast in that nature, but fallen, it is the less, while in virtue of the unity thence retained it keeps some value; multiplicity has value in so far as it tends to return to unity and to abide in it.

But how explain the unlimited? It would seem that either it is among Beings and so is limited, or, if unlimited, is not among Beings but, at best, among things of process such as Time. To be brought to limit it must be unlimited; not the limited but the unlimited is the subject of limitation, since between the limited and the unlimited there is no intermediate to accept the principle of limitation. The unlimited recoils by very nature from the Idea of limit, though it may be caught and held by it from without: the recoil, of course, is not from one place to another; the limitless can have nothing to do with place, which arises only with the limiting of the unlimited. Hence what is known as the flux of the unlimited is not to be understood as local change; nor does any other sort of recognizable motion belong to it in itself; therefore the limitless cannot move: neither can it be at rest: in what, since all place is later? Its movement means little more than that it is not fixed in rest.

Is it, then, suspended at some one point, or rocking to and fro?

No; any such poising, with or without side motion, could be known only by place (which Matter, the unlimited, precedes).

How, then, are we to form any conception of its being?

We must fasten on the bare notion and take what that gives us—opposites that still are not opposed: we think of large and small and the unlimited becomes both, of stationary and moving and it will be both of these. But primarily it can be neither in any defined degree, or at once it is under limit. Limitless in this unlimited and undefined way, it is able to appear as either of a pair of opposites: draw near, taking care to throw no net of limit over it, and you have something that slips away; you come upon no unity for so it would be defined; approach the thing as a unit and you find it manifold; call it a manifold and again you falsify, for when the single thing is not a unity neither is the total a manifold. In one manifestation it takes the appearance of movement, in another of rest, as the mind envisages it.

❙ Its inability to be seen through itself betokens a movement out of Intellectual-Principle, a sliding away. That it cannot break free but is under rigorous compulsion from without and has no possibility of advance, in this would be its rest. Thus it is not true to speak of it[1] as being solely in flux.❙

4. We have to inquire into the existence of the Numbers in the Intellectual. ❙ Are they something added to the Ideas—in other words, necessary concomitants to the Ideas? In that[2] case, ❙ Being, as the first (in the Intellectual), would give us the conception of the Monad; then since Being produces motion and rest, Three exists; and so on for all the other members of the realm of Being.

Or perhaps (secondly) there is one monad for each member, or a monad for the first, with a dyad for its next, since there exists a series, and a corresponding number for every successive total, dekad for ten, and so on.

If, a third possibility, Number is a direct production of the Intellectual-Principle (an Idea in itself), there is the question whether it preceded or followed the other Ideas.

Plato, where he says that men arrived at the conception of Number by way of the changes of day and night—thus making the concept depend upon variation among things—seems to hold that the things numerable precede and by their differences produce number: Number then would consist in a process within the human mind passing onwards from thing to thing; it results by the fact that the mind takes count, that is when the mind traverses things and reports their differences; observing pure identity unbroken by difference, it says 'One'. But there is the passage where he tells us that the veritable Number has Being, is a Being; this is the opposed view that Number is no product of the reckoning mind but a reality in itself, the concept of which is reawakened in the mind by changes in things of sense.

5. What then is the veritable nature of Number?

Is it an accompaniment upon each substance, something seen in the things as in a man we see one man, in a being one being, and in the total of Intellectual beings the total of number?

But how explain the dyad and triad? How comes the total to be unitary and any particular number to be brought under unity? The theory offers a multiplicity of units, and no number is reducible to unity but the simple 'one'. It might be suggested that a dyad is that thing—or rather what is observed upon that thing—which has two powers combined, a compound thing related to a unity: or numbers might be what the Pythagoreans seem to hold them in their symbolic system in which Justice, for example, is a Tetrad: but this is rather to add the number, a number of manifold unity like the dekad, to the multiplicity of the thing which yet is one thing. Now it is not so that we treat the ten things; we bring them together and apply the figure ten to the several items. Or rather in that case we say ten, but when the several items form a unity we say dekad. This would apply in the Intellectual as in the sensible.

But how then can number, observed upon things, rank among Real Beings?

One answer might be that whiteness is similarly observed upon things and yet is real, just as movement is observed upon things and there is still a real existence of movement. But movement is not on a par with number: it is because movement is an entity that unity can be observed upon it. Besides, the kind of real existence thus implied annuls the reality of number, making it no more than an attribute; but that cannot be since an attribute must exist before it can be attributed; it may be inseparable from the subject but still must in itself be something, some entity as whiteness is; to be a predicate it must be that which is to be predicated. Thus if unity is observed in every subject, and 'one man' says more than 'man'—the oneness being different from the manness and common to all things—then this oneness must be something prior to man and to all the rest: only so can the unity come to apply to each and to all: it must therefore be prior also to even movement, prior to Being, since without unity these could not be each one thing: of course what is here meant is not the unity postulated as transcending Being but the unity predicable of each and every Idea. So too there is a dekad prior to the subject in which we affirm it; this prior would be the dekad absolute, for certainly the thing in which the dekad is observed is not that absolute.

Is this unity, then, connate and coexistent to the Beings? Suppose it coexistent merely as an accidental like health in man, it still must exist of itself; suppose it present as an element in a compound, there must first exist unity and the unity absolute that can thus enter into composition; moreover, if it were compounded with an object brought into being by its agency it would make that object only spuriously a unity; its entry would produce a duality.

But what of the dekad? Where lies the need of dekad to a thing which, by totalling to that power, is dekad already?

The need may be like that of Form to Matter; ten and dekad may exist by its virtue; and, once more, the dekad must previously exist of its own existence, dekad unattached.

6. Granted, then, that there exist, apart from things, a unity absolute and a dekad absolute—in other words, that the Intellectual beings, together with their characteristic essence, have also their order, Henads, Dyads, Triads, what is the nature of these numerical entities and how does it come into being? **I** Not that 'coming into being' applies literally to the Intellectual realm.[3]**I**

As a beginning, what is **I** the nature[4] of **I** the Ideas in general? It is not that the thinking principle thought of each Idea and by that act of thought procured their several existences; not because Justice and Movement were thus thought did they come to be; that would imply that while the thought is later than the thing—the concept of Justice must be later than Justice itself—yet the thought precedes what, as founded on the thinking, owes its existence to it. Besides, if Justice is only a certain definite thought we have the absurdity that Justice is nothing more than a definition of Justice. Thinking of Justice or Movement is but grasping their nature; this would mean grasping the non-existent, an impossibility.

We may be reminded that in immaterial objects the knowledge is identical with the thing; but we must not misapply that statement; it does not say that the knowledge is the thing known, or that the reason surveying the thing is the thing, but that the immaterial thing, being an Intellectual object, is also a thought; this does not imply a definition or conception of the object; the thing itself, as belonging to the Intellectual, can be nothing else than Intellect or knowledge. This is not a case of knowledge self-directed; **I** it is that the thing in the Intellectual transmutes the knowledge, which no longer resembles[5] the knowledge of material things; **I** in other words it makes it true knowledge, that is to say no image of the thing but the thing directly.

Thus it is not the conception of movement that brings movement to be; movement absolute produces that conception; it produces itself as at once movement and the concept of movement, for movement as it exists There, bound up with Being, is a concept. It is movement absolute because it is the first movement—there can be none till this exist—and it is the authentic Movement since it is not accidental to something else but is the activity of actual Being in motion. Thus it is a real existent though the notion of Being is different.

Justice therefore is not the thought of Justice but, as we may put it, a state of the Intellectual-Principle, or rather an activity of it—an appearance so lovely that neither evening nor dawn is so fair, nor anything else in all the realm of sense, an Intellectual manifestation self-rising, self-seen, or, rather, self-being.

7. It is inevitably necessary to think of all as contained within one nature; one nature must hold and encompass all; there cannot be as in the realm of sense thing apart from thing, here a sun and elsewhere something else; all must be mutually present within a unity. This is the very nature of the Intellectual-Principle as we may know from Soul which reproduces it and from what we call Nature under which and by which the things of process are brought into their disjointed being while that Nature itself remains indissolubly one.

But within the unity There, the several entities have each its own distinct existence; the all-embracing Intellect sees what is in it, what is within Being; it need not look out upon them since it contains them; need not separate them since they stand for ever distinct within it.

Against doubters we cite the fact of participation; the greatness and beauty of the Intellectual-Principle we know by the Soul's longing towards it; the longing of the rest towards Soul is set up by its likeness to its higher and by the possibility open to them of attaining resemblance through it.

It is surely inconceivable that any living thing be beautiful failing a Life-Form Absolute (an Idea of Living Being) of a wonderful, an ineffable, beauty: this must be the Collective Life-Form, made up of all living things, or embracing all—a unity coextensive with all, as our universe is a unity embracing all the visible.

8. As then there is a Life-Form primal—which therefore is the Life-Form Absolute—and there is Intellectual-Principle or Being, Authentic Being, these, we affirm, contain all living things and all Number, and Absolute Justice and Beauty and all of that order; for we ascribe an existence of their own to Absolute Man, Absolute Number, Absolute Justice. It remains to discover, in so far as such knowledge is possible, how these distinct entities come to be and what is the manner of their being.

At the outset we must lay aside all sense-perception; by Intellectual-Principle we know Intellectual-Principle. We reflect that within ourselves there is life, there is intellect, not in extension but as power without magnitude, that Authentic Being has divested itself of extension and magnitude and is power self-existing, no vacuity but a thing most living and intellective—nothing more living, more intelligent, more real—and producing its effect by contact and in the ratio of the contact, closely to the close, more remotely to the remote. If Being is to be sought, then most to be sought is Being at its intensest; so, too, the intensest of Intellect if the Intellectual act has worth; and so, too, of Life.

First, then, we take Being as first in order; then Intellectual-Principle; then the Living-Form considered as containing all things: Intellectual-Principle, as the Act of Real Being, is a second.

Thus it is clear that Number cannot be dependent upon the Living-Form since unity and duality existed before that; nor does it rise in the Intellectual-Principle since before that there existed Real Being which is both one and numerous.

9. It remains then to consider whether Being by its distinction produced Number or Number produced that distinction. It is certain that either Number was the cause of Being, movement, rest, identity, and difference, or these the cause of Number.

The first question is whether Number can exist in and of itself or is dependent upon things—Two being something observed in two things, Three in three; and so of the arithmetical One, for if this could exist apart from numbered objects it could exist also before the divisions of Being.

But could it precede Being itself?

For the present we must take it that Being precedes Number, is its source. But if Being means one being and Beings two (or more) beings, then unity precedes Being, and Number precedes the Beings.

Mentally, to our approach? Yes: and in reality of existence as well.

Let us consider: When we think of the authentically-existent Man or of the single form of Beauty, the unity is certainly thought of as subsequent in either case; when we group a horse with a dog, the duality is obviously the subsequent. But think of that which brings man or horse or dog into being or produces them, with full intention, from where they lie latent within itself: the producer must say, 'I begin with a first, I pass on to a second; that makes two; counting myself there are three'. Of course there was no such numbering even of Beings for their production since the due number was known from the very beginning; but this consideration serves to show that all Number precedes the very Beings themselves.

But if Number thus preceded the Beings, then it is not included among them?

The truth is that it existed within the Authentic Being but not as applying to it, for Being was still unparted; the potentiality of Number existed and so produced the division within Being, put in travail with multiplicity; Number must be either the substance of Being or its Activity; the Life-Form as such and the Intellectual-Principle must be Number. Clearly Being is to be thought of as Number collective, while the Beings are Number unfolded: the Intellectual-Principle is Number moving within itself, while the Living-Form is Number container of the universe. Even Being is the outcome of the Unity and since the prior is unity the secondary must be Number.

Hence it is that the Forms (Ideas) have been described as Henads and Numbers. This is the authentic ❙(essential)⁶ ❙ Number; the other, the 'monadic', is its image. The Authentic is that made manifest in the Forms and helping to bring them to be; primally it is the Number in the Authentic Being, inherent to it and preceding the Beings, serving to them as root, fount, first principle.

For the Unity is source to Being; Being's Being is stayed upon the Unity as its safeguard from dissolution; the Unity cannot rest upon Being which at that would be a unity before possessing unity; and so with the dekad before possessing dekadhood.

10. When it takes lot with multiplicity, Being becomes Number by the fact of awakening to manifoldness; before, it was a preparation, so to speak, of the Beings, their fore-promise, a total of henads offering a stay for what was to be based upon them.

Here with us a man will say, 'I wish I had such and such a quantity of gold'— or 'such and such a number of houses'. Gold is one thing: the wish is not to bring the numerical quantity into gold but to bring the gold to quantity; the quantity, already present in the mind, is to be passed on to the gold so that it acquire that numerical value.

If the Beings preceded the number and this were discerned upon them at the stirring, to such and such a total, of the numbering principle, then the actual number of the Beings would be a chance not a choice; since that total is not a matter of chance, Number is a causing principle preceding that determined total.

Number then pre-exists and is the cause by which produced things participate in quantity.

The single thing derives its unity by participation in Unity-Absolute; its being it derives from Being-Absolute, which in turn hold its Being from itself and its unity from Unity-Absolute; the particular unity—where the unity is a multiple unity—is one thing only as the Triad is; the collective Being is a unity of this kind, the unity not of the monad but of the myriad or any such collective number.

Take a man affirming the presence of ten thousand things; it is he that produces the number; he does not tell us that the ten thousand have uttered it; they merely exhibit their several forms; the enumerator's mind supplies the total which would never be known if the mind kept still.

How does the mind pronounce?

By being able to enumerate; that is by knowing Number: but in order to this, Number must be in existence and that that Principle should not know its own total content is absurd, impossible.

It is with Number as with Good. When we pronounce things to be good either we mean that they are in their own nature so or we affirm goodness as an accidental in them. Dealing with the primals, the goodness we have in mind is that First Hypostasis; where the goodness is an accidental we imply the existence of a Principle of Good as a necessary condition of the accidental presence; there must be some source of that good which is observed elsewhere, whether this source be an Absolute Good or something that of its own nature produces the good. Similarly with number; in attributing the dekad to things we affirm either the truly existent dekad or, where the dekadhood is accidental, we necessarily posit the self-subsistent dekad, dekad not associated; if things are to be described as forming a dekad, then either they must be of themselves the dekad or be preceded by that which has no other being than that of dekadhood.

It must be urged as a general truth that anything affirmed of a subject not itself either found its way in from outside or is the characteristic Act of that subject; and supposing the predicated attribute to show no variation of presence and absence but to be always present, then, if the subject is a Real Being so also is the accidental in an equal degree; or, failing Real Being, it at least belongs to the existents, it exists. In the case when the subject can be thought of as remaining without its Act, yet that Act is inbound with it even though to our minds it appears as a later; when on the contrary the subject cannot be conceived without the attribute—man, for example, without unity—then the attribute is either not later but concomitant or, being essential to the existence, is precedent. In our view, Unity and Number are precedent.

11. It may be suggested that the dekad is nothing more than so many henads; admitting the one henad why should we reject the ten? As the one is a real existence why not the rest? We are certainly not compelled to attach that one henad to some one thing and so deprive all the rest of the means to unity: since every existent must be one thing, the unity is obviously common to all. This means one principle applying to many, the principle whose existence within itself we affirmed to be presupposed by its manifestation outside.

But if a henad exists in some given object and further is observed in something else, then, that first henad being real, there cannot be only one henad in existence; there must be a multiplicity of henads.

Supposing that first henad alone to exist, it must obviously be lodged either in the thing of completest Being or at all events in the thing most completely a unity. If in the thing of completest Being, then the other henads are but nominal and cannot be ranked with the first henad, or else Number becomes a collection of unlike monads and there are differences among monads (an impossibility). If that first henad is to be taken as lodged in the thing of completest unity, there is the question why that most perfect unity should require the first henad to give it unity.

Since all this is impossible, then, before any particular can be thought of as a unit, there must exist a unity bare, unrelated by very essence. If in that realm also there must be a unity apart from anything that can be called one thing, why should there not exist another unity as well?

Each particular, considered in itself, would be a manifold of monads, totalling to a collective unity. If however Nature produces continuously—or rather has produced once for all—not halting at the first production but bringing a sort of continuous unity into being, then it produces the minor numbers by the sheer fact of setting an early limit to its advance: outgoing to a greater extent—not in the sense of moving from point to point but in its inner changes—it would produce the larger numbers; to each number so emerging it would attach the due quantities and the appropriate thing, knowing that without this adaptation to Number the thing could not exist or would be a stray, something outside, at once, of both Number and Reason.

12. We may be told that unity and monad have no real existence, that the only unity is some definite object that is one thing, so that all comes to an attitude of the mind towards things considered singly.

But, to begin with, why at this should not the affirmation of Being pass equally as an attitude of mind so that Being too must disappear? No doubt Being strikes and stings and gives the impression of reality; but we find ourselves just as vividly struck and impressed in the presence of unity. Besides, is this attitude, this concept itself, a unity or a manifold? When we deny the unity of an object, clearly the unity mentioned is not supplied by the object since we are saying it has none; the unity therefore is within ourselves, something latent in our minds independently of any concrete one thing.

[An objector speaks:] But the unity we thus possess comes by our acceptance of a certain idea or impression from things external; it is a notion derived from an object. Those that take the notion of numbers and of unity to be but one species of the notions held to be inherent in the mind must allow to numbers and to unity the reality they ascribe to any of the others and upon occasion they must be met; but no such real existence can be posited when the concept is taken to be an attitude or notion rising in us as a by-product of the objects; this happens when we say 'This', 'What', and still more obviously in the affirmations 'Crowd', 'Festival', 'Army', 'Multiplicity'. As multiplicity is nothing apart from certain constituent items and the festival nothing apart from the people gathered happily at the rites, so when we affirm unity we are not thinking of some Oneness self-standing, unrelated. And there are many other such cases; for instance 'On the right', 'Above', and their opposites; what is there of reality about this 'On-the-right-ness' but the fact that two different positions are occupied? So with 'Above': 'Above' and 'Below' are a mere matter of position and relative to parts of the universe called by these names.

Now in answer to this series of objections our first remark is that there does exist an actuality implicit in each one of the relations cited; I though this is not the same from one example to another, or the same as the relationship with[7] unity. I

But these objections must be taken singly.

13. It cannot reasonably be thought that the notion of unity is derived from the object since this is physical—man, animal, even stone; a presentation of that order is something very different from unity (which must be a thing of the Intellectual); if that presentation were unity, I the mind could never affirm unity of (an abstract idea like) not-man.[8] I

Then again, just as in the case of 'On the right' or other such affirmation of relation, the mind does not affirm in some caprice but from observation of contrasted position, so here it affirms unity in virtue of perceiving something real; assuredly the assertion of unity is not a bare attitude towards something non-existent. It is not enough that a thing be alone and be itself and not something else: and that very 'not something else' tells of another unity. Besides, Otherness and Difference are later; unless the mind has first rested upon unity it cannot affirm Otherness or Difference; when it affirms Aloneness it affirms unity-with-aloneness; thus unity is presupposed in Aloneness.

Besides, that in us which asserts unity of some object is first a unity, itself; and the object is a unity before any outside affirmation or conception.

A thing must be either one thing or more than one, manifold: and if there is to be a manifold there must be a precedent unity. To talk of a manifold is to talk of what has something added to unity; to think of an army is to think of a multitude under arms and brought to unity. In refusing to allow the manifold to remain manifold, the mind makes the truth clear; it draws a separate many into one, either supplying a unity not present or keen to perceive the unity brought about by the ordering of the parts; in an army, even, the unity is not a fiction but as real as that of a building erected from many stones, though of course the unity of the house is more compact.

If, then, unity is more pronounced in the continuous, and more again where there is no separation by part, this is clearly because there exists, in real existence, something which is a Nature or Principle of Unity. There cannot be a greater and less in the non-existent: as we predicate Substance of everything in sense, but predicate it also of the Intellectual order and more strictly there—since we hold that the greater and more sovran substantiality belongs to the Real Beings and that Being is more marked in Substance, even sensible Substance, than in the other Kinds—so, finding unity to exhibit degree of more and less, differing in sense-things as well as in the Intellectual, we must similarly admit that Unity exists under all forms though still by reference, only, to that primal Unity.

As Substance and Real Being, despite the participation of the sensible, are still of the Intellectual and not of the sensible order, so too the unity observed present in things of sense by participation remains still an Intellectual and to be grasped by an Intellectual Act. The mind, from a thing present to it, comes to knowledge of something else, a thing not presented; that is, it has a prior knowledge. By this prior knowledge it recognizes Being in a particular being; similarly when a thing is one it can affirm unity, as it can affirm also duality and multiplicity.

It is impossible to name or conceive anything not making one or two or some number; equally impossible that the thing should not exist without which nothing can possibly be named or conceived; impossible to deny the reality of that whose existence is a necessary condition of naming or affirming anything; what is a first need, universally, to the formation of every concept and every proposition must exist before reasoning and thinking; only as an existent can it be cited to account for the stirring of thought. If Unity is necessary to the substantial existence of all that really is—and nothing exists which is not one—Unity must precede Reality and be its author. It is, therefore, an existent Unity, not an existent that develops Unity; considered as Being-with-Unity it would be a manifold, whereas in the pure Unity there is no Being save in so far as Unity attends to producing it.

As regards the word 'This', it is not a bare word; it affirms an indicated existence without using the name, it tells of a certain presence whether a substance or some other existent; any This must be significant; it is no attitude of the mind applying itself to a non-existent; the This shows a thing present, as much as if we used the strict name of the object.

14. To the argument touching relation we have an answer surely legitimate:

The Unity is not of a nature to lose its own manner of being only because something else experiences a change which it does not itself share; to stray from its unity it must itself suffer division into duality or the still wider plurality.

If by division the one identical mass can become a duality without loss of quantity, clearly the unity it possessed and by this destructive division lost was something distinct. What may be alternatively present and absent to the same subject must be classed among Real-Beings, regardless of position; an accidental elsewhere, it must have reality in itself whether it be manifested in things of sense or in the Intellectual—an accidental in the Laters but self-existent in the higher, especially in virtue of its primal aspect of Unity developing into Being. We may be told that Unity may lose that character without change in itself, becoming duality by association with something else; but this is not true; unity does not become two things; neither the added nor what takes the addition becomes two; each remains the one thing it was; the duality is predicable of the group only, the unity remaining unchanged in each of those unchanged constituents.

Two and the Dyad are not essentially relative: if the only condition to the construction of duality were meeting and association such a relation might perhaps constitute Twoness and Duality; but in fact we see Duality produced by the very opposite process, by the splitting apart of a unity. This shows that duality—or any other such numerical form—is no relation produced either by scission or association. If one configuration produces a certain thing it is impossible that the opposite should produce the same so that the thing may be identified with the relation.

What then is the actual cause?

Unity is due to the presence of Unity; duality to that of Duality; it is precisely as things are white by Whiteness, just by Justice beautiful by Beauty. Otherwise we must reject these universals and call in relation here also: Justice would arise from a certain attitude in a given situation, Beauty from a certain pattern of the person with nothing present able to produce the beauty, nothing coming from without to effect that agreeable appearance.

You see something which you pronounce to be a unity; that thing possesses also size, form, and a host of other characteristics you might name; size, bulk, sweetness, bitterness, and other properties are actually present in the thing; why not unity? It surely cannot be thought that, while every conceivable quality has being, quantity (Number) has not, and that while continuous quantity exists, discrete quantity does not—and this though continuous quantity is measured by the discrete. No: as size by the presence of Magnitude, so Oneness by the presence of Unity, and similarly with Duality and all the other numerical modes.

As to the How of participation, the inquiry is that of all participation in Ideal Forms; we must note, however, that the presence of the Dekad (for instance) in the looser totals is different from its presence in the continuous; there is difference again in its presence within many powers where multiplicity is concentred in unity; arrived at the Intellectuals, there too we discover Number, the Authentic Number, no longer entering the alien but self-centred, Dekad-

Absolute not Dekad of some particular Intellectual group.

15. We must repeat: The Collective Being, the Authentic, There, is at once Being and Intellectual-Principle and the Complete Living Form; thus it includes the total of living things; the Unity There is reproduced by the unity of this living universe in the degree possible to it—for the sense-nature as such cannot compass that transcendental unity—thus that Living-All is inevitably Number-Entire: if the Number were not complete, the All would be deficient to the extent of some number, and if every number applicable to living things were not contained in it, it would not be the all-comprehending Life-Form. Therefore, Number exists before every living thing, before the collective Life-Form.

Again: Man exists in the Intellectual and with him all other living things, both by possession of Real-Being and because that is the Life-Form Complete. Even the man of this sphere is a member of the Intellectual since that is the Life-Form Complete; every living thing by virtue of having life, is There, There in the Life-Form.

Similarly, the Intellectual-Principle by its very nature contains all intelligences as severally members within itself. Now all this means Number There. Yet even in Intellect Number is not present primally; its presence There is the reckoning of the Acts of Intellectual-Principle; it tallies with the justice in Intellectual-Principle, its moral wisdom, its virtues, its knowledge, all whose possession makes that Principle what it is.

But knowledge—must not this imply presence to the alien? No; knowledge, known, and knower are an identity; so with all the rest; every member of Intellectual-Principle is therefore present to it primally; justice, for example, is not accidental to it as to soul in its character as soul, where these virtues are mainly potential, becoming actual by the intention towards Intellectual-Principle and association with it.

Next we come to Being, fully realized, and this is the seat of Number; by Number Being brings forth the Beings; its movement is planned to Number; it establishes the numbers of its offspring before bringing them to be, in the same way as it establishes its own unity by linking pure Being to the First: the numbers do not link the lower to the First; it suffices that Being is so linked; for Being, in taking form as Number, binds its members to itself. As a unity, it suffers no division, remaining self-constant; as a thing of division, containing its chosen total of members, I it knows that total and so brings forth the number,[9] a phase therefore of its content: I its development of parts is ruled by the powers of Number, and the Beings it produces sum to that Number. Thus Number, the primal and true, is Principle and source of actuality to the Beings.

Hence it is that in our sphere, also, Number accompanies the coming to be of particular things, and to suppose another number than the actual is to suppose the production of something else or of nothing.

These then are the primal numbers; they are numerable; the numbers of the other order are of a double character; as derived from the first numbers they are themselves numerable but as acting for those first they are measures of the rest of things, numbering numbers and numerables. For how could they declare a Dekad save in the light of numbers within themselves?

16. But here we may be questioned about these numbers which we describe as the primal and authentic:

Where do you place these numbers, in what genus among Beings? To everyone they seem to come under Quantity and you have certainly brought Quantity in, where you say that discrete Quantity equally with the continuous holds place among Beings; but you go on to say that there are the numbers belonging to the Firsts and then talk of other numbers quite distinct, those of reckoning; tell us how you arrange all this, for there is difficulty here. And then, the unity in sense-things—is that a quantity or is quantity here just so many units brought together, the unity being the starting-point of quantity but not quantity itself? And, if the starting-point, is it a kindred thing or of another genus? All this you owe it to us to make clear.

Be it so; we begin by pointing out a distinction:

You take one thing with another—for we must first deal with objects of sense—a dog and a man, or two men; or you take a group and affirm ten, a dekad of men: in this case the number affirmed is not a Reality, even as Reality goes in the sphere of sense, but is purely Quantity: similarly when you resolve into units, breaking up the dekad, those units are your principle of Quantity since the single individual is not a unity absolute.

But the case is different when you consider Man in himself and affirm a certain number, duality, for example, in that he is at once living and reasoning.

By this analysis and totalling you get quantity; but there are two objects under consideration and each of these is one; each of the unities contributes to the complete being and the oneness is inherent in each; this is another kind of number, number essential; even the duality so formed is no posterior; it does not signify a quantity apart from the thing but the quantity in the essence which holds the thing together. The number here is no mere result of your detailing; the things exist of themselves and are not brought together by your reckoning, but what has it to do with essential reality that you count one man in with another? There is here no resultant unity such as that of a choir; the dekad is real only to you who count the ten; in the ten of your reckoning there cannot be a dekad without a unitary basis; it is you that make the ten by your counting, by fixing that tenness down to quantity; in choir and army there is something more than that, something not of your placing.

But how do you come to have a number to place?

The Number inherent apart from any enumeration has its own manner of being, but the other, that resulting upon the appearance of an external to be appraised by the Number within yourself, is either an Act of these inherent numbers or an Act in accordance with them; in counting we produce number and so bring quantity into being just as in walking we bring a certain movement into being.

But what of that 'Number within us having its own manner of being?'

It is the Number of our essence. 'Our essence' we read 'partakes of Number and harmony' and, also, is Number and harmony. 'Neither body nor magnitude', someone says: Soul, then, is Number since it is essence. The number belonging to body is an essence of the order of body; the number belonging to Soul constitutes the essences of souls.

In the Intellectuals, also, if the Absolute Living-Form There is a multiple—a triad, let us say—that Triad of the Living-Form is of the nature of essence: and the Triad prior to any living thing, Triad in the realm of Being, is a principle of essence.

When you enumerate two things—say, animal and beauty—each of these remains one thing; the number is your production; it lay within yourself; it is you that elaborate quantity, here the dyad. But when you declare virtue to be a Tetrad, you are affirming a Tetrad which does actually exist; the parts, so to speak, make one thing; you are taking as the object of your act a Unity-Tetrad to which you accommodate the Tetrad within yourself.

17. But what of the Infinite Number we hear of; does not all this reasoning set it under limit?

And rightly so if the thing is to be a number; limitlessness and number are in contradiction.

How, then, do we come to use the term? Is it that we think of Number as we think of an infinite line, not with the idea that any such line exists but that even the very greatest—that of the (path of the) universe, for example—may be thought of as still greater? So it might be with number; let it be fixed, yet we still are free to think of its double, though not of course to produce the doubled quantity since it is impossible to join to the actual what is no more than a conception, a phantasm, private to ourselves.

It is our view that there does exist an infinite line, among the Intellectual Beings: for There a line would not be quantitative and being without quantity could be numerically infinite. This, however, would be in another mode than that of limitless extension. In what mode, then? In that the conception of the Absolute Line does not include the conception of limit.

But what sort of thing is the Line in the Intellectual and what place does it hold?

It is later than Number since unity is observed in it; it rises at one point and traverses one course and simply lacks the quantity that would be the measure of the distance.

But where does this thing lie? Is it existent only in the defining thought, so to speak?

No; it is also a thing, though a thing of the Intellectual. All that belongs to that order is at once an Intellectual and in some degree the concrete thing. There is a position, as well as a manner of being, for all configurations, for surface, for solid. And certainly the configurations are not of our devising; for example, the configurations of the universe are obviously antecedent to ourselves; so it must be with all the configurations of the things of nature; before the bodily reproductions all must exist There, without configuration, primal configurations. For these primals are not shapes in something; self-belonging they are perfect without extension; only the extended needs the external. In the sphere of Real-Being the configuration is always a unity; it becomes discrete either in the Living-Form or immediately before: I say 'becomes discrete' not in the sense that it takes magnitude There but that it is broken apart for the purposes of the Living-Form and is allotted to the bodies within that Form—for instance, to Fire There the Intellectual Pyramid. And because the Ideal-Form is There, the fire of this sphere seeks to produce that configuration against the check of Matter: and so of all the rest as we read in the account of the realm of sense.

But does the Life-Form contain the configurations by the mere fact of its life?

They are in the Intellectual-Principle previously but they also exist in the Living-Form; if this be considered as including the Intellectual-Principle, then they are primally in the Life-Form, but if that Principle comes first, then they are previously in that. And if the Life-Form entire contains also souls, it must certainly be subsequent to the Intellectual-Principle.

No doubt there is the passage, 'Whatever Intellect sees in the entire Life-Form'; thus seeing, must not the Intellectual-Principle be the later?

No; the seeing may imply merely that the reality comes into being in the process of that seeing; the Intellectual-Principle is not external to the Life-Form; all is one; the Act of the Intellectual-Principle possesses itself of bare sphere, while the Life-Form holds the sphere as sphere of a living total.

18. It appears then that Number in that realm is definite; it is we that can conceive the 'more than is present'; the infinity lies in our counting: in the Real is no

conceiving more than has been conceived; all stands entire; no number has been or could be omitted to make addition possible. It might be described as infinite in the sense that it has not been measured—who is there to measure it?—but it is solely its own, a concentrated unit, entire, not ringed round by any boundary; its manner of being is settled for it by itself alone. None of the Real-Beings is under limit; what is limited, measured, is what needs measure to prevent it running away into the unbounded. There every being is Measure; and therefore it is that all is beautiful. Because that is a living thing it is beautiful, holding the highest life, the complete, a life not tainted towards death, nothing mortal there, nothing dying. Nor is the life of that Absolute Living-Form some feeble flickering; it is primal, the brightest, holding all that life has of radiance; it is that first light which the souls There draw upon for their life and bring with them when they come here. It knows for what purpose it lives, towards What it lives, from Whence it lives; for the Whence of its life is the Whither: and close above it stands the wisdom of all, the collective Intellectual-Principle, knit into it, one with it, colouring it to a higher goodness, by kneading wisdom into it, making its beauty still more august. Even here the august and veritably beautiful life is the life in wisdom, here dimly seen, There purely. For There wisdom gives sight to the seer and power for the fuller living and in that tenser life both to see and to become what is seen.

Here attention is set for the most part upon the unliving and, in the living, upon what is lifeless in them; the inner life is taken only with alloy: There, all are Living Beings, living wholly, unalloyed; however you may choose to study one of them apart from its life, in a moment that life is flashed out upon you: once you have known the Essence that pervades them, conferring that unchangeable life upon them, once you perceive the judgement and wisdom and knowledge that are theirs, you can but smile at all the lower nature with its pretension to Reality.

In virtue of this Essence it is that life endures, that the Intellectual-Principle endures, that the Beings stand in their eternity; nothing alters it, turns it, moves it; nothing, indeed, is in being beside it to touch it; anything that is must be its product; anything opposed to it could not affect it. Being itself could not make such an opposite into Being; that would require a prior to both and that prior would then be Being; so that Parmenides was right when he taught the identity of Being and Unity. Being is thus beyond contact not because it stands alone but because it is Being. For Being alone has Being in its own right.

How then can we deny to it either Being or anything at all that may exist within Being's activity, anything that may derive from it?

As long as it exists it produces: but it exists for ever; so, therefore, do its products. And so great is it in power and beauty that it remains the allurer, all things of the universe depending from it and rejoicing to hold their trace of it and through that to seek their good. To us existence is before the good; all this world desires life and wisdom in order to Being; every soul and every intellect seeks to be its Being; but Being is sufficient to itself.

NOTES TO ENNEAD VI.6

1. FIRST EDITION has this paragraph as: "*And there is movement in its lack of consciousness; it has passed* out of Intellectual-Principle, *slid* away. That it cannot break free but is under compulsion from without *to keep to its circling with* no possibility of advance, in this would be its rest. Thus it is not true to speak of *Matter* as being solely in flux."

ARMSTRONG supports the fourth edition completely. GUTHRIE: ". . . its property of being invisible by itself constitutes a movement which distinguishes it from intelligence; its property of not being able to escape, of being exteriorly embraced, of being circumscribed within an unescapable circle constitutes a sort of stability. Movement therefore cannot be predicated of infinity, without also attributing stability to it."

2. FIRST EDITION: "Are they *Ideas* added to the other Ideas? *Or are they no more than* necessary concomitants to the Ideas?

"In the *latter* case . . ."

GUTHRIE: "Are they inherent in the other forms? Or are they, since all eternity, the consequences of the existence of these forms? In the latter case . . ."

ARMSTRONG poses the issue as: "But we must consider how the numbers are in the intelligible, whether as coming into existence after the other Forms or always accompanying them; for instance . . ."

3. FIRST EDITION: "*We cannot but think that some reason accounts for their origin.*"

GUTHRIE: "It must be admitted that a certain Reason presides over the generation of these Numbers."

ARMSTRONG; "But we must understand that we make them come into being only in thought."

4. FIRST EDITION: ". . . the *origin* of . . ."

ARMSTRONG: "substantial nature."

GUTHRIE, in place of the interrogative structure, has the thought as: "It is therefore necessary clearly to understand that in general, if intelligible forms at all exist, it is not because the thinking principle first thought each of them, and thereby gave them hypostatic existence."

5. FIRST EDITION: ". . . it is that the thing in the Intellectual transmutes the knowledge, which *is not fixed like* the knowledge of material things;"

GUTHRIE: ". . . it is the (actual) thing itself which keeps that knowledge (thereof possessed by reason) from remaining different from it, just as the knowledge of a material object remains different from that object;"

ARMSTRONG: ". . . but the thing there makes the knowledge, which does not stay like the knowledge of a thing in matter, to be different:"

6. FIRST EDITION omits "(essential)."

ARMSTRONG has: "substantial number." GUTHRIE has: "Such then is 'essential' Number (number that is 'Being')."

7. FIRST EDITION: "...though this is not the same *for all or the same for correlatives or the same for every reference to* unity."

GUTHRIE: "...not identical in all things, considered either in respect to each other, or each in respect to the One which is in all."

ARMSTRONG: "...not the same in all, either of themselves in relation to each other or in the relation of all to the one."

8. FIRST EDITION: "...the mind could never affirm unity *unless of that given thing, man, for example.*"

ARMSTRONG: "Otherwise reason would not predicate 'one' in the case of a thing which is not man."

GUTHRIE: "...otherwise, our judgement would not be able (as it is) to predicate unity of the non-man."

9. FIRST EDITION: "...it knows that total and so brings forth *Number*, a phase therefore of its content:"

GUTHRIE: "...it saw into how many things it had divided itself; and through this (process) it begat the number that exists within itself;"

ARMSTRONG: "...it looked to see how many it had generated according to number, which were therefore in it;"

SEVENTH TRACTATE

How the Multiplicity of the Ideal-Forms came into Being; and on The Good

1. God, or some one of the gods, in sending the souls to their birth, placed eyes in the face to catch the light and allotted to each sense the appropriate organ, providing thus for the safety which comes by seeing and hearing in time and seeking or avoiding under guidance of touch.

But what led to this provision?

It cannot be that other forms of being were produced first and that, these perishing in the absence of the senses, the maker at last supplied the means by which men and other living beings might avert disaster.

We may be told that it lay within the divine knowledge that animal life would be exposed to heat and cold and other such experiences incident to body and that in this knowledge he provided the senses and the organs apt to their activity in order that the living total might not fall an easy prey.

Now, either he gave these organs to souls already possessing the sensitive powers or he gave senses and organs alike.

But if the souls were given the powers as well as the organs, then, souls though they were, they had no sensation before that giving. If they possessed these powers from the moment of being souls and became souls in order to their entry into process, then it is of their very nature to belong to process, unnatural to them to be outside of process and within the Intellectual: they were made in the intent that they should belong to the alien and have their being amid evil; the divine provision would consist in holding them to their disaster; this is God's reasoned purpose, this the plan entire.

Now what is the foundation of reasoned plan?

Precedent planning, it may be; but still we are forced back to some thing or things determining it. What would these be here?

Either sense-perception or intellect. But sense-perception does not yet exist: intellect is left; yet, starting from intellect, the conclusion will be knowledge, not therefore the handling of the sensible; what begins with the intellectual and proceeds to the intellectual can certainly not end in dealings with the sensible. Providence, then, whether over living beings or over the sensible universe in general, was never the outcome of plan.

There is in fact no planning There; we speak of reasoned purpose in the world of things only to convey that the universe is of the character which in the later order would point to a wise purposing; Providence implies that things are as in the later order a competent foreplanning would produce them. Reasoning serves, in beings not of the order above that need, to supply for the higher power; foresight is necessary in the lack of power which could dispense with it; it labours towards some one occurrence in preference to another and it goes in a sort of dread of the unfitting; where only the fitting can occur, there is no foreseeing. So with planning; where one only of two things can be, what place is there for plan? The alone and one and utterly simplex cannot have an explicated plan, a 'this to avert that': if the 'this' could not be, the 'that' must; the serviceable thing appeared and at once approved itself so.

But surely this is foreseeing, deliberating: are we not back at what was said at the beginning, that God did to this end give both the senses and the powers, however perplexing that giving be?

No: all turns on the necessary completeness of Act; we cannot think anything belonging to God to be other than a whole and all and therefore in anything of God's that all must be contained; God therefore must take in the future, present beforehand. Certainly there is no later in the divine; what is There as present is future for elsewhere. If then the future is present, it must be present as having been fore-conceived for later coming to be; at that divine stage therefore it lacks nothing and therefore can never lack; all existed, eternally and in such a way that at the later stage any particular thing may be said to exist for this or that purpose; the All, in its extension and so to speak unfolding, is able to present succession, but while it is bound up together, it is a single total fact: in other words, it contains its cause (as well as everything else) within itself.

2. Thus we have even here the means of knowing the nature of the Intellectual-Principle, though seeing it more closely than anything else, we still see it at less than its worth. We know that it exists but its cause we do not see, or, if we do, we see that cause as something apart. We see a man—or an eye, if you like—but this is an image or part of an image; what is in that Principle is at once Man and the reason of his being; for There man—or eye—must be, itself, an intellective thing and a cause of its being; it could not exist at all unless it were that cause, whereas here everything partial is separate, and so is the cause of each. In the Intellectual all is at one so that the thing is identical with the cause.

Even here the thing and its cause are often identical—an eclipse furnishes an example—what then is there to prevent other things too being identical with their cause and this cause being the essence of the thing? It must be so; and by this search after the cause the thing's essence is reached, for the essence of a thing is its cause. I am not here saying that the informing Idea is the cause of the thing—though this is true—but that the Idea itself, unfolded, reveals the cause inherent in it.

A thing of inactivity, a lifeless thing,[1] cannot include its own cause; but where could a Forming-Idea, a member of the Intellectual-Principle, turn in quest of its cause? We may be answered, 'In the Intellectual-Principle'; but the two are not distinct; the Idea is the Intellectual-Principle; and if that Principle must contain the Ideas complete, their cause must be contained in them. The Intellectual-Principle itself contains every cause of the things of its content; but these of its content are identically Intellectual-Principle, each of them Intellectual-Principle; none of them, thus, can lack its own cause; each springs into being carrying with it the reason of its being. No result of chance, each must rise complete with its cause; it is an integral and so includes the excellence bound up with the cause. This is how all participants in the Idea are put into possession of their cause.

In our universe, a coherent total of multiplicity, the several items are linked each to the other, and by the fact that it is an all every cause is included in it: even in the particular thing the part is discernibly related to the whole, for the parts do not come into being separately and successively but are mutually cause and caused at one and the same moment. Much more in the higher realm must all the singles exist for the whole and each for itself: if then that world is the conjoint reality of all, of an all not chance-ruled and not sectional, the caused There must include the causes: every item must hold, in its very nature, the uncaused possession of its cause; uncaused, independent, and standing apart from cause, they must be self-contained, cause and all.

Further, since nothing There is chance-sprung, and the multiplicity in each comprehends the entire content, then the cause of every member can be named; the cause was present from the beginning, inherent, not a cause but a fact of the being; or, rather, cause and manner of being were one. What could an Idea have, as cause, over and above the Intellectual-Principle? It is a thought of that Principle and cannot, at that, be considered as anything but a perfect product. If it is thus perfect we cannot speak of anything in which it is lacking nor cite any reason for such lack. That thing must be present and we can say why. The why is inherent, therefore, in the entity, that is to say in every thought and activity of the Intellectual-Principle. Take for example the Idea of Man; Man entire is found to contribute to it; he is in that Idea in all his fullness including every-thing that from the beginning belonged to Man. If Man were not complete There, so that there were something to be added to the Idea, that additional must belong to a derivative: but Man exists from eternity and must therefore be complete; the man born is the derivative.

3. What then is there to prevent man having been the object of planning There?

No: all stands in that likeness, nothing to be added or taken away; this planning and reasoning is based only on an assumption; things are taken to be in process and this suggests planning and reasoning; insist on the eternity of the process and planning falls to the ground. There can be no planning over the eternal; that would imply forgetfulness of a first state; further, if the second state were better, things stood ill at first; if they stood well, so they must remain.

Only in conjunction with their causes are things good; even in this sphere a thing is good in virtue of being complete; form means that the thing is com-plete, the Matter duly controlled; this control means that nothing has been left crude; but something is so left if anything belonging to the shape be missing— eye, or other part. Thus to state cause is to state the thing complete. Why eyes or eyebrows? For completion: if you say 'For preservation', you affirm an in-dwelling safeguard of the essence, something contributory to the being: the essence, then, preceded the safeguard and the cause was inbound with the essence; distinct, this cause is in its nature a part of the essence.

All parts, thus, exist in regard to each other: the essence is all-embracing, complete, entire; the excellency is inbound with the cause and embraced by it; the being, the essence, the cause, all are one.

But, at this, sense-perception—even in its particular modes—is involved in the Idea by eternal necessity, in virtue of the completeness of the Idea; Intellec-tual-Principle, as all-inclusive, contains in itself all by which we are brought, later, to recognize this perfection in its nature; the cause, There, was one total, all-inclusive; thus Man in the Intellectual was not purely intellect, sense-perception being an addition made upon his entry into birth: all this would seem to imply a tendance in that great Principle towards the lower, towards this sphere. Sense-perception is, precisely, perception of the world of sense.

I But surely it is untenable on the one hand that the capacity for sense-perception should exist There, from eternity, and on the other that only upon the debasement of the soul should there be actual[2] sense-perception here I and the accomplishment in this realm of the Act of what was always a power in that?

4. To meet the difficulty we must make a close examination of the nature of Man in the Intellectual; perhaps, though, it is better to begin with the man of this plane lest we be reasoning to Man There from a misconception of Man here. There may even be some who deny the difference.

We ask first whether man as here is a Reason-Principle different to that soul which produces him as here and gives him life and thought; or is he that very soul or, again, the (yet lower) soul using the human body?

Now if man is a reasonable living being and by living being is meant a conjoint of soul and body, the Reason-Principle of man is not identical with soul. But if the conjoint of rational soul and body is the reason-principle of man, how can man be an eternal reality, seeing that it is only when soul and body have come together that the Reason-Principle so constituted appears?

That Reason-Principle will be the foreteller of the man to be, not the Man Absolute with which we are dealing but more like his definition, and not at that indicating his nature since what is indicated is not the Form that is to enter Matter but only that of the known thing, the conjoint. We have not yet found the Man we are seeking, the equivalent of the Reason-Principle.

But—it may be said—the Reason-Principle of such beings must be some conjoint, one element in another (a Form in Matter).

This does not define the principle of either. If we are to state with entire accuracy the Reason-Principles of the Forms in Matter and associated with Matter, we cannot pass over the generative Reason-Principle, in this case that of Man, especially since we hold that a complete definition must cover the essential manner of being.

What, then, is this essential of Man? What is the indwelling, inseparable something which constitutes Man as here? Is the Reason-Principle itself a reasoning living being, or is the living being the conjoint of Form and Matter, while the Reason-Principle is merely a maker of that reasoning life-form? and what is it apart from that act of making?

The living being corresponds to a reasoning life in the Reason-Principle; man therefore is a reasoning life: but there is no life without soul; either, then, the soul supplies the reasoning life—and man therefore is not an essence but simply an activity of the soul—or the soul is the man.

But if reasoning soul is the man, why does it not constitute man upon its entry into some other animal form?

5. Man, thus, must be some Reason-Principle other than soul. But why should he not be some conjoint—a soul in a certain Reason-Principle—the Reason-Principle being, as it were, a definite activity which however could not exist without that which acts?

This is the case with the Reason-Principles in seed which are neither soul-less nor entirely soul. For these productive principles cannot be devoid of soul and there is nothing surprising in such essences being Reason-Principles.

❙ But these principles producing[3] man, ❙ of what phase of soul are they activities? Of the vegetal soul? Rather of that which produces animal life, a brighter soul and therefore one more intensely living.

The soul of that order, the soul that has entered into Matter of that order, is man by having, apart from body, a certain disposition; within body it shapes all to its own fashion, producing another form of Man, man reduced to what body admits, just as an artist may make a reduced image of that again.

It is this soul that holds the pattern and Reason-Principles of Man, the natural tendencies, the dispositions and powers—all feeble since this is not the Primal Man—and it contains also its own kinds of sensation, different from those in the archetype, bright to all seeming, but images and dim in comparison with those of the earlier order.

The higher Man, above this sphere, rises from the more godlike soul, a soul possessed of a nobler humanity and brighter perceptions. This must be the Man of Plato's definition ('Man is Soul') where the addition 'Soul as using body' marks the distinction between the soul which uses body directly and the soul, poised above, which touches body only through that intermediary.

The Man of the realm of birth has sense-perception: the higher soul enters to bestow a brighter life, or rather does not so much enter as simply impart itself; for soul does not leave the Intellectual but maintaining that contact holds the lower life as pendant from it, blending with it by the natural link of Reason-Principle to Reason-Principle: and man, the dimmer, brightens under that illumination.

6. But how can that higher soul have sense-perception?

It is the perception of what falls under perception There, sensation in the mode of that realm: I it is the source of the lower soul's perception of the correspondences in the sense-realm. Man as sense-percipient becomes aware of these correspondences and accommodates the sense-realm to the lowest extremity of its counterpart There, proceeding from the fire here to the fire Intellectual which was perceptible to the higher soul in a manner corresponding to its own nature as Intellectual fire.[4] If material things I existed There, the soul would perceive them; Man in the Intellectual, Man as Intellectual soul, would be aware of the terrestrial. This is how the secondary Man, copy of Man in the Intellectual, contains the Reason-Principles in copy; and Man in the Intellectual-Principle contained the Man that existed before any man. The diviner shines out upon the secondary and the secondary upon the tertiary; and even the latest possesses them all— I not in the sense of identifying itself with[5] them all but I as standing in under-parallel to them. Some of us act by this lowest; in another rank there is a double activity, a trace of the next higher being included; in yet another there is a blending of the third (i.e., highest) grade with the others: each is that Man by which he acts while each too contains all the grades, though in some sense not so. On the separation of the third life and third Man from the body, then if the second also departs—of course not losing hold on the Above— the two, as we are told, will occupy the same place. No doubt it seems strange that a soul which has been the Reason-Principle of a man should come to occupy the body of an animal: but the soul has always been all, and will at different times be this and that.

Pure, not yet fallen to evil, the soul chooses man and is man, for this is the higher and it produces the higher. It produces also the still loftier beings, the Celestials (Daimones), who are of one Form with the soul that makes Man: I higher still stands that Being more entirely of the Celestial rank, in truth a god; and God is reproduced in the Celestial who is as closely bound to God as man to the Celestial. For that Being to which man is bound[6] is not to be called a god; I there remains the difference which distinguishes souls, all of the same race though they be. This is taking 'Celestial' ('Daimon') in the sense of Plato.

When a soul which in the human state has been thus attached chooses animal nature and descends to that, it is giving forth the Reason-Principle—necessarily in it—of the animal as it was in the Intellectual: this it contained and the activity has been to the lower.

7. But if it is by becoming evil and inferior that the soul produces the animal nature, the making of ox or horse was not at the outset in its character; the

Reason-Principle of the animal, and the animal itself, must lie outside of the natural plan?

Inferior, yes; but outside of nature, no. The thing There (the Idea) was in some sense horse and dog from the beginning; given the condition, the soul produces the higher kind; let the condition fail, then since produce it must, it produces what it may: it is like a skilful craftsman competent to create all kinds of works of art but reduced to making what is ordered and what the aptitude of his material indicates.

The power of the All-Soul, as Reason-Principle of the universe, may be considered as laying down a pattern before the effective separate powers go forth from it: this plan would be something like a tentative illumining of Matter; the elaborating soul would follow the tracings and give them minute articulation; every separate effective soul would become that towards which it tended, assuming that particular form as the choral dancer adapts himself to the action set down for him.

But this is to anticipate: our inquiry was, How there can be sense-perception in man without the implication that the Divine addresses itself to the realm of process. We maintained, and proved, that the Divine does not look to this realm but that things here are dependent upon those and represent them and that man here holding his powers from Thence is directed Thither, so that, while sense makes the environment of what is of sense in him, the Intellectual in him is linked to the Intellectual.

What we have called the perceptibles of that realm enter into cognizance in a way of their own, since they are not material, while the sensible sense here is fainter than the perception belonging to that higher world, but gains a specious clarity because its objects are bodies; the man of this sphere has sense-perception because apprehending in a less true degree and taking only enfeebled images of things There: perceptions here are Intellections of the dimmer order, and the Intellections There are vivid perceptions.

8. So much for the faculty of sensation; but it would appear that the prototype There of the whole animal,[7] horse or any other, must look deliberately towards this sphere; and, that being so, the idea of horse must have been worked out in order that there be a horse here?

Yet what was there to present the idea of the horse it was desired to produce? Obviously the idea of horse must exist before there was any planning to make a horse; it could not be thought of in order to be made; there must have been horse unproduced before that which was later to come into being. If then the thing existed before it was produced—if it cannot have been thought of in order to its production—the Being that held the horse as There held it in presence without any looking to this sphere; it was not with intent to set horse and the rest in being here that they were contained There; it is that, I the primal[8] existing, I the reproduction followed of necessity since the total of things was not to halt at the Intellectual. Who was there to call a halt to a power capable at once of self-concentration and of outflow?

But how come these animals of earth to be There? What have they to do within God? Reasoning beings, all very well; but this host of the unreasoning, what is there august in them? Surely the very contrary?

The answer is that obviously the unity of this (the Intellectual) universe must be that of a manifold since it is subsequent to that Unity-Absolute; otherwise it would be not next to that but the very same thing. As a next it could not hold the higher rank of being more perfectly a unity; it must fall short: since the best is a unity, inevitably there must be something more than unity, for deficiency involves plurality.

But why should it not be simply a dyad?

Because neither of the constituents could ever be a pure unity, but at the very least a duality and so progressively (in an endless dualization). Besides, in that first duality of the hypothesis there would be also movement and rest, Intellect and the life included in Intellect, all-embracing Intellect and life complete. That means that it could not be one Intellect; it must be Intellect agglomerate including all the particular intellects, a thing therefore as multiple as all the Intellects and more so; and the life in it would not be that of one soul but of all the souls with the further power of producing the single souls: it would be the 'entire living universe' containing much besides man; for if it contained only man, man would be alone here.

9. Admitted, then—it will be said—for the nobler forms of life; but how can the divine contain the mean, the unreasoning? The mean is the unreasoning since value depends upon reason and the worth of the intellective implies worthlessness where intellection is lacking. Yet how can there be question of the unreasoning or unintellective when all particulars exist in the divine and come forth from it?

In taking up the refutation of these objections, we must insist upon the consideration that neither man nor animals here can be thought of as identical with the counterparts in the higher realm; those ideal forms must be taken in a larger way. And again the reasoning thing is not of that realm: here the reasoning, There the pre-reasoning.

Why then does man alone reason here, the others remaining reasonless?

Degrees of reasoning here correspond to degrees of Intellection in that other sphere, as between man and the other living beings There; and those others do in some measure act by understanding.

But why are they not at man's level of reason: why also the difference from man to man?

We must reflect that since the many forms of lives are movements—and so with the Intellections—they cannot be identical: there must be different lives, distinct intellections, degrees of lightsomeness and clarity: there must be firsts, seconds, thirds, determined by nearness to the Firsts. This is how some of the Intellections are gods, others of a secondary order having what is here known as reason, while others again belong to the so-called unreasoning: but what we know here as unreasoning was There a Reason-Principle; the unintelligent was an Intellect; the Thinker of Horse was Intellect and the Thought, Horse, was an Intellect.

But (it will be objected) if this were a matter of mere thinking we might well admit that the intellectual concept, remaining concept, should take in the unintellectual, but where concept is identical with thing how can the one be an Intellection and the other without intelligence? Would not this be Intellect making itself unintelligent?

No: the thing is not unintelligent; it is Intelligence in a particular mode, corresponding to a particular aspect of Life; and just as life in whatever form it may appear remains always life, so Intellect is not annulled by appearing in a certain mode. Intellectual-Principle adapted to some particular living being does not cease to be the Intellectual-Principle of all, including man: take it where you will, every manifestation is the whole, though in some special mode; the particular is produced but the possibility is of all. In the particular we see the Intellectual-Principle in realization; the realized is its latest phase; in one case the last aspect is horse; at horse ended the progressive outgoing towards the lesser forms of life, as in another case it will end at something lower still. The unfolding of the powers of this Principle is always attended by some abandonment in regard to the highest; the outgoing is by loss and the loss is various, but according to the deficiency of the life-form produced by their failing they find the means of adding various requisites; the safeguards of life becoming inadequate, there appear nail, talon, fang, horn. Thus the Intellectual-Principle re-emerges at the very point of its descent by reason of the perfect sufficiency of its natural constitution, finding there within itself the remedy of the failure.

10. But failure There? What can defensive horns serve to There? To sufficiency as living form, to completeness. That principle must be complete as living form, complete as Intellect, complete as life, so that if it is not to be one thing it may be another. Its characteristic difference is in this power of being now this, now

that, so that, summing all, it may be the completest life-form, Intelligence complete, life in the greatest fullness with each of the particulars complete in its degree while yet, over all that multiplicity, unity reigns.

It is a manifold, but not a manifold of identical parts: that would make it nothing but a self-sufficing unity. Like every compound it must consist of things progressively differing in form and safeguarded in that form. This is in the very nature of shape and Reason-Principle; a shape, that of man let us suppose, must include a certain number of differences of part but all dominated by a unity; there will be the noble and the inferior, eye and finger, but all within a unity; the part will be inferior in comparison with the total but best in its place. I Man is by definition living form and something else, something distinct from living[9] form. I It is so with virtue also; it contains at once the universal and the particular; and the total is good because the universal is not differentiated.

11. The very heavens, patently multiple, cannot be thought to disdain any form of life since this universe holds everything. Now how do these things come to be here? Does the higher realm contain all of the lower?

All that has been shaped by Reason-Principle and conforms to Idea.

But, having fire (warmth) and water, it will certainly have vegetation; how does vegetation exist There? How does fire live? Earth, too? Either these are alive or they are There as dead things and then not everything There has life. How in sum can the things of this realm be also There?

Vegetal life we can well admit, for the plant is a Reason-Principle established in life. If in the plant the Reason-Principle, entering Matter and constituting the plant, is a certain form of life, a definite soul, then, since every Reason-Principle is a unity, either this of plant-life is the primal or before it there is a primal plant, source of its being: that first plant would be a unity; those here, being multiple, must derive from a unity. This being so, that primal must have much the truer life and be the veritable plant, the plants here deriving from it in the secondary and tertiary degree and living by a vestige of its life.

But earth; how is there earth There? What is the being of earth and how are we to represent to ourselves the living earth of that realm?

First, what is earth in the physical realm, what the mode of its being?

Earth, here and There alike, must possess shape and a Reason-Principle. Now in the case of the vegetal, the Reason-Principle of the plant here was found to have life: is there such a Reason-Principle in our earth?

Take the most earthy of things produced and found shaped in earth and they exhibit, even they, the indwelling earth-principle. The growing and shaping of stones, the internal moulding of mountains as they rise, reveal the working of an ensouled Reason-Principle fashioning them from within and bringing them to that shape: this, we must take it, is the creative earth-principle corresponding to what we call the specific principle of a tree; what we know as earth is like the wood of the tree; to cut out a stone is like lopping a twig from a tree, whereas if the stone remains a member of the earth, it is as the twig uncut from the living tree.

Realizing thus that the creative force inherent in our earth is life within a Reason-Principle, we are easily convinced that the earth There is much more primally alive, that it is a reasoned Earth-Livingness, the earth of Real-Being, earth primally, the source of ours.

Fire, similarly, with other such things, must be a Reason-Principle established in Matter: fire certainly does not originate in the friction to which it may be traced; the friction merely brings out a fire already existent in the scheme and contained in the materials rubbed together. Matter does not in its own character possess this fire-power: the true cause is something informing the Matter, that is to say, a Reason-Principle, obviously therefore a soul having the power of bringing fire into being; that is, a life and a Reason-Principle in one.

It is with this in mind that Plato says there is soul in each and every element of this sphere. That soul is the cause of the fire of the sense-world; the cause of fire here is a certain Life of fiery character, the more authentic fire. That transcendent fire being more truly fire will be more veritably alive; the fire absolute possesses life. And the same principles apply to the other elements, water and air.

Why, then, are water and air not ensouled as earth is?

Now, it is quite certain that these are equally within the living total, parts of the living all; life does not appear visibly in them; but neither does it in the case of the earth where its presence is inferred by what earth produces: but there are living things in fire and still more manifestly in water and there are systems of life in the air. The particular fire, rising only to be quenched, **|** eludes the soul animating the totality of fire;[10]**|** it slips away from the magnitude which would manifest the soul within it; so with air and water. If the Kinds could naturally be fastened down to magnitude they would exhibit the soul within them, now concealed by the fact that their function requires them to be loose or flowing. It is much as in the case of the fluids within ourselves; the flesh and all that is formed out of the blood into flesh show the soul within, but the blood itself, not bringing us any sensation, seems not to have soul; yet it must; the blood is not subject to blind force; its nature obliges it to abstain from the soul which none the less is indwelling in it. This must be the case with the three elements; it is the fact that the living beings formed from the close conglomeration of air (the Celestials, or Daimones) are not susceptible to suffering. But just as air, so long as it remains itself, eludes the light which is and remains unyielding, so too, by the effect of its circular movement, it eludes soul—and, in another sense, does not. And so with fire and water.

12. Or take it another way: Since in our view this universe stands to that as copy to original, the living total must exist There beforehand; that is the realm of complete Being and everything must exist There.

The heaven There must be living and therefore not bare of what here are known as stars—for stars are included in the very meaning of the word. Earth too will be There, and not void but even more intensely living and containing all that lives and moves upon our earth and the plants obviously rooted in life; sea will be There and all waters with the movement of their unending life and all the living things of the water; air too must be a member of that universe with the living things of air as here.

The content of that living thing must surely be alive—as in this sphere—and all that lives must of necessity be There. The nature of the major parts determines that of the living forms they comprise; by the being and content of the heaven There are determined all the heavenly forms of life; if those lesser forms were not There, that heaven itself would not be.

To ask how those forms of life come to be There is simply asking how that heaven came to be; it is asking whence comes the living form, and so, whence comes life, whence the All-Life, whence the All-Soul, whence collective Intellect: and the answer is that There no indigence or impotence can exist but all must be teeming, seething, with life. All flows, so to speak, from one fount not to be thought of as some one breath or warmth but rather as one quality englobing and safeguarding all qualities—sweetness with fragrance, wine-quality, and the savours of everything that may be tasted, all colours seen, everything known to touch, all that ear may hear, all melodies, every rhythm.

13. For Intellectual-Principle is not a simplex, nor is the Soul that proceeds from it: on the contrary things include variety in the degree of their simplicity, that is to say in so far as they are not compounds but Principles and Activities; the activity of the lowest is simple in the sense of being a fading-out, that of the First is the total of all activity. Intellectual-Principle is moved in a movement unfailingly true to one course but its unity and identity are not those of the partial; they are those of its universality; and indeed the partial itself is not a unity but divides to infinity.

We know that Intellectual-Principle has a source and advances to some term as its ultimate; now, is the intermediate between source and term to be thought of as a line or as some distinct kind of body uniform and unvaried?

Where at that would be its worth? If it had no change, if no differentiation woke it into life, it would not be a Force; that condition would in no way differ from mere absence of power and, even calling it movement, it would still be the movement of a life not all-varied but indiscriminate; now it is of necessity that life be all-embracing, covering all the realms, and that nothing fail of life. Intellectual-Principle, therefore, must move in every direction upon all, or more precisely must ever have so moved.

A simplex moving retains its character; either there is no change, movement has been null, or if there has been advance it still remains a simplex and at once there is a permanent duality: if the one member of this duality is identical with the other, then it is still as it was, there has been no advance; if one member differs from the other, it has advanced with differentiation, and, out of a certain identity and difference, it has produced a third unity. This production, based on Identity and Difference, must be in its nature identical and different; it will be not some particular different thing but Collective Difference, as its Identity is Collective Identity.

Being thus at once Collective Identity and Collective Difference, Intellectual-Principle must reach over all different things; its very nature then is to modify itself into a universe. If the realm of different things existed before it, these different things must have modified it from the beginning; if they did not, this Intellectual-Principle produced all, or rather was all.

Beings could not exist save by the activity of Intellectual-Principle; wandering down every way it produces thing after thing, but wandering always within itself in such self-bound wandering as authentic Intellect may know; this wandering permitted to its nature is among real beings which keep pace with its movement; but it is always itself; this is a stationary wandering, a wandering within 'the Meadow of Truth' from which it does not stray.

It holds and covers the universe which it has made the space, so to speak, of its movement, itself being also that universe which is space to it. And this Meadow of Truth is varied so that movement through it may be possible; suppose it not always and everywhere varied, the failing of diversity is a failure of movement; failure in movement would mean a failing of the Intellectual Act; halting, it has ceased to exercise its Intellectual Act; this ceasing, it ceases to be.

The Intellectual-Principle is the Intellectual Act; its movement is complete, filling Being complete; and the entire of Being is the Intellectual Act entire, comprehending all life and the unfailing succession of things. Because this Principle contains Identity with Difference its division is ceaselessly bringing the different things to light. Its entire movement is through life and among living things. To a traveller over land all is earth but earth abounding in difference: so in this journey the life through which Intellectual-Principle passes is one life but, in its ceaseless changing, a varied life.

Throughout this endless variation it maintains the one course because it is not, itself, subject to change but on the contrary is present as identical and unvarying Being to the rest of things. For if there be no such principle of unchanging identity to things, all is dead, activity and actuality exist nowhere. These 'other things' through which it passes are also Intellectual-Principle itself; otherwise it is not the all-comprehending principle: if it is to be itself, it must be all-embracing; failing that, it is not itself. If it is complete in itself, complete because all-embracing, and there is nothing which does not find place in this total, then there can be nothing belonging to it which is not different; only by difference can there be such co-operation towards a total. If it knew no otherness but was pure identity its essential Being would be the less for that failure to fulfil the specific nature which its completion requires.

14. On the nature of the Intellectual-Principle we get light from its manifestations; they show that it demands such diversity as is incompatible with its being a monad. Take what principle you will, that of plant or animal: if this principle were a pure unity and not a specifically varied thing, it could not so serve as principle; its product would be Matter, the principle not having taken all those forms necessary if Matter is to be permeated and utterly transformed. A face is not one mass; there are nose and eyes; and the nose is not a unity but has the differences which make it a nose; as bare unity it would be mere mass.

There is infinity in Intellectual-Principle since, of its very nature, it is a multiple unity, not with the unity of a mass but with that of a Reason-Principle, multiple in itself: in the one Intellectual design it includes within itself, as it were in outline, all the outlines, all the patterns. All is within it, all the powers and intellections; the division is not determined by a boundary but goes ever inward; this content is held as the living universe holds the natural forms of the living creatures in it from the greatest to the least, down even to the minutest powers where there is a halt at the individual form. The discrimination is not of items huddled within a sort of unity; this is what is known as I the universal 'Friendship', not of course the friendship[11] known here I which is a copy and prevails amongst beings in separation; I that authentic Friendship[12] I consists in all being a unity and never discriminate. Discrimination, we read, is the mode of the physical universe.

15. That Life, the various, the all-including, the primal and one, who can consider it without longing to be of it, disdaining all the other?

All other life is darkness, petty and dim and poor; it is unclean and polluting the clean, for if you do but look upon it you no longer see nor live this life which includes all living, in which there is nothing that does not live and live in a life of purity void of all that is ill. For evil is here where life is in copy and Intellect in copy; There is the archetype (the Intellectual-Principle) which has the form of Good—we read—as holding the Good in its Forms (or Ideas). That Good is distinct from Intellectual-Principle itself which maintains its life by contemplation (of the Good); and it sees also as good the objects of its contemplation because it holds them in its act of contemplating the Principle of Good. I But the Good comes to it not as it was in its primal state but in accord with the condition of the Intellectual-Principle. The Good is the source from which the objects of contemplation come to be seen in the Intellectual-Principle; Intellectual-Principle has produced them by its vision of the Good.[13] I In the very law, never, looking to That, could it fail of Intellectual Act; never, on the other hand, could its objects be in the Good—otherwise it (the Intellectual-Principle) would not produce them itself. Thence it must draw its power to bring forth, to teem with offspring of itself; I but the Good bestows what itself does[14] not possess. I From that Unity came multiplicity to Intellectual-Principle; it could not sustain the power poured upon it and therefore broke it up; it turned that one power into variety so as to carry it piecemeal.

All its production, effected in the power of The Good, contains goodness; it is good, itself, since it is constituted by these things of good; it is Good made diverse. It might be likened to a living sphere teeming with variety, to a globe of faces radiant with faces all living, to a unity of souls, all the pure souls, not the faulty but the perfect, with Intellect enthroned over all so that the place entire glows with Intellectual splendour.

But this would be to see it from without, one thing seeing another; the true way is to become Intellectual-Principle and be, our very selves, what we are to see.

16. But even there we are not to remain always, in that beauty of the multiple; we must make haste yet higher, above this heaven of ours and even that; leaving all else aside we ask in awe, Who produced that realm and how? Everything There is a single Idea in an individual impression and, I informed by The Good, possesses a common property which extends to all. Everything possesses Being as a common property, and possesses also the Form of Living-Being in virtue of that life which belongs to all alike; and perhaps possesses much else in common.[15] I

But what is the Nature of this Transcendent in view of which and by way of which the Ideas are good?

The best way of putting the question is to ask whether, when Intellectual-Principle looked towards The Good, it had Intellection of that unity as a multiplicity and, itself a unity, applied its Act by breaking into parts what it was too feeble to know as a whole.

At first it was not Intellect looking upon the Good; it was a looking void of Intellection. We must think of it not as looking but as living; dependent upon That, it kept itself turned Thither; all the tendance taking place There and upon That must be a movement teeming with life and must so fill the looking Principle; there is no longer bare Act, there is a filling to saturation. Forthwith it becomes all things, knows that fact in virtue of its self-knowing and at once becomes Intellectual-Principle, filled so as to hold within itself that object of its vision, seeing all by the light from the Giver and bearing that light with it.

In this way the Supreme may be understood to be the cause at once of essential reality and of the knowing of reality. The sun, cause of the existence of sense-things and of their being seen, is indirectly the cause of sight, without being either the faculty or the object: similarly this Principle, The Good, cause of Being and Intellectual-Principle, is a light appropriate to what is to be seen There and to their seer; neither the Beings nor the Intellectual-Principle, it is their source and by the light it sheds upon both makes them objects of Intellection. This filling procures the existence; after the filling the being; the existence achieved, the seeing followed: the beginning is that state of not yet having been filled, though there is, also, the beginning which means that the Filling Principle was in some sense outside and by that act of filling gave shape to the filled.

17. ❙ But how does Intellectual-Principle acquire its content, and how does it come to exist, if the content was not in the Filling Principle? It was not in the filled which before that moment was void of all content.[16] ❙

Giving need not comport possessing; in this order we are to think of a giver as a greater and of a gift as a lower; this is the meaning of origin among real Beings. First there must be an actualized thing; its laters must be potentially their own priors; a first must transcend its derivatives; the giver transcends the given, as a superior. If therefore there is a prior to actuality, that prior transcends Activity and so transcends Life. The Intellectual-Principle contains life, and the giver of this life is therefore a principle of greater good, of greater worth than Life; in gaining life the Intellectual-Principle had no need to look for it to any giver in possession of Life's variety.

The Life was a vestige of that Primal, not a life lived by it; Life, then, as it looked towards That was undetermined; having looked it had determination though That had none. Life looks to unity and is determined by it, taking bound, limit, form. But this form is in the shaped, the shaper had none; the limit was not external as something drawn about a magnitude; the limit was that of the multiplicity of the Life There, limitless itself as radiated from its great Prior; the Life itself was not that of some determined being, or it would be no more than the life of an individual. Yet it is defined; it must then have been defined as the Life of a unity including multiplicity; certainly too each item of the multiplicity is determined, determined as multiple by the multiplicity of Life but as a unity by the fact of limit.

As what, then, is its unity determined?

As Intellectual-Principle: determined Life is Intellectual-Principle. And the multiplicity?

As the multiplicity of Intellectual-Principles: all its multiplicity resolves itself into Intellectual-Principles—on the one hand the collective Principle, on the other the particular Principles.

But does this collective Intellectual-Principle include each of the particular Principles as **|** identical with each other?[17] **|**

No: it would be thus the container of only the one thing; since there are many Intellectual-Principles within the collective, there must be differentiation.

Once more, how does the particular Intellect come to this differentiation?

It takes its characteristic difference by becoming entirely a unity within the collective whose totality could not be identical with any particular.

Thus the Life in the Supreme was the collectivity of power; the vision taking place There was the potentiality of all; Intellectual-Principle, thus arising, is manifested as this universe of Being. It stands over the Beings not as itself requiring base but that it may serve them as base through its vision of that Form of the Firsts, the Formless Form. And it takes position towards the soul, becoming a light to the soul as itself finds its light in the One; whenever Intellectual-Principle becomes the determinant of soul it shapes it into Reasoning Soul, by communicating a trace of what itself has come to possess.

Thus Intellectual-Principle is a vestige of the Supreme; but since the vestige is a Form going out into extension, into plurality, that Prior, as the source of Form, must be itself without shape and Form: if the Prior were a Form, the Intellectual-Principle itself could be only a Reason-Principle. It was necessary that The First be utterly without multiplicity, for otherwise it must be again referred to a prior.

18. But in what way is the content of Intellectual-Principle participant in good? Is it because each member of it is an Idea or because of their beauty, or how?

Anything coming from The Good carries the image and type belonging to that original or deriving from it, as anything going back to warmth or sweetness carries the memory of those originals: Life entered into Intellectual-Principle from The Supreme, for its origin is in the Activity streaming Thence; Intellectual-Principle springs from the Supreme, and with it the beauty of the Ideas; at once all these, Life, Intellectual-Principle, Idea, must inevitably have goodness.

652 | PLOTINUS: THE ENNEADS

But what is the common element in them? Derivation from the First is not enough to procure identical quality; there must be some element held in common by the things derived: one source may produce many differing things as also one outgoing thing may take difference in various recipients: what enters into the First Act is different from what that Act transmits and there is difference, again, in the effect here. None the less every item may be good in a degree of its own. To what, then, is the highest degree due?

But first we must ask whether Life is a Good—bare Life, or only the Life streaming Thence, very different from the Life known here? Once more, then, what constitutes the goodness of Life?

The Life of The Good, or rather not its Life but that given forth from it.

But if in that higher Life there must be something from That, something which is the Authentic Life, we must admit that, since nothing worthless can come❙ Thence, that Authentic Life in which it appears[18] is good; ❙ so too we must admit in the case of Authentic and Primary Intellectual-Principle that it is good; thus it becomes clear that every Idea is good and informed by the Good. The Ideas must have something of good whether as a common property or as a distinct attribution or as held in some distinct measure.

Thus it is established that the particular Idea contains in its essence something of good and thereby becomes a good thing; for Life we found to be good not in the bare being but in its derivation from the Authentic, the Supreme whence it sprung: and the same is true of Intellectual-Principle: we are forced therefore to admit a certain identity.

When, with all their differences, things may be affirmed to have a measure of identity, the matter of the identity may very well be established in their very essence and yet be mentally abstracted; thus life in man or horse yields the notion of animal; from water or fire we may get that of warmth; the first case is a definition of kind, the other two cite qualities, primary and secondary respectively. ❙ The other possibility is that two or more terms might receive the same predicate by an equivocation.[19] ❙

Is The Good, then, inherent in the Ideas essentially? Each of them is good as a whole, but the goodness is not that of the Unity-Good. How, then, is it present?

By the mode of parts?

But The Good is without parts.

No doubt The Good is a unity; but here it has become particularized. The First Activity is good and anything determined in accord with it is good, as also is any resultant. The First Activity is good by origin in the First: the determination is good as an ordered system derived from that Earlier; the resultant is good because it is the resultant of those two. Derived, then, not identical—like the speech and walk and other characteristics of one man, each playing its due part.

Here, it is obvious, goodness depends upon order, rhythm, but what equivalent exists There?

We might answer that in the case of the sense-order the good is imposed since the ordering is of things different from the Orderer but that There the very things are good.

But why are they thus good in themselves? We cannot be content with the conviction of their goodness on the ground of their origin in that realm: we do not deny that things deriving Thence are good, but our subject demands that we discover the mode by which they come to possess that goodness.

19. Are we to rest all on pursuit and on the soul? Is it enough to put faith in the soul's affection and call that good which the soul pursues, never asking ourselves the motive of its pursuit? We marshal demonstration as to the nature of everything else; is the good to be dismissed as choice?

Several absurdities would be entailed. I The good becomes a mere contingency; pursuers are many and pursue different objects,[20] so that I mere choice gives no assurance that the thing chosen is the best; in fact we cannot know the best until we know the good.

Are we to determine the good by the respective values of things?

This is to make Idea and Reason-Principle the test: all very well; but arrived at these, what explanation have we to give as to why Idea and Reason-Principle themselves are good? In the lower we recognize goodness—in its less perfect form—by comparison with what is poorer still; we are without a standard There where no evil exists, the Bests holding the field, alone. Reason demands to know what constitutes goodness; those principles are good in their own nature and we are left in perplexity because cause and fact are identical: and even though we should state a cause, the doubt still remains until our reason claims its rights There. But we need not abandon the search; another path may lead to the light.

20. Since we are not entitled to make desire the test by which to decide on the nature and quality of the good, I we may perhaps have recourse to the Soul's discrimination.

We start from[21] the opposition of things I —order, disorder; symmetry, irregularity; health, illness; form, shapelessness; real-being, decay: in a word, continuity against dissolution. The first in each pair, no one could doubt, belongs to the concept of good and therefore whatever tends to produce these firsts must be ranged on the good side.

Thus virtue and Intellectual-Principle and life and soul—reasoning soul, at least—belong to the idea of good and so therefore does all that a reasoned life aims at.

Why not halt, then—it will be asked—at Intellectual-Principle and make that The Good? Soul and life are traces of Intellectual-Principle; that principle is the Term of Soul which on judgement sets itself towards Intellectual-Principle, pronouncing right preferable to wrong and virtue in every form to vice, and thus ranking by its choosing.

The soul aiming only at that Principle would need a further lessoning; it must be taught that Intellectual-Principle is not the ultimate, that not all things look to that while all do look to The Good. Not all that is outside of Intellectual-Principle seeks to attain it; what has attained it does not halt there but looks still towards good. Besides, Intellectual-Principle is sought upon motives of reasoning, The Good before all reason. And in any striving towards life and continuity of existence and activity, the object is aimed at not as Intellectual-Principle but as good, as rising from good and leading to it: life itself is desirable only in view of good.

21. Now what in all these objects of desire is the fundamental making them good? We must be bold:

Intellectual-Principle and that life are of the order of good and hold their desirability, even they, in virtue of belonging to that order; they have their goodness, I mean, because Life is an Activity in The Good—or rather, streaming from The Good—while Intellectual-Principle is the Activity as already defined; both are of radiant beauty and, because they come Thence and lead Thither, they are sought after by the soul—sought, that is, as things congenial though not veritably good while yet, as belonging to that order, not to be rejected; the related if not good is shunned in spite of that relationship, and even remote and ignobler things may at times prove attractive.

The intense love called forth by Life and Intellectual-Principle is due not to what they are but to their receiving from above something quite apart from their own nature.[22]

Material forms containing light incorporated in them need still a light apart from them that their own light may be manifest; just so the Beings of that sphere, all lightsome, need another and a lordlier light or even they would not be visible to themselves and beyond.

22. That light known, then indeed we are stirred towards those Beings in longing and rejoicing over the radiance about them, just as earthly love is not for the material form but for the Beauty manifested upon it. Every one of those Beings exists for itself but becomes an object of desire by the colour cast upon it from The Good, source of those graces and of the love they evoke. The soul taking that outflow from the divine is stirred; seized with a Bacchic passion, goaded by

these goads, it becomes Love. Before that, even Intellectual-Principle with all its loveliness did not stir the soul; for that beauty is dead until it take the light of The Good, and the soul lies supine, cold to all, unquickened even to Intellectual-Principle there before it. But when there enters into it a glow from the divine, it gathers strength, awakens, spreads true wings, and however urged by its nearer environing, speeds its buoyant way elsewhere, to something greater to its memory: so long as there exists anything loftier than the near, its very nature bears it upwards, lifted by the giver of that love. Beyond Intellectual-Principle it passes but beyond The Good it cannot, for nothing stands above That. Let it remain in Intellectual-Principle and it sees the lovely and august, but it is not there possessed of all it sought; the face it sees is beautiful no doubt but not of power to hold its gaze because lacking in the radiant grace which is the bloom upon beauty.

Even here we have to recognize that beauty is that which irradiates symmetry rather than symmetry itself and is that which truly calls out our love.

Why else is there more of the glory of beauty upon the living and only some faint trace of it upon the dead though the face yet retains all its fullness and symmetry? Why are the most living portraits the most beautiful, even though the other happen to be more symmetric? Why is the living ugly more attractive than the sculptured handsome? It is that the one is more nearly what we are looking for, and this because there is soul there, because there is more of the Idea of The Good, because there is some glow of the light of The Good and this illumination awakens and lifts the soul and all that goes with it, so that the whole man is won over to goodness and in the fullest measure stirred to life.

23. That which soul must quest, that which sheds its light upon Intellectual-Principle, leaving its mark wherever it falls, surely we need not wonder that it be of power to draw to itself, calling back from every wandering to rest before it. From it came all and so there is nothing mightier; all is feeble before it. Of all things the best, must it not be The Good? If by The Good we mean the principle most wholly self-sufficing, utterly without need of any other, what can it be but this? Before all the rest it was what it was, when evil had yet no place in things.

If evil is a Later, there found where there is no trace of This—among the very ultimates, so that on the downward side evil has no beyond—then to This evil stands full contrary with no linking intermediate: This therefore is The Good: either good there is none, or if there must be, This and no other is it.

❙ And to deny The Good[23] ❙ would be to deny evil also; there can then be no difference in objects coming up for choice: but that is untenable.

To This looks all else that passes for good; This, to nothing.

What then does it effect out of its greatness?

It has produced Intellectual-Principle, it has produced Life, the souls which Intellectual-Principle sends forth and everything else that partakes of Reason, of Intellectual-Principle, or of Life. Source and spring of so much, how describe its goodness and greatness?

But what does it effect now?

Even now it is preserver of what it produced; by it the Intellectual Beings have their Intellection and the living their life; it breathes Intellect in, breathes Life in and, where life is impossible, existence.

24. But ourselves—how does it touch us?

We may recall what we have said of the nature of the light shining from it into Intellectual-Principle and so by participation into the soul. But for the moment let us leave that aside and put another question:

Does The Good hold that nature and name because some outside thing finds it desirable? May we put it that a thing desirable to one is good to that one and that what is desirable to all is to be recognized as The Good?

No doubt this universal questing would make the goodness evident but still there must be in the nature something to earn that name.

Further, is the questing determined by the hope of some acquisition or by sheer delight? If there is acquisition, what is it? If it is a matter of delight, why here rather than in something else?

The question comes to this: Is goodness in the appropriate or in something apart, and is The Good good as regards itself also or good only as possessed?

Is any good such, necessarily, not for itself but for something outside? What is the nature for which it is good? Is there a nature for which nothing is a good?

And we must not overlook what some surly critic will surely bring up against us:

What's all this: you scatter praises here, there, and everywhere: Life is good, Intellectual-Principle is good: and yet The Good is above them; how then can Intellectual-Principle itself be good? **I** What good do we gain by contemplating the Ideas? Do we merely see a particular Idea (and not also the Good)?[24] **I** If we are happy in this contemplation we may be deceived into thinking it a good, and life itself a good when it is merely pleasant. But suppose our lot unhappy, why should we speak of good? Is mere personal existence good? What profit is there in it? What is the advantage in existence over utter non-existence—unless goodness is to be founded upon our love of self? It is the deception rooted in the nature of things and our dread of dissolution that lead to all the 'goods' of your positing.

25. It is in view, probably, of this difficulty that Plato in the Philebus makes

pleasure an element in the Term; the good is not defined as a simplex or set in Intellectual-Principle alone; while he rightly refrains from identifying the good with the pleasant, yet he does not allow Intellectual-Principle, in the absence of pleasure, to be The Good, since he sees no attractive power in it. He may also have had in mind that the good, to answer to its name, must be a thing of delight and that an object of pursuit must at least hold some pleasure for those that acquire and possess it, so that where there is no joy the good too is absent; further that pleasure, implying pursuit, cannot pertain to the First and that therefore good cannot.

All this was very well; there the inquiry was not as to the Primal Good but as to ours; the good dealt with in that passage is a quite different good, falling short of that higher and supposedly a mingled thing. We are to understand that good does not hold place in 'the Solitary and Alone' whose being is too great and different for that.

The good must, no doubt, be a thing pursued, not, however, good because it is pursued but pursued because it is good.

The solution, it would seem, lies in priority:

To the lowest of things the good is its immediate higher; each step represents the good to what stands lower so long as the movement does not tend awry but advances continuously towards the superior: thus there is a halt at the Ultimate, beyond which no ascent is possible: that is the First Good, the authentic, the supremely sovran, the source of good to the rest of things.

Matter would have Forming-Idea for its good, since were it conscious it would welcome that; body would look to soul, without which it could not be or endure; soul must look to virtue; still higher stands Intellectual-Principle; above that again is the principle we call the Primal. Each of these progressive priors must have act upon those minors to which they are, respectively, the good: some will confer order and place, others life, others wisdom and the good life: I Intellectual-Principle will draw upon the Authentic Good which we hold to enter into[25] it, I both as being an Activity put forth from it and as even now taking what we designate as light from it. This good we will define later.

26. Any conscious being, if the good come to him, will know the good and affirm his possession of it.

But what if one be deceived?

In that case there must be some resemblance to account for the error: the good will be the original which the delusion counterfeited and whenever the true presents itself we turn from the spurious.

All the striving, all the pain, show that to everything something is a good: the lifeless finds its share in something outside itself; where there is life the longing for good sets up pursuit: the very dead are cared for and mourned for by the living; the living plan for their own good. The witness of attainment is betterment, absence of regret, satisfaction, settlement, suspension of pursuit. Here pleasure shows itself inadequate: its choice does not hold; repeated, it is no longer the same; it demands endless novelty. The good, worthy of the name, can be no such tasting of the casual; anyone that takes this kind of thing for the good goes empty, carrying away nothing but an emotion which the good might have produced. No one could be content to take his pleasure thus in an emotion over a thing not possessed any more than over a child not there; I cannot think that those setting their good in bodily satisfactions find table-pleasure without the meal or love-pleasure without intercourse with their chosen or any pleasure where nothing is done.

27. But what is that whose entry supplies every such need?

Some Form, we maintain. There is a Form to which Matter aspires: to soul moral excellence is this Form.

But is this Form a good to the thing as being apt to it, does the striving aim at the apt?

No: the aptest would be the most resemblant to the thing itself, but that, however sought and welcomed, does not suffice for the good: the good must be something more: to be a good to another a thing must have something beyond aptness; I that only can be adopted as the good which represents a higher worth and standing than the merely apt and is that which the apt [26] tends potentially to be. I

A thing is potentially that to which its nature looks; this, obviously, it lacks; what it lacks, of its better, is its good. Matter is of all the most in need; its next is the lowest Form; Form at lowest is just one grade higher than Matter. If a thing is a good to itself, much more must its perfection, its Form, its better, be a good to it; this better, good in its own nature, must be good also to the quester whose good it procures.

But why should the Form which makes a thing good be a good to that thing? I As being most apt? [27] I

No: but because it is, itself, a portion of the Good. This is why the least alloyed and nearest to the good are most at peace within themselves (have most 'self-aptness').

It is surely out of place to ask why a thing which is good should be good to itself; we can hardly suppose that it must strain outside its essential quality to find goodness, instead of enjoying the good which it effectually is.

There remains the question with regard to the Simplex: where there is utter absence of distinction does this self-aptness constitute the good to that Simplex? Is it good for itself?

If thus far we have been right, the striving of the lower possesses itself of the good as of a thing resident in a certain kind and it is not the striving that constitutes the good but the good that calls out the striving: where the good is attained something is acquired and on this acquisition there follows pleasure. I But the question of whether the good must be chosen though no pleasure ensued demands separate inquiry.[28] I

28. Now to see what all this reasoning has established:

Universally what approaches as a good is a Form; Matter itself contains this good which is Form: are we to conclude that if Matter had will it would desire to be Form unalloyed?

No: that would be desiring its own destruction whereas everything seeks what will do it good. But perhaps Matter would not wish to remain at its own level but would prefer to attain Being and, this acquired, to lay aside its evil.

If we are asked how the evil thing can have tendency towards the good, we answer that we have not attributed tendency to Matter; our argument needed the hypothesis of sensation in Matter—in so far as possible consistently with retention of its character—and we asserted that the entry of Form, that dream of the Good, must raise it to a nobler order. If then Matter is Evil, there is no more to be said; if it is something else—a wrong thing, let us say—then in the hypothesis that its essence acquire sensation would not the appropriate upon the next or higher plane be its good, as in the other cases? But not what is evil in Matter would be the quester of good but that element in it (lowest Form) which is associated with evil.

But if Matter by very essence is evil how could it choose the good?

This question implies that if Evil were self-conscious it would admire itself: but how can the unadmirable be admired; and did we not decline to identify the good with what was apt to the nature?

There that question may rest. But if universally the good is Form and the higher the ascent the more there is of Form—Soul more truly Form than body is and phases of soul progressively of higher Form and Intellectual-Principle standing as Form to soul collectively—then the Good advances by the opposite of Matter and therefore, by a cleansing and casting away to the utmost possible at each stage: and the greatest good must be there where all that is of Matter has disappeared. The Principle of Good rejecting Matter entirely—or rather never having come near it at any point or in any way—must hold itself aloft with that Formless in which Primal Form takes its origin. But we will return to this.

29. Suppose, however, that pleasure did not result from the good but there were something preceding pleasure and accounting for it, would not this be a thing to be embraced?

But when we say 'to be embraced' we say 'pleasure'.

But what if accepting its existence, we think of that existence as leaving still the possibility that it were not a thing to be embraced?

This would mean the good being present and the sentient possessor failing, none the less, to perceive it.

It would seem possible, however, to perceive and yet be unmoved by the possession; this is quite likely in the case of the wiser and least dependent—and indeed it is so with the First, immune not merely because simplex, but because pleasure by acquisition implies lack.

But all this will become clear on the solution of our remaining difficulties and the rebuttal of the stubborn argument brought up against us. This takes the form of the question: What gain is there in the Good to one who, fully conscious, feels nothing when he hears of these things, whether because he has no grasp of them but takes merely the words or because he holds to false values, perhaps being all in search of sense, finding his good in money or such things?

The answer is that even in his disregard of the good proposed he is with us in setting a good before him but fails to see how the good we define fits into his own conception. It is impossible to say 'Not that' if one is utterly without experience or conception of the 'That'; there will generally have been, even, some inkling of the good beyond Intellection. Besides, one attaining or approaching the Good but not recognizing it may assure himself in the light of its contraries; otherwise he will not even hold ignorance an evil, though everyone prefers to know and is proud of knowing, so that our very sensations seek to ripen into knowledge.

If the knowing principle—and specially primal Intellectual-Principle—is valuable and beautiful, what must be present to those of power to see the Author and Father of Intellect? Anyone thinking slightingly of this principle of Life and Being brings evidence against himself and all his state: of course distaste for the life that is mingled with death does not touch that Life Authentic.

30. Whether pleasure must enter into the good, so that life in the contemplation of the divine things and especially of their source remains still imperfect, is a question not to be ignored in any inquiry into the nature of the Good.

Now to found the good upon the Intellect and upon that state of soul or mind which springs from wisdom does not imply that the end or the Absolute Good is the conjunction (of Intellect and state): it would follow merely that Intellect is the good and that we feel happy in possession of that good. That is one theory;

another associates pleasure with Intellect in the sense that the good is taken to be some one thing founded upon both but depending upon our attaining or at least contemplating an Intellect so modified; this theory would maintain that the 'solitary and alone' could not be the good, could not be an object of desire.

But how could Intellect and pleasure combine into one mutually complementary nature?

Bodily pleasure no one, certainly, would think capable of blending in with Intellect; the unreasoning satisfactions of soul (or lower mind) are equally incompatible with it.

Every activity, state, and life will be followed and as it were escorted by the overdwelling consciousness; sometimes as these take their natural course they will be met by hindrance and by intrusion of the conflicting so that the life is the less self-guided; sometimes the natural activity is unmixed, wholly free, and then the life goes brilliantly; this last state of the Intellect is judged the pleasantest, the most to be chosen; so, for lack of an accurate expression, we hear of 'Intellect in conjunction with pleasure'. But this is no more than metaphor, like a hundred others drawn by the poets from our natural likings—'Drunk with nectar', 'To banquet and feast', 'The father smiled'. No: the veritably pleasant lies away in that other realm, the most to be loved and sought for, not something brought about and changing but the very principle of all the colour and radiance and brightness found here. This is why we read of 'Truth introduced into the Mixture' and of the 'measuring standard as a prior condition' and are told that the symmetry and beauty necessary to the Mixture come Thence into whatever has beauty; it is in this way that we have our share in the Good; but in another way, also, we achieve the truly desirable, that is by leading ourselves up to what is best within us; this best is what is symmetry, beauty, incomposite Idea, life clear, intellective, and good.

31. But since the beauty and light in all come from That which is before all, it is Thence that Intellectual-Principle took the brilliance of the Intellectual Energy I which flashed its nature[29] into being; I Thence Soul took power towards life, in virtue of that fuller life streaming into it. Intellectual-Principle was raised thus to that Supreme and remains with it, happy in that presence. Soul too, that soul which as possessing knowledge and vision was capable, clung to what it saw; and as its vision so its rapture; it saw and was stricken; but having in itself something of that principle it felt its kinship and was moved to longing like those stirred by the image of the beloved to desire of the veritable presence. Lovers here mould themselves to the beloved; they seek to increase their attraction of person and their likeness of mind; they are unwilling to fall short in

moral quality or in other graces lest they be distasteful to those possessing such merit—and only among such can true love be. In the same way the soul loves the Supreme Good, from its very beginnings stirred by it to love. The soul which has never strayed from this love waits for no reminding from the beauty of our world: holding that love—perhaps unawares—it is ever in quest, and, in its longing to be borne Thither, passes over what is lovely here and with one glance at the beauty of the universe dismisses all; for it sees that all is put together of flesh and Matter, befouled by its housing, made fragmentary by corporal extension, not the Authentic Beauty which could never venture into the mud of body to be soiled, annulled.

By only noting the flux of things it knows at once that from elsewhere comes the beauty that floats upon them and so it is urged Thither, passionate in pursuit of what it loves: never—unless someone robs it of that love—never giving up till it attain.

There indeed all it saw was beautiful and veritable; it grew in strength by being thus filled with the life of the True; itself becoming veritable Being and attaining veritable knowledge, it enters by that neighbouring into conscious possession of what it has long been seeking.

32. Where, then? where exists the author of this beauty and life, the begetter of the veritable?

I You see the splendour over all the manifold Forms or[30] Ideas; I well might we linger here: but amid all these things of beauty we cannot but ask whence they come and whence the beauty. This source can be none of the beautiful objects; were it so, it too would be a mere part. It can be no shape, no power, nor the total of powers and shapes that have had the becoming that has set them here; it must stand above all the powers, all the patterns. The origin of all this must be the formless—formless not as lacking shape but as the very source of even shape Intellectual.

In the realm of process anything coming to be must come to be something; to every thing its distinctive shape: but what shape can that have which no one has shaped? It can be none of existing things; yet it is all: none, in that beings are later; all, as the wellspring from which they flow. That which can make all can have, itself, no extension; it must be limitless and so without magnitude; magnitude itself is of the Later and cannot be an element in that which is to bring it into being. The greatness of the Authentic cannot be a greatness of quantity; all extension must belong to the subsequent: the Supreme is great in the sense only that there can be nothing mightier, nothing to equal it, nothing with anything in common with it: how then could anything be equal to any part of its content? Its eternity and universal reach entail neither measure nor measurelessness; given either, how could it be the measure of things? So with shape: granted beauty, the absence of shape or form to be grasped is but enhancement of desire and love; the love will be limitless as the object is, an infinite love.

Its beauty, too, will be unique, a beauty above beauty: it cannot be beauty since it is not a thing among things. It is lovable and the author of beauty; as the power to all beautiful shape, it will be the ultimate of beauty, that which brings all loveliness to be; it begets beauty and makes it yet more beautiful by the excess of beauty streaming from itself, the source and height of beauty. As the source of beauty it makes beautiful whatsoever springs from it. And this conferred beauty is not itself in shape; the thing that comes to be is without shape, though in another sense shaped; what is denoted by shape is, in itself, an attribute of something else, shapeless at first. Not the beauty but its participant takes the shape.

33. When therefore we name beauty, all such shape must be dismissed; nothing visible is to be conceived, or at once we descend from beauty to what but bears the name in virtue of some faint participation. This formless Form is beautiful as Form, beautiful in proportion as we strip away all shape, even that given in thought to mark difference, as for instance the difference between Justice and Sophrosyny, beautiful in their difference.

The Intellectual-Principle is the less for seeing things as distinct, even in its act of grasping in unity the multiple content of its Intellectual realm; in its knowing of the particular it possesses itself of one Intellectual shape; but, even thus, in this dealing with variety as unity, it leaves us still with the question how we are to envisage that which stands beyond this all-lovely, beyond this principle at once multiple and above multiplicity, the Supreme for which the soul hungers though unable to tell why such a being should stir its longing—reason, however, urging that This at last is the Authentic Term because the Nature best and most to be loved may be found there only where there is no least touch of Form. Bring something under Form and present it so before the mind; immediately we ask what Beyond imposed that shape; reason answers that while there exists the giver having shape to give—a giver that is shape, idea, an entirely measured thing—yet this is not entire, is not adequate in itself, is not beautiful in its own right but is a mingled thing. Shape and idea and measure will always be beautiful, but the Authentic Beauty, or rather the Beyond-Beauty, cannot be under measure and therefore cannot have admitted shape or be Idea: I the primal Beauty, The First, must be without Form; the beauty of that higher realm must be, simply, the Nature of the[31] Good. I

Take an example from love: so long as the attention is upon the visible form, love has not entered: when from that outward form the lover elaborates within himself, in his own partless soul, an immaterial image, then it is that love is born, then the lover longs for the sight of the beloved to make that fading image live again. If he could but learn to look elsewhere, to the more nearly formless, his longing would be for that: his first experience was loving a great luminary by way of some thin gleam from it.

Shape is an impress from the unshaped; it is the unshaped that produces shape, not shape the unshaped; and Matter is needed for the producing; Matter, in the nature of things, is the furthest away, since of itself it has not even the lowest degree of shape. Thus lovableness does not belong to Matter but to that which draws upon Form: the Form upon Matter comes by way of soul; soul is more nearly Form and therefore more lovable; Intellectual-Principle, nearer still, is even more to be loved: by these steps we are led to know that the primary nature of Beauty must be formless.

34. No longer can we wonder that the principle evoking such longing should be utterly free from shape, even shape Intellectual. The very soul, once it has conceived the straining love towards this, lays aside all the shape it has taken, even to the Intellectual shape that has informed it. There is no vision, no union, for those handling or acting by any thing other; the soul must see before it neither evil nor good nor anything else, that alone it may receive the Alone.

Suppose the soul to have attained: the highest has come to her, or rather has revealed its presence; she has turned away from all about her and made herself apt, beautiful to the utmost, brought into likeness with the divine—by those preparings and adornings which come unbidden to those growing ready for the vision—she has seen that presence suddenly manifesting within her, for there is nothing between: here is no longer a duality but a two in one; for, so long as the presence holds, all distinction fades: it is as lover and beloved here, in a copy of that union, long to blend; the soul has now no further awareness of being in body and will give herself no foreign name, not man, not living being, not being, not all; any observation of such things falls away; the soul has neither time nor taste for them; This she sought and This she has found and on This she looks and not upon herself; and who she is that looks she has not leisure to know. Once There she will barter for This nothing the universe holds; not though one would make over the heavens entire to her; than This there is nothing higher, nothing of more good; above This there is no passing; all the rest however lofty lies on the down-going path: she is of perfect judgement and knows that This was her quest, that nothing higher is. Here can be no deceit; where could she come upon truer than the truth? and the truth she affirms, that she is herself; but all the affirmation is later and is silent. In this happiness she knows beyond delusion that she is happy; for this is no affirmation of an excited body but of a soul become again what she was in the time of her early joy. All that she had welcomed of old—office, power, wealth, beauty, knowledge—of all she tells her scorn as she never could had she not found their better; I linked to This she can fear no disaster, nor even once she has had the vision;[32] let all I about her fall to pieces, so she would have it that she may be wholly with This, so huge the happiness she has won to.

35. Such in this union is the soul's temper that even the act of Intellect once so intimately loved she now dismisses; Intellection is movement and she has no wish I to move; the object of her vision has itself, she says, no Intellection, even though it is by means of the Intellectual-Principle that[33] she has attained the vision, I herself made over into Intellectual-Principle and becoming that principle so as to be able to take stand in that Intellectual space. Entered there and making herself over to that, she at first contemplates that realm, but once she sees that higher still she leaves all else aside. Thus when a man enters a house rich in beauty he might gaze about and admire the varied splendour before the master appears; but, face to face with that great person—no thing of ornament but calling for the truest attention—he would ignore everything else and look only to the master. In this state of absorbed contemplation there is no longer question of holding an object: the vision is continuous so that seeing and seen are one thing; object and act of vision have become identical; of all that until then filled the eye no memory remains. And our comparison would be closer if instead of a man appearing to the visitor who had been admiring the house it were a god, and not a god manifesting to the eyes but one filling the soul.

Intellectual-Principle, thus, has two powers, first that of grasping intellectively its own content, the second that of an advancing and receiving whereby to know its transcendent; at first it sees, later by that seeing it takes possession of Intellectual-Principle, becoming one only thing with that: the first seeing is that of Intellect knowing, the second that of Intellect loving; stripped of its wisdom in the intoxication of the nectar, it comes to love; by this excess it is made simplex and is happy; and to be drunken is better for it than to be too staid for these revels.

But is its vision parcelwise, thing here and thing there?

No; reason unravelling gives process; Intellectual-Principle has unbroken knowledge and has, moreover, an Act unattended by knowing, a vision by another approach. In this seeing of the Supreme it becomes pregnant and at once knows what has come to be within it; its knowledge of its content is what is designated by its Intellection; its knowing of the Supreme is the virtue of that power within it by which, in a later (lower) stage, it is to become 'Intellective'.

As for soul, it attains that vision by—so to speak—confounding and annulling the Intellectual-Principle within it; or rather that Principle immanent in soul sees first and thence the vision penetrates to soul and the two visions become one.

The Good spreading out above them and adapting itself to that union which it hastens to confirm is present to them as giver of a blessed sense and sight; so high it lifts them that they are no longer in space or in that realm of difference where everything is rooted in some other thing; for The Good is not in place but is the container of the Intellectual place; The Good is in nothing but itself.

The soul now knows no movement since the Supreme knows none; it is now not even soul since the Supreme is not in life but above life; it is no longer Intellectual-Principle, for the Supreme has not Intellection and the likeness must be perfect; this grasping is not even by Intellection, for the Supreme is not known intellectively.

36. We need not carry this matter further; we turn to a question already touched but demanding still some brief consideration. We may proceed from the point we have reached and follow the logical development.

I Knowing[34] of The Good or contact with it I is the all-important: this—we read—is the grand learning, the learning, we are to understand, not of looking towards it but attaining, first, some knowledge of it. We come to this learning by analogies, by abstractions, by our understanding of its subsequents, of all that is derived from The Good, by the upward steps towards it. Purification has The Good for goal; so the virtues, all right ordering, ascent within the Intellectual, settlement therein, banqueting upon the divine—by these methods one becomes, to self and to all else, at once seen and seer; identical with Being and Intellectual-Principle and the entire living all, we no longer see the Supreme as an external; we are near now, the next is That and it is close at hand, radiant above the Intellectual.

Here, we put aside all the learning; disciplined to this pitch, established in beauty, the quester holds knowledge still of the ground he rests on, but, suddenly, swept beyond it all by the very crest of the wave of Intellect surging beneath, he is lifted and sees, never knowing how; the vision floods the eyes with light, but it is not a light showing some other object, the light is itself the vision. No longer is there thing seen and light to show it, no longer Intellect and object of Intellection; this is the very radiance that brought both Intellect and Intellectual object into being for the later use and allowed them to occupy the quester's mind. With This he himself becomes identical, with that radiance whose Act is to engender Intellectual-Principle, not losing in that engendering but for ever unchanged, the engendered coming to be simply because that Supreme exists. If there were no such principle above change, no derivative could rise.

37. Those ascribing Intellection to the First have not supposed him to know the lesser, the emanant—though, indeed, some have thought it impossible that he should not know everything. But those denying his knowing of the lesser have still attributed self-knowing to him, because they find nothing nobler; we are to suppose that so he is the more august, as if Intellection were something nobler than his own manner of being, not something whose value derives from him.

But we ask in what must his grandeur lie, in his Intellection or in himself. If in the Intellection, he has no worth or the less worth; if in himself, he is perfect before the Intellection, not perfected by it. We may be told that he must have Intellection because he is an Act, not a potentiality. Now if this means that he is an essence eternally intellective, he is represented as a duality—essence and Intellective Act—he ceases to be a simplex; an external has been added: it is just as the eyes are not the same as their sight though the two are inseparable. If on the other hand by this actualization it is meant that he is Act and Intellection, then as being Intellection he does not exercise it, just as movement is not itself in motion.

But (we are reminded) do not we ourselves assert that the Beings There are essence and Act?

The Beings, yes, but they are to us manifold and differentiated: the First we make a simplex; to us Intellection begins with the emanant in its seeking of its essence, of itself, of its author; bent inward for this vision and having a present thing to know, there is every reason why it should be a principle of Intellection; but that which, never coming into being, has no prior but is ever what it is, how could that have motive to Intellection? As Plato rightly says, it is above Intellect.

An Intelligence not exercising Intellection would be unintelligent; where the nature demands knowing, not to know is to fail of intelligence; but where there is no function, why import one and declare a defect because it is not performed? We might as well complain because the Supreme does not act as a physician. He has no task, we hold, because nothing can present itself to him to be done; he is sufficient; he need seek nothing beyond himself, he who is over all; to himself and to all he suffices by simply being what he is.

38. And yet this 'He is' does not truly apply: the Supreme has no need of Being: even 'He is good' does not apply since it indicates Being: the 'is' should not suggest something predicated of another thing; it is to state identity. The word 'good' used of him is not a predicate asserting his possession of goodness; it conveys an identification. It is not that we think it exact to call him either good or The Good: it is that sheer negation does not indicate; we use the term The Good to assert identity without the affirmation of Being.

But how admit a Principle void of self-knowledge, self-awareness; surely the First must be able to say 'I possess Being'?

But he does not possess Being.

Then, at least he must say 'I am good'?

No: once more, that would be an affirmation of Being.

But surely he may affirm merely the goodness, adding nothing: the goodness would be taken without the being and all duality avoided?

No: such self-awareness as good must inevitably carry the affirmation 'I am the Good'; otherwise there would be merely the unattached conception of goodness with no recognition of identity; any such intellection would inevitably include the affirmation 'I am'.

If that intellection were the Good, then the intellection would not be self-intellection but intellection of the Good; not the Supreme but that intellection would be the Good: if on the contrary that intellection of the Good is distinct from the Good, at once the Good exists before its knowing; all-sufficiently good in itself, it needs none of that knowing of its own nature.

Thus the Supreme does not know itself as Good.

39. As what then?

No such foreign matter is present to it: it can have only an immediate intuition self-directed.

Since the Supreme has no interval, no self-differentiation, what can have this intuitional approach to it but itself? Therefore it quite naturally assumes difference at the point where Intellectual-Principle and Being are differentiated.

Intellect, to act at all, must inevitably comport difference with identity; otherwise it could not distinguish itself from its object by standing apart from it, nor could it ever be aware of the realm of things whose existence demands otherness, nor could there be so much as a duality.

Again, if the Supreme is to have intellection it cannot know only itself; that would not be intellection, for, if it did know itself, nothing could prevent it knowing all things—certainly not lack of power. With self-intellection it would no longer be simplex; self-intellection must be aware of the self as something distinct, otherwise it could never take place at all. Our view is, however, that even if the Supreme chose to see itself as external, it could not have[35] intellection. That act requires a manifold—agent, object, movement, and all the other conditions of a thinking principle. Further we must remember what has been indicated elsewhere that, since every intellectual act in order to be what it must be requires variety, every movement simple and the same throughout, though it may comport some form of contact, is devoid of the intellective.

It follows that the Supreme will know neither itself nor anything else but will hold an august repose. All the rest is later; before them all, This was what This was; any awareness of that other would be acquired, the shifting knowledge of the instable. Even in knowing the stable he would be manifold, for it is not possible that, while in the act of knowing the laters possess themselves of their object, the Supreme should know only in some unpossessing observation.

As regards Providence, that is sufficiently saved by the fact that This is the source from which all proceeds; the dependent he cannot know when he has no knowledge of himself but keeps that august repose. Plato dealing with essential Being allows it intellection but not this august repose: intellection then belongs to Essential Being; this august repose to the Principle in which there is no intellection. Repose, of course, is used here for want of a fitter word; we are to understand that the most august, the truly so, is That which transcends (the movement of) Intellection.

40. That there can be no intellection in the First will be patent to those that have had such contact; but some further confirmation is desirable, if indeed words can carry the matter; we need overwhelming persuasion.

It must be borne in mind that all intellection rises in some principle and takes cognizance of an object. But a distinction is to be made:

There is the intellection that remains within its place of origin; it has that source as substratum but becomes a sort of addition to it in that it is an activity of that source perfecting the potentiality there, not by producing anything but as being a completing power to the principle in which it inheres. There is also the intellection inbound with Being—Being's very author—and this could not remain confined to the source since there it could produce nothing; it is a power to production; it produces therefore of its own motion and its act is Real-Being and there it has its dwelling. In this mode the intellection is identical with Being; even in its self-intellection no distinction is made save the logical distinction of thinker and thought with, as we have often observed, the implication of plurality.

This is a first activity and the substance it produces is Essential Being; it is an image, but of an original so great that the very copy stands a reality. If instead of moving outward it remained with the First, it would be no more than some appurtenance of that First, not a self-standing existent.

As the earliest activity and earliest intellection it can be preceded by no act or intellection: if we pass beyond this being and this intellection we come not to more being and more intellection but to what overpasses both, to the wonderful which has neither, asking nothing of these products and standing its unaccompanied self.

That all-transcending cannot have had an activity by which to produce this activity—acting before act existed—or have had thought in order to produce thinking—applying thought before thought exists—all intellection, even of the Good, is beneath it.

In sum, this intellection of the Good is impossible: I do not mean that it is impossible to have intellection of the Good—we may admit the possibility— but there can be no intellection by The Good itself, for this would be to include the inferior with the Good.

If intellection is the lower, then it will be bound up with Being; if intellection is the higher, its object is lower. Intellection, then, does not exist in the Good; as a lesser, taking its worth through that Good, it must stand apart from it, leaving the Good unsoiled by it as by all else. Immune from intellection the Good remains incontaminably what it is, not impeded by the presence of the intellectual act which would annul its purity and unity.

Anyone making the Good at once Thinker and Thought identifies it with Being and with the Intellection vested in Being so that it must stand as self-intellective: at once it becomes necessary to find another principle, one superior to that Good: for either this act, this intellection, is a completing power of some such principle serving as its ground, or it points, by that duality, to a prior principle having intellection as a characteristic. It is because there is something before it that it has an object of intellection; even in its self-intellection it may be said to know its content by its vision of that prior.

What has no prior and no external accompaniment could have no intellection, either of itself or of anything else. What could it aim at, what desire? To essay its power of knowing? But this would make the power something outside itself; there would be, I mean, the power it grasped and the power by which it grasped: if there is but the one power, what is there to grasp at?

41. Intellection seems to have been given as an aid to the diviner but weaker beings, an eye to the blind. But the eye itself need not see Being since it is itself the light; what must take the light through the eye needs the light because of its darkness. If then intellection is the light and light does not need the light, surely that brilliance (The First) which does not need light can have no need of intellection, will not add this to its nature. What could it do with intellection? What could even intellection need and add to itself for the purpose of its act?

The First has no self-awareness; there is no need. It is no duality—or rather, no manifold consisting of itself, its intellective act distinct from itself, and the inevitable third, the object of intellection. No doubt since knower, knowing, and known are identical, all merges into a unity: but the distinction has existed and, once more, such a unity cannot be the First; we must put away all otherness from the Supreme which can need no such support; anything we add is so much lessening of what lacks nothing.

To us intellection is a boon since the soul needs it; to the Intellectual-Principle it is appropriate as being one thing with the very essence of the principle constituted by the Intellectual Act, so that principle and act coincide in a continuous self-consciousness carrying the assurance of identity, of the unity of the two. But pure unity must be independent, in need of no such assurance.

'Know yourself' is a precept for those who, being manifold, have the task of appraising themselves so as to become aware of the number and nature of their constituents, some or all of which they ignore as they ignore their very principle and their manner of being. The First, on the contrary, if it have content must exist in a way too great to have any knowledge, intellection, perception of it. To itself it is nothing; accepting nothing, self-sufficing, it is not even a good to itself: to others it is good for they have need of it; but it could not lack itself: it would be absurd to suppose The Good standing in need of goodness.

It does not see itself: seeing aims at acquisition: all this it abandons to the subsequent: in fact nothing found elsewhere can be There; even Being cannot be There. Nor therefore has it intellection since Being goes with intellection: the first and true Intellection is identical with Being. Reason, perception, intelligence, none of these can have place in that Principle in which no presence can be affirmed.

42. Faced by the difficulty of placing these powers, you must in reason allocate to the secondaries what you count august: secondaries must not be foisted upon the First or tertiaries upon the secondaries. Secondaries are to be ranged under the First, tertiaries under the secondaries: this is giving everything its place, the later dependent on their priors, circling about them, those priors free.

This is included in that true saying, 'About the King of All, all has being and in view of Him all is': we are to understand from the attribution of all things to Him and from the words 'in view of Him' that He is their cause and they reach to Him as to something differing from them all and containing nothing that they contain: for they will be less than 'all' if anything of the later be in Him.

Thus, Intellectual-Principle, finding place in the 'all', cannot have place in Him. Where we read that He is 'the cause of all beauty' we are clearly to understand that beauty depends upon the Forms, He being set above all that is beautiful here. The Forms are in that passage secondaries, their sequels being attached to them as dependent thirds: 'about the thirds', it is clear, their products are ranged—this world, dependent upon soul.

Soul dependent upon Intellectual-Principle and Intellectual-Principle upon the Good, all is linked to the Supreme by intermediaries, some close, some nearing those of the closer attachment, while the order of sense stands remotest, dependent upon soul.

NOTES TO ENNEAD VI.7

1. FIRST EDITION: "A thing of inactivity, *even though alive,* cannot . . ."

GUTHRIE: ". . . things . . . whose life is without reality, and whose existence is shadowy."

ARMSTRONG: ". . . a thing which is inert and does not have life does not . . ."

COMMENT: Neoplatonism generally holds that only Matter itself is entirely without life. From this perspective, even the extremes of what would be called "tamas" in Hinduism have some degree of life.

2. FIRST EDITION: "But *how could that Principle have such perception, be aware of things of sense?* Surely it is untenable on the one hand that [omits "the capacity for"] sense-perception should exist There, from eternity, and on the other that only upon the debasement of the soul should there be [omits "actual] sense-perception here . . ."

ARMSTRONG: "But how would it not be absurd for there to be sense-perception from eternity, but for it to do its perceiving here below . . ."

3. FIRST EDITION: "But these principles producing *other forms than* man . . ."

ARMSTRONG supports the fourth edition.

GUTHRIE: ". . . these reasons, which do not beget the man (though they do beget the animal) . . ."

4. FIRST EDITION: ". . . it is the source of the [omits "lower"] soul's perception of the *sense-realm in its correspondence with the Intellectual.* Man as sense-percipient becomes aware of that correspondence and accomodates the sense-realm to the lowest extremity of its counterpart There, proceeding from the *fire Intellectual to the fire here* which *becomes* perceptible *by its analogy with that of the higher sphere.* If material things . . ."

ARMSTRONG: "This is the way, therefore, in which the better soul perceives the melody of sense, when the man of the sense-world receives it by sense-perception and comes into tune, to the last and lowest degree, with the melody there in the intelligible, and fire is tuned to the fire there, of which that better soul had a perception which corresponded to the nature of the fire there. For if . . ."

GUTHRIE: "Thus (by this intelligible sense-power) the Soul perceives the supersensual harmony and also the sensual, but in a manner such as the sense-man perceives it, relating it so far as possible to the superior harmony, just as he relates the earthly fire to the intelligible Fire, which is above, and which the superior Soul felt in a manner suitable to the nature of this fire."

5. FIRST EDITION: ". . . not in the sense of *actually living by* them all but . . ."

ARMSTRONG: ". . . not becoming those other men, but set alongside them."

GUTHRIE: ". . . he is not produced by them, he is rather united to them."

6. FIRST EDITION: ". . . higher still stands that *Man* more entirely of the Celestial rank, *almost*

a god, *reproducing God, a Celestial* closely bound to God as a man *is to Man.* For that Being *into which man develops* is not to be called a god;"

GUTHRIE: "The (intellectual) Man, who is anterior to this being, is of a nature still more like that of the guardians, or rather, he is already a divinity. The guardian attached to a divinity is an image of him, as the sense-man is the image of the intellectual man from whom he depends; for the principle to which man directly attaches himself must not be considered as his divinity."

ARMSTRONG: ". . . and he who is before the soul is more of a spirit, or rather is a god, and a spirit is an imitation of a god, dependent on the god as man is on the spirit; for the being on whom man is dependent is not called a god."

7. FIRST EDITION: "So much for the *thing of sense*; but it would appear that the prototype There of the *living form, the universal* horse, must look deliberately towards this sphere;"

GUTHRIE: "Such are our views about sensibility. (Now let us pass to the other question we asked.) How does it happen that all the Animals who, like the Horse itself, are contained in divine Intelligence, do not incline towards the things here below (by generating them)?"

ARMSTRONG: "But so much for the power of sense-perception. But all the same, how do 'horse' and each and every one of the animals not intend to look to the things here below?"

8. FIRST EDITION: ". . . the *universal* existing . . ."

ARMSTRONG: "those intelligibles existed . . ."; GUTHRIE: "the intelligible entities existed already . . ."

9. FIRST EDITION: "*The Reason-Principle, too, is at once the* living form and something else, something distinct from *the being of that* form."

ARMSTRONG: ". . . the rationally defined forming principle is living being and something else, which is not the same as 'living being' . . ."

GUTHRIE: "Reason (the essence of the animal) is animal, and besides, is something different from the animal."

10. FIRST EDITION: ". . . eludes the soul animating the *universe*,"

ARMSTRONG: ". . . moves past the soul in the whole . . ."; GUTHRIE: ". . . do not manifest in the universal Soul . . ."

11. FIRST EDITION: ". . . the Universal *Sympathy*, not of course the *sympathy* known here . . ."

ARMSTRONG: ". . . the love in the All, not the love in this All;"

GUTHRIE: ". . . that union (by Empedocles) called 'friendship'; but such union is very different from that which exists in the sense-world."

12. FIRST EDITION: ". . . that authentic *Sympathy* . . ."

ARMSTRONG: "the true love"; GUTHRIE: "veritable union."

13. FIRST EDITION: "But *these objects* come to it not as *they are There* but in accord with *its own* condition, *for it is their source; they spring thence to be here, and* Intellectual-Principle *it is that* has produced them by its vision *There.*"

GUTHRIE: "Intelligence receives the Good, not such as the Good is in itself, but such as Intelligence is capable of receiving it. The Good is indeed the supreme principle. From the Good therefore, Intelligence derives its perfection; to the Good Intelligence owes its begetting of all the intelligible entities."

ARMSTRONG: "But they came to it, not as they were there, but as Intellect itself possessed them. For that Good is the principle, and it is from that that they are in this Intellect, and it is this which has made them from that Good."

14. FIRST EDITION: ". . . *from* the Good *it takes* what itself *did* not possess."

GUTHRIE: "The Good does not Himself possess the things which He thus donates . . ."

ARMSTRONG: ". . . the Good gave what he did not himself have."

15. FIRST EDITION: ". . . informed by The Good, possesses *the universal good transcendent over* all. *Each possessing that* Being *above,* possesses also the *total Living-Form* in virtue of that *transcendent* life, possesses, *no doubt,* much else *as well.*"

GUTHRIE: "As their common characteristic is to be assimilated to the Good, the consequence is that Intelligence contains all the things conformable to the Good. It possesses therefore the essence which is in all things; it contains all the animals, as well as the universal Life within them, and all the rest."

ARMSTRONG: ". . . being in the form of good, all of them have in common what runs over them all. They of course have also being over them all, and each has the living being as there is a common life over all, and perhaps they have other things [in common]." Brackets are Armstrong's.

16. FIRST EDITION: "*But in what mode are these secondaries, and Intellectual-Principle itself, within the First? They are* not in the Filling Principle; *they are* not in the filled *since* before that moment *it did not contain them.*"

ARMSTRONG: "But how can these be in Intellect, and be Intellect, when they are not there in what fills it, nor, again, in it itself which is filled? For when it was not yet filled, it did not have them."

GUTHRIE: "How can (these beings) exist within Intelligence, and constitute it, if they were neither in that which has given, nor in that which has received this fulness, since, before receiving its fulness from the Good, Intelligence had not yet received (these beings)?"

17. FIRST EDITION: ". . . identical with *itself?*"

GUTHRIE supports the fourth edition.

ARMSTRONG has the question as: "But does the whole Intellect in comprehending each individual comprehend each as the same?"

18. FIRST EDITION: ". . . Thence *Life in itself* is good;"

GUTHRIE: ". . . life as life should be considered good . . ."

ARMSTRONG: ". . . it must be said to be good also in that it is life . . ."

19. FIRST EDITION: "*Both or one part of Intellect, then, would be called by the one term good.*"

GUTHRIE: "Is it by a mere play on words that life, intelligence and ideas are called good?"

ARMSTRONG: ". . . otherwise each of them or each particular one of them would be called good equivocally."

20. FIRST EDITION: "The good becomes a mere *attribute of things; objects of pursuit* are many and *different* so that . . ."

GUTHRIE: "First, the Good would only be an attribute. Then, since our soul has several desires, and each of the latter has different objects . . ."

ARMSTRONG: "First, because the good also will become one of the accompaniments. Then, because there are many that desire, and different ones desire different things . . ."

21. FIRST EDITION: ". . . we may perhaps have recourse to *judgement.*
"We *would apply* the opposition of things . . ."

ARMSTRONG: ". . . should we then turn to judgements and the oppositions of things, for instance . . ."

GUTHRIE: ". . . shall we have recourse to other rules, such as, for instance (the Pythagorean) 'oppositions,' such as . . ."

22. FIRST EDITION: ". . . is due not to what they are but to *the consideration of their nature as something apart, received from above themselves.*"

GUTHRIE: ". . . but that occurs only when they have something more than their natural condition, and when some perfection descends on them from on high."

ARMSTRONG: "But there comes to be the intense kind of love for them not when they are what they are but when, being already what they are, they receive something else from there beyond."

23. FIRST EDITION: "And to deny *the good . . .*" MACKENNA is alone in not capitalizing "good" here; but does "evil" in this context exist in opposition to good—as defined by creatures in the context of duality—or is it meant here to have metaphysical status in opposition to The Good as absolute?

24. FIRST EDITION: "*Or* what do we gain by *seeing* the Ideas *themselves if* we see *only* a particular Idea *and nothing else (nothing 'substantial')?*"

GUTHRIE: "What sort of a good should (a man) have, who thinks the Ideas themselves, contemplating everything in itself?"

ARMSTRONG: "Or what good could the thinker of the Forms have as he contemplates each of them?"

25. FIRST EDITION: "Intellectual-Principle will draw upon the Authentic Good which we hold to *be coterminous with* it . . ."

GUTHRIE: ". . . the Good communicates to Intelligence its influx . . ."

ARMSTRONG: ". . . for Intellect the Good effects something, the Good which we maintain comes also to this . . ."

26. FIRST EDITION: ". . . that only can be adopted as the good which represents *the apt in its better form and is best to what is best in the quester's self, to that which the quester* tends potentially to be."

GUTHRIE: "The determination of what is suitable to a being belongs to the superior Being of whom the lower being is a potentiality."

ARMSTRONG: ". . . one must judge the good by what is higher than what is akin and by what is better than the thing itself, to which it is potentially directed."

27. FIRST EDITION: "As being most *appropriate?*"

ARMSTRONG: ". . . most akin to itself?" GUTHRIE: ". . . eminently suited to it?"

28. FIRST EDITION: "But *the thing* must be chosen even though no pleasure ensued; *it must be desirable for its own sake.*"

GUTHRIE supports the first edition. ARMSTRONG supports the fourth.

29. FIRST EDITION: ". . . which flashed *Nature* into being;"

GUTHRIE: ". . . by which splendor it illuminates nature;"

ARMSTRONG: ". . . with which it illuminated its nature . . ."

30. FIRST EDITION: "You see the splendour over *the things of the universe with all the variety begotten of the* Ideas;"

GUTHRIE: "Do you see the beauty that shines in all these forms so various?"

ARMSTRONG: "You see the beauty which rests upon the very Forms, all of them richly varied."

31. FIRST EDITION: ". . . the primal *existent,* The First, must be without Form; the beauty *in it* must be, simply, the nature of the *Intellectual* Good."

GUTHRIE: "He who then is beauty in the first degree, and primary Beauty, is superior to form, and the splendor of the intelligible (world) is only a reflection of the nature of the Good."

ARMSTRONG: "The primarily beautiful, then, and the first is without form, and beauty is that, the nature of the Good."

32. FIRST EDITION: ". . . linked to This she can fear no disaster nor even *know* it; let all . . ."

GUTHRIE: "Now she fears nothing, so long as she is with Him, and contemplates Him."

ARMSTRONG: ". . . it is not afraid, either, that anything may happen to it, since it does not even see it while it is with that;"

33. FIRST EDITION: ". . . to move; *she has nothing to say of this very Intellectual-Principle by means of which* she has attained the vision . . ."

GUTHRIE: "She does not even assert that it is Intelligence that she sees, though she contemplate only because she has become intelligence . . ."

ARMSTRONG: "For it says that he whom it sees does not move either; yet when this soul has become intellect it contemplates . . ."

34. FIRST EDITION: "*Knowledge* of the Good or contact with it . . ."

GUTHRIE: "Knowledge, or, if it may be so expressed, the 'touch of the Good' . . ."

ARMSTRONG: "The knowledge or touching of the Good . . ."

35. FIRST EDITION: ". . . all things; *but this is impossible.* With self-intellection it would no longer be simplex; *any intellection, even in the Supreme,* must be aware of something distinct; *as we have been saying, the inability to see the self as external is the negation of* intellection."

GUTHRIE: ". . . all things? (Would it not do so) because it was impotent to do so? In short, the principle which thinks itself ceases to be simple, because in thinking itself it must think itself as something different, which is the necessary condition of thinking itself. We have already said that intelligence cannot think itself without contemplating itself as something different."

ARMSTRONG: ". . . all things? Will it not be able to? But in general intellect is not simple when it thinks itself, but its thought about itself must be thought of another if it is to be able to think itself as anything at all. But we said that there is no thinking of this Good, not even if he wanted to see himself as another."

EIGHTH TRACTATE

On Free Will And the Will of The One

1. Can there be question as to whether the gods have voluntary action? Or are we to take it that while we may well inquire in the case of men with their combination of powerlessness and hesitating power, the gods must be declared omnipotent, not merely some things but all lying at their nod? Or is power entire, freedom of action in all things, to be reserved to one alone, of the rest some being powerful, others powerless, others again a blend of power and impotence?

All this must come to the test: we must dare it even of the Firsts and of the All-Transcendent and if we find omnipotence possible work out how far freedom extends. The very notion of power must be scrutinized lest in this ascription we be I really setting up an antithesis of power (potency) and Act, and identifying power[1] with Act not yet achieved. I

But for the moment we may pass over these questions to deal with the traditional problem of freedom of action in ourselves.

To begin with, what must be intended when we assert that something is in our power; what is the conception here?

To establish this will help to show whether we are to ascribe freedom to the gods and still more to God, or to refuse it, or again, while asserting it, to question still, in regard both to the higher and lower, the mode of its presence.

What then do we mean when we speak of freedom in ourselves and why do we question it?

My own reading is that, moving as we do amid adverse fortunes, compulsions, violent assaults of passion crushing the soul, feeling ourselves mastered by these experiences, playing slave to them, going where they lead, we have been brought by all this to doubt whether we are anything at all and dispose of ourselves in any particular.

This would indicate that we think of our free act as one which we execute of our own choice, in no servitude to chance or necessity or overmastering passion, nothing thwarting our will; I the 'free'[2] is conceived I as an event amenable to will and occurring or not as our will dictates. Everything will be 'voluntary' that is produced under no compulsion and with knowledge; our free act is what we are masters to perform.

Differing conceptually, the two conditions will often coincide but sometimes will clash. Thus a man would be master to kill but the act will not be voluntary if in the victim he had failed to recognize his own father. Perhaps, however, that ignorance is not compatible with real freedom: for the knowledge necessary to a voluntary act cannot be limited to certain particulars but must cover the entire field. Why, for example, should killing be involuntary in the failure to recognize a father and not so in the failure to recognize the wickedness of murder? If because the killer ought to have learned, still ignorance of the duty of learning and the cause of that ignorance remain alike involuntary.

2. A cardinal question is where are we to place the freedom of action ascribed to us.

It must be founded in impulse or in some appetite, as when we act or omit in lust or rage or upon some calculation of advantage accompanied by desire.

But if rage or desire implied freedom we must allow freedom to animals, infants, maniacs, the distraught, the victims of malpractice producing incontrollable delusions. And if freedom turns on calculation with desire, does this include faulty calculation? Sound calculation, no doubt, and sound desire; but then comes the question whether the appetite stirs the calculation or the calculation the appetite.

Where the appetites are dictated by the very nature they are either the desires of the conjoint of soul and body and then soul lies under physical compulsions: l or they spring in the soul as an independent, and then much that we take to be free is in reality outside of our free act. Further, does the soul advance any reasoning which is untouched by emotion, and[3] can a l compelling imagination, an appetite drawing us where it will, be supposed to leave us masters in the ensuing act? How can we be masters when we are compelled? Need, inexorably craving satisfaction, is not free in face of that to which it is forced: and how at all can a thing have efficiency of its own when it rises from an extern, has an extern for very principle, thence taking its being as it stands? It lives by that extern, lives as it has been moulded: if this be freedom there is freedom in even the soulless; fire acts in accordance with its characteristic being.

We may be reminded that the Living Being and the Soul know what they do. But if this is knowledge by perception it does not help towards the freedom of the act; perception gives awareness, not mastery: if true knowing is meant, either this is the knowing of something happening—once more awareness—with the motive-force still to seek, or the reasoning and knowledge have acted to quell the appetite; then we have to ask to what this repression is to be referred and where it has taken place. If it is that the mental process sets up an opposing desire we must assure ourselves how; if it merely stills the appetite with no further efficiency and this is our freedom, then freedom does not depend upon act but is a thing of the mind—and in truth all that has to do with act, the very most reasonable, is still of mixed value and cannot carry freedom.

3. All this calls for examination; the inquiry must bring us close to the solution as regards the gods.

We have traced self-disposal to will, will to reasoning and, next step, to right reasoning; perhaps to right reasoning we must add knowledge, for however sound opinion and act may be they do not yield true freedom when the adoption of the right course is the result of hazard or of some presentment from the fancy with no knowledge of the foundations of that rightness.

Taking it that the presentment of fancy is not a matter of our will and choice, how can we think those acting at its dictation to be free agents? Fancy strictly, in our use, takes its rise from conditions of the body; lack of food and drink sets up presentments and so does the meeting of these needs; similarly with seminal abundance and other humours of the body. We refuse to range under the principle of freedom those whose conduct is directed by such fancy: the baser sort, therefore, mainly so guided, cannot be credited with self-disposal or voluntary act. Self-disposal, to us, belongs to those who, through the activities of the Intellectual-Principle, live above the states of the body. The spring of freedom is the activity of Intellectual-Principle, the highest in our being; the proposals emanating thence are freedom; such desires as are formed in the exercise of the Intellectual act cannot be classed as involuntary; the gods, therefore, that live in this state, living by Intellectual-Principle and by desire conformed to it, possess freedom.

4. It will be asked how act rising from desire can be voluntary since desire pulls outward and implies need; to desire is still to be drawn, even though towards the good.

Intellectual-Principle itself comes under the doubt; having a certain nature and acting by that nature can it be said to have freedom and self-disposal—in an act which it cannot leave unenacted? It may be asked, also, whether freedom may strictly be affirmed of such beings as are not engaged in action.

However that may be, where there is such act there is compulsion from without, since, failing motive, act will not be performed. These higher beings, too, obey their own nature; where then is their freedom?

But, on the other hand, can there be talk of constraint where there is no compulsion to obey an extern; and how can any movement towards a good be counted compulsion? Effort is free once it is towards a fully recognized good; the involuntary is, precisely, motion away from a good and towards the enforced, towards something not recognized as a good; servitude lies in being powerless to move towards one's good, being debarred from the preferred path in a menial obedience. Hence the shame of slavedom is incurred not when one is held from the hurtful but when the personal good must be yielded in favour of another's.

Further, this objected obedience to the characteristic nature would imply a duality, master and mastered; but an undivided Principle, a simplex Activity, where there can be no difference of potentiality and act, must be free; there can be no thought of 'action according to the nature', in the sense of any distinction between the being and its efficiency, there where being and act are identical. Where act is performed neither because of another nor at another's will, there surely is freedom. Freedom may of course be an inappropriate term: there is something greater here: it is self-disposal in the sense, only, that there is no disposal by the extern, no outside master over the act.

In a principle, act and essence must be free. No doubt Intellectual-Principle itself is to be referred to a yet higher; but this higher is not extern to it; Intellectual-Principle is within the Good; possessing its own good in virtue of that indwelling, much more will it possess freedom and self-disposal which are sought only for the sake of the good. Acting towards the good, it must all the more possess self-disposal, for by that Act it is directed towards the Principle from which it proceeds, and this its act is self-centred and must entail its very greatest good.

5. Are we, however, to make freedom and self-disposal exclusive to Intellectual-Principle as engaged in its characteristic Act, Intellectual-Principle unassociated, or do they belong also to soul acting under that guidance and performing acts of virtue?

If freedom is to be allowed to soul in its Act, it certainly cannot be allowed in regard to issue, for we are not master of events: if in regard to fine conduct and all inspired by Intellectual-Principle, that may very well be freedom; but is the freedom ours?

Because there is war, we perform some brave feat; how is that our free act, since had there been no war it could not have been performed? So in all cases of fine conduct; there is always some impinging event leading out our quality to show itself in this or that act. And suppose virtue itself given the choice whether to find occasion for its exercise—war evoking courage; wrong, so that it may establish justice and good order; poverty that it may show liberality—or to remain inactive, everything going well, it would choose the peace of inaction, nothing calling for its intervention, just as a physician like Hippocrates would prefer no one to stand in need of his skill.

If thus virtue whose manifestation requires action becomes inevitably a collaborator under compulsion, how can it have untrammelled self-disposal?

Should we, perhaps, distinguish between compulsion in the act and freedom in the preceding will and reasoning?

But in setting freedom in those preceding functions, we imply that virtue has a freedom and self-disposal apart from all act; then we must state what is the reality of the self-disposal attributed to virtue as state or disposition. Are we to put it that virtue comes in to restore the disordered soul, taming passions and appetites? In what sense, at that, can we hold our goodness to be our own free act, our 'fine conduct to be uncompelled'? In that we will and adopt, in that this entry of virtue prepares freedom and self-disposal, ending our slavery to the masters we have been obeying. If then virtue is, as it were, a second Intellectual-Principle, and heightens the Soul to Intellectual quality, then, once more, our freedom is found to lie not in act but in Intellectual-Principle immune from act.

6. How then did we come to place freedom in the will when we made out free action to be that produced—or as we also indicated, suppressed—at the dictate of will?

If what we have been saying is true and our former statement is consistent with it, the case must stand thus:

Virtue and Intellectual-Principle are sovran and must be held the sole foundation of our self-disposal and freedom; both then are free; Intellectual-Principle is self-contained: Virtue in its government of the soul which it seeks to lift into goodness would wish to be free; in so far as it does so it is free and confers freedom; but inevitably experiences and actions are forced upon it by its governance: these it has not planned for, yet when they do arise it will watch still for its sovranty, calling these also to judgement. Virtue does not follow upon occurrences as a saver of the imperilled; at its discretion it sacrifices a man; it may decree the jettison of life, means, children, country even; it looks to its own high aim and not to the safeguarding of anything lower. Thus our freedom of act, our self-disposal, must be referred not to the doing, not to the external thing done but to the inner activity, to the Intellection, to virtue's own vision.

So understood, virtue is a mode of Intellectual-Principle, a mode not involving any of the emotions or passions controlled by its reasonings, since such experiences, amenable to morality and discipline, touch closely—we read—on body.

This makes it all the more evident that the unembodied is the free; to this our self-disposal is to be referred; herein lies our will which remains free and self-disposing in spite of any orders which it may necessarily utter to meet the external. All then that issues from will and is the effect of will is our free action, whether the will is directed outwards or remains unattached; all that will adopts and brings, unimpeded, into existence is in the highest degree at our free disposal.

The contemplating Intellect, the first or highest, has self-disposal to the point that its operation is utterly independent; it turns wholly upon itself; its very action is itself; at rest in its good it is without need, complete, and may be said to live to its will; there the will is intellection: it is called will because it expresses the Intellectual-Principle in the willing-phase and, besides, what we know as will imitates this operation taking place within the Intellectual-Principle. Will strives towards the good which the act of Intellectual-Principle realizes. Thus that principle holds what will seeks, that good whose attainment makes will identical with Intellection.

But if self-disposal is founded thus on the will aiming at the good, how can it possibly be denied to that principle permanently possessing the good, sole object of the aim?

Anyone scrupulous about setting self-disposal so high may find some loftier word.

7. Soul becomes free when it moves without hindrance, through Intellectual-Principle, towards The Good; what it does in that spirit is its free act; Intellectual-Principle is free in its own right. That principle of Good is the sole object of desire and the source of self-disposal to the rest, to soul when it fully attains, to Intellectual-Principle by connate possession.

How then can the sovran of all that august sequence—the first in place, that to which all else strives to mount, all dependent upon it and taking from it their powers even to this power of self-disposal—how can This be brought under the freedom belonging to you and me, a conception applicable only by violence to Intellectual-Principle itself?

It is rash thinking drawn from another order that would imagine a First Principle to be chance-made what it is, controlled by a manner of being imposed from without, void therefore of freedom or self-disposal, acting or refraining under compulsion. Such a statement is untrue to its subject and introduces much difficulty; it utterly annuls the principle of free will with the very conception of our own voluntary action, so that there is no longer any sense in discussion upon these terms, empty names for the non-existent. Anyone upholding this opinion would be obliged to say not merely that free act exists nowhere but that the very word conveys nothing to him. To admit understanding the word is to be easily brought to confess that the conception of freedom does apply where it is denied. No doubt a concept leaves the reality untouched and unappropriated, for nothing can produce itself, bring itself into being; but thought insists upon distinguishing between what is subject to others and what is independent, bound under no allegiance, lord of its own act.

This state of freedom belongs in the absolute degree to the Eternals in right of that eternity and to other beings in so far as without hindrance they possess or pursue The Good which, standing above them all, must manifestly be the only good they can reasonably seek.

To say that The Good exists by chance must be false; chance belongs to the later, to the multiple; since the First has never come to be we cannot speak of it either as coming by chance into being or as not master of its being. Absurd also the objection that it acts in accordance with its being if this is to suggest that freedom demands act or other expression against the nature. Neither does its nature as the unique annul its freedom when this is the result of no compulsion but means only that The Good is no other than itself, is self-complete and has no higher.

The objection would imply that where there is most good there is least freedom. If this is absurd, still more absurd to deny freedom to The Good on the ground that it is good and self-concentred, not needing to lean upon anything else but actually being the Term to which all tends, itself moving to none.

Where—since we must use such words—the essential act is identical with the being—and this identity must obtain in The Good since it holds even in Intellectual-Principle—there the act is no more determined by the Being than the Being by the Act. Thus 'acting according to its nature' does not apply; the Act, the Life, so to speak, cannot be held to issue from the Being; the Being accompanies the Act in an eternal association: from the two (Being and Act) it forms itself into The Good, self-springing and unspringing.

8. But it is not, in our view, as an attribute that this freedom is present in the First. In the light of free acts, from which we eliminate the contraries, we recognize There self-determination self-directed and, failing more suitable terms, we apply to it the lesser terms brought over from lesser things and so tell it as best we may: no words could ever be adequate or even applicable to that from which all else—the noble, the august—is derived. For This is principle of all, or, more strictly, unrelated to all and, in this consideration, cannot be made to possess such laters as even freedom and self-disposal, which in fact indicate manifestation upon the extern—unhindered but implying the existence of other beings whose opposition proves ineffective.

We cannot think of the First as moving towards any other; He holds his own manner of being before any other was; even Being we withhold and therefore all relation to beings.

Nor may we speak of any 'conforming to the nature'; this again is of the later; if the term be applicable at all in that realm it applies only to the secondaries—primally to Essential Existence as next to this First. And if a 'nature' belongs only to things of time, this conformity to nature does not apply even to Essential

Existence. On the other hand, I we are not to deny that the Being of the One is self-derived,[4] for I that would be to take away its existence and would imply derivation from something else.

Does this mean that the First is to be described as happening to be?

No; that would be just as false; nothing 'happens' to the First; it stands in no such relationship; happening belongs only to the multiple where, first, existence is given and then something is added. And how could the Source 'happen to be'? There has been no coming so that you can put it to the question, 'How does this come to be? What chance brought it here or produced it?' Chance did not yet exist; there was no 'automatic action': these imply something before themselves and occur in the realm of process.

9. If we cannot but speak of Happening we must not halt at the word but look to the intention. And what is that? That the Supreme by possession of a certain nature and power is the Principle. Obviously if its nature were other it would be that other and if the difference were for the worse it would manifest itself as that lesser being. But we must add in correction that as Principle of All, it could not be some chance product; it is not enough to say that it could not be inferior; it could not even be in some other way good, for instance in some less perfect degree; the Principle of All must be of higher quality than anything that follows it. It is therefore in a sense determined—determined, I mean, by its uniqueness and not in any sense of being under compulsion; compulsion did not co-exist with the Supreme but has place only among secondaries and even there can exercise no tyranny; this uniqueness is not from outside.

This, then, it is; This and no other; simply what it must be; it has not 'happened' but is what by a necessity prior to all necessities it must be. We cannot think of it as a chance existence; it is not what it chanced to be but what it must be—and yet without a 'Must'.

All the rest waits for the appearing of the king to hail him for himself, not a being of accident and happening but authentically king, authentically Principle, The Good authentically, not a being that acts in conformity with goodness—and so, recognizably, a secondary—but the total unity that he is, no moulding upon goodness but the very Good itself.

Even Being is exempt from happening: of course anything happening happens to Being, but Being itself has not happened nor is the manner of its Being a thing of happening, of derivation; it is the very nature of Being to be; how then can we think that this happening can attach to the Transcendent of Being, That in whose power lay the very engendering of Being?

Certainly this Transcendent never happened to be what it is; it is so, just as Being exists in complete identity with its own essential nature and that of

Intellectual-Principle; otherwise one might go on to say of Intellectual-Principle that it happened to be what it is, on the mistaken assumption that Intellectual-Principle could be anything different from what in fact is its nature. Certainly that which has never passed outside of its own orbit, unbendingly what it is, its own unchangeably, is that which may most strictly be said to possess its own being: what then are we to say when we mount and contemplate that which stands yet higher; can we conceivably say, 'Thus, as we see it, thus has it happened to be'? Neither thus nor in any mode did it happen to be; there is no happening; there is only a 'Thus and No Otherwise than Thus'. And even 'Thus' is false; it would imply limit, a defined form: to know This is to be able to reject both the 'Thus' and the 'Not-Thus', either of which classes among Beings to which alone Manner of Being can attach.

The One, therefore, is beyond all things that are 'Thus': standing before the indefinable you may name any of these sequents but you must say 'This is none of them': at most it is to be conceived as the total power towards things, supremely self-concentred, being what it wills to be or rather projecting into existence what it wills, itself higher than all will, will a thing beneath it. In a word it neither willed its own 'Thus'—as something to conform to—nor did any other make it 'Thus'.

10. The upholder of Happening must be asked how the false attribution of happening can ever come about, taking it that it does, and how the happening can ever be denied. If there is to be made an exception, then he must admit that in this case happening does not apply:[5] for if I we attribute to chance the Principle which is to eliminate chance from all the rest, how can there ever be anything independent of chance? And this Nature does take away the chanced from the rest, bringing in form and limit and shape. In the case of things thus conformed to reason the cause cannot be identified with chance but must lie in that very reason; chance must be kept for what occurs apart from choice and sequence and is purely concurrent. When we come to the source of all reason, order, and limit, how can we attribute the reality there to chance? Chance is no doubt master of many things but is not master of Intellectual-Principle, of reason, of order, so as to bring them into being. How could chance, recognized as the very opposite of reason, be its Author? And if it does not produce Intellectual-Principle, then certainly not that which precedes and surpasses that Principle. Chance, besides, has no means of producing, has absolutely no being at all in the Eternal.

Since there is nothing before Him who is the First, we must call a halt; there is nothing to say; we may inquire into the origin of his sequents but not of Himself who has no origin.

But perhaps, never having come to be but being as He is, He is still not master of his own essence: not master of his essence but being as He is, not self-originating but acting out of his nature as He finds it, must He not be of necessity what he is, inhibited from being otherwise?

No: what He is, He is not because He could not be otherwise but because so is best. Not everything has power to move towards the better though nothing is prevented by any external from moving towards the worse. But that the Supreme has not so moved is its own doing: there has been no inhibition; it has not moved, simply because it is That which does not move; in this stability the inability to degenerate is not powerlessness; here permanence is very Act, a self-determination. This absence of declination comports the fullness of power; it is not the yielding of a being held and controlled but the Act of one who is necessity, law, to all.

Does this indicate a Necessity which has brought itself into existence? No: there has been no coming into being in any degree; This is that by which being is brought to all the rest, its sequents. Above all origins, This can owe being neither to an extern nor to itself.

11. But this Unoriginating, what is it?

We can but withdraw, silent, hopeless, and search no further. What can we look for when we have reached the furthest? Every inquiry aims at a first and, that attained, rests.

Besides, we must remember that all questioning deals with the nature of a thing, its quality, its cause or its essential being. In this case the being—in so far as we can use the word—is knowable only by its sequents: the question as to cause asks for a principle beyond, but the principle of all has no principle; the question as to quality would be looking for an attribute in that which has none: the question as to nature shows only that we must ask nothing about it but merely take it into the mind if we may, with the knowledge gained that nothing can be permissibly connected with it.

The difficulty this Principle presents to our mind in so far as we can approach to conception of it may be exhibited thus:

We begin by posing space, a place, a Chaos; into this container, whether conceived in our imagination as created or pre-existent, we introduce God and proceed to inquire: we ask, for example, whence and how He comes to be there: we investigate the presence and quality of this new-comer projected into the midst of things here from some height or depth. But the difficulty disappears if we eliminate all space before we attempt to conceive God: He must not be set in anything either as enthroned in eternal immanence or as having made some entry into things: He is to be conceived as existing alone, in that existence which the necessity of discussion forces us to attribute to Him, with space and all the rest as later than Him—space latest of all. Thus we conceive, as far as we may, the spaceless; we abolish the notion of any environment: we circumscribe Him within no limit; we attribute no extension to Him; He has no quality since no shape, even shape Intellectual; He holds no relationship but exists in and for Himself before anything is.

How can we think any longer of that 'Thus He happened to be'? How make this one assertion of Him of whom all other assertion can be no more than negation? It is on the contrary nearer the truth to say 'Thus He has happened not to be': that contains at least the utter denial of his happening.

12. Yet, is not God what He is? Can He, then, be master of being what He is or master to stand above Being? The mind utterly reluctant returns to its doubt; some further considerations, therefore, must be offered.

In us the individual, viewed as body, is far from reality; by soul which especially constitutes the being we participate in reality, are in some degree real. This is a compound state, a mingling of Reality and Difference, not therefore reality in the strictest sense, not reality pure. Thus far we are not masters of our being; in some sense the reality in us is one thing and we another. We are not masters of our being; the real in us is the master since that is the principle establishing our characteristic difference; yet we are again in some sense that which is sovran in us and so even on this level might in spite of all be described as self-disposing.

But in That which is wholly what it is—self-existing reality, without distinction between the total thing and its essence—the being is a unit and is sovran over itself; neither the being nor the essence is to be referred to any extern. It is in fact allowed to be self-disposing in virtue of representing the first level of complete reality. Certainly there can be no subjection whatever in That to which reality owes its freedom, That in whose nature the conferring of freedom must clearly be vested, pre-eminently to be known as the liberator. The very mention of subjection in such a Principle is barely tolerable.

Still, is not this Principle subject to its essential Being? On the contrary, it is the source of freedom to Being which is later: itself has no Being.

Even if there be Act in the Supreme—an Act with which it is to be identified—this is not enough to set up a duality within it and prevent it being entirely master of that self from which the Act springs; for the Act is not distinct from that self. If we utterly deny Act in it—holding that Act begins with others moving about it—we are all the less able to allow either mastery or subjection in it: even self-mastery is absent here, not that anything else is master over it but that self-mastery begins with Being while the Supreme is to be set in a higher order.

But what can there be higher than that which is its own master?

Where we speak of self-mastery there is a certain duality, Act against essence; from the exercise of the Act arises the conception of the mastering principle—though one identical with the essence—hence arises the separate idea of mastery, and the being concerned is said to possess self-mastery. Where there is no such duality joining to unity but solely a unity pure—either because the Act is the whole being or because there is no Act at all—then we cannot strictly say that the being has this mastery of self.

13. Our inquiry obliges us to use terms not strictly applicable: we insist, once more, that not even for the purpose of forming the concept of the Supreme may we make it a duality; if now we do, it is merely for the sake of conveying conviction, at some cost of verbal accuracy.

If, then, we are to allow Activities in the Supreme and make them depend upon will—and certainly Act cannot There be will-less—and these Activities are to be the very essence, then will and essence in the Supreme must be identical. This admitted, as He willed to be so He is; it is no more true to say that He wills and acts as his nature determines than that his essence is as He wills and acts. Thus He is wholly master of Himself and holds his very being at his will.

Consider also that every being in its pursuit of its good seeks to be that good rather than what it is; it judges itself most truly to be when it partakes of its good: in so far as it thus draws on its good its being is its choice: much more then must the very Principle, The Good, be desirable in itself when any fragment of it is very desirable to the extern and becomes the chosen essence promoting that extern's will and identical with the will that gave the existence.

As long as a thing is apart from its good it seeks outside itself; when it holds its good it accepts itself as it is: and this presence of the good is no matter of chance; the essence now is not outside of the will; by the good it is determined, by the good it is in self-possession.

If then this Principle is the means of determination to everything else, we see at once that self-possession must belong primally to it, so that through it others in their turn may be self-belonging: what we must call its essence comports its will to possess such a manner of being; we can form no idea of it without including in it the will towards itself as it is. It must be a consistent self willing its being and being what it wills; its will and itself must be one thing, all the more one from the absence of distinction between a given nature and one which would be preferred. What could The Good have wished to be other than what it is? Suppose it had the choice of being what it preferred, power to alter the nature, it could not prefer to be something else; it could have no fault to find with anything in its nature, as if that nature were imposed by force; The Good is what from always it wished and wishes to be. ❙ For the Good is precisely⁶ a willing towards itself, ❙ towards a good not gained by any wiles or even attracted to it by force of its nature; The Good is what it chose to be and, in fact, there was never anything outside it to which it could be drawn.

It may be added that nothing else contains in its essence the principle of its own satisfaction; there will be inner discord: but this hypostasis of the Good must necessarily have self-option, the will towards the self; if it had not, it could not bring satisfaction to the beings whose contentment demands participation in it or imagination of it.

Once more, we must be patient with language; we are forced for reasons of exposition to apply to the Supreme terms which strictly are ruled out; everywhere we must read 'So to speak'. The Good, then, exists; it holds its existence through choice and will, conditions of its very being: yet it cannot be a manifold; therefore the will and the essential being must be taken as one identity; the act of the will must be self-determined and the being self-caused; thus reason shows the Supreme to be its own Author. For if the act of will springs from God Himself and is as it were his operation and the same will is identical with his essence, He must be self-established. He is not, therefore, 'what He has happened to be' but what He has willed to be.

14. Another approach: Everything to which existence may be attributed is either one with its essence or distinct from it. Thus any given man is distinct from essential man though belonging to the order Man: a soul and a soul's essence are the same—that is, in the case of soul pure and unmingled; ❙ Man as Form (or Idea)⁷ is ❙ the same as man's essence; where the thing, man, and the essence are different, the particular man may be considered as accidental; but man, the essence, cannot be so; the ❙ Form of⁷ Man ❙ is self-determined. Now if the essence of man is self-determined, not chanced or accidental, how can we think That to be accidental which transcends the Form of Man, author of the Form, source of all being, a principle more nearly simplex than man's being or being of any kind? As we approach the simplex, accident recedes; what is utterly simplex accident never touches at all.

Further, we must remember what has been already said, that where there is true being, where things have been brought to reality by that Principle— ❙ and this is true also of whatsoever has this character within the order of sense—all that reality has determined condition in virtue of its origin in the divine. By determined condition I mean its ability to contain, inbound with its essence, the reason of its being as it is,⁸ so that, ❙ later, an observer can state the use for each of the constituent parts—why the eye, why feet of such and such a kind to such and such a being—and can recognize that the reason for the production of each organ is inherent in that particular being and that the parts exist for each other. Why feet of a certain length? Because another member is as it is: because the face is as it is, therefore the feet are what they are: in a word the mutual determinant is mutual adaptation and the reason of each of the several forms is that such is the plan (or essence) of man.

Thus the essence and its reason are one and the same. The constituent parts arise from the one source not because that source has so conceived each separately but because it has produced simultaneously the plan of the thing and its existence. This therefore is author at once of the existence of things and of their reasons, both produced at the one stroke. It is in correspondence with the things of process but far more nearly archetypal and authentic and in a closer relation with the Better, their source, than they can be.

Of things carrying their causes within, none arises at hazard or without purpose; this 'So it happened to be' is applicable to none. All that they have comes from The Good; the Supreme itself, then, as author of reason, of causation, and of causing essence—all certainly lying far outside of chance—must be the Principle and as it were the exemplar of things thus independent of hazard: it is the First, the Authentic, immune from chance, from blind effect and happening: God is cause of Himself; for Himself and of Himself He is what He is, the first self, transcendently The Self.

15. Lovable, very love, the Supreme is also self-love in that He is lovely no otherwise than from Himself and in Himself. Self-presence can hold only in the identity of associated with associating; since, in the Supreme, associated and associating are one, seeker and sought one—the sought serving as Hypostasis and substrate of the seeker—once more God's being and his seeking are identical: once more, then, the Supreme is the self-producing, sovran of Himself, not coming to be as some extern willed but existing as He wills it.

And when we say that neither does He absorb anything nor anything absorb Him, thus again we are setting Him outside of all happening—not only because we declare Him unique and untouched by all but in another way also. Suppose we found such a nature in ourselves; we are untouched by all that has gathered round us subjecting us to happening and chance; all that accruement was of the servile and lay exposed to chance and has, so to say, attached itself to us by chance: by this new state alone we acquire self-disposal and free act, the freedom of that light which belongs to the order of the good and is good in actuality, greater than anything Intellectual-Principle has to give, an actuality whose advantage over Intellection is no adventitious superiority. When we attain to this state and become This alone, abandoning all others, what can we say but that we are more than free, more than self-disposing? And who then could link us to chance, hazard, happening, when thus we are become veritable Life, entered into That which contains no alloy but is purely itself?

Isolate anything else and the being is inadequate; the Supreme in isolation is still what it was. The First cannot be in the soulless or in an unreasoning life; such a life is too feeble in being; it is reason dissipated, it is indetermination; only in the measure of approach towards reason is there liberation from happening; the rational is above chance. Ascending we come upon the Supreme, not as reason but as reason's better: thus God is far removed from all happening: the root of reason is self-springing.

The Supreme is the Term of all; it is like the principle and ground of some vast tree of rational life; itself unchanging, it gives reasoned being to the growth into which it enters.

16. We maintain, and it is evident truth, that the Supreme is everywhere and yet nowhere; keeping this constantly in mind let us see how it bears on our present inquiry.

If God is nowhere, then not anywhere has He 'happened to be'; as also everywhere, He is everywhere in entirety: at once, He is that everywhere and everywise: He is not in the everywhere but is the everywhere as well as the giver to the rest of things of their being in that everywhere. Holding the supreme place—or rather no holder but Himself the Supreme—all lies subject to Him; He has not 'happened' to them, but they, all, to Him—or rather they stand there before Him looking upon Him, not He upon them. He is borne, so to speak, to the inmost of Himself in love of that pure radiance which He is, He Himself being that which He loves. That is to say, **I** as self-dwelling Act and in some sense[9] Intellectual-Principle, the most to be loved, He has given Himself existence. **I** Intellectual-Principle is the issue of Act: God therefore is issue of Act, but since no other has generated Him He is what He made Himself: He is not, therefore, 'as He happened to be' but as He acted Himself into being.

Again; if He pre-eminently is because He holds firmly, so to speak, towards Himself, looking towards Himself, so that what we must call his being is this self-looking, He must again, since the word is inevitable, make Himself: thus, not 'as He happens to be' is He but as He Himself wills to be. Nor is this will a hazard, a something happening; the will adopting the Best is not a thing of chance.

That his being is constituted by this self-originating self-tendance—at once Act and repose—becomes clear if we imagine the contrary; inclining towards something outside of Himself, He would destroy the identity of his being. This self-directed Act is therefore his peculiar being, one with Himself. Thus, He created Himself because his Act was inseparable from Himself. If then this Act never came to be but is eternal—a waking without an awakener, an eternal wakening and a supra-Intellection—He is as He waked Himself to be. This awakening is before being, before Intellectual-Principle, before rational life, though He is these; He is thus an Act before Intellectual-Principle and thought and life; these come from Him and no other; his being, then, is a self-presence, issuing from Himself. Thus not 'as He happened to be' is He but as He willed to be.

17. Or consider it another way: We hold the universe, with its content entire, to be as all would be if the design of the maker had so willed it, elaborating it with purpose and prevision by reasonings amounting to a Providence. All is always so and all is always so reproduced: therefore the reason-principles of things must lie always within the producing powers in a still more perfect form; these beings of the divine realm must therefore be previous to Providence and to preference; all that exists in the order of being must lie for ever There in their Intellectual mode. If this regime is to be called Providence it must be in the sense that before our universe there exists, not expressed in the outer, the Intellectual-Principle of all the All, its source and archetype.

Now if there is thus an Intellectual-Principle before all things, their founding principle, this cannot be a thing lying subject to chance—multiple, no doubt, but a concordance, ordered so to speak into oneness. Such a multiple—the co-ordination of all particulars and consisting of all the Reason-Principles of the universe gathered into the closest union—this cannot be a thing of chance, a thing 'happening so to be'. It must be of a very different nature, of the very contrary nature, separated from the other by all the difference between reason and reasonless chance. And if the Source is precedent even to this, it must be continuous with this reasoned secondary so that the two be correspondent; the secondary must participate in the prior, be an expression of its will, be a power of it: that higher therefore (as above the ordering of reason) is without part or interval (implied by reasoned arrangement), is a one-all Reason-Principle, one number, a One greater than its product, more powerful, having no higher or better. Thus the Supreme can derive neither its being nor the quality of its being. God Himself, therefore, is what He is, self-related, self-tending; otherwise He becomes outward-tending, other-seeking—He who cannot but be wholly self-poised.

18. Seeking Him, seek nothing of Him outside; within is to be sought what follows upon Him; Himself do not attempt. He is, Himself, that outer, He the encompassment and measure of all things; or rather He is within, at the innermost depth; the outer, circling round Him, so to speak, and wholly dependent upon Him, is Reason-Principle and Intellectual-Principle—or becomes

Intellectual-Principle by contact with Him and in the degree of that contact and dependence; for from Him it takes the being which makes it Intellectual-Principle.

A circle related in its path to a centre must be admitted to owe its scope to that centre; it has something of the nature of that centre in that the radial lines converging on that one central point assimilate their impinging ends to that point of convergence and of departure, the dominant of radii and terminals: the terminals are of one nature with the centre, feeble reproductions of it, since the centre I is, in a certain sense, the source[10] of terminals and radii I impinging at every point upon it; these lines reveal the centre; they are the development of that undeveloped.

In the same way we are to take Intellectual-Principle and Being. This combined power springs from the Supreme, an outflow and as it were development from That and remaining dependent upon that Intellective nature, showing forth that, so to speak, Intellect-in-Unity which is not Intellectual-Principle since it is no duality. No more than in the circle are the lines or circumference to be identified with that centre which is the source of both: radii and circle are images given forth by indwelling power and, as products of a certain vigour in it, not cut off from it.

I Thus the Intellective power circles around the Supreme which stands to it as archetype to image; the archetype is Intellect-in-Unity;[11] the image I in its manifold movement round about its prior has produced the multiplicity by which it is constituted Intellectual-Principle: that prior has no movement; it generates Intellectual-Principle by its sheer wealth.

Such a power, author of Intellectual-Principle, author of being—how does it lend itself to chance, to hazard, to any 'So it happened'?

What is present in Intellectual-Principle is present, though in a far transcendent mode, in the One: so in a light diffused afar from one light shining within itself, the diffused is vestige, the source is the true light; but Intellectual-Principle, the diffused and image light, is not different in kind from its prior; and it is not a thing of chance but at every point is reason and cause.

The Supreme is cause of the cause: it is cause pre-eminently, cause as containing cause in the deepest and truest mode; for in it lie the Intellective causes which are to be unfolded from it, author as it is not of the chance-made but of what the divine willed: and this willing was not apart from reason, was not in the realm of hazard and of what happened to present itself but of what must needs be, since hazard is excluded from that realm.

Thus Plato applies to it the words 'necessary' and 'appropriate' because he wished to establish beyond a doubt that it is far removed from hazard and that what it is is what it must be: if thus its existence is 'necessary' it does not exist without reason: if its manner of being is the 'appropriate', it is the utterly self-disposing in comparison with its sequents and, before that, in regard to itself: thus it is not 'as it happened to be' but as it willed to be: all this, on the assumption that God wills what should be and that it is impossible to separate right from realization and that this Necessary is not to God an outside thing but is, itself, his first Activity manifesting outwardly in the exactly representative form. Thus we must speak of God since we cannot tell Him as we would.

19. Stirred to the Supreme by what has been told, a man must strive to possess it directly; then he too will see, though still unable to tell it as he would wish.

One seeing That as it really is will lay aside all reasoning upon it and simply state it as the self-existent, such that if it had essence that essence would be subject to it and, so to speak, derived from it; none that has seen would dare to talk of its 'happening to be', or indeed be able to utter word. With all his courage he would stand astounded, unable at any venture to say where This might be, with the vision everywhere before the eyes of the soul so that, look where one may, there it is seen unless one deliberately look away, ignoring God, thinking no more upon Him. So we are to understand the Beyond-Essence darkly indicated by the ancients: it is not merely that He generated Essence but that He is subject neither to Essence nor to Himself; his Essence is not his Principle; He is Principle to Essence and not for Himself did He make it; producing it He left it outside of Himself: He had no need of being, who brought it to be. Thus his making of being is no 'action in accordance with his being'.

20. The difficulty will be raised that God would seem to have existed before thus coming into existence; if He makes Himself, then in regard to the self which He makes He is not yet in being and as maker He exists before this Himself thus made.

The answer is that we utterly must not speak of Him as made but sheerly as maker; the making must be taken as absolved from all else; no new existence is established; the Act here is not directed to an achievement but is God Himself unalloyed: here is no duality but pure unity. Let no one suspect us of asserting that the first Activity is without Essence; on the contrary the Activity is the very reality. To suppose a reality without activity would be to make the Principle of all principles deficient; the supremely complete becomes incomplete. To make the Activity something superadded to the Essence is to shatter the unity. If then Activity is a more perfect thing than Essence and the First is all perfect, then the Activity is the First.

I By acting He is at once Activity,[12] and I there is no question of 'existing before coming into existence'; when He acted He was not in some state that could be described as 'before existing'. He was already existent entirely.

Now assuredly an Activity not subjected to Essence is utterly free; God's self-hood, then, is of his own Act. If his being has to be ensured by something else, He is no longer the self-existent First: if it be true to say that He is his own container, then He inducts Himself, since from the beginning He caused the being of all that by nature He contains.

If there had been a moment from which He began to be, it would be possible to assert his self-making in the literal sense; but since what He is He is from before eternity, his self-making is to be understood as simultaneous with Himself; the being is one and the same with the making, the eternal 'bringing into existence'.

This is the source also of his self-disposal—strictly applicable if there were a duality, but conveying, in the case of a unity, a disposing without a disposed, an abstract disposing. But how a disposer with nothing to dispose? In that there is here a disposer looking to a prior when there is none: since there is no prior, This is the First—but a First not in order but in sovranty, in power purely self-controlled. Purely; then nothing can be There that is under any external disposition; all in God is self-willing. What then is there of his content that is not Himself, what that is not his Act, what not his work? Imagine in Him anything not of his Act and at once his existence ceases to be pure; He is not self-disposing, not all-powerful: in that at least of whose doing He is not master He would be impotent.

21. Could He then have made Himself otherwise than as He did?

If He could we must deny Him the power to produce goodness for He certainly cannot produce evil. Power, There, is no producer of opposites; it is that steadfast constant which is most decidedly power by inability to depart from unity: ability to produce opposites is inability to hold by the perfect good; that self-making must be definite once for all since it is the right: besides, who could upset what is made by the will of God and is itself that will?

By his will—before He existed? Can He exercise will when, so far as existence goes, He is without will? Whence then does He draw that will, seeing that essence, source of will, is inactive in Him?

The will was included in the essence; they were identical: or was there something, this will for instance, not existing in Him? All was will, nothing unwilled in Him. There is then nothing before that will: God and will were primally identical.

God, therefore, is what He willed, is such as He willed; and all that ensued upon that willing was what that definite willing engendered: but it engendered nothing new; all existed from the first.

As for his 'self-containing', this rightly understood can mean only that all the rest is maintained in virtue of Him by means of a certain participation; all traces back to the Supreme; God Himself, self-existing always, needs no containing, no participating; all in Him belongs to Him or rather He needs nothing from them in order to being Himself.

When therefore you seek to state or to conceive Him, put all else aside; abstracting all, keep solely to Him; see that you add nothing; be sure that there is not something which you have failed to abstract from Him in your thought. Even you are able to take contact with Something in which there is no more than That Thing itself to affirm and know, Something which lies away above all and is—it alone—veritably free, subject not even to its own law, solely and essentially That One Thing, while all else is thing and something added.

NOTES TO ENNEAD VI.8

1. FIRST EDITION: "... really *making power identical with Essential Act, and even* with Act not yet achieved."

> GUTHRIE: "Besides, in respect to this omnipotence, we shall have to distinguish possibility from actualization, present or future."

> ARMSTRONG: "And we must investigate as well what this 'potent' means, in case by using this term we intend to say that it sometimes means potency and sometimes actual activity, and an activity which belongs to the future."

2. FIRST EDITION: "... the *voluntary* is conceived ..."

> ARMSTRONG and GUTHRIE both translate "voluntary" here. Guthrie follows through to explicitly distinguish between "free" action and "voluntary" action, the latter being action for which we are "responsible." In the case of ignorantly killing one's own father, he says a few lines down, "the action was free, but not voluntary."

3. FIRST EDITION: "... *if* they spring in the soul as an independent, then much that we take to be *voluntary* is in reality outside of our free act. Further, *every emotion is preceded by some meagre reasoning; how then* can a ..."

> ARMSTRONG: "... but if they are of the kind that belongs to the soul alone, many of the things which are now said to be in our power will be outside it. Then also, what bare calculation precedes our passions? Or when ..."

> GUTHRIE: "... if they belong to the soul alone, many of the things which are generally attributed to the domain of our free will will have to be withdrawn therefrom. Besides, passions are always preceded by some sort of abstract reasoning."

4. FIRST EDITION: "... we are not to deny that *it* is derived *from Essential Existence* for ...

> GUTHRIE: "... for to say that 'being' does not exist by itself would be to affect its existence;"

> ARMSTRONG: "Nor indeed must we say this nature 'is not from itself ';"

5. FIRST EDITION: "If there is to be *a natural scheme at all, it must be admitted that this happening does not and cannot exist:* for if . . ."

ARMSTRONG: "And if there is a nature, will he then say that the 'happened to be' does not fit? For if . . ."

GUTHRIE: "If there be a nature (such as the nature of the one Unity), which makes (chance) disappear, it itself could not be subject to chance."

6. FIRST EDITION: "For the *really existent* Good is a willing towards itself . . ."

ARMSTRONG: "For the nature of the Good is in reality the will of himself . . ."

GUTHRIE: "The nature of Good is really His will;"

7. FIRST EDITION: "Man as *type* is . . ."

ARMSTRONG: ". . . the human being as such"; GUTHRIE: ". . . the Man-in-himself."

8. FIRST EDITION: ". . . and this is true of whatsoever has *determined condition* within the order of sense—all that reality *is brought about* in virtue of *something emanating from* the divine. By *things of* determined condition I mean *such as* contain, inbound with *their* essence, the reason of *their* being as *they are,* so that . . ."

ARMSTRONG: ". . . and anything among the things of sense which is of this kind, is of this kind by what comes from those higher beings: I mean by 'of this kind' having together with their substance also the cause of their existence, so that . . ."

GUTHRIE gives the whole thought as: ". . . beings which exist genuinely . . . and which have received their form of hypostatic existence from the Good, likewise owe it to Him that they are individual, as are the similarly situated sense-beings. By such individual beings is here meant having in one's own being the cause of his hypostatic existence."

9. FIRST EDITION: ". . . as self-dwelling Act and [omits "in some sense"] Intellectual Principle, the most to be loved, He has given Himself existence."

GUTHRIE: ". . . giving Himself a hypostatic form of existence, because He is an immanent actualization, and what is most lovable in Him constitutes the higher Intelligence."

ARMSTRONG: ". . . he gives himself existence, supposing him to be an abiding active actuality and the most pleasing of things in a way rather like Intellect."

10. FIRST EDITION: ". . . is, in a certain sense, the *total* of terminals and radii . . ."

ARMSTRONG: ". . . has power to produce them . . ."

GUTHRIE: ". . . the latter's [i.e., those of the 'centric extremities' of the radii—ed.] potentiality includes both the radii and their (distal) extremities;"

11. FIRST EDITION: "Thus the Intellective power circles *in its multiple unity* around the Supreme which stands to it as archetype to image; the image . . ."

GUTHRIE: "Similarly, the One is the higher archetype of the intellectual power which moves around Him, being His image. For in the Unity there is a higher Intelligence . . ."

ARMSTRONG: ". . . so also is that too, as the intellectual power runs round it, a kind of archetype of the image of itself, Intellect in one . . ."

12. FIRST EDITION: "By *having acted,* He is *what He is* and . . ."

GUTHRIE: "He is what He is as soon as He actualizes."

ARMSTRONG: "In his activity, therefore, he is already this first, and . . ."

NINTH TRACTATE

On The Good, or The One

1. It is in virtue of unity that beings are beings.

This is equally true of things whose existence is primal and of all that are in any degree to be numbered among beings. What could exist at all except as one thing? Deprived of unity, a thing ceases to be what it is called: no army unless as a unity: a chorus, a flock, must be one thing. Even house and ship demand unity, one house, one ship; unity gone, neither remains: thus even continuous magnitudes could not exist without an inherent unity; break them apart and their very being is altered in the measure of the breach of unity.

Take plant and animal; the material form stands a unity; fallen from that into a litter of fragments, the things have lost their being; what was is no longer there; it is replaced by quite other things—as many others, precisely, as possess unity.

Health, similarly, is the condition of a body acting as a co-ordinate unity. Beauty appears when limbs and features are controlled by this principle, unity. Moral excellence is of a soul acting as a concordant total, brought to unity.

Come thus to soul—which brings all to unity, making, moulding, shaping, ranging to order—there is a temptation to say, 'Soul is the bestower of unity; soul therefore is the unity.' But soul bestows other characteristics upon material things and yet remains distinct from its gift: shape, Ideal-Form, and the rest are all distinct from the giving soul: so, clearly, with this gift of unity; soul to make things unities looks out upon the unity just as it makes man by looking upon Man, realizing in the man the unity belonging to Man.

Anything that can be described as a unity is so in the precise degree in which it holds a characteristic being; the less or more the degree of the being, the less or more the unity. Soul, while distinct from unity's very self, is a thing of the greater unity in proportion as it is of the greater, the authentic, being. Absolute unity it is not: it is soul and one soul, the unity in some sense a concomitant; there are two things, soul and soul's unity, as there is body with body's unity. The looser aggregates such as a choir are furthest from unity, the more compact are the nearer; soul is nearer yet but still a participant.

Is soul to be identified with unity on the ground that unless it were one thing it could not be soul? No; unity is equally necessary to every other thing, yet unity stands distinct from them; body and unity are not identical; body, too, is a participant.

Besides, the soul, even the individual soul, is a manifold, though not composed of parts:[1] it has diverse powers—reasoning, desiring, perceiving—all held together by this chain of unity. Itself a unity, soul confers unity, but also accepts it.

2. It may be suggested that, while in the unities of the partial order the essence and the unity are distinct, yet in collective existence, in Real Being, they are identical, so that when we have grasped Being we hold unity; Real Being would coincide with Unity. Thus, if Essential Being is the Intellectual-Principle, Unity also is the Intellectual-Principle which is at once Primal Being and Pure Unity, purveying, accordingly, to the rest of things something of Being and something, in proportion, of the unity which is itself.

There is nothing (we may be told) with which the unity would be more plausibly identified than with Being; either it is the same as Being—a man and one man are identical—or it will correspond to the Number which rules in the realm of the particular; it will be a number applying to a certain unique thing as the number two applies to others.

Now if Number is a thing among things, then clearly so this unity must be; we would have to discover what thing of things it is. If Number is not a thing but an operation of the mind moving out to reckon, then the unity will not be a thing.

We found that anything losing unity loses its being; we are therefore obliged to inquire whether the unity in particulars is identical with the being, and Unity Absolute identical with Collective Being.

Now the being of the particular is a manifold; unity cannot be a manifold; there must therefore be a distinction between Being and Unity. Thus a man is at once a reasoning living being and a total of parts; his variety is held together by his unity; man therefore and unity are different—man a thing of parts against unity partless. Much more must Collective Being, as container of all existence, be a manifold and therefore distinct from the unity in which it is but participant.

Again, Collective Being contains life and intelligence—it is no dead thing—and so, once more, is a manifold.

If Being is identical with Intellectual-Principle, even at that it is a manifold; all the more so when count is taken of the Ideal-Forms in it; for the Idea, particular or collective, is, after all, a numerable agglomeration whose unity is that of a cosmos.

Above all, unity is The First: but Intellectual-Principle, Ideas, and Being, cannot be so; for any member of the realm of Forms is an aggregation, a compound, and therefore—since components must precede their compound—is a later.

Other considerations also go to show that the Intellectual-Principle cannot be the First. Intellect must be about the Intellectual Act: at least in its higher phase, that not concerned with the outer universe, it must be intent upon its Prior; its introversion is a conversion upon the Principle.

Considered as at once Thinker and Object of its Thought, it is dual, not simplex, not The Unity: considered as looking beyond itself, it must look to a better, to a prior: looking simultaneously upon itself and upon its Transcendent, it is, once more, not a First.

There is no other way of stating Intellectual-Principle than as that which, holding itself in the presence of The Good and First and looking towards That, is self-present also, self-knowing and knowing itself as All-Being: thus manifold, it is far from being The Unity.

In sum: The Unity cannot be the total of beings for so its oneness is annulled; it cannot be the Intellectual-Principle, for so it would be that total which the Intellectual-Principle is; nor is it Being, for Being is the total of things.

3. What then must The Unity be, what nature is left for it?

No wonder that to state it is not easy; even Being and Form are not easy, though we have a way, an approach through the Ideas.

The soul or mind reaching towards the formless finds itself incompetent to grasp where nothing bounds it or to take impression where the impinging reality is diffuse; in sheer dread of holding to nothingness, it slips away. The state is painful; often it seeks relief by retreating from all this vagueness to the region of sense, there to rest as on solid ground, just as the sight distressed by the minute rests with pleasure on the bold.

Soul must see in its own way; this is by coalescence, unification; but in seeking thus to know the Unity it is prevented by that very unification from recognizing that it has found; it cannot distinguish itself from the object of this intuition. None the less, this is our one resource if our philosophy is to give us knowledge of The Unity.

We are in search of unity; we are to come to know the principle of all, the Good and First; therefore we may not stand away from the realm of Firsts and lie prostrate among the lasts: we must strike for those Firsts, rising from things of sense which are the lasts. Cleared of all evil in our intention towards The Good, we must ascend to the Principle within ourselves; from many, we must become one; only so do we attain to knowledge of that which is Principle and Unity. We shape ourselves into Intellectual-Principle; we make over our soul in trust to Intellectual-Principle and set it firmly in That; thus what That sees the soul will waken to see: it is through the Intellectual-Principle that we have this vision of The Unity; it must be our care to bring over nothing whatever from sense, to allow nothing from that source to enter into Intellectual-Principle:

with Intellect pure, and with the summit of Intellect, we are to see the All-Pure.

If the quester has the impression of extension or shape or mass attaching to That Nature he has not been led by Intellectual-Principle which is not of the order to see such things; the activity has been of sense and of the judgement following upon sense: only Intellectual-Principle can inform us of the things of its scope; I its competence is upon its priors and upon its content:[2] but I even its content is outside of sense; and still purer, still less touched by multiplicity, are its priors, or rather its Prior.

The Unity, then, is not Intellectual-Principle but something higher still: Intellectual-Principle is still a being but that First is no being but precedent to all Being: it cannot be a being, for a being has what we may call the shape of its reality, but The Unity is without shape, even shape Intellectual.

Generative of all, The Unity is none of all; neither thing nor quantity nor quality nor intellect nor soul; not in motion, not at rest, not in place, not in time: it is the self-defined, unique in form or, better, formless, existing before Form was, or Movement or Rest, all of which are attachments of Being and make Being the manifold it is.

But how, if not in movement, can it be otherwise than at rest?

The answer is that movement and rest are states pertaining to Being, which necessarily has one or the other or both. Besides, anything at rest must be so in virtue of Rest as something distinct: Unity at rest becomes the ground of an attribute and at once ceases to be a simplex.

Note, similarly, that when we speak of this First as Cause we are affirming something happening not to it but to us, the fact that we take from this Self-Enclosed: strictly we should put neither a This nor a That to it; we hover, as it were, about it, seeking the statement of an experience of our own, sometimes nearing this Reality, sometimes baffled by the enigma in which it dwells.

4. The main source of the difficulty is that awareness of this Principle comes neither by knowing nor by the Intellection that discovers the Intellectual Beings but by a presence overpassing all knowledge. In knowing, soul or mind abandons its unity; it cannot remain a simplex: knowing is taking account of things; that accounting is multiple; the mind thus plunging into number and multiplicity departs from unity.

Our way then takes us beyond knowing; there may be no wandering from unity; knowing and knowable must all be left aside; every object of thought, even the highest, we must pass by, for all that is good is later than This and derives from This as from the sun all the light of the day.

'Not to be told; not to be written': in our writing and telling we are but urging towards it: out of discussion we call to vision: to those desiring to see, we point the path; our teaching is of the road and the travelling; the seeing must be the very act of one that has made this choice.

There are those that have not attained to see. The soul has not come to know the splendour There; it has not felt and clutched to itself that love-passion of vision known to the lover come to rest where he loves. Or struck perhaps by that authentic light, all the soul lit by the nearness gained, we have gone weighted from beneath; the vision is frustrate; we should go without burden and we go carrying that which can but keep us back; we are not yet made over into unity.

From none is that Principle absent and yet from all: present, it remains absent save to those fit to receive, disciplined into some accordance, able to touch it closely by their likeness and by that kindred power within themselves through which, remaining as it was when it came to them from the Supreme, they are enabled to see in so far as God may at all be seen.

Failure to attain may be due to such impediment or to lack of the guiding thought that establishes trust; impediment we must charge against ourselves and strive by entire renunciation to become emancipate; where there is distrust for lack of convincing reason, further considerations may be applied:

5. Those to whom existence comes about by chance and automatic action and is held together by material forces have drifted far from God and from the concept of unity; we are not here addressing them but only such as accept another nature than body and have some conception of soul.

Soul must be sounded to the depths, understood as an emanation from Intellectual-Principle and as holding its value by a Reason-Principle thence infused. Next, this Intellect must be apprehended, an Intellect other than the reasoning faculty known as the rational principle; with reasoning we are already in the region of separation and movement: our sciences are Reason-Principles lodged in soul or mind, having manifestly acquired their character by the presence in the soul of Intellectual-Principle, source of all knowing.

Thus we come to see Intellectual-Principle almost as an object of sense: it is perceptible as standing above soul, father to soul, and it is one with the Intellectual Cosmos; we must think of it as a quiet, unwavering motion; containing all things and being all things, it is a multiple but at once indivisible and comporting difference. It is not discriminate as are the Reason-Principles, which can in fact be known one by one: yet its content is not a confusion; every item stands forth distinctly, just as in a science the entire content holds as an indivisible and yet each item is a self-standing verity.

Now a plurality thus concentrated like the Intellectual Cosmos is close upon The First—and reason certifies its existence as surely as that of soul—yet, though of higher sovranty than soul, it is not The First since it is not a unity, not simplex as unity, principle over all multiplicity, must be.

Before it there is That which must transcend the noblest of the things of Being: there must be a prior to the Intellectual-Principle which aiming towards unity is yet not unity but a thing in unity's likeness. From this highest it is not sundered; it too is self-present: so close to the unity, it cannot be articulated: and yet it is a principle which in some measure has dared secession.

That awesome Prior, The Unity, is not a being, for so its unity would be vested in something else: strictly no name is apt to it, but since name it we must there is a certain rough fitness in designating it as unity with the understanding that it is not the unity of some other thing.

Thus it eludes our knowledge, so that the nearer approach to it is through its offspring, Being: we know it as cause of existence to Intellectual-Principle, as fount of all that is best, as the efficacy which, self-perduring and undiminishing, generates all beings and is not to be counted among these its derivatives, to all of which it must be prior.

This we can but name The Unity, indicating it to each other by a designation that points to the concept of its partlessness while we are in reality striving to bring our own minds to unity. We are not to think of such unity and partless-ness as belong to point or monad; the veritable unity is the source of all such quantity which could not exist unless first there existed Being and Being's Prior: we are not, then, to think in the order of point and monad but to use these—in their simplicity and their rejection of magnitude and partition—as symbols for the higher concept.

6. In what sense, then, do we assert this Unity and how is it to be adjusted to our mental processes?

Its oneness must not be belittled to that of monad and point: for these the mind abstracts extension and numerical quantity and rests upon the very minutest possible, ending no doubt in the partless but still in something that be-gan as a partible and is always lodged in something other than itself. The Unity was never in any other and never belonged to the partible: nor is its impartibility that of extreme minuteness; on the contrary it is great beyond anything, great not in extension but in power, sizeless by its very greatness as even its immedi-ate sequents are impartible not in mass but in might. We must therefore take the Unity as infinite not in measureless extension or numerable quantity but in fathomless depths of power.

Think of The One as Mind or as God, you think too meanly; use all the resources of understanding to conceive this Unity and, again, it is more au-thentically one than God, even though you reach for God's unity beyond the unity the most perfect you can conceive. For This is utterly a self-existent, with no concomitant whatever. This self-sufficing is the essence of its unity. Something there must be supremely adequate, autonomous, all-transcending, most utterly without need.

Any manifold, anything beneath The Unity, is dependent: combined from various constituents, its essential nature goes in need of unity; but unity cannot need itself; it stands unity accomplished. Again, a manifold depends upon all its factors; and furthermore each of those factors in turn—as necessarily inbound with the rest and not self-standing—sets up a similar need both to its associates and to the total so constituted.

The sovranly self-sufficing principle will be Unity-Absolute, for only in this unity is there a nature above all need whether within itself or in regard to the rest of things. Unity seeks nothing towards its being or its well-being or its safehold upon existence; cause to all, how can it acquire its character outside of itself or know any good outside? The good of its being can be no borrowing: This is The Good. Nor has it station; it needs no standing-ground as if inadequate to its own sustaining; what calls for such underpropping is the soulless, some material mass that must be based or fall. This is base to all, cause of universal existence and of ordered station. All that demands place is in need; a First cannot go in need of its sequents: all need is effort towards a first principle; the First, principle to all, must be utterly without need. If the Unity be seeking, it must inevitably be seeking to be something other than itself; it is seeking its own destroyer. Whatever may be said to be in need is needing a good, a preserver; nothing can be a good to The Unity, therefore.

Neither can it have will to anything; it is a Beyond-Good, not even to itself a good but to such beings only as may be of quality to have part with it. Nor has it Intellection; that would comport diversity: nor Movement; it is prior to Movement as to Intellection.

To what could its Intellection be directed? To itself? But that would imply a previous ignorance; it would be dependent upon that Intellection in order to knowledge of itself; but it is the self-sufficing. Yet this absence of self-knowing, of self-intellection, does not comport ignorance; ignorance is of something outside—a knower ignorant of a knowable—but in the Solitary there is neither knowing nor anything unknown. Unity, self-present, it has no need of self-intellection: indeed this 'self-presence' were better left out, the more surely to preserve the unity; we must eliminate all knowing and all association, all intellection whether internal or external. It is not to be thought of as having but as being Intellection; Intellection does not itself perform the intellective act but is the cause of the act in something else and cause is not to be identified with caused: most assuredly the cause of all is not a thing within that all.

This Principle is not, therefore, to be identified with the good of which it is the source; it is good in the unique mode of being The Good above all that is good.

7. If the mind reels before something thus alien to all we know, we must take our stand on the things of this realm and strive thence to see. But in the looking beware of throwing outward; this Principle does not lie away somewhere leaving the rest void; to those of power to reach, it is present; to the inapt, absent. In our daily affairs we cannot hold an object in mind if we have given ourselves elsewhere, occupied upon some other matter; that very thing, and nothing else, must be before us to be truly the object of observation. So here also; preoccupied by the impress of something else, we are withheld under that pressure from becoming aware of The Unity; a mind gripped and fastened by some definite thing cannot take the print of the very contrary. As Matter, it is agreed, must be void of quality in order to accept the types of the universe, so and much more must the soul be kept formless if there is to be no infixed impediment to prevent it being brimmed and lit by the Primal Principle.

In sum, we must withdraw from all the extern, pointed wholly inwards; no leaning to the outer; the total of things ignored, first in their relation to us and later in the very idea; the self put out of mind in the contemplation of the Supreme; all the commerce so closely There that, if report were possible, one might become to others reporter of that communion.

Such converse, we may suppose, was that of Minos, thence known as the Familiar of Zeus; and in that memory he established the laws which report it, enlarged to that task by his contact with the Divine. Some, on the other hand, there will be to disdain such citizen service, choosing to remain always in the higher: these will be those that have seen much.

God—we read—is outside of none, present unperceived to all; we break away from Him, or rather from ourselves; what we turn from we cannot reach; astray ourselves, we cannot go in search of another; a child distraught will not recognize its father; to find ourselves is to know our source.

8. Every soul that knows its history is aware, also, that its movement, unthwarted, is not that of an outgoing line; its natural course may be likened to that in which a circle turns not upon some external but on its own centre, the point to which it owes its rise. The soul's movement will be about its source; to this it will hold, poised intent towards that unity to which all souls should move and the divine souls always move, divine in virtue of that movement; for to be a god is to be integral with the Supreme; what stands away is man still multiple, or beast.

Is then this 'centre' of our souls the Principle for which we are seeking?

We must look yet further: we must admit a Principle in which all these centres coincide: it will be a centre by analogy with the centre of the circle we know. The soul is not a circle in the sense of the geometric figure ❙ but in that its primal nature (wholeness) is within it and about it, that it owes its origin to what is whole, and that it will be still more entire when severed from body.³❙

In our present state—part of our being weighed down by the body, as one might have the feet under water with all the rest untouched—we bear ourselves aloft by that intact part and, in that, hold through our own centre to the centre of all the centres, just as the centres of the great circles of a sphere coincide with that of the sphere to which all belong. Thus we are secure.

If these circles were material and not spiritual, the link with the centres would be local; they would lie round it where it lay at some distant point: since the souls are of the Intellectual, and the Supreme still loftier, we understand that contact is otherwise procured, that is by those powers which connect Intellectual agent with Intellectual object; indeed soul is closer to the Supreme than Intellect to its object—such is its similarity, identity, and the sure link of kindred. Material mass cannot blend into other material mass: unbodied beings are not under this bodily limitation; their separation is solely that of otherness, of differentiation; in the absence of otherness, it is similars mutually present.

Thus the Supreme as containing no otherness is ever present with us; we with it when we put otherness away. It is not that the Supreme reaches out to us seeking our communion: we reach towards the Supreme; it is we that become present. We are always before it: but we do not always look: thus a choir, singing set in due order about the conductor, may turn away from that centre to which all should attend; let it but face aright and it sings with beauty, present effectively. We are ever before the Supreme—cut off is utter dissolution; we can no longer be—but we do not always attend: when we look, our Term is attained; this is rest; this is the end of singing ill; effectively before Him, we lift a choral song full of God.

9. In this choiring, the soul looks upon the wellspring of Life, wellspring also of Intellect, beginning of Being, fount of Good, root of Soul. It is not that these are poured out from the Supreme, lessening it as if it were a thing of mass. At that the emanants would be perishable; but they are eternal; they spring from an eternal principle, which produces them not by its fragmentation but in virtue of its intact identity: therefore they too hold firm; so long as the sun shines, so long there will be light.

We have not been cut away; we are not separate, what though the body-nature has closed about us to press us to itself; we breathe and hold our ground because the Supreme does not give and pass but gives on for ever, so long as it remains what it is.

Our being is the fuller for our turning Thither; this is our prosperity; to hold aloof is loneliness and lessening. Here is the soul's peace, outside of evil, refuge taken in the place clean of wrong; here it has its Act, its true knowing; here it is immune. Here is living, the true; that of today, all living apart from Him, is but a shadow, a mimicry. Life in the Supreme is the native activity of Intellect; in virtue of that silent converse it brings forth gods, brings forth beauty, brings forth righteousness, brings forth all moral good; for of all these the soul is pregnant when it has been filled with God. This state is its first and its final, because from God it comes, its good lies There, and, once turned to God again, it is what it was. Life here, with the things of earth, is a sinking, a defeat, a failing of the wing.

That our good is There is shown by the very love inborn with the soul; hence the constant linking of the Love-God with the Psyches in story and picture; the soul, other than God but sprung of Him, must needs love. So long as it is There, it holds the heavenly love; here its love is the baser; There the soul is Aphrodite of the heavens; here, turned harlot, Aphrodite of the public ways: yet the soul is always an Aphrodite. This is the intention of the myth which tells of Aphrodite's birth and Eros born with her.

The soul in its nature loves God and longs to be at one with Him in the noble love of a daughter for a noble father; but coming to human birth and lured by the courtships of this sphere, she takes up with another love, a mortal, leaves her father and falls.

But one day coming to hate her shame, she puts away the evil of earth, once more seeks the father, and finds her peace.

Those to whom all this experience is strange may understand by way of our earthly longings and the joy we have in winning to what we most desire—remembering always that here what we love is perishable, hurtful, that our loving is of mimicries and turns awry because all was a mistake, our good was not here, this was not what we sought; There only is our veritable love and There we may unite with it, not holding it in some fleshly embrace but possessing it in all its verity.[4] Any that have seen know what I have in mind: the soul takes another life as it draws nearer and nearer to God and gains participation in Him; thus restored it feels that the dispenser of true life is There to see, that now we have nothing to look for but, far otherwise, that we must put aside all else and rest in This alone, This become, This alone, all the earthly environment done away, in haste to be free, impatient of any bond holding us to the baser, so that with our being entire we may cling about This, no part in us remaining but through it we have touch with God.

Thus we have all the vision that may be of Him and of ourselves; but it is of a self wrought to splendour, brimmed with the Intellectual light, become that very light, pure, buoyant, unburdened, raised to Godhood or, better, knowing its Godhood, all aflame then—but crushed out once more if it should take up the discarded burden.

10. But how comes the soul not to keep that ground?

Because it has not yet escaped wholly: but there will be the time of vision unbroken, the self hindered no longer by any hindrance of body. Not that those hindrances beset that in us which has veritably seen; it is the other phase of the soul that suffers, and that only when we withdraw from vision and take to knowing by proof, by evidence, by the reasoning processes of the mental habit. Such logic is not to be confounded with that act of ours in the vision; it is not our reason that has seen; it is something greater than reason, reason's Prior, as far above reason as the very object of that thought must be.

In our self-seeing There, the self is seen as belonging to that order, or rather we are merged into that self in us which has the quality of that order. It is a knowing of the self restored to its purity. No doubt we should not speak of seeing; but we cannot help talking in dualities, seen and seer, instead of, boldly, the achievement of unity. In this seeing, we neither hold an object nor trace distinction; there is no two. The man is changed, no longer himself nor self-belonging; he is merged with the Supreme, sunken into it, one with it: centre coincides with centre, for centres of circles, even here below, are one when they unite, and two when they separate; and it is in this sense that we now (after the vision) speak of the Supreme as separate. This is why the vision baffles telling; we cannot detach the Supreme to state it; if we have seen something thus detached we have failed of the Supreme which is to be known only as one with ourselves.

11. This is the purport of that rule of our Mysteries: 'Nothing Divulged to the Uninitiate': the Supreme is not to be made a common story, the holy things may not be uncovered to the stranger, to any that has not himself attained to see. There were not two; beholder was one with beheld; it was not a vision compassed but a unity apprehended. The man formed by this mingling with the Supreme must—if he only remember—carry its image impressed upon him: he is become the Unity, nothing within him or without inducing any diversity; no movement now, no passion, no outlooking desire, once this ascent is achieved; reasoning is in abeyance and all Intellection and even, to dare the word, the very self: caught away, filled with God, he has in perfect stillness attained isolation; all the being calmed, he turns neither to this side nor to that, not even inwards

to himself; utterly resting he has become very rest. He belongs no longer to the order of the beautiful; he has risen beyond beauty; he has overpassed even the choir of the virtues; he is like one who, having penetrated the inner sanctuary, leaves the temple images behind him—though these become once more first objects of regard when he leaves the holies; for There his converse was not with image, not with trace, but with the very Truth in the view of which all the rest is but of secondary concern.

There, indeed, it was scarcely vision, unless of a mode unknown; it was a going forth from the self, a simplifying, a renunciation, a reach towards contact and at the same time a repose, a meditation towards adjustment. This is the only seeing of what lies within the holies: to look otherwise is to fail.

Things here are signs; they show therefore to the wiser teachers how the supreme God is known; the instructed priest reading the sign may enter the holy place and make real the vision of the inaccessible.

Even those that have never found entry must admit the existence of that invisible; they will know their source and Principle since by principle they see principle and are linked with it, by like they have contact with like and so they grasp all of the divine that lies within the scope of mind. Until the seeing comes they are still craving something, that which only the vision can give; this Term, attained only by those that have overpassed all, is the All-Transcending.

It is not in the soul's nature to touch utter nothingness; the lowest descent is into evil and, so far, into non-being: but to utter nothing, never. When the soul begins again to mount, it comes not to something alien but to its very self; thus detached, it is in nothing but⁵ itself; self-gathered it is no longer in the order of being; it is in the Supreme.

There is thus a converse in virtue of which the essential man outgrows Being, becomes identical with the Transcendent of Being. The self thus lifted, we are in the likeness of the Supreme: if from that heightened self we pass still higher—image to archetype—we have won the Term of all our journeying. Fallen back again, we waken the virtue within until we know ourselves all order once more; once more we are lightened of the burden and move by virtue towards Intellectual-Principle and through the Wisdom in That to the Supreme.

This is the life of gods and of the godlike and blessed among men, liberation from the alien that besets us here, a life taking no pleasure in the things of earth, the passing of solitary to solitary.

NOTES TO ENNEAD VI.9

1. FIRST EDITION: "Besides, the soul, *even the collective soul for all its absence of part,* is a manifold: it has . . ."

> GUTHRIE: "Further, the soul is manifold as well as one, though she be not composed of parts. She possesses . . ."

> ARMSTRONG: ". . . and then the soul is many, even the soul which is one, even if it is not composed from parts; for there are . . ."

> TAYLOR: ". . . each soul is a multitude, though it does not consist of parts. For there are . . ."

2. FIRST EDITION: ". . . its competence is upon its priors, *its content and its issue:* but . . ."

> TAYLOR: "Intellect, however, is able to see either things prior to itself, or things pertaining to itself, or things effected by itself."

> GUTHRIE: "Intelligence can see both the things that are above it, those which belong to it, and the things that proceed from it."

> ARMSTRONG: "Intellect is competent to see its own things and the things before it."

3. FIRST EDITION: ". . . but in that *it at once contains the Primal Nature (as centre) and is contained by it (as circumference),* that it owes its origin to *such a centre and still more that the soul, uncontaminated, is a self-contained entity.*"

> TAYLOR: ". . . but because an ancient nature is in and about it. And because the soul is suspended from a thing of this kind, and in a still greater degree when it is wholly separated from the body."

> ARMSTRONG: ". . . but because there is in it and around it the ancient nature, and because it comes from an origin of this kind, and because souls are wholly separated."

> GUTHRIE: ". . . but that in her and around her subsists primordial nature. (By saying that she has a centre, we mean that) the soul is suspended from the primary Principle (by the highest part of her being), especially when she is entirely separated (from the body)."

4. FIRST EDITION: ". . . There we may *hold it and be* with it, *possess it in its verity no longer submerged in alien flesh.*"

> GUTHRIE: ". . . the only one with which we could unite or identify ourselves, which we could intimately possess, because it is not separated from our soul by the covering of our flesh."

> TAYLOR: ". . . with which we may be conjoined, which we may participate, and truly possess, and which is not externally enveloped with flesh."

> ARMSTRONG: ". . . with whom also we can be united, having a part in him and truly possessing him, not embracing him in the flesh from the outside."

5. FIRST EDITION: ". . . thus detached, it is *not in nothingness* but *in* itself;"

> ARMSTRONG: ". . . and in this way since it is not in something else it will not be in nothing, but in itself;"

> GUTHRIE: "From the fact that she then is not in anything different from herself, it does not result that she is within anything, for she remains in herself."

> TAYLOR: "And thus not being in another thing, it is not on that account in nothing, but is in itself."

APPENDIX I

A Suggestive Outline of Plotinian Metaphysics

⟦ THE ENNEADS *are formulations of Plotinus' intuitive realizations of ultimate truths to which only our inner being may respond. We must let the logos in our soul absorb the impact and assimilate the meaning of his intuitions before allowing our critical and egotistical intellect to pounce upon them. In other words, our mental activity must be stilled so that the silence within can receive the passage in question without coloration.*

The Sage, then, has gone through a process of reasoning when he expounds his act to others; but in relation to himself he is Vision. (III.8.6)

The *Enneads* are born of such vision. The uncanny precision and skillful dialectic of Plotinus' creative exposition is a result of the final stages of human intelligence. At the core of his work is a path—profound and encompassing—beckoning us to follow the highest philosophic ideals with the goal of self-knowledge.

Central to his method is contemplation—a "Seeing that lives"—the mind rapt in intense awareness, knowing without image.

Because his words are formulated from this state of profound insight, we can participate in the vision to some degree by following his reasoning process with concentrated thought. As we meditate on the passages, the ideas will begin to permeate our being, awakening in us a love for the Divine and an aspiration to experience these eternal verities. Eventually we can be brought to recollection, contemplation of their subsistence within our own soul.

These seeds for meditation which Plotinus provides are of inestimable value to beginners and proficients alike. But the *Enneads* also present a powerful challenge to our intellects. Written in response to questions from students, many of the tractates presuppose a familiarity with the philosophic basis of Plotinus' whole teaching and the context in which he worked. To help the modern reader see more deeply into the world-view and presuppositions implicit in the *Enneads*, we have organized the following brief commentary with diagrams. It is drawn mainly from writings of the contemporary American philosopher Anthony Damiani (1922–1984), whose major work *Astronoesis* (as yet unpublished) relates the philosophy of Plotinus with a creative vision of cosmology. Damiani's sympathetic viewpoint of Neoplatonism, combined with an extensive knowledge of ancient and modern philosophy, revitalizes a world-view which has been obscured by time.

We offer this as a suggestive interpretation, an inspiration to fellow travelers. While we should not look for complete solutions to Mind's ultimate Mystery, we can offer some precise and detailed statements. The outline begins with an examination of the One and follows Damiani's thread of meaning from primal realities to their manifestation. Like Ariadne's thread, this flow of meanings may also serve us well in retracing our nature—both conceptually and experientially—to its Source.

. . .

In compiling this outline we use, as often as possible, direct excerpts from Mr. Damiani's writings: such paragraphs in the text are preceded by a ⎕. Passages from Plotinus are identified by tractate and often set off as block quotations. The remainder of the text is our own, based on—and we believe true to—Damiani's writings. Diagrams are tailored from among hundreds which he used. Words we have inserted either into the text of Plotinus or into the Damiani extracts are indicated by square brackets. References to John Deck's translations of Plotinian passages come from the Larson edition of Mr. Deck's text *Nature, Contemplation, and the One.*

1. THE ONE

⎕ *In seeking by means of these passages a glimpse of the incomprehensible nature of the One, the intellect must be like a bird which in flying through the air leaves no trace: the intellect's operation must dissolve back into the stillness into which it is advancing. We must think very intensely on what the nature of the One is, and then there is a point at which you let go of everything. But do not think that the discussions of this are pointless, for the One is the only important thing you can discuss ever in your life—at any time, anywhere—there is nothing more important.*

Plotinus presents a philosophy of Unity: unity as unfathomable and transcendent, and unity as omnipresent and immanent.

⎕ First in the order of importance are statements about the existence of God, the One-Only; for following upon this certitude that is the very core of all that he will say, Plotinus transmits for our benefit a wisdom-knowledge or *prima philosophia* conascent with the foundations of our world and our being.

"In what sense, then," Plotinus asks in vi.9.6, "do we assert this Unity and how is it to be adjusted to our mental processes?" This question initiates our inquiry into the nature of the One.

⎕ The One is absolute positivity: pure universal existence inbound with the totality of possibilities and infinity of power. Perhaps it might be more meaningful and provocative to say that it is intelligence—or, better still, pure intelligence. Sufficient and complete in itself, *the only Perfection* is without peer and is beyond any limitation, dependence, need, or multiplicity of any kind:

> Standing before all things . . . transcending Being. . . . Untouched by multiplicity, it will be wholly self-sufficing, an absolute First . . . (v.4.1)

⬙ This affirmation of its transcendence does not imply that the One is a blank homogeneity or zero; rather, that it is unlimited fullness. To aim the understanding "beyond being" does not mean that it must at some point fall into an abyss of nothingness. On the contrary, remove whatever aseity [unique essence] characterizes any principle or idea, and the infinity of the transcendent is then conceptually available.

Although the One is beyond knowledge in the ordinary sense, Plotinus indicates that it is a Supra-Knowledge in an extraordinary sense. It is "not, so to speak, imperceptive, but everything of it is in it and with it; it is entirely self-discerning." (v.4.2, Deck, page 33) It is not by excluding qualities that the One is beyond all qualities, but rather because no distinct character can remain intact in its infinite atmosphere.

⬙ In vi.8.16 [Deck translation], Plotinus speaks of an eternal "wakefulness" (or a consciousness). . . . The statement that the One "will *be* in the way it is awake" (Deck, page 32) is a particularly emphatic assertion of the identity of wakefulness (consciousness) with existence. . . . But first we must fully encounter the uniqueness of this conception of the Absolute: our minds should be brought to a halt by what we are being asked to consider. Pure unconditioned being in all its universality is conceived here as [in] identity with intrinsically appropriate super-intelligence: eternal stasis reigns.

⬙ Obviously, no symbol is adequate to this Absolute. But . . . Plotinus assures us that "there is a certain rough fitness in designating it as unity." (vi.9.5) Plotinus clearly states that the One's simplicity is not that of a spatial point or a quantitative unit to be enumerated with others:

> . . . nor is its impartibility that of extreme minuteness; on the contrary it is great beyond anything, great not in extension but in power . . . infinite . . . in fathomless depths of power. (vi.9.6)

⬙ In a preliminary fashion, he dismisses the elementary associations that the word "One" may have. . . . this very positive description of the Unity's power as beyond any determination or limitation means that unlimited power should be understood as an indivisible aspect that is identical with Unity. . . . In this sense, it is beyond Divine Mind, or Being. Such a total affirmation . . . points beyond to an ultimateless Ultimate "utterly a self-existent, with no concomitant whatever. This self-suffing is the essence of its unity. . . . supremely adequate, autonomous, all-transcending, most utterly without need." (VI.9.6) It is the Alone.

▢ This One is not, therefore, an abstraction from other principles. On the contrary, all other principles are *literally* divine outflowings from the superabundance of its Perfection. The later principles are all dependent on It; but the One depends on none. For any principle or being to be at all, it must first be a unity: the first principle of all principles is Unity itself . . .

▢ We are presented with a Supreme Intelligence that does not loosen, dwindle, or divide itself, nor is it modified or spread out among the lower orders of reality. This is the initial premise. Appreciating this intact perfection is a necessary and absolute prerequisite to arrive at a proper understanding of emanation.

A second question arises:

> . . . from such a unity as we have declared The One to be, how does anything at all come into substantial existence . . . ? (v.1.6)

Plotinus' initial answer is so beautiful and simple that it merits a pause to appreciate its precise solution to the problem:

> All existences, as long as they retain their character, produce—about themselves, from their essence, in virtue of the power which must be in them—some necessary, outward-facing hypostasis continuously attached to them and representing in image the engendering archetypes. . . . Again, all that is fully achieved engenders: therefore the eternally achieved engenders eternally an eternal being. (v.1.6)

This approach to the One accounts for the arisal of Beings without lessening the One.

▢ For Plotinus the One-and-its-Power stands first and foremost above all and simultaneously sustains and includes lesser levels of reality which are neither self-sufficient nor illusory. Through an understanding of this principle of Power, we can make available to our minds what we refer to as the double truth—that is, the nondual reality does not exclude the dualistic but includes and supports it.

> If The First is perfect, utterly perfect above all, and is the beginning of all power, it must be the most powerful of all that is, and all other powers must act in some partial imitation of it. . . . the First Good, the Power towards all, how could it grudge or be powerless to give of itself, and how at that would it still be the Source? (v.4.1)

▢ In considering this Power which we conceive as identical with the One's own nature, a twofold character of the One is observable. There is utter stillness or passive perfection of the Transcendent and there is its infinite Act: "his being is constituted by this self-originating self-tendance—at once Act and repose." (VI.8.16)

These two ultimate complementaries—active and passive perfection—although unavoidably polarized by our own thought, must nonetheless be recognized as coinciding within the One's absolute completion. In order to understand such descriptions of the ultimate, it is essential for our minds to become acclimated to a logic of paradox. For here we are indeed aspiring to knowledge beyond (*para*) the proper realm of what Plato calls *doxa*, that is, the intellectual processes corresponding with sense-experience.

▢ Plotinus characterizes the infinite and indeterminate Power of the One as both identical with the pure undifferenced [super-] knowledge of the One and radiating from it.

There is in everything the Act of the Essence and the Act going out from the Essence: the first Act is the thing itself in its realized identity, the second Act is an inevitably following outgo from the first, an emanation distinct from the thing itself. . . .

So it is in the divine also: or rather we have there the earlier form of the double act: the divine remains in its own unchanging being, but from its perfection and from the Act included in its nature there emanates the secondary or issuing Act which—as the output of a mighty power, the mightiest there is—attains to Real Being as second to that which stands above all Being. (V.4.2)

▢ Power, as spoken of here, has this twofold meaning. When Plotinus refers to it as a completing power which produces no new thing within the One, it coincides with and is indistinguishable from the One. Secondly, that same power flows forth or emanates from the One [taking shape as the Intellectual-Principle].

▢ Excluded from the Godhead is any personal volition; the process is completely impersonal. Within the One itself there can be no change or process, no operation, arrangement, or combination of any sort—not even the universal relativity of Forms found in the Intellectual-Principle. Bearing all this in mind, we must hold firmly that the One is in no way becoming anything. . . . Throughout all the production that inevitably ensues, the One remains unmoved; all possible production is already transcendentally actual and accomplished within its own infinite power.

▢ From the sheer intensity of this perfection, there emanates, as a distinct and lower existent, the Intellectual-Principle, the aggregate of eternally-existing Ideas and Beings. . . . This emanating power contains and reflectively includes the transcendent models or paradigms and the ideas . . . an externalization or efflux of the complex interiority of the indivisible aspects of the Supreme Perfection.

> The only reasonable explanation of act flowing from it lies in the analogy of light from a sun. The entire intellectual order may be figured as a kind of light with the One in repose at its summit as its King: but this manifestation is not cast out from it . . . but the One shines eternally, resting upon the Intellectual Realm; this, not identical with its source, is yet not severed from it . . . (v.3.12)

The sun itself has an internal power or energy, and the radiating light is its outgoing act. From the sun's point of view, the light is not other than itself, but the emanating rays can be taken as its expression, revealing in their spectrum something of the sun itself.

▯ The Divine Mind [Intellectual-Principle] is a reflex . . . an image of an infinite original of such power and perfection that the very copy, so-called, stands a reality. The Intellectual-Principle and its emanation, Soul, are not illusory in any sense; they are also eternal. . . . we have to consider them as distinct realities of different degrees.

> There is, accordingly, from the first principle to ultimate an outgoing in which unfailingly each principle retains its own seat while its offshoot takes another rank, a lower, though on the other hand every being is in identity with its prior as long as it holds that contact. (v.2.2)

▯ Even if we view the three primal Hypostases—the One, Intellectual-Principle and Soul—as forming an integral whole (which is often referred to as the Absolute when considered from the side of manifestation), the distinctions cannot be dissolved in such a way that the Nous and Soul, so carefully defined, become illusory principles. In our understanding of the metaphysical Infinite, we retain the view of the One as the pure and only perfect reality, as well as the view of real and distinct emanations from it. We do not violate the One's sovereignty by granting to each of the other levels of reality their proper status; they do not become null and void in the face of the One which they eternally contemplate.

▯ These principles or wisdom emanations [the pure hypostases in themselves] . . . constitute a spiritual hierarchy that is broader and more inclusive than can ever be adequately suggested by any verbal schema. [They] exist in a distinctionless mode . . . a self-suffing and eternally august nature, the grandeur of authenticity. In truth they are an inscrutable abyss—a blinding darkness to our intellect, a radiance and joy that can suffocate the unprepared but illuminate and enlighten permanently the proficient, the adept. Their own proper subsistence constitutes a realm that is beyond the reach of any imaginative activity, heights that are *literally* unimaginable. Nonetheless, they are precisely what constitute the content of philosophic wisdom.

For Plotinus, the three primals together with their manifestation, the system of Nature, constitute the fourfold nature of Reality. On the basis of these distinctions, Plotinus presents the entire breadth of his vision of reality.

> There exists a Principle which transcends Being; this is The One, whose nature we have sought to establish, in so far as such matters lend themselves to proof. Upon The One follows immediately the Principle which is at once Being and the Intellectual-Principle. Third comes the Principle, Soul.
>
> Now just as these three exist for the system of Nature, so, we must hold, they exist for ourselves. (v.1.10)

The remarks in v.1.10 lend themselves to a pictorial form. These principles can be diagrammed as a circle divided into four quadrants, offering a simple static representation of his meaning. The first quadrant represents the One; the second, Intellectual-Principle (Nous); the third symbolizes Soul; and the fourth, the entire System of Nature or Universal Manifestation in its totality—the Body of God.

 FIG. 1

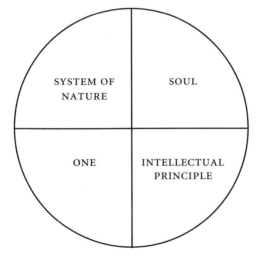

We see this quadrature as representing four "substantial" levels of reality, each of which entails a distinct level of Consciousness or Mind. This same reality may be portrayed in terms of its "functional" modes. Plotinus suggests two ways to imagine the dynamic relation of the One to its emanations.

There is, we may put it, something that is centre; about it, a circle of light shed from it; round centre and first circle alike, another circle, light from light; outside that again, not another circle of light but one which, lacking light of its own, must borrow. (IV.3.17)

FIG. 2

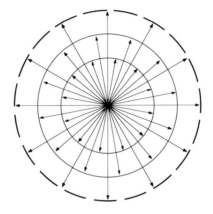

Reversing the order of the circles, the entire background intelligence represents the One, and the other principles are seen as successive circles nested within it—all encompassed by the uncircumscribed Good.

But Soul is not in the universe, on the contrary the universe is in the Soul . . . Soul is contained in Intellectual-Principle and is the container of body. The Intellectual-Principle in turn is contained in something else; but that prior principle has nothing in which to be. . . . But all the rest must be somewhere; and where but in the First?

. . . the First is neither remote from things, nor directly within them; there is nothing containing it; it contains all. It is The Good to the universe if only in this way, that towards it all things have their being, all dependent upon it . . . (V.5.9)

FIG. 3

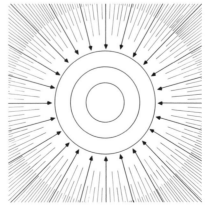

By superimposing the two perspectives of quadrants and circles, we get a diagram which visually suggests the paradoxical nature of Reality—intelligence and its activity, or substance (quadrants) and function (rings) as simultaneous. The image of the contracting circles is used here, though the radiating sequence would be equally compelling. We show four rings to indicate the functioning of reality: the two outermost rings represent Being and Intellection (cf. v.1.10 above), the third represents soul, and the innermost represents body.

FIG. 4

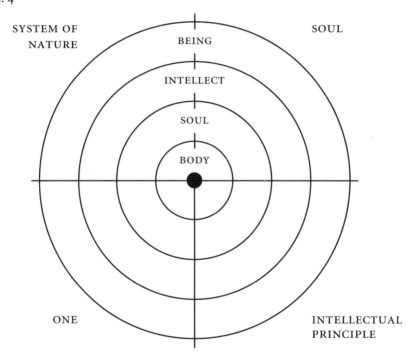

SYSTEM OF NATURE

SOUL

BEING

INTELLECT

SOUL

BODY

ONE

INTELLECTUAL PRINCIPLE

As passing through all four quadrants, the rings represent a dynamic or active view connecting the substance represented by the quadrants. This interweaving emphasizes that the primals are simultaneous as well as hierarchical.

This symbol also helps us to see the simultaneous views of the One as transcendent and immanent. We represent the One as transcendent by the first quadrant, while the other quadrants symbolize those principles that emanate from the One. The presence of the rings in the first quadrant indicates that the One prefigures the other levels within itself in a transcendent and mysterious mode. "What is present in Intellectual-Principle," Plotinus says in vi.8.18, "is present, though in a far transcendent mode, in the One."

We represent the One as immanent by the presence of the entire circular disc in each of the successive rings. It is, as Plotinus says, "wonderful" that "while it [the One] is nowhere, nowhere is it not." (v.5.8)

This image of the fourfold nature of Reality provides us with a paradigm: for any authentic existent will participate in unity, intellection, soul, and body (manifestation). This teaching on the nature of the One applies not only to the transcendent One, but to any authentic being which is a one—such as we ourselves are in our inner nature.

> Every particular thing has a One of its own to which it may be traced; the All has its One, its Prior but not yet the Absolute One; through this we reach that Absolute One, where all such reference comes to an end.
>
> Now when we reach a One—the stationary Principle—in the tree, in the animal, in Soul, in the All—we have in every case the most powerful, the precious element: when we come to the One in the Authentically Existent Beings—their Principle and source and potentiality—shall we lose confidence and suspect it of being—nothing?
>
> Certainly this Absolute is none of the things of which it is the source. . . . But possess yourself of it by the very elimination of Being and you hold a marvel. . . . understanding it by that intuitive thrust alone, but knowing its greatness by the Beings that follow upon it and exist by its power. (III.8.10)

2. INTELLECTUAL-PRINCIPLE

⬚ *Out of the ocean of infinite possibilities present in the ineffable undifferenced intelligence of the One, there pours forth a radiant display of glorious revelations— the Divine Mind and its Ideas. These luminous existences, emanating on the surface of the One's voidness, exhibit the inner nature, the inherent perfection of the unique and unknowable God.*

⬚ The power of the One is so great that the Divine Mind [Intellectual-Principle], though an "image One," is itself authentic reality. . . . as the "outward" expression of the One, it paradoxically stands as a distinct hypostasis midst the One without a second. [We will subsequently treat the terms Intellectual-Principle, Divine Mind, and Nous as interchangeable.]

> Seeking nothing, possessing nothing, lacking nothing, the One is perfect and, in our metaphor, has overflowed, and its exuberance has produced the new: this product has turned again to its begetter and been filled and has become its contemplator and so an Intellectual-Principle. (v.2.1)

⬚ The concentrated unity of the One is reflected in the Intellectual-Principle, which Plotinus characterizes as no longer a unity but a "One-Many" (v.1.8) [and a "unity in duality" (v.6.1)].

> . . . this is pure being in eternal actuality . . . everything, in that entire content, is Intellectual-Principle and Authentic-Existence. . . . Intellectual-Principle by its intellective act establishes Being, which in turn, as the object of intellection, becomes the cause of intellection and of existence to the Intellectual-Principle . . . (v.1.4)

Authentic Being (divine substance) and Knowing (divine function) are the twofold nature of Intellectual-Principle. Although the One is beyond being and knowing, it grants the power of being and knowing to the Intellectual-Principle. Intellectual-Principle draws its "power to bring forth" from the Good, but "the Good bestows what itself [the Good] does not possess." (vi.7.15) But Intellectual-Principle is also self-determining.

> The Intellectual-Principle, thus, is informed of itself by the fact of being a multiple organ of vision. . . . in its outgoing to its object it is not (fully realized) Intellectual-Principle; it is an eye that has not yet seen; in its return it is an eye possessed of the multiplicity which it has itself conferred . . . (v.3.10,11)

Prefigured as an "eye that has not yet seen," Intellection is an impression of the One. Arising as an eye filled with vision, Intellectual-Principle is the entirety of knowledge and Ideas, a determination of the absolute infinity of the One. These two perspectives are simultaneous, like the stereoscopic vision of our eyes in which two images coalesce.

> Thus the Intellectual-Principle, in the act of knowing the Transcendent, is a manifold. It knows the Transcendent in very essence but, with all its effort to grasp that prior as a pure unity, it goes forth amassing successive impressions. . . . If it had not possessed a previous impression of the Transcendent it could never have grasped it, but this impression, originally of unity, becomes an impression of multiplicity . . . (v.3.11)

Intellectual-Principle, itself originally included or prefigured in the One in a transcendent mode, has a "previous impression"—direct super-essential contact with Unity. The "successive impressions" which result from its self-determining vision are the Divine Ideas, which constitute its own nature as a distinct hypostasis.

The following picture illustrates Plotinus' description of the Intellectual-Principle as a One-Many: the encompassing circle represents its Oneness and the many divisions are the Ideas, or "successive impressions" of unity. Although they are here drawn as distinct, imagine also that all the Ideas interpenetrate one another, much as the many notes of a musical chord permeate all of auditory space. The modes of Intelligence here portrayed are aspects of the whole Intellectual-Principle, as well as the structure of specific instances of knowledge.

FIG. 5

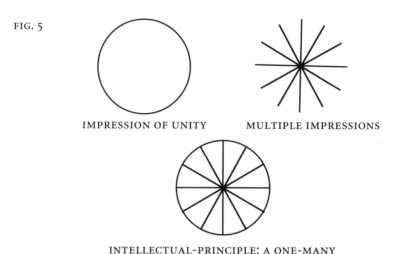

IMPRESSION OF UNITY   MULTIPLE IMPRESSIONS

INTELLECTUAL-PRINCIPLE: A ONE-MANY

If we superimpose the picture above (Fig. 5) onto our image of fourfold reality (Fig. 4), the divisions of the circle represent the Ideas as the substantial aspect of the Intellectual-Principle, and the two rings of Being and Intellection indicate its active (functional) nature.

FIG. 6

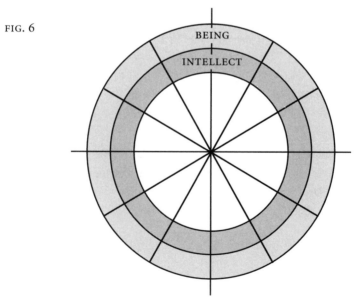

❡ The various levels of Reality which are included in the ultimate Truth can and do maintain a distinct degree of Being because they are "ones" in their own right. Therefore, insofar as anything is a "one" or a unity, it has a principle that is indivisible and without parts, a self-identity which does not enter into relationship with anything else. . . . The Intellectual-Principle is such a "one." It is Intellection pure and simple, the ecstatic activity of Ideation: the thoughts that it thinks are the many-membered parts of itself. This activity of Ideation does not cancel out that uniqueness, its indivisible self-identity; it does not introduce any element of duality or predication into itself, but it does have many thoughts (parts) and these together [with its self-identity] constitute a whole. This oneness is both the same as and different from the sum of its parts. [See Plato's *Parmenides* for a detailed exploration of this logic of unity and participation.]

This manifold unity of Intellection has an intrinsic and timeless order: "The First must be without form, and, if without form, then it is no Being; Being must have some definition and therefore be limited." (v.5.6) Definition and order is determined by the principle which Plotinus calls Authentic Number.

> The Authentic [Number] is that made manifest in the Forms and helping to bring them to be; primally it is the Number in the Authentic Being, inherent to it and preceding the Beings, serving to them as root, fount, first principle. (vi.6.9)

Authentic or Divine Number can be understood in the sense used by the Pythagoreans, where each number is thought of as a wholeness, a quality, a way that unity is expressed. At the highest level, Number is concerned with the unfoldment and reintegration of all things from and into the One. Through the operation of Number, Intellectual-Principle's indeterminate vision of Unity is determined and ordered as a simultaneous multiplicity of Ideas, unfolding in a hierarchy of forms:

> Clearly Being is to be thought of as Number collective, while the Beings are Number unfolded: the Intellectual-Principle is Number moving within itself, while the Living-Form is Number container of the universe. (vi.6.9)

Thus Number determines the interrelation of Ideas among themselves and to the whole of Intellection and Life, so that each and every Idea will reflect and duplicate the organization and structure of the entire Intellectual-Principle.

> What, then, is that content [of the Intellectual-Principle]?
> An Intellectual-Principle and an Intellective Essence, no Idea distinguishable from the Intellectual-Principle, each actually being that Principle. The Intellectual-Principle entire is the total of the Ideas, and each of them is the (entire) Intellectual-Principle in a special form. (v.9.8)

Divine Ideas in their totality are the Being of the Intellectual-Principle—substantial existences with power and intelligence. Each Idea is a form of the Good as apprehended in the vision of Intellectual-Principle. Ideas interpenetrate and commune—they are not isolated—but each idea is itself and not another. An Idea can be contracted into a central unity or essence in which all knowing and naming ceases, and can expand to indefinite living expressions. They are deific and dynamic powers, shaping the internality of all individual souls. Each instance or manifestation of an Idea participates in the authenticity of the Idea entire, but cannot exhaust the mystery of the Idea-essence. They are not bound to place and time, but can be present at every level of experience.

Any one of the Ideas can represent the unity of the Intellectual-Principle or Intellection; and each of the Ideas can unfold the profound depths of its possibilities. "Each of them is the (entire) Intellectual-Principle in a special form"—much as each authentic quality of our mind, such as justice, pervades the entire mind yet retains its unique character.

Of particular importance for us, as human beings, is what Plotinus calls the "Idea of Man"—expressed in the human realization that the One is immanent in Life. This Idea imparts uniqueness and intrinsic self-cognition to the individual. It is a special version of the Intellectual-Principle, imprinted upon or within the soul and determining it as human. This spark of the Nous within us is the divine channel for life, intelligence, and goodness: "This light shining within the Soul enlightens it; that is, it makes the Soul intellective, working it into likeness with itself, the light above." (v.3.8) Thus the Idea of Man is the higher knower within us, continuously operative at every level; it includes all that is necessary for its manifestation and actualization in innumerable individuals.

Take for example the Idea of Man; Man entire is found to contribute to it; he is in that idea in all his fullness including everything that from the beginning belonged to Man. If Man were not complete There, so that there were something to be added to the Idea, that additional must belong to a derivative: but Man exists from eternity and must therefore be complete; the man born is the derivative. (vi.7.2)

FIG. 7

⏚ The sages who have plumbed the depths of that source of Wisdom which lies within their souls and ours, if we could attain the vision, have told us, as Plotinus does, of the blinding beauty of the Ideas, their living Power, and yet the essential mystery which is their core.

> (Perfect Wisdom:) for all the Principles of this order, dwelling There, are as it were visible images projected from themselves, so that all becomes 'an object of contemplation to contemplators immeasurably blessed.' The greatness and power of the wisdom There we may know from this, that it embraces all the real Beings, and has made all and all follow it, and yet that it is itself those beings, which sprang into being with it, so that all is one and the essence There is wisdom. (v.8.4)

We do not possess the Ideas: rather they are the guiding principles or logoi within our soul, drawing us to deeper participation and contemplation. "Contemplation and its object constitute a living thing, a Life, two inextricably one." (III.8.8) True cognition or consciousness is authentic Being, not a derivative or effect, and every being as well as Being *per se* is consciousness—is knowing. For the individual seeker, the consequences of the union are profound. In order to attain self-knowledge we must participate in Nous: "by our part in true knowledge we are those Beings" for "to know without image is to be." (VI.5.7) To know an Idea is to Be the Idea, for "in proportion to the truth with which the knowing faculty knows, it comes to identification with the object of its knowledge." (III.8.6)

The power of contemplation is to be brought to all experience. The world of Intelligence is not sundered from manifestation except by our mistaken perception. Amidst the flux of experience, Ideas provide meaning to the individual and its world.

In *Nature, Contemplation, and the One* (page 110), John Deck explains:

> His world of true being is not, except metaphorically, a world above the everyday world. It *is* the everyday world, not as experienced by sense, by opinion, or by discursive reasoning, but as known by intellect, the Nous, the Knower.
>
> Plotinus' world of true being is, therefore, the real world of everyday experience when the latter is known by the best knowing power.

To the perception of the sage, the world of sense is known to be the unfoldment of Divine Ideas: "side by side with the primal knowledge . . . we have also as it were a sense-perception of their operation." (1.4.10)

3. Soul

Our venerable friend and guide reveals that he has penetrated into the mysteries of soul, its greatness and wonder, its graded powers and divinity. This is not a knowledge by acquaintance—the intellect's capacity for remembering created concepts—but a knowledge that goes beyond the imagination's formulation of thoughts, beyond even the categories of thought. For the capacity of the lower mind to formulate thoughts and concepts is objective to the experience of the sage. We are now speaking of the sage's intimacy with the innermost recesses of his being . . .

The grandeur and sublimity of this principle [Soul] cannot be retold but must be experienced. . . . Nor can the reading of mystical literature be accepted as a substitute for such inner experience. . . . This unobjectifiable and immaterial principle, which is illuminating the ego's functioning, is to be differentiated from it and isolated in the meditational practices. . . . What is required is an intimacy and a recognition of this pure principle as our "Isness."

When Plotinus considers Soul as inseparable from the One and the Intellectual-Principle, he does so in order to emphasize its transcendence and inconceivability—a mysterious Void. But looked at as a distinct essence, Soul is living intelligence, the outgoing activity of the Supreme, and our inner divinity.

> . . . Soul does not take its essence from its ultimates [i.e., its lowest reaches] or from its parts, but from the Primals; it has its source in the First and thence, along an unhindered path, it flows into a total of things, conferring grace . . . (IV.4.10)

Because of its scope and diversity of activity, Soul is in some sense the most complex of the primals. A brief outline will help to reveal the hierarchy implicit in Plotinus' exposition of Soul. This overview will organize our understanding of the many meanings of the term Soul as used in the *Enneads*, so that we may place individual passages in a proper context.

Soul is a single essence with distinct aspects: it flows from the infinite nature of the One, through Absolute Soul, Universal Soul, Cosmic and human individual souls.

> A single Existent, it makes itself many by what we may call its motion: it is one entire, but by its striving, so to speak, to contemplate itself, it is a plurality; for we may imagine that it cannot bear to be a single Existent, when it has the power to be all that it in fact is. The cause of its appearing as many is this contemplation, and its purpose is the Act of the Intellect . . . (VI.2.6)

Soul as a continuous essence can be pictured as a ring passing through the four levels of substantial intelligence represented by the four quadrants.

FIG. 8

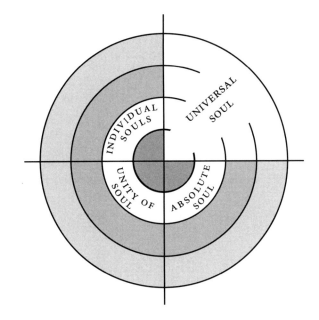

⟐ At the highest level we must understand Soul as an indivisible aspect of the One itself. Here the formless form of the unsullied Life [the unity of Soul] may be recognized as the transcendent paradigm or immaculate version of this principle from which flows a whole hierarchy.

⟐ From the One's perfection there radiates the life of the Intellectual-Principle, Absolute Soul, which is the recipient of all the Ideas. Just as the life of the Intellectual-Principle is determined by all the Ideas, so reciprocally are all the Ideas made living and permanent possibilities or presences within the Intellectual by Soul.

> And before the particular Soul there is another Soul, a universal, and, before that, an Absolute-Soul, which is the Life existing in the Intellectual-Principle before Soul came to be and therefore rightly called (as the Life in the Divine) the Absolute-Soul. (v.9.14)

⟐ Considered most precisely as the Intellect of the Soul, Absolute Soul is an eternal Presence, totally and unextendedly present in the Now: "Life—instantaneously entire" (III.7.3), Soul as passive perfection. It does not descend, for as descending it would annul its own Perfection. Yet the super-abundance of Soul gives of itself ceaselessly; it is the "entire stream of life sent forth by that Principle." (v.1.3)

The primal phase of the Soul—inhabitant of the Supreme and, by its participation in the Supreme, filled and illuminated—remains unchangeably There; but in virtue of that first participation . . . a secondary phase . . . goes forth ceaselessly as Life streaming from Life. . . . But, travel as far as it may, it never draws that first part of itself from the place whence the outgoing began . . . (III.8.5)

▢ The next hierarchical level of Soul . . . is the Soul of the Universe [Universal Soul] or the Demiurge: Zeus.

But Zeus—ordering all, governor, guardian, and disposer, possessor for ever of the 'kingly soul' and the 'kingly intellect', bringing all into being by his providence, and presiding over things as they come . . . unfolding the periods of the Cosmos. . . . Zeus knows his own unlimited life, and, in that knowledge, knows the activity that flows from him to the Cosmos; but he knows it in its unity not in its process. (IV.4.9)

The ordering principle is twofold; there is the principle known to us as the Demiurge and there is the Soul of the All [Universal Manifestation]; we apply the appellation Zeus sometimes to the Demiurge and sometimes to the principle conducting the universe. (IV.4.10)

▢ Here Soul is the principle of Universal manifestation and it is referred to as twofold: on the one hand, eternally contemplating the Ideas or the wisdom of God, a timeless and abiding wisdom, and on the other hand organizing the past traces of universal manifestation into a basic or primitive plan of the universe to be [which Plotinus calls the Reason-Principle of the Universe (cf. III.3.3 and III.2.16)]. This vast and cosmic sweep of its intellectual fabrication is referred to as the "tentative illumining of Matter." (VI.7.7)

Finally we come to individual souls, and in this category are included cosmic, planetary, and human souls. Although Plotinus distinguishes different kinds of soul by their power, wisdom, and relation to the manifest universe, he points out that all souls have their source in and are direct emanations of the Divine Mind.

In the Intellectual Cosmos dwells Authentic Essence, with the Intellectual-Principle (Divine Mind) as the noblest of its content, but containing also souls, since every soul in this lower sphere has come thence. . . . Soul, there without distinction and partition, has yet a nature lending itself to divisional existence . . . (IV.1.1)

▢ Here, Soul or Mind is included in an undifferentiated unity and . . . has a tendency or desire towards secession. We may also rephrase this in accordance with his previous statements that what is authentically real has an outwardly facing hypostasis [and that] what is perfect engenders and the eternally perfect engenders eternally. We may take this to mean that Absolute Soul eternally engenders souls. Each and every soul, offspring of the Absolute Soul, is similar to but not identical with its prior.

> Thus the gist of the matter is established: one soul the source of all; the many founded in that one, on the analogy of the Intellectual-Principle; those many are at once divided and undivided; that Soul which abides in the Supreme is the one expression or Logos of the Intellectual-Principle, and from it spring other Reason-Principles, partial but immaterial . . . (IV.3.5)

◌ It is this emanation, this thought of the Mind of God—our Absolute Self—that must be investigated, for this is the key to the mysteries. This unit of Being-Life-Consciousness goes forth, "formed from the undivided essence and the essence divided among bodies." (IV.1.1) We may refer to this . . . as the individual soul or mind . . . our absolute individuality . . . [Continuing in IV.1.1:]

> . . . this description of Soul must therefore mean that it has phases above and below, that it is attached to the Supreme and yet reaches down to this sphere, like a radius from a centre.
>
> Thus it is that, entering this realm, it possesses still the vision inherent to that superior phase in virtue of which it unchangingly maintains its integral nature. Even here it is not exclusively the partible soul: it is still the impartible as well: what in it knows partition is parted without partibility . . . (IV.1.1)

◌ Regardless with what it is occupied, with the idea of the universe or a body within it, soul gives itself to either or both "without abdicating its unity." (IV.2.1) In other words, its omnipresence does not fragment its identity, for it is at once both divisible and indivisible.

> . . . its divisibility lies in its presence at every point of the recipient, but it is indivisible as dwelling entire in the total and entire in any part.
>
> To have penetrated this idea is to know the greatness of the Soul and its power, the divinity and wonder of its being, as a nature transcending the sphere of Things. (IV.2.1)

◌ The recitation of these words is not a guarantee that the meaning accompanies their repetition. Plotinus is referring here to the mystical experience of this illuminating principle as egoless Being-Consciousness . . . both a one or unity and "multi-present" in its graded powers.

> There is, therefore, no escape: soul is, in the degree indicated, one and many, parted and impartible. We cannot question the possibility of a thing

being at once a unity and multi-present, since to deny this would be to abolish the principle which sustains and administers the universe . . . (IV.2.2)

⬚ This conception of Soul or mind may be likened to a transparent crystalline sphere of life-radiating consciousness, which is a reflex or emanation from the Absolute Soul. The individual souls are associated with the light of the Cosmic Soul, and in this undivided awareness the souls hold together, not separated by any boundaries, and indifferently referred to as one or many.

. . . each separate life lives by the Soul entire, omnipresent in the likeness of the engendering father, entire in unity and entire in diffused variety. (V.1.2)

⬚ Plotinus describes each individual soul as omnipresent, indivisible in its unity; as indivisible, it manifests the entire heavenly system as a unit within itself. If this point is not seized, any interpretation of his epistemology will go astray. The life of each unit soul is the medium in which this reality [the Ideas] is being manifested. [This point will be developed in the Nature section.]

⬚ It is this unit soul, the God within us, that may be referred to as our soul, our ultimate individuality and the true knower. It is man made in the image of God. . . . this formless and infinite consciousness of the unit soul gets contracted and starts on a journey of self-realization. This contracted consciousness may be referred to as an impersonal or witnessing consciousness, and is associated with the planetary mind from which it receives the image of the World-Idea.

. . . we are not to think of it as going forth from itself (losing its unity by any partition): the fact is simply that the element within it, [soul] which is apt to entrance into body, has the power of immediate projection any whither . . . (IV.3.8)

⬚ Soul or mind is "reduced" and will ultimately become identified with bodily vehicles that are being fabricated for its use in order to experience the sensible [world], i.e., complete its contemplation.

Soul is living consciousness: simultaneously transcendent and immanent as our very awareness. Based on this distinction of formless infinite consciousness and embodying consciousness, each individual unit of life has potentially two kinds of knowledge: insight and understanding.

⬚ For Plotinus, the unit soul or mind is a double knower—that is, it has self-cognition, undifferentiated being-consciousness [insight], which includes cognition of its source or origin. The lower knower or secondary phase—that is, the faculty of understanding and reasoning—will evolve by its journey through the cosmic circuit which is providing the circumstances, situations, and events that educe its potential and make it actual through experience.

4. THE SYSTEM OF NATURE

❡ *THIS, THE sensible universe, is the primordial scripture, the vision referred to, and as such it embodies the wisdom of the primal principles which are beyond it. Who has not thrilled to the excitement of the starry skies—the silent unanswered questions?*

᪥

The entire universe, including all levels and all possible worlds, is the body of God manifested within Soul. For Plotinus, this is the system of Nature. Our universe as thus conceived is not inert matter, nor is it an illusion:

> . . . this All is one universally comprehensive living being, encircling all the living beings within it, and having a soul, one soul, which extends to all its members in the degree of participant membership held by each . . . (IV.4.32)

For Plotinus, the Cosmos is not only an image of divinity, but also the presence of divinity. The primal principles are immanent in and for the system of Nature. In successive order: while the One "is nowhere, nowhere is it not" (v.5.8); Intellectual-Principle communicates the Reason-Principle of the Universe (III.2.2); Soul is said to be "the author of all living things" (v.1.2). And in III.8.4, Nature herself says: "I gaze and the figures of the material world take being as if they fell from my contemplation."

FIG. 9

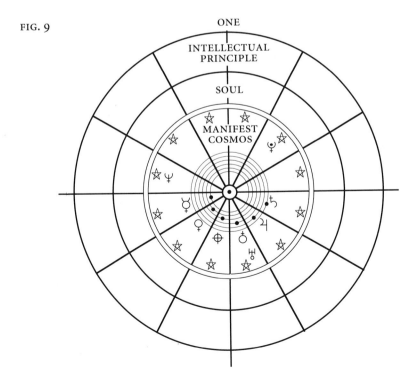

In sum: the loveliness that is in the sense-realm is an index of the nobleness of the Intellectual sphere, displaying its power and its goodness alike: and all things are for ever linked; the one order Intellectual in its being, the other of sense; one self-existent, the other eternally taking its being by participation in that first, and to the full of its power reproducing the Intellectual nature. (IV.8.6)

⬓ Our hope is that we will be led to a superior understanding, or rather to a qualitatively different kind of understanding of our being here—an understanding that does not sidestep or deny the anomaly of sense perception, but, rather, reveals something of the meaning implicit in the orderly and evolving transformation that our minds and bodies undergo. In short, we are going to enter sympathetically into an analysis of experience as conceived by some of the ancient philosophers. We will try to understand and appreciate the philosophic insight which they summarized in the dictum: "The world is full of Gods."

To unfold this vision of the cosmos, we begin with the "Reason-Principle" or Idea of the Universe in the mind of the Demiurge, as the background within which a hierarchy of souls will manifest a cosmos.

All living things, then—all in the heavens and all elsewhere—fall under the general Reason-Principle of the All . . . (II.3.13)

⬓ To try to pictorialize this realm, we can imagine the stars as statues of the gods, or the Ideas, that radiate a guiding influence throughout boundless space. . . . The energy of their intelligence lays down the basic pattern within which our world, among others, develops and unfolds.

If the stars live a blessed life in their vision of the life inherent in their souls, and if, by force of their souls' tendency to become one, and by the light they cast from themselves upon the entire heavens, they are like the strings of a lyre which, being struck in tune, sing a melody in some natural scale: if this is the way the heavens, as one, are moved, and the component parts in their relation to the whole—the sidereal system moving as one, and each part in its own way, to the same purpose, though each too hold its own place—then our doctrine is all the more surely established; the life of the heavenly bodies is the more clearly an unbroken unity. (IV.4.8)

The Idea of the cosmos—the World-Idea—and its inhabitants, evolving and manifesting, can be traced ultimately to this circle of stars (Ideas). In this view, the stars are not only the source of physical light, but are the embodiment of divine souls. Our sensible sun is such a star. As a unit Soul it proceeds to unfold a vast intelligence. Through its contemplation, there arises within it the Idea of the world.

IV.3.11 brings a Himalayan panorama into view:

> The sun of that sphere—let us return to it as our example—is an Intellectual-Principle, and immediately upon it follows the Soul depending from it, stationary Soul from stationary Intelligence. But the Soul borders also upon the sun of this sphere, and becomes the medium by which it is linked to the over-world; it plays the part of an interpreter between what emanates from that sun down to this lower, and what rises—as far as, through Soul, anything can—from the lower to the higher. (IV.3.11)

The "sun of that sphere" is the Intellectual-Principle, the Ideas shining in the intelligible world, inseparable from the "stationary Soul"—which is the Absolute Soul. But "the Soul borders also upon the sun of this sphere"—soul is not of a nature to be in the Nous only. Soul, as emanating from the Divine Mind, is present with the entire world it manifests within itself. Cosmic Soul is the unbroken link, the eternal continuity of Being and Becoming. For Plotinus, the Soul of the sun is the God of our solar system.

FIG. 10

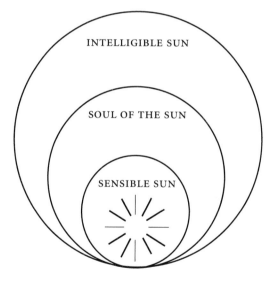

Behind the visible sun is the Cosmic Soul [the Sun Soul]—an inconceivable immaterial boundless light and life, the substratum of the cosmos. . . . The infinite life-intelligence of the Sun Soul is interpenetrating with all the other [star] souls. Through their mutual omnipresence, each cosmic soul's intellection or contemplation constitutes its World-Idea. . . . When the Sun Soul interprets to itself its infinite inner vision, through its own universal reasoning, it brings about within itself an archetypal form of the World-Idea. . . . This celestial wisdom is symbolized by the Sun's sidereal zodiac, and constitutes its intellectuality ["Ideal-Forms . . . unrolled and separate" (1.1.8)]. . . . Symboli-cally, the Sun's travel through the cosmos represents to us the universal rea-soning through which our Sun too is assimilating facets of the unfathomable divinity of Nous. [Note the parallel of this passage to the sixth book of the *Republic,* where Plato bases his grand epistemology on an analogy between the sensible sun with its light, and the Idea of the Good—the "intelligible sun"—author of being and knowing.]

In sum, this infinite light, the soul of the sun, is a principle of consciousness and intelligence which thinks the world into existence. Together with the living system of planetary souls, our sun unfolds its World-Idea as the solar system (which Plotinus refers to as the Cosmos, and the "circuit").

> . . . the entire Cosmos puts its entire life into act, moving its major members with its own action and unceasingly setting them in new positions; by the relations thus established, of these members to each other and to the whole, and by the different figures they make together, the minor members in turn are brought under the system as in the movements of some one living being, so that they vary according to the relations, positions, configurations . . . (IV.4.33)

◻ Each of the planets is also a god manifesting or unfolding the master plan inherent in the Sun's intellectuality.

> These Beings (the heavenly bodies) are divine in virtue of cleaving to the Supreme, because, by the medium of the Soul thought of as descending, they remain linked with the Primal Soul, and through it are veritably what they are called and possess the vision of the Intellectual Principle . . . (IV.3.11)

In particular, our Earth is spoken of as a god, with a divine intellect and soul.

> We must conclude, then, that every part and member of the earth carries its vestige of this principle of growth . . . next in order is the nature . . . concerned with sensation . . . then the higher soul and the Intellectual-Principle, constituting together the being known as Hestia (Earth-Mind) and Demeter (Earth-Soul)—a nomenclature indicating the human intuition of these truths . . . (IV.4.27)

Through the bodies it mysteriously fashions for us, our earth provides the world-image appropriate for the human souls inhabiting it.

This encompassing view of the cosmos as an unfolding of the World-Idea provides the epistemological background needed to understand how Plotinus sees the arisal of knowledge for the individual human entity. We summarize the levels within the cosmos by drawing a parallel to the fourfold metaphysical principles.

FIG. 11

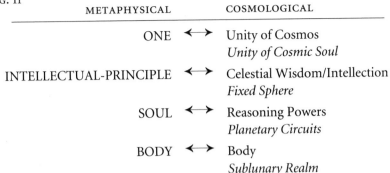

METAPHYSICAL		COSMOLOGICAL
ONE	←→	Unity of Cosmos *Unity of Cosmic Soul*
INTELLECTUAL-PRINCIPLE	←→	Celestial Wisdom/Intellection *Fixed Sphere*
SOUL	←→	Reasoning Powers *Planetary Circuits*
BODY	←→	Body *Sublunary Realm*

Tractate III.4.6 emphasizes the immense scope of the individual Soul or mind and its intimate relation to the cosmos.

> We must understand that, while our souls do contain an Intellectual Cosmos, they also contain a subordination of various forms like that of the Cosmic Soul. The World Soul is distributed so as to produce the fixed sphere and the planetary circuits corresponding to its graded powers: so with our souls; they must have their provinces according to their different powers, parallel to those of the World Soul . . . (III.4.6)

The individual soul's undivided awareness is omnipresent as a unity with the Cosmic Soul. Through participation in the Cosmic Soul's powers, the individual soul or mind is modalized into three grades of life: life intellectual, rational, and embodied—represented respectively by the starry sphere, planetary spheres, and sublunar sphere.

FIG. 12

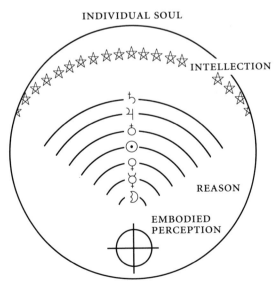

INDIVIDUAL SOUL

INTELLECTION

REASON

EMBODIED
PERCEPTION

When the individual souls remain at the level of the Cosmic Soul's contemplation, the power immanent in them pervades the entire archetypal thought-form of the solar system held by the Cosmic Soul. Our Intellection is a participation in this formless, universal reasoning of the Cosmic Soul.

Simultaneous with this Intellection, our soul participates also in the productive planetary reasoning powers. This intermediary phase of the soul's understanding is what Plotinus means by reason.

> Perhaps reason, whose actualization always accompanies thought, has the function of receiving it and transmitting it to imagination. Indeed, thought is indivisible, and so long as it is not evoked from the depths of intelligence, it remains as it were hidden within it. (IV.3.30, Guthrie transl., p. 437)

Because of its desire for embodiment or experience—the complete differentiation of thought—soul presides over successive embodiments on this planet, shining its light and power into the psychosomatic organism, the Animate. Ego subjectivity emerges.

> . . . from the organized body and something else, let us say a light, which the Soul gives forth from itself, it forms a distinct Principle, the Animate; and in this Principle are vested Sense-Perception and all the other experiences found to belong to the Animate.
>
> . . . We are not separate from the Animate so constituted, even though certainly other and nobler elements go to make up the entire many-sided nature of Man. (I.1.7)

☐ The entrance of the soul into the world, to associate with a particular body, is determined by the root tendencies inherent in the soul. . . . The human soul is now a fated member of the Circuit. [A detailed application of these principles to human life is developed in *Astronoesis*. There, Anthony Damiani juxtaposes philosophy and astrology so as to reveal metaphysical principles in act, and to show that the basis of classical astrology is an acquaintance with the wisdom-knowledge that sustains the cosmos.]

> In the Timaeus the creating God bestows the essential of the Soul, but it is the divinities moving in the Cosmos (the stars) that infuse the powerful affections holding from Necessity. . . . By this statement our personality is bound up with the stars, whence our Soul takes shape; and we are set under necessity at our very entrance into the world: our temperament will be of the stars' ordering, and so, therefore, the actions which derive from temperament, and all the experiences of a nature shaped to impressions. (II.3.9)

Having explained the process of embodiment and the experience of the sensible world, Plotinus shows us that the purpose of the journey through the cosmic circuit is to acquire some good. What possible good could this be? The experiences provided through many lifetimes will develop soul's faculties of understanding, feeling, reason, and imagination.

> . . . by exhibiting those activities and productions which, remaining merely potential in the unembodied, might as well never have been even there, if destined never to come into actuality, so that the Soul itself would never have known that suppressed and inhibited total.
>
> The act reveals the power, a power hidden, and we might almost say obliterated or non-existent, unless at some moment it became effective: in the world as it is, the richness of the outer stirs us all to the wonder of the inner whose greatness is displayed in acts so splendid. (IV.8.5)

Ultimately, the purpose is the acquisition of Ideas by the mind, to complete the vision resident in the logos.

> Action, thus, is set towards contemplation and an object of contemplation, so that even those whose life is in doing have seeing as their object; what they have not been able to achieve by the direct path, they hope to come at by the circuit. . . .
>
> Hence the Reason-Principle must not be left to lie outside, but must be made one identical thing with the Soul of the novice so that he finds it really his own. (III.8.6)

 So it is rather a straightforward affair to discern that the purpose of all this activity is to ultimately possess the object of contemplation, the ideas or reason-principles that are being manifested by life.

 Soul incarnates or participates in the ideas of the planetary mind by perceiving the world and experiencing through a body what the gods think. Thus Earth—footstool of the Gods—nurses our soul to heavenly maturity and humanity. What is becoming explicit in this exegesis is a theory of the endless evolution of the content of an individual soul's awareness. Through reasoning on the content of the World-Idea which it is manifesting, the soul evolves its understanding until intellection becomes predominant, and this is brought to bear on its own self-nature. If the inquiry is pursued, this process will result in intrinsic self-awareness.

5. A Sequence of Quotes from The *Enneads*

The following sequence of key passages on the One, Intellectual-Principle, Soul, and the system of Nature is provided to complement the preceding outline. It is arranged in an order following the progression of the One to manifestation. Excerpts given are key or opening phrases in the passages to be read.

The section "On the Path of Contemplation in Plotinus" offers, in order of appearance in the *Enneads*, a selection of inspiring passages on Plotinus' path to reality.

ON THE ONE

c∾

V.1.10: There exists a Principle which transcends Being . . .
[paragraphs 1-3]

V.1.8:   This is the explanation of Plato's Triplicity . . . [all]

V.4.1:   Standing before all things, there must exist a Simplex . . .
[paragraph 2]

VI.9.6: In what sense, then, do we assert this Unity . . . ? [paragraphs 1-3]

VI.8.16: That his being is constituted by this self-originating self-
tendance . . . [paragraph 4, also 1-3]

VI.8.14: . . . He is what He is, the first self, transcendentally The Self.
[last paragraph]

VI.7.38: . . . we use the term The Good to assert identity without the
affirmation of Being. [end of first paragraph]

V.3.13: Thus The One is in truth beyond all statement . . . [paragraph 1]

V.5.6:   Its definition, in fact, could only be 'the indefinable' . . .
[last paragraph]

VI.9.5: That awesome Prior, The Unity . . . strictly no name is apt to it . . .
[last three paragraphs]

V.5.12: The Good is gentle and friendly and tender . . . [paragraph 6]

v.4.2: ... the One is "not, so to speak, imperceptive ..."
[Deck translation of paragraph 6; see Deck, page 33]

v.2.1: Seeking nothing, possessing nothing, lacking nothing, the One is perfect and, in our metaphor, has overflowed ... [paragraph 3]

v.4.2: So it is in the divine also: or rather we have there the earlier form of the double act ... [next to last paragraph]

vi.8.18: The Supreme is cause of the cause ... in it lie the Intellective causes ... [paragraphs 6,7]

vi.7.16: In this way the Supreme may be understood to be the cause at once of essential reality and of the knowing of reality. [last paragraph]

v.1.6: All existences, as long as they retain their character, produce. . . . the eternally achieved engenders eternally an eternal being. [last three paragraphs]

v.3.15: All that is not One is conserved by virtue of the One ... [paragraph 4]

iii.8.10: Every particular thing has a One ... [last three paragraphs]

v.5.8: No doubt it is wonderful that The First should thus be present ... while it is nowhere, nowhere is it not ... [last paragraph]

vi.9.8: Thus the Supreme as containing no otherness is ever present with us ... [last paragraph]

ON THE INTELLECTUAL-PRINCIPLE

v.2.1: ... the One is perfect and ... has overflowed ... [paragraph 3]

v.2.1: That station towards the One ... establishes Being; that vision directed upon the One establishes the Intellectual-Principle ... [paragraph 4]

v.4.2: (on Intellectual-Principle as the outcome of a mighty power) [last two paragraphs]

v.1.6:   This greatest, later than the divine unity, must be the Divine
          Mind . . . [next to last paragraph]

v.1.8:   . . . the distinction is made between the Primal One . . . and a
          secondary One which is a One-Many . . . [last paragraph]

vi.7.15: The Good is the source from which the objects of contemplation
          come to be seen . . . [paragraph 2]

vi.7.16: In this way the Supreme may be understood to be the cause at once
          of essential reality and of the knowing of reality. [last paragraph]

vi.7.17: The Life was a vestige of that Primal . . . determined Life is
          Intellectual-Principle. [paragraphs 3-5]

v.1.4:   That archetypal world. . . . this is pure being in eternal actuality. . . .
          its intellective act establishes being, which in turn . . . becomes
          the cause of intellection and of existence to the Intellectual-
          Principle . . . [paragraphs 3,4]

v.6.6:   In a Being, then, the existence, the intellection, the life are present
          as an aggregate. [paragraph 4]

v.5.2:   Thus we . . . must provide for knowledge and for truth . . .
          [all; also first paragraph of v.5.3]

v.3.11:   Thus the Intellectual-Principle, in the act of knowing the
          Transcendent, is a manifold. [paragraphs 1-3]

v.3.10:   The Intellectual-Principle, thus, is informed of itself . . . [paragraph 3]

vi.7.35: Intellectual-Principle, thus, has two powers . . . [paragraph 2]

vi.6.9,10: The truth is that it [Number] existed within the Authentic
          Being. . . . Hence it is that the Forms (Ideas) have been described as
          Henads and Numbers.
          [last three paragraphs of vi.6.9 and first of vi.6.10]

v.9.6:   We take it, then, that the Intellectual-Principle is the authentic
          existences . . . [paragraph 1]

v.9.8:   The Intellectual-Principle entire is the total of the Ideas, and each of them is the (entire) Intellectual-Principle in a special form. [paragraph 3]

v.1.4:   Thus the Primals (the first 'Categories') are seen to be . . . [last three paragraphs]

vi.2.7,8: What, then, are the several entities observable in this plurality? [all]

v.8.3:   For assuredly all the gods are august and beautiful . . . [paragraph 3]

v.8.4:   To 'live at ease' is There. . . . for all the Principles of this order, dwelling There . . . [all]

vi.7.2:   . . . the Idea itself, unfolded, reveals the cause inherent in it. [paragraph 2]

vi.7.2:   Take for example the Idea of Man . . . [last paragraph]

ON SOUL

iv.4.10: . . . it has its source in the First and thence, along an unhindered path, it flows into a total of things, conferring grace . . . [last paragraph]

v.9.14:   And before the particular Soul there is another Soul, a universal, and, before that, an Absolute-Soul . . . [last paragraph]

iii.8.5: The primal phase of the Soul—inhabitant of the Supreme and . . . a secondary phase . . . goes forth ceaselessly as Life streaming from Life . . . [paragraph 2]

vi.2.6:   A single Existent, it [Soul] makes itself many by what we may call its motion. . . . its purpose is the Act of the Intellect . . . [last paragraph]

iv.4.9,10: . . . Zeus . . . possessor for ever of the 'kingly soul' and the 'kingly intellect' . . . [all]

IV.1.1: In the Intellectual Cosmos . . . containing also souls. . . . this description of Soul must therefore mean that it has phases above and below . . . [all]

IV.2.1,2: (on soul essence as indivisible and divisible) [all]

IV.3.5: By their succession they are linked to the several Intellectual-Principles . . . [last two paragraphs]

V.1.2: Let every soul recall, then, at the outset the truth that soul is the author of all living things . . . [paragraph 1]

V.1.2: . . . each separate life lives by the Soul entire . . . [paragraph 5]

VI.4.1: How are we to explain the omnipresence of the Soul? [paragraph 1]

VI.4.4: For Soul is not articulated . . . there is integral omnipresence . . . [last two paragraphs]

IV.8.4: So it is with the individual souls . . . [paragraph 1]

IV.8.8: And—if it is desirable to venture . . . even our human Soul has not sunk entire . . . [paragraph 1]

V.3.4: Thus the self-knower is a double person . . . [paragraph 4]

V.3.6: Our way is to teach our Soul . . . [paragraph 7]

V.3.8: That which sees. . . . This light shining within the Soul enlightens it . . . [paragraph 6]

IV.3.8: This means that it is no external limit . . . [Soul] has the power of immediate projection any whither . . . [next to last paragraph]

III.5.3: But besides this purest Soul. . . . every soul is striving towards The Good . . . [last paragraph]

VI.9.9:   In this choiring, the soul looks upon the wellspring of Life . . .
            [paragraph 1]

VI.7.34:   Suppose the soul to have attained . . . [paragraph 2]

ON NATURE

∽

III.2.1:   Of course the belief that after a certain lapse of time. . . . the
            providence ruling in the Universe as a universal consonance with
            the divine Intelligence . . . [paragraph 6]

III.2.2:   The Intellectual Principle, then . . . has brought the universe into
            being . . . [paragraph 5]

III.2.11:   No: the Reason-Principle is the sovereign, making all . . .
            [paragraph 2]

III.2.16:   This Reason-Principle, then . . . this Logos . . .
            [paragraphs 6-11]

II.3.13:   The gist of the whole matter lies in the consideration that Soul
            governs this All by the plan contained in the Reason-Principle . . .
            [paragraphs 2,6,7,8]

II.3.17:   But these Reason-Principles, contained in the Soul . . . [all]

II.3.18:   Rightly, therefore, is this Cosmos described as an image continu-
            ously being imaged . . . [paragraphs 5,6]

III.3.3:   Certainly not: the inequality is inevitable by the nature of things . . .
            [next to last paragraph]

IV.4.32:   The secret is . . . that this All is one universally comprehensive living
            being . . . [paragraph 2]

IV.4.33:   The Circuit does not go by chance but under the Reason-Principle
            of the living whole . . . [paragraphs 1,4]

IV.4.35: The being we are considering is a living unity, and therefore necessarily self-sympathetic . . . all the members of this living whole in their choral dance are under a rule of Number. [paragraph 5]

IV.8.6: In sum: the loveliness that is in the sense-realm . . . [last paragraph]

VI.4.2: Side by side exist the Authentic All and its counterpart, the visible universe. [first two paragraphs]

IV.3.11: I think, therefore. . . . every particular entity is linked to that Divine Being in whose likeness it is made. . . . The sun of that sphere . . . [all]

III.4.6: We must understand that, while our souls do contain an Intellectual Cosmos . . . [sixth paragraph from end]

VI.7.6: It is the perception of what falls under perception There . . . [paragraph 2]

II.3.9: This brings us to the Spindle-destiny. . . . our personality is bound up with the stars. . . . For every human Being is of twofold character . . . [paragraphs 1,2,6-8]

IV.3.9: The entry of soul into body takes place under two forms. [paragraphs 1-4]

VI.4.14: Before we had our becoming Here we existed There . . . [last paragraph]

I.1.7: No; from the organized body and something else, let us say a light . . . [all]

IV.3.30: (Reason takes Thought and spreads it out for our imagination) [see endnote with Guthrie translation of paragraphs 2,3]

IV.8.5: The act reveals the power, a power hidden . . . [last paragraph]

II.9.18: Attaining to something of this immunity, we begin to reproduce within ourselves the Soul of the vast All and of the heavenly bodies . . . [paragraph 4]

III.8.6:   Action, thus, is set towards contemplation. . . . Hence the Reason-
            Principle must not be left to lie outside . . . [all]

ON THE PATH OF CONTEMPLATION
IN PLOTINUS

I.3.4,5:   Is Dialectic, then, the same as Philosophy? It is the precious part of
            Philosophy. [all]

I.6.7-9:   Therefore we must ascend again towards the Good . . . [all]

II.3.9:   Our task, then, is to work for our liberation from this sphere,
            severing ourselves from all that has gathered about us. . . . There is
            another life, emancipated, whose quality is progression towards the
            higher realm . . . by deliberate usage . . . [paragraph 5]

III.8.6:   Hence the Reason-Principle must not be left to lie outside . . .
            [paragraphs 7,8]

V.1.1:   A double discipline must be applied if human beings in this pass are
            to be reclaimed, and brought back to their origins . . .
            [paragraphs 4,5]

V.1.12:   Possessed of such powers . . . [all]

V.3.6:   Our way is to teach our Soul how the Intellectual-Principle
            exercises self-vision . . . [paragraph 7]

V.3.8:   If the Soul is questioned as to the nature of that Intellectual-
            Principle . . . it has but to enter into that Principle, or to sink all its
            activity into that, and at once it shows itself to be in effective
            possession of those priors whose memory it never lost . . .
            [last paragraph]

V.3.17:   No: the Soul is yet, and even more, in pain. . . . We may know we
            have had the vision when the Soul has suddenly taken light. . . . to
            see the Supreme by the Supreme. . . . Cut away everything.
            [last four paragraphs]

v.8.9: Let us, then, make a mental picture of our universe. . . . Keep this sphere before you, and from it imagine another, a sphere stripped of magnitude and of spatial differences; cast out your inborn sense of Matter . . . [first two paragraphs]

v.8.11: Similarly any one, unable to see himself, but possessed by that God, has but to bring that divine-within before his consciousness . . . [paragraph 1]

vi.5.7: Of what is There we have direct knowledge . . . and to know withoutimage is to be; by our part in true knowledge we are those Beings. . . . If a man could but be turned about—by his own motion or by the happy pull of Athene—he would see at once God and himself and the All. [all]

vi.5.12: In that you have entered into the All, no longer content with the part; you cease to think of yourself as under limit but, laying all such determination aside, you become an All. [third from last paragraph]

vi.7.31-34: In the same way the soul loves the Supreme Good, from its very beginnings stirred by it to love. [all]

vi.7.36: Knowing of The Good . . . is the grand learning . . . [paragraph 2]

vi.8.7: Soul becomes free when it moves without hindrance, through Intellectual-Principle, towards The Good . . . [paragraph 1]

vi.9.3: The soul or mind reaching towards the formless . . . [all]

vi.9.4: Our way then takes us beyond knowing . . . [paragraph 2]

vi.9.8-11: (the aspiring of the Alone to the Alone) [all]

APPENDIX II

Concordance of the Systematic and Chronological Orders of the Tractates

chron.	Enn.	chron.	Enn.	chron.	Enn.	chron.	Enn.	chron.	Enn.	chron.	Enn.
1	I.6	10	V.1	19	I.2	28	IV.4	37	II.7	46	I.4
2	IV.7	11	V.2	20	I.3	29	IV.5	38	VI.7	47	III.2
3	III.1	12	II.4	21	IV.1	30	III.8	39	VI.8	48	III.3
4	IV.2	13	III.9	22	VI.4	31	V.8	40	II.1	49	V.3
5	V.9	14	II.2	23	VI.5	32	V.5	41	IV.6	50	III.5
6	IV.8	15	III.4	24	V.6	33	II.9	42	VI.1	51	I.8
7	V.4	16	I.9	25	II.5	34	VI.6	43	VI.2	52	II.3
8	IV.9	17	II.6	26	III.6	35	II.8	44	VI.3	53	I.1
9	VI.9	18	V.7	27	IV.3	36	I.5	45	III.7	54	I.7

———— ～ ————

Enn.	chron.	Enn.	chron.	Enn.	chron.	Enn.	chron.	Enn.	chron.	Enn.	chron.
I.1	53	II.1	40	III.1	3	IV.1	21	V.1	10	VI.1	42
I.2	19	II.2	14	III.2	47	IV.2	4	V.2	11	VI.2	43
I.3	20	III.3	52	III.3	48	IV.3	27	V.3	49	VI.3	44
I.4	46	II.4	12	III.4	15	IV.4	28	V.4	7	VI.4	22
I.5	36	II.5	25	III.5	50	IV.5	29	V.5	32	VI.5	23
I.6	1	II.6	17	III.6	26	IV.6	41	V.6	24	VI.6	34
I.7	54	II.7	37	III.7	45	IV.7	2	V.7	18	VI.7	38
I.8	51	II.8	35	III.8	30	IV.8	6	V.8	31	VI.8	39
I.9	16	II.9	33	III.9	13	IV.9	8	V.9	5	VI.9	9